D1591681

Routledge Handbook of Political Marketing

With the Obama campaign universally acknowledged as the most successfully marketed presidential campaign of all time, the future of political marketing is fiercely contested, provoking a wealth of high-quality scholarship from across the globe. This work provides an accessible introduction to the field, international in both content and authorship, which will set the direction of future research.

The *Routledge Handbook of Political Marketing* contains cutting-edge contributions written by academic experts and informed practitioners but also has a cohesive structure, containing emerging areas and authors alongside established ones. The *Handbook* addresses the practicalities as well as the broader impact of political marketing on politics including its role in the changing relationship between political leaders, parties and voters. With each chapter providing a comparative and carefully structured discussion of a key topic, the *Handbook* examines issues within the following broad themes:

- Understanding the market, gathering ideas and debate
- Product development, branding and strategy
- Internal marketing
- Communicating and connecting with the public
- Government marketing – delivery, policy and leadership

With each chapter written to a common template presenting new research and contemporary case studies, the *Handbook* combines a succinct presentation of the latest research with an accessible and systematic format, which will be of great interest to scholars and practitioners alike.

Jennifer Lees-Marshment (University of Auckland, New Zealand) is an international expert in political marketing and author/editor of 10 books, including *Political Marketing: principles and applications* (2009) and *Global Political Marketing* (2010).

Routledge Handbook of Political Marketing

Edited by
Jennifer Lees-Marshment

LONDON AND NEW YORK

First published 2012
by Routledge
2 Park Square, Milton Park, Abingdon, Oxon, OX14 4RN

Simultaneously published in the USA and Canada
by Routledge
711 Third Avenue, New York, NY 10017

Routledge is an imprint of the Taylor & Francis Group, an informa business

British Library Cataloguing in Publication Data
A catalogue record for this book is available from the British Library

Library of Congress Cataloging in Publication Data
Routledge handbook of political marketing / edited by Jennifer Lees-Marshment.
p. cm.
Includes bibliographical references and index.
1. Public relations and politics. 2. Campaign management. 3. Political campaigns.
4. Communication in politics. 5. Government publicity. I. Lees-Marshment, Jennifer.
JF2112.P8R68 2012 324.7'3–dc23
2011020377

ISBN: 978-0-415-57993-3 (hbk)
ISBN: 978-0-203-34990-8 (ebk)

Typeset in Bembo
by Taylor & Francis Books

Printed and bound in the USA by
Edwards Brothers, Inc, Lillington NC

This book is dedicated to my daughter Hazel Anna Greenaway

Contents

Figures

Tables

Contributors

Editor

Jennifer Lees-Marshment (University of Auckland, New Zealand) is a researcher in political marketing. Her books include *Political Marketing: Principles and Applications* (Routledge 2009), *Global Political Marketing* (Routledge 2010), *The Political Marketing Game* (Palgrave Macmillan 2011), and *Political Marketing in Canada* (UBC 2012). See www.lees-marshment.org for further details. Email j.lees-marshment@auckland.ac.nz.

Editorial board

Kenneth M. Cosgrove (Suffolk University, US) is Associate Professor of Government at Suffolk University in Boston, Massachusetts. He is the author of *Branded Conservatives* (Peter Lang 2007), which examined the way in which Republicans developed a branding strategy that included both the brand and the use of a marketing model to distribute it, and what resulted therefrom. His research interests centre on political marketing with a focus on branding in North American politics. His teaching interests centre on political marketing, the US Congress, US foreign policy in general, and specifically North American relations.

Nigel A. Jackson (Plymouth University, UK) is Reader in Persuasion and Communication at the Plymouth Business School, University of Plymouth. Dr Jackson has published widely on online political communication, political marketing and political public relations, including *The Marketing of Political Parties* (MUP 2006), *Politics: The Basics* (Routledge 2008) with Steve Tansey, and *Political Campaigning, Elections and the Internet* (Routledge 2011). Email: nigel.jackson@plymouth.ac.uk.

Alex Marland (Memorial University, Canada) researches and teaches political communications and Canadian politics. He was the lead editor with Thierry Giasson and Jennifer Lees-Marshment of *Political Marketing in Canada* (UBC 2012). He has also practised media relations and opinion research in the public, private and political sectors. See www.mun.ca/posc for further details.

Roger Mortimore (Ipsos Mori, UK) is Director of Political Analysis. He has worked for MORI since 1993, specialising in political polling. He has written numerous books and papers on British elections and political marketing. Since 2003 he has been Journals Review Editor of the *International Journal of Public Opinion Research*, and is also a member of the editorial boards of the *Journal of Elections, Public Opinion, and Parties* and the *Journal of Political Marketing*.

Robin T. Pettitt (Kingston, UK) is a researcher in comparative party politics. He specialises in the role of party members and the challenges and opportunities of intra-party democracy. For further details see www.robinpettitt.co.uk.

Claire Robinson (Massey University, New Zealand) is an Associate Professor of Communication Design, and Associate Pro Vice-Chancellor of the College of Creative Arts. Her research interests include political marketing and political communication, with specific emphasis on the visual communication of political messages. Claire is a regular writer and media commentator on political marketing, political advertising and political leadership in New Zealand.

Khariah Salwa-Mohktar (USM, Malaysia) works in the Political Science Section in the School of Distance Education and her areas of specialisation include public policy, new public management, political marketing and distance education, and she is currently working on ethnic-/religious-based political marketing. She has several book and journal publications and can be reached by email at khairiah@usm.my.

Jesper Strömbäck (Mid-Sweden University, Sweden) is Professor in Media and Communication and Ludvig Nordström Professor and Chair in Journalism at Mid-Sweden University. He has published more than 30 articles in journals such as *Political Communication, European Journal of Political Research* and *Journal of Political Marketing*. His books include *Political Public Relations: Principles and Applications* (Routledge 2011), *Global Political Marketing* (Routledge 2010), and *Handbook of Election News Coverage Around the World* (Routledge 2008).

Authors

Robert H. Binstock (Case Western Reserve University, US) is Professor of Aging, Health and Society. A former President of the Gerontological Society of America, he has served as director of a White House Task Force on Older Americans and frequently testified before the US Congress. Binstock is the author of over 300 articles, book chapters and monographs, most of them dealing with politics and policies related to aging. His 26 authored and edited books include seven editions of the *Handbook of Aging and the Social Sciences* (the latest in 2011). His Ph.D. is in political science from Harvard University.

Lisa Birch (Laval University, Québec City, Canada) completed her Ph.D. at Laval University in July 2010 with a thesis on the utilisation of public opinion research in Canadian tobacco control policy. She has recently published work on the use of focus groups in health policy, and forthcoming publications are regarding the utilisation of government-sponsored opinion research. She currently teaches at Champlain-St Lawrence College and collaborates with the Center for Public Policy Analysis (CAPP) at Laval University.

Alexander Braun (PSB Associates, Washington DC, US) is a vice-president at communications firm Penn Schoen Berland. He specialises in consulting on international political campaigns, primarily on issues of strategy and polling. His political clients span four continents and have included British and Czech prime ministers, Ukrainian and Philippines presidents, and numerous other heads of state, high-level candidates and media outlets. A former news reporter, he holds degrees from universities in New York, Budapest and Prague.

Michael John Burton (Ohio University, US) is an Associate Professor of Political Science. He teaches campaign management, public leadership and quantitative methods. With Daniel M. Shea, he has written *Campaign Craft: The Strategies, Tactics, and Art of Political Campaign Management* (fourth edition; Praeger 2010) and *Campaign Mode: Strategic Vision in Congressional Elections* (Rowman & Littlefield 2003). Dr Burton worked in the office of Vice-President Al Gore as special assistant to the chief of staff and assistant political director.

Robert Busby (Liverpool Hope University) researches on political populism and social aspects of political marketing. His interests centre on contemporary British and American politics. His recent publications include *Marketing the Populist Politician: The Demotic Democrat* (Palgrave 2009).

Brian M. Conley (Suffolk University, US) is an Assistant Professor in Government at Suffolk University in Boston, MA, USA. His principal research interests are in the areas of US electoral politics, political and public policy. He received his Ph.D. in political science from the New School for Social Research in New York City.

Kenneth M. Cosgrove (Suffolk University, US) See above under *Editorial Board*.

Scott Davidson (De Montfort University, UK) is Senior Lecturer in Public Relations and Media, building upon a professional career in public affairs and campaigns management – including for Age Concern England. He is the author of *Going Grey: The Mediation of Politics in an Ageing Society* (Ashgate 2012), and has also published on the impact of the internet on elections, and on how non-governmental organisations and bloggers network online to expose human rights abuses.

Anna Esselment (University of Waterloo, Canada) is an Assistant Professor in the Department of Political Science. She has published in the *Canadian Journal of Political Science* and *Canadian Public Administration*. Her research interests include the role of partisanship in intergovernmental relations, political professionals and partisan advisers, campaigns and elections, and Canadian institutions.

Paul Fawcett (University of Sydney, Australia) is a Lecturer in the Department of Government and International Relations. He has published in the areas of network governance theory, executive government, policy transfer, the use of branding in public policy, and political participation. Email: paul.fawcett@sydney.edu.au.

Émilie Foster (Université Laval, Canada) is a Ph.D. student at the Department of Information and Communication. She is a student researcher with the Research Lab on Political Communication (GRCP) and she is also a student member of the Centre for the Study of Democratic Citizenship. Émilie coordinates the activities of Political Marketing Canada network. Her research revolves around marketing practices by interest groups and political parties and the impacts of marketing on democracy. She has published several articles on the use of political marketing by interest groups. She can be contacted at emilie.foster@com.ulaval.ca.

Susan Harada (Carleton University, Canada) is an Associate Professor of Journalism and a former national Parliamentary Correspondent who has charted the progress of the Green Party of Canada since its breakthrough election in 2004. Her chapters about the Greens include 'Great expectations: the Green Party of Canada's 2006 campaign', in J.H. Pammett and C. Dornan (eds) *The Canadian Federal Election of 2006* (Dundurn Press 2006); and 'The promise of May: the Green Party of Canada's campaign 2008', in J.H. Pammett and C. Dornan (eds) *The Canadian Federal Election of 2008* (Dundurn Press 2009).

Raymond Hudon (Université Laval, Canada) teaches political science. His main research interests are in political sociology and in public policies, and are focused, in particular, on interest groups, lobbying and representation in democracies. In recent years his most important research projects have been coalitions, lobbies in the health sector and the development of private initiatives in the health system. He has published more than 100 articles, book chapters and books in these fields and on these subjects.

Nigel A. Jackson (University of Plymouth, UK) See above under *Editorial Board*.

Dennis W. Johnson (The George Washington University, US) is Professor of Political Management at the Graduate School of Political Management. His books include *No Place for Amateurs: How Political Consultants Are Reshaping American Democracy* (second edition; Routledge 2007) and *Campaigning in the Twenty-first Century* (Routledge 2011). He is editor of the *Routledge Handbook of Political Management* (2008) and *Campaigning for President 2008* (Routledge 2009). He served as a Fulbright Professor in China, 2010–11. For a decade he was a political consultant working for a variety of gubernatorial and senatorial candidates in the US.

Mathias König (Universität Koblenz-Landau, Campus Landau, Germany) is a researcher in the field of Governance, Communication and Society. He was a scientific consultant of the government in the German Federal *Land* of Rhineland-Palatinate to design Deliberative Governance Arenas (DGA) in a deliberative political marketing process. In 2011 he received an award for his theory of Deliberative Governance Arenas by the Foundation for the Rights of Future Generations (FRFG). FRGF is a think-tank on the interface of science, politics and the business world. Email: koenig-mathias@live.de.

Wolfgang König (Universität Koblenz-Landau, Campus Landau, Germany) is a researcher in the field of Governance, Communication and Society. His previous work includes being a scientific consultant of the government in the German Federal *Land* of Rhineland-Palatinate to design Deliberative Governance Arenas (DGA) in a deliberative political marketing process. He received an award for his theory of DGA by the Foundation for the Rights of Future Generations (FRFG) in 2011. FRGF is a think-tank on the interface of science, politics and the business world. Email: koenig-wolfgang@live.de.

Ruud Koole (Leiden University, the Netherlands) is Professor of Political Science/ Dutch Politics. His research and publications concentrate on Dutch political history and comparative political parties. In 2001–07 he was a practitioner as well (chair of a Dutch political party). With Professor Dr J. van Holsteyn he coordinates the Leiden Party Membership Project.

Roy Langmaid (Langmaid Practice, UK) is a consultant in the UK who worked for the company Promise, which advised the Blair Labour government in 2004–05. He now runs The Langmaid Practice – see the website www.langmaidpractice.com.

Jennifer Lees-Marshment (University of Auckland, New Zealand) See above under *Editor.*

Darren G. Lilleker (University of Bournemouth, UK) is Director of the Centre for Public Communication and Senior Lecturer in The Media School, Chair of the PSA Political Marketing Specialist Group and Convenor for political communication for the ECPR. Dr Lilleker has published widely on the professionalisation and marketisation of political communication including the textbook *Key Concepts in Political Communication* (Sage 2006) and *Political Campaigning, Elections and the Internet* (Routledge 2011), and has co-edited *The Marketing of Political Parties* (MUP 2006), *Voters or Consumers* (CSP 2008) and *Political Marketing in Comparative Perspective* (MUP 2005). Email: dlilleker@bournemouth.ac.uk.

Jenny Lloyd (University of the West of England, UK) is a Senior Lecturer in Marketing at the University of the West of England, in Bristol. Over the past 10 years she has researched and published extensively in the field of political branding, political communication and voter insight.

Alex Marland (Memorial University, Canada) See above under *Editorial Board.*

David Marsh (Australian National University, Australia) is Professor of Political Sociology in the School of Sociology at the Australian National University. He has published in the areas of public policy, political sociology and comparative politics. For his sins, he supports Bristol Rovers.

Stephen Mills (University of Sydney, Australia) is a lecturer in the Graduate School of Government, University of Sydney, and is undertaking doctoral research in the Department of Government and International Relations at that university. The research deals with campaign professionals within Australia's major parties. He is the author of *The New Machine Men* (Penguin 1986) and *The Hawke Years* (Viking 1993). See www.stephen-mills.com.au for further details.

Helen M. Morris (Carleton University, Canada) is Liaison Officer for the Canada-Europe Transatlantic Dialogue. Publications include 'Human rights and international organizations', in J. Hiden, V. Made and D.J. Smith (eds) *The 'Baltic Question' during the Cold War* (Routledge 2009); and 'The future non-citizens of the EU', in D.J. Smith (ed.) *Baltic States: New Europe or Old?* (Rodopi 2005).

François Pétry (Laval University, Québec City, Canada) is Professor in the Department of Political Science. His research and his teaching focus on public policy, polls and public opinion, and methodology. He is co-author of *Les sondages et la démocratie* (second edition; 2010) and of *Le guide pratique d'introduction à la régression en sciences sociales* (second edition; 2009). He is currently studying the role of public opinion research in health policy-making. See www.pol.ulaval.ca/?pid=234 for further details.

Robin T. Pettitt (Kingston University, London, UK) See above under *Editorial Board.*

Claire Robinson (Massey University, New Zealand) See above under *Editorial Board.*

Chris Rudd (University of Otago, New Zealand) is a Senior Lecturer in the Department of Politics at the University of Otago, New Zealand. His research interests include political communications in local and national politics.

Eva Johanna Schweitzer (Johannes Gutenberg-Universität, Germany) is a doctoral candidate in the Department of Communication at the University of Mainz, Germany. Her research interests include political communication and online communication. Recent work has appeared in the *European Journal of Communication*, *German Politics*, the *Encyclopedia of Political Communication* (Sage), and the *Sage Handbook of Public Opinion Research*. Email: eva.schweitzer@web.de.

Jesper Strömbäck (Mid-Sweden University, Sweden) See above under *Editorial Board*.

Jens Tenscher (University of Augsburg, Germany and University of Innsbruck, Austria) is a political scientist and communications scholar. He co-chairs the political communications section of the German Political Science Association. His books include *Campaigning in Europe – Campaigning for Europe* (Lit 2006), *100 Tage Schonfrist* (VS Publishers 2008) and *Superwahljahr 2009* (VS Publishers 2011). See www.tenscher.de for further details.

Peter N. Ubertaccio (The Martin Institute at Stonehill College, US) is Chair of the Political Science Department and Director of the Joseph W. Martin Institute for Law and Society. His specialities are the US presidency, US political history, Massachusetts state politics, and political parties. He is also a political blogger and public speaker on the state of US politics. See www.professorpolitics.com for more information.

Peter Van Aelst (University of Antwerp, Belgium) is Associate Professor of Political Science and founding member of the research group, Media, Movements and Politics (www.M2P.be). His research focuses on elections, campaigns and political communication. He coordinates a five-year research project on media and politics in comparative perspective at Leiden University, funded by the Dutch Research Council.

Joop van Holsteyn (Leiden University, The Netherlands) is Professor of Electoral Research. His principal research and publications are in the fields of elections and voting behaviour, direct democracy, party membership and the far right. See socialsciences.leiden.edu/politicalscience/organisation/faculty/holsteyn-dr-jjm-van.html#publications for a list of publications and further details.

Georg Winder (Austrian National Election Study, University of Innsbruck, Austria) is a pre-doc researcher in political communication and media studies. His main interests of research are political communication in election campaigns, media research and populism.

Stéphanie Yates (Université du Québec à Montréal, Canada) is an Assistant Professor at the Department of Social and Public Communication of UQAM. She specialises in lobbying, and studies the role of interest groups and citizens in state and market governance. As such, her current research focuses on participatory mechanisms, public acceptance processes and corporate social responsibility. For a summary of her main publications, see www.dcsp.uqam.ca/Profil/yates_stephanie.aspx.

1

Introduction

Political marketing in the 21st century

Jennifer Lees-Marshment

The *Routledge Handbook of Political Marketing* offers cutting-edge, fresh perspectives on how politicians, parties and governments can use political marketing to develop a more productive relationship with the public. Each chapter outlines a different topic, previous research in that area, presents new research, and then reflects on what works, the impact on politics and democracy and the way forward for research or practice. The chapters are written by leading and emerging scholars around the world, ensuring that the content is international in outlook. Aside from the worth of individual chapters, collectively this produces advice for practitioners, considerations for academics, and a sense not just of the field's progress to date but how it may develop in future. This provides a flagship work in the field that will not only be an accessible introduction to the field but will set the direction of research in the years to come.

The *Handbook* was guided by an editorial board whose role was to provide input such as suggestions for topics and authors, and to review submissions. They were selected because of particular expertise in a particular area of political marketing, to ensure a broad geographical spread, and their ability to provide constructive critique:

Dr Ken Cosgrove (Suffolk University, US)
Dr Nigel Jackson (Plymouth University, UK)
Dr Alex Marland (Memorial University, Canada)
Dr Roger Mortimore (Ipsos Mori, UK)
Dr Robin T. Pettitt (Kingston University, UK)
Dr Claire Robinson (Massey University, New Zealand)
Dr Khariah Salwa-Mohktar (USM, Malaysia)
Professor Jesper Strömbäck (Mid-Sweden University, Sweden)

Their expertise spans market research, branding, political parties, political communication, candidate electioneering, market orientation, journalism, e-marketing, public relations, political advertising and Asian political marketing. I would like to express my thanks to the board. Not only did they read and comment on the first draft of the chapters submitted for review, but their contribution to the framework for the book, the open call for contributions, and their suggestions of topics and authors contributed significantly to ensuring that the handbook was groundbreaking, rather than just a summary of previous research.

All chapters in this book went through three processes: submission of an initial outline, the first draft of the chapter in October 2010, and the second draft at the end of February 2011. Authors were both invited individually to submit an outline, and to respond to an open advertisement via Professor Phil Harris's mailing list and the Political Marketing Group. Initially over 30 chapters were invited to proceed to first draft, with the overall process resulting in 27 chapters. All chapters were required to follow the set structure, so that the sum of the book would be greater than the parts. I would like to record my thanks to authors for not only their hard work but the quality and originality of content, and their appropriate response to review comments.

I would also like to thank Routledge for the opportunity to edit this handbook, and for possessing a both practical and intellectual vision that now is the right time not just for a textbook such as *Political Marketing: Principles and Application*, but for a new handbook in political marketing.

The *Handbook* is divided into five sections (see Figure 1.1). Part I, on understanding the market, gathering ideas and debate, discusses a range of market research methods, including polling, focus groups, segmentation, voter selection and targeting, but also deliberation and co-creation; more importantly, how they are or could be used in politics. Part II, on product development, branding and strategy, explores market orientation, niche marketing and political branding. Part III, on internal marketing, considers relationship marketing and direct marketing to members and volunteers, marketing fundraising, and the role of party officials in political marketing. Part IV, on communicating and connecting with the public, explores changes in marketing over time, the branding and positioning of candidates, populism and marketing, political communication in elections, how leaders can interact with voters, political public relations, and short- and long-term online relationships. Part V, on government marketing – delivery,

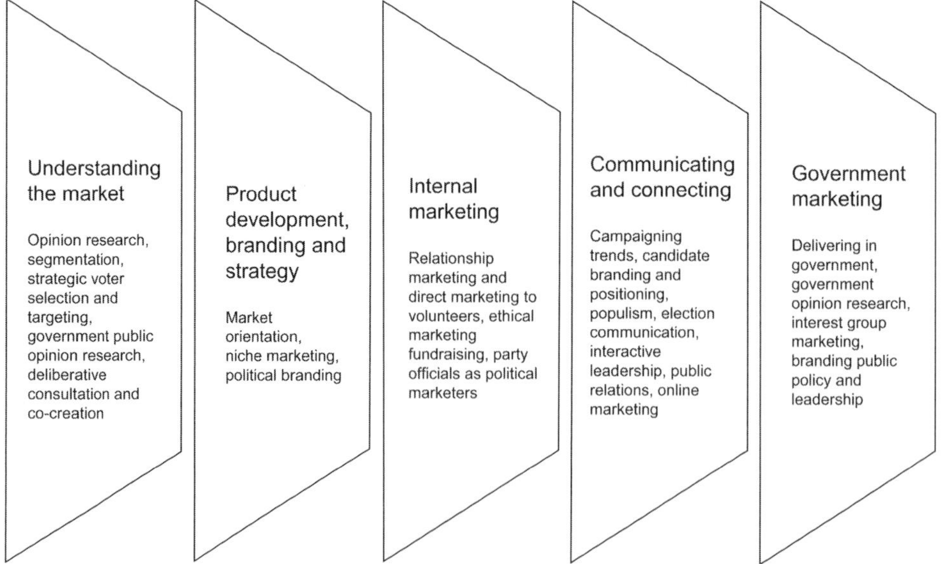

Figure 1.1 Topics in the *Routledge Handbook of Political Marketing*

policy and leadership, discusses delivering in government, how governments use public opinion research, the use of marketing by interest groups, branding public policy and making space for leadership. The concluding chapter sets out new directions in political marketing practice, discusses political marketing and democracy, and outlines future trends in political marketing research and practice.

Part I
Understanding the market, gathering ideas and debate

2

The role of opinion research in setting campaign strategy

Alexander Braun

The topic: opinion research-based strategy

Should our candidate focus on healthcare or on education in next week's televised debate? Campaigns have to consider and decide myriad such questions every day. This chapter is about how good campaigns find the right answer to that question.

While the question seems simple and straightforward, answering it immediately requires answering a host of other questions first. Should the candidate participate in the debate at all? How will the debate fit with what voters think about the candidate and with the image the candidate wants to project? Should the debate be used to explain the candidate's positions or to point out opponents' weaknesses?

There is no way a campaign can afford the time to start deliberating about each of these issues from scratch as they arise. Rather, campaigns rely on a number of assumptions and prior decisions that all stem from an overall strategy. All decisions in the campaign, from messaging to scheduling to resource allocation, should be based on a core strategy plan. Such a plan is simply the blueprint that lays out the route to victory for the campaign, but it can be successful only if it is based on good information, rather than assumptions. A campaign plan based on instinct and anecdotal evidence is likely to fail.

That's why research should play a crucial role in good campaigns. It minimizes guessing and provides answers necessary for campaigns to effectively create strategies and keep them on track. Research also raises the alert for possible risks and opportunities, and provides answers to questions where campaigns simply don't know or opinions differ. Good campaigns use the acquired knowledge to develop the right message that reaches the right target though the right vehicles. This chapter argues that voter research is an indispensible tool for creating an effective campaign strategy, and explains the different methods and approaches available and how they can be used most effectively in politics.

Previous research on opinion research-based strategy

Surprisingly, there is relatively little focused academic research on the use of market research in politics, although its normative impact on politics has been debated significantly (e.g. see Savigny

2008) and it increasingly plays an important role in political marketing models (for example Lees-Marshment 2001). One reason for that may be that polling is usually one of the most closely guarded secrets of campaigns and political parties, and as such is generally unavailable for closer academic scrutiny. There is non-political marketing literature on which we can draw, such as those who discuss polling in campaigns from the practical perspective (Stonecash 2008; Thurber and Nelson 1995), work on the methods and science of opinion research (see Fowler 2002; Schuman 2008), and insider accounts such as Gould (1998) and Morris (1995). One thing all this literature has in common is agreement on the importance and power of research. For example, Stonecash notes how without research,

> campaigns become guessing games. Campaign managers and supporters are reduced to speculating and arguing about what is important, but with little basis for assessing where the race stands, what issues are important, and what strategy they should follow to win a race. With information, a politician can formulate a plan.
>
> *(Stonecash 2008: 11)*

Research is used to create the strategy and campaign plan, and as Shea and Burton (2001: 100) note, 'polling has become the most efficient means by which campaigns come to understand the hearts and minds of voters'. This chapter will draw on some of this work, as well as practical experience, to provide an informed explanation of the different forms and uses of opinion research.

New research: explaining the utility of opinion research in strategy development

While research in campaigns is most useful to inform communications and understand who the voters are, its utility extends well beyond that and can be useful for virtually all aspects of campaigns.

Positioning

The most important part of every campaign strategy, and one where research is indispensible, is the central positioning of the candidate or party. Positioning is the core rationale that the candidate will use to convince voters to vote for him or her over opponents. Will the candidate run mainly on left- or right-wing ideology, on the concept of change, or on a specific policy issue like immigration? Or will the positioning focus on the candidate's personal ability to connect with voters or on their competency?

Knowing answers to these questions is critical, because while voters have views on most issues, they care meaningfully only about some fraction of them, and base their voting decisions on even fewer of them. Basing a positioning on a concept that voters agree with but don't find particularly relevant to their needs will result in a losing campaign. Similarly, a positioning that voters care about but don't find believable when delivered by a particular candidate will not result in success on election day. Constructing an effective positioning depends on the ability to gauge and quantify voters' basic attitudes, and to put them in the right context of the race and candidates.

Good voter polling does exactly that. One of the first areas on which voter research measurement focuses is people's general disposition and the most basic campaign communications archetypes. Do voters think that the country and economy are on the right or wrong track? Are they looking for a change or do they just prefer building on the current course of things? Are they looking for strong leaders or for candidates who easily connect with regular voters? These questions provide the broadest framework within which voters might think about the election.

The next area that positioning research covers is the political actors, whether they are individual candidates, current politicians, parties, other institutions, or all of the above. What, if anything, do voters already know and think about the candidate? How does that perception compare with that of the opponents? What attributes do voters associate with the candidate? Do they like the leader better than the party, or vice versa? These questions help to narrow down the possible options for positioning to those that are actually applicable to a given candidate.

The third area of research focus is the issues. With what are voters satisfied and with what are they dissatisfied? What issues do voters care about the most? Do they care more about a specific issue or about the state of politics in general? Do the candidate and opposition have a particular strength or weakness on some of these issues? These questions help with calibrating the actual content of the positioning.

It is important to keep in mind that positioning never exists in a vacuum. It will always be evaluated not only on its own but also in the competitive context of the race. This means that a candidate's positioning is not just his own, but is also measured against other candidates' positioning concepts, and also has to contend with voters' general lack of attention to politics. Joel Bradshaw nicely summarizes the characteristics a good positioning should have (Thurber and Nelson 1995: 43). It needs to be:

- clear, to be easy to communicate and understand;
- concise, to reach voters in the short time they might pay attention;
- compelling, to have a sense of emotional urgency;
- connected to voters to reflect their needs;
- credible, so that voters believe it; and
- contrasting, to establish difference among candidates.

Since campaigns face the fact that they have limited financial and human resources and limited time in which to appeal to voters, it is important that they only select one positioning and stick with it. Also, building a candidate's image in voters' minds is a hard task, but changing an existing one can be even harder. Popkin offers a great analysis of voters' psychology and why the first framing of an issue, candidate or race is so important: 'Narratives are more easily compiled and are retained longer than facts. Narratives, further, require more negative information before they change' (Popkin 1994: 78). That, of course, doesn't mean that the narratives or context of the race cannot change, especially if there is new compelling information. Popkin specifically highlights that personal information is more powerful in being able to change voters' views than new information about issues. However, trying to change a candidate's positioning halfway through the campaign is always a difficult task.

Messaging architecture

Although there should be just one positioning and that positioning should not change through the course of the campaign, candidates of course need to speak to a broad range of issues. Additionally, a positioning can rarely stand on its own and needs to be substantiated by specifics. Also, various target groups will require different levels of customization of communications, both in terms of issues and tone of messaging. A good communications strategy will, therefore, be based on a messaging architecture that prioritizes themes, messages and support points in a way that accentuates the candidate's positives and the opponents' negatives, while laddering up to the overall positioning.

What this means can be best illustrated on a message house, a diagram that is often used in corporate marketing for brand positioning of a product or service. On top, as a roof over everything, is the central positioning statement. It rests on themes, which give positioning more content and meaning. Themes, in turn, rest on 'pillars' of messages, which are concrete statements on a particular topic. Last, messages are backed by support points, which can be very specific pieces of information, figures or past events that validate the messages. (While there is general consensus on this theory, different authors might use the terms positioning, theme and messaging interchangeably.)

Thinking of messaging architecture this way is useful not only because it helps to structure communications, but also because it gives communication a hierarchy and context. While candidates will be forced to react to a host of specific issues, they should always strive to connect their communication to a concrete theme. This way their communication will not only reinforce the overall positioning, but will also put the discussed issue in a context that is favorable to the candidate, or at least help mitigate its potential negative impact.

The example in Figure 2.1 shows a schematic message house for the Czech Social Democrats (CSSD) in their 2008 gubernatorial campaign. CSSD was in opposition both on the national and on the regional level, having no governors in office. Its main opponent, ODS, led a national government and had 13 out of 14 governors. CSSD was in a tough position because its little-known candidates didn't have any strong issues in their favor and were running against very popular ODS incumbents. CSSD, therefore, made a strategic decision not to run individual regional campaigns, but rather to run on a central national positioning. The goal was to frame the election as an opportunity for voters to send a message to the central government that they disagreed with controversial new social policy reforms.

The positioning rested on roughly three themes: recently introduced healthcare fees that were very unpopular; an overall feeling of being left behind among large parts of the population; and an emphasis on the connection between governors and their national party. The theme of healthcare fees was actually so powerful that it needed support from only one simple message, and the media widely recognized the debate over health fees as a symbol of the election. The second and third themes were each supported by several messages, some of which were positive and some negative. Each message was backed by various support points.

Positioning	Making These Individual Elections a National Referendum on Government's Radical Policies				
Themes	Healthcare Fees	Ignored Voters' Needs		Connecting ODS Governors with National ODS	
Messages	Fees need to be abolished	Central govt cares about numbers, not people	CSSD will provide hope and social security	Governors condone their party's national policies	Need to put checks on ODS hegemony
Support Points and Figures					

Figure 2.1 Positioning of Czech Social Democrats in 2008 gubernatorial elections

Research was instrumental in developing this communications strategy. The campaign conducted multiple polls that clearly identified high job approval of local governors but low job approval of the national government and resentment toward the central government's reforms. Additionally, healthcare consistently topped the lists of most important issues and voters were especially riled up about the newly instituted fees. The strategy was developed based on these research findings and the campaign continued regular polling until the election day to stay on top of the situation and the campaign strategies of other parties, and to refine CSSD's messages and their tone. The success of this approach is evident from the final results: CSSD, which originally had no governors, won every single gubernatorial seat in the country, as well as 23 out of 27 Senate seats that were in play that year.

Understanding voters' makeup

No positioning can be successful if it tries to appeal to everyone. Campaigns have limited time and limited budgets with which to reach voters. Even if this were not the case, candidates could never be able to come up with a positioning that would both appeal to everyone and at the same time be compelling enough to move them. Rather, a positioning needs to be targeted only at a limited group of voters to achieve resource and message efficiency (Faucheux 2002: 141). Failing to sufficiently narrow down the campaign's audience will only result in money and resources being wasted on people who will not end up voting for the candidate, and will dissolve the strength of the campaign messaging.

The process of targeting begins with the relatively straightforward step of looking at the broadest universe possible, at all people living in the area where the race takes place. The next step is to remove from the consideration set those who are and will be ineligible to participate in the given election. For example, in Estonia all inhabitants of the country can vote in municipal elections but only those who have Estonian citizenship can vote in national elections. Since almost one-third of the population is Russian without an Estonian passport, parties appeal to substantially different audiences depending on the type of election. In the US, too, it is always important to keep in mind the differences between the general population and registered voters.

Next, the campaign needs to narrow down the audience to only likely voters. Turnout is one of the key variables in any campaign and always needs to be carefully accounted for in any strategy. Typically, only about half of registered voters vote in US presidential elections, and only about one-third in mid-term congressional elections. From the campaign perspective, it is irrelevant what the other half or two-thirds of registered voters think, since they will not show up on election day. An effective campaign will therefore only look at the opinions of the one-half or one-third of voters identified as likely to turn out. The only exception should be if the campaign believes it can successfully alter the turnout levels, either by increasing turnout among supporters or depressing turnout among supporters of other candidates.

Eventually, every good campaign will want to divide likely voters into three basic groups: current supporters, persuadable or 'swing' voters, and unreachable voters. Similar to the principles above, the campaign doesn't want to waste resources on those voters who will never vote for the party or candidate no matter what the campaign does or says. As long as there are enough voters in the base and persuadable groups to make victory possible, effective campaigns should focus their strategic communications on these two sets of voters. At this point, the campaign has narrowed down its target audience to maybe 20 percent of the overall population, which clearly makes campaigning easier, more efficient and more impactful.

Research is indispensible to the process of narrowing down the audiences and figuring out who they are. Even long-term incumbents can't be sure that the voters who elected them many times before have not changed their view of the candidate, come to prioritize different issues, taken a liking to a new contender, become discouraged from turning out, or simply thinned out in number until there are no longer enough of them. It is critical that campaigns always start with assessing the lay of the electoral land, and that they develop their strategies only after they understand who the key voter groups are and what their size is (see Figure 2.2). That knowledge will allow the campaign to develop targeted strategic tracks to keep base voters in its fold and increase turnout among them, and to persuade the largest possible share of swing voters to become supporters.

Besides measuring size and voting intensity, there are multiple ways in which research can describe the makeup of these voter blocs. First, target groups can be described through their geography. Are the base voters located in specific areas or they are spread more or less evenly? What share of persuadable voters live in large cities versus rural areas? Are there any favorable trends when looking at different habitat sizes in different regions?

Second, it is essential to get a reading of the demographic information of different voter groups. The most obvious and common are gender and age. Do supporters tend to be younger or older? Is there a gender gap? Are there differences when age and gender are combined so that, for example, research might discover great opportunities among middle-aged women? Depending on the race and country, other demographic criteria might be also important, such as income, education, ethnicity and race, marital status, children, occupation or religion.

Third, campaign research needs to go beyond the descriptors of what voters are and also know who they are by understanding their attitudes and beliefs. What are the most important issues among our base voters? What do swing voters think about a person who could possibly endorse the candidate? Where do voters stand on the question of cutting government spending

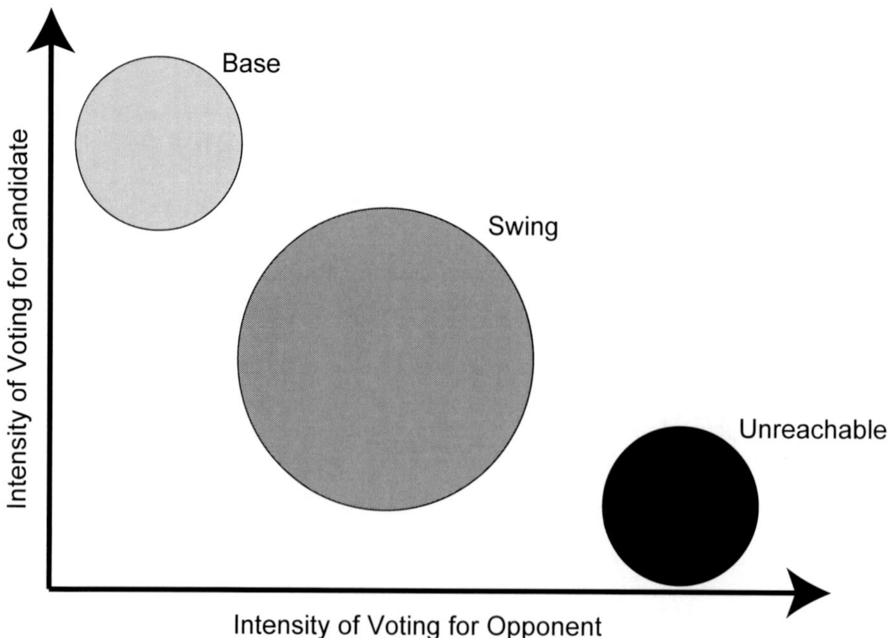

Figure 2.2 Example of basic voter division (unlikely voters already filtered out)

versus increasing taxes? Of course, it is critical that the campaign fully understands the views of the voting blocs of all the candidates and parties.

Fourth, it is very useful if the campaign can develop an understanding of the information sources and media consumption habits of voters. What percentage of current supporters is online? Where do swing voters get their political information? Which TV network do they consider most credible?

Fifth, it is helpful if campaigns take steps to understand the values and lifestyles of voting groups, sometimes referred to as psychographics. Regrettably, many campaigns do not pay sufficient attention to this step. Branding and corporate reputation campaigns have learned that understanding these 'softer' and seemingly unrelated attributes about customers (voters) can often uncover hidden commonalities and unmet needs that can play a huge role in motivating people's purchase intent (voting behavior). Is a significant segment of swing voters afraid to walk outside after dark? How happy are they in their current careers?

For example, research conducted by Mark Penn for Bill Clinton in the run-up to the 1996 elections found that values were a more powerful predictor of voting behavior than most demographics. Clinton therefore shifted his focus from more traditional pocketbook issues to questions of school discipline, tobacco advertising and TV violence. Famously, the president was also urged into taking an outdoorsy vacation in Jackson Hole, Wyoming, to reconnect with swing voters whose favorite pastime, polling showed, was camping (Morris 1999: 212–38). The background for these strategy moves was based on a large 'neuropersonality' poll, which included a number of lifestyle and behavior-related questions, as well as a modified Meyers-Briggs classification module designed to measure psychological preferences in how people perceive the world and make decisions.

In another race, Mark Penn's company conducted a unique micro-targeting project for Michael Bloomberg's election campaign for mayor of New York City in 2001. Since Bloomberg, who was running as a Republican, needed to overcome the fact that 70 percent of registered voters in the city were Democrats, he targeted them based on a combination of demographics, party affiliation and established attitudes and needs. This resulted in often counterintuitive but powerful findings where, for example, older, affluent Jewish males on Wall Street and younger, low-socio-economic status, Hispanic waitresses shared concerns on the effects of terrorism on their business and income. The campaign therefore sent these seemingly widely different groups similar communications on Bloomberg's security plan.

The more detail that campaigns have about their voters, the more targeted and more effective their communications can be. Since the possible combinations could be endless, researchers sometimes apply various statistical tools such as cluster or factor analysis to identify the more pertinent trends and groups. The electorate might eventually be divided into several segments based on combined information sources such as demographics, lifestyles and stance on select issues, allowing campaigns to better prioritize and develop more individualized communications. That said, campaigns must not fail to see the forest for the trees, and must always understand where segment groups fall on the crucial base/swing/unreachable spectrum (while statistical exercises will usually produce groups that overlap, in practice campaigns will mostly need to decide whether a particular group is 'base', 'swing' or 'unreachable' – see Figure 2.3).

The ability to target voters through smaller groups allows a campaign to have better reach and impact with its communication. At the same time, the law of diminishing returns applies here. In most cases, the crucial distinctions are in basic demographic or geographic information. While detailed slicing and dicing of the electorate can sometimes detect a very important trend, the findings also need to be applicable to large enough groups to be actionable and make a difference.

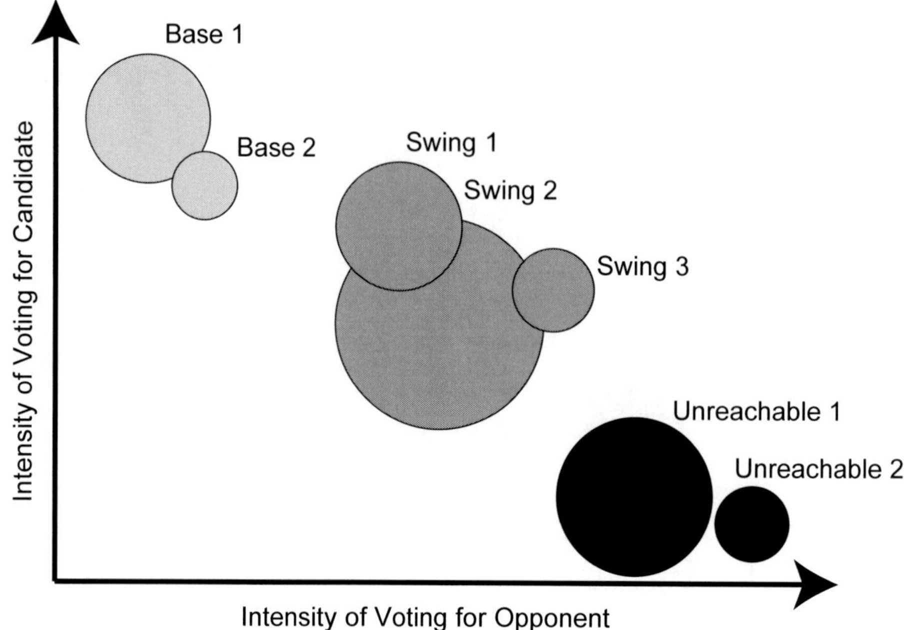

Figure 2.3 Example of voter segmentation

Timing and delivery

While the overall positioning should not change as long as the fundamentals of the race stay consistent, communications and tactics will inevitably evolve throughout any campaign. The dynamic nature of campaigns requires that candidates constantly update their information and adjust their 'lower-level' communication strategies and tactics depending on the changing situation. Besides just being reactive, campaigns also want to actively shape the race and therefore need to have a plan for sequencing and timing their communications.

Once again, research can be very helpful for all this. Let's say a candidate is accused by an opponent of accepting a campaign contribution from a businessman of questionable reputation. Besides a rapid-response reaction, the campaign needs to assess relevance and longer-term impact of the attack and decide on the best answer to the accusation. It might be that voters don't know or care about the issue and that overreacting to the charge would be harmful, but it could also be that unless the issue is cleared up, the charge will lower turnout intent among the base voters and therefore the campaign must do all it can to address the issue. Knowing which is the case is clearly critical for the campaign, and only research can provide a definitive answer. Research can also indicate how different voter groups react to different possible responses to the charge.

Conversely, if the candidate gains information, for example, about tax evasion by one of his or her opponents, research can help with the strategic use of this information. Will voters react negatively to hearing such accusations? Does the candidate with the information have sufficient credibility to level the charge? Is it in the candidate's strategic interest to attack that particular opponent? Or might it shift the focus of the campaign away from a topic that is more favorable to the candidate?

Research allows campaigns to understand the impact of new developments, to test different attacks and possible answers, and to game out scenarios. Rather than making missteps, campaigns can test different approaches and their effects in the microcosm of voter research before taking the steps in the real world. This extends beyond crisis communications. For example, it can include testing different executions of advertising: rather than spending huge sums of money on advertising that doesn't work, it is wise for a campaign to test the advertisements first on focus groups to determine their effectiveness.

Types of research

Campaign research can take many forms. Each form's usefulness depends on the current needs of a campaign and how much time is left before election day. Selecting a particular type of research should never be a mechanical process, and should always be done based on what best advances the campaign goals at that moment. For example, a candidate considering a run for office clearly has different research needs than a candidate running neck-and-neck with two other opponents a few weeks before polling sites open.

Before discussing individual methodologies, it should be noted that there are two strategic dimensions to any opinion research. First, research is almost always descriptive, meaning that it provides a current picture of the political landscape. This is valuable for campaigns because it tells them what the current horse race is, explains who supporters are, who are undecided voters, what are the most important issues, etc. Often, campaigns are satisfied with just this dimension, because it supplies them with the crucial pieces of information that campaigns need to develop their strategy or keep it on track.

However, research can go further and have also a predictive (some might even say prescriptive) dimension. What that means is that campaigns can use research not only to describe the current situation and be left to interpret it, but also to directly inform them about how best to move in order to gain advantage. This can include message and slogan testing, gaming out different scenarios, and testing for the most effective responses to attacks or for voters' reactions to changes in communications.

Besides these two strategic dimensions, research is usually classified into two basic methodological approaches: quantitative and qualitative. As the names indicate, the former deals with numbers and measurements and the latter strives to shed light on the meaning and context of issues. While there have been attempts to combine the two approaches (for example, I used a hybrid approach during the British Labour Party's 2005 election campaign), the two methodologies generally remain distinct from each other. Campaigns must understand the power and limitations of both methodologies in order to be able to fully harness the utility of each.

Qualitative research

The most common type of qualitative research by far is focus groups. These are controlled discussions of usually 8–12 participants selected to either encompass a wide demographic profile of voters or, conversely, to consist of only participants who fit certain criteria, such as undecided female voters or voters from swing districts. The discussions are guided by a moderator who loosely follows a script designed to elicit a broad range of opinions, reactions, emotions and associations on given topics. The discussions are recorded for analytic purposes and often are observed by consultants or candidates from behind a one-way mirror.

Other types of qualitative research include dial groups, in which participants turn a knob to indicate their current satisfaction with a speech or advertisement they are watching. Campaigns also sometimes opt for 'jury groups', which resemble court trials with two sides arguing over an issue and a jury deciding which argument was stronger. Rarely, campaigns might also employ one-on-one, in-depth interviews, although this is usually only reserved for elite interviews rather than 'average voter' interviews. Such qualitative exercises can be great in understanding language and arguments that voters might use on particularly contentious problems. Additionally, as online penetration grows, campaigns increasingly turn towards various online chats as an easier and cheaper way of conducting qualitative research.

Qualitative research is an often misunderstood and sometimes overrated approach when it comes to developing strategies. It can be powerful in some situations and ineffective or downright misleading in others. Therefore, it is important to recognize both what this type of research can do and what it can't do.

First, qualitative research is very useful in situations when campaigns simply don't know what to do or are looking for a completely new and untried approach. Because of its open-ended nature, campaigns can explore new hypotheses at a level of depth and nuance that would be harder to achieve in a quantitative survey, understand and probe around the context of issues, and uncover both hidden obstacles and new ideas. This is why focus groups are mostly used in the beginning of the campaign and when radical new developments arise.

Second, qualitative research is great to comprehensively understand the language and terminology used by various voter groups, as opposed to campaign professionals or other elites. Being able to understand the issues through the words of voters allows for better and more accessible communication that takes the proper tone. Third, qualitative research offers the opportunity to game out scenarios based on a number of positions that could be taken by different sides in a race, allowing the campaign to drill down to the most salient arguments. Besides suggesting which way an argument can go, it provides the crucial insight into why voters might react in a certain way.

The fourth and fifth most important benefits are less immediately tangible. Qualitative research can help narrow down lists of options that might be too large, and thus generate and refine content for quantitative research. Additionally, since candidates and consultants tend to live in a bubble of self-enforcing views and opinions, being able to observe focus groups is often a great way for the campaign leadership to start thinking differently and get back in touch with voters.

At the same time, qualitative research has severe limitations. First and foremost, it is not representative of a population as a whole, and campaigns must resist the urge to draw major conclusions based only on several focus groups. Even if large numbers of focus groups are conducted across multiple demographics and geographies, they still remain just discussions of several small groups of people, which never reach the size of a moderately large poll and 'are only slightly more reliable than anecdotes' (Greenberg 2009: 13). They provide insights, flavor and ideas for testing, but not a measurement of the situation or decision-grade data.

Additionally, focus groups often suffer from 'groupthink', a phenomenon where people adjust their statements to align with those of the majority of the group or with the loudest participants. In the real world, where voters don't have to publicly discuss their ideas, those participants might not change their positions and their opinions. It is therefore important to keep in mind that the conclusions of the group might be unreflective not only of the overall population but also even of the participants sitting in the room. To that point, both Warren and Asher describe how opinions in focus groups often spiral out and end up being more negative than in reality (Asher 2004: 132; Warren 2003: 207).

Quantitative research

While campaigns might decide not to employ qualitative research without necessarily putting themselves at a dire disadvantage, no responsible campaign manager could do without quantitative voter research, or polling. 'Today's politicians live and die by polls' (Warren 2003: 195), and being able to quantitatively measure voters' moods is critical for any campaign's strategy.

Typically, the first poll that campaigns conduct is also the largest and most important one. The benchmark poll is a comprehensive survey in which many questions are asked of a large group of respondents sampled to be representative of the overall electorate. It covers a lot: it describes the makeup of the electorate, gauges voters' attitudes toward candidates and issues, tests possible messaging and positioning, and allows for examination of the results by various demographic and other groups. The results are usually presented to the campaign leadership in great detail, and the information gleaned from the benchmark is used for nothing less than developing the overall strategic plan of the campaign, its positioning, targeting and framework for communications.

An important thing to realize about either type of opinion research – qualitative or quantitative – is that it provides a snapshot of voters' minds at a particular time. Since voters' perceptions change and react to new developments, campaigns need to regularly update their research information, which is why they conduct multiple polls throughout the campaign.

After the benchmark poll, subsequent polls are generally designed to contain two parts. One part keeps re-testing the key metrics, such as the candidate horse race and favorability ratings, to track and measure any movement that has taken place over the course of the campaign. The second part contains new questions that the campaign wants answered, whether on past events or possible future changes. These questions allow campaigns to anticipate emerging key issues and enable them to develop messages that address these issues as effectively as possible.

Whereas campaigns might conduct these issue polls once every month or two, many campaigns decide to do daily or weekly tracking on the most important questions in the last weeks of the campaign. As campaign professionals know, the period shortly before election day is often marked by increased shifts among the electorate, as campaign communications reach maximum volume and undecided voters start making up their minds. Being able to keep up with the volatile electorate in the last days of the campaign, and adjust strategy accordingly, can mean the difference between success and failure. These tracking polls typically have only a few questions and use rolling averages to keep the base size statistically viable.

Additionally, campaigns can commission message-testing polls that focus specifically on refining communications. These measure the appeal and believability of different themes and messages from both the candidate and his or her opponents. Often, these polls employ split-sampling, a method in which matched halves or thirds of respondents are exposed to different messages or stimuli, and answers are compared and evaluated. The analysis can consist of simple rankings of aggregate responses on individual questions, but can also include creating scores that rate messages on multiple metrics or higher-level statistical analysis where responses are correlated to key metrics to reveal true derived, rather than stated, effectiveness.

Flash polls are quick, often overnight surveys used to provide an immediate read of the impact that major or unexpected news has had on the campaign. With the advent of online polling, campaigns also increasingly use quantitative research to test advertising. Typically, advertisement testing surveys use a pre/post method in which they benchmark voters' basic attitudes, show the execution and get top-of-mind reaction to it, and then re-test the initial key questions to measure shifts. In this way, advertisements are not only evaluated for likeability but, more importantly, for their effect on voting intention. Online testing allows for many new possibilities, such as respondents highlighting the most compelling parts of messaging or advertising, which was previously only possible through unrepresentative qualitative research.

As powerful as polling is, it of course also has its limits and campaigns are wise to keep them in mind. Just like in qualitative research, responses can become biased if the questionnaire doesn't have good structure or if questions are not worded neutrally. While in qualitative research a good moderator can try to fix issues with poorly worded questions or interview flow, no such recourse is possible in fully structured quantitative interviews. The axiom of 'garbage in, garbage out' holds true in polling more than anywhere else.

The basic principle of polling rests on the fact that if a randomly selected sample of voters is interviewed, those voters will have proportionately the same characteristics and opinions as the whole universe from which they were chosen. Yet there is, of course, a host of very important caveats. There is always a margin of error, which grows as the sample gets smaller, and the principle of sample representativeness works only if the selection is truly random. A number of other possible problems exist that are beyond the scope of this chapter (see, for example, Schuman 2008; Fowler 2002). Nevertheless, as long as a poll is conducted by a reputable pollster, the sample size stays above a certain level (often a minimum of 400 respondents is considered to be statistically reliable) and the sample composition fits major demographic and geographic parameters (through quotas or weighting), polling yields surprisingly precise results.

Advice for practitioners

Voter research is a powerful tool but it is important to keep in mind that it is not a panacea that guarantees victory. Polls are just a tool that can empower campaigns, and if they are not conducted well or if erroneous conclusions are drawn from the results, they can actually mislead. Good polls should never just end up as mountains of data, but must provide a clear picture and actionable conclusions. Research that doesn't advance the campaign strategy is just a waste of money. Nevertheless, good research is the best method that campaigns have to get the necessary information for a victorious strategy.

In general, no campaign should start without a benchmark understanding of who the voters are and what they think; their perceptions of candidates, institutions and issues; the hierarchy of their pain points; and how this all translates into their voting decisions. A good campaign will continue to update this knowledge through continued voter research until the election day and will develop its messaging and targeting based on research. Even when campaigns have a clear plan, there will be situations when they don't know how to proceed or unexpected situations arise, and research is very useful in such situations. Overall, campaigns can use research to develop or update positioning and messaging, timing, sequencing, intensity and the means of their communications.

The impact on politics

There is no doubt that research-driven campaigns are becoming more prevalent and that they have an impact on politics. While it is clear that 'polling has become the cornerstone of new-style electioneering' (Shea and Burton 2001: 100), this type of campaigning is also sometimes criticized for reducing the focus to only a narrow set of issues and small groups of swing voters, or for encouraging politicians to follow the moods of the public as opposed to lead them (see Savigny 2008). Although these issues are certainly worth a deep and continuous academic debate, a lot of the criticism is also misinformed and misplaced.

While research is a powerful campaign tool, it is always up to the individual politicians how they use it. The reality is that in most cases politicians don't change their policies based on research but rather change the way in which they talk about the policies. Their communication can't also just be simply aimed at a narrow group of swing voters, but needs to balance enough appeal to the base not to alienate them and not to mobilize the opposition. Additionally, as market-oriented parties become more commonplace, they also need to be able to keep delivering on their promises rather than just focus on short-term gains (see Lees-Marshment 2001: 223).

The fact that research informs politicians about what people think might carry some negative connotations, but is overall a positive and democratic benefit. Politicians in democracies should listen to the people and represent their voters. The central question shouldn't be about research but about how modern politicians find the right balance between principled leadership and understanding people's needs. The good news is that in democracies, the politicians and the whole system have to undergo regular tests in the form of elections in which voters are the ultimate judges.

The way forward: the future of research-based strategy

Clearly, research helps to make better campaigns and there should be little doubt that modern campaigns will use more rather than less research. As more campaigns employ research to inform their strategies, the pressure to use ever more opinion research to stay competitive increases for all campaigns. Having advised campaigns on four continents, I have seen that research-based strategies have an edge over other methods regardless of the region, culture or situation, and that every year the amount of campaign research worldwide seems to increase.

As such, it is important that politicians and candidates become more informed about the strengths and weaknesses of voter research and understand how to conduct it properly. On the academic side, there is a lot of room for further investigation of the impact that research-based campaigns have both on political practice and on voter behavior. A more detailed academic analysis of how research-based strategies are actually used in reality would provide a more informed debate, one that isn't merely based on outside critiques, and one that would benefit academics and practitioners alike.

Bibliography

Asher, H. (2004) *Polling and the Public. What Every Citizen Should Know*, 6th edn, Washington DC: CQ Press.

Faucheux, R.A. (2002) *Running for Office. The Strategies, Techniques and Messages Modern Political Candidates Need to Win Elections*, New York: M. Evans & Company.

Fowler, F.J., Jr (2002) *Survey Research Methods*, 3rd edn, Thousand Oaks: Sage Publications.

Gould, P. (1998) *The Unfinished Revolution: How the Modernisers Saved the Labour Party*, London: Little, Brown and Co.

Greenberg, S.B. (2009) *Dispatches from the War Room: In the Trenches with Five Extraordinary Leaders*, New York: St Martin's Press.

Lees-Marshment, J. (2001) *Political Marketing and British Political Parties: The Party's just Begun*, Manchester and New York: Manchester University Press.

Morris, D. (1999) *Behind the Oval Office*, Los Angeles: Renaissance Books.

Popkin, S.L. (1994) *The Reasoning Voter. Communication and Persuasion in Presidential Campaigns*, 2nd edn, Chicago and London: The University of Chicago Press.

Savigny, H. (2008) *The Problem of Political Marketing*, New York: Continuum International Publishing Group.

Schuman, H. (2008) *Method and Meaning in Polls and Surveys*, Cambridge, MA: Harvard University Press.

Shea, D.M. and Burton, M.J. (2001) *Campaign Craft: The Strategies, Tactics, and Art of Political Campaign Management*, Westport, CT: Praeger Publishers.

Stonecash, J. M. (2008) *Political Polling: Strategic Information in Campaigns*, 2nd edn, Lanham, MD: Rowman and Littlefield Publishers.

Thurber, J.E. and Nelson, C.J. (eds) (1995) *Campaigns and Elections American Style*, Boulder, CO: Westview Press.

Warren, K.F. (2003) *In Defense of Public Opinion Polling*, Boulder, CO: Westview Press.

3

Political marketing and segmentation in aging democracies

Scott Davidson and Robert H. Binstock

The topic: segmentation

Developed countries throughout the world are experiencing population aging characterized by unprecedented national proportions of older persons (see Table 3.1). This phenomenon has brought to the fore various policy reforms regarding benefits for older persons that have long been provided by established old-age welfare states (see Kohli and Arza 2010). It has also increasingly brought the attention of politicians to strategies for marketing themselves to older voters in the context of both policy decisions and election campaigns.

This chapter focuses on political marketing in aging democracies in the contexts of what we know about older voters and campaigns to attract them, in the context of the special emphasis on segmentation within political marketing theory. It begins with a brief exposition regarding segmentation in political marketing and an assessment of the strengths and weaknesses of the 'senior power' model of voting. It then reviews the recent research literature on segmentation and marketing, with attention to issues related to older age groups. Next, it presents case studies of segmenting and marketing to older voters in the US and Britain. There follows a discussion of the importance of attention to life stages, the life cycle, and concomitant values in marketing to older populations. Three final sections suggest: first, some implications of this chapter for practitioners; second, the impact on politics in general of efforts to market to senior voters; and third, future considerations for those who segment and market politically to older voters.

Previous research on segmentation

Parties and candidates segment the electorate – the process of defining and targeting identified sub-sections of voters – in their search for competitive advantages over their opponents. Segmentation allows a more efficient allocation of communication resources and is an increasingly sophisticated dimension to the most basic of campaign objectives – the need to identify target audiences and then get them out to vote. As such segmentation represents a key element in the wider adoption of strategic communications and marketing in the campaigns and elections process, the incorporation of these principles has been recorded and theorized widely (Kavanagh 1995; Baines 1999; Newman 1999; Smith and Hirst 2001; Wring 2005).

Table 3.1 Percentage of the population aged 65+ in 2009 and 2030

	2009	*2030*
Germany	20.4	27.9
Italy	20.1	26.4
Japan	22.7	31.8
US	12.9	19.3

Source: Vienna Institute of Demography 2010.

Increasingly, campaigns bypass first-order segmentation such as gender and class and concentrate on second-order variables such as media habits or lifestyle choices (Butler and Harris 2009). While there may be many different approaches to segmenting a market, Bannon (2004) identified two overarching approaches. First, *a priori*, which in this context is the utilization of prior political intelligence, such as the knowledge that seniors are more likely to vote than younger voters. This historical intelligence is then combined with cluster analysis techniques that search for common traits such as behavior or attitudes that are shared by sub-groups, but may cut across more general demographic categorizations. Within these processes Bannon then identified four common methods for identifying sub-segments of the electorate:

- Geographic: Voters with similar characteristics tend to congregate in the same geographic location.
- Demographic: Age, gender and family status are all variables that could indicate potential political preferences.
- Behavioral: Grouping voters based on their actual actions, such as the benefits they may seek from a government.
- Psychographic: The development of segments through combining data on lifestyle choices such as leisure pursuits, media habits, etc., with social attitudes and dispositions towards candidates and parties.

Mattinson has described how in 2009 the British Labour Party adopted a segmentation process that began first with identifying voters who were most likely to swing to or from the party, and then analyzed the demographics, attitudes and lifestyles of these voters to ascertain who were the 'winnable' or most 'persuadable' segments (Mattinson 2010: 16). In the US the parties are combing their proprietary information in combination with consumer or demographic data from companies such as Experian or Claritas to refine their segments into smaller units for micro-targeting (Johnson 2011).

These trends have raised a number of concerns that segmented groups of voters achieve a privileged status within the political process at the expense of politics representing the public as a whole. Savigny (2005) argues that segmentation elevates the potential of a minority of voters to disproportionately influence political actors, and that this process takes place through research instruments such as focus groups rather than through open public engagement. Lilleker (2005) has described this process as creating a division between those to whom politics belongs, and those it has abandoned, and can be responsible for alienating voters, including those who once considered themselves partisan loyalists.

Demographic trends in combination with the increasing use of segmentation have influenced the tone and direction of debate on the impact of the growing number of older voters. Implicit in concerns about 'the gray peril' is a 'senior power' model for interpreting the politics of aging. The model rests on the assumption – influenced by traditional economic theory – that older persons are likely to vote to preserve or enhance their material self-interests. The model also assumes: that older people constitute a numerically important proportion of the electorate; that all or most of them perceive their stakes in old-age benefits similarly (regardless of their diverse economic and social situations); and that because of material self-interest older people are homogeneous in political attitudes and voting behavior and will thereby clash sharply with younger age groups in the electoral process. The senior power model also includes the notion that interest groups that purport to represent older people are influential forces that can 'swing' the votes of older persons and thereby 'intimidate' politicians (for example, see Pratt 1976).

Various analysts use different age ranges when defining *older voters*. US analysts customarily use those aged 65 and older because 66 is the age at which individuals become eligible for full retirement benefits under social security and 65 the age for getting Medicare, the national health insurance program for older people. In contrast, many European analysts include persons aged in their 50s. This is justified on several grounds. First, people in their 50s start to personally experience the many manifestations of age discrimination in society, most critically in employment. Moreover, persons aged 55 and older have reached a stage in their life courses where they have to consider retirement and 'old-age' as issues requiring practical, sometimes urgent, personal attention. In addition, the family structure of many in their late 50s and early 60s is likely to include parents who are in their 70s or 80s, heightening awareness among the former regarding issues involving the quality of health and social care provision for those in later life.

Regardless of which age categories are used, many of the senior power model's assumptions regarding older voters are contradicted by the following facts and observations: Although older persons participate in elections at a higher rate than younger voters, they are not necessarily the largest age group in the electorate. In the 2008 US presidential election, for example, Americans aged 45–64 cast 38 percent of the vote and those aged 25–44 accounted for 36 percent, compared with only 16 percent by people aged 65 and older (Campbell and Binstock 2011). Despite election campaign efforts to target older voters with 'senior issues' and 'senior desks,' old-age benefit issues do not seem to have much impact on their electoral choices; as shown in Figure 3.1,

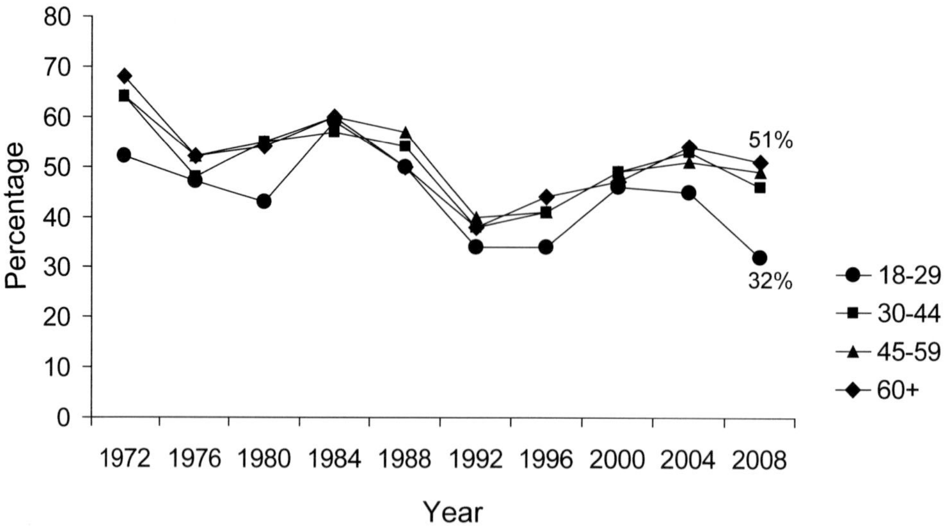

Figure 3.1 Percent voting for Republican US presidential candidates, by age groups, 1972–2008

in the last 10 US presidential elections, all age groups except the youngest (aged 18–29) distributed their votes among candidates in roughly the same proportions.

Old age is only one of many personal characteristics of older people with which they may identify themselves; there is little reason to expect that a birth cohort – diverse in economic and social status, labor force participation, gender, race, ethnicity, religion, education, health status, family status, residential locale, political party attachments and every other characteristic in society – would suddenly become homogenized in self-interests and political behavior when it reaches the old-age category.

Candidates are on the ballot, not old-age benefit policies; candidates usually identify themselves with their political parties, as well as a broad range of issue positions of which old-age benefits may be only one of many. Older voters, like all voters, respond to a variety of candidate traits, such as their personalities, appearances, career backgrounds, performances and even religions, ethnicity and race. In the 2008 US presidential election, for instance, all age groups of whites aged 30 and older voted heavily in favor of John McCain over Barack Obama, in contrast with African-Americans and Hispanics (Binstock 2009). For fuller discussions and documentation of these and related matters involving the voting behavior of older persons, see Campbell and Binstock (2011).

Nonetheless, for several reasons the image of older persons as bloc voters swayed by 'senior issues' persists. First, it helps journalists to reduce the intricate complexities of politics. Second, and more important, politicians share the widespread perception that there is a huge, monolithic senior citizen army of voters (Peterson and Somit 1994). This perception is reinforced by the fact that a great many older citizens are active in making their views known to members of their legislatures, especially when proposals arise for cutting back old-age benefits (Campbell 2003). Hence, politicians are wary of 'waking a sleeping giant' of angry older voters. They strive to position themselves in a fashion that they think will appeal to the self-interests of older voters, and usually take care that their opponents do not gain an advantage in this arena. So even though older persons do not vote as a bloc, they do have an impact on election campaign strategies and often lead incumbents to be concerned about how their actions in the governing process, such as votes in Congress, can be portrayed to older voters in subsequent re-election campaigns. Third, the image of a senior voting bloc is marketed by the leaders of old age-based interest groups. These organizations have a strong incentive to inflate perceptions of the voting power of the constituency for which they purport to speak.

Yet, as Walker concluded in summarizing an overview of political participation and representation of older people in European nations, '[old] age per se is not a sound basis for political mobilization' (Walker 1999: 7). Similarly, regarding US politics, Heclo concluded, 'The elderly is really a category created by policy analysts, pension officials, and mechanical models of interest group politics' (Heclo 1988: 393).

New research

The quality of the segmentation process will be a key determinant in deciding which campaigns successfully build bonds of trust with the aging electorate. With seniors aged in their 50s and older likely to count for approaching, or even exceeding half of turnout in many contests, a campaign plan that groups together all older voters into one segment is unsophisticated in the extreme and likely to fail.

The process of segmentation will require parties to adopt a process of ongoing adjustments of their positioning in order to maximize the benefits of their own perceived strengths as well as the weaknesses of their opponents. In practical terms, this requires brand adjustments and, informed by market research, the selection of issues, images, language and policies to foreground in their campaigning.

The aging electorates of the 21st century will see the continuation of social trends that began in the previous century, which have combined to increase the levels of voter volatility. Citizens across all age groups are increasingly disloyal to political brands (Dalton 2002) and more likely to switch their preferences across first- and second-order elections (Carrubba and Timpone 2005). This decline in partisan allegiances means that campaign managers cannot make the kind of firm assumptions of voter support based on first-order variables such as class or ethnicity that were common in the middle of the 20th century. A further challenge to strategists will be presented by building the capacity to research and understand senior voters as a sub-group of the electorate because senior cohorts will change profoundly from one general election to the next. As Butler and Stokes famously noted in 1969, every year millions of voters die and leave the electorate, millions join the ranks of the retired and millions enter the electorate for the first time. The electorate as a whole changes every five years, as does the composition of senior voters, as cohorts join and slowly leave this category. As such, generational replacement can be argued as a key variable behind social political changes in the electoral market (Hooghe 2004).

The following are examples of where governmental and commercial organizations have deployed research in order to develop segmentation categories of older people.

In research commissioned by the UK Central Office of Information (Darnton 2005), to assist in the refinement of their communication with older people, social and market research knowledge was synthesized to produce a list of key life stages or events that are highly relevant to the segmentation process. These are listed in Table 3.2.

Snyder (2002) argues that attitudes and opinions will constantly change during a voter's lifetime, but that values developed over time through accumulated personal experience and confirmed in interactions with peers and family members are less likely to change and act as guiding rules for living and decision-making, and form the basis of personal identity. Snyder's value-based segmentation research breaks older voters into eight value 'portraits':

- True-blue Believers: good health, fun, faith.
- Hearth and Homemaker: good health, relationships, active in community.
- Fiscal Conservative: worried about financial security and health.
- Intense Individualists: possessions, travel, independence.
- Active Achievers: active, online, intellectual.
- Liberal Loners: healthy, lower income, value social equality.
- In-Charge Intellectuals: intellectual, affluent, physically active.
- Woeful Worriers: lower income, financial security worries, family.

Table 3.2 Life stages

Life stage/event	*Short description*
Finishing work	planned retirement seen as a gain, but a loss when forced through redundancy
Bereavement	a shock to couples can entail loss of support and identity
Giving up driving	considered a major loss of independence
Experiencing crime	instils fear and reduces social activity
Experiencing ill health	reduced mobility: spending more time in the home
Giving up home	widely differing experiences: some feel loss of independence, others benefit from support

The Understanding Fifties and Over (UFO) project in 2004 was a collaboration between media agency OMD and businesses such as the *Daily Telegraph* newspaper and Peugeot cars. Its research identified seven segments of older persons based on lifestyle and attitudes in areas such as media, brands and politics:

- Live Wires: busy, health-conscious, income to spend on holidays and cars.
- Happy and Fulfilled: financially secure, against change.
- Super Troopers: positive outlook, often lost a partner, high TV viewing.
- Rat Race Junkies: still working, but may have financial worries.
- Living Day to Day: low income but interested in buying brands.
- Unfulfilled Dreamers: often with loans or reliant on social security benefits.
- Anchored in the Past: risk-averse, traditional outlooks, lack interest in new trends.

Although all of these approaches represent valuable attempts to go beyond clumsy segmentation by age alone, it should be noted that there is good evidence to suggest that voters will reject attempts to target them purely on the basis of their age. Indeed, many seniors actively resent being targeted because of their age (RHC Advantage 2010). People age at different rates, and a voter's cognitive age – how they feel and see themselves – will usually be younger than their chronological age. They will ignore or actively resist any message that explicitly states *you should agree because you are old.*

The lesson for political marketers is that segmentation by chronological age alone is unlikely to gain a competitive edge for their candidates. A more intelligent development of age-related voter segments based on variables such as life stage, values, generational identities and media consumption habits will be required to achieve strategic advancement. There will be no easy short cuts in the process. The necessary research will require financial and time resources to ultimately develop the ostensibly age-neutral political brands that, nonetheless, resonate strongly with older voters.

This can be illustrated by two case studies, one in the UK and one in the US.

Case study 1: segmenting and marketing to US older voters

Since John F. Kennedy's campaign for president in 1960, senior-citizen committees, 'senior desks' and other types of special structures targeting older voters have been established within US election campaigns (see Binstock and Riemer 1978; Pratt 1976; MacManus 2000). Their aims are to register older voters, maintain and enhance the allegiance of older voters through the substance of issue appeals, and then ensure that they turn out to vote. To do this, senior campaigns promulgate issues intended to appeal to older persons through methods commonly used to target other voting constituencies – robocalls, email blasts, direct mail, and television and radio advertisements; letters to the editor; and appearances by the candidate or surrogates before targeted audiences. Surrogates, typically, are elected officials, celebrities and academics.

Such common efforts to reach out to particular groups of voters have some dimensions that are special in the case of seniors. One such dimension is that events featuring candidates and surrogates can be held in a great many venues where retired older voters can be easily targeted and (unlike non-retired voters) are available as audiences on weekdays. These venues include senior centers, congregate meal sites, retirement communities, public housing projects for the elderly, assisted-living facilities, nursing homes, conferences sponsored by old-age organizations, and the like. One of the reasons that legislators readily agree to government support for senior centers and congregate meal programs is that these provide pre-assembled, targeted audiences when candidates are running for re-election.

Although senior voters have been more difficult to reach through the use of social media in the past, the percentage of internet users in each new cohort that reaches old-age categories increases. For example, just over one-fourth of Americans aged 70–75 were online in 2005, but by 2009 45 percent of that age group was online (Jones and Fox 2009). While instant messaging, social networking and blogging have gained ground as communications tools, the most popular online activity among older internet users is email. Three-quarters of US users aged 64 and older send and receive email (Jones and Fox 2009).

Another dimension of strategies to target older voters is that some swing states with large numbers of electoral votes also have a higher proportion of older persons than the national average. Consequently, campaign efforts there to capture the votes of seniors are potentially more rewarding than elsewhere. For instance, Florida had 27 electoral votes in 2008 and 25 percent of its voting-age population was aged 65 and older; Pennsylvania had 21 electoral votes and 23 percent of its voting-age population was in this age range. In contrast, although 22 percent of West Virginia's voting-age population was aged 65 and over, that state had only five electoral votes (Project Vote Smart 2010; US Census Bureau 2010).

Still another special dimension of planning strategies is to target senior voters who have distinct concerns and political leanings. For instance, poor and wealthy older Americans have substantially different stakes in issues concerning Social Security. Social Security benefits account for 83 percent of income for older persons in the lowest income quintile, while they are only 18 percent for those in the highest quintile (Federal Interagency Forum on Aging-Related Statistics 2010). Similarly, in planning campaigns aimed at seniors in specific geographical locales, it is important to pay attention to differing long-term political attachments of the elders residing there. Older persons who have migrated to the east coast of Florida to retire, for example, have preponderantly come from the northeastern states and have Democratic leanings. Retiree migrants on the west coast of the state are more likely to have come from other, more Republican-leaning parts of the country.

Although these various strategies and efforts to sway older voters have become standard practice in US election campaigns, their impact is problematic despite perennial proclamations by journalists and political consultants (e.g. Penn 2008) that older persons are a pivotal battleground in determining the outcome of elections. In the 2008 US presidential election, for instance, older voters were the only age group to vote for the loser, John McCain; those aged 60 and older gave him 51 percent of their votes, and those aged 65 and above gave him 53 percent (Binstock 2009).

Case study 2: age and campaigning in Britain – the 2010 general election

Recent general elections have seen noteworthy campaigns where the parties outlined new policy commitments, sought to frame issues and managed adjustments in their strategic political positioning and response to an aging electorate.

Over the next 10–15 years, demographic aging in conjunction with higher turnout rates of older people will translate into a new political geography of Britain, with most parliamentary seats estimated to possess over half of turnout on polling day coming from voters aged 55 and over (Davidson 2010). The main parties have responded to the growing significance of older voters by making clear attempts to set the campaign agenda at the national level. Aging issues have been framed in order to maximize perceived valence opportunities, although the parties appeared to lack the tactical sophistication that would be expected in highly segmented communications.

The Labour government entered the 2010 election pledging to introduce free residential care for older people who had already self-funded for the first two years, and to then roll out universal free care at some point after 2015. In contrast, the Conservatives' policy on social care limited its extension to those who could elect to make a one-off payment of around £8,000 on retirement. Policy on social care became the main battleground between the parties in the pre-campaign exchanges three months before polling day. In this regard, 2010 followed a similar pattern to the 2005 election, with high-profile clashes on aging issues between the parties gaining wide media coverage before these issues become submerged by other concerns in the month before polling day. This was exemplified when the Conservatives published billboard posters claiming Labour's potential funding mechanism for universal care would amount to a 'death tax', with the strapline 'now Gordon (Brown) wants £20,000 when you die'. Labour strategists accused the Conservatives of 'driving a wrecking ball through attempts to reach cross-party consensus' (Wintour 2010). Accordingly, in the melee pre-campaign hopes to establish cross-party agreement on social care reforms subsided.

The most recent UK elections have demonstrated that the parties now attach strategic importance to their positioning on aging issues and proactively seek to frame and foreground the campaign agenda to their perceived advantage. Segmentation suggests strategic sophistication. However, in essence, and despite the rise of digital media, the British parties were primarily engaged in exercises of mass communications. Campaign sub-brands aimed at older voters or other associated tactical initiatives have been so far largely absent. The main focus of localized segmentation financed by the national parties comes through the extensive use of direct mail. Both the Conservative and Labour parties used the data management company Experian's Mosaic geo-demographic software to organize mail shots to older voters. Local candidates were able to build relationships with older voters through regular visits to day centers and church groups that tend to have older users and members. Additionally, information gathered from doorstep or telephone canvassing would often be used to generate more direct mail. Nonetheless, these local efforts were ad hoc, with little to no national coordination, and largely left to the initiative of individual candidates.

Table 3.3 shows that the Conservative Party was able to win the most seats in 2010 with the considerable assistance of the large leads over Labour that they enjoyed with older voters. However, it should also be noted that while the Conservatives enjoyed their largest leads

Table 3.3 How Britain voted 2010

	Con	*Lab*	*LD*	*Oth*	*Con lead over labour*	*Turnout*	*Con*	*Lab*	*LD*	*Turnout*	*Con-Lab swing*
	%	*%*	*%*	*%*	*% change*		*% change*	*% change*	*% change*	*% change*	*% change*
All	37	30	24	10	7	65%	4	–6	1	4	5
Gender											
Male	38	28	22	12	10	66%	4	–6	0	4	5
Female	36	31	26	8	4	64%	4	–7	3	3	5.5
Age											
18–24	30	31	30	9	–2	44%	2	–7	4	7	4.5
25–34	35	30	29	7	4	55%	10	–8	2	6	9
35–44	34	31	26	9	4	66%	7	–10	3	5	8.5
45–54	34	28	26	12	6	69%	3	–7	1	4	5
55–64	38	28	23	12	10	73%	–1	–3	1	2	1
65+	44	31	16	9	13	76%	3	–4	–2	1	3.5

Source: IPSOS/MORI. How Britain voted 2010. Base: 10,211 British adults aged 18+ (of whom 5,927 were 'absolutely certain to vote' or said that they had already voted), interviewed 19 March–5 May 2010.

amongst seniors, they had only managed to achieve below average swings with this age group; indeed, with voters aged 55–64, the oldest boomers who were about to retire, their vote share declined. The results are also contextualized by observing that Labour, in what was a historically poor result in terms of percentage-of-vote share, scored slightly better with older voters aged 65+ than they did nationally. In fact, Britain's main party of the left drew almost equal levels of support from the country's oldest and youngest voters. In contrast, the Conservatives performed much better with older voters than they did with younger age groups, a mirror image of the Liberal Democrats, who draw more of their votes from younger voters and perform relatively poorly amongst older voters.

Advice for practitioners

The relationship between birth certificates and ballot can be a surprisingly complex variable for understanding political behavior. Age is simultaneously a fixed chronological value, a relative concept, a probability indicator of morbidity, and a shared as well as a highly individualized personal experience. Any given individual's attitudes and behaviors are likely to be forged by the dominant influences in childhood, the main political cleavages experienced as a young adult, and the impact of social trends during the life span. Also important are the cumulative impact of advantages and disadvantages experienced throughout the life course (Dannefer 2003).

To understand how political strategists can research, create and target segments of older voters the role of differing generational characteristics and the influence of an individual's progress through the life cycle needs to be carefully considered. Historical events or social changes frequently leave lasting impressions on significant sections of society. Such changes would include the Second World War, stark economic recessions or social movements such as feminism. A consistent theme in the debates on political generations is the notion that effects that take place when voters are younger tend to be profound and long-lasting. This is because youth is seen as a formative period in a person's life, when they are relatively more open to new ideas (Mannheim 1952), as opposed to middle-aged and older voters who reflect new experiences through a much more defined prism of existing views and experiences. However, it would be a mistake to assume that voters from particular generations hold fixed party political allegiances. Van der Brug (2010) argues that people do not get 'stuck in their ways' in terms of party preference, but rather there are small but discernible differences in the criteria in how different generations evaluate parties and candidates.

Political behaviors can also be expected to evolve as the individual leaves home for full-time education, enters the labor market, develops adult relationships and/or starts new family units, re-locates into new communities, retires and eventually enters later life. Each successive stage in the life cycle produces different networks and economic contexts (Norris 2003). So both younger and older voters will not only be from different generations, but they will also be in distinctly different life stages. One life cycle effect that sharply differentiates the young and the old is that the average retired person is on a lower income than the average younger worker in their 30s who is in full-time employment; the incomes of the retired are also more likely to be fixed in the form of state or secondary pension payments (Blundell and Tanner 1999; Hills 2006) unless they are adjusted for inflation.

Impact on politics

The increasing practice of segmenting older voters means that political parties and individual office holders are increasingly conscious during the governing process (not just during election

Table 3.4 Ten implications for the practitioner

1	The electorate is greying – can you justify to your candidate/party NOT prioritizing older voters as a strategy?	Older voters are more likely to vote, pay attention to campaigns, volunteer or donate. They are increasing as a proportion of the electorate and in many areas will form the majority of voters. A strategy that prioritizes young, rather than older voters will need a compelling logic.
2	Discard all stereotypes and media myths regarding 'senior power'.	Although older voters are increasingly critical, the senior power model is not a sound basis for campaign strategy. Older voters do not vote as a bloc, but significant numbers will respond to clear weaknesses or strengths in any given candidate.
3	Segmenting by age is the very least you can do.	Age may tell you that social security and healthcare are more likely to matter, but it does not give insights into the range of political values and opinions among older voters. Nationally, from election to election, millions on the electoral roll will die and millions from another generation will join the ranks of the retired. The senior vote is always changing.
4	You risk losing out to your competitors if they develop stronger insights into seniors.	Campaigns that only segment by broad age groups will increasingly be at a competitive disadvantage to those who will invest in building stronger insights and relationships with seniors. Are you planning to be the electoral beneficiaries of an aging electorate, or will you lose out to your more pro-active competitors?
5	Successful segmentation of seniors requires a commitment to research and will be a process of ongoing discovery.	To generate clusters of older voters for targeting, age will need to be combined with data on lifestyle, social attitudes, local political intelligence, life stage, generational identities and aspirations for later life.
6	Campaigns that target seniors will need to ensure an age-neutral appeal.	Campaign communications that only appeal on the basis of age are likely to be rejected by your target voters. Seniors will actively resist any message that explicitly states that they should agree purely because they are 'old'.
7	Digital and social media are providing increasingly important communication channels to reach senior voters.	Older voters remain strong consumers of traditional media such as the press and TV, but the fastest rates of growth in internet and social media usage are to be found in older age groups.
8	Understand that the meaning of retirement is being transformed.	Voters now retiring helped to forge the consumer society and are increasingly indiscernible from younger age groups in terms of the link between consumerism and identity. Retirement is no longer about disengagement. Voters hold aspirations that this is a period to realize goals of personal fulfilment. Your appeal must go beyond old-age benefits and concessions.
9	Be aware that seniors, as with other age groups, are increasingly disloyal to political brands and more likely to switch their preferences across local and national elections.	Another stereotype that needs to be discarded is that of the highly loyal-to-one-party older voter. Seniors may be more likely to be partisan supporters of one party, but an increasing proportion regularly switch their votes. For politicians in office delivery on policy and quality of life issues will matter.

Table 3.4 (continued)

10	Recognize and address the wide inequalities between different groups of older voters.	While it is generally true that seniors are better off now than in the past, older voters are highly diverse and a significant proportion will be struggling due to an interplay of factors such as low income, ill-health, family bereavement, etc. These will be a significant proportion of active senior voters and their needs should be central to your strategy.

campaigns) of the potential reaction of seniors to policy decisions. This goes beyond traditional concerns with pensions and healthcare and applies to a wider range of policy issues than in the past.

A sign of the increased importance of older voters may not be evidenced through high-profile clashes between the parties on senior issues during the last weeks of any given campaign, but rather through a strategic imperative to ensure before any formal campaign that no valence opportunity on an aging issue will be presented for exploitation by opponents. A perception that one party has the best chance of delivering policies that are generally considered by most older voters to be important, would be highly significant. This strategic imperative is likely to intensify as the proportion of older voters in the electorate grows.

As society takes on a demographic profile never seen before in human history, segmentation can help politics understand the needs of this diverse and growing section of older citizens. It can serve as a tool to open up a dialogue about the meaning of retirement and later life, negotiating a response to the transformation of older voters from excluded minority to a position where politics and government delivers a socially equitable response to the new policy challenges.

However, the danger remains that segmentation will further exaggerate inequalities amongst older people, if only the more literate and more active are attended to. Any perceived disregard of the needs of some sections of older voters as part of a process of privileging others may result in alienating from future politics significant sections of the senior vote. Seniors currently show the healthiest levels of civic engagement, but if their participation rates were to fall towards those of younger voters, this would represent a considerable blow to democratic legitimacy.

Another threat may come from wilder media narratives about 'greedy geezers', 'selfish boomers' and 'the gray peril', as they will hamper the tone and quality of public policy debates. Aging issues such as social care and pensions often require long-term solutions, strong cross-party consensuses and multi-generational support.

The way forward

All the major democracies are going through a prolonged period of population aging. There will be an additional 32 million Americans aged 65 and over in the 20 years from 2010 to 2030 (US Census Bureau 2010). In Britain a large number of parliamentary constituencies will see a majority of turnout coming from voters aged 55 and over (Davidson 2010). The significance and potential of voter segmentation for democracies that are now experiencing an age transformation will not be limited to the application of scientific persuasion and the selling of policy programs. The normative application of segmentation will see a process of discovery of the political needs and aspirations of the aging electorate, and provide the evidence base for the communicative and policy responses from governments and parties.

It is now a feature of modern campaigns for commentators to proclaim seniors as one of the pivotal battlegrounds in determining the final outcome. Certainly, it has been the variation in age-group turnout rates internationally that has accelerated the impact of population aging. For example, in the UK younger age groups in the 1970s showed lower turnout rates, but in subsequent elections, as they grew older, their turnout increased. However, this trend seems to have been broken in the 1990s and first-time voters in 2001 maintained their low participation rates in 2005 (Phelps 2005).

Older people are also more likely to vote, join campaigns and contact elected representatives. They have high levels of political literacy and are more likely to follow the campaign closely in the mainstream media. However, as demonstrated in this chapter, the senior power model – and the overly simplistic rational choice-based predictions of 'gerontocracy' (Sinn and Uebelmesser 2002) – hold only limited value and are ultimately flawed. They downplay the diversity of older voters and falsely assume that they vote as a single bloc that perceives a single shared economic interest. This model also ignores older voter concerns regarding the prospects for their own children and grandchildren and how they are divided by hugely varying personal social and economic circumstances.

That said, it is clear that there are issues that particularly impact on the quality of life for older voters. If gray voters were to perceive one party to be discernibly stronger, or weaker, on those issues, this is likely to be significant. Any candidate that performs poorly with seniors is going to have to do remarkably well with younger age groups to compensate. For strategists there is a clear choice: to either be the beneficiaries or the victims of long-term demographic change.

The lesson for political marketers is that segmentation by chronological age is crude and unlikely to gain a competitive edge for their candidates. A more intelligent development of age-related voter segments based on variables such as life stage, values, generational identities and media consumption habits will be required to achieve significant strategic advancement. There will be no easy short cuts in the process. The necessary research will require financial and time resources to ultimately develop the ostensibly age-neutral political brands that, nonetheless, resonate strongly with older voters.

Bibliography

Baines, P.R. (1999) 'Voter segmentation and candidate positioning', in B. Newman (ed.) *Handbook of Political Marketing*, Thousand Oaks, CA: Sage.

Bannon, D. (2004) 'Marketing segmentation and political marketing', paper presented to the UK Political Studies Association conference, University of Lincoln, Lincoln, UK, 2004.

Binstock, R.H. (2009) 'Older voters and the 2008 election', *The Gerontologist* 49: 697–701.

Binstock, R.H. and Riemer, Y. (1978) 'Campaigning for "the senior vote": A case study of Carter's 1976 campaign', *The Gerontologist* 18: 517–24.

Blundell, R. and Tanner, S. (1999) 'Labour force participation and retirement in the UK', paper prepared for the National Academy of Science. Institute for Fiscal Studies, December.

Butler, P. and Harris, P. (2009) 'Considerations on the evolution of political marketing theory', *Marketing Theory* 9: 149–64.

Butler, D. and Stokes, D. (1969) *Political Change in Britain: Forces Shaping Electoral Choice*, London: Macmillan.

Campbell, A.L. (2003) 'Participatory reactions to policy threats: Senior citizens and the defense of Social Security and Medicare', *Political Behavior* 55: 29–49.

Campbell, A.L. and Binstock, R.H. (2011) 'Politics and aging in the United States', in R.H. Binstock and L.K. George (eds) *Handbook of Aging and the Social Sciences*, seventh edn. San Diego, CA: Academic Press, 265–79.

Carrubba, C. and Timpone, R. (2005) 'Explaining vote switching across first- and second-order elections: evidence from Europe', *Comparative Political Studies* 38, 3: 260–81.
Coates, S. (2007) 'First Lib Dem candidate happy to be an underdog', *The Times*, 18 October.
Dalton, R.J. (2002) 'The decline of party identifications', in R.J. Dalton and M.P. Wattenburg (eds) *Parties Without Partisans: Political Change in Advanced Industrial Democracies*, Oxford and New York: Oxford University Press.
Dannefer, D. (2003) 'Cumulative advantage and the life course: cross-fertilizing age and social science knowledge', *Journal of Gerontology* 58b, S327–S337.
Darnton, A. (2005) 'Common good research. Communicating with older people', Central Office of Information Research Unit, May. Online, coi.gov.uk/documents/commongood/commongood-older-deskcommentary.pdf (accessed 20 March 2011).
Davidson, S. (2010) 'Quantifying the changing age structure of the British electorate 2005–25: researching the age demographics of the new parliamentary constituencies', Age Concern England. Online, www.civilsociety.co.uk/docs/Quantifying_the_Changing_Age_1.pdf (accessed 20 March 2011).
Federal Interagency Forum on Aging-Related Statistics (2010) 'Older Americans 2010. Key indicators of well being'. Online, www.agingstats.gov/agingstatsdotnet/Main_Site/Data/2010_Documents/Docs/OA_2010.pdf (accessed 19 October 2010).
Heclo, H. (1988) 'Generational politics', in J.L. Palmer, T. Smeeding and B. Boyle Torrey (eds) *The Vulnerable*, Washington, DC: Urban Institute Press, 381–411.
Hills, J. (2006) 'A new pension settlement for the twenty-first century? The UK Pensions Commission's analysis and proposal', *Oxford Review of Economic Policy* 22, 1: 113–32.
Hooghe, M. (2004) 'Political socialization and the future of politics', *Acta Politica* 39: 331–41.
Johnson, D.W. (2011) *Campaigning in the Twenty-first Century: A Whole New Ballgame?* New York: Routledge.
Jones, S. and Fox, S. (2009) 'Generational differences in online activities'. Online, www.pewinternet.org/Reports/2009/Generations-Online-in-2009/Generational-Differences-in-Online-Activities/2-Internet-use-and-email.aspx (accessed 19 October 2010).
Kavanagh, D. (1995) *Election Campaigning: The New Marketing of Politics*, Oxford and Cambridge, MA: Blackwell.
Kohli, M. and Arza, C. (2010) 'The political economy of pension reform in Europe', in R.H. Binstock and L.K. George (eds) *Handbook of Aging and the Social Sciences*, seventh edn. San Diego, CA: Academic Press, 251–64.
Lilleker, D. (2005) 'Political marketing: the cause of the democratic deficit?', in W.W. Wymer and J. Lees-Marshment (eds) *Current Issues in Political Marketing*, New York: Haworth Press, 5–26.
MacManus, S.A. (2000) *Targeting Senior Voters: Campaign Outreach to Elders and Others with Special Needs*, Lanham, MD: Rowman & Littlefield Publishers, Inc.
Mannheim, K. (1952 [1928]) 'The problem of generations', in D. Kecskemeti (ed.) *Essays on the Sociology of Knowledge*, London: Routledge and Kegan Paul, 276–322.
Mattinson, D. (2010) *Talking to a Brick Wall*, London: Biteback Publishing Ltd.
Morgan, K. (1990) *The People's Peace: British history 1945–1989*, Oxford and New York: Oxford University Press.
New York Times (2008) 'Election results 2008'. Online, elections.nytimes.com/2008/results/president/national-exit-polls.html (accessed 26 February 2009).
Newman, B. (ed.) (1999) *A Handbook of Political Marketing*, London: Sage.
Norris, P. (2003) 'Young people and political activism: from the politics of loyalties to the politics of choice?' Report for the Council of Europe: Strasbourg, 27–28 November.
Penn, M.J. (2008) '"Active grannies" are the new Soccer Moms', *Politico.com*. Online, dyn.politico.com/printstory.cfm?uuid=6B988EAC-3048-5C12-0039834BCE101D33 (accessed 7 July 2008).
Peterson, S.A. and Somit, A. (1994) *Political Behavior of Older Americans*, New York: Garland.
Phelps, E. (2005) 'Young voters at the 2005 British general election', *The Political Quarterly* 76, 4: October: 482–87.
Pratt, H.J. (1976) *The Gray Lobby*, Chicago: University of Chicago Press.
Project Vote Smart (2010) 'U.S. Electoral College 2008 – list of states and votes'. Online, www.votesmart.org/election_president_electoral_college.php (accessed 19 October 2010).
RHC Advantage (2010) 'Marketing and older audiences: a review of data, research and literature', London: RHC Advantage.
Russell, A., Pattie, C. and Johnston, R. (1992) 'Thatcher's children: exploring the link between age and political attitudes', *Political Studies* 40, 742–50.

Savigny, H. (2005) 'Labour, political marketing and the 2005 election: a campaign of two halves', *Journal of Marketing Management* 21, 9/10: 925–41.

Sinn, H.-W. and Uebelmesser, A. (2002) 'Pensions and the path to gerontocracy in Germany', *European Journal of Political Economy* 19, 153–58.

Smith, G. and Hirst, A. (2001) 'Strategic political segmentation: a new approach for a new era of political marketing', *European Journal of Marketing* 35, 9/10: 1058–73.

Snyder, R. (2002) 'Market segmentation: successfully targeting the mature population', *The Journal on Active Aging*. March/April: 11, 49–50. Online, www.aahf.info/sec_news/section/pdf/market-segmentation2.pdf (accessed 20 March 2011).

Thurow, L.C. (1996) 'The birth of a revolutionary class', *New York Times Magazine* 19 May, 46–47.

US Census Bureau (2010) 'Interim projections under age 18 and 65 and older'. Online www.census.gov/population/www/projections/projectionsagesex.html (accessed 19 October 2010).

Van der Brug, W. (2010) 'Structural and ideological voting in age cohorts', *West European Politics* 33, 3: 586–607.

Vienna Institute of Demography (2010) 'European demographic data sheet, 2010'. Online, www.oeaw.ac.at/vid/datasheet/index.html (accessed 12 September 2010).

Walker, A. (1999) 'Political participation and representation of older people', in A. Walker and G. Naegele (eds) *The Politics of Old Age in Europe*, Philadelphia, PA: Open University Press, 7–24.

Wintour, P. (2010) 'Tory "death tax" poster condemned', *Guardian*, 12 February. Online, www.guardian.co.uk/society/2010/feb/12/tory-death-tax-bakewell-insult.

Wring, D. (2005) *The Politics of Marketing the Labour Party*, New York: Palgrave Macmillan.

4

Strategic voter selection

Michael John Burton

The topic: strategic voter selection

Abraham Lincoln and his Whig colleagues had a clear strategy for gathering votes in the run-up to the 1840 elections. Operatives were instructed:

> 1st. To divide their county into small districts, and to appoint in each a sub-committee, whose duty it shall be to make a perfect list of all the voters in their respective districts, and to ascertain with certainty for whom they will vote … 2nd. It will be the duty of said sub-committee to keep a CONSTANT WATCH on the DOUBTFUL VOTERS, and from time to time have them TALKED TO by those IN WHOM THEY HAVE THE MOST CONFIDENCE, and also to place in their hands such documents as will enlighten and influence them. 3d. It will also be their duty to report to you, at least once a month, the progress they are making, and on election days see that every Whig is brought to the polls.
>
> *(Henry* et al. *1840: 202)*

The Whig strategy, laborious in implementation, would count as state-of-the-art voter selection for generations.

Shoe-leather duties inevitably gave way to professionalized research. In the late 1980s British Labour strategists reportedly 'launched an extensive analysis of the Green Party's European election vote, with the aim of improving the targeting of Labour's own environmental policy package' (Hughes 1989). In the early 1990s Bill Clinton's presidential campaign attended to the comparative costs of reaching different parts of the US electorate (Kurtz 1992). The following decade, a US firm called Aristotle International played a role in the 2004 Ukrainian presidential election, later advertising that it had '[d]esigned and deployed a voter turnout system – collecting and analyzing voter participation in each region and at 250 pre-selected bellwether voting locales' (Aristotle International no date a). In 2008 the voter selection operation that backed Senator Barack Obama's bid for the presidency was so innovative that it won respect from some Republicans (see Wayne 2008). Many campaigns still emulate the Whig model with 'voter ID' calls – phoning voters one at a time – but in a contemporary campaign such an effort might be aided by technologically sophisticated 'predictive dialers'.

Strategic voter selection is the act of prioritizing members of the voting-eligible population, as individuals or as groups, in order to guide the allocation of outreach expenditures. Many campaign organizations select, first, likely supporters who should be mobilized to cast their ballots, and second, likely voters who should be persuaded to cast their ballots the 'right way'. Reaching out to people who are unalterably backing the opposition would be a waste of scarce resources, and people who will surely cast a supportive vote can safely be ignored. However, such individuals are outliers. People generally fall somewhere between the poles, so voter selection procedures may wisely deal in mere probabilities as they seek optimal distributions of campaign time, money and effort.

Political strategists have resorted to a variety of selection methods. Techniques include the analysis of demographics and electoral history, along with survey research, and more recently the use of information-rich voter lists, 'microtargeting', and absentee 'chase' programs. This chapter will seek to explain strategic voter selection, both in concept and in practice, and to discuss implications for democratic politics.

Previous research on strategic voter selection

The core concepts of strategic voter selection were expressed in the 1970s. Daniel M. Gaby and Merle H. Treusch (1976) detailed the workings of demographic and precinct research, as did successive versions of a workbook circulated by the National Women's Education Fund (see 1978). By the 1980s and 1990s, basic selection methods had essentially become public domain (see Allen 1996; Fishel 1998a; Fishel 1998b). In the 21st century this tradition continues with manuals such as Catherine Shaw's popular handbook, *The Campaign Manager* (Shaw 2010). Hal Malchow, a leader in the American political consulting industry, has supplemented his authoritative *The New Political Targeting* (Malchow 2008) with software that lets readers try the process for themselves.

The scholarly literature is more sparse, but its findings are instructive. Experimental research by Joshua D. Clinton and John S. Lapinski (2004) provides modest support for the notion that the effects of campaign advertising may vary by voter characteristics, a result that suggests the importance of sending the appropriate message to the appropriate voters. Daron R. Shaw (2006), a political scientist who helped strategize the George W. Bush campaigns of 2000 and 2004, has found that targeted campaign messaging can have an impact. Bruce Hardy, Chris Adasiewicz, Kate Kenski and Kathleen Hall Jamieson (2010) have examined the role of targeted messaging in the 2008 presidential campaign. Early efforts to calculate optimal selection (e.g. Kramer 1966) have been given contemporary form by Kosuke Imai and Aaron Strauss (2011). Scholarly research has thus gained traction on the effects of strategic voter selection; still, much work remains.

Daron Shaw's analysis merits special attention. Shaw found that state-level electioneering had a measurable, but small, impact on weekly presidential 'trial heat' polls. The minimal nature of the effect might be a function of the dynamic nature of electoral strategy. The political adversaries in that contest were, in effect, counterprogramming each other, reaching out to voters selected by the other side: '[P]ooled time series data', Shaw says, show that campaign organizations 'appear to limit campaign effects by matching the opposition's TV advertising and appearances' (Shaw 2006: 138). A favorable shift (actual or anticipated) within a selected segment can prompt opposition forces to reallocate spending in order to shore up support. For researchers, this sort of activity can mean that the combined expenditures of electoral competitors may, to some greater or lesser degree, wash each other out – and the effect of voter selection might therefore be hard to detect even when it exists.

New research

While practitioners might have a gut-level understanding of strategic voter selection, recent thinking on the topic has led to a more detailed articulation of underlying principles.

Strategic voter selection in concept

Generally speaking, the efficacy of strategic voter selection is gleaned from its rationale: An outreach effort that indiscriminately spreads its campaign communications across the electorate will tend to underperform an outreach effort that masses the same quantum of resources on segments of the electorate with high proportions of moveable voters; campaign communications should therefore be directed toward those high-proportion segments. Catherine Shaw distinguishes supportive 'saints' from oppositional 'sinners' – 'but', she says, 'we focus on the third group, the savables' (Shaw 2010: 3). Simply stated, strategic voter selection is an effort to break up the whole and prioritize the parts.

Segmentation and ranking

Segmentation is the process of identifying heterogeneity within the overall population and carving the electorate into distinct groups that can be ranked according to their electoral value.

Figure 4.1 represents an *un*-segmented electorate that is facing, say, a ballot issue. This notional population comprises YES voters (25 percent), undecided voters (50 percent), and NO voters (25 percent). Assume this electorate can be partitioned into six mutually exclusive segments. Differentiation might run along geographic boundaries; demographic characteristics such as gender, race and ethnicity; party registration; or some other combination of politically meaningful features. Figure 4.2 represents the same notional electorate as Figure 4.1, but disaggregated into six discrete segments that range in their proportions of undecideds from 100 percent in the top segment to zero in the bottom.

For a persuasion strategy that seeks to move undecided voters to YES, one approach might be to rank the segments as shown here. For a get out the vote ('GOTV') strategy, segments having large percentages of supporters who skip elections might be placed on top. Whether supporters or undecideds or some other group is deemed most desirable, the point of strategic voter selection is to locate segments of the electorate with high concentrations of the desired individuals.

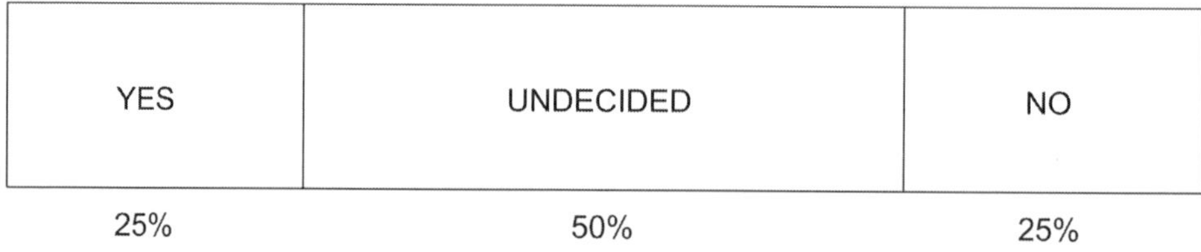

Figure 4.1 Notional electorate – unsegmented

Efficiency and coverage

Assume that each of the six segments holds 1,000 voters, and assume further that the campaign wants to persuade undecided voters. Mailing postcards to everyone in the electorate would result in 50 percent of these cards going to the desired voters, the undecideds – recall that half of the voters have already made up their minds – whereas mailing to the voters in only the top two segments would result in 1,800 of the 2,000 postcards going to undecideds. In other words, the narrow effort directed at the top two segments would see 90 percent of those postcards going to desired voters, improving efficiency by 40 percentage points. Malchow affirms that efficiency 'is the most important measurement of the effectiveness of your targeting' (Malchow 2008: 8).

Enhancing efficiency is important, sometimes critically so. However, fixating on this aspect of voter selection to the exclusion of all others can amount to a losing strategy. The most efficient mailing for the electorate represented in Figure 4.2 would have the campaign restricting its outreach to the top-ranked group, an approach that would offer 100 percent efficiency; however, such an effort would reach just 1,000 of the 3,000 undecided voters in the electorate, or 33 percent of the total number of undecideds. Many of the other 2,000 available undecideds might wind up siding with the opposition. Thus, in addition to enhancing efficiency, a strategist should also ensure proper 'coverage' (Malchow 2008: 9). If the campaign expanded its mailing to the *three* most efficient groups, it would be contacting 2,400 of the desired undecideds, achieving 80 percent coverage. While efficiency is a good thing, its

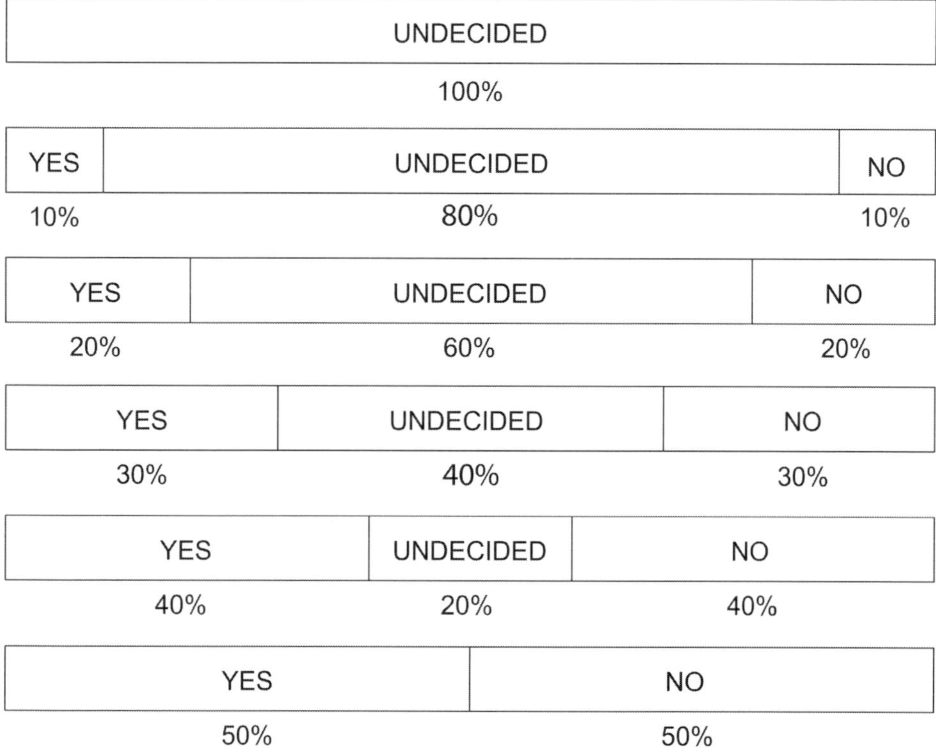

Figure 4.2 Notional electorate – segmented

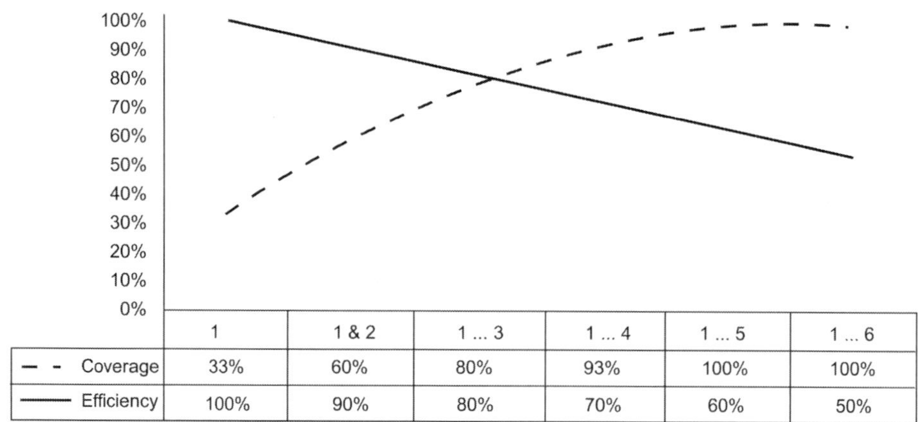

	1	1 & 2	1 ... 3	1 ... 4	1 ... 5	1 ... 6
– - Coverage	33%	60%	80%	93%	100%	100%
—— Efficiency	100%	90%	80%	70%	60%	50%

Figure 4.3 Efficiency *versus* coverage

ultimate utility is wedded to coverage, and a campaign that calculates efficiency alone might properly be asked, in Malchow's words, '[H]ow many target voters are you missing?' (Malchow 2008: 9).

This last point highlights the trade-off between efficiency and coverage, as illustrated in Figure 4.3. When segments comprise varying proportions of desired voters and are ranked accordingly, increased coverage will mean decreased efficiency. If the campaign sends postcards to the top two groups in Figure 4.2, coverage is 60 percent and efficiency is 90 percent. Reaching out further to the top five groups maximizes coverage but reduces efficiency by 30 percentage points – while every desired voter would be hit, the mailing would incur a higher cost per desired voter because more undesired voters would be in the mix.

Yield

A standard problem in strategic voter selection is that of optimizing efficiency and coverage in light of outreach costs – in other words, determining the most advantageous yield scenario. Yield is the net number of votes returned per unit of expenditure (see Burton and Shea 2010: 88–89; Green and Gerber 2008: 13). One way to illustrate a winning yield strategy is to, first, assume (for simplicity) that both sides of the electoral contest will select the same exact segments, and then second, estimate how far, and in which direction, the moveable voters in a targeted segment will in fact move. The central question would be: Who will gather how many moveable voters on election day, and at what cost?

Begin with the notional scenario illustrated above – the 6,000-voter electorate carved into six equal-sized segments. Assume that the proportion of moveable undecideds can be estimated but the identities of individual undecideds cannot be determined. If sending one postcard to a voter costs 25¢, then incorporating that same voter into a 10-postcard mailing program will cost $2.50. With 3,001 votes being the threshold for victory, recalling that 1,500 sure YES votes are already 'in the bank', it would appear that 1,501 additional votes will be needed for the win. The difficulty is as follows: If all the undecideds could be personally identified and if each undecided voter included in a postcard program would be persuaded to vote YES, then the cost of victory would be equal to the cost of 10 postcards ($2.50) multiplied by the number of additional votes needed to win (1,501) – and so the cost would be $3,752.50; but because the identity of the undecideds is unknown, the campaign will have to tolerate some measure of inefficiency as it seeks adequate coverage.

Table 4.1 Yield accumulations

Group (by rank)	*Desired voters*	*Accumulated contacts*	*Votes gained*	*Accumulated votes*	*Accumulated cost*
Base vote			1,500	1,500	
1	1,000	1,000	700	2,200	$2,500
2	800	2,000	560	2,760	$5,000
3	600		300	3,060	
4	400		200	3,260	
5	200		100	3,360	
6	0		0	3,360	

Yield estimates can help optimize the trade-off between efficiency and coverage. Assume, as previously mentioned, that 1,500 voters will surely vote YES – call that the 'base' vote. Then add two more assumptions: First, 70 percent of undecided voters included in the postcard program will swing to YES; and second, undecided voters who are *not* included will split evenly between YES and NO. Sending postcards to all the voters in the two top-ranked segments would be expected to deliver new YES votes as shown in Table 4.1. Fully 700 votes are gathered from the 1,000 undecideds in the first segment at a cost of $2,500, and another 560 votes come in from the 800 undecideds in the second segment for another $2,500. With the rest of the segments – the ones populated by smaller shares of undecideds, which are not targeted for mail and therefore are expected to split their undecideds evenly between YES and NO – the accumulation of YES votes slows considerably. The third segment produces only 300 votes; the fourth segment brings 200; the fifth segment adds only 100 votes; and no new votes come in from the last segment. The final accumulation envisions success with 3,360 out of 6,000 votes for the price of $5,000 – more than $3,752.50, the price of the ideal campaign, but far less than the $15,000 cost of reaching out to all 6,000 voters in the electorate. (For a Bayesian approach, see Imai and Strauss 2011.)

Caveats

Precarious assumptions (such as segment-level movement estimates) go into this sort of analysis, some or all of which might be wrong. Also, in the real world outreach costs might vary across segments. If one group of voters is best reached by internet advertisements while another is only reachable by television commercials, then the comparative value of these segments would seem to depend on the unequal pricing. Additionally, strategists would want to consider that a piece of mail will be delivered, not necessarily into the hands of the desired voter, but at the door of an entire household. Transforming individual-level selection into a household-level mailing demands its own sort of expertise. Finally, the price of analysis itself must be taken into account. If the selection process consumes more money for research than it saves in efficiency, then the process might fail a strict cost-benefit analysis.

Strategic voter selection in practice

A scholar would be hard-pressed to find large numbers of strategists computing efficiency, coverage and yield, and indeed there are many ways to run a strategic analysis (see Burton and

Shea 2010: 88–91; Fishel 1998a; Fishel 1998b; Malchow 2008; Shaw 2010: 391–409). Calculations like these merely reconstruct the underlying logic of strategic voter selection – an idealized vision of reality. Such computations form a set of principles that becomes manifest when strategists patch together a target list based on demographic analysis, the study of electoral history and survey research.

Demographic analysis

Segmentation by way of demographic research is one of the best-known methods of voter selection. If a high proportion of suburban women are not committed to any particular political party, that segment might be ripe for persuasion. In the US national electorate, black voters are as a rule loyal to the Democratic Party, but they turn out to vote in comparatively small numbers, so a Democratic candidate may want to focus its GOTV operation on African Americans.

Demographic segmentation is made possible in the US by scrupulous efforts to learn about the populace. The US Census Bureau tries to acquire information on all individuals living in the country, and it publishes aggregate data on the nation, states, counties, cities and even city blocks. With time and effort, a campaign strategist can use Census data to draw a revealing portrait of an electorate. These data can be merged with additional information acquired from economic development agencies, municipal offices and private data firms. Many demographic characteristics are generally presumed salient, from race to gender to income to education, and a variety of other factors may be gleaned from research and insight. Of course, a political strategist using national-level data should remember that district-level realities can vary drastically. Demography also might be less helpful in a non-partisan contest (such as an initiative or referendum) or a within-party contest (such as a US primary) where less might be known about the relationship between demographic characteristics and political behavior.

Unfortunately, using aggregated data can lead to a difficulty called the 'ecological inference problem' – the idea that the characteristics of a general population accurately represent the individual members of that population, when perhaps they do not. In one formulation of the problem, a county showing a median household income of $80,000 might contain few upper-middle-class voters. It could well be that 45 percent of households are barely hedging above the poverty line while another 45 percent are supremely wealthy, with just 10 percent in the middle. A less obvious problem is illustrated by the 'Red-State, Blue-State' divide in US politics. Paradoxically, downscale *states* tend to vote Republican ('Red') while downscale *people* tend to vote Democratic ('Blue') (Gelman *et al.* 2008). Believing that individuals look just like the groups to which they belong is a risky proposition. Nevertheless, analysts may be compelled from a paucity of individual-level information to discount or deal with the problems attending ecological inference.

Electoral history

A 1976 campaign manual by Gaby and Treusch advised campaign organizations to view electoral precincts according to voting age population, number of registered voters, turnout in general elections, partisanship, gaps between high and low vote-getters within a given election, and partisan differences across time, the strength of the parties by precinct and voter turnout in primary elections (Gaby and Treusch 1976: 74–76). Gaby and Treusch reasoned that:

> If a precinct is classified as highly persuadable, it will then contain a large concentration of voters who are persuadable. Similarly, if a district has been highly supportive of your party in the past but has shown low turnouts of voters on election day, we assume that nonvoters would also be supporters of your party.
>
> *(Gaby and Treusch 1976: 74)*

The logic of precinct analysis makes sense if neighborhoods are faithful to their political predispositions. Even as a new family moves into a precinct, it is reasonable to assume that the incoming household will be similar in political bearing to the one that is leaving; similarly, the departing family may be transitioning into a new stage of life – say, by marriage, child-rearing or retirement – and these changes may at the same time be altering that family's political preferences as it moves away.

Instructions for precinct selection can be found in numerous electioneering manuals, perhaps due to the method's palpable advantages. First, precinct analysis is based on votes actually cast in elections rather than broad-spectrum demographic characteristics or self-reports from a survey sample. Second, precinct-based voter selection can save money, as data entry might be relegated to volunteers. Third, it can be highly specific. An electorate that contains 200 precincts is rankable into just as many discrete segments, letting analysts draw fine-grained distinctions among geographic units.

The method has weaknesses, however. In addition to risking ecological inference problems, precinct analysis can be demanding when boundaries change, forcing strategists to carve up and reallocate bits of old precincts to represent the new configuration. While historical analysis may be useful in a two-way partisan race, strategizing a primary election or a ballot issue can be more challenging. There may be no clear precedent to use as a basis of comparison. In any case, strategists should look at the politics beneath the numbers. Gaby and Treusch noted that these kinds of 'targeting operations … are intended to supplement regular political knowledge, not to substitute for it', and strategists are advised to consult 'a person familiar with the politics of the area' (Gaby and Treusch 1976: 70, 74).

Survey research

Campaign strategists look at survey research from a different perspective than, say, the news media or members of the community at large. For those outside the campaign industry, polling often serves a human-interest function. Who is ahead today? Which races are most compelling? For campaign operatives, survey research is commonly employed to address a wider set of questions. Strategists want to know, for example, which segments of the electorate should be selected for persuasion or mobilization.

Conventional wisdom holds that the middle ground should be the focus of persuasion, the idea being that centrist voters are amenable to political messaging. Alternatively, a campaign might look at how much respondents 'move' after hearing the campaign's argument. Toward the beginning of a survey, a respondent might be asked, 'If the election were held today, would you vote YES, NO, or are you undecided at this time?' After the answers are recorded, the respondent might be read a series of arguments, both for and against. Then the respondent might be queried one more time, 'Now that you've heard more about the issue, I'd like to ask again: If the election were held today …' The difference between the results on the first reading of the ballot question and the second, 'informed' ballot shows movement on the issue. Whether a strategist looks at where voters position themselves or how they might move, the findings of a campaign poll can help identify persuadable segments of the electorate.

Table 4.2 Survey results – raw responses

Response	*Upstate*			*Downstate*		
	Dem	*Unaff.*	*Repub*	*Dem*	*Unaff.*	*Repub*
Yes	76	14	28	20	20	22
Undecided	31	29	33	97	100	70
No	13	77	59	3	0	28

Segments can be presented as crosstabulated data. Table 4.2 represents a minimalistic crosstab for some notional ballot question, showing in raw numbers how the views of upstate and downstate respondents might be presented. Partisanship seems to make little difference among downstaters on YES (though it makes a big difference on NO); upstate, however, partisanship is a strong explainer for YES. Many downstaters seem undecided, particularly Democrats and unaffiliated voters; most upstaters appear to have made up their minds. A persuasion campaign that looks for undecideds might be drawn to downstate voters while a prominent Democratic official hoping to mobilize co-partisans – specifically, the ones who are ready to vote YES – might want to contact upstate Democrats to make sure they cast their ballots.

Unfortunately, individual columns in a crosstab may contain distressingly small subsamples. If a survey performed within a large population of 1 million voters includes 720 respondents (which would be a large number for a 'benchmark' poll), the survey's sampling error for topline results at 95 percent confidence is typically calculated at about ±3.7 percent. If respondents are evenly distributed among the table's six columns (as shown here), then each column will have 120 respondents, with a reported sampling error of about ±8.9 percent. If the columns are evenly subdivided by yet another variable (for example, type of community: urban, suburban or rural), paring column size to 40 respondents, the error might be reported at about ±15.5 percent. Quite often, variables are not so evenly distributed and some columns will hold only a handful of respondents, making inference to a larger population hazardous. Finally, sampling error is only one of many problems that might crop up, and a smart consumer of opinion polls will be mindful of the hurdles facing survey researchers (see Weisberg 2005). (For an important issue related to the practice of cherry-picking survey results, see Jones *et al.* 2001.)

Innovations in strategic voter selection

Recent developments in voter selection reflect the increasing power and decreasing cost of information technology, as seen in the production of information-rich voter lists, microtargeting and absentee ballot chasing.

Information-rich voter lists

Many US jurisdictions offer lists of registered voters, complete with addresses, ages and voting histories – not showing *which way* the individuals voted, of course, but *in which elections* they voted – maybe including the political affiliations of those voters. This is valuable data. People who have cast ballots in two consecutive primary elections might safely be counted as likely voters for an upcoming general election; someone who voted in the most recent general election, but not in the primary, may need some reminding. A wise campaign might supplement its basic voter list with data from fundraising rosters, 'voter ID' calls and comments heard on neighborhood walks.

Campaigns have long maintained 'house lists', but in recent years, both major US political parties have stepped up their efforts to gather individual-level data on members of the electorate. Commercial firms have also been accumulating facts and figures. Aristotle International – the company that was involved with the Ukrainian election – has advertised that, in addition to political data, it 'maintains a list of over 5.4 million voters who hold hunting and fishing licenses, as well as individuals who subscribe to a wide array of magazine subscriptions including family, religious, financial, health, culinary and Do-It-Yourself publications' (Aristotle International no date b).

Microtargeting

In the 1980s some Republican operatives were linking consumer information to their datasets and, as the years passed, the party refined its techniques and kept up with technological developments. In 2003, following a senior strategist's PowerPoint presentation (title: 'Standard Precinct Targeting versus Micro-Targeting'), the party redoubled its efforts. By looking at a wide range of characteristics it was found that:

> In fifteen battleground states, there were some 5 million 'suspect Republicans' (likely to vote [Republican] if properly motivated), 6.7 million 'unreliable Republicans' (people who like the [Republican] brand but are infrequent voters), and 2 million 'registration targets' (likely Republicans who are not registered to vote).
>
> *(Sosnik, Dowd and Fournier 2006: 41)*

This analysis showed far more potential supporters than did traditional methods. A decision was quickly made to invest $3 million in a ground-breaking microtargeting program (Sosnik *et al.* 2006: 41).

Microtargeting techniques are by and large proprietary, and they surely differ, but Ken Strasma of Strategic Telemetry has provided a functional definition:

> Micro-targeting works by taking whatever individual-level information is available (e.g., IDs, contributor information, vote history) and combining it with demographic, geographic and marketing data about those individuals to build statistical models that predict the attitudes and behaviors of voters for whom that individual-level information is not known.
>
> *(Strasma no date)*

The general idea is to collect information about the electorate and then attempt to profile voters (and prospective voters) in terms of their likelihoods to cast a ballot and to be supportive. This task might be aided by high-end algorithms. With mounting quantities of information becoming available, computational power increasing and targeting operations gaining experience with complex modeling procedures, it is reasonable to suppose that microtargeting will soon become a standard fixture of down-ballot political campaigns.

Absentee chase programs

Some US states have begun instituting absentee ballot ('AB') or vote-by-mail ('VBM') programs; likewise, some allow for early voting ('EV') in ordinary voting booths for a few weeks prior to election day. If local boards of elections publish the names of voters who have requested absentee ballots – some US jurisdictions do exactly that – then early voting offers a new marketing opportunity. When a ballot request is reported, the campaign can rush literature into the mail. The voter might receive the ballot and a campaign flyer on the very same day, as if, from the voter's point of view, by magic. Moreover, people who have already voted might be struck from mailing lists, preserving campaign cash for better use elsewhere. Such efforts can be labor-intensive. While some reports are available online, ready to merge into the campaign's database, others demand considerable processing.

Chasing ballots combines the oft-conflicting ideals of high efficiency and broad coverage. A campaign is able to send its message at the moment when many voters are in 'buy mode', hitting every selected voter who requests a ballot. 'The importance of running an AB chase program', according to Michael Beach of Targeted Victory, 'is only going to increase as more states make AB/EV an easier option and more voters grow accustomed to casting their ballots that way'. Likewise, says Beach, the data required for a chase program is becoming more and more obtainable: 'If you look at a state like Nevada that has had significant AB/EV voting in the past you will see that they have made great strides in producing clean files on a daily basis and posting them directly to their web site' (personal communication).

Advice for practitioners

The guiding steps of an ideal voter selection procedure can be stated simply:

- Disaggregate the electorate into politically meaningful segments.
- Estimate the benefit of reaching each segment.
- Estimate the cost of reaching each segment.
- Then find the most cost-effective means of accumulating enough votes to win the election.

In the abstract, each step flows smartly, one to the next, and maybe the arithmetic can be done by hand. Still, politics being the art of the possible, it is not clear that a single, parsimonious method exists to handle every voter-selection problem.

In some jurisdictions, privacy considerations might preclude the use of otherwise valuable individual-level data. For some campaigns, survey research might be prohibitively expensive. In any event, the efficiencies gained from a selection procedure may or may not justify the costs of running the procedure itself, and the value of such an endeavor might not become clear until after all the ballots have been cast, if then. Trade-offs abound. Given the variety of data scenarios and strategic conditions that a strategist could possibly confront, it might be true that selection procedures should be custom-tailored for each electoral contest – though customized solutions may themselves bring overhead costs that a campaign is unable to afford.

The upshot is that 'what works' remains an open question. To say that strategists should disaggregate electorates and optimize expenditures sidesteps the need for concrete advice; however, getting too deep into specifics implies that an overarching solution might endure the shifting sands of electoral politics.

Impact on politics: strategic voter selection and democracy

Strategic voter selection procedures have been developed not to promote a national conversation, but to win elections. Increasing a campaign's operational efficiency often means *excluding* large numbers of voters from political communications. If this effort results in narrow outreach programs directed toward unrepresentative fragments of the electorate, pulling communications away from the vast bulk of the citizenry, then any benefit to the overall political conversation would seem little more than an unintended consequence.

Critics of strategic voter selection can find support in Heather Savigny's discussion of recent campaigns in the UK. Savigny notes that 'new' Labour has been concentrating its efforts on small segments of that electorate (Savigny 2008: 52–60). In 1997 the party gave its attention to 'Tory switchers', and this sort of narrow-gauge selection continued in 2001 with 'Operation Turnout', which 'targeted weak and wavering Labour voters' (ibid.: 55, 60). In 2005 Labour used advanced databasing to select target groups from among dozens of electoral segments (ibid.: 59). Writes Savigny, 'The practice of marketing in campaigning suggests that rather than the demands of the polity being at the centre of the political process, it was the voters whose votes mattered to the election outcome' (ibid.: 59). Further, if voter segmentation prompts a left-leaning party to look more like its right-leaning competitor by targeting groups like Tory-switchers, then one may reasonably conclude that some degree of voter choice has been lost in the bargain (ibid.: 56).

Strategic voter selection might therefore deepen the feeling that candidates are being sold like breakfast cereal. A commercial product needs only a small market share to gain an honorable profit, so tightly focused advertising is unproblematic from a business perspective. However, with political campaigns, which participate in a struggle that purports to confer some kind of public mandate, selective outreach might prompt well-meaning citizens to conclude once and for all that the electoral process lacks authenticity.

It is conceivable that treating voters like data points could depress turnout or could otherwise erode the legitimizing role of elections. Another way to understand voter segmentation, however, would be to view targeted outreach as a means of smoothing over gaps in participation. The ideal selection model ignores voters who have already made up their minds and opts for those who would put campaign-generated information to good use. In contrast, reaching out to an entire electorate would likely result in fewer resources directed toward moveable voters – less GOTV outreach to under-motivated citizens, less political information to the undecideds. Indeed, if one's own partisans start to drift, smart selection could plausibly locate these voters so that they can be motivated once again.

All of which is to suggest that new methods of voter selection do not settle ongoing debates about campaigns and democracy; they merely throw important questions into sharper relief. Matters become even more complicated with the rise of new channels of communication that allow citizens neglected by a campaign's selection procedure to engage with like-minded individuals in the blogosphere, to post comments regarding web-published news stories, and to find information on official campaign websites, in social media and through micro-blogs. If the rise of new-style campaigning in the 1960s and 1970s, which soon spread professionalized campaign management practices around the globe, had the effect of motivating a debate over the participatory nature of elections that has yet to be resolved (Burton and Shea 2010: 215–19), then ongoing refinements to political marketing are unlikely to settle larger disputes about democratic governance.

The way forward: future research into voter selection

Decades of political research have gone toward studying voter behavior, with a great deal of attention being paid to the ways in which members of certain groups arrive at their respective decisions. Some of this work relates to strategic voter selection. Scholars have demonstrated cutting-edge segmentation techniques (Green and Kern 2010; Imai and Strauss 2011; Murray and

Scime 2010) and they have analyzed controlled field experiments in ways that suggest practical applications (Arceneaux and Nickerson 2009; Green and Kern 2010). However, questions remain. Is demographically based voter selection superior to geographically based or survey-based voter selection? How might these dimensions of an electorate be combined? Considering the price of research and the savings putatively gained from efficiency, which voter selection procedures tend to be most useful? Which demographic segments show meaningful distinctions over time and across jurisdictions, and which are more local and time-bound, restricted to certain campaigns and candidates?

These questions are hard to answer, partly owing to the close-held nature of the methods used in political campaigns, partly because scientific experimentation generally requires that a control group be left out (and campaign organizations do not always like to leave promising voters 'untreated'), but also because political campaigns are ever-changing. The practice of electioneering is under relentless pressure to evolve. Any electoral system that is free and fair invites strategic innovation, and major developments such as the introduction of microtargeting tend to change the way campaigns are run. The study of political campaigns must therefore appreciate the dynamism of a political world constituted by an 'upward spiral of measure, countermeasure, and counter-countermeasure, in which new strategies give rise to new electoral environments, and vice versa' (Burton and Shea 2003: 10).

What has *not* changed is the ultimate goal of campaign strategy – *winning elections* – and the subordinate requirement of winning those elections on budget. At least as far back as Lincoln's time, campaign organizations have seen the path to victory in the perfect list, the talking to, the constant watch and the effort to get supporters out to vote. Nineteenth-century operatives used the tactics available to them, however quaint those tactics would later appear. The methods now emerging in the political marketplace have merely extended a time-honored logic to the information, expertise and technologies that have become available to campaign strategists in the new millennium.

Bibliography

Allen, C. (1996) *Taking Back Politics: An Insider's Guide to Winning*, Seattle, WA: Jalepeño Press.

Arceneaux, K. and Nickerson, D.W. (2009) 'Who is mobilized to vote? A re-analysis of 11 randomized field experiments', *American Journal of Political Science* 53: 1–16.

Aristotle International (no date a) 'We salute the triumph of the Ukrainian people'. Online, www.aristotle.com/content/view/115/120 (accessed 14 February 2011).

—— (no date b) 'Premium enhancement matrix'. Online, www.aristotle.com/content/view/57/191 (accessed 16 February 2011).

Burton, M.J. and Shea, D.M. (2003) *Campaign Mode: Strategic Vision in Congressional Elections*, Lanham, MD: Rowman & Littlefield.

—— (2010) *Campaign Craft: The Strategies, Tactics, and Art of Political Campaign Management*, fourth edn, Santa Barbara, CA: Praeger.

Clinton, J.D. and Lapinski, J.S. (2004) '" Targeted" advertising and voter turnout: An experimental study of the 2000 presidential election', *Journal of Politics* 66: 69–96.

Fishel, M. (1998a) 'Electoral targeting, part I: Do-it-yourself', in R. Faucheux (ed.) *The Road to Victory*, second edn, Dubuque, IA: Kendall/Hunt, 171–80.

—— (1998b) 'Electoral targeting, part II: Analyzing the data', in R. Faucheux (ed.) *The Road to Victory*, second edn, Dubuque, IA: Kendall/Hunt, 181–203.

Gaby, D.M. and Treusch, M.H. (1976) *Election Campaign Handbook*, Englewood Cliffs, NJ: Prentice-Hall.

Gelman, A., Park, D., Shor, B. and Cortina, J. (2008) *Red State, Blue State, Rich State, Poor State: Why Americans Vote the Way They Do*, Princeton, NJ: Princeton University Press.

Green, D.P. and Gerber, A.S. (2008) *Get Out the Vote: How to Increase Voter Turnout*, second edn, Washington, DC: Brookings Institution Press.

Green, D.P. and Kern, H.L. (2010) 'Detecting heterogeneous treatment effects in large-scale experiments using Bayesian additive regression trees', Working Paper dated 24 May.

Hardy, B., Adasiewicz, C., Kenski, K. and Jamieson, K.H. (2010) 'Spending differences and the role of microtargeting', in K. Kenski, B.W. Hardy and K.H. Jamieson (eds) *The Obama Victory: How Media, Money, and Message Shaped the 2008 Election*, New York: Oxford.

Henry, A.G., Baker, E.D., Barrett, R.F., Speed, J.F. and Lincoln, A. (1840) 'Campaign circular from Whig committee', in *The Collected Works of Abraham Lincoln, Volume 1*, 201–3. Online, quod.lib.umich.edu/cgi/t/text/text-idx?c=lincoln;idno=lincoln1;rgn=div1;view=text;cc=lincoln;node=lincoln1%3A214 (accessed 16 February 2011).

Hughes, C. (1989) 'Parliament and politics: Labour sets sights on green voters', *Independent*, 29 June: 8.

Imai, K. and Strauss, A. (2011) 'Estimation of heterogeneous treatment effects from randomized experiments, with application to the optimal planning of the Get-Out-The-Vote campaign', *Political Analysis* 19: 1–19.

Jones, L.V., Lewis, C. and Tukey, J.W. (2001) 'Hypothesis tests, multiplicity of', in N.J. Smelser and P.B. Baltes (eds) *International Encyclopedia of the Social and Behavioral Sciences*, Oxford: Elsevier.

Kramer, G. (1966) 'A decision-theoretic analysis of a problem in political campaigning', in J. L. Bernd (ed.) *Mathematical Applications in Political Science II*, Dallas, TX: Southern Methodist University Press.

Kurtz, H. (1992) 'Clinton, Bush ads go separate ways; while Democrat targets specific states, Republican uses nationwide approach', *Washington Post*, 23 September: A12.

Malchow, H. (2008) *The New Political Targeting*, second edn, Washington, DC: Predicted Lists.

Murray, G.R. and Scime, A. (2010) 'Microtargeting and electorate segmentation: Data mining the American National Election Studies', *Journal of Political Marketing* 9: 143–66.

National Women's Education Fund (1978) *Campaign Workbook*, second edn, Washington, DC: National Women's Education Fund.

Savigny, H. (2008) *The Problem of Political Marketing*, New York: Continuum.

Shaw, C. (2010) *The Campaign Manager: Running and Winning Local Elections*, fourth edn, Boulder, CO: Westview Press.

Shaw, D.R. (2006) *The Race to 270: The Electoral College and the Campaign Strategies of 2000 and 2004*, Chicago: University of Chicago Press.

Sosnik, D.B., Dowd, M.J. and Fournier, R. (2006) *Applebee's America: How Successful Political, Business, and Religious Leaders Connect with the New American Community*, New York: Simon & Schuster.

Strasma, K. (no date) 'Micro-targeting: New wave political campaigning', in *Winning Campaigns*. Online, www.winningcampaigns.org/Winning-Campaigns-Archive-Articles/Micro-Targeting-New-Wave-Political-Campaigning.html (accessed 16 February 2011).

Wayne, L. (2008) 'Democrats take page from their rival's playbook', *New York Times*, 1 November: A15.

Weisberg, H.F. (2005) *The Total Survey Error Approach: A Guide to the New Science of Survey Research*, Chicago: University of Chicago Press.

5

Government public opinion research and consultation

Experiences in deliberative marketing

Mathias König and Wolfgang König

The topic: the deliberative marketing approach

Political marketing can help governments and political parties to respond to the specific needs of the citizens and avoid superficial or undifferentiated protest, but rather than just conducting market research, another form of consultation or dialogue is through a deliberative political marketing process. The intelligent involvement of citizens in political decision-making processes can also increase the effectiveness of governance. The multifaceted knowledge of citizens is an additional resource that should be utilized. This idea is based on the concept of communicative action (Habermas 1984) respondent deliberative democracy (Habermas 1996: 287–328) and rests upon the argument that through the participation of the public and the citizens in political processes, it becomes possible to make better decisions and thus also to communicate them more easily. Not only from a philosophical standpoint, but also directly from practice-oriented administrative science there have been efforts to increase citizen participation in administrative politics and decision-making at least since the discussions of New Public Management and Good Governance (Scott 2003: 55–69). After all, what is striven for is an increasingly efficient constitutional and citizen-friendly administrative practice and that is dependent upon democratic quality and legitimacy (Dahl 1994). From the viewpoint of political marketing, deliberative communicative processes represent new forms of dialogue and marketing. Furthermore, deliberative political marketing can develop beyond a technique to a form of governance.

Previous research on deliberative political marketing

In political marketing literature, few studies have linked deliberation to marketing, other than Lees-Marshment and Winter (2009), Henneberg *et al.* (2009), and Lees-Marshment (2011). Lees-Marshment and Winter pointed out that political marketing is associated with deliberative democracy and so deliberative politics may therefore offer greater insight into how governments can consult the public and make that consultation more worthwhile (Lees-Marshment 2009: 282).

Henneberg *et al.* (2009) point to terminological inexactitudes and difficulties when it comes to the delineation of 'political marketing', 'political management' and 'political communication'. From a democratic-theoretical perspective, the concept of political marketing runs the risk of appearing like a discursive instrument of power to be used for the achievement of short-term political goals, e.g., during elections. However, from the very same point of view a more positive conception may be adopted, i.e., political marketing as an opportunity to establish and maintain a trustful relationship between voters on the one hand and political parties and administration on the other. To practicians, and hence realists, the truth lies somewhere in between. Thus, Henneberg *et al.* (2009: 165–88) subdivide 'political marketing' into three practical concepts:

- selling-oriented political marketing management (PMM);
- instrumentally oriented PMM; and
- relational PMM.

A selling-oriented approach 'puts an ideology or conviction first', whereas 'instrumentally-oriented PMM is focused on a deep understanding of primary stakeholders'. However, a relational approach 'also incorporates the interests of stakeholders who are not direct exchange partners and assesses the trade-offs between short-term and long-term effects' (Henneberg *et al.* 2009: 171–72).

From a democratic-theoretical perspective, the strategic use of political marketing instruments seems closely linked to the logic of Joseph Schumpeter's 'competitive elitism'. According to Schumpeter, democracy is a procedure for the selection of elites by means of regular elections. Thus, his theory is based on the assumption that it is not the citizens who rule, but the elites. However, the term 'elite' has positive connotations in Schumpeter's approach, and from his point of view political marketing can be understood as management by and through elites. Hence, political marketing is predominantly perceived as an instrument. At the same time, arguments from the theory of deliberative democracy are gaining more and more significance within the context of political marketing. Whoever wants to win elections nowadays must win the 'political marketing game'. That means that politicians:

> need to offer responsive leadership that responds to but does not just follow public opinion; authentic reflectiveness that shows genuine considerations of different demands but does not change positions without justification. Furthermore, they need to move towards a partnership relationship with the public where both citizens and government work together to find solutions.
>
> *(Lees-Marshment 2011: 209)*

Lees-Marshment's (2011) new theory of a partnership democracy argues that market analysis needs to become more deliberative and even form an institution in its own right.

The political decision-makers and leaders who must decide upon a strategy are still a central factor. 'They need to balance leading and following the public …' (Lees-Marshment 2011: 213). If one understands politicians as a brand (Lees-Marshment 2011: 213), the decision on the kind and manner of the chosen political marketing then is a key element of the brand. Accordingly, the level of deliberation of the chosen political marketing is a key element of the brand. Thus, deliberative market analysis is 'the new system of voter input in politics' (Lees-Marshment 2011: 220).

However, the idea to link political marketing and deliberation needs further development and application. First, it is important to make the link between political marketing and deliberative politics. Habermas explained a key factor of deliberative politics and communication: 'The communication circulation in the public sphere is especially vulnerable to the selective pressure of social inertia; the influence thus generated, however, can be converted into political procedure and penetrates the constitutionally organized political system in general' (Habermas 1996: 327). Second, although much of the literature has discussed the need for politicians to become market-oriented, even if a politician wanted to meet the wishes of the voters, it is always possible that he or she will fail. Therefore, a market orientation cannot ensure a long-term relationship, because the voters are addressed as customers and not as citizens. Customers expect a good product, and will switch producers if the product is deficient. Empowered citizens, however, can understand why and how political decisions were made, and so failures do not destroy a long-term relationship. 'Parties should not treat voters solely as consumers, but as both consumers and citizens' (Lees-Marshment 2008: 12). In order to emphasize the citizen perspective, a new form of marketing is necessary, namely deliberative marketing, which would enable the circulation of communication in the public sphere.

New research on deliberative political marketing

Elite discussion of deliberative marketing: President Obama and the EU Commission

The focus shift in political marketing became evident in the Obama campaign. The chief campaign manager for Barack Obama's 2008 presidential campaign in the US, David Plouffe, pointed out that the so-called grassroots focus is the key to success. 'There is no more effective courier for a message than people who believe in it and have authentically embraced it' (Plouffe 2009: 379). The grassroots approach makes campaigners less like foot soldiers and more like the passionate minutemen of the American Revolution because the campaign creates a user-generated brand culture (Bryant 2008). This made it possible to connect with voters on a different level. The internet has proven to be of great value here. The further development of political marketing is reflected in the Open Government initiative:

> On his first day in Office, President Obama signed the Memorandum on Transparency and Open Government, ushering in a new era of open and accountable government meant to bridge the gap between the American people and their government:
>
> The Administration is reducing the influence of special interests by writing new ethics rules that prevent lobbyists from coming to work in government or sitting on its advisory boards.
>
> The Administration is tracking how government uses the money with which the people have entrusted it with easy-to-understand websites like recovery.gov, USASpending.gov, and IT.usaspending.gov.
>
> The Administration is empowering the public – through greater openness and new technologies – to influence the decisions that affect their lives.
>
> *(White House Open Government Initiative no date)*

This initiative is predominantly implemented through the internet. One example is the website Data.gov. Data.gov enables the public to participate in government and deliberate on political issues by providing downloadable federal datasets to build applications, conduct analyses and perform research. The site also allows the communication between citizens and administration. 'The site will continue to improve based on feedback, comments, and recommendations from the public and therefore we encourage individuals to suggest datasets they'd like to see, rate and comment on current datasets, and suggest ways to improve the site' (Data.gov no date). The internet allows citizens to become active participants and opens the opportunity for a more robust, sustainable level of involvement of citizens in the governance of their society (Benkler 2008: 53). The cost structure of the internet enables the creation of a deliberative arena through political marketing. These arenas will be increasingly important because people always want more things to decide. 'For it's clear we're living in a new age, where millions of people can participate directly in governance and policy making, not just in ratifying the results on Election Day' (Fine *et al.* 2008: 1).

One reason for Obama's latest crisis can be seen in the fact that his government did not succeed in the institutionalization of deliberative political marketing, which has led to the loss of the communicative impetus that had accompanied his election campaign. What Obama's case shows is the necessity to employ deliberative marketing not only as a way to short-term success, but as a philosophy in itself. The constituents know if they are dealing only with a simple technique or with an authentic and credible philosophy. When used solely as a technique, deliberative political marketing may evoke exaggerated expectations on the part of the constituents and thus lead to a spiral of disappointment with the government.

In Europe there is a dawning realization that deliberative political marketing needs to become an inherent part of European governance. In its White Paper on European Governance, the European Union (EU) Commission aims to help reinforce the culture of consultation and dialogue in the EU. The democratic institutions and the representatives of the people, at both national and European levels, must try to connect Europe with its citizens (Commission of the European Communities 2001: 3).

> The Commission believes that the processes of administration and policy-making must be visible to the outside world if they are to be understood and have credibility. This is particularly true of the consultation process, which acts as the primary interface with interests in society.
> *(Commission of the European Communities 2002: 17)*

Extensive consultation should take place in all political arenas. In this context, good consultation serves a dual purpose by helping to improve the quality of the policy outcome, while at the same time increasing the involvement of interested parties and the public at large. A further advantage is that transparent and coherent consultation processes run by the Commission do not only allow the general public to be more involved, they also give the legislature greater power to scrutinize the Commission's activities (Commission of the European Communities 2002). The intention of the so-called 'European Citizens' Initiative' (ECI), enacted in December 2010, is to push citizen involvement. A central element of the ECI is the political and legal institutionalization of a new instrument of deliberative marketing, the opportunities and benefits of which are known. That is, the public is mobilized while being well aware of the fact that although the results are not binding, they will definitely help produce political pressure:

> The ECI will introduce a whole new form of participatory democracy to the EU. It is a major step forward in the democratic life of the Union. It's a concrete example of bringing

> Europe closer to its citizens. And it will foster a cross border debate about what we are doing in Brussels and thus contribute, we hope, to the development of a real European public space …
>
> *(Maroš Šefčovič, Vice-President for Inter-institutional Relations and Administration)*

Implementation of deliberation: examples of citizens' juries

The precursor to the European Citizens' Initiative was the European Citizens' Consultations, which represent the only EU-wide deliberation until the introduction of the ECI in 2012. The first transnational, EU-wide citizens' juries, namely the European Citizens' Consultations, serve as the first case study. These were established in order to increase the involvement of citizens after the failed referenda on the EU Constitution, and at the same time to boost the support of the general public for the EU project. The European Citizens' Consultations have been awarded several PR prizes.

In the second case, a citizens' jury (*Planungszelle* in German) is utilized in the framework of a controversial communal and general administrative reform in Germany, in addition to two other forms of deliberative communication. This had great impact on citizens. Figure 5.1 illustrates the 'change dynamics' of the attitudes (beliefs) of the participants as assessed in the examined procedure in Rhineland-Palatinate.

Figure 5.1 summarizes the results from six *Planungszellen*. It becomes clear that citizens' beliefs change through the procedure. They demand in particular the support of voluntary work by citizens and gain trust in the political process of the reform. Transparency and knowledge

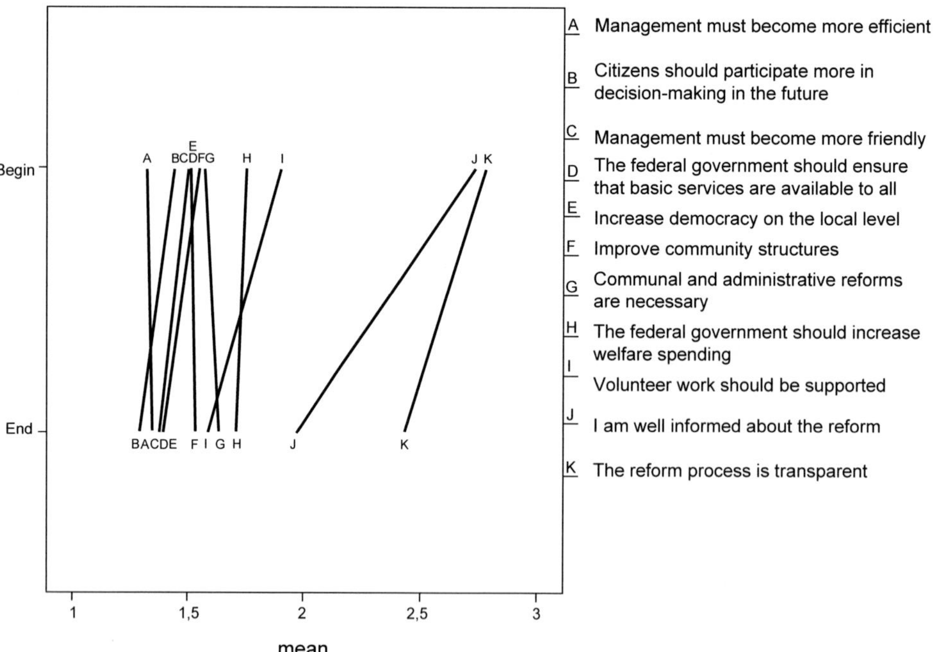

Figure 5.1 Changes in ratings of statements concerning reforms in the course of the planning procedure (*Planungszelle*) (N=140)

improve the most; from the viewpoint of political marketing this result should be interesting for further research. Changes and possible mergers of cities and communities in the state (*Land*) of Rhineland-Palatinate are the issue here. Such reforms have previously failed in other German states because of poor political marketing, among other things. For the example of Rhineland-Palatinate, its own extensive qualitative and quantitative data is available on the basis of which it is possible to formulate conclusions concerning the success of deliberative political marketing beyond the citizens' jury. The main result is that in general as participation increases, so does the satisfaction of the citizens. In any case, it is clear that in principle there is a need for reform. Citizens who are in further participation in the Reform process show interest (Sarcinelli *et al.* 2009: 2).

A look at Japan shows that a citizens' jury can also proceed bottom-up. In Japan, citizens discuss with experts and representatives from the administration and policy, enforced by non-governmental organizations. This *shimintōgikai*[1] promotes interest in the political process and contributes to changes in Japanese public culture previously characterized by the rejection of politics in Japan (Shinoto 2009: 18).

Due to their global utilization in the meantime, citizens' juries are well suited to serve as an empirical case (see Table 5.1). This empirical finding makes clear that the deliberative marketing phenomenon should be explored from the perspective of governance theory.

Deliberative marketing and governance

Governance theory addresses the further development of political institutions, national-global linkages and transnational public-private cooperation (Kooiman 2003: 5), and thus can be linked to deliberative political marketing. Stoker notes how 'theoretical work on governance reflects the interest of the social science community in a shifting pattern in styles of governing' (Stoker 1998: 17). It is all about 'new patterns of interaction', that is, new 'interactive' forms of governance between actors from government, society and economy to observe and explain. 'These new patterns are apparently aimed at discovering other ways of coping with new problems or of creating new possibilities for governing' (Kooiman 1994: 1). Governance is a theory about the changing ways of governing, and governance is understood as an interaction of or with society. However, the impact of change in the relationship of rulers to the ruled has not been adequately explored

Table 5.1 Deliberative political marketing and the citizens' jury

	USA	*EU*	*Japan*	*Rhineland-Palatinate (Germany)*
Name	Citizens' jury	'European Citizens Consultation'	Shimintōgikai	Planungszelle
Organized by administration	+	-	+	+++
Media campaign	+	+++	-	+++
Organized by non-governmental organizations administration	+++	+++	+++	+++
Administrative input	++	+	+++	+++
Problem formulation/ Solution proposals	National, state and local	Transnational	Local	State and local

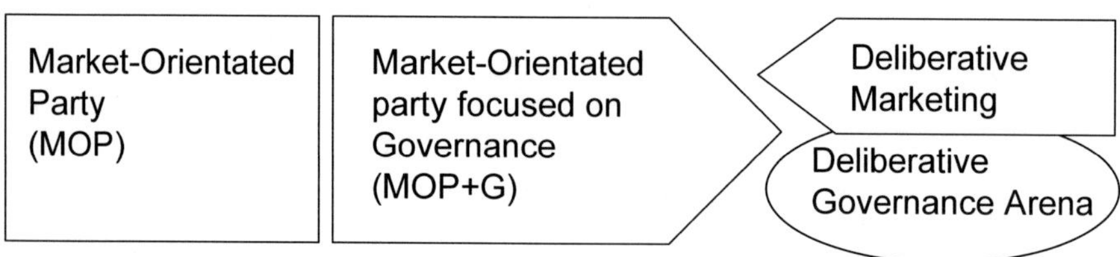

Figure 5.2 Governance focused market-orientated party (MOP+G)

(Kooiman 1994: 249). Governance can explore how elites develop their own ideas and use different instruments and measures to achieve their goals (Kooiman 2003: 10), and how new methods and modes can create socio-political interaction including problem solving (Kooiman 2003: 133).

Governance can also be concerned with the citizen-state relationship and include both more participation and 'extra-formal democracy' (Heinrich *et al.* 2010: 9). Communitarianism and deliberative democracy are two accepted forms of democracy which try to create the smallest possible decision arenas, as these have a low threshold to get citizens involved in decision-making (Pierre and Peters 2000: 148). Citizens are no longer just taxpayers and consumers of public services but participate in the production of public services and contribute to the welfare of society (Bouckaert 1994: 157). It is about the joint development of solutions. Dialogue involves communication, argumentation, deliberation, persuasion and choice (Pekonen 1994: 217).

Thus, given the increased use of deliberative marketing, we can put forward a new theory of 'governance-oriented deliberative political marketing'. 'Market-oriented party' (MOP) can adopt a governance perspective (MOP+G), with deliberative marketing playing a central role. 'Deliberative governance arenas' allow institutional space for the deliberation process (see Figure 5.2).

These deliberative governance arenas also allow the inclusion of different components of knowledge. According to van Buuren, this increases the success of collaborative governance. Fact-finding and framing are the essential ingredients (van Buuren 2009: 230–32).

However, each level of government will be different, of course. The following matrix (see Table 5.2) illustrates the interrelated elements of different kinds of deliberative governance arenas and deliberative political marketing in the decision-making process. In an ideal world, elites would choose the activities that that are most appropriate for the respective partnership.

Advice for practitioners: success factors for deliberative political marketing

The following steps represent the key factors in realizing deliberative political marketing:

The ability of deliberative governance

The first step is to check if there is something to decide and to deliberate. If not, then deliberative political marketing is not helpful.

Designate the responsible leader: The second step is to identify and to name the leader or leaders who are responsible for the deliberative marketing process. At this point it is necessary to clarify the strategic significance of deliberative political marketing for the party.

Table 5.2 Overview of different deliberative governance arenas in the context of the process of political decision-making

Deliberative political marketing focus	*Variations of deliberative governance arenas in the context of the steps in the political decision making process*					
	Agenda setting	*Drafting*	*Decision*	*Implementation*	*Monitoring*	*Reformulation*
Partnership	Work group or committee	Co-drafting	Joint decision-making Co-decision making	Strategic partnerships	Work groups or committee	Work groups or committee
Dialogue	Hearings and public forums Citizens' forums and future councils Key government contact	Hearings and Q&A panels Expert seminars Multi-stakeholder committees and advisory bodies	Open plenary or committee sessions	Capacity building seminars Training seminars	Work groups or committee	Seminars and deliberative forums
Consultation	Petitioning Consultation online or other techniques	Hearings and Q&A panels Expert seminars Multi-stakeholder committees and advisory bodies	Open plenary or committee sessions	Events, conferences, forums, seminars	Feedback mechanisms	Conferences or meetings Online consultation
Information	Easy and open information access Research campaigning and lobbying Website for key documents	Open and free access to policy documents Website for key documents Campaigns and lobbying Web casts Research input	Campaigning and lobbying	Open access to information Website for information access E-mail alerts FAQ Public tendering procedures	Open access to information Evidence gathering Evaluations Research studies	Open access to information

Choose the right deliberative governance arena wisely: The third step is to identify the most useful deliberative governance arena in the context of the decision-making process and the strategic goals. The 'Matrix of Civil Participation' in Conference of INGOs of the Council of Europe (2009: 17) is useful for this step.

Check the deliberative political marketing focus: The fourth step is to ensure that the chosen deliberative governance arena is in line with the strategy of the party.

What happens with the results? The fifth step focuses on the output. In planning the deliberative marketing strategy, it is essential to know which steps will be taken after the results of the deliberation have been obtained. This is also important for the people who deliberate because they want to know if the time they are investing in a deliberative governance arena is worthwhile.

Design the deliberative marketing communication: The sixth step is to design and choose marketing instruments that are useful for implementing the specific form of deliberative governance by considering the outcomes and impacts.

Use the deliberative governance arena as a marketing event: The seventh step is to use the communicative power of the deliberative governance arena. Voters and party members can be mobilized to deliberate and find collaborative solutions which give new perspectives for political solutions. This fact is particularly interesting for the media because new perspectives may collide with established ways of thinking

Conflicting results

Challenge for leadership: Dealing with conflicting results is the greatest challenge for leadership in deliberative political marketing. At this step the importance of step 2 becomes clear, because that is where personal accountability and responsibility for ensuring and monitoring outcomes are determined.

Communicate your decision

The final step is to communicate the decision wisely. This is one of the most challenging tasks in deliberative political marketing. The decision (especially when there are conflicting results) must be transparent and comprehensible, so the stakeholders can understand why the leader prefers a different solution.

A lifecycle approach: Steps one to nine can be considered a lifecycle model when deliberative political marketing is used continuously over time.

Deliberative political marketing: a governance philosophy

Under a holistic perspective, deliberative political marketing must be seen as a governance philosophy for market-oriented parties, so that they will be able to handle the problem of complexity.

Impact on politics: deliberative political marketing and leadership

The market-orientation model is a valuable heuristic guideline, but no party can be 'truly' market-oriented (Temple 2010: 274–75). The concept of market orientation is not just about following the market demands, but using market intelligence (Lees-Marshment *et al.* 2010: 295). Deliberative marketing, however, may make it work more effectively if it is integrated into a new leadership style whereby policy-makers or parties must align marketing intelligence with governance. The consequence for political leaders or marketing managers is that they find themselves in the middle of a new kind of strategic collaboration for which they need respective skills. Collaboration-related competencies include the ability to work productively both within and outside of hierarchy and to act deliberatively and strategically (Norris-Tirrell and Clay 2010a: 2–10). They also should attend carefully to the development of the collaboration's structure, focusing on the rules of deliberative governance and the political decision-making process (Norris-Tirrell and Clay 2010b: 36). The existence of a champion or highly visible and well-known leader or leadership group helps citizens to join or to engage in deliberative governance arenas (Clay and Norris-Tirrell 2010: 64). Voters must trust governments to deal with the unexpected as well as the expected, and a party or government will be more highly regarded when it is seen as being responsive to public opinion. However, in the long term it is necessary to develop leadership systems because leaders will someday leave the organization. Thus, operational guidelines should encompass leadership development programs so that future leaders can acquire experience in key roles before stepping up to higher positions (Norris-Tirrell and Clay 2010c: 81). Consequently, deliberative political marketing needs to undergo a transformation from a mere idea to an entire philosophy. If deliberative political marketing is accepted and applied within the federal institutional system, then it will become part of the logic of the political culture. This will lead to a new form of trust in the citizen–leader relationship.

The way forward

There is a growing awareness of the need for participation to be valued in democratic systems. This has implications for policy-making and decision-making, in that participation and multi-perspectives are the ingredients for a more informed debate over policy issues and the basis for the analysis of policy options (White 2002: 158–59). Through deliberative governance arenas, policy-makers get the whole system into one room which could result in creative solutions for a particular issue that are quantitatively different from solutions found by a small group. The use of such processes could activate citizens and strengthen their faith in democratic processes. The following practical criteria must be considered on a permanent basis:

- Reasonable time frame: This is necessary in order to increase the willingness of the individual to invest time in common interests.
- Partnership: Cooperation with the participants on a level playing field.
- Intrinsic motivation: Ensuring that participants motivate themselves.
- Personal interest/self-interest: The topic must interest the citizen and appear meaningful.
- Plausibility: Easy comprehensibility of the processes from the beginning until the end.
- Integrative aspects: Integration of diversity to make use of its potentials.

Exactly to attain these quality criteria, deliberative marketing analyses are necessary. The next steps in research are to learn about how to work with large groups in deliberative governance arenas and apply the results in order to optimize deliberative marketing, because constant combining and adapting will be necessary to produce the most powerful dynamic of methods of deliberative governance arenas (Carson and Hartz-Karp 2005: 135) and deliberative political marketing. The challenge is to build decision-making processes in which participatory action is possible with a fully engaged leadership or leadership group that accurately reflects the diverse views and values and can still make effective decisions (Murell 2000: 811–12).

Note

1 The concept consists of *shimin* (citizen), *tōgi* (discourse) and *kai* (discussion).

Bibliography

Ansell, C. and Gash, A. (2008) 'Collaborative governance in theory and practice', *J Public Adm Res Theory* 18: 543–71.

Aquina, H. and Bekke, H. (1994) 'Governance in interaction: public tasks and private organisations', in J. Kooiman (ed.) *Modern Governance: New government-society interactions*, London: Sage.

Barnes, S.H. (1979) *Political Action: Mass participation in five western democracies*, Beverly Hills, CA: Sage.

Benkler, Y. (2008) 'Participation as sustainable cooperation in pursuit of public goals', in A.H. Fine, M.L. Sifry, A. Rasiej and J. Levy (eds) *Rebooting America: Ideas for redesigning American democracy for the internet age*, New York: Personal Democracy Press.

Bouckaert, G. (1994) 'Governance between legitimacy and efficiency: citizen participation in the Belgian fire service', in J. Kooiman (ed.) *Modern Governance. New government-society interactions*, London: Sage.

Bryant, I. (2008) *An Inside Look at Obama's Grassroots Marketing*. Online, www.adweek.com/aw/content_display/community/columns/other-columns/e3i714b5acb6525107fda1eb890ff94a48a (accessed 7 June 2010).

Bütschi, D. and Nentwich, M. (2002) 'The role of participatory technology assesment in the policy-making process', in S. Joss and S. Belucci (eds) *Participatory Technology Assessment. European perspectives*, London: Center for the Study of Democracy.

Carson, L. and Hartz-Karp, J. (2005) 'Adapting and combining deliberative designs: juries, polls and forums', in J. Gastil and P. Levine (eds) *The Deliberative Democracy Handbook: Strategies for effective civic engagement in the twenty-first century*, New York: Jossey-Bass.

Cho, C.-L., Kelleher, C.A., Wright, D.S. and Yackee, S.W. (2005) 'Translating national policy objectives into local achievements across planes of governance and among multiple actors: second-order devolution and welfare reform implementation', *J Public Adm Res Theory* 15: 54–31.

Choi, Y.-T. (2007) 'Strategic marketing issue', in C.A. van Deusen, S. Williamson and H.C. Babson (eds) *Business Policy and Strategy: The art of competition*, seventh edn, Boca Raton, FL: Auerbach.

Clay, J.A. and Norris-Tirrell, D. (2010) 'Assesing collaborative readiness: the missing strategic step', in D. Norris-Tirrell and J.A. Clay (eds) *Strategic Collaboration in Public and Nonprofit Administration: A practice-based approach to solving shared problems*, Boca Raton, FL: CRC.

Commission of the European Communities (2001) *European Governance: A White Paper: COM (2001) 428 final*, Brussels. Online, ec.europa.eu/civil_society/consultation_standards (accessed 25 June 2010).

—— (2002) *General Principles and Minimum Standards for Consultation of Interested Parties by the Commission: COM(2002)704 final*, Brussels. Online, ec.europa.eu/civil_society/consultation_standards (accessed 12 December 2003).

Conference of INGOs of the Council of Europe (2009) *Code of Good Practice for Civil Participation in the Decision-making Process*. Adopted by the Conference of INGOs at its meeting on 1 October 2009, CONF/PLE(2009)CODE1, Stockholm, Istanbul, Kiev. Online, www.coe.int/t/ngo/Source/Code_English_final.pdf (accessed 24 May 2011).

Dahl, R.A. (1994) 'A democratic dilemma: system effectiveness versus citizen participation', *Political Science Quarterly* 109: 34–23.

Data.gov (no date) 'About'. Online, www.data.gov/about (accessed 21 March 2011).

Duclaud-Williams, R. (1994) 'The governance of education: Britain and France', in J. Kooiman (ed.) *Modern Governance. New government-society interactions*, London: Sage.

Fine, A.H., Sifry, M.L., Rasiej, A. and Levy, J. (2008) 'Preface', in Personal Democracy Forum, A.H. Fine, M.L. Sifry, A. Rasiej and J. Levy (eds) *Rebooting America. Ideas for redesigning American democracy for the internet age*, New York: Personal Democracy Press.

Habermas, J. (1984) *The Theory of Communicative Action*, Boston, MA: Beacon Press.

—— (1996) *Between Facts and Norms: Contributions to a discourse theory of law and democracy*, Cambridge, MA: MIT Press.

Heinrich, C.J., Lynn, L.E. and Milward, H.B. (2010) 'A state of agents? Sharpening the debate and evidence over the extent and impact of the transformation of governance', *J Public Adm Res Theory* 20: i3–19.

Henneberg, S.C., Scammell, M. and O'Shaughnessy, N.J. (2009) 'Political marketing management and theories of democracy', *Marketing Theory* 9: 188–65.

Hill, L.B. (1991) 'Who governs the American administrative state? A bureaucratic-centered image of governance', *J Public Adm Res Theory* 1: 294–61.

Kaplan, R.S. and Norton, D.P. (2001) *The Strategy-focused Organization: How balanced scorecard companies thrive in the new business environment*, Boston, MA: Harvard Business School Press.

Kooiman, J. (1994) 'Social-political governance: introduction', in J. Kooiman (ed.) *Modern Governance. New government-society interactions*, London: Sage.

—— (2003) *Governing as Governance*, London: Sage.

Lees-Marshment, J. (2004) *The Political Marketing Revolution: Transforming the government of the UK*, Manchester: Manchester University Press.

—— (2008) *Political Marketing and British Political Parties*, Manchester and New York: Manchester University Press.

—— (2009) *Political Marketing: Principles and applications*, London and New York: Routledge.

—— (2010) 'Global political marketing', in J. Lees-Marshment, J. Strömbäck and C. Rudd (eds) *Global Political Marketing*, London and New York: Routledge.

—— (2011) 'Conclusion: political marketing, democracy, and partnership', in J. Lees-Marshment (ed.) *The Political Marketing Game*, London and Basingstoke: Palgrave Macmillan.

Lees-Marshment, J., Strömbäck, J. and Rudd, C. (2010) 'Global political marketing: analysis and conclusions', in J. Lees-Marshment, J. Strömbäck and C. Rudd (eds) *Global Political Marketing*, London and New York: Routledge.

Lees-Marshment, J. and Winter, S. (2009) 'Reconciling political marketing market-oriented party theory with deliberative democracy: initial conceptual thoughts', in J. Lees-Marshment (ed.) *Political Marketing: Principles and Applications*, London and New York: Routledge.

Lilleker, D.G. (2003) 'Political marketing: the cause of an emerging democratic deficit in Britain?' Paper presented at the UK Political Studies Association conference, Leicester University, UK, 2003. Online, www.psa.ac.uk/journals/pdf/5/2003/Darren%20Lilleker.pdf (accessed 1 June 2010).

Metcalfe, L. (1994) 'Public management: from imitation into innovation', in J. Kooiman (ed.) *Modern Governance. New government-society interactions*, London: Sage.

Moloney, K. (2004) 'Is political marketing new words or new practice in UK politics?' Paper presented at the UK Political Studies Association conference, University of Lincoln, Lincoln, UK, 2004. Online, www.psa.ac.uk/journals/pdf/5/2004/Moloney.pdf (accessed 14 June 2010).

Mortimore, R. and Gill, M. (2010) 'Implementing and interpreting marketorientation in practice. Lessons from UK', in J. Lees-Marshment, J. Strömbäck and C. Rudd (eds) *Global Political Marketing*, London and New York: Routledge.

Murell, K.L. (2000) 'Organizational change as applied art. Blending pace, magnitude, and depth', in R.T. Golembiewski (ed.) *Handbook of Organizational Consultation*, second edn, New York: Dekker.

Norris-Tirrell, D. and Clay, J.A. (2010a) 'A new lens: the life cycle model of collaboration', in D. Norris-Tirrell and J.A. Clay (eds) *Strategic Collaboration in Public and Nonprofit Administration: A practice-based approach to solving shared problems*, Boca Raton, FL: CRC.

—— (2010b) 'The promise of strategic collaboration', in Norris-Tirrell and J.A. Clay (eds) *Strategic Collaboration in Public and Nonprofit Administration: A practice-based approach to solving shared problems*, Boca Raton, FL: CRC.

—— (2010c) 'Strategic collaboration in action: six principles', in D. Norris-Tirrell and J.A. Clay (eds) *Strategic Collaboration in Public and Nonprofit Administration: A practice-based approach to solving shared problems*, Boca Raton, FL: CRC.

Ostrom, E. (2010) 'The institutional analysis and development framework and the commons', *Cornell Law Review* 103: 807–15.

Pekonen, K. (1994) 'Governance and the problem of representation in public administration: the case of Finland', in J. Kooiman (ed.) *Modern Governance: New government-society interactions*, London: Sage.

Pierre, J. and Peters, B.G. (2000) *Governance, Politics, and the State*, New York: St Martin's Press.

Plouffe, D. (2009) *The Audacity to Win: The inside story and lessons of Barack Obama's historic victory*, New York: Viking.

Sarcinelli, U., König, M. and König, W. (2009) *Bürgerbeteiligung im Rahmen der Kommunal-und Verwaltungsreform in Rheinland-Pfalz. Gutachten zur ersten und zweiten Stufe der Bürgerbeteiligung Oktober 2007–September 2009*, Mainz/Landau: Staatskanzlei und Ministerium des Inneren und für Sport Rheinland-Pfalz. Online, www.buergerkongresse.de/Verwaltungsreform/med/b75/b7550951-8454-0621-aeb6-df186 5a3eafa,11111111-1111-1111-1111-111111111111.pdf (accessed 1 December 2009).

Scott, G. (2003) 'The learning government', *OECD Journal on Budgeting* 2/3.

Shinoto, A. (2009) *Deliberatives Bürgerforum in Japan. Ein Kompaktmodell?* Manuscript. *Universität Beppu (Japan)*, Beppu.
Skelcher, C. (2010) 'Fishing in muddy waters: principals, agents, and democratic governance in Europe', *J Public Adm Res Theory* 20: i161–75.
Stenvall, K. (1994) 'Public policy planning and the problem of governance: the question of education in Finland', in J. Kooiman (ed.) *Modern Governance. New government-society interactions*, London: Sage.
Stoker, G. (1998) 'Governance as theory: five propositions', *International Social Science Journal* 50/155: 28–17.
Strömbäck, J. (2010) 'A framework of comparing political market-orientation', in J. Lees-Marshment, J. Strömbäck and C. Rudd (eds) *Global Political Marketing*, London and New York: Routledge.
Temple, M. (2010) 'Political marketing, party behaviour and political science', in J. Lees-Marshment, J. Strömbäck and C. Rudd (eds) *Global political marketing*, London and New York: Routledge.
van Buuren, A. (2009) 'Knowledge for governance, governance of knowledge: inclusive knowledge management in collaborative governance processes', *International Public Management Journal* 12: 208–35.
van Deusen, C.A., Williamson, S. and Babson, H.C. (2007) 'The importance of business strategy and the external business environment', in C.A. van Deusen, S. Williamson and H.C. Babson (eds) *Business Policy and Strategy: The art of competition*, seventh edn, Boca Raton, FL: Auerbach.
White, L. (2002) 'Size matters: large group methods and the process of operational research', *The Journal of the Operational Research Society* 53: 160–49.
White House Open Government Initiative (no date) 'About open government'. Online, www.whitehouse.gov/open/about (accessed 4 May 2010).

6

Co-creating the future

Roy Langmaid

The topic: co-creation as a market research tool

Market research is a crucial part of political marketing, but is commonly thought of in terms of standard tools such as polls and focus groups. This chapter explores a more innovative method, co-creation, which uses a range of techniques that involve the user, or voter, in creating the solution to the problem, rather than simply voicing their demands and issues. This is more realistic because so many of our desires emerge and take shape as we become more fully aware of both external circumstances and inner motives.

Standard market research draws on the human potential movement in psychology in supporting the idea that rather than controlling the vicissitudes of desire, we should instead celebrate them and through goods and services find ways to indulge them. Politics, albeit possibly without realising it, adopted this idea of a voter as an individual customer who may exchange his vote and his taxes for the rewards of the goods and services that he covets rather than a citizen who votes out of duty and obligation or to maintain the status quo. Correspondingly political parties began to be referred to as brands (the Tory brand, the New Labour brand) and marketed in similar fashion.

Focus groups in particular had proved extremely successful in the sphere of commercial marketing – particularly in uncovering unmet needs and pathways to their fulfilment. This chapter criticises focus groups and puts forward an alternative method which addresses many of the weaknesses of market research in politics: co-creation. Co-creation takes more time to explore an issue and uses more creative and effective methods. It holds the potential to provide higher-quality information which will be more valuable to politicians and thus offers a new direction in market intelligence that political marketing needs to embrace.

Previous research on co-creation

Political marketing has not discussed co-creation, with debate focusing on focus groups (see Savigny 2007, 2008; Wring 2007) and polling. The rare exception is Scammell (2008), who wrote about the work of Promise in using methods such as role-play to create a reconnection strategy for Tony Blair towards the end of his office. This chapter puts forward an original perspective, drawing on practitioner experience in both business and politics to explain the technique of co-creation. There are now several books that discuss relevant topics such as creativity, collaborative creativity and crowd sourcing (see Csikszentmihalyi 1996, Amabile 1996 and Sternberg 1999 on creativity; and Langmaid and Andrews 2003, Johansson 2004, Shirky 2008, Putnam *et al.* 2003, Howe 2008, Earls 2009, Leadbeater 2008, Surowiecki 2004 and Sawyer 2007 on collaborative creativity). This work is not to be confused with deliberative inquiry, which shares some of the elements of co-creation but lacks the core component – the creation of a micro-culture that allows for free expression of vulnerability, together with hidden, selfish or aggressive desires. The next section will explain the background to co-creation, the concept and methods, and illustrate it using the example of the work done for Tony Blair when he was the British prime minister.

The road to co-creation: realising the limitations of the focus group

The personal experience of more than 2,000 focus groups had pointed to some major problems with the method. The key insight was not that focus groups are not useful – for many things they are – but that in an era when diversity, modernity, competition for resources and the impact of globalisation and mediated communication were mushrooming, you could no longer rely on this kind of 'small talk' setting to generate any level of authenticity, depth of contact or reflexivity within the group. Reflexivity – or self-awareness – has become an increasingly important aspect of modern identities in that these are not derived solely from the traditions of parents or the indigenous culture.

Co-creation moves beyond the focus group and uses a more creative reflective and productive methodology that aims to reduce many of the weaknesses in the focus group method. If we summarise those now, they are:

- Time: the standard focus group has eight participants and lasts for 90 minutes. Without pauses, given a perfectly efficient Q&A and counting the facilitator or moderator as a ninth member, that gives 10 minutes to each person. What kind of depth can you expect in these circumstances?
- The size of the problem: if the issue under discussion is which of three opening mechanisms you might prefer for a new sauce bottle, 10 minutes is adequate, even luxurious. However, if you are gathered to talk about your life, your family, education, welfare, the evolution of our society or almost any topic that is complex, how can 10 minutes give you anything but a superficial exploration?
- The nature of the invitation: most focus groups are recruited anonymously with no prior information on the topic or the structure of the group. People show up without any prior contemplation.
- Group dynamics: most people in the group have this one, main, question in their heads through which all of their answers are filtered: 'What will they think of me if I say that?'

  There are lots of minor variations here: someone who hasn't spoken for 10 minutes will be driven to speak because, 'If I don't say something everyone will think I'm dumb.'

In other words, all the participants are reacting to prompts from their inner voices based on past experiences in groups. The distortion of this kind of influence was illustrated by Irving Janis in his book *Groupthink*. Here he describes how even the most intelligent and informed people rush to consensus and form conclusions based on little evidence to avoid tensions between each other.

- Their relationship with the topic: people must have an opportunity to express what is on *their* minds, what *their* concerns are, if they are to take *your* topic seriously.
- Reduced autonomy and creative freedom: focus groups are run to an agenda that is not shared with participants. In our experience these agendas are increasingly long and full of detail. This immediately creates a dependent mindset where the group takes direction from the moderator. This in turn increases conformity.
- Mixed messages and confusion: in the hurry to get through the agenda it is impossible to know whether people are talking about the same thing in the same time frame or not.
- The embodiment problem: we live in our bodies and our feelings are first realised physically. Yet focus groups do not allow physical movement, or the cathexis of emotion and expressive responses.

So, if focus groups have so many limitations, what can take their place?

The road to co-creation: Big Talk

Big Talk was the name coined to distinguish the first co-creation process from the self-centred small talk that dominated focus groups. Big Talk had several important differences from focus groups, namely:

- It featured large groups (15–100 participants) of people talking together both in plenary and smaller sessions.
- It took place on two consecutive days, running for up to eight hours each day.
- It focused on an inspiring or salient topic in human affairs.
- It had as little power structure or fixed structure as was reasonably necessary to move a large group forward in a collaborative manner.
- It comprised more than just customers or citizens. Commercial, institutional or political people were there, staff of corporations or public services were invited, as were experts, specialists and any other instrumental or influential parties.
- All participants were invited to take the role of members of a society or neighbours in a city or country from which to discuss the topic – from personal, not professional perspectives.

This prototype co-creation process was designed to avoid many of the pitfalls and inadequacies of focus groups.

Co-creation: early definitions

This is the first definition of co-creation that emerged in those early days:

> Co-creation is a methodology that involves both the producer and the customer who, together, create and build solutions, products and services that truly meet the evolving needs of all parties. In essence co-creation places the customer alongside the producer at the center of business decision making.
>
> *(Langmaid and Forsythe 2003)*

Initially the tools of *pragmatism* and *empiricism* were used to develop this work in an improvisational fashion. As it progressed, a key principle underlying this approach became clear: 'Relationships are the source of results – more than what you know!'

In many ways this is just the good old-fashioned notion that building trust, empathy and shared values and experience is a good foundation for openness, trust and collaboration. Underlying this principle is our observation that humans in groups are torn by the desire both to be separate and individual *and* to join together for a bigger sense of connection and comfort. It was a key feature of our co-creation work, right from the start, that conflicting desires were allowed legitimate expression and that time and facilitation was devoted to working through these to find a higher solution.

What kind of relationships are most helpful in co-creation? There were four main types of relationships, first distinguished by my fellow co-creator, Mac Andrews, illustrated in Figure 6.1.

Most activities in the workplace or among strangers are carried out at levels one and two, the Professional and the Public. Yet the practice of co-creation has taught that a group that can move fluently between all four levels is easily the most productive creatively. It became important to develop tools and techniques to help facilitate such mobility.

Co-creation: the essential process

It's difficult to convey a meaningful impression of a group of 60 or so people working together over two days. To help get a sense of what a co-creation or Big Talk process is like, here is an outline of the process: the key steps.

- Invitation and enrolment
- Creating relationship
- Creating safety and warm-ups
- Creating permission
- Completing the past
- Creativity on the topic – exercises, techniques, demonstrations, practice

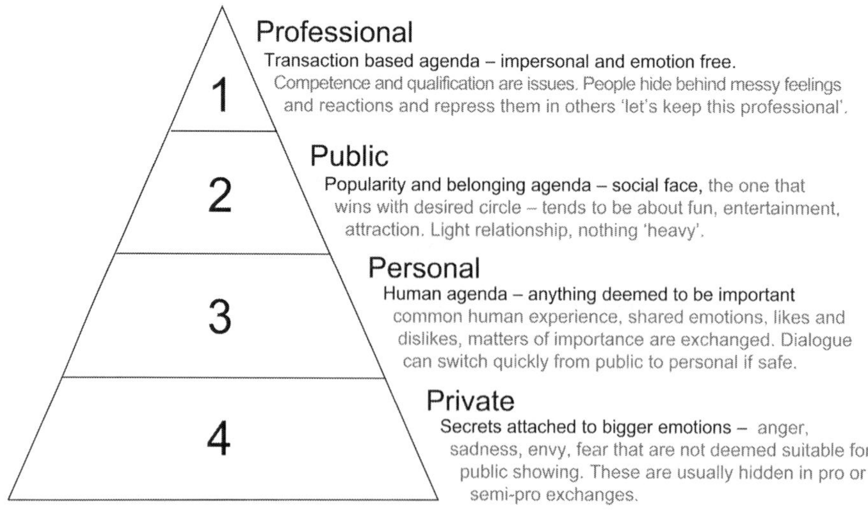

Figure 6.1 The four primary levels of relationships

- Celebrating accomplishment – the power of completion and reward
- Building and structuring the creativity
- From creativity to action (planning)
- Enrolling the community (or the organisation)

The role taken by the author in co-creation has been primarily as designer and facilitator. Now, with more than 100 live co-creation projects completed, both big and small, on commercial and social topics, it is easier to create a list of the steps followed in these projects. The way these steps emerged was empirical: things were tried, what worked was kept and what did not was discarded or amended.

Creative techniques

Whenever I talk of co-creation anywhere people are fascinated by the creative techniques. Figure 6.2 presents some of them.

Whichever techniques are used, it is important to maintain a playful non-judgmental atmosphere in the room and to celebrate and acknowledge accomplishment regularly. At least every two hours creative teams should come together to share their emerging ideas so that everyone can both applaud them and build on them. The more energy and goodwill is put into building this creative culture, the more it will flourish. This encouragement is lacking in the outside world and people are accustomed to becoming quickly discouraged, giving up and calling themselves and their ideas 'rubbish'.

Figure 6.2 Creative techniques

Co-creation in politics: the Blair project

In February 2005 we were invited by a group of people including Philip Gould, Alan Milburn and Alastair Campbell to run a diagnostic process using co-creative techniques to understand and repair the disconnection between the UK electorate and Prime Minister Blair.

It was Nicky Forsythe, another co-creator, who came up with the idea of using 'two chair work' as a means of exploring in an open research session the underlying feelings about Blair and what, if anything, could be done to repair his relationships with key groups of the electorate. In the crucial session we were working with female 'undecideds' – women between 35 and 50 who had voted New Labour in the 2001 election but were not reconsidering and were, at present, undecided.

The interesting feature of 'two chair work' is that it brings a surprisingly real representation of an absent person into the room and allows individuals and the whole group to work with that person in a creative way. To start with, a volunteer is chosen to be the main protagonist in the experiment. Next, two chairs are set facing each other about four feet apart. The volunteer is asked to sit in one chair, away from the other participants, and to close her eyes and imagine that Tony Blair is sitting in the chair opposite. Next the volunteer is asked to fully experience her feelings and what she would like to say to Blair, sitting in front of her. Then, opening her eyes, she is invited to say what came to mind in the genuine and appropriate tone (i.e. with feeling) to the chair opposite. What came out took us all by surprise:

> I loved you and thought you were one of us. A people person. Yet you were more interested in sucking up to people more famous than yourself. To do that you even put our boys' lives at risk in Iraq even though more than a million people had marched against that war. Why didn't you listen? Why are you spending so much time away from us? Why didn't you come home straight away after the Tsunami? How could you stay on holiday when our people were dying?

The speaker finished to cheers from the group. Next Nicky asked her to move over to Mr Blair's chair and speak as him: how would he answer? What would he say? She was given time to practise his posture, gestures, tone of voice and expressions with help from the group. Then she started:

> I'm afraid you've only got part of the picture. From where I sit the war in Iraq was crucial to the cause of world peace. But I understand that it's difficult to see the whole thing for you [boos from the group!]. You put me in charge and I must do what I think to be the right thing. I am sure that history will prove us right in the end.

Next Nicky solicited reactions from the volunteer and the whole group. Everyone felt that the volunteer had provided an accurate representation of her own feelings and Blair's likely response – and that they were dissatisfied with that. Then Nicky asked the volunteer to go back to her chair and speak again as Mr Blair, who this time was saying what she really needed to hear: this is what emerged:

> I understand your feelings and realize there are many who do not agree with me over Iraq. I realized this as I listened to more and more people over the past months. I still believe that on balance we did the right thing, though I have been shocked to appreciate the depth of frustration among those who disagree. I solemnly promise to spend more time at home

> in contact with our own people and to debate these issues more seriously before we launch on such an endeavour again.

In many ways the difference between the two Blair responses is not huge, but the first is patronizing and justificatory while the second remains open to the expression of disagreement and other points of view. In the view of the women this was crucial: they felt heard by the second Blair, not by the first.

In other words, a reparative response which owned the fact that there had been a breakdown in both relationships and agreements and that Blair was committed to repairing and attending to that relationship was needed to reconnect the prime minister. This reflection and commitment became the basis of his speech at the Sage Centre in Gateshead on 13 February 2005, and was reported on the BBC with the words:

> Well, if a romantic weekend in Gateshead – at the classiest venue in town – can't fix a troubled marriage, what can? And, as Tony Blair acknowledged on Sunday in his closing speech at Labour's spring conference, he has plenty of fixing to do.
>
> *(Wheeler 2005)*

The very next day on the front page of the *Sun* newspaper (which has 8 million primary and secondary readers), a St Valentine's Day card with a heart with the following words emblazoned on it read: 'You think I'm not listening. I think you're not hearing. You raise your voice, I raise mine and some of you throw a bit of crockery'. Slightly less flippantly below, the writer kicked off with:

> Tony Blair last night made a Valentine Day's plea to Britain to fall in love with him again. Blair admits that his journey has taken him from being 'all things to all people' to 'I know I'm right' and that he has now arrived at 'we can only do this together'.
>
> (The Sun, *14 February 2005)*

As ever a consummate communicator, Blair was able to appreciate the distance that needed closing between him and frustrated and disappointed female voters – and to offer an olive branch along the road to reparation. In the seven weeks remaining until polling day on 5 May, the support among females intending to vote Labour increased by four full percentage points.

At the core of this example is the idea of working *with* people and taking on board their concerns rather than *on* them by deciding what would be best for them and announcing it. This is the crucial distinction that underpins co-creation and offers supreme value to politicians who must inevitably negotiate choppy seas, divided opinions, frustrated voters and disaffected supporters.

Advice for practitioners

To explain what works, this section will propose a political example and the practical steps in how to do co-creation.

Invitation and enrolment

What idea would most excite you to come and share your views and ideas? How about this: 'Come and help us build the future for a better Britain. For the first time, ordinary people, who belong to no interest or power group and who represent our diverse and multi-cultural society, are gathering together for two days to co-create a design for a better future.'

Or this: 'They say that a Big Society is the answer; that we need to come together and take responsibility for making things better. This is an opportunity to form a prototype of that Big Society with 50 others drawn from all classes, races, geographies and cultures. For two days we will co-create a Better Britain together. Will you come and take part?'

Enrolment and attendance

However exciting or promising the invitation sounds, there will be doubts and hesitation among those to whom it is issued. Even before this point there is the problem of who should be invited. So, we face the issues of who to invite and how to encourage their attendance.

There are a few important considerations from our experience of co-creation projects here:

- The more naïve the group, the richer the co-creation will be.
- Two days is a lot of time to give up in modern life; you may have to start with one-day events and introductory evenings to whet appetites and dispel doubts and concerns about selling and manipulation.
- Experts should be in the minority. They should not have any more power in their opinions than anyone else.
- We need to consider the question of incentives. In commercial projects we pay cash to ensure attendance. In political or business forums, the advantages of networking or the proximity to power are often incentives to attend. It is necessary to avoid engaging only those with interest in power or lobbying. We need naïve members of the public to ensure authenticity.
- Experience has shown that cash is the cleanest incentive. Everyone gets the same, and it can be presented as an honorarium to cover expenses, which to some considerable extent it is. It is also more generally acceptable to naïve attendees and these are crucial to success.
- Co-creation, like any form of creativity, is meaningless unless the results find an audience. As the well-known writer on creativity Mihalyi Csikszentmihalyi points out:

  > Originality, freshness of perceptions, divergent-thinking ability are all well-known and good in their own right, as desirable personal traits. But without some form of public recognition they do not constitute creativity … Therefore it follows that what we call creativity is a phenomenon that is constructed through an interaction between producer and audience. Creativity is not the product of single individuals but of social systems making judgments about individuals' products.
  >
  > *(Mihalyi Csikszentmihalyi 1996: 314)*

- Thus it is vital to give participants a clear understanding of how and via what process their ideas might see the light of day or be input into further development. The tendency of politicians only to attend to people and their needs while seeking their votes is well known. All are sceptical of politicians' ability to keep them in mind once in power. Co-creation can help to close this gap.
- As far as possible everyone should speak from 'I'. It is their personal speaking that we need, not their ability to quote from learned texts or statistics.
- Everyone in the room has something in common – they live in the society that we are trying to improve. They all have both personal and social needs. These are often in conflict

and this must be introduced early. People have already devised ways of working through these conflicts: what are the techniques already available in the room?

The next part of enrolment is *setting the scene*. This is the first session of the co-creation workshop itself. Usually this is done in a theatre-style layout with curved rather than straight rows of chairs. We are trying not to look too regimented in approach.

Once everyone is seated a facilitator introduces the session by welcoming everyone. Next, people are reminded of the purpose of gathering here in the form of the objectives of the session and told a little about how they will work together.

The main forms of engagement will be:

Plenary sessions

These will tend to begin and end each topic and the workshop overall. In these we will get together as we are now as a large group and people will be invited to describe anything that has had an impact on them in their experience and to reflect upon insights, discoveries or puzzles. These sessions will not be debates; we will take it in turn to offer our perspectives if we have something we wish to make public.

Individual work

We may ask you to venture on your own into an exploration. We might ask you to go out into the locality with a topic in mind and notice what you see that throws light or perspective on that topic. We might ask you to draw or compose something that expresses a subject. We might do a creative visualisation.

Group work

This will happen in twos, fours, eights or any other appropriate size of groupings for the task at hand.

Large group work

We may create tribes or teams to look at diversity or conflict or competition for resources or ascendancy.

Whatever the style of work we will feedback to the whole workshop so that we all learn together and have the advantage of each other's progress or the benefit of knowing that we are not alone with a knotty problem. The essential fact here is that all knowledge quickly becomes the resource for the entire group.

Creating relationships

Our thesis is that people do not or cannot bring all of themselves to a creative process because fundamentally they are torn by conflicting desires and do not wish this turmoil to be seen by others. Not only are they worried that others might see it, but we all find it makes us self-conscious while we are speaking from one side of ourselves whilst denying the other. In these circumstances it often seems best to toe the line or say little.

Figure 6.3 Creating relationships

Figure 6.3 shows the process that we developed in our past co-creation programmes. A good idea is to use flip charts once foursomes have been formed so that people can note their discoveries as they go round the group. The purposes of this session are fourfold:

- We immerse people quite quickly in engaging with the selfish and social sides of their natures through participation with everyone else. All are in the same boat. At the same time the exercises are short and simple. You only have to speak and listen for a little while.
- We subtly train people to listen and report accurately on what others are saying. Taking responsibility for introducing your partner in his/her presence ensures that people are doing that. In the instructions each group member is encouraged to correct mistaken details in their partner's description of them.
- The idea of splits and divisions as a normal part of living is created in the room and normalised. Everyone has these parts. We don't need to spend the rest of the session pretending we are straightforward, nice or tough people.
- The groups work together to examine the consequences of these splits and the workarounds that individuals have constructed to help to manage them.

Having fun with our different sides

Now it's time to play with these sides and allow them to express themselves creatively. Here is a typical exercise that we might use to embody these distinctions and let people practise them:

In groups of eight, your task is to invent a game that has never been played before, that you can demonstrate to us in five minutes. Your game must include an instrumental role for both the selfish side and the social sides of us. In other words you must have to use both to win. The game must have a name and you have 15 minutes to do it.

The purpose here is to give the group both instant practice and a successful experience of co-creating from an open brief in a very short time.

Creating safety and permission

Usually the task of creating permission – in other words of expanding the social and personal possibilities for people within this group – is accomplished by these opening procedures. If not, there are a variety of things you can do to expand permissions.

Safety is another matter. We're not talking about physical safety here; the sense of safety with which we are concerned is fairness – that everyone has the opportunity to make their contribution without being bullied, put down or scorned by others.

Completing the past

Most of us simply do not realise day to day the influence that the past has on the future. This influence is so great that much of the future is already written – it is waiting to happen based usually on what happened in the past. The efficiencies of habit, adaptation and routine make it so. We are prone to doing it the way we did it last time. It is like the drift or current of a great river running through our lives that we cannot see if we look only at the smooth surface of the water. Unless we take into account the effects and strength of the current we cannot hope to get free of it. We must distinguish its nature and force for co-creation to be able to step outside of it.

Let's imagine that our workshop is tasked with the development of a useable, affordable, high-quality co-creation programme for the electorate and politicians to engage together in designing policy and practice. In such an event a suitable topic for completing the past might be:

Let's imagine that this workshop never happened and that things carried on pretty much as they are today. Let's think about the future, say two years from today. What will have happened? How will the relationship between the general public and politics be two years from now? What will people be saying? What will be the story of the day in the news? What will have changed?

If you have time, project a little further forward to the next election. How will that be? Use the same sort of framework: i.e. 'If we carry on as we always have, change nothing, what will be the main themes and emotional climate of the election, five years from now?'

This exercise is best done in groups of not more than eight. Ask each group to use a flip chart to list the features of the outcome they predict based on the past. Once the exercise is complete, each group has a couple of minutes to feedback its findings to the whole room.

Creating a clearing

The essence of the clearing created by completing the past is simple. Once the feedback has happened, everyone is no longer standing in the flow, or floating in the river to maintain the metaphor, but is standing on the bank, outside of the water. The minute a mindset or 'groupthink' loses its grip then it is possible to create something new. Now, before the current re-asserts its grip, we must put some new information into the room and launch a creative session. One of the central struggles for politics is that people are so cynical and sceptical about politicians and their self-serving agendas that it is vital to complete the past to create any new possibilities in this arena.

We don't need to look too far for this new information. We already have some from the creating relationships exercise.

Creativity on the topic

Setting a creative brief

In co-creation projects the brief is always set in collaboration with the sponsor of the project. We have imagined our brief as we would wish it to be and in so doing mention some of the problems we find in live briefs. In our theoretical co-creation session, the group has learned that our natures contain fundamental conflicts. The creative task here is: to find a way of doing politics, making choices and decisions, that takes account of these conflicts, includes and manages them. Managing conflicts and finding workarounds is such a part of everyday life that we must include it in our co-creation processes if we are to reflect reality.

Structuring creativity

After several hours, usually working in teams of up to 10 individuals, you will have a room packed with ideas. The first thing to do is to have a feedback session where all of the ideas are shared with the whole group and made available for everyone to build with/work up. Then, after a break to let the energy settle, it is time to build the ideas into a complete manifesto.

Ideas occur at different levels. There are ideas that are visionary, that seek to change the world, others that are about process, doing things differently to make things better, others that are about product features or details, small improvements that can make a big difference, like say the courtesy light that stays on for 15 seconds when you close the car door or being able to renew licences online. Even more detailed are ideas to do with guarantees/promises that affect delivery and what people can count on in this respect. In other words there is a wealth of ideas and a series of different domains or levels of human activity where they may have an effect.

We noticed that these levels are not completely discrete; they are and must be allowed to be interlocking, much as a political manifesto needs to cover the main domains of society's activities and concerns. This interlocking hierarchy is what came to be called the Total Communications Technology. A series of five interlocking levels of expression for an idea that

Table 6.1 The different levels of ideas

Level	*Desired effect*	*Example*
Vision	Inspiration	'A world where no-one goes to bed hungry'
Stand (commitment)	To call to others, rally support	'I will not eat or drink until the fighting stops' [Mahatma Gandhi]
Proposition	To enrol customers, stakeholders, funders	'If you can find a better offer we'll give you your money back'
Menu	To excite prospective customers and allow them to see what they will get	A list of services and ingredients like a menu in a restaurant – each with some well-crafted description to attract interest and desire
Delivery	To show that you aim to deliver, and how	A timetable, coupled with a commitment to measurable results and budgets – and including a review process

permitted the proponent of the idea to talk about it, both to a front-line worker operating at the level of transactions or to a CEO who wished to impress the City with his vision for the future.

In any project or set of ideas these were the crucial elements that needed to be present to assure both communicability and capability. If an idea cannot inspire, enrol and propose well, it is unlikely to excite and sustain interest. If an idea cannot be viewed as a menu of things that can be delivered according to a plan, it is unlikely ever to happen.

We all understand these levels and the distinctions contained within them, but each of us is practised in some and less skilful at others. That is why so many ideas do not see the light of day, or get distorted and diminished between insight and implementation. The well-known Belbin typology used in business acknowledges that any team that wishes to make things happen needs to feature people skilled in different elements of the process.

To illustrate their qualities and their commonplace occurrence in everyday life, there is a set of film clips available online that shows each of the levels in action (see www.langmaidpractice.com and links to VSPMD movies). This is helpful because many people react to this matrix as if it is unnatural, complicated and difficult to use, without realising that they use it every day: they just have not put it all together!

After the creativity sessions, it is crucial that the co-creators work in new teams to select the ideas they are most inspired by and subject them to formulation in this or a similar matrix. As well as fleshing out the complete hierarchy from inspiration to delivery, this formulation process will also encourage condensation of the ideas into words and phrases that can be said in a moment.

From creativity to action (planning)

Many people do not have much commitment to detailed planning. This is especially noticeable in a group that has spent a number of hours building relationships in order to create together. Planning – and indeed to some extent building the VSPMD matrix above – requires convergent energy rather than the divergent energy of creativity, together with a high degree of condensation of the sort in which copy writers and editors are skilled.

Because of this, we usually recommend another day for planning, some 7–10 days after the creative work. In this detailed session, plans and projects are designed that answer the questions, 'what', 'who', 'when', 'how' and 'how much'?

Enrolling the community: the listening programme

One of the most powerful elements of co-creation and its process is the amount of time and value given to the activity of listening. The listening programme described below can be rolled out as far as is necessary. It is very hard for people to sustain objections in the face of a better argument if their opinions have been heard. Here, the co-creators seek out those with strong opinions and vested interests within the domain of work, be it health, education or social care, and arrange to listen to 20 or so prominent figures from the relevant domain. These interviews should be recorded so that content analysis can point out synergies between these views and the co-creation and highlight differences that need to be resolved or aligned. It is important that those selected to be listened to are given a similar brief to those who participated in the co-creation sessions – so that they focus on the same sorts of big questions and also bring their experiences and preferences to bear on providing some detailed ideas and answers.

It is extraordinary the degree of correspondence and agreement that emerges between the pure co-created ideas and those of experts and pundits in the field of inquiry. In many ways we all want the same things but are reluctant to share our viewpoints for fear of ridicule. We have, after all, created an oppositional system where power and incumbency rather than 'the force of the better argument' (Habermas) hold sway.

Once the results of co-creation are completed, after the listening programme it is time to write up the findings in the form of a description, analysis and recommendations for the vision, commitments and menu of possibilities for the project.

The impact on politics

Co-creation, conducted and revisited regularly, provides an ideal tool for keeping up to date with the preoccupations, concerns and needs of the electorate and a means of fostering genuine engagement and input into policy and politics. Co-creation is not just about using a more innovative market research method. It holds the potential to change the relationship between government and the people. Its central idea is to work *with* people rather than *on* them to find solutions. This kind of collaborative activity is the future. Just look at the rise in academic papers mentioning co-creation on Google since 1990, illustrated in Figure 6.4.

I am grateful to my friend and colleague, Dr Nick Coates, for this piece of analysis. The collaborative spirit of co-creation is reinforced by allowing time for possibilities to emerge and evolve rather than reacting to a pre-prepared set of 'options' as is so often the case in standard research methods – even if they do include the minister's favourite! Time and again our work has shown that if such a favourite is a great idea it will emerge from the group.

When you consider that any new administration is full of elected representatives who may never have run a large department, let alone a country, who have only a partial picture of the vested interests of different elements of the community and have not considered how the

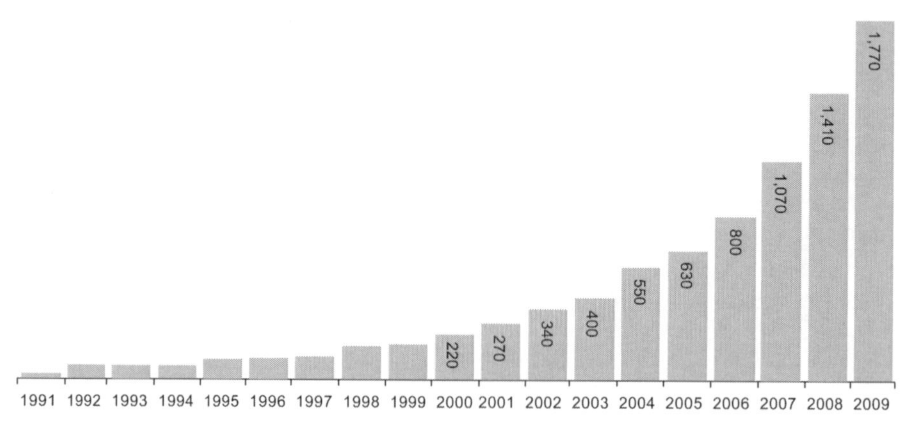

Figure 6.4 Co-creation articles in Google Scholar 1991–2009

political consequences of decisions might play out on the larger stage, it is only too obvious a methodology to bring light where currently there is ignorance and at the same time to allow experience to the inexperienced. Above all, it is a forum where creativity and innovation can shine and politicians can get a real sense of the winds of opinion, desires and fears blowing through their communities. It is also a place to witness the conflict between expert and lay opinion that underlies so many policy issues in modern societies.

Not only does it move away from the idea that elites know best, but it moves beyond the idea that politicians find out what people want and then develop a product to give it to them. Instead, politicians and public are both creators of the solution. If adopted more widely in politics, it could potentially transform citizen–state relationships and increase trust in politicians, as they will be no longer expected to find the answer to everything.

The way forward

One of the laments of the political classes is that the electorate is detached or dissociated from politics. That is largely because politics seems to take place at such a distance and uses a discourse ('the Right Honourable Member …') that is incomprehensible to most of us. Co-creation offers a practical, even inspirational means of solving this problem. Policy-making, fact-finding, conflict resolution, allocating priorities can all be done together.

Political marketing needs to conduct further research into the use of more innovative research tools, especially co-creation, and be open to new forms and approaches beyond the simple focus group or poll. Politicians and governments should consider using processes that are co-creative, as it would help them to develop more positive long-term relationships with their public as well as better policies.

Bibliography

Amabile, T.M. (1996) *Creativity in Context*, Boulder, CO: Westview Press.

Csikszentmihalyi, M. (1996) *Creativity: Flow and the psychology of discovery and invention*, New York: Harper Collins.

Earls, M. (2009) *Herd: How to change mass behavior by harnessing our true nature*, Chichester, UK and Hoboken, NJ: John Wiley & Sons.

Howe, J. (2008) *Crowdsourcing: How the power of the crowd is driving the future of business*, New York: Crown Business.

Johansson, F. (2004) *The Medici Effect: Breakthrough insights at the intersection of ideas, concepts and cultures*, Boston, MA: Harvard Business School Press.

Langmaid, R. and Andrews, M. (2003) *The Breakthrough Zone: Harnessing consumer creativity for business innovation*, Hoboken, NJ: John Wiley & Sons.

Langmaid, Roy and Forsythe, Nicky (2003) internal document, Promise London.

Leadbeater, C. (2008) *We-Think: Mass innovation, not mass production*, London: Profile Books Ltd.

Putnam, R.D. and Feldstein, L.M. with Cohen, D. (2003) *Better Together*, New York: Simon and Schuster.

Savigny, H. (2007) 'Focus Groups and Political Marketing: science and democracy as axiomatic?' *British Journal of Politics and International Relations* 9: 122–37.

—— (2008) *The Problem of Political Marketing*, New York: Continuum International Publishing Group Ltd.

Sawyer, K. (2007) *Group Genius: The creative power of collaboration*, New York: Basic Books.

Scammell, M. (2008) 'Brand Blair: marketing politics in the consumer age', in D. Lilleker and R. Scullion (eds) *Voters or Consumers: Imagining the contemporary electorate*, Newcastle: Cambridge Scholars Publishing, 97–113.

Shirky, C. (2008) *Here Comes Everybody: The power of organizing without organizations*, New York: Penguin Books.

Sternberg, R.J. (1999) *Handbook of Creativity*, Cambridge, UK and New York, NY: Cambridge University Press.

Surowiecki, J. (2004) *The Wisdom of Crowds: Why the many are smarter than the few and how collective wisdom shapes business, economies, societies, and nations*, New York: Doubleday.

Wheeler, Brian (2005) 'Rekindling the Labour Love Affair', *BBC News*, 13 February. Online news.bbc.co.uk/1/hi/uk_politics/4262333.stm.

Wring, D. (2007) 'Focus Group Follies? Qualitative research and British Labour Party strategy', *Journal of Political Marketing* 5, 4: 71–97.

Part II
Product development, branding and strategy

7

Political party market orientation in a global perspective

Jesper Strömbäck, Jennifer Lees-Marshment and Chris Rudd

The topic: global political market orientation

Political party market orientation is about how parties behave in response to the electorate; it is a way of thinking. Whilst all parties might use different marketing techniques such as polling and focus groups, voter segmentation, direct mail, telemarketing, sophisticated voter databases and opposition research, what is important is the way they use these, and the influence this has on the way they create their political product and communicate. Parties may fall into one of three orientations and be product-oriented, sales-oriented or market-oriented (Lees-Marshment 2001; see also Newman 1994; Ormrod 2009 for further discussion of a market orientation). These concepts suggest that some parties use marketing techniques to sell themselves and their policies, and that some also use marketing to decide what to offer the public in the first place – what policies to adopt, which leaders to select to best present those policies, and how to best communicate policy delivery. It is distinct from other campaign or media management because of the potential influence of marketing tools on the communication and the political 'product'. The defining characteristics of these orientations are summarized in Table 7.1 (see Lees-Marshment 2001; Lees-Marshment 2010a; Strömbäck 2007a; Strömbäck 2010a).

Such behavior has developed in response to changes in voting behavior and communication whereby in many, albeit not all, countries party identification has declined; voters switch parties more often than they used to and decide later what party to vote for; political distrust has increased; political parties have lost members (Dalton and Wattenberg 2000); and media environments have become more competitive and commercial (Hamilton 2004). Political communication and campaign studies show how political parties worldwide have increased their efforts to professionalize their campaign strategies and tactics. This chapter seeks to explore the extent to which political party market orientation has also gone global, by presenting a summary of results from new research in *Global Political Marketing* (Lees-Marshment *et al.* 2010) which conducted a comparative analysis of party behavior, and examining the extent to which variation in party behavior is due to a wide range of systemic differences (such as the electoral and party system).

Table 7.1 Defining characteristics of product-, sales- and market-oriented parties

	Product-oriented party	*Sales-oriented party*	*Market-oriented party*
Defining characteristic	Argues for its own ideas and policies; assumes that voters will realize that its ideas are the best and therefore vote for it.	Believes in its own ideas and policies, but realizes that they must be 'sold' to the public; does not change its behavior or policies to give people what they want, but tries to make people want what the party offers.	Uses market intelligence to identify voter needs and demands, and design its policies, candidates and behavior to provide voter satisfaction; does not try to change what people want, but give people what they want.
If the party does not succeed in elections	Believes that the voters just do not realize that the party's policies are the best ones; refuses to change policies.	Tries to make better use of market intelligence and persuasion techniques, i.e., become more professionalized in its campaigning.	Uses market intelligence to re-design the product so that it becomes better suited to the wants and needs of targeted people.

Previous research on global political market orientation

Whilst the spread of professionalization and modernization in campaigning has been studied extensively (Farrell and Webb 2000; Norris 2000; Plasser and Plasser 2002), there has never been a systematic and scientific comparative analysis of political marketing behavior in the sales- and market-oriented sense. Previous research (Lees-Marshment 2001; Lilleker and Lees-Marshment 2005) suggested that parties may be moving towards the market-oriented party model to achieve electoral success, but that this could be influenced by systemic factors such as party and electoral system. It was, however, not clear how. The interest in this at a comparative global level was aided by several well-known world examples of marketing the product, with the most famous being the transfer and adaptation of the product used by Bill Clinton's New Democrats in 1992 to Tony Blair's New Labour in the UK in 1997, to the German SPD and Labour in New Zealand in 1999. These examples illustrate the use of targeting on new markets and represented a move away from selling ideologically driven policy to using a voter-responsive strategy. More recent additions increased such interest: for example, in 2007 Australian Labor leader Kevin Rudd's successful campaign was likened to Tony Blair's.

On the surface, parties seemed to be moving universally towards market-oriented strategies where political marketing is employed *before* the electoral campaign. However, the cumulativity of research on political marketing from a comparative perspective has been limited. One reason is that most studies are single-country studies. A second reason is that many studies focus on only a limited number of parties within the chosen country, typically the largest or the most successful parties. A third reason is that most studies are British or American in their origins, which limits the generalizability of the results. We thus wanted to produce a broader study. Whilst there are other models of market-orientation (e.g. O'Cass 1996; Newman 1994; Lees-Marshment 2001; Ormrod 2009), as we were not focusing on just this form of orientation we decided to use the Lees-Marshment (2001) framework for a global, more comprehensive project. We also needed to find a way to examine the impact of systemic features on party behavior in order to explore not just the extent to which parties have become increasingly market oriented, but also *why*.

This new project therefore sought to address this first by conducting carefully selected case studies including 14 countries, and more specifically Australia (Hughes and Dann 2010), the

Czech Republic (Matuskova *et al.* 2010), Germany (Maier *et al.* 2010), Ghana (Mensah 2010), Greece (Kotzaivazoglou and Zotos 2010), Hungary (Kiss and Mihályffy 2010), Japan (Asano and Wakefield 2010), New Zealand (Lees-Marshment 2010b), Peru (Galindo 2010), Russia (Hutcheson 2010), Sweden (Strömbäck 2010b), Taiwan (Fell and Cheng 2010), the UK (Lees-Marshment and Pettitt 2010), and the US (Knuckey 2010). Second, the analysis applied a framework for comparing political market-orientation, developed by Strömbäck (2010a). The framework builds on Sjöblom (1968) and argues that political parties are active on at least four different markets or arenas, each accompanied by specific strategic goals and sets of key stakeholders: a parliamentary arena, an electoral arena, an internal arena and a media arena (Sjöblom 1968; Strömbäck 2007a, 2007b). The next section will explain this framework and the results of the research.

New research: global political market orientation

The framework (Strömbäck 2010a) suggests that on the parliamentary arena the strategic goal is to maximize parliamentary influence, while the primary stakeholders are members of parliament of different parties. On the electoral arena the strategic goal is to maximize the number of votes, and the primary stakeholders are the voters. On the internal arena the strategic goal is to maximize internal cohesion, and the primary stakeholders are members, activists, staff and representatives of the party. On the media arena the strategic goal is to maximize positive publicity, and the primary stakeholders are journalists and editors. Whether parties should strive to be a mainly product-, sales- or market-oriented party is thus not a decision taken in isolation of the surrounding environment. It is shaped in particular contexts, and is dependent on history and traditions as well as factors both internal and external. In addition, all party behavior is shaped in dynamic processes, and it is simply not the case that a party can just make a decision to follow any of the orientations. To the extent that the party leadership wants the party to follow a particular orientation, it must be implemented through processes that take time and are vulnerable to reactions both internal and external.

Therefore, there is a large range of factors related to differences across countries, such as whether the political and electoral system is candidate- or party-centered; whether the electoral system is majoritarian or proportional; the strength of the left–right ideological continuum; the number of parties; the degree of electoral volatility, which follows from the strength of party identification; how commercialized the media are; how adversarial the journalistic culture is; whether there are deep social or political cleavages; whether the political culture is egalitarian rather than hierarchical; the degree of political distrust; and whether there are linkages between the parties and the media and the strength of these.

With respect to differences between parties within countries, the most important factors according to the framework are the size of the parties in terms of voter support and resources; the influence of activists and middle-level elites within the parties; how ideologically committed on the left–right ideological continuum members of and activists in the parties are; how strongly supporters identify with the parties; whether parties are part of or have a competitive chance of forming government; how long parties have been in government; how strongly linked the parties are to certain policy positions related to major issues; whether parties have suffered successive or major electoral defeats; whether the internal party culture is egalitarian rather than hierarchical; how strong parliamentary party discipline is; whether the parties are mainly office-, vote- or policy-seeking; and how strong ties the parties have to particular social or political cleavages or interest groups. Thinking about these factors as independent variables, and the likelihood that parties are market-oriented as dependent variable, the framework suggests 12 research propositions related to differences between countries, and 12 research propositions related to differences between parties within countries. These are summarized in the appendix, Table 7A.1, at the end of the chapter.

The results of the empirical study were that first, political marketing in a broad sense is a global activity. Political parties around the world all make use of a diverse set of marketing strategies, tactics and techniques. However, most parties use marketing techniques to facilitate the selling of the party, its policies, its image or its brand, but not to design the political product, and not to adapt to voters' wants and needs. There were examples of parties behaving in a more market-oriented fashion, but it was more to *win* rather than to *maintain* office. When in office, they tend to revert to being sales-oriented. As a consequence, there is no evidence that major office-seeking parties in established democracies around the world successively move towards the market-oriented party model and that parties in developing democracies eventually follow; and it appears as if there are significant barriers to becoming consistently market-oriented. Parties tend to shift from sales to market orientation and back. Additionally, most parties are *more or less* product-, sales- or market-oriented: party orientation appears to be a matter of degree rather than of type.

Furthermore, research found that a number of parties were behaving in a more market-oriented fashion, but not comprehensively so, whilst others attempted to become market-oriented but failed. Attempts to be market-oriented floundered at the product adjustment phase. In a number of our case studies we noted that party members or core voters often blocked the willingness and ability of a party leadership to pursue a market-oriented approach. In other words, a party leadership can employ marketing professionals, conduct marketing exercises – focus groups and the like – but the market intelligence gathered may not be acted upon if members or external support groups are unwilling to respond positively. Parties trying to be market-oriented are related to how to carry out product adjustment in practice. They want to be responsive but still credible, authentic and retain some principles, so that they can satisfy internal as well as external markets. There was also a trend that many parties did not maintain a market orientation when in power. Thus the comparative study demonstrated that whilst political marketing is being used on a global scale it is in a much more diverse and rich way than previously thought. In relation to why this is so, the research found that the framework helped to explain this to some extent, although the study also uncovered other factors that impact on political marketing orientation.

The political system

The framework predicted that multi-party systems tend to foster sales-oriented parties as the multiplicity of parties makes for a crowded political landscape, making it harder for parties to 'shift to the center'. However, even in countries dominated by two parties there was no clear pattern for the dominant parties to be predominantly market-oriented. Instead, major parties shifted back and forth between sales and market orientations, with the main factor pushing a party towards market orientation being successive electoral defeats or prolonged periods in opposition, while the shift back to a sales orientation usually resulted from a long period of incumbency. Those studies that examined minor parties found that gathering information about their potential market appears to be even more important for small parties, which need to use their limited resources effectively. This is perhaps not surprising, as all parties, even those that cater to a niche market, need to have some idea as to who their likely voters are. Importantly, market intelligence can be used to inform not just product development and strategy, but also the communication and selling of a party and its programs. What makes market-oriented parties differ from product- and sales-oriented parties is not their use of market intelligence per se, but *how* they use it.

Parliamentary arena

With respect to the parliamentary (or legislative) arena, evidence from a number of countries confirms that parties that suffer declining vote share in successive elections are more likely to become more market-oriented as a means to recover lost support. Furthermore, a long tenure of government incumbency, just like a long spell in opposition, can weaken a party's market-orientation. Parties in office face a number of constraints. For example, it is difficult to deliver and to keep using market intelligence to cater for the wants and needs of only selected target groups, as a governing party has a responsibility to consider a much wider group of voters. Parties may also find themselves in a government with coalition partners, and to retain the support of such partners a party may need to compromise on some of its promises. In a sense there is a 'curse of incumbency' where governing parties are placed in a position where logic dictates they must defend those policies that they have been responsible for implementing, irrespective of whether the policies are popular or not. There was one exception to this pattern, where the governing UK Labour Party tried to reverse a drift away from being market-oriented by reconnecting.

Single-party majority governments are usually in a better position to deliver on promises than coalition governments. This ability to deliver on promises is reinforced where members of the governing party or parties in parliament can be guaranteed to support government legislation. However, this holds for all types of parties in government, not just market-oriented ones. Its significance lies more in the internal party arena, where members of parliament are viewed as just one of the stakeholders who must be brought on board *if* the party leaders should seek to become more market-oriented.

Electoral arena

Almost all countries have experienced a decline in party identification and party membership, greater electoral volatility, and a weakening of left–right ideology as a basis for voting. The country studies suggest that electoral de-alignment is a *necessary* condition for the development of market-oriented parties. If parties still compete along the socio-economic cleavage, drawing their support largely from clearly identified and stable social groupings where party choice is largely the product of socialization, then a market orientation would seem unnecessary if not even counter-productive. Yet if electoral de-alignment is a *necessary* condition for the development of market-oriented parties, it is not a *sufficient* condition and does not automatically lead to more market-oriented parties. A party can also respond to the above developments by intensifying its use of marketing techniques and becoming more sales-oriented. Highly important also are factors related to the internal party arena.

Internal party arena

The internal party arena imposes significant constraints on the party's freedom to choose orientation and in particular become market-oriented. The country studies suggested several examples where internal opposition retarded a movement towards increasing market orientation, particularly in established democracies. Therefore, parties in newer democracies without firmly established party cultures might have greater flexibility to introduce radical change in the party direction. In general terms, the more centralized and hierarchical the party, the easier to make the shift in orientation; the more decentralized, the harder.

This also shows the importance of adjusting the product to suit the internal market to ensure effective implementation. A party's history means that the party cannot approach an election as if it had a blank sheet on which to write party policy. If the party strays too far from its historically defined image or brand, it runs the risk of losing credibility and its core voters, without necessarily being able to attract new ones. For most party activists, the idea of deviating from what is perceived as the core ideology or the core values is at odds with the reasons for which they once became active in politics. Most people join parties because they have a goal to change society in a particular way. To abandon that goal based on the argument that some voters want something else may be difficult for an activist to accept.

Such concerns may, however, be reduced when the party has little core vote to lose or its core support is so loyal that a party can reposition without fear of losing many stalwart supporters; or the party may have a party organization sufficiently centralized or sufficiently demoralized by lack of success, that party leaders are able to impose more market-oriented measures despite opposition from the rank and file. The costs of becoming more market-orientated may, however, be less where parties adopt a more comprehensive implementation of the concept and properly consider the internal market. For example, Kevin Rudd in Australia (Hughes and Dann 2010) attempted to appeal to external *and* internal markets while trying to shift his party towards more market orientation, although he was then usurped as a result of internal factions after a loss of public support before he faced re-election. Being more market-oriented need not mean abandoning internal supporters; the more effective party leaders are at managing the demands of the different markets, the more successful they can become at implementing a market-oriented strategy.

Media arena

The research found the media arena to be of less importance as an antecedent of political market orientation. This does not mean that the media have no effect on political marketing (Sellers 2010; Strömbäck and Kaid 2008): as Temple (2010: 266) suggests, the role of the media is 'crucially different for politicians than for companies'. The media matter more for political marketing than political market orientation, however, and in terms of comparative analysis there was too little variance to isolate the media's effects on political market orientation. All parties in our study placed emphasis on the use of the free media with which to communicate with voters, and in highly competitive and deregulated media markets there are a multitude of media channels available for politicians to use.

Additional factors: leadership

There was, though, one factor that the framework did not take into consideration, but which was shown to be of major importance: individual party leaders and whether there was a change of party leader following an electoral shock. It is clear that in many of the country studies, the role of a new leader was a critical factor in bringing about major change in a party's orientation. Examples include, for example, Tony Blair (UK Labour), Kevin Rudd (Australian Labor), Junichiro Koizumi (Japanese LDP), George Papandreou (Greek Pasok) and Fredrik Reinfeldt (Swedish Moderates). At the same time, while electoral defeats and change of leadership may facilitate changes in party orientation, they do not necessarily cause them. Crucial is how the electoral defeat is interpreted by party members and activists, and whether the costs to a party becoming more market-oriented are perceived to outweigh the perceived benefits or not. This may happen when a party has suffered electoral defeats of such a magnitude or with such frequency that this is not viewed as a temporary setback. Examples of where electoral defeats pushed parties towards a *more* market-oriented strategy would be the UK Conservatives (2005–10), Swedish

Moderates (2003–), and New Zealand National (2005–08). However, the Swedish Moderates suffered losses in just one election before adopting a more market-oriented approach (Strömbäck 2010b), whereas the other parties suffered three defeats. This suggests that it is important to understand how the parties perceive electoral defeats. Is the defeat viewed as a temporary setback or the start of a long-term decline? Or might it even be the case that an *absence of electoral victories* can have an effect similar to electoral defeats? A party may have expected to perform well in successive elections, but in reality failed to expand its vote share. Such a party may react as if it had in fact suffered electoral defeats.

Summary

The *Global Political Marketing* project yielded several conclusions, some which call 'conventional wisdom' into question:

- The use of marketing techniques does not equal being market-oriented.
- The dominant trend is sales orientation rather than market orientation: it is not the case that all major parties become market-oriented, or that parties have to become market-oriented to achieve electoral success.
- There is no linear progression of party development, and parties shift from sales- to market-oriented, and back again.
- Product, sales and market orientation should not be considered as categories, but rather as positions along a continuum ranging from product orientation through sales orientation to market orientation.

Considering the comparative framework and differences between countries, the research suggested that the reasons behind this varying pattern of political marketing are:

- A decline in party identification and party membership as well as greater electoral volatility increases the *potential* for a move towards greater sales or market orientation, depending on where the parties start out, but does not mean that all parties will be market-oriented.
- The degree of party unity and discipline on the parliamentary (legislative) arena also has an impact on ability to deliver and, crossing over into the internal arena, maintain a higher *degree* of market orientation.
- The internal arena is highly influential on the success of party strategy and leaders' ability to implement a higher *degree* of market orientation, because members and activists can exert significant influence on party direction and orientation. In general terms, the more centralized and hierarchical the party, the easier to make a shift in orientation.
- Fluid and time-bound factors have a great impact, namely electoral loss and new leadership. Parties that suffer successive electoral defeats are more likely to become more market-oriented as a means to recover lost support, and a long tenure of government incumbency can weaken a party's *degree* of market orientation while new party leaders who want to push a market-oriented strategy need to gain control of the party and attract public support. However, these two factors need to occur simultaneously and thus their causality is more situational than is often assumed, and this may explain the fluidity in parties' orientation.

Instead, the project has shown that there are variations across both space and time, and the complex interactions at different levels of analysis that contribute to political parties' behavior and orientations. Political marketing is undoubtedly a worldwide phenomenon, and the use of marketing strategies, tactics and techniques is both ubiquitous and here to stay. Parties adapt, but they adapt based on the particular circumstances relevant to, and constrained by the structural and semi-structural factors present in their country at any particular point in time. On the basis of this research, we can therefore suggest a revised framework to predict the degree of political market orientation: see Table 7.2.

Table 7.2 Revised framework to explain degree of political market orientation

Propositions related to differences between countries

1 Parties in candidate-centered political systems are likely to be more market-oriented than parties in party-centered political systems.
2 Parties in countries with majoritarian electoral systems are likely to be more market-oriented than parties in countries with proportional electoral systems.
3 Parties in countries where the left–right ideological dimension is of less importance in the minds of voters are likely to be more market-oriented than parties in countries where it is of major importance.
4 Parties in countries with few competing parties are likely to be more market-oriented than parties in countries with many competing parties.
5 Parties in countries with a low degree of party identification are likely to be more market-oriented than parties in countries with a high degree of party identification.
6 Parties in countries with high electoral volatility are likely to be more market-oriented than parties in countries with low electoral volatility.
7 Parties in countries with deep social or political cleavages are likely to be less market-oriented than parties in countries without such deep cleavages.

Propositions related to differences between parties within countries

1 Larger parties in terms of voter support and resources are likely to be more market-oriented than smaller parties.
2 Parties where activists and middle-level elite have a strong influence on the political product are likely to be less market-oriented than parties where they have a limited influence as compared with the central leadership and ordinary members.
3 Parties where the members and activists are ideologically committed on the left–right ideological dimension are likely to be less market-oriented than parties where they have a more value-oriented outlook.
4 Parties whose voters are strongly identified with the party are likely to be less market-oriented than parties whose voters are weakly identified with the party.
5 Parties that have a competitive chance of forming the next government are likely to be more market-oriented than parties that do not have a competitive chance of forming a government.
6 Parties that have been in government for a longer period of time are likely to be less market-oriented than parties that have not been in government but have a competitive chance of forming the next government.
7 Parties that are historically linked with certain policy positions regarding major issues are likely to be less market-oriented than parties that are historically not linked to certain policy positions in major issues.
8 Parties that have suffered successive or major electoral defeats are likely to become more market-oriented than parties that have not suffered such defeats.
9 Parties that have had a change of party leadership are likely to become more market-oriented than parties that have had no change of party leadership.
10 Parties with a hierarchical internal culture are likely to be more market-oriented than parties with an egalitarian internal culture.
11 Parties whose members of parliament mainly answer to the central leadership of the party are likely to be more market-oriented than parties without a strong parliamentary party discipline.
12 Office- and vote-seeking parties are likely to be more market-oriented than policy-seeking parties.
13 Parties with strong ties to particular social or political cleavages are likely to be less market-oriented than parties with weak ties to particular social or political cleavages.

Advice for practitioners

Based on the above analysis, there is no universal answer to the question of what works in terms of electoral success. For practitioners, politicians and parties have a choice: it is not inevitable that they have to take on any particular orientation. There are almost no general lessons as party behavior varies so much and the effectiveness is not pre-determined. Leaders of major parties might still want to aim to become market-oriented as it can aid electoral success, but lots of factors including the competition affect this and sales-oriented parties do still win and maintain power. If a party wants to become market-oriented it can do so in all countries, as it is not just suitable for one type of system, but the leadership must drive the process for it to be successful, and it must manage internal markets effectively and adjust the product. Most failed attempts at becoming more market-oriented are thwarted by party figures and members. Once in power, if parties want to maintain support they need to maintain a market orientation or try to reconnect – but as yet, few have succeeded at this.

Impact on politics

On one hand this study suggests that political marketing, in one form or another, is truly global, and thus has changed politics itself. This could threaten ideology and value and seem bad for democracy as it reduces politics to commercial-like transactions. Politicians around the world continually seek to use market research and other tools to help them win elections. On the other hand, the orientation that parties take up, which does not follow a linear pattern from product to sales to market orientation, but is more flexible, suggests that politicians still have room to choose how they are going to respond to the electorate. This leaves room for leadership and creativity, with market-oriented parties most often losing their responsiveness in power in order to pursue change-making policies.

The way forward

With respect to research, we have two main suggestions for the way forward. First, instead of conceptualizing product-, sales- and market-oriented parties as three different party types, they should be perceived on a continuum with product orientation marking one end of the scale and sales orientation marking the other (see Figure 7.1). Conceptualizing the party orientations on a scale would allow more nuanced and rich understandings of parties' orientations and positions; how their orientations and positions are affected by structural and semi-structural factors; and how they move, reorient and reposition themselves in reaction to contextual factors that are more specific in time and place to particular parties.

Second, there is the need for a broader range of methods to be used when studying political marketing and political marketing orientation comparatively. Up to now, most research on the

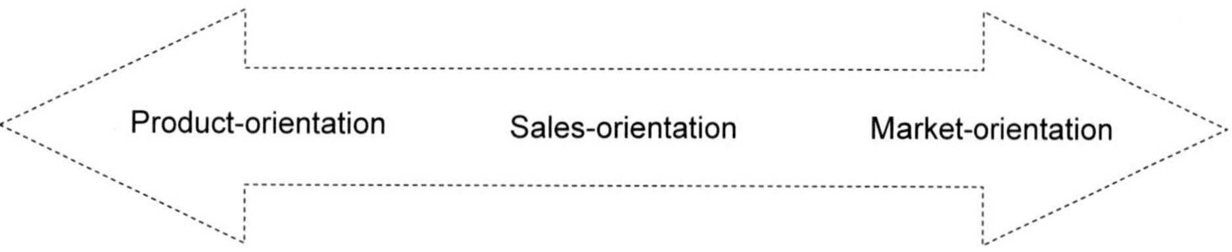

Figure 7.1 Product-, sales- and market-oriented parties along a continuum

use of marketing techniques and political product, sales and market orientation is based on single-country case studies, where the preferred methodology is qualitative interviews and analyses of party behavior or documents. Studies including a greater number of parties and countries and using quantitative methodologies are rare, and studies using methodologies that can be replicated across time or countries are virtually non-existent (but see Ormrod 2009). From the perspective of comparative research and of increasing research cumulativity, this is a problem. In-depth case studies and qualitative research holds great value, but to increase research cumulativity, there is a great need for quantitative research using standardized research instruments that can be applied in different settings (for an example see Gibson and Römmele 2009, who developed an index for research on the professionalization of political campaigning). Quantitative methodologies using operationalizations of key independent and dependent variables that can be applied across both time and countries would make research more systematic. Only then will it also be possible to draw firm conclusions with respect to what works in terms of electoral success. This calls for a new global study of political marketing and political market orientation, based on quantitative methodology.

In terms of practice, practitioners need to continue to share ideas through global knowledge transfer, but they should also be aware of the need to adapt techniques and strategies to suit not even just the particular country, but the particular election. Whilst political marketing is indeed global, each election is unique.

Bibliography

Asano, M. and Wakefield, B. (2010) 'Political market-orientation in Japan', in J. Lees-Marshment, J. Strömbäck and C. Rudd (eds) *Global Political Marketing*, London: Routledge, 234–48.

Blumler, J.G. and Gurevitch, M. (1995) *The Crisis of Public Communication*, London: Routledge.

Dalton, R.J. and Wattenberg, M.P. (eds) (2000) *Parties without Partisans: Political Change in Advanced Industrial Democracies*, New York: Oxford University Press.

Farrell, D.M. and Webb, P. (2000) 'Political parties as campaign organizations', in R.J. Dalton and M.P. Wattenberg (eds) *Parties without Partisans: Political Change in Advanced Industrial Democracies*, New York: Oxford University Press, 102–28.

Fell, D.J. and Cheng, I. (2010) 'Testing the market-oriented model of political parties in a non-Western context: the case of Taiwan', in J. Lees-Marshment, J. Strömbäck and C. Rudd (eds) *Global Political Marketing*, London: Routledge, 175–88.

Galindo, P.P. (2010) 'Political marketing in a weak democracy: the Peruvian case', in J. Lees-Marshment, J. Strömbäck and C. Rudd (eds) *Global Political Marketing*, London: Routledge, 202–17.

Gibson, R.K. and Römmele, A. (2009) 'Measuring the professionalization of political campaigning', *Party Politics* 15, 3: 265–93.

Gummesson, E. (2002) *Total Relationship Marketing: Marketing Management, Relationship Strategy and CRM Approaches for the Network Economy*, Oxford: Butterworth Heinemann.

Hamilton, J.T. (2004) *All the News That's Fit to Sell: How the Market Transforms Information Into News*, Princeton NJ: Princeton University Press.

Henneberg, S.C.M. (2002) 'Understanding Political Marketing', in N.J. O'Shaughnessy and S.C.M. Henneberg (eds) *The Idea of Political Marketing*. Westport CT: Praeger, 93–170.

—— (2006) 'Leading or following? A theoretical analysis of political marketing postures', *Journal of Political Marketing* 5, 3: 29–46.

Hughes, A. and Dann, S. (2010) 'Australian political marketing: substance backed by style', in J. Lees-Marshment, J. Strömbäck and C. Rudd (eds) *Global Political Marketing*, London: Routledge, 82–95.

Hutcheson, D.S. (2010) 'Political marketing techniques in Russia', in J. Lees-Marshment, J. Strömbäck and C. Rudd (eds) *Global Political Marketing*, London: Routledge, 218–33.

Kiss, B. and Mihályffy, Z. (2010) 'Political salesmen in Hungary', in J. Lees-Marshment, J. Strömbäck and C. Rudd (eds) *Global Political Marketing*, London: Routledge, 143–56.

Knuckey, J. (2010) 'Political marketing in the United States: from market-towards sales-orientation?', in J. Lees-Marshment, J. Strömbäck and C. Rudd (eds) *Global Political Marketing*, London: Routledge, 96–112.

Kohli, A.K. and Jaworski, B.J. (1990) 'Market orientation: the construct, research propositions, and managerial implications', *Journal of Marketing* 54, 2: 1–18.

Kotzaivazoglou, I. and Zotos, Y. (2010) 'The level of market-orientation of political parties in Greece', in J. Lees-Marshment, J. Strömbäck and C. Rudd (eds) *Global Political Marketing*, London: Routledge, 128–42.

Lees-Marshment, J. (2001) *Political Marketing and British Political Parties*, Manchester: Manchester University Press.

—— (2004) *The Political Marketing Revolution: Transforming the Government of the UK*, Manchester: Manchester University Press.

—— (2009) *Political Marketing: Principles and Applications*, New York: Routledge.

—— (2010a) 'Global political marketing', in J. Lees-Marshment, J. Strömbäck and C. Rudd (eds) *Global Political Marketing*, London: Routledge.

—— (2010b) 'New Zealand political marketing: marketing communication rather than the product?', in J. Lees-Marshment, J. Strömbäck and C. Rudd (eds) *Global Political Marketing*, London: Routledge, 113–27.

Lees-Marshment, J. and Pettitt, R.T. (2010) 'UK political marketing: a question of leadership?', in J. Lees-Marshment, J. Strömbäck and C. Rudd (eds) *Global Political Marketing*, London: Routledge, 113–95.

Lees-Marshment, J., Strömbäck, J. and Rudd, C. (eds) (2010) *Global Political Marketing*, London: Routledge.

Lilleker, D. and Lees-Marshment, J. (eds) (2005) *Political Marketing: A Comparative Perspective*, Manchester: Manchester University Press.

Maier, M., Tenscher, J. and Schüller, K. (2010) 'Political marketing in Germany', in J. Lees-Marshment, J. Strömbäck and C. Rudd (eds) *Global Political Marketing*, London: Routledge, 16–33.

Matuskova, A., Eible, O. and Braun, A. (2010) 'The Czech case: a market-oriented party on the rise?', in J. Lees-Marshment, J. Strömbäck and C. Rudd (eds) *Global Political Marketing*, London: Routledge, 157–74.

Mensah, K. (2010) 'Political marketing in Ghana', in J. Lees-Marshment, J. Strömbäck and C. Rudd (eds) *Global Political Marketing*, London: Routledge, 189–201.

Newman, B.I. (1994) *The Marketing of the President: Political Marketing as Campaign Strategy*, Beverley Hills CA: Sage.

—— (ed.) (1999a) *Handbook of Political Marketing*, Thousand Oaks CA: Sage.

—— (1999b) *The Mass Marketing of Politics: Democracy in an Age of Manufactured Images*, Thousand Oaks CA: Sage.

Newton, K. and van Deth, J.W. (2005) *Foundations of Comparative Politics*, New York: Cambridge University Press.

Norris, P. (2000) *A Virtuous Circle: Political Communications in Postindustrial Societies*, New York: Cambridge University Press.

—— (2004) *Electoral Engineering: Voting Rules and Political Behavior*, New York: Cambridge University Press.

O'Cass, Aron (1996) 'Political marketing and the marketing concept', *European Journal of Marketing* 30 (10/11): 37–53.

Ormrod, R.P. (2009) *Understanding Political Market Orientation*, Ph.D. thesis, Aarhus: University of Aarhus.

Pfetsch, B. and Esser, F. (2004) 'Comparing political communication: reorientations in a changing world', in F. Esser and B. Pfetsch (eds) *Comparing Political Communication: Theories, Cases, Challenges*, New York: Cambridge University Press, 3–22.

Plasser, F. and Plasser, G. (2002) *Global Political Campaigning: A Worldwide Analysis of Campaign Professionals and Their Practices*, Westport CT: Praeger.

Sellers, P. (2010) *Cycles of Spin: Strategic Communication in the U.S. Congress*, New York: Cambridge University Press.

Sjöblom, G. (1968) *Party Strategies in a Multiparty System*, Lund: Studentlitteratur.

Slater, S.F. and Narver, J.C. (1998) 'Customer-led and market-oriented: let's not confuse the two', *Strategic Management Journal* 19, 10: 1001–6.

Strömbäck, J. (2007a) 'Political marketing and professionalized campaigning: a conceptual analysis', *Journal of Political Marketing* 6, 2/3: 49–67.

—— (2007b) 'Antecedents of political market orientation in Britain and Sweden: analysis and future research propositions', *Journal of Public Affairs* 7, 1: 1–11.

—— (2010a) 'A framework for comparing political market-orientation', in J. Lees-Marshment, J. Strömbäck and C. Rudd (eds) *Global Political Marketing*, London: Routledge, 16–33.

—— (2010b) 'Political market-orientation in a multi-party system: the Swedish case', in J. Lees-Marshment, J. Strömbäck and C. Rudd (eds) *Global Political Marketing*, London: Routledge, 52–64.

Strömbäck, J. and Kaid, L.L. (eds) (2008) *Handbook of Election News Coverage Around the World*, New York: Routledge.

Temple, M. (2010) 'Political marketing, party behaviour and political science', in J. Lees-Marshment, J. Strömbäck and C. Rudd (eds) *Global Political Marketing*, London: Routledge, 263–77.

Wring, D. (2005) *The Politics of Marketing the Labour Party*, Hampshire: Palgrave.

Table 7A.1 Framework for comparing political market orientation: research propositions

Propositions related to differences between countries	*Propositions related to differences between parties within countries*
1 Parties in candidate-centered political systems are more likely to be market-oriented than parties in party-centered political systems.	1 Large parties in terms of voter support and resources are more likely to be market-oriented than small parties.
2 Parties in countries with majoritarian electoral systems are more likely to be market-oriented than parties in countries with proportional electoral systems.	2 Parties where activists and middle-level elite have a strong influence on the political product are less likely to be market-oriented than parties where they have a limited influence as compared with the central leadership and ordinary members.
3 Parties in countries where the left–right ideological dimension is of less importance in the minds of voters are more likely to be market-oriented than parties in countries where it is of major importance.	3 Parties where the members and activists are ideologically committed on the left–right ideological dimension are less likely to be market-oriented than parties where they have a more value-oriented outlook.
4 Parties in countries with few competing parties are more likely to be market-oriented than parties in countries with many competing parties.	4 Parties whose voters are strongly identified with the party are less likely to be market-oriented than parties whose voters are weakly identified with the party.
5 Parties in countries with a low degree of party identification are more likely to be market-oriented than parties in countries with a high degree of party identification.	5 Parties that are part of or have a competitive chance of forming the next government are more likely to be market-oriented than parties that are not part of government or do not have a competitive chance of forming the next government.
6 Parties in countries with high electoral volatility are more likely to be market-oriented than parties in countries with low electoral volatility.	6 Parties that have been in government for a longer period of time are less likely to be market-oriented than parties that have not been in government but have a competitive chance of forming the next government.
7 Parties in countries with a highly commercialized media system are more likely to be market-oriented than parties in countries with a less commercialized media system.	7 Parties that are historically linked with certain policy positions regarding major issues are less likely to be market-oriented than parties that are historically not linked to certain policy positions in major issues.
8 Parties in countries with an adversarial journalistic culture are more likely to be market-oriented than parties in countries with a less adversarial journalistic culture.	8 Parties that have suffered successive or major electoral defeats are more likely to become market-oriented than parties that have not suffered such defeats.

Table 7A.1 (continued)

Propositions related to differences between countries	*Propositions related to differences between parties within countries*
9 Parties in countries with deep social or political cleavages are less likely to be market-oriented than parties in countries without such deep cleavages.	9 Parties with a hierarchical internal culture are more likely to be market-oriented than parties with an egalitarian internal culture.
10 Parties in countries with an egalitarian political culture are more likely to be market-oriented than parties in countries with a hierarchical political culture.	10 Parties whose members of parliament mainly answer to the central leadership of the party are more likely to be market-oriented than parties without a strong parliamentary party discipline.
11 Parties in countries with a high level of political distrust are more likely to be market-oriented than parties in countries with a lower level of political distrust.	11 Office- and vote-seeking parties are more likely to be market-oriented than policy-seeking parties.
12 Parties in countries with news media independent of the party-political system are more likely to be market-oriented than parties in countries where the news media form part of the party-political system.	12 Parties with strong ties to particular social or political cleavages are less likely to be market-oriented than parties with weak ties to particular social or political cleavages.

8

Niche marketing the Greens in Canada and Scotland

Susan Harada and Helen M. Morris

The topic: niche marketing

In May 2010 the Green Party of England and Wales made history when party leader Caroline Lucas won the Brighton Pavilion seat in the UK-wide Westminster election. The victory demonstrated that a niche party could win wider support in a first-past-the-post electoral system. Green Party of Canada (GPC) strategists jumped on the Lucas bandwagon, emailing GPC e-newsletter subscribers, calling for donations so that their leader might emulate Lucas (interview with Cantin 2010). The Scottish Green Party (SGP) said the victory 'changes everything', providing an excellent platform for the 2011 Scottish parliamentary election (Scottish Green Party 2010a). The SGP and GPC reactions may suggest they were consolidating base support through standard political communications methods, or – viewed through a political marketing lens – may reveal an attempt by either party to rework their niche appeal, using the Lucas victory for political validation.

The concept of political niche marketing builds on fundamental business model characteristics. Although Toften and Hammervoll note a lack of a 'widely accepted single conceptual definition of niche marketing' (Toften and Hammervoll 2007: 1380), niche markets are mainly seen as being compact, with specialized appeal for a small defined group whose members are distinguished by common needs and/or interests (Keegan *et al.* 1992; Dalgic and Leeuw 1994; Kara and Kaynak 1997). A producer aiming to cultivate such a group positions the product(s) to satisfy the narrowly defined interest (Porter 1980; Bantel 1997; Hezar *et al.* 2006). According to Bantel, this allows for producers to deploy sparse resources strategically (Bantel 1997: 246). Overall, it follows that niche marketing can generally be described as 'positioning into small, profitable homogeneous market segments which have been ignored or neglected by others' (Dalgic and Leeuw 1994: 42). This chapter will explore a niche marketing approach by studying the Canadian and Scottish national Green parties.

Previous research on niche marketing

The range of political choice in many democratic countries widened in the latter decades of the 20th century, as a significant number of new political parties – including niche parties – were formed (Meguid 2008). The new niche parties, including some Green parties, focused on non-traditional issues or identities, appealed across left–right divisions, and offered a narrow range of policies (Meguid 2005, 2008). Although Green parties are not homogeneous (Burchell 2002), and some have attempted to broaden their perceived 'single issue' policy base, they share political and policy antecedents that justify the niche categorization (Müller-Rommel 1989; Burchell 2002; Talshir 2002).

Acknowledging Lees-Marshment's caution that 'politics cannot simply be fitted into a marketing framework that stems from analysis of the business world' (Lees-Marshment 2003: 9), it is still valuable to highlight a number of parallels between niche market conditions in both spheres. In the business sphere, an increasing range of products and shifting consumer expectations fundamentally altered the largely one-size-fits-all marketing landscape (McKenna 1988; Kotler 1989; Dalgic and Leeuw 1994). This focused attention on the concept of niche marketing. The balance of power had shifted; the marketplace was required to respond more nimbly to specific consumer desires. The resulting acceleration of niche marketing had a significant impact on wider culture (Anderson 2006; McKenna 1988).

In the political sphere, Butler and Collins (1996) utilized marketing elements to reconsider the categorical framework – which included the 'nicher', along with the market leader, the challenger and the follower – set by various scholars (Porter 1980; Kotler 1994). Butler and Collins (1996: 29) described a nicher party as the 'leader in [a] narrowly defined market or niche', with 'specialist appeal'. It is not solely issue-based; successful nichers have also targeted specific linguistic groups, voters within a defined geographic area, and recent immigrants (ibid.: 33). Similarly, in business, Kotler (1989) noted that a niche market specialization could run the gamut from product to geography to quality/price.

There are also parallels with respect to successful strategic nicher behaviours. In business, Dalgic and Leeuw (1994: 45–46) and McKenna (1988: 93–94) noted the necessity of marketing the company as well as its product, treating customers as individuals, responding to their unique needs, and establishing strong long-term relationships. In politics, Butler and Collins (1996: 32) cited the importance of strong, lasting relationships between nichers and their targeted political consumers. Raynor (1992) concluded that a successful niche strategy in the business sphere cannot be communications-driven. Instead, a genuine niche must first be identified, and only then can a specialization, tailored to meet consumer expectations, be effectively delivered. Similarly, political marketing theories (Lees-Marshment 2001; Newman 1994; Wring 1997) generally posit that successful market-oriented political parties identify constituent wants/needs through market research before tailoring their product/policy accordingly.

Following Butler and Collins, who identified the importance of a 'create, expand and defend' nicher strategy (Butler and Collins 1996: 32), it can be said that a political niche party must adopt specific behaviours, as outlined in Figure 8.1, if it hopes to engage in niche market-oriented politics.

These identified behaviours are utilized as a guide for analysis that first explores whether the GPC and SGP can be categorized as niche market-oriented political groups, and then considers the possible implications of our conclusions.

New research: niche marketing the Greens in Canada and Scotland

Research analysed strategies employed by the GPC during the 2004 and 2008 Canadian federal election campaigns, and by the SGP during the 2003 and 2007 Scottish parliamentary election campaigns (for the sake of comparative consistency with the SGP, the 2006 Canadian federal election, for which GPC strategies were largely an expansion of those used in 2004, is excluded

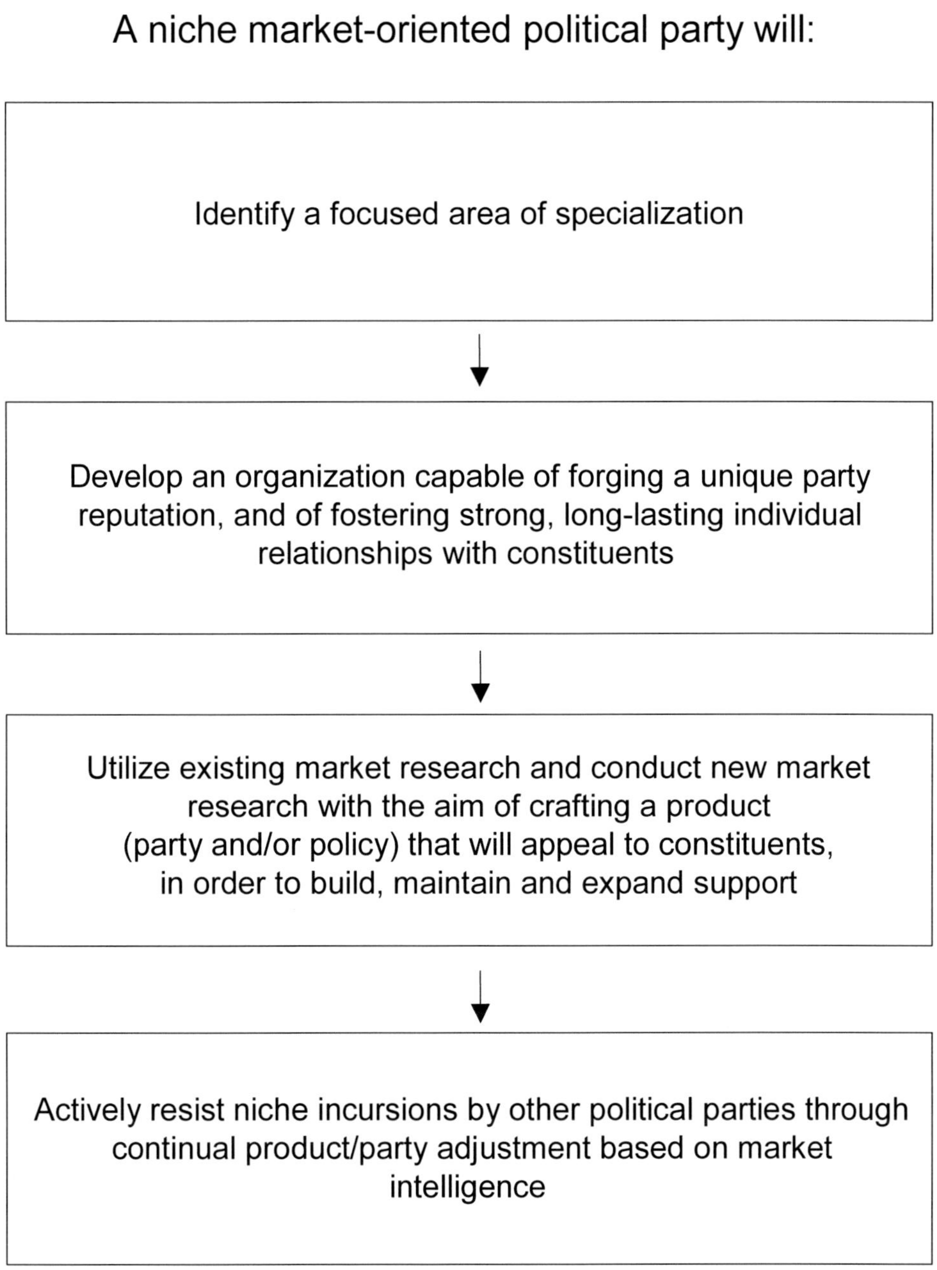

A niche market-oriented political party will:

Identify a focused area of specialization

↓

Develop an organization capable of forging a unique party reputation, and of fostering strong, long-lasting individual relationships with constituents

↓

Utilize existing market research and conduct new market research with the aim of crafting a product (party and/or policy) that will appeal to constituents, in order to build, maintain and expand support

↓

Actively resist niche incursions by other political parties through continual product/party adjustment based on market intelligence

Figure 8.1 Indicators of niche market-oriented political behaviour

from analysis). To date, their most meaningful party activity has been organized around those elections. The authors conducted semi-structured qualitative interviews over five months in 2010 with nearly a dozen senior GPC and SGP members in key decision-making roles. The questions were open-ended, focusing on organization, technology, research, strategies and political niche marketing concepts. The findings were triangulated with information gathered from party manifestos/platforms and slogans produced for the studied campaigns, alongside news reports, press releases and the authors' existing research material.

The Greens in Canada and Scotland

The Green parties in Canada and Scotland are niche parties with similar philosophical roots and areas of specialization. Both emerged from ecology-based campaigning movements and faced the challenge of how to transform themselves into successful, functioning political parties, while retaining their unique political identities. Since its formation in 1983, the GPC has attempted to develop as a force for environmentally focused social and political change. It first attracted notable support in 2004, winning 4.3 percent of the popular vote – still marginal compared with the leading parties (12.4–36.7 percent), and still short of electing members, but significantly higher than its own 0.8 percent in 2000. The GPC's geographically dispersed popular vote rose to 6.8 percent in 2008 but it again failed to win a seat. The SGP formed in 1990 by amicably moving away from the UK party and, in 1999, elected a member to the re-established Scottish Parliament and gained 3.6 percent of the vote. In 2003 it won seven seats (6.9 percent of the vote), reduced to two (4.0 percent of the vote) after the 2007 election (when assessing vote share, note that the SGP stood in the regional list and did not compete for constituency votes).

However, the GPC and SGP have faced differing challenges. Canada's national first-past-the-post or single member plurality (SMP) political landscape is dominated by four parties (Conservative, Liberal, New Democrat and Bloc Québécois). SMP favours parties with concentrated support over smaller parties which tend to have dispersed backing. In contrast, members of the Scottish Parliament are elected by an Additional Member System whereby each elector has two votes: one to elect a regional member – 56 across eight regions – and one to vote for a constituency Member of the Scottish Parliament (MSP) (73 members) using first-past-the-post. The number of MSPs elected under the regional list portion aims to reflect broadly the portion of votes won by that party, acting as a top-up for parties who may have received substantial numbers of votes at the constituency level but secured few or no seats (Herbert *et al.* 2007). The SGP was constrained financially to contesting the regional list (interview with Harvie 2010). No party gained a majority in the first three elections to the re-established Scottish Parliament. The Labour and the Scottish National parties are the two leading parties, with the Liberal Democrat and Conservative parties each garnering a decent share of seats. The smaller parties, including the Greens, took three seats in 1999 and 2007 and 17 seats in 2003, a direct contrast with Canadian smaller parties, which remain sidelined and seatless.

With six times as many eligible voters spread unevenly across territory more than 125 times the size of Scotland, Canadian political life plays out in unique ways. The influence of regional interests and the resources required to campaign nationally loom large in Canadian party fortunes (Carty *et al.* 2000). The 2004 changes to the electoral funding system, which subsidized parties winning a minimum of 2 percent of the national vote, had an impact on the behaviour of political parties (Flanagan and Jansen 2009). The GPC, as will be discussed, was no exception. It qualified for state funding in 2004, receiving approximately (CDN) $1,000,000 annually; this rose to around (CDN) $1,800,000 after the 2008 election. The SGP has limited funds, mostly from individual small donors. In 2003 they had £63,864 (Electoral Commission 2003) to fight their campaign; in 2007 this was boosted by Green MSPs donating 20 percent of their salary to party funds.

The similarities and differences allow us to examine GPC and SGP campaign behaviour from a niche market-oriented perspective, while considering variables that might influence success, including electoral systems, geography and funding. Accepting that both parties satisfy the first indicator of political niche marketing through their focused area of appeal, our case studies will analyse the extent to which they engage the remaining three indicators as evidenced by their governance and campaign decision-making structure, candidate selection process, and platform/manifesto development process, as well as their application of existing and new polling data and other feedback mechanisms during two campaign periods. If we find evidence of political niche market-oriented techniques, we will ask what this means for the cohesion of their parties and democracy. If we find no such evidence, we will ask if adoption is possible, and if greater electoral success would result.

Green Party of Canada (GPC) – federal elections 2004–08

The GPC's governance structure was designed to facilitate decentralized decision-making, a Green party feature that allows Greens to portray themselves as unique entities dedicated to promoting a non-traditional approach to politics (Müller-Rommel 1989; Burchell 2002). However, the GPC has been evolving towards a more traditional centralized and leader-centric structure during campaign periods. Its first significant shift occurred in 2004 (interviews with Crookes 2010a, Travis 2010b), when it attempted a more 'professionalized' campaign style (Gibson and Römmele 2001). Emulating larger parties, the GPC ran its first full-blown national leader's tour, and aimed for consistent and more top-down party messaging through the provision of national campaign materials to Electoral District Associations (EDAs). However, limited resources hampered consistent cohesion between the two levels (interviews with Travis 2010a, 2010b).

With the possibility of qualifying for post-election public subsidies, the party secured funding at the national level through private loans and donations, before and during the campaign period (Elections Canada 2004a, 2004b). The money enabled it to top up its one part-time staff member with nearly five dozen paid staff and volunteers (interview with Travis 2010b). It set up a more centralized campaign structure with paid staff in key decision-making roles; this was reprised in 2008. The professionalization attempts arguably caused some erosion of the GPC's claim to the unique political behaviour that was part of its original niche attraction. During both campaigns the party experienced internal tensions and subsequent media coverage reminiscent of the traditional political parties from which it was seeking to set itself apart (Harada 2006, 2009).

Two measurements of the GPC's ability to forge strong relationships with its constituents are common political participatory methodologies: candidate selection (Erickson and Carty 1991; Cross 1998); and policy development (Carty *et al.* 2000). In 2004 the GPC had a decentralized structure for candidate selection. It lacked resources to develop a rigorous central process, leaving it to EDAs and local volunteers whenever possible (interview with Travis 2010b). Still, a significant new top-down strategy of running a full slate of candidates was imposed. This had a two-fold objective: to attain the popular vote level necessary for state funding (which resulted in a number of parachute candidates), and to recast its minor party status. Post-2008 there was talk of requiring central party pre-screening of local nominations, in order to minimize the possibility of candidates who might damage party credibility. However, it was recognized that significantly centralizing candidate selection could alienate the party's grassroots (Harada 2009). Allowing local members to largely retain candidate selection power enabled the GPC to conserve a crucial element of its unique identity, which likely helped preserve relations with core niche constituents.

The participatory nature of the GPC's policy development process is examined within the framework of its campaign platforms. In 2004 the GPC used the internet to maximize voter engagement. The platform chair designed an interactive 'wiki' that allowed party members to create and edit the platform's policy planks; non-members could view and comment only. Three rules governed plank development: existing party policy, passed at convention, could not be contradicted; existing policy need not be included; and policy gaps could be filled with new planks (interview with Pilling 2010). By 2008 the largely decentralized process was appreciably altered, although the intent – to seek as much input as possible while building constituent–party relationships – remained the same. The GPC held a series of pre-campaign policy conferences across the country, involving party members, subject-area experts and the general public. The GPC's leader and shadow cabinet crafted an omnibus policy document, which incorporated results from the conferences alongside existing party policy: the planks of the subsequent 2008 campaign platform were pulled from that document. That process provided a more indirect connection between grassroots participation and the final platform than did the 2004 process. However, the final 2004 product had attracted critics, notably environmentally focused non-governmental organizations (NGOs), one reason the interactive 'wiki' experience was not repeated (interview with Travis 2010b).

Lees-Marshment (2001, 2003) notes that market intelligence is crucial for political parties seeking to become market-oriented. As outlined above, it is also crucial for niche political parties seeking to defend and expand their niche support. Limited resources meant that the GPC largely relied on public market research. In 2004 it parlayed its growing support levels in public polls into mainstream media coverage – a bid to build credibility and create a sense of momentum. This strategy continued in 2008. In 2004 other strategies included attempts to change public perceptions that the GPC was a left-leaning, single-issue party: it embraced more fiscally conservative policy planks (interview with Pilling 2010), and made efforts to ensure that its leader discussed a wide range of issues, not just the environment (interview with Crookes 2010b). By 2008, with a new, high-profile leader, the GPC had repositioned itself into a more leader-centric entity. The national campaign and television advertisements focused on leader Elizabeth May; she led GPC efforts to muster public support for her eventual inclusion in the nationally televised debates, which traditionally involved only the leaders of the larger political parties. As participation was largely restricted to parties with seats, May's inclusion was also strategically enabled by the GPC's pre-campaign recruitment of an independent Member of Parliament, who later failed to keep his seat under the Green banner.

Informal market intelligence was gathered through internet outreach. The website was increasingly professionalized and the GPC grew more adept between 2004 and 2008 at utilizing its website and emails for campaigning and fundraising. Feedback mechanisms such as blogs were linked into the site. An internal system of voter ID management was developed and made available to local campaigns, and was used at the national level to target support more efficiently (Harada 2009).

The GPC had sufficient resources to commission some limited formal market research in 2004 and 2008. In 2004 national surveys were conducted by Oraclepoll Research before and just after the election call, probing issues of importance to voters, as well as their openness to alternatives such as proportional representation and tax shifting. EDA-specific surveys were also undertaken to identify support levels (interviews with Crookes 2010a, 2010b). The market research influenced messaging in news releases, some of the leader's speeches and resource investments in one EDA. It had no impact on the platform, mainly because polls were anathema to some GPC members (interview with Travis 2010c). Although information released by the party about 2008 market research is limited, it acknowledged hiring an external expert to analyse polling data to help it make decisions about resource concentration. It also surveyed popular support in half a dozen key ridings. During the campaign, it conducted market research to gauge support levels for the GPC leader's electoral bid (Labchuk 2008). Overall, the strategy of funnelling additional funding and human resources support into specific EDAs in 2004 and 2008 was a tactical departure for a party with a philosophy of decentralization, as was the decision to actively commission market research. The latter move was particularly significant. Even so, the information garnered from the research seemed to direct campaign strategies rather than lead to product adjustment.

The fourth characteristic of a niche market-oriented political party is its ability to resist incursions by other parties through continual product/party adjustment based on market intelligence. The incursion threat was greatest in 2008, when public opinion surveys identified the environment as one of the main issues concerning Canadians. The major parties staked substantial claims on the climate change file, given its prominence as an issue of concern (Ellis and Woolstencroft 2009; Jeffrey 2009; Erickson and Laycock 2009). The left-of-centre New Democrats, in particular, were cognizant that they could lose crucial support from young voters attracted to the GPC's environmental emphasis (Erickson and Laycock 2009: 99). Although the opportunity existed, the GPC did not consistently meet the incursion threat by promoting its own unique identity. On the one hand, the party tied the top-of-mind environmental issue to its tax shift policy; when the Liberals adopted a similar 'green tax shift' programme the GPC portrayed it as a marker of its own political relevance. On the other hand, the party leader aligned herself with the Liberal leader (who personally championed climate change issues), when the two struck a deal to not run candidates in each other's ridings. The deal ignited a controversial internal/external debate about strategic voting, and about GPC identity as a movement versus a political party (Harada 2009); it did little to assist the GPC with incursion resistance.

Scottish Green Party (SGP)

In 2003 the SGP enjoyed its greatest electoral success, gaining seven regional list members of the Scottish Parliament. The party's '2nd vote Green' election campaign sought to differentiate the traditional first-past-the-post constituency vote from the regional list vote. Voters had two votes; the SGP campaign suggested that people could follow 'tribal loyalties' with the first, but that the second was the conscience or freedom vote (interview with Baird 2010). This campaigning technique was employed by the SGP and the Scottish Socialist Party, while larger parties appeared to stick to traditional constituency-based tactics (Ministry of Justice 2008). The campaign encouraged the idea of vote-splitting (interview with Harvie 2010) – backing a different party on the constituency and list ballots. The political landscape in 2003 leant itself to this campaign; when the party manifestos were launched, political commentators struggled to differentiate between the parties (MacWhirter 2003). Arguably, the main division between the parties was over the war in Iraq, a policy area not devolved to the Scottish Parliament (Burnside *et al.* 2003: 26). One candidate said that given the similarities between the main parties, constituents were willing to give smaller ones, such as the SGP, a chance with their regional list vote (interview with Ballance 2010). Of those who voted, between one-fifth and one-quarter cast their second vote for someone – including the SGP – other than one of the four parties that had dominated the 1999 parliament (Curtice 2003).

The 2007 Scottish parliamentary election presented a very different political landscape. The election was viewed as a two-horse race between the pro-independence Scottish National Party (SNP) and the Labour Party, which supports Scotland remaining a part of the United Kingdom. The possibility and cost of Scottish independence were constant campaign themes. Voters had clear choices between the parties on issues that were devolved to the Scottish Parliament. The outcome of the vote was expected to be very close, prompting speculation that voters were less willing to risk their second vote with smaller parties such as the SGP (Curtice 2007). In the first two elections there were two separate ballot papers: one for the regional vote and one for the constituency vote. In 2007 a single ballot contained both. Arguably this worked against smaller parties seeking to focus on list votes. The new format may also have contributed to the abnormally high number of spoilt ballots. In 16 constituency contests the number of spoilt ballots was greater than the winning candidate's majority (Denver 2007: 62). The single ballot paper containing both regional and list contests precluded a repeat of '2nd vote Green'. In 2007 some 146,099 ballots were rejected (Electoral Commission 2007c). The 2003 SGP vote was around 150,000. The head of SGP communications for the 2003 election argued that given the margins with which the SGP was getting elected, the loss of spoilt ballots was enough to almost wipe it out in 2007 (interview with Burgess 2010).

The SGP operates from four principles: ecology, equality, radical democracy, and peace and non-violence (Scottish Green Party 2007a). The party functions democratically such that the final manifesto can be a distillation of ideas from all party members. In reality there is a small core of active members (Bennie 2004), and drafts go through party committees before one person pulls the ideas together into one coherent policy platform (interview with Baird 2010). Traditionally, the gathering and use of market intelligence has not played a role in the development of party policy.

The election of seven MSPs in 2007 dramatically changed the party's ability to forge a unique identity between election periods. The SGP was a relative unknown to many voters, and MSPs worked to build credibility throughout the parliament, possibly neglecting public campaigning and local branch development (interview with Harvie 2010).

The SGP ramps up activities ahead of a Scottish parliamentary election. Scarce party resources are concentrated upon elections where there is a perceived stronger chance of winning seats (interview with Ballance 2010). Local parties take the lead on candidate selection in line with the SGP principle of decentralization. The national party will act as an overseer to try to ensure gender balance and, as one former MSP put it, 'avoid rogue elements embarrassing the party' (interview with Baird 2010).

The seven SGP MSPs elected in 2007 boosted party funds by contributing 20 percent of their parliamentary salary. Local party branches also had an MSP to hold accountable and to communicate with voters through the media. The party had access to policy research conducted by SGP staff employed by parliamentarians. Harvie likened it to a loose association of local societies suddenly having the staff and resources of a sizeable national NGO (interview with Harvie 2010). The additional money and resources enabled the national party to have a degree of influence on, for example, locally issued press releases. However, with the strong principle of decentralization, local parties and individual MSPs continued to act independently on local concerns (interview with Baird 2010), suggesting that there was no clear single party message.

Decision-making by members at the SGP conference, as well as at a series of meetings throughout the year, can be lengthy and complex. There has been some internal debate about reforming the policy process to make it more responsive and nimbler, but no specific changes have been made (interview with Harvie 2010). The main relationships that the party forges are with its own membership through the policy-making and campaigning stages. List candidates must campaign across substantially larger regions than their constituency candidate counterparts. South of Scotland stretches across the width of the country encompassing around 30 market towns (interview with Ballance 2010), while the Highlands and Islands is a region the size of

Belgium (interview with Scott 2010). Rather than using a marketing strategy, Scott said that campaigning would likely be conducted where volunteers were available. In 2007 those MSPs not holding down outside jobs were able to dedicate themselves to 'campaigning twenty-four-seven'. They also had enhanced knowledge and resources, having served in parliament (interview with Ballance 2010).

In 2003 restricted funds meant that public outreach was limited to the party election broadcast (assembled by a friend of a party member with an edit suite (interview with Harvie 2010)), the free delivery of an SGP-financed leaflet to every household, activists putting up street placards, and maximum possible media coverage (interview with Burgess 2010). The SGP received more limited media coverage than the four main parties. Media attention was focused on the Iraq war and, as one journalist put it, multi-party politics between all-male, middle-aged leaders who agree on more nurses, teachers and police is hard to fit into media news values (Fraser 2003). For the 2007 election the SGP had much more money (£437,107), but still a fraction of the SNP's £1.4 million (Electoral Commission 2007b). The shortage of funds meant that the party struggled with a lack of information about voters. One MSP noted that in 2007 the SNP had a clearer idea of who Green voters were than the SGP, and deliberately targeted their vote. The size and funding of the party limited its options ahead of the 2007 poll (interview with Ballance 2010). The SGP was still very much at the building stage of conducting market research, largely to reinforce existing SGP positions and help to shape internal policy debate (interview with Harvie 2010).

There is a concern that the party must stick to its core principles, communicating these to voters rather than adapting them to popular sentiment (interview with Baird 2010; Bennie 2004). The SGP is confident that it has the true environmental and social justice credentials and directly criticizes other parties' environmental rhetoric (Scottish Green Party 2007a, 2007b). A long-serving member of the party argued that, rather than changing the SGP to meet popular opinion, there is a need to let the public know that the SGP addresses wider issues and that the environment is a core issue, not a fringe concern (interview with Baird 2010). The SGP appears to operate under the assumption that it is too small to set the political agenda but can use circumstances to further its cause, be it the electoral system or the victory of the Greens south of the border. As the next SGP conference approached, the victory by Caroline Lucas, leader of the Green Party of England and Wales, was front and centre in the publicity material (Scottish Green Party 2010b).

The GPC and the SGP did not wholly conform to our theoretical framework for political niche market-oriented parties, as noted in Figure 8.2.

A number of factors limit the ability of the GPC and SGP to operate as true niche market-oriented parties, including:

- Money: market intelligence is crucial, but expensive (Marland 2005). The GPC has some means to conduct limited market research and has shifted closer to a marketing model in that sense. However, it was the SGP, with fewer resources, that won representation, suggesting that although money is a factor, the electoral system is also critical to success.
- Green principles: being a niche political party in a marketing age can be a double-edged sword. Non-traditional party behaviours help create niche support, while adopting traditional marketing techniques may be equated with traditional political party behaviour. Parties face tension between core beliefs and their somewhat elaborate democratic structures versus a growing realization of a need to streamline operations and be more responsive to public opinion in order to be electable.

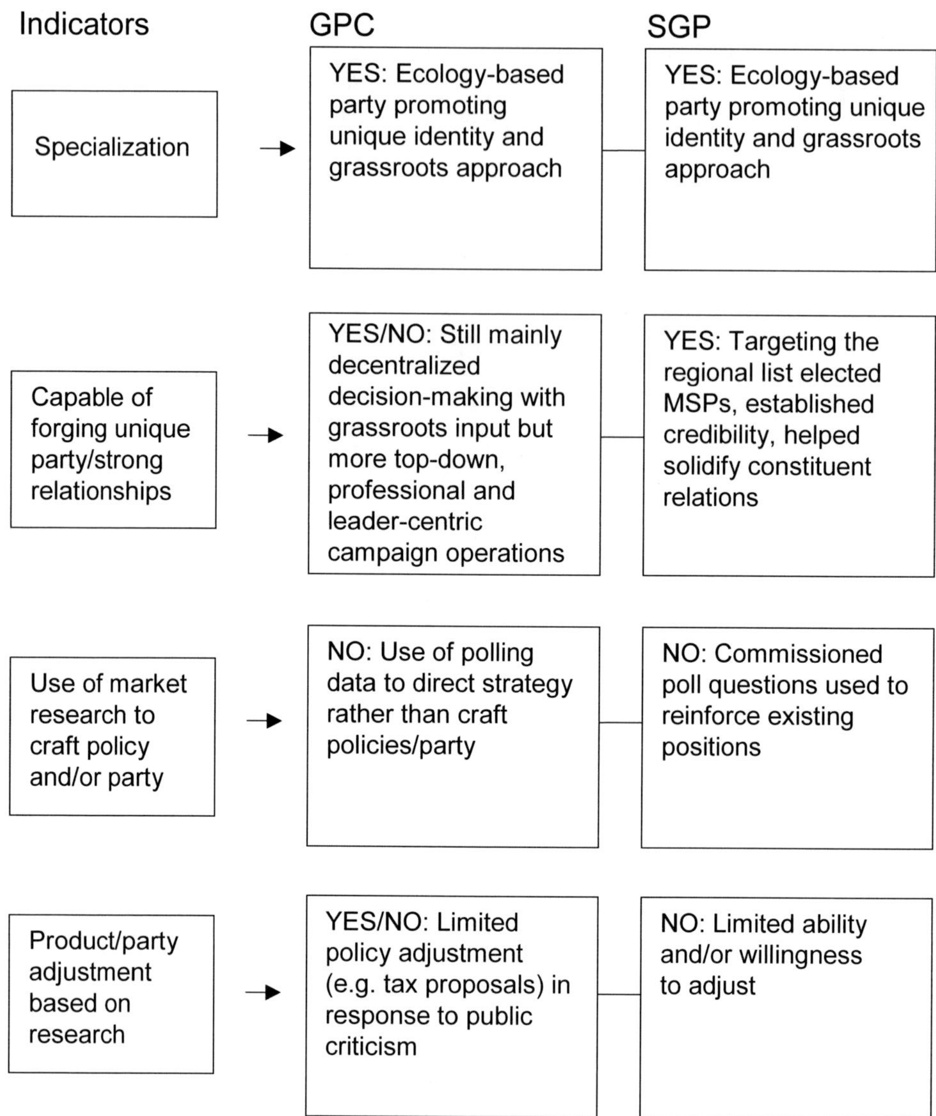

Figure 8.2 Indicators of GPC and SGP niche market-oriented political behaviour

Advice for practitioners

Noting Bantel's (1997) earlier point about niche firms having the ability to employ scarce resources strategically, niche parties may consider a variation of Anderson's 'Long Tail' model, which involves marketing to individual niches rather than mass marketing (Anderson 2006). This variation could aim to selectively deepen the niche rather than expand it in ways that might alienate core support or deviate from fundamental party principles. As such, it would differ from 'segmentation', which Shani and Chalasani define as a 'top-down approach' to dividing up a large market, and instead more closely resemble what they term a 'bottom up' niche marketing approach (Shani and Chalasani 1992: 35). In our view, a niche market-oriented party could present unique aspects of itself to portions of the population rather than marketing the party as a whole to the entire electorate. This includes:

- Marketing a leader as a distinct and winning brand rather than marketing the whole niche party;
- Marketing the niche party at a lower level of government to establish credibility; electing even one member can demonstrate that the party has legitimate, productive representatives, and is not simply a campaigning group;
- Exploiting aspects of the electoral system which lend themselves to niche parties, such as regional list voting and proportional systems, rather than trying to compete head to head with mainstream parties.

Impact on politics

Political parties may be able to adopt some niche market-oriented behaviours while minimizing the need to drastically retool their unique party identities. They might retain their core niche vote while attracting new support and giving the political consumer a wider range of choice. Circumstances and electoral systems would dictate how that would translate into concrete post-election political and policy action. An electoral system such as a regional list system may give citizens access to a greater variety of political representation to advocate on their behalf. Within a traditional SMP system, the impact of niche party representation would depend on the parliamentary makeup. Unless the elected niche party members had sufficient representation to hold the balance of power in a minority parliament, members may have limited influence on policy. On the other hand, the election of even one representative, such as the leader, could have great symbolic value for the issue(s) or political philosophy championed by the niche party. The representative could be deployed strategically, to deepen the party's support.

It may be that the framework of the political environment will ultimately limit the choices of niche parties and compel them to play within the rules of the game set by the larger parties. Although that limitation can hinder democracy, in a certain sense it can also encourage the push towards democratic values. If the end result is that niche parties are forced to gain a fuller understanding of their constituents in order to elect representatives within established frameworks, their hard-won understanding might lead, in the end, to a more meaningful representation of minority interests.

The way forward

It is possible that Green parties in particular need to consider marrying a market-oriented mindset with more pragmatic electoral strategies. A closer study of the UK and Australian electoral successes may provide assistance for niche party campaigners elsewhere, enabling them to adapt successful Green strategies.

Market-oriented basics – professionalizing and building credibility – could sharpen the niche party's ability to tap into existing 'green' supporters and gain their vote. This could be more effective than attempting to change unduly its product in the search for a new support base. Further research could assess the feasibility of applying a version of the Long Tail model to niche parties. A political variation of the model has already been popularly defined within the context of US politics as being 'every variety of political belief that does not fit within the two major parties' (Kling 2005). This goes full circle to the question of whether Green parties can expand their support base to reach those who hold a variety of political beliefs, and whether, in doing so, they can still retain their original niche constituents. It would be painstaking work to set a Long Tail-type framework and then track support across differing systems and through several campaigns in order to answer that question, but it would be an interesting and worthwhile pursuit that could ultimately encourage political participation.

Bibliography

List of interviewees

Baird, S. (2010) MSP (2003–07) Scottish Green Party. Telephone interview with Morris, H. from Dundee, Scotland, 7 July.

Ballance, C. (2010) MSP (2003–07) Scottish Green Party. Telephone interview with Morris, H. from Moffat, Scotland, 12 August.

Burgess, S. (2010) Green Party, Head of Communications 2003 Scottish election campaign. Telephone interview with Morris, H. from Edinburgh, Scotland, 25 June.

Cantin, C. (2010) then-Interim Executive Director, Green Party of Canada. Telephone interview with Harada, S. from Ottawa, Canada, 29 June.

Crookes, W. (2010a) former Campaign Manager, Green Party of Canada. Telephone interview with Harada, S. from British Columbia, Canada, 13 August.

—— (2010b) former Campaign Manager, Green Party of Canada. Telephone interview with Harada, S. from British Columbia, Canada, 29 August.

Harvie, P. (2010) MSP, Scottish Green Party. Telephone interview with Morris, H. from Glasgow, Scotland, 12 July.

May, E. (2010) Leader, Green Party of Canada. News conference attended by Harada, S. in Toronto, Canada, 21 August.

Murphy, M. (2010) former Executive Director, Green Party of Canada. Interview with Harada, S. in Ottawa, Canada, 7 May.

Pilling, M. (2010) former Platform Chair, Green Party of Canada. Telephone interview with Harada, S. from Thunder Bay, Canada, 13 August.

Scott, E. (2010) former MSP (2003–07) Scottish Green Party. Telephone interview with Morris, H. from Scottish Highlands, 29 June.

Travis, D. (2010a) former Director of Media Relations, Green Party of Canada. Telephone interview with Harada, S. from Montreal, Canada, 2 July.

—— (2010b) former Director of Media Relations, Green Party of Canada. Telephone interview with Harada, S. from Montreal, Canada, 7 August.

—— (2010c) former Director of Media Relations, Green Party of Canada. Telephone interview with Harada, S. from Montreal, Canada, 1 September.

Secondary

Anderson, C. (2006) *The Long Tail: Why the Future of Business is Selling Less of More*, New York: Hyperion.

Bantel, K.A. (1997) 'Performance in adolescent, technology-based firms: product strategy, implementation and synergy', *Journal of High Technology Management Research* 8: 243–62.

Bennie, L. (2004) *Understanding Political Participation: Green Party Membership in Scotland*, Aldershot: Ashgate.

Burchell, J. (2002) *The Evolution of Green Politics: Development and Change within European Green Parties*, London: Earthscan Publications.

Burnside, R., Herbert, S. and Curtis, S. (2003) *Election Briefing 03/25*, Edinburgh: Scottish Parliament Information Centre (SPICe). Online, www.scottish.parliament.uk/business/research/briefings-03/sb03-25.pdf (accessed 29 September 2010).

Butler, P. and Collins, N. (1996) 'Strategic analysis in political markets', *European Journal of Marketing* 30: 25–36.

Carty, R.K., Cross, W. and Young, L. (2000) *Rebuilding Canadian Party Politics*, Vancouver: UBC Press.

Cross, W. (1998) 'The conflict between participatory and accommodative politics: the case for stronger parties', *International Journal of Canadian Studies* 17: 37–55.

Curtice, J. (2003) 'Turnout, electoral behaviour and fragmentation of the party system', in R. Burnside, S. Herbert and S. Curtis, *Election Briefing 03/25*, Edinburgh: Scottish Parliament Information Centre

(SPICe). Online, www.scottish.parliament.uk/business/research/briefings-03/sb03-25.pdf (accessed 28 September 2010).

—— (2007) 'Turnout and electoral behaviour', in S. Herbert, R. Burnside, M. Earle, T. Edwards, T. Foley and I. McIver, *Election Briefing 07/21*, Edinburgh: Scottish Parliament Information Centre (SPICe). Online, www.scottish.parliament.uk/business/research/briefings-07/SB07-21.pdf (accessed 28 September 2010).

Dalgic, T. and Leeuw, M. (1994) 'Niche marketing revisited: concept, applications and some European cases', *European Journal of Marketing* 28: 39–55.

Denver, D. (2007) 'A historic moment? The results of the Scottish Parliament elections 2007', *Scottish Affairs* 60.

Elections Canada (2004a) *Return Details – Statement of Contributions Received: Details of Operating Loans* (Part 2c). Online, www.elections.ca/scripts/webpep/fin/detail_report.aspx (accessed 13 August 2010).

—— (2004b) *Returns Details – Statement of Contributions Received: Details of Contributions from Individuals* (Part 2a). Online, www.elections.ca/scripts/webpep/fin/detail_report.aspx (accessed 13 August 2010).

Electoral Commission (2003) *Register of Campaign Expenditure, Scottish Parliament Election, 1 May*. London.

—— (2007a) *Scottish Elections 2007, Electoral Administration Issues Arising from the Scottish Parliamentary and Local Government Elections 3 May 2007*. Online, www.electoralcommission.org.uk/-data/assets/electoral_commission_pdf_file/0012/13224/Scottish-Election-Report-B-Final-For-Web_27602-20317-E-N-S-W-.pdf (accessed 27 August 2010).

—— (2007b) *Register of Campaign Expenditure, Scottish Parliament Election, 3 May*, London.

—— (2007c) *The Independent Review of the Scottish Parliamentary and Local Government Elections, 3 May*, London.

Ellis, F. and Woolstencroft, P. (2009) 'Stephen Harper and the Conservatives campaign on their record', in J.H. Pammett and C. Dornan (eds) *The Canadian Federal Election of 2008*, Toronto: Dundurn Press, 16–62.

Erickson, L. and Carty, R.K. (1991) 'Parties and candidate selection in the 1988 Canadian general election', *Canadian Journal of Political Science* 24: 331–49.

Erickson, L. and Laycock, D. (2009) 'Modernization, incremental progress, and the challenge of relevance: the NDP's 2008 campaign', in J.H. Pammett and C. Dornan (eds) *The Canadian Federal Election of 2008*, Toronto: Dundurn Press.

Flanagan, T. and Jansen, H.J. (2009) 'Election campaigns under Canada's party finance laws', in J.H. Pammett and C. Dornan (eds) *The Canadian Federal Election of 2008*, Toronto: Dundurn Press, 195–216.

Fraser, D. (2003) 'The media campaign', in R. Burnside, S. Herbert and S. Curtis, *Election Briefing 03/25*, Edinburgh: Scottish Parliament Information Centre (SPICe). Online, www.scottish.parliament.uk/business/research/briefings-03/sb03-25.pdf (accessed 28 September 2010).

Gibson, R.K. and Römmele, A. (2001) 'Changing campaign communications: a party-centred theory of professionalized campaigning', *Harvard International Journal of Press/Politics* 6: 31–43.

Harada, S. (2006) 'Great expectations: the Green Party of Canada's 2006 campaign', in J.H. Pammett and C. Dornan (eds) *The Canadian Federal Election of 2006*, Toronto: Dundurn Press, 143–70.

—— (2009) 'The promise of May: the Green Party of Canada's campaign 2008', in J.H. Pammett and C. Dornan (eds) *The Canadian Federal Election of 2008*, Toronto: Dundurn Press, 162–93.

Herbert, S., Burnside, R., Earle, M., Edwards, T., Foley, T. and McIver, I. (2007) *Election Briefing 07/21*, (8 May 2007) Edinburgh: Scottish Parliament Information Centre (SPICe). Online, www.scottish.parliament.uk/business/research/briefings-07/SB07-21.pdf (accessed 13 August 2010).

Hezar, I., Dalgic, T., Phelan, S. and Knight, G. (2006) 'Principles of global niche marketing strategies: an early conceptual framework', in T. Dalgic (ed.) *Handbook of Niche Marketing: Principles and Practice*, Binghampton, NY: The Haworth Reference Press.

Jeffrey, B. (2009) 'Missed opportunity: the invisible Liberals', in J.H. Pammett and C. Dornan (eds) *The Canadian Federal Election of 2008*, Toronto: Dundurn Press, 63–97.

Kara, A. and Kaynak, E. (1997) 'Markets of a single customer: exploiting conceptual developments in market segmentation', *European Journal of Marketing* 31: 873–95.

Keegan, W., Moriarty, S.E. and Duncan, T.R. (1992) *Marketing*, Englewood Cliffs, NJ: Prentice-Hall.

Kling, A. (2005) *Incumbent Politicians vs. the Long Tail*, Grace Creek Media and the George W. Bush Institute. Online, www.ideasinactiontv.com/tcs_daily/2005/08/incumbent-politicians-vs-the-long-tail.html (accessed 24 September 2010).

Kotler, P. (1989) 'From mass marketing to mass customization', *Planning Review*, September–October: 11–47.

—— (1994) *Marketing Management: Analysis, Planning, Implementation and Control*, eighth edn, Englewood Cliffs, NJ: Prentice-Hall International.

Labchuk, C. (2008) 'Elizabeth May closes gap in Central Nova'. Online, greenparty.ca/en/node/8315 (accessed 27 August 2010).

Lees-Marshment, J. (2001) *Political Marketing and British Political Parties: The Party's just Begun*, Manchester: Manchester University Press.

—— (2003) 'Political marketing: how to reach that pot of gold', *Journal of Political Marketing* 2: 1–32.

McKenna, R. (1988) 'Marketing in an age of diversity', *Harvard Business Review*, September–October: 88–95.

MacWhirter, I. (2003) 'Who ate all the policies?', *Sunday Herald*, 13 April.

Marland, A. (2005) 'Canadian political parties: market-oriented or ideological slagbrains?', in J. Lees-Marshment and D.G. Lilleker (eds) *Political Marketing: A Comparative Perspective*, Manchester: Manchester University Press, 57–78.

Meguid, B.M. (2005) 'Competition between unequals: the role of mainstream party strategy in niche party success', *American Political Science Review* 99: 347–59.

—— (2008) *Party Competition between Unequals: Strategies and Electoral Fortunes in Western Europe*, Cambridge: Cambridge University Press.

Ministry of Justice (2008) *The Governance of Britain Review of Voting Systems: The Experience of New Voting Systems in the United Kingdom since 1997*, London.

Müller-Rommel, F. (1989) 'Green parties and alternative lists under cross-national perspective', in F. Müller-Rommel (ed.) *New Politics in Western Europe: The Rise and Success of Green Parties and Alternative Lists*, Boulder, CO: Westview Press, 5–19.

Newman, B.I. (1994) *The Marketing of the President: Political Marketing as Campaign Strategy*, Thousand Oaks, CA: Sage Publications.

Porter, M.E. (1980) *Competitive Strategy: Techniques for Analysing Industries and Competitors*, New York: The Free Press.

Raynor, M.E. (1992) 'The pitfalls of niche marketing', *Journal of Business Strategy* 13: 29–32.

Scottish Green Party (2010a) 'Scottish Greens over the moon about first Green MP'. Online, www.scottishgreens.org.uk/news/show/6401/scottish-greens-over-the-moon-about-first-green-mp (accessed 20 June 2010).

—— (2010b) *Greenprint: News from the Scottish Green Party*, Summer 2010. Online, greenprint.scottishgreens.org.uk/greenprint_summer2010_online_lowres.pdf (accessed 27 August 2010).

—— (2007a) *Manifesto Holyrood*. Online, www.scottishgreens.org.uk/uploaded/Holyrood2007.pdf (accessed 27 August 2010).

—— (2007b) *Election Broadcast*. Online, www.youtube.com/watch?v=3muIYf2oWs8&feature=related.

Shani, D. and Chalasani, S. (1992) 'Exploiting niches using relationship marketing', *The Journal of Consumer Marketing* 9: 33–42.

Talshir, G. (2002) *The Political Ideology of Green Parties: From the Politics of Nature to Redefining the Nature of Politics*, Houndmills, England: Palgrave Macmillan.

Toften, K. and Hammervoll, T. (2007) 'Niche firms and marketing strategy: an exploratory study of internationally oriented niche firms', *European Journal of Marketing* 43: 1378–91.

Wring, D. (1997) 'Reconciling marketing with political science: theories of political marketing', *Journal of Marketing Management* 13: 651–63.

9

Political branding in the modern age

Effective strategies, tools and techniques

Kenneth M. Cosgrove

The topic: branding strategies and tools

Branding is a common marketing strategy and technique, and this chapter discusses the different ways in which it is used by the mainstream political parties in the US and, by way of comparison within North America, the Conservative Party of Canada. Branding offers important advantages to the political practitioner because it can sum up a complicated series of events or ideas, give meaning to an individual or incident, and provide a consistency of message over time with which one-off efforts simply can't compete. The brand's importance has grown during the past three decades as the number of political enterprises and the amount of background noise generated through the transformation of media from mass to niche has occurred. Branding represents a summary for the consumer about a product or, in this case, a party, candidate or policy, which can be subject to significant input by the user based on experience or perception. Branding works with positioning and differentiation because it helps to answer the questions of what market space the product should occupy in the mind of the consumer, how it differs from other products in the same space, and which consumers should and should not be interested in the product being supported. Based on the positioning, branding ensures that values, benefits and specific attributes all tie together, which allows for a consistent message. Branding requires a wholesale commitment to building a complete offering, ideally over time. Branding done well can add value far beyond just a single marketing campaign as each successive initiative builds on the existing strength of the brand. However, when poorly executed, it can make it all too easy for the opposition to attack, because the implementation no longer matches the brand promises communicated to the voter/consumer.

There are multiple branding strategies just as there are multiple uses for the brand. This chapter will focus specifically on the brand hierarchy concept because it is a good way to examine the way in which the brand reaches the consumer on a number of different levels. One commonly implemented strategy includes focusing on a top level (or house brand in consumer marketing lingo), then layering specific platforms and products under that brand. Another common strategy is to focus on the platform and product brands, and de-emphasize

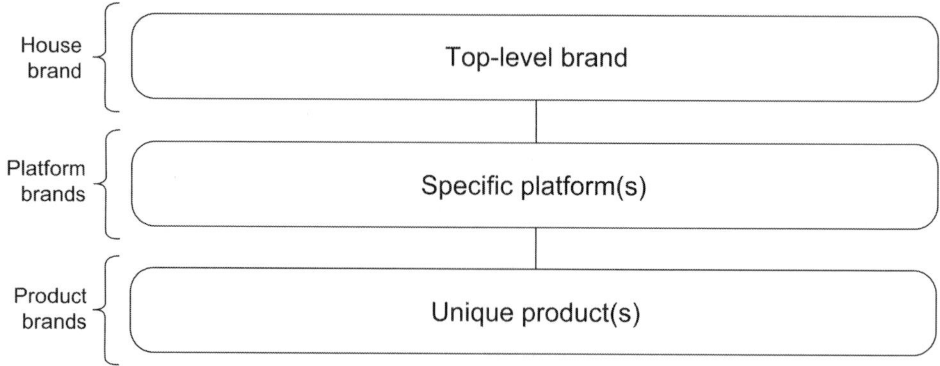

Figure 9.1 A typical brand hierarchy

the top level. These techniques allow us to look at the way in which the high-level brand vision is translated into the specific brand attributes and these guide the way in which the brand is translated to the consumer.

Two relevant examples of effective implementation of these strategies from the consumer world are BMW and Proctor & Gamble. BMW uses a strong centralized brand with a consistent message, emotion and product – high-end products for people who enjoy driving. This goes across multiple product categories, such as cars, motorcycles and commercial trucks. Mini is the one notable exception to this strategy, and is essentially a stand-alone brand with a narrow product line that is tightly aimed at a specific audience to which the BMW brand may not appeal. In contrast, Proctor & Gamble markets its products under a variety of brand names. Many consumers may not realize that the parent company of two competing brands of detergent is, in fact, the same. For BMW, the targeted focus allows them to launch new products under the same umbrella, while using fewer resources. For Proctor & Gamble, the emphasis on the platform brands, such as Tide or Swiffer, allows them to create a unique message for each product, without worrying about how well it fits with the top-level brand. Figure 9.1 illustrates a typical brand hierarchy.

Branding tools

Once the branding strategy has been selected, the next step is to develop the implementation plan. Branding incorporates values, benefits and attributes for a specific product, candidate or policy. While the execution can focus on any of these key areas, the most successful brands over the long term resonate with the voter/consumer's core values, and allow the messages to be framed in terms of high-level values and emotions, versus specific benefits or attributes that can be more easily countered by the opposition. Benefits ladders offer a graphic illustration of this concept and are used repeatedly throughout this chapter. See Figure 9.2 for an example of this tool.

Positioning: How a candidate – or policy initiative – is different and better than the alternative(s)

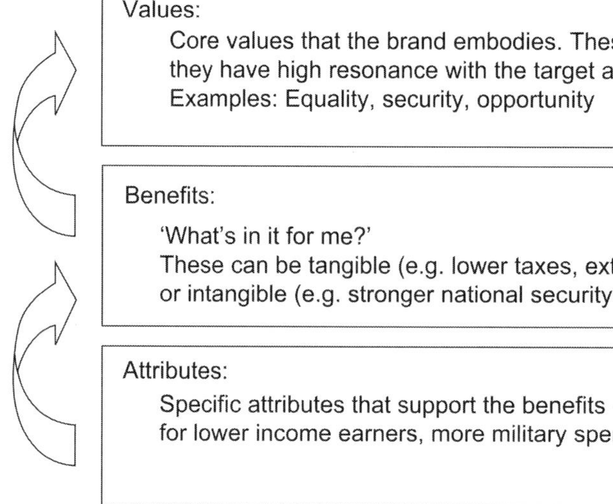

Figure 9.2 Benefits ladder

Previous research on branding strategy

The use of branding in peer-reviewed political science literature is growing but the literature is still very heavy with analysis centered on framing and public relations or one-off incidents. The US media, on the other hand, is filled with references to the concept of political branding but these lack the broader analytical framework provided by the political marketing literature.

Of particular value and interest are the work of Catherine Needham, Bruce I. Newman and Kenneth M. Cosgrove. Each of these scholars has written extensively about the use of branding in different areas, using different methods and in distinctly different contexts.

Writing primarily in the context of British politics with some comparison to the Clinton years in the US, Needham has looked at the brand in terms of explaining leader popularity in a variety of ways. A good brand should have six attributes: simplicity, uniqueness, reassurance, aspiration, values and credibility (Needham 2005). Her work on Blair and Clinton indicates that the brand can help a party leader build a relationship. As incumbents, facing challenges in shifting strategic and institutional environments, she argues the value of the brand in terms of candidates and services, and the changing nature of the brand in the modern fragmented age. While Needham argues that parties engage in branding, she also suggests that this could cause potential problems down the road during leadership changes. Needham rightly points out that branding can help parties make the original sale and can be a key customer relationship management tool, especially in this age of declining customer loyalty (Needham 2006). What she does not examine is the extent to which some of the branding around Clinton had to do with Clinton or the work of his opponents. She further suggests that branding is heavily bundled up with customer relationship marketing in a way that does not seem to be supported by the political world as consistently as she suggests is the case. Further, she does not look at the George W. Bush Administration, which was so enamored of the permanent campaign that an entire book appeared on the topic (Edwards 2006).

More recently, Smith and French (2009) argued that the brand can be a key way in which consumers learn about politics. They argue that the brand's importance can change depending on the presence of competitors, the person leading the party, its ability to keep promises and its perceived importance (Smith and French 2009). They look at the brand from the perspective of the consumer more than the marketer and argue that it can build community and provide cultural identity, rational benefits that really seem to differentiate between one set of proposals and another, psychological benefits and a reinforcement of self-perception, while allowing voters to seek out variety in their consumption. However, they close by asserting that the emerging global anti-brands movement may limit the value of the brand itself (ibid.). This last line of argument was anticipated in Heath and Potter (2004), who argued that such movements, far from undermining the branded consumerism about which they are complaining, tend to reinforce it.

Writing from the US perspective, Bruce I. Newman (1999) also examined the Clinton Administration's effort to build an image. While Newman's work is most interesting in terms of the way image building works in general, it only looks at a single case and suffers at this point, as would any contemporaneous examination of the Clinton strategy, from the shift away from mass to niche marketing. Newman's work is interesting because it acknowledges that image building is occurring, but it is limited by its orientation toward mass marketing. It would remain applicable as a guide for that, but is silent about the new media world that exists at present because it was written only at the dawn of it.

Writing several years later than Newman and well into the era of niche narrow-casting, Cosgrove (2007) argues that branding is a key tool to smooth over such leadership transitions and this has been proven by the multi-decade success of the Republican Party in building a brand that has Ronald Reagan as its heritage. The use of Reagan as a heritage has allowed, in general, the Republicans to avoid the kinds of succession problems that have been seen in the UK. Needham has written that the intra-partisan contest has become one of who can align best with the Reagan heritage and how quickly can they do this. The candidates that have done so – George H.W. Bush in 1988 and his son in 2000 and 2004 – have had an easier path to election and legitimacy within the party than have the two candidates who demonstrated that they didn't share the Reagan product heritage – John McCain in 2008 and George W. Bush in 2000. The Republican Party has applied its brand not just to all of its activities but to its customer relationship management plan, and has attracted support from swing voters as a result.

There are a number of excellent works from the business literature that would be of use to anyone seeking to expand their understanding of the concept and its applications. Of particular note are the works of Trout and Ries, individually and collectively, as well as Ries and Reis (2002) on the creation of successful brands. Ries and Trout's (2001) work *Positioning* shows the way in which a brand comes to occupy a specific market space. Also, from the commercial branding perspective, the works of Sergio Zyman and his co-authors make for a good read (Zyman 2000; Zyman and Brott 2002) about the transformation of the marketing and advertising worlds and their subsequent impact on branding. Mark and Pearson's (2000) work on the power of narrative and archetype in branding building, as well as Travis's (2000) work on emotional branding have considerable relevance for political marketers, despite their orientation toward psychology and commercial applications. This is because tapping into cultural narratives and emotional appeals have probably never had more value than at present. Political activists have written extensively about branding from the left and the right. Their work tends to reflect their partisan bias; however, the words of Viguerie and Franke (2004) and Trippi (2004) show how brands get created and used, and their work also focuses on mechanics or ego far more than does the academic literature.

New research: party branding

There are fundamental differences in how an organization, such as a political party, strategically chooses to brand itself. While many branding strategies are viable, some are more consistently effective than others. This chapter compares and contrasts several different branding strategies. These strategies run the gamut from unified party branding with supporting branding for policy initiatives, to more decentralized branding with candidates and policies being uniquely branded. Specific examples include: candidate Obama, the Obama Administration, Nancy Pelosi and the New Democratic Congress, Canada's New Government and the Republicans' bundled policy initiatives.

The next sections will look at two, of many, different ways to brand. The methods used by the Democrats and Republicans illustrate two different approaches to using the brand. The Republicans have been branding for a long time with a focus on their high-level partisan brand. The benefits of focusing on the top-level house brand include consistency in messaging and efficiency in launching a new campaign, because it is tied-in closely with the existing brand, which is already recognized by the voter/consumer. Trade-offs of this strategy include more difficulty in establishing a unique identity beyond that of the party. It is also difficult for an individual candidate or the party as a whole to move away from a failed party strategy. In contrast, the Democrats have chosen to put more emphasis on the individual platform and product brands. The benefits of this strategy are that individual candidates and policies get more focus and a unique message can be crafted to sell the voter/consumer on the benefits of said candidate or policy. The most significant trade-off is an increase in the amount of resources needed to successfully execute this strategy. Because it does not tie in with a strong high-level brand, the brand and its associated message must be built from scratch. This means time and money must be repeatedly spent to effectively develop and communicate a strong message. The two brand hierarchy charts in Figure 9.3 and Figure 9.4 show the divergent strategies of the parties.

The Democratic Party's branding efforts have been far more scattershot in terms of composition, consistency and intensity than have the Republican (especially Conservative) branding campaigns. Additionally, for most of the period the Republicans enjoyed a significant advantage in marketing architecture. The Republicans were further advantaged by the fact that one of their movement leaders, Ronald Reagan, had significant experience as a product marketer and was far more familiar with the means through which product marketing works than was any Democrat. One can argue that it was, in fact, not until after the 2004 election that liberals, in particular, became concerned with these matters.

Select case studies help to illustrate these points, as well as offer insight into effective and less effective branding execution.

Effective branding examples

- Candidate Obama
- Republican Party (1980–2006)
- Canada's New Government and the Harper Government
- The War on Terror

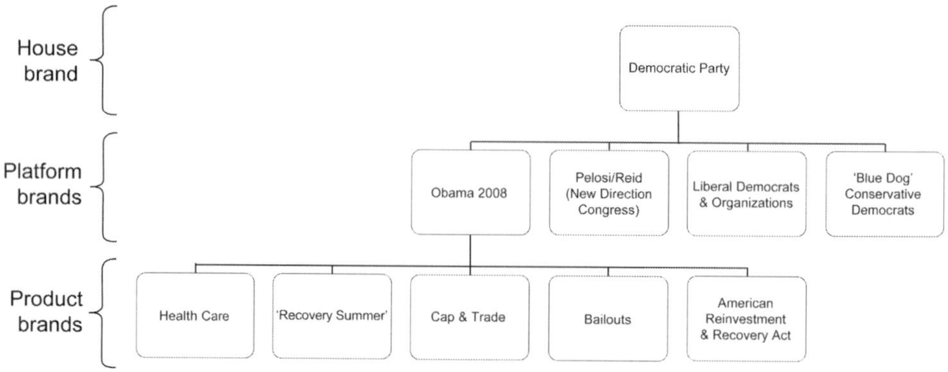

Figure 9.3 Democrat brand hierarchy

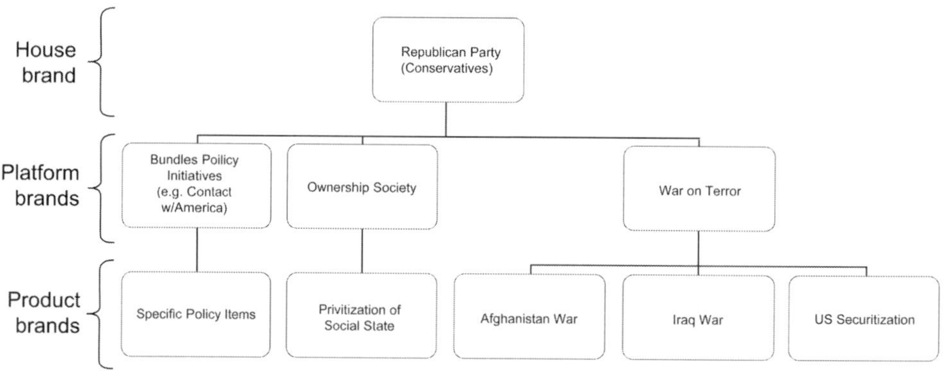

Figure 9.4 Republican brand hierarchy

Ineffective branding examples

- The Obama Administration
- New Direction Congress
- Opportunity Society

Advice for practitioners

Candidate Obama: building an effective personal brand as party brand

While there is no doubt that the Obama campaign had a policy agenda, it is not clear that this was the driving force behind Obama's election. The policies were akin to the product line that the

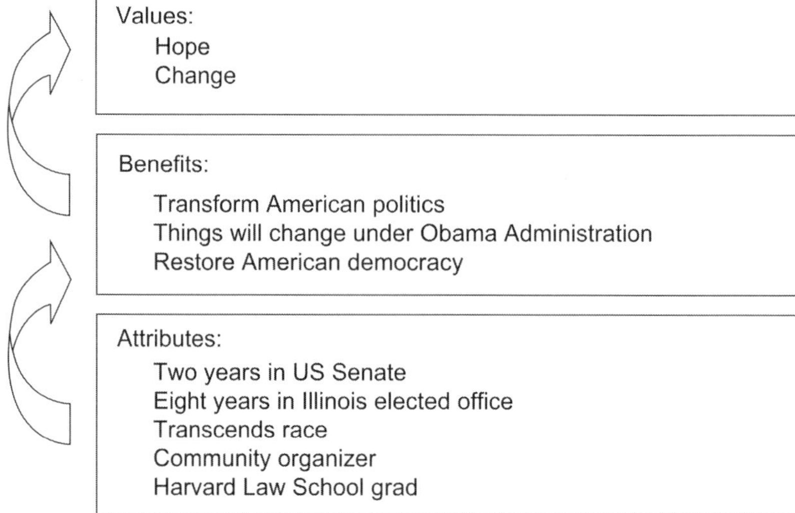

Figure 9.5 Obama benefits ladder

brand supports. The brand was very much about aspirations and values. The core Obama brand could be summed up as containing the values of hope and change, but also a heavy dose of the idea of new politics to move beyond the partisan division of the Bush years. Candidate Obama was a focused, effective communicator who usually made his case in the terms that are commonly employed by successful product spokespeople. When he did not do so, one could see the communication problems that would emerge in the Obama Administration, when his more professorial traits emerged. The brand supporting Barack Obama's campaign changed little from the beginning of the primary and caucus season to the end of the general election.

Obama was heavy on brand values, had a clear set of brand benefits and attributes that positioned him very favorably for the circumstances within which the 2008 contest was held. As the *New York Times* reported, the visual representation of the brand featured a red, white and blue color scheme, a consistent font and a logo specifically created for it. It was designed by a commercial design studio and a designer with a background in corporate marketing who explained that he first treated Obama like any other corporate client, but then read his two books and wanted to position the candidate as a uniter of the red and blue states and a clean break with the past (Hellner 2008). The logo and the message sourced from Obama's own writing created a highly authentic brand and in this Obama bears a striking resemblance to that Conservative heritage brand, Ronald Reagan. The net result was to build a strong personal brand but, as the results of the 2010 election proved, personal brands may not translate to the rest of a political party.

Republican Party (1980–2006)

The Republican Party used branding in conjunction with a product-marketing model to sell its candidates and its issues to the voters during the 1980–2006 period. Its brand featured Ronald Reagan as its face and, eventually, its heritage. Its brand promise and core were focused on a specific version of Conservatism that emphasized a strong national defense, free market economics, weak regulatory and social states, and family (meaning traditional Christian) values. The Republican brand became the political equivalent of total entertainment marketing at sporting events, in that the voters were presented with it at every opportunity in policy and political terms, as well as through a variety of policy issues. The Republican Party had a very long run of success with its core brand. It really only ran into trouble when it presided over a massive economic downturn, two wars and a series of scandals, meaning that its product no longer appeared to work as the brand promised. The downside to the Republican strategy of branding the party then harmed the party's electoral fortunes because all Republicans were tied on some level with its brand failure. While many Republicans may have wanted to distance themselves from George W. Bush, the branding strategy that they had collectively used to win elections and sell policies tied them all together in the public mind. The Republican solution at this point has been to, first, oppose Obama's agenda, second, debate repositioning themselves, or third, launch the branded 'Tea Party' movement that is very much employing the conservative branding strategy associated with Ronald Reagan and the 1980–2006 period.

Republicans had great but not perfect success branding public policy issues, as the examples of the Bush Administration's War on Terror and the Opportunity Society show. The first sold because it responded to market conditions, could incorporate a variety of policies and presented the Administration as responding to a pressing public problem about which people knew little, as Cosgrove (2007) reports. The Bush team placed its policy proposals into a coherent narrative that enabled it to build fellowship between unrelated events abroad and implement sweeping changes in US domestic policy. The opposite was true in its Opportunity Society brand because the problem it sought to deal with was not obvious to the consumer, who already knew a lot about social spending, and because the Administration expended little effort in selling it, didn't tie it to the higher party brand and many opponents had their own branded alternatives ready to contest it. The result was success in one case and failure in the other. Branding policy works well when introducing new things or things about which the US public knows little and for which the proposal can be presented as the obvious solution.

Canada's New Government: a comparative case that worked

Branding is employed by the Conservative Party of Canada in a way that resembles the branding style employed by the US Republican Party. Early on in their work with branding, the Canadians received help from some of the same people who perfected that strategy in the US. For example, the very successful US political consultant Frank Luntz instructed a conservative Canadian civic group on how to go about branding the Conservatives (Canwest News Service 2006). Consistent with the brand strategy, he suggested centering the effort on taxes and accountability, stressing images and pictures, tapping into national symbols and tying their activities to Canada's national sport, hockey (ibid.). In his speech, Luntz ran through what constitutes the core of the Conservative branding strategy (taxes, accountability, justice and personal traits of the candidate, especially honesty), before pointing out the need to tie the branded government's policy actions to the daily lives of average folks (ibid.). One key difference is that Canada as a nation is quite consciously branded, as Potter (2010) has noted.

The Conservative Party has a face for its brand, Stephen Harper, just as the Republicans did in the US. Once elected, the Conservative Party of Canada instructed bureaucrats and political staff to refer to the Conservative Government. As the *Ottawa Citizen* reported in 2006, an email from Natural Resources Canada told employees to substitute the brand for the former government title and gave formatting instructions for how the term was to be written (*Ottawa*

Citizen 2006). Doing so fits the branding strategy because a consistent face was put on all aspects of a relatively amorphous institution: the Canadian Government.

A web search using Google featuring the terms 'Canada's New Government launches' produced a number of results in very different policy areas, each using this branding. For slightly over the first year and a half of the Conservative reign the term was used, being eventually replaced by an emphasis on the Harper Government, as the CBC reported in 2007 (*Canadian Press* 2007 and Wikipedia no date). This transition should not be taken as a sign of failure but rather of success, because the 'new' branded product had survived long enough that it was no longer so new and it could be branded in a different way: the Harper Government.

A second Google search was conducted for the terms 'The Harper Government launches' and it, too, produced a number of results across different policy areas. The Harper Government has also pursued a branding campaign around a high stimulus issue: economic policy. It has done so by launching 'Canada's Economic Action Plan'. The Plan has its own logo (featuring multicolored arrows upward and a consistent font for its verbiage with both official languages); it appears on signage at funded projects, which also note how many jobs were created at the site in question or how much money the federal government has invested in the relevant policy area; and there is a nationwide media advertising campaign in support of it. Thus, the Plan's impact is tied directly to the site on which the work is being done or to the policy area in which money is being spent, and to the economic fortunes of the community in which it is being implemented. This, as we will see, is a very different approach to the topic of economic stimulus than was taken by the Obama Administration in the US. The Harper Government placed its branded economic recovery plan within the higher-ranking brand of the country of Canada.

What didn't work: the Obama Administration and the New Direction Congress

While branding is a wonderfully useful tool for political marketers, it is not without its problems. This section will examine some of the downsides of branding beyond what we saw above in the case of the Bush Administration. It will look most specifically at the transition from Candidate Obama to the Obama Administration. The Obama campaign brand raised public expectations and emotions in a way that President Obama has found difficult to satisfy. We can see this in its core message that Huffington reports was described by David Axelrod as being 'change versus a broken status quo; people versus the special interests; a politics that would lift people and the country up; and a president who would not forget the middle class' (Huffington 2009). The Obama experience shows the downside to the way in which the Democrats are trying to brand, because the candidate was branded but was unable to show results right away or communicate on a daily basis with the public as candidates do. Further, neither the party nor the Administration's policy proposals were clearly branded. Branding works best when it is part of a well thought out marketing plan; it is less effective on an ad hoc basis.

Although Obama had articulated a policy agenda and had been consistent in selling it, this was neither the bulk of his campaign activity nor, especially after early October, the focus of the election, which became the economic crisis of the moment and which candidate would deal better with the crisis. Obama had an ambitious policy agenda but much of the campaign was either about aspirations or economics. Once in office, the campaign's policy laundry list did not produce a house brand for the Obama Administration or the Democratic Party. Thus, the policies and the Administration itself lack the brand value proposition that the Obama campaign very much had. Instead, individual issues have been dealt with, but there is no coherent story around them within which to understand them, and there is no structuring device like a house brand for the Democratic Party through which these could be sold to the voter. The lack of a single set of core values that run throughout all of the marketing campaigns surrounding policy and the lack of an overall narrative built around the whole are striking when compared to either the Obama campaign or the Republican branding strategy. It is difficult to identify where the Administration has used branding while in office. This may reflect the above-noted split between the heavy emphasis on consumer relationship marketing and brand building undertaken by the Democratic Congress at present and the Republicans during the Age of Reagan and a heavier orientation on governance issues favored by Obama's chief of staff, or it may simply be the result of a White House that is pushing so many policies at once that it is difficult to market any of them well. There are many different takes on this problem. Three include Alter (2010) or Peters and Simon-Rosenthal (2009), who look at Rahm Emmanual's theories on branding; Jonathan Alter (2010), who discusses the first year of the Obama Administration; and Mat Bai (2005), who examines the role of linguist George Lakoff in shaping Obama's message. The clear product brands that have been developed have been around the stimulus bill and the first lady (see Borelli 2010), but nothing more.

This failure meant that the significant policy and political accomplishments of the first two years of the Administration have not received much public acclaim or registered much public awareness. The lack of a Democratic house brand has not helped. Other Democrats and third-sector groups have used a tag-along strategy to promote their own agendas under the guise of supporting Obama's. The Administration's inconsistency has created this situation and has made it seem more reactive than was the case for its more branded Republican predecessors. Even worse, it has promoted ideas, not initiatives, and has no way to brand those, as was the case during the healthcare debate. Candidate Obama represents an excellent model of what works in branded politics, but President Obama is more of a cautionary tale about branding's pitfalls.

The stimulus bill: promises made, not kept

The most branded undertaking of the Obama Administration has been the American Investment and Recovery Act of 2010, frequently called 'the stimulus bill'. Its name positioned public spending as 'investments', it was marketed through the use of signs on sites that had received funding, which featured a logo and the name, but no mention of how much money was being spent there or how many jobs were being created (that information could be found by examination of the market-oriented website that tracked the number of jobs it created, the amount of 'tax relief it provided' and showed users where the money was spent, recovery.gov). The overall logo focused on green energy and manufacturing, alongside an American flag, and was placed on $5 million-worth of signage which often included a figure of a worker with shovel (Condon 2010).

At no point did the words 'Obama' or 'Democrats' appear on the signage. The problem with this program was that Obama made specific statements about its impact in terms of employment and time of recovery. Branding generally does not work well with such specifics and can set up the political actor using it for a brand failure should product performance not match brand promises. Something like this happened in the Bush Administration with 'Mission Accomplished', and again with the Obama 'Recovery Summer'. The White House rolled out the term in June 2010, as ABC News reported (Dwyer 2010). While this may have been an attempt to get the public to emotionally engage with the Administration and its policies while showing that promises had been kept, the obvious difference between the brand narrative and realities in

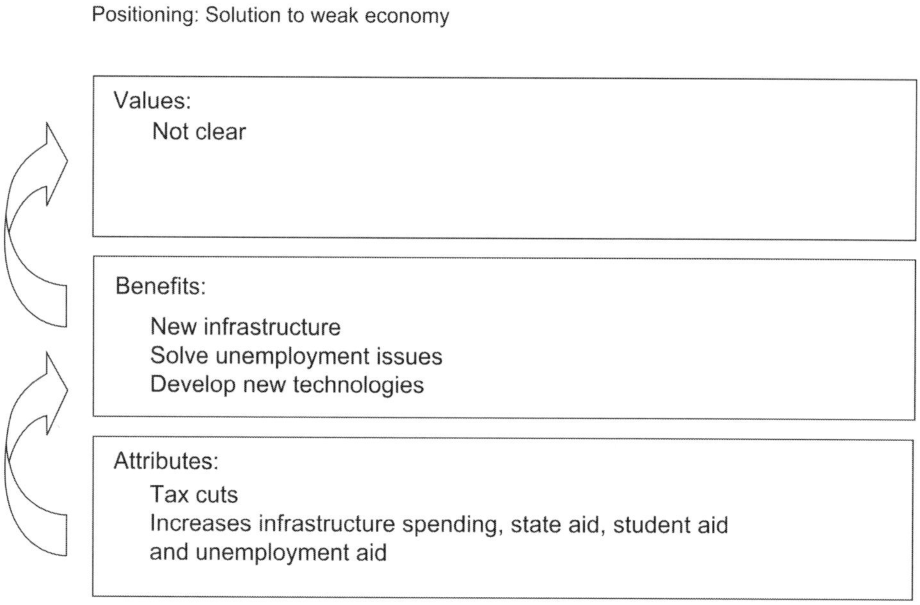

Positioning: Solution to weak economy

Values:
Not clear

Benefits:
New infrastructure
Solve unemployment issues
Develop new technologies

Attributes:
Tax cuts
Increases infrastructure spending, state aid, student aid and unemployment aid

Figure 9.6 Benefits ladder – American Reinvestment and Recovery Act

the economy instead raised questions about the Administration's competence. While the consensus position on the stimulus bill and the bailouts is that they staunched the economic bleeding, this required the Obama team to try to prove a negative and thus limited the number of ways in which it could visually show that its promises had been kept, as is required in an effective branding campaign. This experience illustrates the downsides of using specifics in branding and of using branding in situations where the marketer doesn't have a great deal of control over events, as is the case with economic policy in the globalized world. Thus, the Republicans were able to introduce the narrative that they had built for several decades about Democrats in general and liberals in particular, and their reluctance to embrace free market economics. The Administration, meanwhile, was left to talk about gradual instead of dramatic improvements to initiate a positioning and differentiation exercise to shift most of the blame for the current circumstances onto the GOP (the Republican Party) and the Bush Administration. It has sometimes branded the Republicans as the 'party of No', something that many of its core Conservative activists readily embraced.

Healthcare: no consistency in branding

Achieving a national health system that covers all Americans has been a goal of the Democratic Party since at least the 1950s. During the first 18 months the Obama Administration and Congressional Democrats got much closer to that goal. They did so using the term 'reform', but this was not one specific proposal, meaning that there were multiple plans and differing benefits that would flow from the passage of a bill. These were, in a nutshell: better access, better care and lower costs.

The problem is that there isn't a single Democratic product and this fight exposed the deep differences within the party over ideology. The Republicans had a much simpler message of opposition, which was deeply based in the values and emotions of their targets: Obamacare.

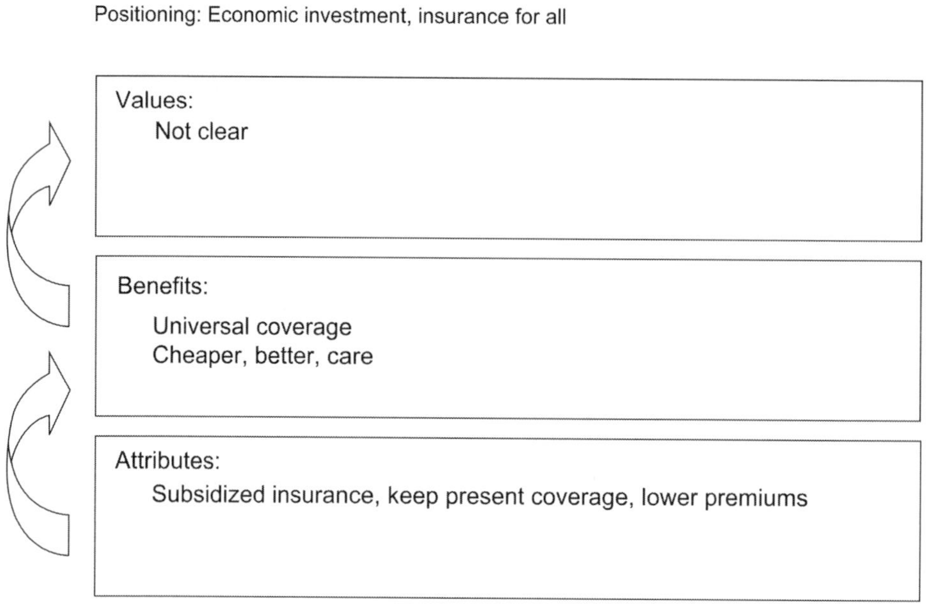

Positioning: Economic investment, insurance for all

Values:
Not clear

Benefits:
Universal coverage
Cheaper, better, care

Attributes:
Subsidized insurance, keep present coverage, lower premiums

Figure 9.7 Benefits ladder – healthcare

The Democrats, who debated and revised, ended up with a policy but not a brand because they lacked the top-level values with which they could sell the policy to the voters. Their final argument seemed to be that passing this policy change was a way to stick it to greedy insurance companies and, indeed, their case for doing so was aided when several insurers announced large rate hikes in the spring of 2010. While the Democrats attempted to market this policy as a huge victory and sent the president on a post-passage roadshow as a post-selection device, this episode represented a defeat because the Republican brand gained credibility with party identifiers and swing voters.

Cap and trade: no immediate benefit

Because of the economic and healthcare battles, there was little time to produce the other two major initiatives that had been touted during the 2008 campaign. Cap and trade, a platform brand that combined energy and environmental policies, and comprehensive immigration reform. These promises mattered to key constituencies but they also mattered to Republicans who, once again, might not have the best intellectual policy and may not have helped their own brand but have certainly won the emotions and values surrounding both issues.

The bill passed the House but a combination of effective conservative marketing and a lack of a consistent Democratic campaign doomed it. As one of its opponents explained, cap and trade was turned into 'cap and tax', and the entire trading system's favorable impact on the balance sheets of large economic enterprises was pointed out, according to Myron Ebell of the Competitive Enterprise Institute, one of the leading opposition groups to the proposal who spoke to the *New York Times* in March 2010 on the topic (Broder 2010). The opponents blocked the bill because they picked two stimulus issues that were both visible to and tied into the lives of average Americans. The Democrats, in contrast, promised new jobs

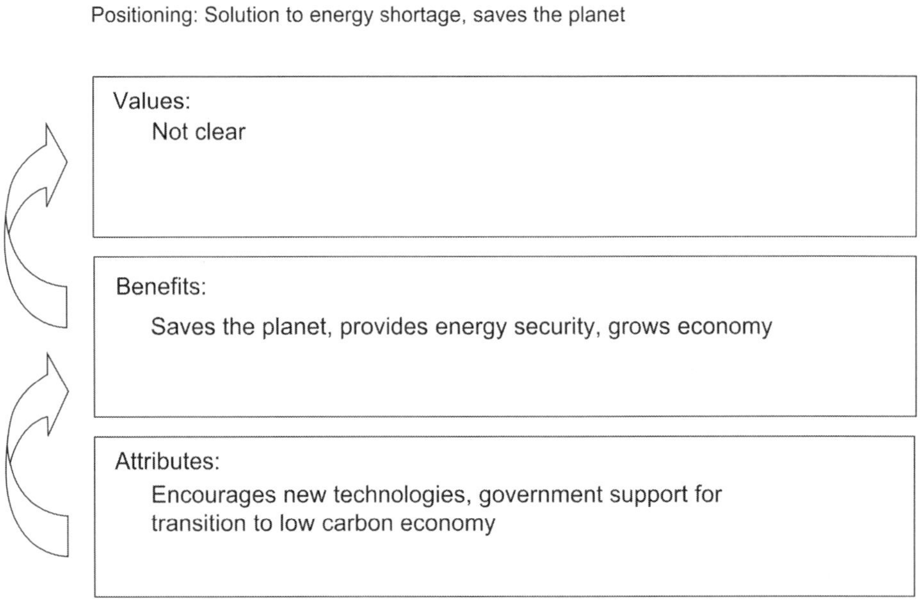

Positioning: Solution to energy shortage, saves the planet

Values:
Not clear

Benefits:
Saves the planet, provides energy security, grows economy

Attributes:
Encourages new technologies, government support for transition to low carbon economy

Figure 9.8 Benefits ladder – cap and trade

and more reliable energy, but couldn't say when those things would come about or what their cost might be. Good branding requires that one be aware of market conditions in order to succeed.

The New Direction Congress: failure to build public awareness

The Congressional Democrats also had a substantive interest in selling policy and that was done through a different vehicle to the Democratic campaign committees: The Party Congressional leadership. They had multiple problems in executing the brand strategy during their first four years of attempts. This was because: during the first two years they had no strategic incentive to do so because of the fixed electoral calendar; there was no agreed-upon Democratic product or core principles, so there was no single Democratic brand.

Eventual speaker Nancy Pelosi's effort shows one possible way in which the Democrats could build a consistent brand, but it also shows how difficult it is to do so on a stand-alone basis. Pelosi also met repeatedly with branding and marketing legend Jack Trout and linguist George Lakoff to shape a message, as Peters and Simon-Rosenthal (2009) and Bai (2005) reported independently. They used positioning and differentiation to brand the 110th Congress as the 'New Direction Congress'. As Peters and Rosenthal and a CNN report in August 2006 show, they branded their policies by developing the 'Six for 06' platform and 'The Contract with America', with the intention of making that year's elections a referendum on the Bush Administration. The items were very similar to the kinds of value-driven appeals that Republicans normally make. The items were, according to materials found on the House website: real security at home and overseas; prosperity – better American jobs, better pay; opportunity – college access for all; energy independence – lower gas prices; affordable healthcare – life-saving science; and retirement security and dignity (www.speaker.gov/pdf/thebook.pdf). While nobody could oppose these goals on their face value, they showed how branding could be used

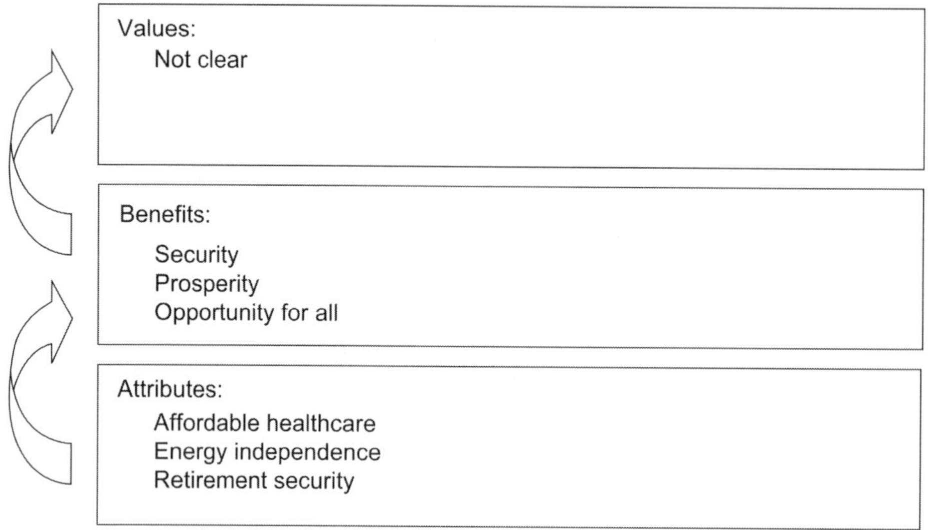

Figure 9.9 Benefits ladder – Congressional Democrats

to mask the contents of a party's policies while at the same time differentiating the party from its opponents. The benefits ladder that Pelosi and the Democrats used in 2006 can be seen in Figure 9.9.

Once in office, the Democrats held a 100 session in order to show that they were keeping their promises and, as a result, ensuring credibility in their brand.

Their strategic problem was the fixed electoral calendar in the US. It became very much in their interests not to try to fully execute their brand strategy and to avoid dealing with controversial topics, because doing so would give Republicans an opportunity to differentiate themselves from an unpopular incumbent president and revitalize their brand. The use of a brand strategy can limit the willingness of political leaders to take on difficult issues. We can see this in the subjects taken up during the period: national security, the minimum wage, student loan costs and energy policy, as the *New York Times* reported on 3 January 2007 (Hulse 2007). The term 'New Direction Congress' became the dominant feature of the House leadership's communicative efforts during the remainder of that Congress, and Speaker Pelosi was outstanding at staying on message, as the same article reported. The internet retained traces of this throughout the Democrats' Congressional majority, with web pages bearing a box containing blue stars and white text reading 'A NEW DIRECTION'. Behind that, in smaller white text but clearly visible, were the kind of vague value-driven terms with which branding works well. Examples included 'restore accountability', 'preserve our planet', 'defend our country' and 'strengthen our families'. The entire website was clearly set up with a marketing and branding model in mind, as it noted what had been 'accomplished', what was 'on the President's desk for approval', what was 'headed for the President's desk for approval', what had 'passed the House and Senate', 'passed the House', and what had 'been blocked by Senate Republicans', and finally what had been 'vetoed by the President over the Will of the American People'. The New Direction Congress continued to be used by some Democrats throughout their majority, as the author found during the course of this research (see www.speaker.gov/legislation?

id=0053). As Peters and Simon-Rosenthal (2009) note, at the end of its first term the speaker herself presented the list of accomplishments of the branded Democratic Congress by listing the promises it had kept, by noting that it had achieved a rate of 70 percent bipartisanship in its activities, by noting that more could have been done but for President Bush and his Congressional allies, and by noting the continuing need for 'A New Direction for America' (www.speaker.gov/legislation?id=0053). The problem was that nobody ever heard of it beyond Capitol Hill and this was partially a result of the unwillingness of the Democrats to use their brand in the service of large policy battles that would build more public awareness of and equity within it. Branding, then, works better when public attention is called to the brand through both free and paid media.

Branding as a power tool: what works and the care to be taken

The brand is the key communicative tool of contemporary politics. It is a real power tool because it can be the key to gaining and using power to great effect. It is a must have in order to effectively communicate with the voter/consumer. However, the politician or party using the brand is wise to take care that one would with any powerful tool because, while very useful, its use comes with some risk. Mistakes that limit its effectiveness include: having a great brand but a weak product or no product at all; inconsistency in using the brand; not undertaking the actions that will build awareness and equity; failing to see the brand as part (but not all) of one's customer relationship management strategy; and failing to use the brand as a device to keep the consumer engaged, and instead settling for a one-time purchasing decision. The brand can be a key tool to stimulate longer-term activism provided the mistakes noted above are not made and a branding strategy is in place prior to initiating its use. Successful branding requires consistent messaging across candidates and policies and having the product being sold in place before launching the branding effort. It involves a stronger appeal to values than to specific knowledge, in an effort to win over emotions rather than facts. It requires a clear decision about branding strategy to be made in terms of the choice between branding a party and branding individuals or specific policy proposals. While both can work, there are significant resource trade-offs involved. In the case of building an overriding house brand and then applying it to everything, the problem is that it becomes difficult to reposition away from policy and personal failures.

Branding works best when the brand is clearly and consistently positioned, when supported by strong messaging, and when it moves up the benefits ladder from specific attributes to high-level values. All of the successful brands in our case studies did these things well. The failures have been those that have failed in at least one of these elements. Branding is too powerful a tool to use casually or lightly but, as is true with all powerful tools, a little planning and thought can produce a very impressive result.

Impact on politics

The brand is a double-edged sword in democratic terms because it has the potential to ensure effective communication between politicians and citizens, but it can expose a political actor as a failure and can be seen as a manipulative device. It seems to work best when introducing new policy ideas, new political movements or individual candidates. It seems to be of less use when trying to introduce changes to an entrenched status quo that is well understood by the public, as both George W. Bush (ownership society) and Barack Obama (administration policy branding) discovered. This is driven by the fact that a key component of branding is the positioning, and once the consumer/voter has categorized a candidate or policy initiative, it is far more difficult to change that mental assessment.

Overall, it is a powerful tool when used properly, and it is capable of helping people to understand their world and to join together to solve public problems, as its use in the US and Canada shows. Its effectiveness in introducing new commodities to public life is profound, but seems more limited when trying to change public perceptions of a familiar status quo. It requires a significant amount of time and energy to build and consistent effort to maintain, but doing so can strengthen the organization by making it easier to launch new candidates and policy proposals. A well-built brand can create enduring ties between citizens and the politician and can be one way through which citizen education about politics and policy can occur.

The way forward

Branding is a key and growing area of political market research. Some of the issues that research could address are the branding of leaders, the knowledge and understanding of consultants of political branding, and democratic implications.

Bibliography

Alter, J. (2010) *The Promise: President Obama, Year One*, New York: Simon and Schuster.

Bai, M. (2005) 'George Lakoff and the Framing Wars', *New York Times*, 17 July. Online, www.nytimes.com/2005/07/17/magazine/17DEMOCRATS.html?pagewanted=all (accessed 18 May 2011).

—— (2007) *The Argument: Billionaires, Bloggers and the Battle to Remake Democratic Politics*, New York: Penguin.

Borelli, Mary Anne (2010) 'High Culture, Popular Culture and Policy Outreach: The (Early) First Ladyship of Michelle Obama', unpublished paper presented at the 2010 New England Political Science Association meeting.

Broder, J.M. (2010) 'Cap and Trade Loses Its Standing as Energy Policy of Choice', *New York Times*. Online, www.nytimes.com/2010/03/26/science/earth/26climate.html (accessed 4 April 2011).

Brott, A. and Bryman, S. (2002) *The End of Advertising As We Know It*, New York and Chichester: Wiley.

Canadian Press, The (2007) '"New" Government Becomes Old News for Tories', *CBC News Canada*. Online, www.cbc.ca/canada/story/2007/10/16/new-government.html (accessed 4 April 2011).

Canwest News Service (2006) 'American Political Strategist Teaches Tories Tips for Keeping Power', *Canada.com*. Online, www.canada.com/reginaleaderpost/news/story.html?id=e0a004b7-31a1-4925-bb2c-dc34e911aceb&k=25352 (accessed 26 May 2006).

Condon, S. (2010) 'Labor Union: Stimulus Signs Create Jobs', *CBS News*. Online, www.cbsnews.com/8301-503544_162-20010692-503544.html (accessed 4 April 2011).

Cosgrove, K.M. (2007) *Branded Conservatives: How the Brand Brought the Right from the Fringes to the Center of American Politics*, New York: Peter Lang.

Dean, H. (2004) *You Have the Power: How to Take Back Our Country and Restore Democracy in America*, New York: Simon and Schuster.

Dwyer, D. (2010) 'GOP Targets Obama's "Recovery Summer" Amid Economic Gloom', *ABC News*. Online, abcnews.go.com/Politics/president-obama-recovery-summer-stimulus-projects-fail-yield/story?id=11463344 (accessed 4 April 2011).

Edsall, T. and Edsall, M.B. (1992) *Chain Reaction*, New York: W.W. Norton.

Edwards, G.C. (2006) *Governing by Campaigning: The Politics of the Bush Presidency*, AB Longman.

Feld, L. and Wilcox, N. (2008) *Netroots Rising: How a Citizen Army of Bloggers and Online Activists Is Changing American Politics*, Westport, CT: Praeger.

Heath, J. and Potter, A. (2004) *The Rebel Sell: Why The Culture Can't Be Jammed*, Ontario: HarperCollins Canada.

Heilmann, J. and Halperin, M. (2010) *Game Change*, New York: Harper.

Hellner, M. (2008) 'The "O" in Obama', *New York Times*. Online, campaignstops.blogs.nytimes.com/2008/11/20/the-o-in-obama (accessed 20 May 2009).

Huffington, A. (2009) 'Obama One Year Later: The Audacity of Winning vs. the Timidity of Governing', *Huffington Post*. Online, www.huffingtonpost.com/arianna-huffington/obama-one-year-later-the_b_343209.html (accessed 4 April 2011).

Hulse, Carl (2007) 'Democrats Plan First 100 Hours, Give or Take a Speech', *New York Times*, 3 January. Online, www.nytimes.com/2007/01/03/washington/03cong.htm.

Kingdon, J. (2002) *Agendas, Alternatives and Public Policymaking*, New York: AB Longman.

Lewis, M. (2010) *The Big Short*, New York: W.W. Norton.

McGir, L. (2001) *Suburban Warriors: The Origins of the New American Right*, Princeton, NJ: Princeton University Press.

Mark, M. and Pearson, C. (2000) *The Hero and the Outlaw: Building Extraordinary Brands through the Power of Archetypes*, New York: McGraw-Hill.

Micklewaith, J. and Woolridge, A. (2005) *The Right Nation: Conservative Power in America*, New York: Penguin.

Needham, C. (2006) 'Customer Relationship Marketing: Brands and Political Loyalty', *The Journal of Brand Management* 13, 3: 178–87.

—— (2005) 'Brand Leaders: Clinton, Blair and the Limitations of the Permanent Campaign', *Political Studies* 53, 2: 343–61.

Newman, B.I. (1999) *The Mass Marketing of Politics: Democracy in an Age of Manufactured Images*, Thousand Oaks, CA: Sage.

Ottawa Citizen, The (2006) 'Tories Rebrand Government to Reflect Change of Guard', *Canada.com*. Online, www.canada.com/ottawacitizen/news/story.html?id=6662bfbd-3aba-424b-94e4-901bcfc36b13 (accessed 4 April 2011).

Peters, R.M. and Simon-Rosenthal, C. (2009) *Speaker Nancy Pelosi and the New American Politics*, New York: Oxford University Press.

Potter, Evan H. (2010) *Branding Canada: Projecting Canada's Soft Power Through Public Diplomacy*, Montreal: McGill-Queens University Press.

Ricci, D. (1993) *The New Washington*, New Haven, CT: Yale University Press.

Ries, A. and Ries, L. (2002) *The 22 Immutable Laws of Branding*, second edn, New York: HarperCollins.

Ries, A. and Trout, J. (2001) *Positioning: The Battle for Your Mind*, New York: McGraw-Hill.

Schoenwald, J. (2002) *A Time for Choosing*, New York: Oxford University Press.

Smith, G. and French, A. (2009) 'The Political Brand: A Consumer Perspective', *Marketing Theory* 9, 2: 206–26.

Travis, D. (2000) *Emotional Branding: How Successful Brands Get the Irrational Edge*, Roseville, CA: Prima Venture.

Trippi, J. (2004) *The Revolution Will Not Be Televised*, New York: Regan Books.

Trout, J. and Ries, A. (2000) *Positioning: The Battle for Your Mind*, New York and London: McGraw-Hill.

Viguerie, R.A. and Franke, D. (2004) *America's Right Turn: How Conservatives Used New and Alternative Media to Take Over America*, Chicago: Bonus Books.

Wattenberg, M. (2007) *Is Voting for Young People*, New York: AB Longman.

Wikipedia (no date) 'Canada's New Government', *Wikipedia*. Online, en.wikipedia.org/wiki/Canada%27s_New_Government (accessed 4 April 2011).

Winograd, M. and Hais, M. (2008) *Millenial Makeover*, New Brunswick, NJ: Rutgers University Press.

Zyman, S. (2000) *The End of Marketing as We Know It*, New York: Collins Business Books.

Zyman, S. and Brott, A. (2002) *The End of Advertising as We Know It*, Hoboken, NJ: John Wiley and Sons.

10

The politics of hope

The Democratic Party and the institutionalisation of the Obama brand in the 2010 mid-term elections

Brian M. Conley

The topic: institutionalising the party brand

The branding of Obama as an agent of hope and change was central to the successful strategy of marketing the Democratic presidential candidate as an appealing alternative to the Republican status quo in 2008. However, unlike either the re-election of Bush in 2004 in the US, or Tony Blair in 2001 in the UK, which were also characterised by the use of branding strategies, it is not clear whether the Obama brand was, or will become the Democratic Party brand. In both the Blair and Bush re-elections, the candidate's message reflected ideas central to an established party brand (Gould 1998; Lilleker 2005; Cosgrove 2007). This was less the case with Obama's election, given the absence of a similar, market-oriented effort to brand the Democratic Party over the last decade. The Obama election, then, raises questions about why candidates, parties and other political organisations are increasingly using branding strategies. It also raises questions about how and when branding strategies are formally incorporated into the functioning of a party, and specifically whether or not the Obama brand will be adopted by the Democratic Party or will remain, as it originated, the product of a highly successful political entrepreneur.

The development and use of more market-oriented strategies, including branding, is a relatively new trend in US and UK politics. In the US, for example, the presidencies of Ronald Reagan, Bill Clinton and George Bush were each characterised, with varying degrees of success, by the development of branded political personalities and stories. In the UK, Tony Blair and the Labour Party's ability to defeat the Conservatives in 1997 after more than a decade out of power also illustrates how the development of a market-based brand story can change a party's or a candidate's fortunes. Now Barack Obama, and his story of hope and change, has provided one of the most pronounced examples to date of the manner in which a branded politics is redefining how political leaders interact with and are perceived by the public. What is equally clear is that some parties have been more successful than others at designing and implementing unique brand stories. This is particularly true in the US, where despite the Republican Party's success at institutionalising a conservative political brand, the Democrats have largely been unable to brand themselves (Cosgrove 2007). The Democratic Party has had branded candidates, party leaders and, more recently, electoral campaigns. What Democratic leaders have struggled to do is brand the party itself, or to institutionally codify a consistent and differentiating political narrative, with associated policies, symbols and images.

However, with the approach of the 2010 mid-term elections, the Democratic Party hoped to capitalise on Obama's branding success by incorporating themes central to his brand story into the party's core message. It was unlikely, I would argue, that the Democrats would be able to replicate the Republican Party's branding success in 2010 owing to persistent institutional and cultural differences between the parties. While the Republicans have traditionally been a more centrally organised, top-driven party organisation, dominated by an institutional culture that prioritises party unity over dissension, the Democrats, by contrast, have historically been less organisationally cohesive (Freeman 1986). The practical consequences of this are that the Democrats, as a party and as individual office holders and candidates, have been less able than the Republicans or Labour to cohere around a unifying political narrative.

The focus of the chapter will be on the Obama brand and the extent to which the brand was or was not institutionalised by the Democratic Party during the mid-term 2010 elections. To analyse this, the chapter will look first at the concepts of political and party brands. I will do so as an entry point into a broader discussion of how differences in political culture might help to explain variations between Republican, Labour and Democratic Party branding. Do differences in internal political culture and the degree of party centralisation help explain why the Democrats, unlike either the Republican or Labour Parties have been unable to institutionalise a unique political brand? To test this question, I will look at the degree to which the Democratic Party and its candidates who ran to retain party seats in the US Senate in the 2010 mid-term election were able to run a coordinated campaign, centred on a unifying brand story. I will do so by examining the degree to which they adopted two policies central to the Obama brand: economic recovery and tax relief.

Previous research on political and party branding

Branding has emerged as one of the most common tools used by market-oriented political parties to both respond to the shifting needs of the market as well as to potentially build loyalty among targeted voters. In politics, brands are essentially unique political narratives or stories designed to link in an enduring way the interests and aspirations of the market with the product promises of a particular party, candidate or organisation. When successful, political brands are experienced as an affirmation of the beliefs and values of the targeted audience, which can create a durable association in the voter's mind between themselves and a party. However, their use also highlights precisely how targeted and party-driven a market approach to politics can be. The brand experience, whether in business or politics, is intended to be an exclusive one. It forms a bond with certain audiences by reflecting their values, but also by contrasting them with other beliefs or practices in society. At the same time, brands are not fully participatory. They are based on market needs, but are designed by and for candidates, parties and other entities as a means of building loyalty, and thus enhancing competitiveness within the electoral market place.

What distinguishes a branding strategy, then, from other approaches in politics is the ability of the brand to foster an exclusive association in the minds of a targeted audience between their preferences and that of a party's product. What a brand does, explains Ken Cosgrove in his study of the rise of a Conservative Republican Party brand in the US, is 'build images in people's minds about a product or … politicians or public policies' (Cosgrove 2007: 16). Brands are for the most part 'intangible', explains Gareth Smith, and consist mainly of 'the knowledge about a product that is held in the memory of consumers' (Smith 2009: 211). For instance, 'a name is not a brand', as Daryl Travis contends, 'neither is a logo' (Travis 2000: 4). Rather, a brand is 'what these symbols mean and the feelings they engender', Travis explains (ibid.: 4). Such imagery and feelings are intended to 'set a brand apart', Cosgrove writes, in order to 'attract the right audience to it', and to 'give that audience a set of feelings about using and being affiliated with it' (Cosgrove 2007: 10). Political brands are able to elicit such strong feelings by invoking ideas, values, aspirations or 'frames' inherent to the market in which the party or candidate is situated. Frames, Cosgrove writes, may be defined as the 'means through which the target audience sees the event' (ibid.: 24). The power of such framing, Cosgrove and others note, can be seen in the emotional connections that some customers develop toward brands 'that [are] much deeper than the product being sold' (ibid.: 19; Mark and Pearson 2001; Travis 2000).

The use of a targeted branding strategy in the 1970s and 1980s helped Conservative Republicans, Cosgrove explains, to build a loyal base of supporters sufficient to move the Republican Party from a minority to a majority status in US politics. The development of a distinct conservative brand story helped the Republicans to 'produce a consistent message about themselves' and in doing so, 'build lasting relationships with their audience targets' Cosgrove (2007: 7) explains. The Republican brand resonated, he contends, because it 'tells a story, makes promises [and] is specifically positioned to appeal to targeted audiences' (ibid.: 11). The brand effectively explained to a select audience how conservatism reflected their values, was distinct from Democratic policies and would, if afforded the chance to govern, provide a new type of leadership for the country. The brand worked, in other words, because it did what most successful brands have done, as Catherine Needham has argued: namely, it offered 'simple and reassuring messages, effectively differentiated [itself] from their opponents, established a value basis for [its] claims, built aspirational appeals and delivered on their promises' (Needham 2005: 348). Successful brands, Needham explains, not only simplify consumer choice, they offer a unique and affirming product experience.

As Cosgrove notes, the branding of the Republican Party was initially promoted by party conservatives, and the brand's institutionalisation within the party in many ways parallels the rise of the Republican right in the 1980s and 1990s (Cosgrove 2007; Brennan 1995). The first real political success of the Conservative Republican brand came in 1980, when Ronald Reagan was able to draw on the emerging conservative brand narrative to win the presidency. Reagan became, in the process, what scholars refer to as a 'brand personality' (Smith 2009). In 2000, and especially in 2004, George W. Bush was able to follow Reagan's example, which has now become a 'heritage brand' for the Republicans, and present himself as a line extension of the Conservative Republican brand (Cosgrove 2007: 72). We saw something similar in 1997 when Tony Blair and the Labour Party won a landslide victory over the Conservatives. Again, a candidate was able to win office, at least in part, by successfully 'personifying' an appealing party brand narrative (Lilleker 2005; White and de Chernatony 2002).

In both cases, individual candidates used simple, differentiating and aspirational ideas, images and rhetoric developed by their party, along with specific promises to brand their candidacy. Bill Clinton and, to a greater extent, Barack Obama have also been able to do so, but unlike the Republicans or Blair, neither Clinton nor Obama had an enduring party brand narrative on which to draw (Newman 1999; Morris 1997). The conservative brand story upon which Reagan rested his presidential candidacy in 1980, for example, had been developed over more than a decade by a conservative political movement that extended beyond the Republican Party, but that had also become a dominant force within the GOP (the Republican Party) in the 1960s and 1970s (Cosgrove 2007; Brennan 1995). Indeed, Reagan's own emergence as a political figure in the mid-1960s sprang directly from his prominence within the historic, but failed conservative campaign to elect Barry Goldwater president in 1964 (Schoenwald 2001). Tony Blair's leadership, first within the party and then as prime minister, was also shaped by an ongoing effort to rebrand the Labour Party in the early 1990s (Gould 1998; Lilleker 2005; White and de Chernatony 2002). After finding itself in an historically weak position following repeat Conservative Party victories in the 1980s, the Labour Party sought to reverse its fortunes in the 1990s by rebranding itself as 'New Labour'. The goal of this initiative was to 'modernise' the party, write White and de Chernatony, and to 'reconnect [it] to the electorate, and overcome the electorate's doubts and fears about Labour as a party of government' (White and de Chernatony 2002: 48). The result was a repositioning of the Labour Party that aligned it more firmly with the aspirational and individualist values of the growing 'working middle-class' in Britain, as Philip Gould describes it, while at the same time distancing the party from its traditional commitment to working-class interests (Gould 1998: 173). It was a narrative that Blair, as a young, savvy politician, was readily able to appropriate as a means of casting himself as personally indicative of a new, more forward-looking and less class-based style of Labour politics in Britain (Lees-Marshment 2001a; King 1998).

In both the Republican and Labour cases, then, the branding of individual politicians followed from the branding of a party. Yet, as President Obama's branding success illustrates, candidates and politicians are capable of branding themselves independent of an established party brand. What is less clear, however, is whether a candidate or politician can brand a party. The Democratic Party leadership has, since Obama's 2008 victory, sought to institutionalise the unique features of the Obama brand narrative. However, evidence suggests that the party is again failing to effectively brand either itself or its policies. It is a circumstance that raises questions not only about whether or not a candidate brand can become a party brand, but also about whether or not there is something distinct about the Democratic Party itself that limits its ability to institutionalise a unifying brand narrative?

Comparative research on the Republican and Democratic parties in the US has pointed to a number of differences between the parties, including differences in party goals and party organisation (Aldrich 1995). Arguably, however, the most persistent difference between the parties, though one of the least studied, is the difference in political culture. In her seminal essay on the topic, for instance, Jo Freeman (1986) argues that the two major parties in the US essentially share the same goal of winning elections, but differ fundamentally in terms of their internal political culture. The source of this difference, she argues, is at once 'structural', and relates to how power or decision-making authority is exercised within the respective parties, as well as 'attitudinal' or how the parties perceive themselves. 'In the Democratic Party power flows upward', Freeman explains, while 'in the Republican Party power flows downward' (Freeman 1986: 328). The result, she continues, is a 'Democratic Party [that] is pluralistic and polycentric' and 'has multiple power centers', and a Republican Party that is more 'unitary' and one where 'great deference is paid to the leadership, activists are expected to be "good soldiers", and competing loyalties are frowned upon' (ibid.: 329). Cultural differences between the parties also follow, she claims, from the fact that Republicans see themselves as representing dominant cultural values in the US, while the Democrats perceive themselves as outsiders, or representative of more marginalised groups. We know, as Cosgrove discovered in his study of the Republican Party, that brands can help unify a party (Cosgrove 2007: 54–55). However, it may also be true, as Lees-Marshment's (2001a) analysis of market-orientated parties suggests, that some heightened level of party centralisation may be critical to the successful design, adjustment and implementation of a market-driven branding strategy. Certainly, the Labour Party, under Blair, as Lees-Marshment notes, exhibited a highly centralised party structure, which was used to bring the party leadership and membership in alignment, at times quite forcefully, with the New Labour brand narrative (Lees-Marshment 2001a: 184–86). A similar pressure to adhere to the party brand was applied from on high by the Republican leadership during both the recent period of Republican dominance in Congress, and the Bush presidency (Sinclair 2006; Hacker and Pierson 2006; Schickler and Pearson 2005).

To examine what impact, if any, political culture, particularly in terms of party organisation, has had on the Democrats' ability to institutionalise a unifying brand narrative, I will look at the degree to which the party's effort to retain its majority in the US Senate in 2010 was or was not based on a repositioning of the populist economic policy that was central to Obama's brand narrative. In this context, institutionalisation may be defined much as Lees-Marshment has defined 'implementation' in the marketing process, that is, a policy has been institutionalised when it has been both formally adopted by the party leadership as well as in practice by the party rank-and-file (Lees-Marshment 2001a: 37–39). Did the party use promises of economic recovery and tax relief in 2010, much as Obama had successfully done in 2008, in order to highlight how continued Democratic rule in the Senate would differ from a return to Republican control and thus what voters would get if they supported the Democratic Party in 2010? Moreover, to what extent were these ideas embraced by Democratic senators running for re-election in 2010?

New research: the Obama brand

Obama's branding strategy effectively encapsulated many of the key variables that Cosgrove, Travis, Needham and others associate with successful branding. His brand story was at once simple and reassuring, centred as it was on a rhetoric of 'hope' and possibility, while also being implicitly differentiating. Obama was an agent of hope, but also of change in a time marked by Republican excess. The power of Obama's brand can been seen in his extraordinary appeal, as a candidate and as a person. The enthusiasm that Obama supporters felt about his candidacy, for instance, was twice that felt by McCain's supporters (Todd and Gawiser 2009: 42). Obama's core message – 'Yes We Can' – reflected the optimism that many core Democratic voters wanted to have about the direction of the country, the prospects of rebuilding the economy and ending or somehow winning the war in Iraq. It was a level of message clarity that was largely absent from the McCain campaign. The Obama brand targeted specific segments of the electoral market, made promises and explained how change could be made (Plouffe 2010: 377–78). For the audience, it was a unique branding experience facilitated by an unprecedented uniformity in policy pronouncements, rhetoric, imagery and stylistic nuances that informed everything the campaign did, said and published.

Such continuity in content and delivery was particularly true with regard to the populist thrust of Obama's economic policy. As polls indicated throughout the 2008 election, the American public regarded problems with the economy, including slowed job growth, the loss of employment benefits and a rapidly contracting housing market, as the most pressing issues facing the country (Kenski *et al.* 2010: 16–17). These concerns became particularly acute after the near collapse of the financial markets in September 2008. As the candidate of hope and change, Obama was able to strike a chord with the public by successfully linking the lax regulatory and regressive tax policies of the Bush presidency to the excesses of Wall Street, while also proposing middle-class tax relief, specifically a tax cut for 95 percent of Americans (Kenski *et al.* 2010: 186–87; Obama 2008: 35–36).

That the Democratic Party would adopt Obama's brand follows not only from his electoral success and charisma, but also from his place now as the formal head of the party. The party, moreover, has become increasingly open to the branding idea, having successfully used a branding strategy during the 2006 mid-terms to characterise itself as distinct from a Republican 'Culture of Corruption' in Washington (Cosgrove 2009: 17–19). In terms of the party leadership, notably the White House, the Democratic Congressional Campaign Committee (DCCC) and the Democratic Senatorial Campaign Committee (DSCC), the adoption of Obama's brand narrative was clear during the run-up to the 2010 election, as evidenced by the party's policy statements and rhetoric, imagery and official websites. This is particularly true with regard to economic policy. When talking about the economy, jobs or taxes, the party leadership sought to capitalise on Obama's narrative of a changed politics in Washington by casting the Democrats as defenders of the interests of the 'average American', and 'main-street', in contrast to a Republican Party that is out of touch, ideologically extreme and subservient to the interests of corporate power. They have particularly highlighted the economic benefits of the Recovery or 'stimulus' Act.

However, the party has faced real problems both repositioning the economic rhetoric of Obama's brand to appeal to mid-term voters, as well as implementing it party-wide. Most of the 19 Democrats running to retain party seats in the US Senate in 2010 ignored or effectively ran away from President Obama and his brand with regard to economic issues. Indeed, an analysis of their campaign websites – where research suggests that candidates and campaigns tend to offer the most 'unmediated, holistic and representative portrait' of their principles and policy positions – reveals a lack of any uniform presentation of the Recovery Act, either in terms of simplified rhetoric, differentiating policy statements, affirming imagery, particularly images of the president, or, for that matter, claims of promises made and promises kept that highlight what the Act delivered for middle-class Democratic voters (Druckman *et al.* 2009: 346). Instead, during the fall campaign only nine, or 47 percent, of the candidate websites even referred to the Recovery Act, while only four, or 22 percent, made any reference to Obama when discussing economic policy. Moreover, only three (16 percent) and 10 (52 percent), respectively, referred to such signature features of Obama's economic narrative as the tax cut for 95 percent of working families, or middle-class tax relief, in general. These trends are illustrated in Figure 10.1. Overall, the websites of Senate Democrats seeking to retain party seats in 2010 suggested no unity of content; and no simplified, differentiating political narrative modelled on Obama's branding success. Indeed, among the websites examined, there was only one example – Harry Reid of Nevada – of a candidate seeking to differentiate their position or the Democratic Party position from Republican policies by contrasting themselves with the economic policies of the Bush era, as both the White House and the DSCC had actively done.

The Republicans, by contrast, have for the most part lined up, as a party, behind a critique of big government and a renewed endorsement of the principles of the free market. As the Republican National Committee (RNC) website succinctly states, the Republican Party 'believes in the power and opportunity of America's free market economy' and thus 'oppose[s] interventionist policies that put the federal government in control of industry and allow it to pick winners and losers in the marketplace' (GOP 2010). Both claims animated the campaigns of nearly all the 18 candidates running to retain Republican seats in the Senate, as can be seen from their nearly uniform critique of oversized government (94 percent), taxes (83 percent) and government spending (88 percent), as is demonstrated in Figure 10.1.

To be sure, there are a number of possible reasons for this contrast, and specifically the failure of the Democrats to cohere around a more unifying, market-based message. The president's sliding popularity, which reached a low of 43 percent in August 2010, may help account for the absence of a more coordinated party strategy. It is not uncommon for candidates to distance themselves from unpopular presidents in mid-term elections. It happened to both Reagan and

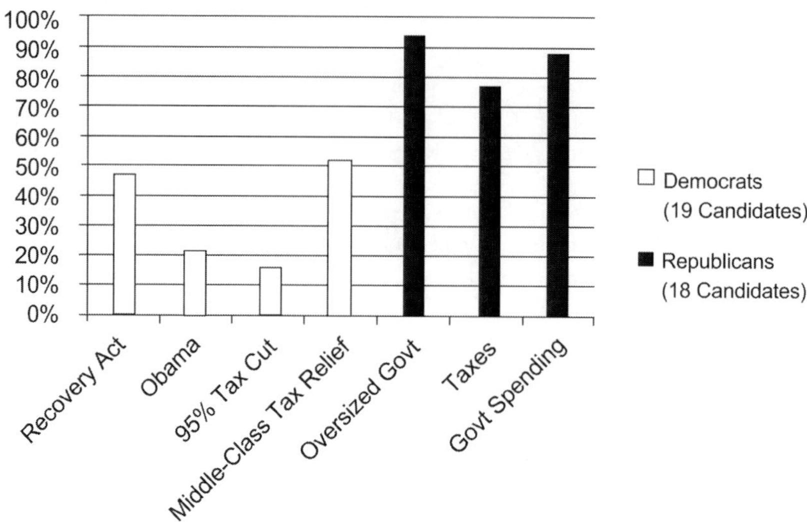

Figure 10.1 Candidate messaging by issue: US Senate election, 2010

Clinton during their second year in office, for instance. However, there was no correlation between competitiveness of the election and cases where Democratic candidates distanced themselves from the president. Candidates were on message in several competitive races, including Mike Bennet in Colorado, Harry Reid in Nevada and Barbara Boxer in California, and not on message in several states that were considered safe for the Democrats, notably Richard Blumenthal in Connecticut and Ron Wyden in Oregon. Moreover, the tenets of Obama's economic populism remained moderately popular in the US in the summer and fall of 2010. Support for the 'stimulus' (American Recovery and Reinvestment Act), for example, reached its highest point (38 percent) in August 2010 since the law's passage in 2009 (Rasmussen Reports 2010). Obama also retained the approval of roughly 80 percent of registered Democrats right up to the 2010 election (Jones 2010a). Taken together, what these variables again suggest is that the lack of coherent Democratic branding strategy follows as much from ineffective centralised party organisation as it does from political uncertainty. Some Democrats were on message, in competitive races and won, and Obama remains quite popular among Democrats; yet the party still lacked a coordinated campaign.

Advice for practitioners

For political branding to be successful, parties need to become more responsive to internal stakeholders as well as voters. There are five steps that parties can take to create an effective brand: see Table 10.1.

Impact on politics

Scholars have questioned the degree to which simplified and targeted brand narratives designed by parties actually contribute to voter awareness of the issues, or generate solutions to complex policy challenges, like economic recovery, or whether they simply exaggerate differences between parties, primarily for short-term electoral gain, and ultimately discourage voter participation (Smith and French 2009; Needham 2005). A brand story can strengthen a party, but the

Table 10.1 Five steps to successful party branding

1 Market research: A party must become more systematic in its study and understanding of the changing contours of public opinion as they relate to the party, its policy and politics in general. The party must learn how it is perceived by the public and what the public expects from the government in order to begin the process of identifying those segments of the public with which the party can and cannot relate and thus possibly build a lasting relationship.
2 Brand design: The market research process will enable a party to design and modify brand concepts based on market desires as well as the party's unique history and political identity.
3 Brand implementation: To be effective, the brand concept must be as organic to a party as possible, to the extent that it must reflect the input and then receive the support of a broad section of a party's leadership and membership. To work, a political brand cannot be imposed from above, nor resisted from below, but once established the brand will function as a mechanism for coordinating the party's activities. Hence, those who initiate or manage the brand process within a party must develop internal mechanisms through which they test and gather feedback on working brand concepts from all stakeholders.
4 Brand communication and management: Once a party brand has been developed, it must become the main prism through which the party interacts with and is understood by the public. It is the brand that will represent the party in the public mind whether it is during, after or between elections. As such, the brand is also the vehicle through which the party will, when necessary, reposition itself with its target audiences.
5 Brand delivery: A party's brand, its promises, ideals and images must permeate the party's behaviour and decision-making process once in government. A brand will only engender loyalty if it seen as successfully delivering on its promises.

loyalty it fosters, as Cosgrove discovered in his study of Conservative Republicans, may be grounded as much on core values and a grasp of the issues as it is on emotionally charged characterisations of an opponent (Cosgrove 2007). Though the development of a Republican Party brand 'has served the Conservative movement very well', Cosgrove writes, 'it is not at all clear that it has served the people or the government of the United States nearly as well' (ibid.: 8). The strength of the Conservative Republican brand, he explains, rests on the 'feelings' that it can engender in its target audience, 'rather than to substantive impact of the policies [it] proposes or the soundness of their analysis of current events' (ibid.: 8). The result, he concludes, is that 'large numbers of average Americans have … voted for politicians who enact policies that work against their substantive interests because of the highly visible, emotive way in which … policy has been presented to them' (ibid.: 8).

However, a brand may also weaken a party, as Lilleker argues about New Labour. As part of their rebranding efforts in the mid-1990s, Labour leaders began focusing the party's targeting efforts on less committed 'swinger' and 'doubter' voters, Lilleker writes, rather than on party 'loyalists'. The party's subsequent victory in the 1997 and 2001 elections have generally been seen as validating this strategy, Lilleker writes, but the election results also reveal its weaknesses. The party was able to reach out to new swing voters, and won both elections in landslide fashion, but it did so, Lilleker explains, at the expense of some of its most loyal supporters, who, the evidence suggests, were confused and ultimately demobilised by the party's rebranding efforts (Lilleker 2005: 19). During the 2001 election, for instance, which saw a record-low turnout nationwide in the UK, 'the constituencies that witnessed the lowest turnout, on average, were safe Labour seats in those areas regarded as the party's heartland', he explains (ibid.: 19). Such is the risk, Lilleker asserts, of a market-oriented party and politics that becomes too narrow in its targeting, and abandons other segments of the public (ibid.: 24).

The way forward

The solution, however, is not for parties and candidates to distance themselves from branding, but to take the brand premise more seriously. The conditions of a successful brand are in many ways quite demanding, requiring not only a keen appreciation for changing market needs, as well as effective implementation and communication, but also successful delivery once in government. Unless each is satisfied, the voting public will not be. That, as Lees-Marshment notes, gives political marketing and branding the potential to be a powerful force in favour of a more robust form of democratic governance (Lees-Marshment 2009: 275).

Unfortunately, in the case studied in this chapter, the US Democrats have struggled with every step of the marketing process, from design to delivery. As such, the way forward for the Democratic Party is to develop a more compelling brand narrative that affirms what it means to be a Democrat and specifically what Democratic politics offer the US in contrast to the Republican alternative. This process starts with market research, through focus groups and internal and external polling, as well as less formal means, to determine what a receptive audience wants and needs from the Democratic Party. Such market research will enable the party to not only target certain market segments but also, when needed, reposition itself with these audiences. The party must then design a party brand story that responds to and reflects the concerns, issues and aspirations gleaned from potential target audiences. The design process may entail, as Lees-Marshment notes, minimal change to a party, or alternatively, 'changing … not just the policy of a party, but aspects such as its leaders … the behavior of … candidates for office, organizational structures and membership rights' (Lees-Marshment 2001a: 33). As importantly, however, the party must also 'adjust' its brand product, as Lees-Marshment contends, to ensure that it is consistent and complementary with the party's values and strengths; that it is acceptable to the party's base; achievable in terms of policy implementation; and strategic, or likely to help the party win elections (Lees-Marshment 2001a: 33–34). Doing so helps with the institutionalisation of the brand, or ensuring that the party as a whole, and not just party leaders, 'accept' both the party's brand identity and, as importantly, a market-driven process of determining its contours. Only then can the Democratic Party begin to use a brand story to communicate with the public in a more focused and compelling way, and thus more effectively convey what it represents and how it differs from the Republican Party.

The Democrats' difficulties with the branding process stem in large part from the party's decentralised and federated institutional culture. As such, it may prove difficult for the Democrats to institutionalise a unifying brand narrative. However, confronted as the party is by a highly effective opposition Republican brand, designing a clearly differentiated brand product based on market and party needs that can then be communicated to the public may be essential both to bring the Democratic Party together and to ensure that it remains politically competitive.

Bibliography

Aldrich, J. (1995) *Why Parties? The Origin and Transformation of Political Parties in America*, Chicago: University of Chicago.

Bell, P. (2010) 'Public Puts Higher Priority on Cutting Budget Deficit', *National Journal*. Online, nationaljournal.com/congressdaily/cda_20100720_8896.Php (accessed 31 March 2011).

Brennan, M. (1995) *Turning Right in the 1960s: The Conservative Capture of the GOP*, Chapel Hill: University of North Carolina Press.

CBS News (2009) 'Bush's Approval Rating: 22 Percent', 16 January. Online, www.cbsnews.com/stories/2009/01/16/opinion/polls/main4728399.shtml (accessed 31 March 2011).

Cohen, J., Kassa, M. and Hamman, J. (1991) 'The Impact of Presidential Campaigning on Midterm U.S. Senate Elections', *American Political Science Review* 85, 1: 165–78.

Cosgrove, K. (2009) 'Barack Obama, Howard Dean and the Transformation of Democratic Politics', Paper Presented at the Annual Canadian Political Association Meeting, Ottawa, Ontario, 27–29 May.

—— (2007) *Branded Conservatives: How the Brand Brought the Right From the Fringes to the Center of American Political Life*, New York: Peter Lang.

Dowd, M. (2006) 'Campaign Organization and Strategy', in K. Hall Jamieson (ed.) *Electing the President, 2004: The Insiders' View*, Philadelphia: University of Philadelphia Press, 20–28.

Druckman, J.N., Kifer, M.J. and Parkin, M. (2009) 'Campaign Communications in U.S. Congressional Elections', *American Political Science Review* 103, 3: 343–66.

Dutton, S., De Pinto, J., Backus, F. and Salvanto, A. (2010) 'Poll: Public Opinion of Democratic Party at All-Time Low', *CBS News*, 25 May. Online, www.cbsnews.com/8301-503544_162-20005961-503544.html (accessed 31 March 2011).

Freeman, J. (1986) 'The Political Culture of the Democratic and Republican Parties', *Political Science Quarterly* 101, 3: 327–56.

GOP (2010) *Republican National Committee*. Online, www.gop.com/index.php/issues/issues (accessed 28 September 2010).

Gould, P. (1998) *The Unfinished Revolution: How the Modernizers Saved the Labour Party*, London: Little, Brown and Company.

Hacker, J. and Pierson, P. (2006) *Off Center: The Republican Revolution and the Erosion of American Democracy*, New Haven, CT: Yale University Press.

Jones, J.M. (2010a) 'Obama Approval Averages 45% in September', *Gallup* 4 October. Online, www.gallup.com/poll/143354/Obama-Approval-Averages-September.aspx (accessed 31 March 2011).

—— (2010b) 'Record Midterm Enthusiasm as Voters Head to Polls', *Gallup* 2 November. Online, www.gallup.com/poll/144152/record-midterm-enthusiasm-voters-head-polls.aspx (accessed 31 March 2011).

Kenski, K., Hardy, B.W. and Hall Jamieson, K. (2010) *The Obama Victory: How the Media, Money, and Message Shaped the 2008 Election*, Oxford: Oxford University Press.

King, A. (1998) 'Why Labour Won – At Last', in A. King, P. Norton, I. McLean, P. Norris, P. Seyd, D. Sanders and D. Denver (eds) *New Labour Triumphs: Britain at the Polls*, Chatham: Chatham House Publishing, 177–207.

Knuckey, J. and Lees-Marshment, J. (2005) 'American Political Marketing: George W. Bush and the Republican Party', in D. Lilleker and J. Lees-Marshment (eds) *Political Marketing: A Comparative Perspective*, Manchester: Manchester University Press.

Kohli, A.K. and Jaworski, B.J. (1990) 'Market Orientation: The Construct, Research Propositions and Managerial Implications', *Journal of Marketing* 54: 1–18.

Kotler, P. (1979) 'Strategies for Introducing Marketing into Non-Profit Organizations', *Journal of Marketing* 43: 37–44.

Lafferty, B. and Hult, T. (2001) 'A Synthesis of Contemporary Market Orientation Perspectives', *European Journal of Marketing* 35: 92–109.

Lancaster, G. and Massingham, L. (1993) *Essentials of Marketing*, New York: McGraw-Hill.

Lees-Marshment, J. (2001a) *Political Marketing and British Political Parties: The Party's Just Begun*, Manchester: Manchester University Press.

—— (2001b) 'The Product, Sales and Market-Oriented Party', *European Journal of Marketing* 35, 9/10: 1074–84.

—— (2009) *Political Marketing: Principles and Applications*, London: Routledge.

Levitt, T. (1960) 'Marketing Myopia', *Harvard Business Review* (July–August): 45–56.

Lewis-Beck, M.S., Jacoby, W.G., Norpoth, H. and Weisberg, H.F. (eds) (2008) *The American Voter Revisited*, Ann Arbor: University of Michigan Press.

Lilleker, D.G. (2005) 'Political Marketing: The Cause of an Emerging Democratic Deficit in Britain?' in W. Wymer and J. Lees-Marshment (eds) *Current Issues in Political Marketing*, Binghamton, NY: Best Business Books.

Lilleker, D.G. and Negine, R. (2003) 'Not Big Brand Names But Corner Shop: Marketing Politics to a Disengaged Electorate', *Journal of Political Marketing* 2 (1): 55–75.

Lloyd, J. (2005) 'Square Peg, Round Hole? Can Market-based Concepts such as the "Product" and the "Marketing Mix" Have a Useful Role in the Political Arena?', in W. Wymer and J. Lees-Marshment (eds) *Current Issues in Political Marketing*, Binghamton, NY: Best Business Books.

Mark, M. and Pearson, C. (2001) *The Hero and the Outlaw: Building Extraordinary Brands Through the Power of Archetypes*, New York: McGraw-Hill.
Morris, D. (1997) *Behind the Oval Office*, New York: Random House.
Needham, C. (2005) 'Brand Leaders: Clinton, Blair and the Limitations of the Permanent Campaign', *Political Studies* 53: 343–61.
Newman, B.I. (1999) *The Mass Marketing of Politics: Democracy in an Age of Manufactured Images*, Thousand Oaks, CA: Sage Publications.
Obama, B. (2008) *Change We Can Believe In*, New York: Three Rivers.
Ormrod, R.P. (2005) 'A Conceptual Model of Political Marketing Orientation', in W. Wymer and J. Lees-Marshment (eds) *Current Issues in Political Marketing*, Binghamton, NY: Best Business Books.
—— (2006) 'A Critique of the Lees-Marshment Market-Oriented Party Model', *Politics* 26, 2: 110–18.
Plouffe, D. (2010) *The Audacity to Win*, New York: Penguin Books.
Rasmussen Reports (2010) '38% Say Stimulus Plan Helped Economy, 36% Say It Hurt', 24 August. Online, www.rasmussenreports.com/public_content/business/economic_stimulus_package/august_2010/38_say_stimulus_plan_helped_economy_36_say_it_hurt (accessed 31 March 2011).
Scammell, M. (1999) 'Political Marketing: Lessons for Political Science', *Political Studies* 47 (4): 718–39.
Schickler, E. and Pearson, K. (2005) 'The House Leadership in an Era of Partisan Warfare', in L.C. Doss and B.I. Oppenheimer (eds) *Congress Reconsidered*, eighth edn, Washington, DC: CQ Press.
Schoenwald, J.M. (2001) *A Time for Choosing: The Rise of Modern American Conservatism*, New York: Oxford University Press.
Sinclair, B. (2006) *Party Wars: Polarization and the Politics of National Policy Making*, Norman: University of Oklahoma Press.
Smith, G. (2009) 'Conceptualizing and Testing Brand Personality in British Politics', *Journal of Political Marketing* 8: 209–32.
Smith, G. and French, A. (2009) 'The Political Brand: A Consumer Perspective', *Marketing Theory* 9: 209–26.
Todd, C. and Gawiser, S. (2009) *How Barack Obama Won*, New York: Vintage Books.
Travis, D. (2000) *Emotional Branding*, Roseville, CA: Prima Venture.
Wattenberg, M. and Brians, C. (2002) 'Partisan Turnout Bias in Midterm Legislative Elections', *Legislative Studies Quarterly* 27, 3: 407–21.
White, J. and de Chernatony, L. (2002) 'New Labour: A Study of the Creation, Development and Demise of a Political Brand', *Journal of Political Marketing* 1, 2–3: 45–52.

Part III
Internal marketing

11

Internal party political relationship marketing

Encouraging activism amongst local party members

Robin T. Pettitt

The topic: internal party relationship marketing

Local party member activism is an area of growing importance for electoral success, and parties and scholars alike often debate how participation can be encouraged within increasingly centralised party organisations. Modern political marketing in some ways creates an obstacle to local activism: a carefully crafted product, based on extensive marketing analysis carried out by experts hired by the party leadership, and delivered in a centrally controlled campaign, inevitably means centralisation of key functions – especially, quite obviously, designing the product. We therefore have a situation where the making of the product is increasingly seen as a something done centrally, but where local activists have a key part in bringing that product to the voters. This creates a problem, especially if the local volunteers are not happy with the product. It is a well-established idea that activists need to be incentivised. What is the incentive for delivering a product that activists have had no stake in producing? However, relationship or stakeholder marketing offers new tools and concepts to analyse and potentially overcome this problem. This chapter will focus on how *internal* stakeholder relationships can be nourished and explores what strategies can be used to incentivise internal stakeholders in a centralised organisation.

Previous research on internal party marketing

Although Hughes and Dann (2009) have discussed the importance of stakeholders in political parties generally, little has been written about the relationships between internal stakeholders. The few exceptions are Dean and Croft 2001 and Lees-Marshment 2001. In the model of a market-oriented party, Lees-Marshment notes the importance of adjusting the product to suit the internal market to aid implementation, and criticises UK 'New' Labour under Blair in the lead-up to 1997 for failing to do this effectively (Lees-Marshment 2001: 181). Of course, the failure to view party members as key stakeholders could have been a deliberate attempt to illustrate that the party had changed. A clash with internal stakeholders is sometimes seen, not as a necessary evil, but as being outright beneficial. According to the New Labour pollster Philip Gould, Blair said in 1994 that 'Past Labour leaders failed because they compromised. I will never compromise. I would rather be beaten and leave politics than bend to the party. I am going to take the party on' (Gould 2001: 216). The former Danish prime minister, Anders Fogh Rasmussen, who read Philip Gould's book with the intention of 'doing a New Labour' to his own Liberal Party (Pettitt 2009: 249–51), has argued that a (victorious) confrontation with internal critics not only shows the strong leadership necessary for high political office, but also shows the voters that change has taken place and is firmly entrenched (see Larsen 2003: 263–64, 266–68). However, this chapter will consider both the importance of bringing internal stakeholders on board and how it might be achieved.

As for relationship marketing, one of its key points is the importance of building relationships that go 'beyond the immediacy of market transactions' (Payne *et al.* 2004: 856). Dean and Croft argue that relationship marketing in politics is about having a 'focus … on building lifetime relationships with voters instead of intermittent, short-lived promotional *blitzkrieg* every four to five years' (Dean and Croft 2001: 1212). Having such relationships will make it easier to ensure repeat 'buying' and also has the potential to lead to a better product through a more intimate understanding of voters' demands.

However, the most important aspect of relationship marketing is the idea that a particular organisation, be it a company or a political party, does not just have to consider the ultimate buyer of the product, but also all the stakeholders, both external and internal, involved in making and delivering the product. In the context of local activism the issue of internal stakeholders is particularly important. One of the key texts in the field of relationship marketing stresses that 'Relationship marketing also focuses on the internal (staff) relationships critical to the success of (external) marketing plans' (Christopher *et al.* 1991: viii). Christopher and colleagues argue that a company has six markets (Christopher *et al.* 1991: 21).[1] This model has been found to be, with some modifications, useful in analysing company behaviour (see e.g. Payne *et al.* 2004). Dean and Croft recognise the potential in the multiple market model employed by Christopher for understanding political parties, but also stress that merely relabelling the original model to approximate a political party rather than a company would be a mistake. Instead they suggest starting from scratch when adapting the idea to political parties (Dean and Croft 2001: 1205, 1206–7).

This chapter will propose a multiple market model for political parties by drawing on the literature on political parties and campaigning.

New research: new theories of internal marketing

This section will outline a model for understanding the multiple markets or stakeholders that a party has, particularly internally, and discuss empirical illustrations. Figure 11.1 presents the model that argues that a party has eight markets, three internal and five external.

When it comes to the internal markets it makes sense to work with Katz and Mair's idea that a party has three 'faces' (see Katz and Mair 1993, 2002). These three faces are: the party in public office – i.e. elected parliamentarians and government ministers; the party on the ground – i.e. volunteers in the party, be they card-carrying and fee-paying members or 'merely' regular supporters; the party in central office – i.e. anyone paid to be working for the party. These three faces make up the internal markets or stakeholders of a party. On the external front there are obviously and most importantly the voters, analogous to buyers/consumers in the commercial world. In the context of party politics the media must be seen as a separate market

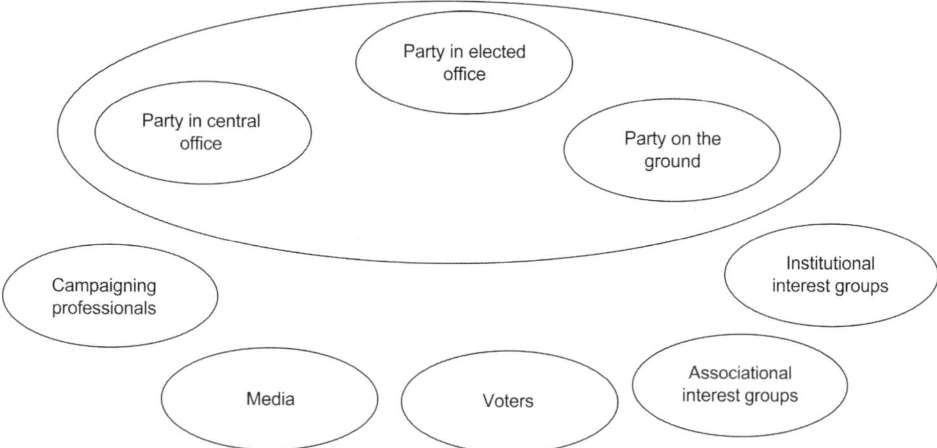

Figure 11.1 Multiple market model for political parties

that needs careful attention. In addition there are what can be broadly be defined as 'interest groups', which make demands of political parties and can in turn be useful as influencers of the primary market of the electorate. According to Almond *et al.* (2007) there are two types of interest groups that are or more or less permanently organised (as opposed to brief surges of activism): associational groups – i.e. named groups set up with the specific purpose of promoting a specific cause or section of society, with examples including trade unions, Amnesty International, Greenpeace and the World Wide Fund for Nature; and institutional groups, e.g. organisations that were not set up with the purpose of promoting certain interests, but nevertheless have interests of which they want parties to take account. In addition, they may be able to affect the electorate. The main example of institutional groups is national and international businesses and companies. The final market, and one which has become increasingly important in recent decades, consists of external experts in political campaigning.

Having outlined the multiple market model for political parties, the section will now outline how the relationships between these different markets have changed. Much of the literature on campaigning regards parties as having moved through three stages (see Table 11.1), each with different relationships between the various party stakeholders (see Figure 11.2 – the arrows indicate the strength of the relationship. Interest groups have been put to one side here as they do not feature prominently in the party political campaigning literature).

Looking at the developments from the first to the second stage there is a clear centralising trend and a move away from activist involvement in campaigning. Two factors created this trend. The first is the increased centralisation of the making of the product. As parties become increasingly focused on surviving in an ever more volatile electoral market the leadership starts to turn away from old ideological certainties and towards designing a product that is tuned to the demands of the voters. In doing so they turn to polling experts and away from the members. The second factor is the rise of national television in the late 1950s and 1960s. This led to the focus moving away from local 'shoe leather' campaigning and towards national media campaigning, often focused on the leader. Again, experts were brought in to help to the detriment of party membership involvement.

However, in the third stage there is a strong counter-trend towards local activism (see e.g. Whiteley and Seyd 2003; Denver *et al.* 2003; Green and Gerber 2008). The conclusion of

Table 11.1 Stages of campaigning

Stages	*Characteristics*				
	'Style' of campaigning	*Personnel*	*Voter feedback*	*Voter segmentation*	*Communication channels*
1 Pre-modern; Product-oriented party; mass party	'Propaganda' approach; rallying the 'masses' behind a pre-existing product	Decentralised local campaigning by volunteer activists	Local canvassing returns. Impressions and 'gut instincts'	Heavy emphasis on specific class (class-mass party)	Party press, posters, billboards, pamphlets, word of mouth via volunteers. Little if any focus on press management
2 Modern; Sales-oriented; catch-all party	'Selling' approach; research to find out which voters might be interested in pre-existing product and explore which elements of the product might resonate with the potential voters at a given time	Highly centralised campaign organised by internal media and polling experts; heavy focus on a leadership-driven national media campaign	Extensive nationwide polling	Catch-all approach; attempting to attract voters from across society irrespective of social background	Heavy focus on national media, especially television. Decreased emphasis on local channels. Rise of media management; building relationship with journalists
3 Post-modern; market-oriented; cartel party	'Marketing' approach; less about attracting voters to a pre-existing product and more about discovering voter needs and designing a product accordingly	Highly centralised campaign making increased use of external campaign professionals contracted in on an ad-hoc basis. Return of the local campaign relying on volunteer activists to sell the product door to door, but local campaign co-ordinated from the centre	Increasingly advanced polling and use of focus groups	Continued use of catch-all approach; also increased use of detailed voter segmentation according to array of social and demographic factors	Targeted direct mail to carefully selected sectors of the electorate; return of volunteer-driven word of mouth; increasingly intense media management 'spinning' the message

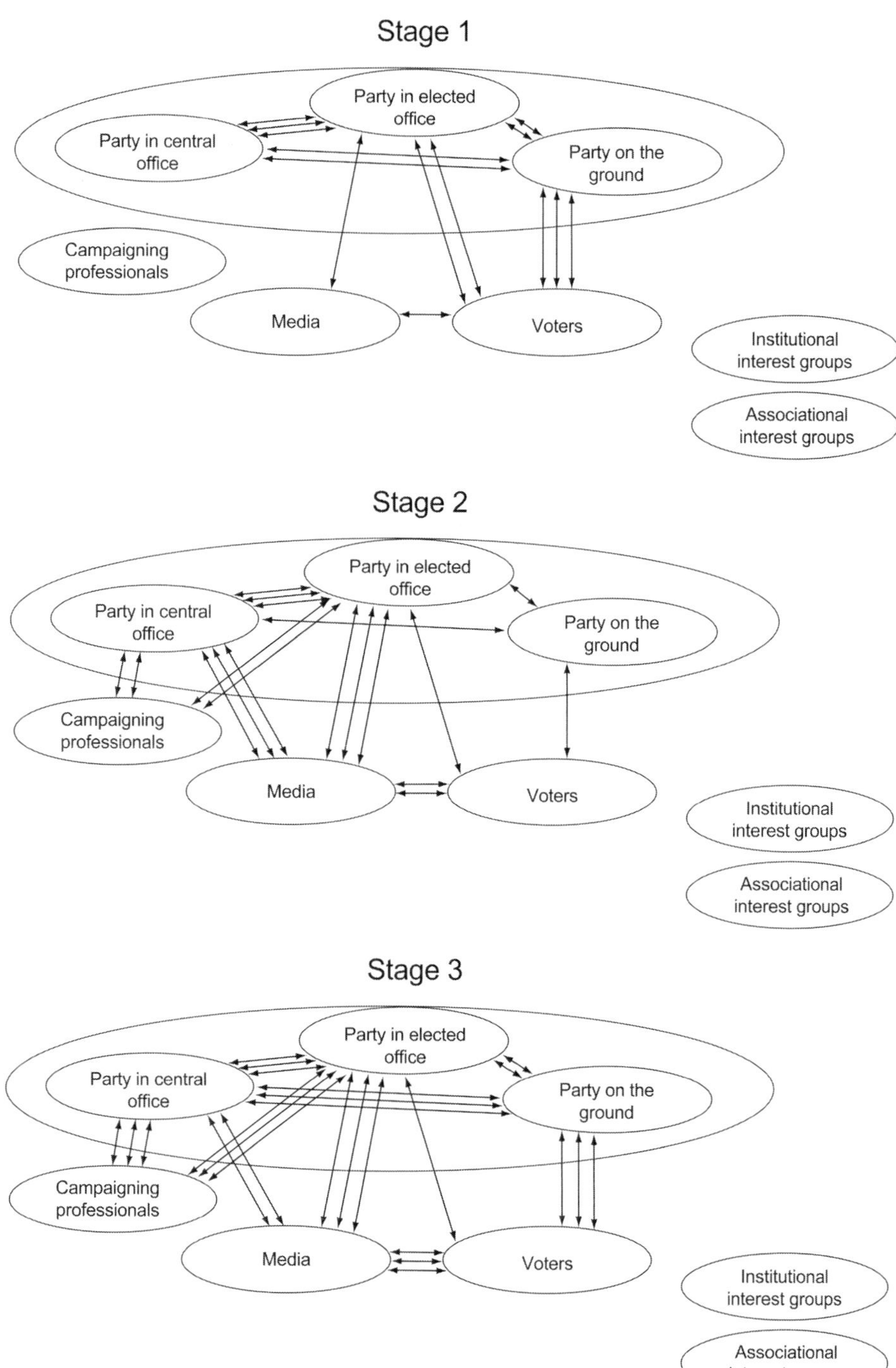

Figure 11.2 Stages of campaigning with relationships between stakeholders

one group of scholars in their work on the UK is that 'there is no doubt that constituency campaigning is now seen as more significant than ever by the parties and possibly even more significant than the national campaign focussed on the mass media' (Fisher *et al.* 2005: 18).

The importance of local campaigning has also been recognised across the Atlantic, as exemplified by the 2008 Obama presidential election campaign. In his book on the campaign Plouffe writes: 'Our secret weapon, day in and day out, was our army of volunteers, real people who brought Obama's message and ideas to their neighbors, co-workers, and fellow citizens, guided by our extraordinary staff' (Plouffe 2009: 379–80).

What we are left with in the third stage is a strong central product designed by the leadership with help from external experts. That product is then 'sold' to a large extent through the centrally co-ordinated efforts of local activists.

However, these two trends – the centralisation of the making of the product and the importance of local activism in modern campaigning – creates a problem. One key line in Plouffe's book is the argument that there 'is no more effective courier for a message than people who believe in it and have authentically embraced it' (Plouffe 2009: 379). In this he is no doubt right, but that has important implications when it comes to political marketing. As we saw above, the making of the message has become centralised and the local participation in the making of the product is limited. The question for party leaders then becomes how they give volunteers a stake in a product they were not invited to help create.

That brings us to the issue of incentives for activism. Clark and Wilson (1961: 130) in their seminal paper on incentives argue that all 'viable organizations must provide tangible or intangible incentives to individuals in exchange for contributions of individual activity to the organizations'. Further, it has been argued that such incentives cannot be collective goods – that is, available to everybody irrespective of membership or activism (Olson 1965). Hence, arguing that a member of, for example, the working class should be active in a working-class party because it would be beneficial for the working class to have such a party in power would not work. All workers would benefit from having a working-class party in power, regardless of whether they helped put that party in power or not. On a cost-benefit analysis it would make more sense *not* to be active, since the benefits of party victory can be enjoyed without having been active. What are required then are 'selective' incentives – that is incentives that are only available through activism (Olson 1965).

Clark and Wilson (1961: 134–36) identify three broad categories of incentives:

- Material incentives: these are rewards for activism that have tangible and often monetary value, e.g. a salary.
- Solidary incentives: these are intangible rewards associated with the process of being active. Examples include the pleasure derived from socialising and the feeling of group membership – of being part of something bigger than oneself through one's activism. Clark and Wilson (1961: 134, note 8) also include feelings of loyalty towards the organisation (as distinct from its purpose) in this category. Seyd and Whiteley (1992: 60) use the term 'process incentives' to describe the idea that 'for some people, the political process is interesting and stimulating in itself, regardless of the outcomes or the goals' (Seyd and Whiteley 2002: 52).
- Purposive incentives: these are related to the stated ends of the organisation. Hence a committed socialist will be active in a socialist party because of their strong belief in socialism. A socialist may not seek socialist ends because they would benefit personally, but because they believe in the idea of socialism. The same would go for a committed conservative, liberal, religious believer or strong atheist.

The argument being made here, then, is that for successful internal relationship/stakeholder marketing to be implemented in relation to local activists it must be based on one or more of these incentive types. The following will explore how this might be done.

There are five approaches that party leaders can take to internal stakeholder marketing aimed at motivating local activists to carry out their role in external marketing.

Material incentives (pay them)

The simplest and easiest option, but perhaps also the one that will lead to the least convincing or energetic local campaigning, is to pay activists. That is, employing straightforward material incentives. This would certainly involve the least amount of effort in terms of the quid pro quo involved, i.e. once the money has been handed over and the activities carried out there are no further mutual obligations by either party leaders or activists.

However, there are also several problems with this approach. First, paying sufficient numbers of activists to make a difference in a campaign is expensive, and in some countries there are limits on how much a party is allowed to spend before and during an election campaign (see, for example, the several contributions in Lees-Marshment *et al.* 2010). Hence, there will have to be a balance between paying for local activists and for all the other parts making up a modern election campaign. Even if there are no limits on what can be spent, the money has to come from somewhere. State funding is very generous in some countries (see again Lees-Marshment *et al.* 2010), but not limitless and relying on private donations brings with it its own problems in terms of favours being bought and suspicions of outright corruption (see, for example, the several contributions in Williams 2000).

However, perhaps most importantly in relationship marketing terms, relying on paid activists could undermine the effect of having personal contact between the party and voters. As Plouffe argues, genuine volunteers can work better than paid labour (Plouffe 2009: 182, 379). It is worth reiterating his comments that there 'is no more effective courier for a message than people who believe in it and have authentically embraced it' (ibid.). If the 'courier' is paid, the authenticity of the message could well be undermined by the impression that the activist is only in it for the money, whether that is true or not. Hence, material incentives are simple and straightforward, but also carry cost, both in terms of money (obviously) and in loss of the 'authenticity' of personal campaigning.

Base strategy (give the internal stakeholders what they want)

The second option is to rely on purposive incentives, that is, go for what Panagopoulos and Francia (2009: 320–21) refer to as a 'mobilise the base' strategy. In this situation the party leaders will incentivise their (potential and actual) activists by pushing a product that is very much to the liking of the party's most committed supporters. As Clark and Wilson argue, one of the reasons for being active in a party is the commitment to the stated aims of the party. If the leadership pursues policies and rhetoric very much in line with the party's official ideological foundations they can mobilise the ideologues amongst the party's supporters. This is what Lees-Marshment would refer to as a sales-oriented party (Lees-Marshment 2001: 29–30), that is, a party that has a product in place first, and then focuses on selling that product to the voters, hoping that they can be made to like it. According to Panagopoulos and Francia (2009: 321), this was the approach followed by the Republicans in 2002 (successfully in electoral terms) and again in 2008 (with somewhat less success, at least electorally). It has also been argued that the British Conservative Party followed this approach from 1997 until about 2005, with notable lack of electoral success

(Lees-Marshment and Pettitt 2010). This option will certainly make it easier to get the internal stakeholder on board, but as exemplified by the British Conservatives from 1997 to 2005 and the Republicans in 2008, whilst it may successfully mobilise activists, there is only so much that 'authentically committed couriers' can do to pass on a message if it is something the voters really do not want to hear. Arguably, it is also a strategy that is less likely to work for a catch all-style party that is basing its strategy on attracting a wide range of voters across several societal groups. Hence, this approach may be more appealing to smaller parties, especially in multi-party systems, which can have a very successful life appealing to fairly narrow groups. As a prime example of this can be mentioned radical parties on both the left and the right in the Scandinavian consensus-style democracies. In these highly fragmented party systems radical parties have successfully mobilised fairly narrow sections of the electorate with base strategies, but have still managed to achieve a significant level of legislative influence due to the tendency towards coalition and/or minority governments.

Empty vessel (glittering generality)

A related approach is what might be referred to as an empty vessel or 'glittering generality' strategy. As with the base strategy, the appeal is to purposive incentives. However, rather than trying to appeal to the base with a strongly ideological product, the idea is to use a vague and more or less empty product, which sounds appealing to a wide group of people, but mainly because it is so vague that people can project onto the product their own ideas, wants and demands. The idea of 'glittering generality' is taken from Lee and Lee's (1939) work on propaganda techniques, in which 'associating something with a "virtue word" – is used to make us accept and approve the thing without examining the evidence' (ibid.: 23). A 'virtue word' is essentially any word or phrase with positive connotations which is then used to build support for someone or something, but without explaining the exact meaning of that word. Examples include the Labour Party's 1997 slogan 'New Labour, New Britain', followed shortly after by 'Cool Britannia'. In an age seen as suspicious of overt ideological appeal, Blair's and Schroder's use of the idea of a 'third way' or 'new centre' (see, for example Hombach 2000), copied from Bill Clinton, falls into the same category. Whilst extensive attempts have been made to flesh out what the third way means (e.g. Giddens 1998), it has been repeatedly used and often in very vague ways to appeal to a non-ideological electorate. Obama's use of 'yes we can' and 'change we can believe in' would also count as a 'glittering generality' strategy. Indeed, any appeals to 'change' not followed by a detailed plan would count as a 'glittering generality'. The advantage of this strategy is that it can appeal to purposive incentives, but without the same risk of alienating non-ideologues inherent in a base strategy. In short, it is a purposive strategy for the catch-all party.

There are, however, two downsides. The first is that the glitter of the generality will fade very quickly, either when the emptiness of the virtue word is exposed, or, especially in the case of gaining power on the back of a glittering generality strategy, the flesh has to be put on the bone. As soon as a new government has to actually start doing 'things' many people will very quickly discover that what they had imagined was meant by the glittering generality does not match the actions of the new government. In other words, the formerly empty vessel of the glittering generality will be filled with the solid evidence of government action, thus driving out what people thought was meant by a particular virtue word or phrase. Arguably, this is exactly what happened to Blair and Schroder, both immensely popular at the time of their first victory, but who over time faced a sustained decline in popularity. The same could be said to have been happening to Obama since his inauguration in 2009.

Dignified/empty democracy

The next strategy relies on solidary incentives, i.e. the satisfaction derived from feeling part of a greater whole through activism, in this context the satisfaction of being involved in creating the party's product through, apparently, democratic processes. The idea of 'dignified democracy' comes from Walter Bagehot's 1867 description of the British political system. Bagehot separates the British political system into a 'dignified' and an 'efficient' part. The efficient part is where power really lies; the dignified part is where the show of consultation takes place and where the legitimacy of the efficient part is created. In the context of party politics the dignified part is the powerless conference, the 'listening' tour of the party leader or the membership-wide ballot carefully timed and worded to ensure the greatest possible likelihood of leadership success. In one memorable phrase Bagehot writes that the dignified parts of a political system 'may not do anything definite that a simpler polity would not do better; but they are the preliminaries, the needful presentations of all work. *They raise the army*' (Bagehot 1963: 62 – emphasis added). According to the UK Labour Party politician R.H.S. Crossman, this is highly relevant for political parties. In the case of the Labour Party he writes that:

> Since it could not afford, like its opponents, to maintain a large army of paid party workers, the Labour Party required militants – politically conscious socialists to do the work of organising the constituencies. But since these militants tended to be the 'extremists' a constitution was needed which maintained their enthusiasm by apparently creating a full party democracy while excluding them from effective power.
>
> *(Crossman 1963: 41–42)*

This has the advantage of, potentially, resolving the battle identified by Lilleker between internal membership and external voter opinion should the two diverge (Lilleker 2005: 577). By making a show of consulting internal opinion, but still following external opinion, the leadership of a party can use solidary incentives to mobilise activists for external marketing purposes whilst still designing a product that will attract an election-winning cross-section of the voters. As Crossman suggests, this is the approach followed by the Labour Party for a significant part of its history. The downside, apart from the morally dubious nature of the approach, is that activists will eventually notice that their views are not actually reflected in the party's product. Hence, dignified democracy will only work for so long before it starts to wear off. This is particularly the case if the leadership wants to change the party's product. Again, this is something which can be seen at several times in the Labour Party's history, especially with the rise of 'New Labour'.

Effective/real democracy/consultation

The final option is the other side of the coin of Bagehot's dignified democracy – the effective element, i.e. real democratic consultation and joint creation and ownership of the product by all internal stakeholders. Plouffe's remark that the most effective courier for a message are people who believe in it and have authentically embraced it (see above) is relevant here. It is reasonable to argue that people are most likely to embrace and believe in a product they have themselves had a hand in creating. Whiteley and Seyd (2002: 215) show in the context of the British Labour Party that those most active in the party are also the ones most likely to favour participatory models of democracy. This suggests that genuine democratic product development can be a powerful tool for mobilisation.

Table 11.2 Levels of policy

Policy level	*Consists of*
1 Long term	Basic principles, statements on ideology
2 Medium term	Electoral period, election manifestos
3 Short term	Annual, parliamentary year
4 Day to day	Daily negotiations internally and externally, crisis management

The most important argument against internal party democracy is that the political struggle requires fast decision-making and that democracy is simply too slow to cope with the requirements of political life. This is something that has been recognised at least since the work of Michels (1915) almost 100 years ago. However, whilst this may be true for some aspects of political life it is not universally so. Policy can be divided into several layers as illustrated in Table 11.2. The daily cut and thrust of politics (Level 4) certainly requires very fast turnaround times, especially in the world of 24/7/365 news. Extensive consultation is clearly not possible on the day-to-day rough and tumble of politics, but provided the right mechanisms are in place there should be nothing fundamental to stop fairly extensive consultation taking place at the other three levels. By right mechanisms is meant forums for debate and consultation between leaders and activists. For a democratic consultative product development process to lead to a sellable product, leaders need to understand what activists are willing to sell, and activists need to understand what voters are willing to buy. This mutual understanding is best achieved through a process of consultation and sharing of information, including the leadership sharing party polling data with the activists and activists feeding back on how local party branches are reacting to early product designs. Hence, a democratic product-development process is not simply about the party on the ground telling the party in elected office what to do, but about developing a relationship between the internal stakeholders that will allow them to share information on what the voters will buy and the activists will sell, and if there is a divergence, agree on a compromise. As Sheth and Parvatiyar argue, when stakeholders deal directly with each other they are likely to 'understand and appreciate each other's needs and constraints better, are more inclined to cooperate with one another, and thus, become more relationship oriented' (Sheth and Parvatiyar 1995: 398).

Advice for practitioners

When considering how to mobilise local party activists, party leaders need to be aware of the implications of taking one path to local mobilisation rather than another. To assist in making the choice between the different incentive strategies the following two points should be taken into account:

- Regardless of what approach is chosen there will be benefits and costs. When deciding on their approach the party leadership therefore needs to consider what kinds of benefits are important to them and what kinds of costs they are willing to bear. Table 11.3 gives a brief summary of the costs and benefits of each approach.
- As with all marketing, market intelligence is key. Traditionally in the context of political parties 'market intelligence' has meant understanding the electoral market. What the idea of multiple markets highlights is the need for intelligence on more than just the electoral market. In the context of internal relationship marketing in a political party what is also

Table 11.3 Costs and benefits of different incentive strategies

Strategy	*Costs and benefits*
Material incentives	Gives a high degree of product design flexibility and makes a catch-all strategy easy to pursue. However, it will also result in a low level of authentic commitment to the product, and the relationship will last only as long as the money continues to flow, and can therefore in effect be switched on and off.
Base strategy	Gives a very low level of design flexibility and pursuing a catch-all approach will therefore be difficult. On the other hand, activist commitment to the product will be high and will last as long as the product is relatively unchanged.
Empty vessel	Gives a high degree of product design flexibility making a catch-all strategy easy to pursue. Activist commitment to the product will be high, but also short term once they realise the disjuncture between what they thought they were getting and what they are actually getting. Building new relationships will subsequently be very hard indeed, in contrast to the relatively easy 'on/off' nature of material incentives.
Dignified democracy	Leads to a high degree of product design flexibility and a high degree of activist commitment to the product. However, whilst it may be easier to hide the emptiness of dignified democracy than of the empty vessel, once it is exposed the relationship will end and be very difficult to rebuild.
Effective democracy	Reduces the flexibility of the product design as the product will have to be adjusted to take into account activist views. Product design flexibility is likely to be enhanced if the leadership shares information on voter demands and therefore increases activist awareness of what is required to increase the electoral attractiveness of the product. Activist commitment will be high, and the relationship between the party in elected office and the party on the ground will continue for as long as democratic consultation continues.

needed is intelligence on the 'party on the ground' market. For example, if a catch all-oriented party leadership is faced with a 'party on the ground' market which is more concerned with ideological purity than electoral success, then they will have to decide between trying to change the internal market to a more catch-all-oriented stance or choose either the empty vessel or the dignified democracy strategies. Material incentives are unlikely to work on ideologically motivated activists and neither a base strategy nor effective democracy is likely to lead to a catch-all product. However, these decisions can only be made if adequate internal and external market intelligence is available.

Impact on politics

The ways in which parties mobilise activists and voters have potentially major implications for the future path of democracy. Mair has argued that there is a worrying trend in both the practice and normative views on democracy away from popular participation in democratic life (Mair 2006: 33). Amongst his evidence for this he cites the widespread decline in voter turnout at election time and the equally widespread decline in party membership numbers. The result, he argues, is that we are increasingly seeing a 'notion of democracy that is being steadily stripped of its popular component – democracy without a demos' (Mair 2006: 25). Needless to say, he does not see this as a thing to be celebrated. However, the rediscovery of the importance of local campaigning, and the role of local activists in that campaigning, does appear to present a counter-trend. Not only does local campaigning involve a greater level of direct interaction between parties and voters, but also a need for party leaders to (re-)engage with local activists, further strengthening the local connection. Both these factors would appear to lead to a greater level of popular participation in and contact with democratic processes, either as voters being engaged by parties or as party activists. This being the case, the increased focus on local campaigning does hold the potential for a re-engagement between parties and voters and through that lead to parties that are more closely tied in with civil society and therefore more responsive to its demands – something which political marketing has always hoped to achieve.

However, whether or not and how well this actually becomes a reality will depend to a considerable extent on the ways in which internal relationship marketing is carried out, especially the method(s) chosen to incentivise local party stakeholders. Each of the five approaches to incentivising internal party stakeholders at the local level offers different levels of potential and danger when it comes to sustained party/civil society interaction.

Relying on money is perhaps the simplest option, but also one that is unlikely to achieve any sustained interaction between parties and civil society, or even between party and activists beyond the election campaign. As Payne *et al.* argue, relationship marketing involves 'an emphasis on stakeholder collaboration beyond the immediacy of market transactions' (Payne *et al.* 2004: 856). Relying purely on material incentives in the form of payment for activism is not likely to build such collaboration in the context of political parties.

A base strategy should certainly be able to achieve Plouffe's 'authentic' activism, but also runs the risk of undermining any catch-all profile. Hence, it may rally the activists, but turn off many voters when they are offered a product not to their taste.

The problem with both the glittering generality and the dignified democracy approaches is that, whilst they certainly have the potential to generate authentically motivated activism, they are also inherently short term. Sheth and Parvatiyar (1995: 398) argue that a key part of relationship marketing is an emotional bonding between stakeholders that transcends the immediate exchange. However, Plouffe also argues that such bonds are based on fragile sinews of trust which are easily broken (Plouffe 2009: 380). Hence, whilst both glittering generalities and dignified democracy can undoubtedly create excitement and engagement to counteract the growth in the gap between politicians and voters, there is a price to pay later. The inevitable disappointment that will come when the vessel is filled with something not quite right (as is almost bound to happen when people fill in the blanks themselves) or when the hollow nature of dignified democracy is exposed, is likely to destroy the relationship between internal stakeholders and quite possibly accelerate the rate of separation between (by now probably former) local citizen activists and politicians.

The last option, i.e. genuine democratic internal relations, is therefore the option that is most likely to counteract the rise of a democracy without a demos in a sustained manner. Democratic relations between internal stakeholders will make all parts of the party aware of what is required to create a product that has enough catch-all appeal to be electorally attractive and still able to mobilise local activists. Hence, a democratic process of product design is the incentive system most likely to generate a product that will be 'sellable' and also generate sustainable local party activism and thereby long-term relationships between voters and parties.

The way forward

The main issue to take forward is how best to put into practice incentives for local activism that are sustainable, and will not lead to either a loss of electoral appeal through a too narrow product or to later disappointment, loss of trust and resultant decline in activism. It has been suggested that internal democratic processes are most likely to achieve this, but there are significant challenges that would have to be overcome to implement such a system. What is clear is that more needs to be done to understand how effective internal political marketing can be carried out in the context of party politics.

A number of key areas need to be explored:

- What combinations of the five incentive strategies are currently being used to build (more or less) lasting relationships with local activists?
- How well do they work? There are problems with all five strategies, and how these are overcome, or not as the case may be, will be important to understand.
- For how long do they work? As already mentioned, glittering generalities and dignified democracy have limited shelf lives. This is particularly important, and interesting, in the context of Obama in 2012, who will have to decide what comes after 'yes we can'.

Internal relationship marketing is crucial to maintain activism, something that is increasingly central to electoral success, and important lessons could be learnt through documenting and developing good practice in this area.

Note

1 They are customer markets; internal markets; referral markets; supplier markets; employee (recruitment) markets; and influence markets.

Bibliography

Almond, G.A., Powell Jr, J.B., Dalton, R.J. and Strom, K. (2007) *Comparative Politics Today: a theoretical framework*, London: Pearson.

Bagehot, W. (1963) *The English Constitution*, London: Collins.

Christopher, M., Payne, A. and Ballantyne, D. (1991) *Relationship Marketing: bringing quality, customer service and marketing together*, Oxford: Butterworth-Heineman.

Clark, P.B. and Wilson, J.Q. (1961) 'Incentive Systems: A Theory of Organizations', *Administrative Science Quarterly* 6, 2: 129–66.

Crossman, R.H.S. (1963) 'Introduction', in Walter Bagehot, *The English Constitution*, London: Collins.

Dean, D. and Croft, R. (2001) 'Friends and Relations: Long-term Approaches to Political Campaigning', *European Journal of Political Marketing* 35, 11: 1197–217.

Denver, D., Hands, G., Fisher, J. and MacAllister, I. (2003) 'Constituency Campaigning in Britain, 1992–2001: Centralisation and Modernisation', *Party Politics* 9, 5: 541–59.

Fisher, J., Denver, D., Fieldhouse, E., Cutts, D. and Russell, A. (2005) *Constituency Campaigning in the 2005 British General Election*, Paper presented at the Annual Conference of the PSA Specialist Group on Elections, Public Opinion and Parties, University of Essex, September.

Giddens, A. (1998) *The Third Way: the renewal of social democracy*, Cambridge: Polity.

Gould, P. (2001) *The Unfinished Revolution: how the modernisers saved the Labour Party*, London: Abacus.

Green, D.P. and Gerber, A.S. (2008) *Get Out the Vote: how to increase voter turnout*, second edn, Washington, DC: Brookings Institution.

Hombach, B. (2000) *The Politics of the New Centre*, Cambridge: Polity.

Hughes, A. and Dann, S. (2009) 'Political Marketing and Stakeholder Engagement', *Journal of Marketing Theory* 9, 2: 243–56.

Katz, R.S. and Mair, P. (1993) 'The Evolution of Party Organizations in Europe: The Three Faces of Party Organization', *The American Review of Politics* 14, 4: 455–77.

—— (2002) 'The Ascendency of the Party in Public Office: Party Organisational Changes in Twentieth-Century Democracies', in R. Gunther, J. Ramon Montero and J.J. Linz (eds) *Political Parties: old concepts and new challenges*, Oxford: Oxford University Press.

Larsen, T. (2003) *Anders Fogh Rasmussen: i godtvejr og storm*, Copenhagen: Gyldendal.

Lee, A.M. and Lee, E.B. (1939) *The Fine Art of Propaganda: a study of of Father Coughlin's speeches*, New York and Harcourt: Brace and Company.

Lees-Marshment, J. (2001) *Political Marketing and British Political Parties: the party's just begun*, Manchester: Manchester University Press.

Lees-Marshment, J. and Pettitt, R.T. (2010) 'UK Political Marketing: A Question of Leadership', in Jennifer Lees-Marshment, Jesper Strömbäck and Chris Rudd (eds) *Global Political Marketing*, Abingdon: Routledge.

Lees-Marshment, J., Strömbäck, J. and Rudd, C. (eds) (2010) *Global Political Marketing*, Abingdon: Routledge.

Lilleker, D.G. (2005) 'The Impact of Political Marketing on Internal Party Democracy', *Parliamentary Affairs* 58, 3: 570–84.

Mair, P. (2006) 'Ruling the Void: The Hollowing of Western Democracy', *New Left Review* 42, Nov.–Dec.

Michels, R. (1915) *Political Parties: a sociological study of the oligarchical tendencies of modern democracy*, New York: Hearst's International Library.

Olson, M. (1965) *The Logic of Collective Action: public goods and the theory of groups*, Cambridge, MA: Harvard University Press.

Panagopoulos, C. and Francia, P.L. (2009) 'Grassroots Mobilization in the 2008 Presidential Election', *Journal of Political Marketing* 8, 4: 315–33.

Payne, A., Ballantyne, D. and Christopher, M. (2004) 'A Stakeholder Approach to Relationship Marketing Strategy: The Development and Use of the "Six Markets" Model', *European Journal of Marketing* 39, 7: 855–71.

Pettitt, Robin T. (2009) 'Learning from the Master: The Impact of New Labour on Political Parties in Denmark', in J. Lees-Marshment (ed.) *Political Marketing: principles and applications*, London, Routledge, 249–53.

Plouffe, D. (2009) *The Audacity to Win: the inside story and lessons of Barack Obama's historic victory*, New York: Viking.

Seyd, P. and Whiteley, P. (1992) *Labour's Grass Roots: the politics of party membership*, Oxford: Oxford University Press.

—— (2002) *New Labour's Grassroots: the transformation of the Labour Party membership*, Basingstoke: Palgrave.

Sheth, J.N. and Parvatiyar, A. (1995) 'Relationship Marketing in Consumer Markets: Antecedents and Consequences', *Journal of the Academy of Marketing Science* 23, 4: 255–71.

Whiteley, P. and Seyd, P. (2002) *High-Intensity Participation: the dynamics of party activism in Britain*, Ann Arbor: Michigan University Press.

—— (2003) 'How to Win a Landslide by Really Trying: The Effects of Local Campaigning on Voting in the 1997 British General Election', *Electoral Studies* 22, 2: 301–24.

Williams, Robert (ed.) (2000) *Party Finance and Political Corruption*, Basingstoke: Macmillan Press.

12

Party members as part-time marketers

Using relationship marketing to demonstrate the importance of rank-and-file party members in election campaigns

Peter Van Aelst, Joop van Holsteyn and Ruud Koole

The topic: party members as part-time marketers

Modern election campaigns consist of two elements: a centralized media campaign around the leadership of the political party and a campaign involving the participation of active party members or campaign activists. The literature on parties and campaigns emphasizes the importance of the first element, the media campaign, while at least until recently downplaying the importance of members. Political marketing literature itself has paid little attention to the role of members. This chapter will address that omission by combining insights derived from relationship marketing with ideas on party members and grassroots campaigning. Using the concept of part-time marketers, we demonstrate the potential importance of party members in modern or postmodern election campaigns. This will be illustrated through a case study of Dutch parties and party members.

Previous research: the dominant literature on professionalization rather than on member activity

Within the political party literature, research on the media side of election campaigns describes various aspects of professionalization of parties (e.g. Panebianco 1988), including the introduction of campaign professionals (e.g. Plasser and Plasser 2002), opinion pollsters and market intelligence (e.g. Butler 1996), centralization of decision-making (e.g. Farrell and Webb 2000), improving media strategies (e.g. Norris *et al.* 1999), and a candidate-centered approach (e.g. Poguntke and Webb 2005). The idea is that professionalization and innovation has become a prerequisite for success and survival in contemporary campaigns and elections (Butler and Ranney 1992; Swanson and Mancini 1996). To sketch the line of reasoning roughly: elections are won by a small group of professional strategists who craft a central message, and a 'charismatic' party leader who subsequently 'sells' this message successfully in front of television cameras. This handful of professionals and the political leader are in close contact with each other, operating from a 'war room'. They have little contact with the rest of the party, let alone with the rank-and-file party activists and members: 'parties have begun to transform themselves more and more into centralized and professional campaigning organizations, in which the scope for the amateur politician has been curtailed and in which the weight and direction of party strategy have tended increasingly to be located within the party leadership as such' (Mair *et al.* 2004: 265).

This literature seems to ignore party members as a potentially valuable link to voters. In their 'modern model of campaigning', Swanson and Mancini (1996: 252) mention as its defining elements 'personalization of politics; adapting campaign practices to media logic and priorities; and employing technical experts to advise parties on public relations, opinion polling and marketing strategies'. No mention is made of the rank-and-file party membership. By some scholars, party members are seen as a barrier to reach the general electorate since they are less flexible and 'still bound to the traditions of their party' (Mair *et al.* 2004: 266). Also, following the work of, among others, Duverger (1951) and May (1973), active party members are considered as more extreme and not representative of a party's electorate and potential support. Notwithstanding the fact that this thesis lacks convincing empirical evidence, according to this line of reasoning a party that listens too much to its members runs the risk of being out of touch with ordinary voters and will subsequently lose elections.

In recent years the idea that party members and local campaigns are irrelevant or a hindrance for electoral success has been challenged. Especially in the UK, scholars have proven that traditional local campaigning, including the efforts of party members, may lead to better performance (for an overview see Fisher *et al.* 2006). Whiteley and Seyd (2003) have shown that local campaigning contributed to success in the 1997 British elections: without the efforts of local members, the Labour victory would have been more modest. The authors warn parties that alienating their members may come with a price (Seyd and Whiteley 2002). '[M]embers are as important as election campaigners … Parties with fewer active constituency campaigners will suffer electoral consequences' (Seyd and Whiteley 2004: 361). Denver and colleagues present concurring results for both the 1992 and 2001 British elections. Admittedly, the electoral benefits of the efforts of ordinary party members are marginal, but they are significant (Denver *et al.* 2004) – in times when each and every vote is worth fighting for, it would be ill-advised not to use all auxiliary troops that are at one's disposal (Fisher and Denver 2009). The overall positive argument on contribution of local 'labour-intensive' campaign activities based on UK findings concurs with findings in other countries such as Canada (Carty and Eagles 1999), Ireland (Marsh 2004) and the US (Wielhouwer 1999; Green *et al.* 2003).

The work of Scarrow (1994) on parties and party members theoretically underpins pro-membership arguments. They may operate as 'vote multipliers' or as ambassadors to their respective communities. If party members are willing to express their political views and preferences in their daily contacts this may result in a benefit for the party, especially if they are able to circulate the message to a 'non-party milieu'. Since party membership is a communication channel that works both ways, party leaders may be able to learn about voters' opinions via their members. Moreover, the more parties provide opportunities for their members to impact on party policies, the more members may be willing to be active as local ambassadors for their party (e.g. Ware 1992; Van Holsteyn and Koole 2009).

Political marketing research helps to expand these arguments by utilizing relationship marketing theories. The concept of part-time marketers was developed by the founding fathers of the so-called Nordic school (Gummesson 1987; Gummesson 1990; Grönroos 1994; Grönroos 2000). These scholars contributed substantially to the emerging theory of relationship marketing, with roots in service and non-profit marketing. They stress the need of creating mutually satisfying exchanges and long-term relationships between customers and organizations (Grönroos 1994). Establishing such relationships should be realized by the organization and *all* of its members, not solely by a separate marketing or sales department. As Gummesson (1987: 17) puts it: 'The work to create and maintain market relationships is divided between the full-time professional marketers in the marketing department and the omnipresent (non-professional) "part-time marketers" '. According to Grönroos (1990), this demands a specific management philosophy and a commitment of the organization so that employees as amateur part-time marketers have the attitudes and skills to perform this task. This implies attention to internal marketing and a view of employees as an important channel for promotion of the organization.

Relationship marketing has been applied to politics to only some extent (see Henneberg 2002; Bannon 2005; Henneberg and O'Shaughnessy 2009). In the work of Johansen (2005) the idea of the part-time marketer has been most explicitly applied to the world of parties. In order for a party (the organization) to create a relationship with its voters (the customers), a special role should be attributed to its members (the employees). In Johansen's organizational perspective these members have a crucial input and output function. This is why she questions the increasing role of focus groups and surveys to gauge public opinion while at the same time 'the potentially effective feedback channel of party membership' is neglected (Johansen 2005: 95). By communicating daily experiences to the party leadership and campaign professionals within the organization, members can be a valuable help from an input or bottom-up perspective, acting as an 'early-warning system' for societal developments that may be about to hit the party (Koole 2000). Moreover, their contribution is less costly than the services of professional pollsters and consultants (Müller 2000). Lees-Marshment states that parties should be aware of the 'internal reaction' when employing a market-oriented strategy, but that taking members seriously does not conflict with the goal of electoral success (Lees-Marshment 2001; Lees-Marshment and Quayle 2001: 211). Also Strömbäck (2007) stresses the importance of 'the internal arena' in party-centred democracies.

New research: the theory and practice of part-time marketers

Towards a model of members as part-time marketers

This new research thus argues that rank-and-file party members have been overlooked as valuable, employable auxiliary forces in the fight for the volatile voter of the 21st century. Based on the insights of relationship marketing we develop and empirically explore the idea of party members as part-time marketers: marketing is not a separate task solely performed by a specialized department of the organization, but involves *all* parts of the organization. In the political and electoral context party members are those who operate close to the electoral market, which offers them the opportunity to have multiple contacts with ordinary voters. These contacts could be useful both as a way to persuade people to vote for their party and as a feedback channel to inform the party leadership about the concerns and preferences of ordinary citizens and potential supporters. Drawing on these ideas, we argue two principles:

- Members provide an important feedback function, i.e. a form of market intelligence: Parties may learn from their members as they interact on a daily basis with citizens and voters, as employees on a day-to-day basis interact with customers. Moreover, ordinary party members are more than the professional politicians present and active in different parts of society, e.g. in a sports club, school board, or interest group (Van Holsteyn *et al.* 2002). As a consequence of this omnipresence in society the rank-and-file members receive plenty of information about the opinions, the preferences and the general mood of ordinary citizens.

- Members contribute to the electoral success of their party by promoting its candidates and platform: Using members as local campaigners can be considered as a contribution from an output or top-down perspective. This, of course, can hardly be considered an original idea, but rather an idea that seems to have been forgotten by political parties and scholars alike. In their effort to control, market and 'sell' their products, parties have centralized and professionalized their power structures, especially during election campaigns. Parties have indirectly discouraged their ordinary members to be active.

Johansen (2005) stresses both principles and points to the fact that the party membership as input (feedback) and output (promotion) channel may interact and strengthen each other. Moreover, the more ordinary members have the feeling that they are co-producers of 'their' product, the more willing they are to convince others to taste and buy it. It is like the employee of Volkswagen who drives a Volkswagen and positively discusses the company and the car with friends, family and acquaintances as well.

If members have, potentially, such major benefits for parties both in the short and long run, how come they are given so little attention? Previous research suggests that the reluctance to include individual party members in modern election campaigns may have to do with their opinions and attitudes (see Lees 2005; Lilleker 2005a). Are members representative of potential voters of their party and for the party as a whole? If in particular the active members have more extreme positions (cf. May 1973; Jacobs and Shapiro 2002: 59; but see Norris 1995; Granik 2005; Koole and Van Holsteyn 2000; Scarrow and Gezgor 2010), there is a danger in having them act as marketers. They may chase off moderate supporters and attract the wrong, 'extremist' voters. More generally, the fact that this small group of citizens have become party members makes them the exception to the rule and different from all those citizens who did not become members. This may impact negatively on their capacity to act as party ambassadors, in particular in times when new political entrepreneurs are picturing a negative image of parties and party members. Politicians such as Berlusconi in Italy have created organizationally thin parties that more or less serve as the leaders' personal instrument (Mazzoleni 2000). The successful Dutch populist Wilders has created a party with only one individual member: himself.

Finally, that some people did become party *members* does not mean that they want to be active and want to become a party *activist*. The notion of party members as part-time marketers implies that members are willing and able to play an active role, in particular in the run-up to elections, in meeting and persuading potential voters. This is far from obvious. It is one thing to become a party member, but it is another thing to become active on behalf of this party in a discordant context – competitive democratic elections are about differences of opinion and conflicting preferences and interests.

To address these concerns about the electoral potential of ordinary party members we present a model (see Table 12.1), which includes three preconditions for the idea of members as part-time marketers: representativeness, connectedness and willingness. Representativeness refers to the position and attitudinal make-up of members as two-way communication channels between potential voters and the party. In this capacity, i.e. 'members can be political communicators, both upwards and downwards' (Seyd and Whiteley 2004: 362), they have to know and represent political opinions correctly (e.g. Scarrow 2007). Probably for party members the best way to possess this knowledge is to have identical or at least similar opinions compared to (potential) voters as well as to the party more generally. If in this way members are representative, then this precondition for acting as party ambassadors and intermediaries between the mass and elite

Table 12.1 A model of members as part-time marketers

Representativeness	– Members know and can communicate public opinion and preferences from mass to elite level – Members have identical or at least similar opinions compared to (potential) voters for the party
Connectedness	– Members are connected to society at large, not just party elites – Members are connected to various other organized parts of civil society
Willingness	– Members are open about their political affiliation and willing to spread the word – Members are willing to campaign for the party in election time

levels will be fulfilled. Connectedness means that members are active in society at large, not only in their party organization. Modern party organizations are sometimes referred to as cartel parties, linked to the state but detached from civil society and acting as 'semi-state agencies' (Katz and Mair 1995: 16). If this were indeed the case this would be problematic for the idea of party members as marketers. If neither parties nor individual party members are related to other parts of society, then any activities of individual members as part-time marketers would be impossible or ineffective. Willingness, finally, implies that members have the drive and motivation to be active for their party. Studies have shown that this is not always the case (e.g. Granik 2005; Scarrow 2000). If members are to take up their role as part-time marketers they should be open about their party affiliation and willing to actively promote their party.

The model of members as part-time marketers: the Dutch case

We explore our model of party members as part-time marketers by inspecting the Dutch case in more depth. The Netherlands is a parliamentary democracy with an extreme proportional electoral system, a fragmented party system, a tradition of coalition governments and a polity that has been typified as a consensus or consociational democracy (Lijphart 1999). The Netherlands fits the general pattern of advanced Western democracies, with major changes in the political landscape in recent decades (Pennings and Keman 2008). As regards party membership, a slight reversal of the downward trend was noticeable following the exciting political situation with the rise and success of the controversial Pim Fortuyn in 2002 (Den Ridder *et al.* 2011a). The number of party members is about 3 percent (Andeweg and Irwin 2009: 76; see for a comparative overview Mair and van Biezen 2001).

The analysis is based on a survey among a sample of party members. Seven (out of ten) parties that were represented in the second chamber of parliament after the general elections of November 2006 participated in this Leiden Party Member Survey (LPMS) 2008.[1] The questionnaire contained several questions that were similar to questions of the Dutch National Election Study 2006, to compare members with ordinary voters. With response rates ranging between over 30 percent and over 60 percent, and a total number of 4,251 members participating, ample information on party members was collected.

- Representativeness: Do party members resemble voters? From a socio-demographic perspective this is not the case: members are old, male and highly educated. However, the picture for substantive representation tells a different story. On several issues members have almost identical opinions to the voters of their party. Only with regards to the issues of the integration of ethnic minorities and European integration were there slight but significant differences between both groups for a few parties, but the overall conclusion is that the ideas of members correspond closely with those of the voters (see Den Ridder *et al.* 2011b; Koole and Van Holsteyn 2000). Moreover, in general ideological positions, i.e. with respect to their self-placement in terms of left and right, voters and members are similar. On a 10-point scale, the mean ideological position of the two groups of the same party never differs by more than one point; for several parties the difference is less than half a point.

For our model this substantive similarity should be considered much more important than the socio-demographic differences. As long as the older, educated male members express the same political opinions as the voters and potential supporters, as well as the party, they can act as both the party's input and output channel. Although similar issue and ideological positions, of course, do not conclusively prove that individual party members and other relevant actors within and for these parties are on exactly the same ideological wavelength, they do strongly suggest that members are suitable to act as part-time marketers from the perspective of representativeness.

- Connectedness: Pim Fortuyn, the political entrepreneur who was murdered only days before the general elections in 2002, referred to the Dutch political process as 'a completely incestuous scene of self-appointing and co-opting political and administrative elites' (Fortuyn 2002: 135–36, translation by the authors). This is another way of stating that parties have developed into cartel parties with strong ties to the state but only weak ties to civil society (Katz and Mair 1995). The fear that parties are disconnected from society is not warranted, however, if we look at their members. We asked them whether or not they were a member or supporter of a number of different interests and other groups, ranging from labour unions to sports clubs and from women's organizations to organizations for the conservation of nature, and whether or not they were active as a volunteer worker for these groups. These indicators of societal connectedness clearly prove that party members are not clinging exclusively to their party but are involved in other groups and organizations. Only a tiny minority of 5 percent were *not* members or supporters of any other group. In general, over 40 percent were members of one to three other organizations and an almost equal percentage were members or supporters of four to six organizations (see Table 12.2, final column). Moreover, passive involvement is more frequent than activism, but the majority of party members indicate that they have done voluntary work for one to three groups or organizations.

Even more important and relevant from the point of view of the respective parties is that there is no negative relationship between being active as a party member and both passive and active forms of involvement in other organizations within civil society. According to the rival structure hypothesis (e.g. Sainsbury 1983; Ware 1996), we should expect that as a result of the competition for scarce resources of time, money and energy, activism inside and outside the party would be correlated negatively. This is not the case. Indeed, if there is any correlation it is a (weak) positive one. Over 30 percent of the members who 'confess' to be inactive as a party member are not doing any voluntary work in any other organization either, compared with 15 percent of the members who consider themselves very active. In the latter group, one in ten members is engaged in voluntary work in at least four groups, whereas this is true for almost one in four of the most active party members.

Our data show support for the second precondition: party members are no unworldly citizens, isolated from and unaware of the wider society, and swallowed by the activism for or

Table 12.2 Indicators of societal connectedness of party members, by level of activism (%)

	Level of (subjective) activism as a party member				
	(Almost) not active	*Not very active*	*Fairly active*	*Very active*	*All members*
Number of organizations of which party members are a member or supporter:					
0	7	4	4	3	5
1–3	51	48	42	45	48
4–6	41	44	48	45	43
7 +	2	4	6	8	4
Number of organizations for which party members are a voluntary worker:					
0	32	20	16	15	24
1–3	59	63	56	63	60
4–6	10	17	27	22	16
7 +	0	1	2	1	1

Source: Leiden Party Member Survey 2008 for seven parties (see note 1) (weighted data).

within their party. Contrary to the idea of a cartel party being isolated from society, members of Dutch parties are rooted in society at large and connected as members or volunteers to other organized parts of civil society. As such, they are able to constitute the linkage between their party and society. At election time they may canvass in the various societal environments and groups with which they are connected. All in all, many party members have the potential to play the role of ambassador, salesman or foot soldier – but are they willing to do so?

- Willingness: According to our third precondition, party members should be willing to be active as part-time marketers. As said, this is not obvious. First, many members are not active in their party. In the LPMS 2008 a plurality of 44 percent of the members considered themselves inactive; only 25 percent was in their own estimation fairly or very active. The fact that not all Dutch party members are or want to be active is not exceptional from a comparative perspective (Scarrow 2000).
- The concept of part-time marketers, however, implies that members are first of all open about their political affiliation and willing to spread the word. Our data show that many Dutch party members are willing to speak out about their party membership (Table 12.3, final column). For over 90 percent it is true that their acquaintances know about their membership and a large majority of 72 percent of the party members talk about their party at work. Moreover, about 80 percent do not think that being active for their party would cause any discomfort in everyday life.
- Party members also think that they can be a source of information for their party (at the input side of the communication channel). A large majority of over 70 percent agrees with the statement that rank-and-file members may have good ideas about what their party should do, and a non-negligible minority of about 20 percent even think that they know the minds of the people better than elected representatives. Since less than 10 percent of members think that activities of people like themselves are of no use since the party leadership decides everything, the potential for fuelling the leadership with information from the mass level very likely does exist.

- If it is true that future behaviour is best predicted from past performance, parties still have some encouraging to do. In Table 12.3 findings for three separate campaign activities are presented, i.e. for actions that indicate the willingness of members to show their political preference and to actually canvass at elections. The data show that four out of every ten members have shown a poster or window bill at home; over 20 percent tried to persuade others to vote for their party, and distributed leaflets or other campaign information. But the glass appears to be half empty rather than half full: some party members already act as part-time marketers for their party, but for all parties included in our study the majority is *not* active, or at least not at recent election campaigns.

To sum up, party members who are less active internally do not differ strongly from their more active fellow members with respect to their willingness to speak out as a member or in their self-confidence as a party member. What makes the difference – and this may come as no surprise – is that those members who are less active within their party also appear to have been less active as auxiliary troops for their party at previous election campaigns. Apparently, those members who consider themselves to be very active already act as part-time marketers: 65 to 75

Table 12.3 Indicators of potential willingness of members to be active for their party, by level of activism

	Level (subjective) of activism as a party member				
	(Almost) not active	*Not very active*	*Fairly active*	*Very active*	*All members*
Willingness to speak out as a party member					
'At work I never talk about my party' (% not true)	62	74	83	90	72
'The people among my acquaintances know that I am a member of [party]' (% true)	87	95	99	99	92
'People who are active for their party experience discomfort in their everyday life' (% (fully) disagree)	78	78	82	76	79
Self confidence of party members					
'Rank-and-file party members know the minds of the people better than elected representatives' (% (fully) agree)	21	24	20	18	22
'Often rank-and-file party members have good ideas about what the party should do' (% (fully) agree)	69	72	78	81	72
'Activities of party members like me are of no use since the party leadership decides everything' (% (fully) agree)	9	9	6	8	8
Prior campaigning experience : percentage of party members who during the previous five years (very) often...					
...showed a poster or window bill at home	24	40	65	77	40
...tried to persuade others to vote for the party	9	19	39	64	22
...distributed leaflets or other information	5	19	51	76	23

Source: Leiden Party Member Survey 2008 for seven parties (see note 1) (weighted data).

percent of those members did show a poster, tried to persuade others and/or distributed campaign information. Those members who are less active within their party are also (much) less active in the run-up to elections. So according to our data, a substantial number of reserve troops are still at rest. Dutch parties have tried to mobilize these troops, but apparently not effectively and without convincing results as yet. However, the party that succeeds in getting them into action will be able to employ an impressive number of extra marketers in future campaigns.

Advice for practitioners

What lessons can parties learn from the general idea of members as part-time marketers, and the Dutch case in particular? We showed that the alleged unrepresentativeness of members is to a large extent – in the Netherlands and from a substantive point of view – a myth. Dutch party members' opinions on major political issues and in terms of left–right ideological self-placement hardly differ from their parties' electorate. Furthermore, party members are active in and connected to other parts of civil society as members and active participants in various societal organizations. This makes these members well positioned to provide feedback about the general mood of the electorate. Our study supports the idea of devoting structural attention to this valuable and relatively cheap form of market intelligence, for instance by organizing regular surveys among members and providing members with easy online and offline ways to express their opinions to the party headquarters. This feedback channel is the first benefit of treating members as part-time marketers.

Besides the market intelligence that it provides, the input channel strengthens the second benefit of the part-time marketer concept: members as active ambassadors and foot soldiers for their party. Our case study showed that the representativeness and connectedness of members does not imply that they have been active in campaigning. A majority of members has not canvassed for their party in recent years. This means that there may be new ground to develop among the party membership. Parties should try to mobilize this group of potential foot soldiers, who remain necessary in order to meet with potential voters face to face and make the party visible on the street. This is not an easy assignment, but it might be an effective undertaking. In our survey over 40 percent of members stated that they were never asked by their party to get involved in any activity for their party, but of those 60 percent who were contacted, over 90 percent appreciated this. Among the 40 percent who were never contacted, over 50 percent thought this would be a good idea. Among the party membership there is virgin territory as regards party activism.

Finally, we believe that regarding members as part-time marketers is not only useful in the short run, i.e. to win the next election, but also in the long run. Parties that neglect their rank-and-file members may attract new voters, but simultaneously lose their traditional base of support. In the case of UK New Labour, Lilleker (2005b) found that members felt that there had been a lack of consultation when their party modernized in the 1990s and they had been disenfranchised. Labour had won votes, but lost two-thirds of its members since the mid-1990s (Pettitt 2009). As voters become more disloyal, a party that loses a significant amount of members loses some of its lifeblood. Moreover, '[b]y taking measures to extend the role of individual members in party decision-making, cartel parties can defend themselves against accusations of elitism and detachment from society' (Hopkin 2001: 345).

Impact on politics

Parties are not the only beneficiary of the part-time marketer model: democracy as a whole might benefit. The idea of members as part-time marketers means that ordinary people are actually involved, not only as spectators but as co-producers. In this respect, the part-time marketer model is in line with theories that stress the importance of a participatory democracy (e.g. Verba *et al.* 1995).

As party members become an integrated part of an electoral strategy in a market-oriented modern election campaign, our model might also adjust the (incorrect) idea that political marketing is necessarily in conflict with traditional party activism. The concept of part-time marketers should not be seen in contrast to the centralized media campaign, but rather as a crucial part of it. We even argue that without the party's central organization involvement and coordination, the idea of part-time marketers has little chance of being truly effective. On the one hand, the input and knowledge from wider society would never reach party headquarters, and on the other hand, party leaders' attempts to activate their members would be unheard or left unanswered. In short, successful election campaigns require an integration of modern and traditional methods. As Marsh (2004: 263) aptly puts it, 'elections take place on the airwaves, but they also take place on the doorsteps'.

The way forward

Future research should try to test more cases to explore whether party members are really unwilling, or rather unable, to be more active in a campaign context. Are these members simply not mobilized, or consciously neglected by party headquarters? Whatever may be the case, with at least two of the three preconditions fulfilled in the Dutch case, there is ample reason to further explore and develop the possibilities for political parties to increase the grassroots potential of party members in election campaigns, in particular in a time where the internet has dramatically increased the opportunities for parties and candidates to connect more easily with their core supporters, as was shown by the primary campaign of Howard Dean in 2004 (Hindman 2005) and again by Barack Obama in 2008. 'It is clear that parties are here to stay, an unavoidable part of democracy. Whether, as Schattscheider believed, political parties make modern democracy, or whether they are an inextricable weed in its garden, is a question that social science research does not answer yet' (Stokes 1999: 263–64). Indeed, political parties are here to stay, as are their members, so why not make the best of it?

Note

1 The parties that participated were: the Christian Union (ChristenUnie, CU); the Christian Democratic Appeal (Christen Democratisch Appèl, CDA); D66 (Democraten 66, or Democrats 66); the GreenLeft (GroenLinks, GL); the Labour Party (Partij van de Arbeid, PvdA); the Liberal Party (Volkspartij voor Vrijheid en Democratie, VVD); and the Dutch Reformed Party (Staatkundig Gereformeerde Partij, SGP). Three parties did not want to participate: The Party for Freedom (Partij voor de Vrijheid, PVV); the Socialist Party (Socialistische Partij, SP); and the Party for the Animals (Partij voor de Dieren, PvdD).

Bibliography

Andeweg, R.B. and Irwin, G.A. (2009) *Governance and Politics of the Netherlands*, Houndmills: Palgrave.

Bannon, D.P. (2005) 'Relationship Marketing and the Political Process', *Journal of Political Marketing* 4, 2: 85–102.

Butler, D. (1996) 'Polls and Elections', in L. LeDuc, R.G. Niemi and P. Norris (eds) *Comparing Democracies. Elections and voting in global perspective*, London: Sage Publications, 236–53.

Butler, D. and Ranney, A. (1992) *Electioneering*, Oxford: Clarendon Press.

Carty, R.K. and Eagles, M. (1999) 'Do local campaigns matter? Campaign spending, the local canvass and party support in Canada', *Electoral Studies* 18, 1: 69–87.

Den Ridder, J., Van Holsteyn, J. and Koole, R. (2011b) 'De representativiteit van partijleden in Nederland', in R.B. Andeweg and J. Thomassen (eds) *Democratie Doorgelicht*, Leiden: Leiden University Press, 165–84.

Den Ridder, J., Koole, R. and Van Holsteyn, J. (2011a) 'Join the party! Party members of Dutch political parties', Centre for Voting and Parties, University of Copenhagen, Denmark, 3–4 February, 18 pp.

Denver, D., Hands, G. and MacAllister, I. (2004) 'The electoral impact of constituency campaigning in Britain, 1992–2001', *Journal of Politics* 52: 289–306.

Duverger, M. (1951) *Les partis politiques*, Paris: Collin.

Farrell, D. and Webb, P. (2000) 'Political parties as campaign organizations', in R. Dalton and M. Wattenberg (eds) *Parties Without Partisans. Political change in advanced industrial democracies*, Oxford: Oxford University Press, 102–28.

Fisher, J. and Denver, D. (2009) 'Evaluating the electoral effects of traditional and modern modes of constiuency campaigning in Britain 1992–2005', *Parliamentary Affairs* 62 2: 196–210.

Fisher, J., Denver, D. and Hands, G. (2006) 'The relative electoral impact of central party coordination and size of party membership at constituency level', *Electoral Studies* 25, 4: 664–76.

Fortuyn, P. (2002) *De puinhopen van acht jaar paars*, Rotterdam: Karakter Uitgevers.

Granik, S. (2005) 'Membership benefits, membership action: why incentives for activism are what members want', *Journal of Nonprofit and Public Sector Marketing* 14, 1/2: 65–90.

Green, D.P., Gerber, A.S. and Nickelson, D.W. (2003) 'Getting out the vote in local elections: results from six door-to-door canvassing experiments', *Journal of Politics* 65: 1083–96.

Grönroos, C. (1990) 'Relationship approach to marketing in service contexts: The marketing and organizational behavior interface', *Journal of Business Research* (20): 3–11.

—— (1994) 'Quo vadis, marketing? Towards a relationship marketing paradigm', *Journal of Marketing Management* 10: 347–60.

—— (2000) 'Relationship marketing: the Nordic School perspective', in J.N. Sheth and A. Parvatiy (eds) *Handbook of Relationship Marketing*, Thousand Oaks, CA: Sage, 95–118.

Gummesson, E. (1987) 'The New Marketing – developing long-term interactive relations', *Long Range Planning* 20, 4: 10–20.

—— (1990) 'Marketing-orientation revisited: the crucial role of the part-time marketer', *European Journal of Marketing* 25, 2: 60–75.

Henneberg, S.C. (2002) 'Understanding political marketing', in N.J. O'Shaughnessy and S.C. Henneberg (eds) *The Idea of Political Marketing*, Westport, CT: Praeger, 93–170.

Henneberg, S.C. and O'Shaughnessy, N. (2009) 'Political relationship marketing: some micro/macro thoughts', *Journal of Marketing Management* 25, 1/2: 5–29.

Hindman, M. (2005) 'The real lessons of Howard Dean: reflections on the first digital campaign', *Perspectives on Politics*: 121–28.

Hopkin, J. (2001) 'Bringing the members back in? Democratizing candidate selection in Britain and Spain', *Party Politics* 7, 3: 343–61.

Jacobs, L. and Shapiro, R. (2002) 'Politics and policymaking in the real world. Crafted talk and the loss of democratic responsiveness', in J. Manza, F.L. Cook and B.I. Page (eds) *Navigating Public Opinion*, Chicago, IL: University of Chicago Press, 54–85.

Johansen, H.P.M. (2005) 'Political marketing: more than persuasive techniques, an organizational perspective', *Journal of Political Marketing* 4, 4: 85–105.

Katz, R.S. and Mair, P. (1995) 'Changing models of party organization: the emergence of the cartel party', *Party Politics* 1, 1: 5–28.

Koole, R.A. (2000) 'De toekomst van democratische ledenpartijen', *Socialisme and Democratie* 57/58: 588–99.

Koole, R.A. and van Holsteyn, J. (2000) 'Partijleden in perspectief, Kiezers en leden vergeleken', in G. Voerman (ed.) *Jaarboek DNPP 1999*, Gröningen: DNPP, 93–124.

Lees, C. (2005) 'Political marketing in Germany: the case of the Social Democratic Party', in D. Lilleker and J. Lees-Marshment (ed.) *Political Marketing in Comparative Perspective*, Manchester: Manchester University Press.

Lees-Marshment, J. (2001) *Political Marketing and British Political Parties. The party's just begun*, Manchester: Manchester University Press.

Lees-Marshment, J. and Quayle, S. (2001) 'Empowering the members or marketing the party? The conservative reforms of 1998', *The Political Quarterly* 72, 2: 204–12.

Lijphart, A. (1999) *Patterns of Democracy. Government forms and performance in thirty-six countries*, New Haven, CT: Yale University Press.

Lilleker, D.G. (2005a) 'Political marketing: the cause of an emerging democratic deficit in Britain?', in W. Wymer and J. Lees-Marshment (eds) *Current Issues in Political Marketing*, Binghamton, NY: Best Business Books.

—— (2005b) 'The impact of political marketing on internal party democracy', *Parliamentary Affairs* 58, 3: 570–84.

Mair, P., Müller, W.C. and Plasser, F. (2004) 'Conclusion: political parties in changing electoral markets', in P. Muir, W.C. Müller and F. Plasser (eds) *Political Parties and Electoral Change: Responses to electoral markets*, London: Sage, 264–74.

Mair, P. and van Biezen, I. (2001) 'Party membership in twenty European democracies, 1980–2000', *Party Politics* 7: 5–21.

Marsh, M. (2004) 'None of that post-modern stuff around here: grassroots campaigning in the 2002 Irish general election', *Journal of Elections, Public Opinion and Parties* 14, 1: 245–67.

May, J. (1973) 'Opinion structure of political parties: the special law of curvilinear disparity', *Political Studies* 21, 2: 135–51.

Mazzoleni, G. (2000) 'A return to civic and political engagement prompted by personalized political leadership?', *Political Communication* 17: 325–28.

Müller, W.C. (2000) 'Political parties in parliamentary democracies: making delegation and accountability work', *European Journal of Political Research* 37: 309–33.

Norris, P. (1995) 'May's Law of Curvilinear Disparity revisited: leaders, officers, members and voters in British political parties', *Party Politics* 1, 1: 29–47.

Norris, P., Curtice, J., Sanders, D., Scammell, M. and Semetko, H.A. (1999) *On Message. Communicating the campaign*, London: Sage.

Panebianco, A. (1988) *Political Parties: Organization and power*, Cambridge: Cambridge University Press.

Pennings, P. and Keman, H. (2008) 'The changing landscape of Dutch politics since the 1970s: a comparative exploration', *Acta Politica* 43, 2/3: 154–79.

Pettitt, R. (2009) 'Case study 6.3, resisting marketing: the case of the British Labour Party under Blair', in J. Lees-Marshment (ed.) *Political Marketing: Principles and applications*, London and New York: Routledge.

Plasser, F. and Plasser, G. (2002) *Global Political Campaigning. A worldwide analysis of campaign professionals and their practices*, London: Praeger.

Poguntke, T. and Webb, P. (2005) *The Presidentialisation of Politics. A comparative study of modern democracies*, Oxford: Oxford University Press.

Sainsbury, D. (1983) 'Functional hypothesis of party decline: the case of the Scandinavian Social Democratic parties', *Scandinavian Political Studies* 4: 241–60.

Scarrow, S.E. (1994) 'The "paradox of enrollment": assessing the costs and benefits of party memberships', *European Journal of Political Research* 25: 41–60.

—— (2000) 'Parties without members? Party organization in a changing electoral environment', in R.J. Dalton and R.M. Wattenberg (ed.) *Parties Without Partisans. Political change in advanced industrial democracies*, Oxford: Oxford University Press, 79–101.

—— (2007) 'Political activism and party members', in R. Dalton and H. Klingemann (eds) *The Oxford Handbook of Political Behavior*, Oxford: Oxford University Press, 636–54.

Scarrow, S.E. and Gezgor, B. (2010) 'Declining memberships, changing members? European political party members in a new era', *Party Politics* 16, 6: 822–43.

Seyd, P. and Whiteley, P. (2002) *New Labour's Grass Roots*, Basingstoke: Palgrave Macmillan.

—— (2004) 'British party members: an overview', *Party Politics* 10, 4: 355–66.

Stokes, S.C. (1999) 'Political parties and democracy', *Annual Review of Political Science* 2: 243–67.

Strömbäck, J. (2007) 'Antecedents of political market orientation in Britain and Sweden: analysis and future research propositions', *Journal of Public Affairs* 7: 79–89.

Swanson, D. and Mancini, P. (1996) *Politics, Media and Modern Democracy: An international study of innovations in electoral campaigning and their consequences*, Westport, CT: Praeger.

Van Holsteyn, J. and Koole, R. (2009) *Is It True what They Say? Dutch party members and their opinion on internal party democracy*, Lisbon: ECPR Joint Sessions.

Van Holsteyn, J., Koole, R. and Elkink, J. (2002) 'Marginaal of midden in de maatschappij? Leden van CDA, D66, PvdA en VVD en hun activiteiten in de samenleving', *Beleid en Maatschappij* 29, 2: 67–80.

Verba, S., Schlozman, K.L. and Brady, H.E. (1995) *Voice and Equality: Civic volunteerism in American politics*, Cambridge, MA: Harvard University Press.

Ware, A. (1992) 'Activist-leader relations and the structure of political parties: "exchange" models and vote-seeking behaviour in parties', *British Journal of Political Science* 22, 1: 71–92.

—— (1996) *Political Parties and Party Systems*, Oxford: Oxford University Press.

Whiteley, P. and Seyd, P. (2003) 'How to win a landslide by really trying: the effects of local campaigning on voting in the 1997 British general election', *Electoral Studies* 22, 3: 301–24.

Wielhouwer, P. (1999) 'The mobilization of campaign activists by the party canvass', *American Politics Quarterly* 27, 2: 177–200.

13

Yes we can (fundraise)

The ethics of marketing in political fundraising

Alex Marland

The topic: fundraising

Fundraising, according to Wilcox (2008: 3), is 'the art and science of approaching potential donors with the right appeals at the right time'. It involves directly asking for money and other gifts or indirectly raising funds such as through special events or product sales. Sponsors use publicity techniques to attract attention to the fundraising cause or to persuade giving. Alternatively, they may use marketing whereby research has identified an objective shared with target groups and donations are solicited for that mutual cause. Unlike philanthropy, which is a one-way exchange, political fundraising likely involves the donor receiving a benefit, be it material, social or ideological.

Little wonder, then, that political fundraising is often equated with 'prostitution and extortion' (Steen 1999: 160). The interrelated role of marketing, campaigning and money sparks ethical alarm among academics and journalists who worry about potentially nefarious implications for democracy (O'Shaughnessy 1990, 2002; Smith and Bakvis 2000; Wilcox 2008). This chapter considers the ethics of marketing strategy and tactics in political fundraising.

It can be unclear what constitutes a legitimate concern about fundraising marketing. To discuss this we must first unpack a number of these terms, beginning with ethics, before we can apply theoretical principles of marketing to the recent practice of political fundraising.

Humans consider various norms, particularly legal and moral standards within a given society, to assess their own and others' behaviour, including that of professional organizations (Audi 2010; Brenkert 2008; Duska 2007; Murphy *et al.* 2005; O'Shaughnessy 2002; Rosen 2005; Stoker 1992; Wueste 1994). There is no one set of norms, nor an agreed upon morality, and thus there is variation in the judgement of the degree of acceptability of ethical, legal and social behaviours. Ethics, then, involves a philosophical and cultural interpretation of these standards to differentiate between good and bad behaviour. At times, this can be straightforward and normative, as in the case of laws or a written code. Even so, ethics can be controversial and subjective, invoking one's personal standards of right and wrong. As a result, as O'Shaughnessy (2002: 1092–93) has concluded, 'no ethical debate is ever final' since there are no answers, just critiques, and therefore there is 'no final resting place for the ethical debates on political marketing'. Since all answers to ethical questions are subjective and necessarily biased, we are faced with developing objective questions to help individuals self-adjudicate the ethics of political marketing applications. In other words, assessing the ethics of utilizing marketing in political fundraising typically involves little more than culture-specific educated guesses.

In theory, political actors ought to act on behalf of the collective interests that they represent, and therefore be of virtuous character. In practice, however, often their self-interests prevail; this is the egoism that is also found in the sphere of business marketing. Moreover, as any fan of Machiavelli will attest, for political actors the conundrum of so-called 'dirty hands' emerges whereby morally unpalatable actions are carried out in an effort to achieve a greater moral good (Wueste 1994). Ethical theories such as utilitarianism are used to sort out such 'damned if you do and damned if you don't' dilemmas (Duska 2007: 20; also Audi 2010; Murphy *et al.* 2005; Rosen 2005). Any such discussion of political ethics, or of fundraising or marketing for that matter, can thus pit idealists against realists (Audi 2010; Duska 2007; Singer 2007; Stoker 1992).

Previous research on fundraising

There is no standard model of ethics to test against cases of using political marketing for fundraising purposes. Fundraisers worldwide might simply observe the universal fundraising principles of empathy, honesty, integrity, respect and transparency (European Fundraising Association 2006). However, there are ethics questions in the marketing literature (such as Audi 2010; Brenkert 2008; Murphy *et al.* 2005) from which we can identify questions for elements of the marketing mix that can be used by a fundraising organization to develop a code of ethics and a decision-making framework.

In theory ethical fundraising is likely to build trustworthiness which should lead to future donations; the opposite is also true (Rosen 2005). In politics, fundraising regulations are intended to uphold democratic ideals by aiming to reduce political corruption, by promoting electoral competition, by upholding freedom of speech and by preventing collusion (Smith and Bakvis 2000). The primary concern about marketing is that it involves manipulation and persuasion, particularly through the communication of falsehoods (Brenkert 2008; Kelly 1991; O'Shaughnessy 2002; Sheth and Sisodia 2006). Marketers are thought to exploit market intelligence for their own purposes rather than for those of consumers. This risks taking advantage of the most vulnerable in society and ranges from pushing the boundaries of good taste to criminal acts.

According to Kelly (1991: 157–60), the theoretical ideal of political marketing in fundraising is unattainable: organizational change is unlikely to result in response to donors' preferences. Too often financial calculations, rather than positive donor relations, are used to measure fundraising success and, as a two-way exchange relationship, political donors seek gains in return for their gifts whether they do so in their own interests or whether they seek benefits for the public good. There is thus an expectation for political actors to deliver on their pledges which, as the dirty hands dilemma indicates, is frequently impossible given that politics occurs in an environment of daily policy tradeoffs. Moreover, ethical issues for marketing research include data collection that violates privacy, that lacks informed consent, or which involves the covert gathering of competitive intelligence (Brenkert 2008; Murphy *et al.* 2005). Given such a wide scope of behaviours we must analyse the ethics of political marketing on a case-by-case basis and resist the temptation to dismiss the entire genre (O'Shaughnessy 2002; also O'Cass 2009: 190).

There are even ethical dilemmas involved with marketing and marketing communications' use of audience segmentation. This grouping of like-minded electors through geodemography, behavioural data and/or psychography is used to support product differentiation and to identify promotional efficiencies (Baines *et al.* 2003), but the resulting favouritism of select audiences can entail an ethical condition such as exclusionary segmentation (Brenkert 2008: 83–87). Thinking of this from a political fundraising perspective, on the grounds of social desirability a marketer might opt to ignore citizens whose statistical profile indicates that they are likely to want to donate, such as a conservative candidate who wants to avoid receiving funds from church-goers for fear of being labelled beholden to the Christian right.

Segmentation also inevitably results in the practice of beneficial targeting. This is described by Brenkert (2008: 84) as marketers treating members of the most desirable segments better than the members of other segments. The most salient prospective donors may receive additional information, often through direct marketing, which is of benefit to the recipient if the information is wanted, but which presents an ethical harm if privacy is violated. Note that this is different to the practice of benefit segmentation, whereby electors are segmented along the benefits they seek or stand to receive, which speaks to the opportunity for fundraising marketers to hone in on the personal values of potential donors (Baines *et al.* 2003; Steen 1999). Ethical concerns emerge here if cognitive and emotional levers are employed to motivate donations. Murphy *et al.* (2005) have signalled that the resulting target marketing is unethical chiefly if it focuses on vulnerable populations, such as people who fear for their physical safety, those who lack the ability to understand information, those who cannot resist enticements and people who face significant pressure to conform. Often this involves people at either end of the age spectrum, but also those occupying the less favourable end of the socio-economic spectrum who may be ignorant of the marketplace, such as some recent immigrants.

A communications element of political marketing is the marketing mix. Successful political fundraising involves 'repetition, reinforcement, and relentlessness' (Steen 1999: 171). To that end the marketing mix comprises a strategic combination of marketing communications methods and tactics such that messages are reinforced via different media to which the target audience is likely to be favourably exposed. Components that have particular relevance to fundraising are advertising, direct marketing, endorsements, the internet, media relations, personal sales and pricing. These are briefly described below.

Advertising

There is a plethora of ethical criticisms of advertising, ranging from broad social harms to case-specific deceptive advertising (Murphy *et al.* 2005). Typically only cost-efficient targeting such as online banner advertisements are viable for fundraising purposes, but given the potential harms of advertising, it is incumbent upon fundraisers to inform donors about the campaign advertising that their money will support, particularly if it is of the negative or attack variety.

Direct marketing

At the core of most fundraising campaigns are direct mail and telemarketing, potentially as part of a relationship marketing campaign that conveys feelings of group membership (O'Shaughnessy 1990; Schnur 1999; also Graves 1997). For instance, fundraisers customize appeal letters and develop postcards with stimulating imagery designed to generate a response from market segments of prospective donors, a technique that has been most successful for ideologues who promote fear, particularly conservatives (D'Aprile 2010; Wilcox 2008). Technological innovations mean that direct marketing is quickly evolving, however, such as email being sent to mobile smart phones, or fundraising appeals issued via social networking websites ('socnets') such as Facebook and LinkedIn. This is adding to concerns about the profit margins of conventional direct mail given the high costs (e.g. creative fees, list rental, postage, printing, prospecting), the battles with fundraising consultants over who owns a list and the post-campaign solicitation of funds to reduce debts (D'Aprile 2010).

Endorsements

Political marketers may encourage opinion leaders such as celebrities as well as regular folk to publicly endorse a political party or candidate. This attention-grabbing practice transfers the endorser's positive attributes to the sponsor's image and provides assurances of trustworthiness to audiences (Meenaghan 2001; Veer *et al.* 2010). For example, a high-profile politician might record a supportive voice message which is distributed by auto-diallers, or a Hollywood celebrity might issue an online video appeal for donations. A more personal approach is to engage prominent political supporters at special events, such as at breakfast and barbeque fundraisers (Steen 1999).

The internet

Online fundraising has exponentially increased the quantity of donors and funds, even among second-tier candidates (Wilcox 2008). The use of information and communication technologies (ICTs) in fundraising is cheaper, more efficient and more inclusive than telemarketing or direct mail, reaching a donor pool of citizens who are younger, less affluent and who hold more moderate world views. Moreover, a range of messages can be circulated by text, still images, audio and/or video, conveying feelings of being part of an interactive online community, something that Wilcox (2008: 14) refers to as a 'virtual solidary benefit'. However, the self-regulated nature, low cost and global reach of the internet means that there are a plethora of ethical considerations, including online privacy protections, excessive solicitation, reduced control over who is asked and the potential for fraud.

Media relations

An inexpensive and credible way to appeal for political donations is to attract coverage in mainstream news media and on political blogs (Schnur 1999). Generating such earned media can, for example, entail issuing press releases that inform news editors of staged publicity events such as a candidate speech or a fundraising gala.

Personal sales

Many potential donors, particularly those donating large amounts, respond well to a 'retail approach' of personal solicitations (Steen 1999: 170), such as receiving a phone call from the candidate, socializing with members of a finance committee, or being persuaded by the politically connected 'bundlers' who collect many donations. Prospective donors might receive an exclusive invitation to pay a sizeable fee to attend a special event, such as a dinner at a supporter's home, where the candidate makes a public appearance. Photographs of the candidate with the donor may be purchased and then be shared with other potential donors, such as over socnets, turning the donor into an endorser.

Pricing

How much to ask a supporter to donate is carefully researched. Specific dollar amounts are proposed because vague requests are less successful and for the same reason the amount requested tends to be higher rather than lower (Steen 1999). Major donors will want personal interaction with the candidate and may ask questions about why the money is needed. Other donors may need to be encouraged that even tiny amounts are wanted.

From this review of the literature, a new theory – principles of ethical marketing fundraising – can be created which can then be tested empirically.

New research: a new framework of ethical marketing fundraising and its application to Barack Obama's fundraising

Drawing on the understanding from literature, a new theoretical framework of ethical marketing fundraising has been created, which is detailed in Table 13.1.

These ethical theories and core principles can be applied to a modern model of fundraising marketing employed by the Barack Obama campaign team. When Obama declared his presidential candidacy in February 2007 his party nomination campaign faced a significant financial challenge given that Hillary Clinton had the backing of many of the Democratic Party's major donors. Moreover, while US election spending is notoriously under-regulated as a matter of free speech, fundraising regulations are reasonably strict: in the 2008 election cycle Americans were allowed to give a maximum of $4,600 ($2,300 during the primaries, $2,300 for the general election) to a presidential candidate (Corrado and Corbett 2009). So, while the 'splashy social events' such as the fundraising dinners described by Wilcox (2008: 4) continued to be a vehicle for large contributions, particularly from white males who were older, educated, white collar and affluent, these donor limits necessitated an emphasis on fundraising small amounts from a large quantity of individuals.

While the political fundraising undertaken by the Obama presidential campaign was innovative and made strong use of the marketing mix it did so in a manner that prioritized the organization's needs over the interests of donors (i.e. it did not uphold the highest ethical standards). Its fundraising objective was to provide supporters with marketing tools to become mini-bundlers (Burch 2009; Corrado and Corbett 2009; Green 2008; Smith and Bratt 2009; Wilcox 2008). In other words, it was insufficient to donate funds: the Obama team wanted volunteers to become brand advocates and, using ICTs, to donate their labour independently to raise even more money from their peers. To accomplish this, feelings of an insider status needed to be conveyed, citizens needed to be empowered, and donation 'asks' would have to be balanced with social participation invitations. This was not so much a commitment to deliver donor value as it was an effort to exploit supporters' positive feelings about Barack Obama.

Software experts and amateurs offered up their ideas and services for developing and promoting My.BarackObama.com, a website that was very user-friendly. The site's URL address and an online donate button, with its simplified donation checkout, was promoted in various elements of the marketing mix: in online advertising including interactive display advertisements, search engine advertisements via paid keywords, positioning in blogs and links from YouTube videos; in direct mail and emails; in speeches by celebrities such as Oprah Winfrey; and in mainstream news media coverage (micro-blogging, such as via Twitter, was still in its infancy in the 2008 campaign). An e-communications campaign was initiated that conveyed immediacy, intimacy and preferred customer status, especially to mobile phone users as part of a 'mobile marketing' programme (Smith and Bratt 2009). The traditional list of potential donors used in direct marketing was regularly updated with email, cellphone, text messaging and social networking contact information, as well as zip codes to aid in segmentation. Such personal data were provided by online donors, by attendees at political events and by people who purchased or entered contests to win campaign merchandise; it is unclear to what extent standards of informed consent were observed. List members were segmented into groups who regularly received tailored e-messages, such as breaking campaign news, customized repeat

Table 13.1 Core principles of ethical marketing fundraising

1 Donors do not feel pressured
Donors can easily opt out of verbal agreements and out of receiving further requests
Inbound calls to the campaign office do not result in sales pressure tactics
Telemarketing does not unduly interrupt potential donors; people are not over-solicited
The amount solicited does not take advantage of a donor's financial situation; justification is given for asking for larger amounts from wealthier or more motivated donors
The sales pitch is not overly familiar, flattering or aggressive; fundraisers do not suggest that a trustworthy personal relationship really exists
2 Donors give their informed consent
Donors are aware of how their funds will be used
Intrusive methods such as email spam are avoided
Privacy principles are upheld; only relevant personal information is solicited and kept on file; databases of donor information and giving history are secure; if donor information is shared with others, the donor's consent is obtained first
Web tracking cookies are not used as spyware
3 Fundraising communications are truthful
Communications claims are based on evidence and embellishment is justifiable; information is shared with journalists even if it is sometimes negative; attempts at spin control are reasonable
Fundraisers answer questions honestly and provide relevant information
Only authorized invoices are issued; envelopes do not look like they contain official government information
The candidate or party is not misrepresented; testimonials are not taken out of context
4 Fundraising research follows high industry standards
Offers by an opponent's former employee to provide competitive intelligence are refused
Opponents' fundraising practices are not monitored under unscrupulous conditions
Research is objective and necessary; segmentation is not discriminatory
Telemarketers do not pose as researchers
5 No harm results from political fundraising
Cognitive and/or emotional appeals do not exceed accepted norms
Endorsements are not given under duress
Offensive remarks and negative social impacts are avoided; disturbing images are not used
Online transactions are secure
Publicity tactics are within the boundaries of good taste
Vulnerable groups are not contacted and are protected
6 There is a commitment to deliver donor value
Fundraisers are well-trained to observe ethical principles
Fundraisers do not receive commission that might spur sales pressure tactics; if a fundraising firm or endorser is paid, this is disclosed
Fundraising expenses are monitored and reported; the firm that processes donations is not affiliated with the fundraising firm
If inducements are offered, such as a gift, the retail value is identified; lower-quality products are not sold for fundraising; policy promises are not unreasonably made as an inducement
There is significant concern for the donor's interests

solicitations including requests for pledges of as little as $5, and encouragement to match the donation of a peer. Donors could 'subscribe' to a pledge programme of making regular small e-donations until they reached the annual limit and could direct friends to monitor their fundraising progress on socnets.

What did the online platform look like? The personalized experience for members of the 'Organizing for America' campaign, including 'Obama '08' graphics, continued to be used two years later in the 2010 congressional elections. Supporters who created their own fundraising page were encouraged to upload a personal photo, to write a testimonial and to identify a financial goal ($1,000 was the suggested amount). A graphic of a thermometer displayed their progress towards their stated financial objective. Each supporter was encouraged to enter friends' email addresses, up to 20 at a time, so that they could receive the following message:

> President Obama and I are committed to changing the political process by growing an organization founded on a broad base of support from ordinary Americans. This organization is about putting the people's interests ahead of the special interests, but to do that, Barack needs help from people like you and me. I've set my own personal fundraising goal for the organization, which you can see in the thermometer to the right. Will you click the thermometer to make a donation and help me reach my goal?
>
> *(Organizing for America 2010)*

Some suggestion could be made that this technique knowingly exerted social pressure on peers to donate, that commitments to deliver donor value were not expressly communicated, and that the Obama campaign may have developed an email database of supporters' friends without their consent; however, fundraising communications were truthful and no significant harms resulted. The benefits of fundraising and donating were both psychological and material, generating an emotional 'fun' connection (Green 2008) that created 'an online fundraising psychology that empowered' donors (Corrado and Corbett 2009: 138). The social benefits of insider status included receiving campaign updates, downloadable 'yes we can' ringtones and news widgets; obtaining more socnet friends and the phone numbers of potential supporters; and showing off donation status and items purchased in the Obama online store. Psychological motivations included the campaign creating a sense of urgency, insider involvement and personal responsibility, through statements such as, 'Your own personal fundraising page will put the financial future of this organization in your hands. You set your own goal, you do the outreach, and you get credit for the results' (Organizing for America 2010). Material inducements included virtual gifts, such as e-wallpaper, and qualifying to win paraphernalia such as Obama t-shirts and calendars, backstage passes at campaign events and, later, a flight to Chicago for election night celebrations. Such incentives continued to be extended post-election, with donation inducements ranging from Obama coffee mugs in exchange for a $15 donation, to a chance to win one of 10 tickets to the Presidential Inauguration. These sorts of enticements may be considered fair game: whilst a mug may cost the organization less than a dollar its retail value might be $10 and some might believe that an insider trip to Obama's historical Inauguration would be priceless, though contest entries should not necessarily be dependent on donating.

We can assess the ethics of the Obama campaign's fundraising by applying the theoretical framework of ethical marketing fundraising. In all areas we can see that the campaign behaved in an ethical manner in that no harm appears to have resulted, though it could have done better: the campaign office used ICTs to exert peer pressure on donors; standards of informed consent were wanting; and inducements may have capitalized on some supporters' heightened emotional state. This application also demonstrates that the model needs to be tested using original data such as elite interviews because much fundraising information requires insider knowledge, such as evaluating the protection of donor databases, identifying whether vulnerable groups are contacted, or establishing the appropriateness of expenses.

Table 13.2 Factoids about Obama campaign fundraising (21-month total, as of election day 2008)

Money raised (total)	over $600 million
Money raised online	over $500 million
Money raised through online advertising	$20 million (est.)
Number of email addresses in campaign database	13 million
Number of individual donors	over 3.95 million
Number of online donors	3 million (est.)
Number of online donations	6.5 million (est.)
Value of average online donation	$80
Percentage of online donations in increments of $100 or less	92%

Source: Smith and Bratt (2009); Vargas (2008). Information about the money raised by all campaigns in 2008 can be found elsewhere, such as Corrado and Corbett (2009) and Green (2008).

Advice for practitioners

Conceptually speaking, the use of ICTs, particularly social networking sites, should be one of the most successful tactics for political fundraising. This is due to more than just time, labour and cost efficiencies, which are compelling advantages in their own right. Writing before the era of socnets, Steen (1999: 167) remarked that fundraising is best when it entails 'an army of volunteers or members of the community who solicit contributions', which is exactly what the Obama team demonstrated in their use of ICTs. For brand advocates to become mini-bundlers, a campaign not only needs to provide internet-savvy volunteers with software tools, but with a sustained psychological motivation that leads them to respond favourably to 'asks' related to campaign objectives. As with all two-way fundraising, this can be achieved by offering ideological, material and/or social benefits, which the Obama '08 campaign did for many electors by capitalizing on the campaign's competitive advantages, not the least of which was the candidacy of an historic political figure who motivated an army of followers.

Online fundraising has quickly become preferred over conventional methods because it is a single technique that leverages many of the positive features of direct marketing, endorsements, personal sales and pricing. Using ICTs, the administrative costs of fundraising can be directed foremost to market research to inform target marketing decisions and advertising to reinforce donation messages. This must complement, and not replace, traditional fundraising methods which may reach other audiences such as non-users of ICTs or socnets and the big donors who expect personal attention. The institutionalization of online activities among direct mail, telemarketing and public appearances by the candidate will be important as the competition for, and complexity of, e-donations grows.

The overarching comparative implication for political marketers outside of the US is that they must customize American fundraising techniques to their own markets, including local campaign regulations, cultural norms and donor capacity. For instance, in the UK civic volunteerism and political donations are lower than in the US, and the financial regulatory framework provides fewer incentives for political parties to fundraise (Anstead 2008). The crafting of a written fundraising appeal involves style differences even in the Canadian market, where compared with its southern neighbour there are variations in cultural meanings and power distance, appeals to vanity or patriotism *versus* economics, as well as regional and language considerations (Graves 1997). In authoritarian and totalitarian regimes, as well as in developing economies, the use of ICTs for fundraising may be inappropriate and/or impossible. Moreover, domestic fundraising opportunities may be quite limited, except in more developed areas of the country, and the closeness of a philanthropic organization's relationship with the state must be considered. In Latin America, for example, civil society organizations can be so cash-strapped that they often serve an institutionalized public policy function, and people may donate to charities because of perceptions of government inefficiency, corruption or regression (Bailey 1999). Brenkert (2008: 184) has remarked on the ethical relativism of customs, morals and rules in other societies, such as the tolerance of bribery and gift-giving. This reinforces the point made at the outset of this chapter that there is considerable variation in what constitutes acceptable ethical, legal and social behaviours in political fundraising and marketing, though presumably political marketers should strive to uphold common ideals in all markets.

The impact on politics

O'Shaughnessy (1990) has long warned of the democratic harms of political marketing on democracy: public apathy, demise of community, political fragmentation, superiority of minority interests over the majority, the growth of false issues, etc. This may be briefly tempered by the era of e-democracy, wherein citizens are encouraged to engage in online political debate, are consulted by government elites and are urged by their peers to participate in elections. Using internet marketing for fundraising purposes results in a democracy that is more egalitarian than one that prioritizes backroom personal deals and where donating is concentrated among the rich. The overall effect of the Obama campaign's ICT strategy was to reduce the effort necessary for supporters' political participation and which thus increased civic engagement (Burch 2009). Optimists may then point to how marketing is growing closer to democratic ideals than the politics of days gone by.

Realists, however, will suggest that elites will eventually control any new grassroots technology, as illustrated already by the contrast in quality of the websites of well-financed campaigns as compared with those of underfinanced upstarts. The most significant legal problem appears to be policing internet fraud. Approximately 1 percent of donations in Obama's campaign were scrutinized as being received from donors using fake names and from non-US citizens, a concern related to outdated election rules that did not require the collection of the names and addresses of people giving less than $200 (Mosk 2008). As well, the problem of perpetual fundraising may contribute to donor fatigue and a diminished interest in civic engagement. Donors in 2008 continued to be solicited well after Obama had taken office, to the point that emails could be perceived as spam and requests for money as insensitive to citizens' financial situations in a troubled US economy. It is even worse when such messages are reinforced in the news media which reports on the latest party fundraising gala event. As president, Obama has engaged in dozens of fundraising events that coincide with official presidential trips, and the prices for special event tickets, such as dinner at a museum or a reception at the mansion of singer Gloria Estefan, have reached as high as $34,200 and the price of a photo with the president has been a reported $10,000 (Weisman 2010).

To this end we can apply some of the dualist perspectives of business ethics (Singer 2007; also Stoker 1992) to political fundraising. From an idealist's perspective, fundraising practices should be mindful of the societal implications, and should uphold moral standards that are consistent with the sponsor's ideals. Group rights should be upheld and, when faced with barriers, institutional changes should be pursued for the benefit of all. Financial efficiency is thus less important than is a social choice perspective of following ethical practices that exceed established norms. This long-term promotion of community through distributive justice and care-based ethics is more likely to be championed by left-wing political actors (i.e., liberal and social democrats, socialists) and presumably by most fundraising charities.

Conversely, a realist will point to the need for political fundraising to deliver maximum profits so as to fund the war chest needed to run a credible campaign. The most rational behaviour is thus the one that delivers, within acceptable norms and laws, the best return on investment in a competitive marketplace. This pursuit may involve unconventional proprietary practices resulting in a competitive advantage that inflicts damage on the political system. Capitalist selfishness and ruthless strategizing prevails over collectivism and altruism. This sort of short-term approach to the concentration of resource advantage and freedom from government restraint tends to be the domain of the political right (i.e., conservatives, libertarians).

The dualist perspectives of idealism *versus* relativism mirror contrasts between the marketing concept (TMC) and its more paternalistic counterpart, the social marketing concept (SMC) (Brenkert 2008). Looking at fundraising from TMC and SMC perspectives, a marketer who solicits funds should prioritize donor satisfaction while avoiding perceptions of political corruption as a means towards securing profitability, and efforts to ensure this satisfaction should be promoted throughout the organization. In seeking to satisfy donors' wants and desires, a TMC fundraiser does not make any ethical judgement about the broader societal implications of the fulfilment of those desires: that is the donor's prerogative, within the boundaries of the law, though even an amoral marketer may need to inform and motivate prospective and existing donors. An SMC fundraiser, however, is concerned with the societal implications of meeting a donor's wants and desires. The broader moral implications for the community at large are pitted against the profit motive. Thus lucrative fundraising opportunities might be turned down because of the marketer's concern for social values.

Raising money provides a political organization with some autonomy to pursue its objectives and with flexibility to respond to emerging situations, but a challenge for political marketers is that the unethical behaviours of others sour the political marketplace and thus have a negative impact on politics. Marketing fits nicely with fundraising because the solicitor is often concerned about the donor's interests, and there is thus a mutual satisfaction of wants and needs. In politics TMC and SMC encourages a 'constructive dialogue' between parties and electors towards achieving shared economic and social objectives (O'Cass 2009: 198). However, Sheth and Sisodia (2006) have cautioned that marketing is losing effectiveness amidst a consumer marketplace that is as dissatisfied, disloyal and alienated as the elector marketplace, which is partly a consequence of the unscrupulous marketing that takes advantage of customers and which harms society.

The way forward

Having identified ethical questions and issues for political marketers involved with political fundraising, we can consider these in the context of the Obama fundraising machine, and identify a framework of best practices applicable to other case studies. We can see that the stakes are high in an election, especially a race to become president of the US, and so the act of raising money may matter more than the ethics of how it is raised. The tactics used in the 2007–08 period, and repeated in 2010, were innovative and highly successful, but they still involved egoism, a plethora of policy proposals, peer pressure, persuasion and inducements. This was followed by over-solicitation that may have bordered on intrusion. In short, concerns for collecting money superseded the donors' interests, under a collective philosophy that presumed agreement that the election of Barack Obama was for the greater public good.

The two-way approach employed by the Obama Democrats whilst they were governing is a more exemplary model for political marketers. In 2009 the Democratic Party organized a contest to receive citizen-generated 30-second videos supporting health insurance policy reform. These were uploaded to YouTube and 20 finalists' videos were available for public and expert voting. With the congressional vote on the controversial legislation looming, visitors to BarackObama.com were shown videos that had not yet been broadcast in mainstream media, and were encouraged to donate so that the winning video could be aired to a television audience:

> Help put the final ad on the air. In the next few days, we'll be using the winning video as the basis for a new television ad that will air across the country – and you can help, by ensuring we have the resources to make the biggest impact. With only weeks to go before the final vote on health insurance reform, we need to make sure Congress hears this grassroots message. Can you help get this message out, just when it's most critical? Please donate today, using the form on the right.
>
> *(Organizing for America 2009)*

This tactic is the way forward for ethical practitioners, researchers and for trainers: a rational method to achieve idealist fundraising that exemplifies the SMC approach without sacrificing the competitive or financial priorities of a TMC marketer. It is a fantastic blend of organizational responsiveness and use of the marketing mix, democratizing the fundraising process while generally observing the aforementioned universal fundraising principles. Donors were reasonably informed what their donations would be used to finance. Positive civic engagement inducements included a chance to become the author of profiled advertisements and an offer to participate in the selection of the televised advertisement. Certainly data collection privacy concerns may persist, there are audience limitations insofar as access to ICTs is concerned, and perhaps fear was used to motivate donations from the disadvantaged. However, such an appeal to fund a clear policy objective is democratic, addresses the dirty hands dilemma and reduces many vexations about audience segmentation. As a publicly available practice it encourages competitors to monitor its success and to follow this as the way forward.

The material presented in this chapter can inform a broad framework of best practices for other case studies (Table 13.3). Political marketers should collect and analyse research about the general public, develop policies that are important to key segments, and openly ask for money to support the promotion of specific policy proposals that funding can help lead to their implementation. This should be performed in a transparent manner that provides audiences with policy details while disclosing trade-offs, with information about the promotional tactics that their funding will support, while engaging and empowering them in the collection of funds and creation of promotional materials. By bearing in mind the fine line between good and questionable practices, fundraisers may be more prone to not only practise non-intrusive and transparent tactics, but to also hold to account those who employ deceptive and/or intrusive methods.

In theory, generally, if selectively, following the core principles of ethical marketing fundraising (donors do not feel pressured; donors give their informed consent; fundraising communications are truthful; fundraising research follows high industry standards; no harm results from political fundraising; and there is a commitment to deliver donor value) and embracing good practices that are non-intrusive and transparent should help raise more money. A balance of idealism and relativism is needed, however, for in politics practising good ethics does not necessarily equate to success. Based on the information presented in this chapter, though, especially the 2009 health reform case, it would seem that campaigns do stand to benefit from employing innovative methods while observing higher ethical standards.

Table 13.3 Framework for best practices when using marketing in political fundraising

Questionable practices: non-intrusive, but deceptive	*Good practices: non-intrusive and transparent*
Data mining	Clear, achievable policy promises made
Excessively friendly requests	Donors choose/informed how money spent
False impressions of insider status	Donors voluntarily connect with each other
Hyperbole in press releases	Easy to opt out of pledges
Low odds of winning an inducement	Factual websites with objective information
Media spin	Information shared with inquiring journalists
Poor quality products for sale	Monitoring of fundraising progress
Wealthy citizens given special access	User-requested mobile marketing
Bad practices: deceptive and intrusive	*Questionable practices: transparent, but intrusive*
Aggressive sales pitches	Actions justified as for the greater good
Donor information shared without consent	Appeals to vulnerable populations
Embellished advertising	Images of sex or violence
Endorsements given under pressure	Inducements offered
False sense of urgency/responsibility	Opinion research
Fundraisers hide commission earnings	Oversolicitation/spam
Hiring of opponents' staff	Peer solicitation
Preying on people's emotions	Pop-up online advertising
Pushy telemarketing	Positioning in blogs and online videos
Unauthorized invoices	Truthful advertising

Bibliography

Anstead, N. (2008) 'The Internet and campaign finance in the U.S. and the UK: an institutional comparison', *Journal of Information Technology and Politics* 5: 285–302.

Audi, R. (2010) 'The place of ethical theory in business ethics', in G.G. Brenkert and T.L. Beauchamp (eds) *The Oxford Handbook of Business Ethics*, New York: Oxford University Press.

Bailey, M. (1999) 'Fundraising in Brazil: the major implications for civil society organisations and international NGOs', *Development in Practice* 9: 103–16.

Baines, P.R., Worcester, R.M., Jarrett, D. and Mortimore, R. (2003) 'Market segmentation and product differentiation in political campaigns: a technical feature perspective', *Journal of Marketing Management* 19: 225–49.

Brenkert, G.G. (2008) *Marketing Ethics*, Malden, MA: Blackwell Publishing.

Burch, T. (2009) 'Can the new commander in chief sustain his all-volunteer standing army?' *Du Bois Review* 6: 153–71.

Corrado, A. and Corbett, M. (2009) 'Rewriting the playbook on presidential campaign financing', in D.W. Johnson (ed.) *Campaigning for President 2008*, New York: Routledge.

D'Aprile, S. (2010) 'The staggering price of money', *Politics* May: 28–33.

Duska, R. (2007) *Contemporary Reflections on Business Ethics*, Dordrecht: Springer.

European Fundraising Association (2006) *International Statement of Ethical Principles in Fundraising*. Online, efa-net.bosh.me/wp-content/uploads/2010/03/International_Statement_of_Ethical_Principles_in_Fundraising_16_October_2006.pdf (accessed 15 August 2010).

Graves, R. (1997) '" Dear friend" (?): culture and genre in American and Canadian direct mail letters', *Journal of Business Communication* 34: 235–52.

Green, J. (2008) 'The amazing money machine', *The Atlantic*, June. Online, www.theatlantic.com/magazine/archive/2008/06/the-amazing-money-machine/6809 (accessed 12 August 2010).

Kelly, K.S. (1991) *Fund Raising and Public Relations: A Critical Analysis*, Hillsdale, NJ: Lawrence Erlbaum Associates.

Meenaghan, T. (2001) 'Understanding sponsorship effects', *Psychology and Marketing* 18: 95–122.

Mosk, M. (2008) 'Campaign finance gets new scrutiny', *Washington Post*, 26 October. Online, www.washingtonpost.com/wp-dyn/content/article/2008/10/25/AR2008102502302.html (accessed 20 September 2010).

Murphy, P.E., Lackniak, G.R., Bowie, N.E. and Klein, T.A. (2005) *Ethical Marketing*, Upper Saddle River, NJ: Pearson Prentice Hall.

O'Cass, A. (2009) 'A resource-based view of the political party and value creation for the voter-citizen: an integrated framework for political marketing', *Marketing Theory* 9: 189–208.

Organizing for America (2009) 'Contribute'. Online, donate.barackobama.com/page/contribute/dnc08viddonatends?source=FB (accessed 20 November 2009).

—— (2010). 'Personal Fundraising'. Online, donate.barackobama.com/page/outreach/login/main (accessed 29 October 2010).

O'Shaughnessy, N. (1990) *The Phenomenon of Political Marketing*, New York: St Martin's Press.

—— (2002) 'Toward an ethical framework for political marketing', *Psychology & Marketing* 19: 1079–94.

Rosen, M.J. (2005) 'Doing well by doing right: a fundraiser's guide to ethical decision-making', *International Journal of Nonprofit and Voluntary Sector Marketing* 10: 175–81.

Schnur, D. (1999) 'Greater than the sum of its parts: coordinating the paid and earned media message', in B.I. Newman (ed.) *Handbook of Political Marketing*, Thousand Oaks, CA: Sage Publications.

Sheth, J.N. and Sisodia, R.S. (2006) 'Introduction', in J.N. Sheth and R.S. Sisodia (eds) *Does Marketing Need Reform? Fresh Perspectives on the Future*, Armonk, NY: M.E. Sharpe.

Singer, A.E. (2007) 'Introduction', in A.E. Singer (ed.) *Business Ethics and Strategy, Volume I*, Aldershot, Hampshire: Ashgate Publishing.

Smith, J. and Bakvis, H. (2000) 'Changing dynamics in election campaign finance: critical issues in Canada and the United States', Institute for Research on Public Policy. *Policy Matters* 1: 1–40.

Smith, K. and Bratt, E. (2009) 'The Obama playbook: how digital marketing and social media won the election', MarketingProfs. Online, www.marketingprofs.com/store/product/20/the-obama-playbook-how-digital-marketing-and-social-media-won-the-election (accessed 20 September 2010).

Steen, J.A. (1999) 'Money doesn't grow on trees: fund-raising in American political campaigns', in B.I. Newman (ed.) *Handbook of Political Marketing*, Thousand Oaks, CA: Sage Publications.

Stoker, L. (1992) 'Interests and ethics in politics', *The American Political Science Review* 86: 369–80.

Vargas, J.A. (2008) 'Obama raised half a billion online', *Washington Post*, 20 November. Online, voices.washingtonpost.com/44/2008/11/obama-raised-half-a-billion-on.html (accessed 4 September 2010).

Veer, E., Becirovic, I. and Martin, B.A.S. (2010) 'If Kate voted Conservative, would you? The role of celebrity endorsements in political party advertising', *European Journal of Marketing* 44: 436–50.

Weisman, J. (2010) 'Obama revs up fund-raising machine', *The Wall Street Journal*, 15 April. Online, online.wsj.com/article/SB10001424052702304159304575184432834891108.html (accessed 6 September 2010).

Wilcox, C. (2008) 'Internet fundraising in 2008: a new model?' *The Forum* 6, 1: Article 6. Online, www.bepress.com/forum/vol6/iss1/art6 (accessed 20 July 2010).

Wueste, D.E. (1994) 'Introduction', in D.E. Wueste (ed.) *Professional Ethics and Social Responsibility*, Lanham, MD: Rowman and Littlefield.

14

Political parties and direct marketing

Connecting voters and candidates more effectively

Peter N. Ubertaccio

The topic: parties and direct marketing

At the end of the 20th century political parties worldwide followed a trend towards the centralization of campaigning. In the US, for example, political parties centralized certain fundraising and marketing efforts in their Washington, DC arms – the two national committees and their counterparts for House and Senate candidates – even as the local organizations that once served to connect citizens to government became less important to voters and to nominations. At the same time, political campaigning used the more sophisticated tools of political marketing, particularly direct marketing. Direct marketing, a pioneering tactic of international companies such as Amway and Tupperware, micro-targeting and social networking replaced the tactics of the old party system and, when aggressively used in political campaigns, hold out the promise for a return to locally active organizations. In the US, they were first seen in the Republican congressional campaign of 2002 and the Bush re-election campaign of 2004, which demonstrated that highly effective micro-targeting of voters combined with direct marketing strategies could find more and turn out a greater number of partisan voters. The same principals of direct marketing were also used by Vermont governor Howard Dean during the 2004 Democratic primaries, and then to form the social media strategy of the Obama for President campaign.

Nevertheless, despite the way that the Obama campaign was said to mobilize grassroots campaigning, as a new round of campaigns for Congress and president get underway in advance of the 2012 national elections, the US party system remains largely candidate-centered, with fundraising and messaging centralized in Washington. This chapter will both discuss the nature of direct marketing and its use by parties so far, as well as debating its potential to reconnect voters to local party organizations and campaigns, making the conversations among citizens and between them and candidates much more vibrant.

Previous research on party decline and direct marketing

Political marketing research has commented on the centralizing effect of marketing (Lees 2005) and the potential downgrading of party members (Lilleker 2005; Pettitt 2009), as well as the transformation of party organization (Newman 1994). Lilleker (2005) argued that the UK's New Labour lost volunteers because its promises became more oriented 'towards the middle-class swingers, rejecting working-class based politics' (Lilleker 2005: 573). Political marketing can change internal power: as strategists together with the leadership determine policy direction in relation to market intelligence, this 'can leave ordinary members feeling alienated' (ibid.) if they see no response to their demands within that product development process. In the UK Labour case, Lilleker (2005) found that members felt that there had been a lack of consultation and they had been disenfranchised. In other sub-fields of political science, such as parties, there is an extensive literature on the decline of the US party system. Indeed, parties have always found their centralizing thrust to be difficult in the US system of separation of powers, federalism, and checks and balances, all part of what historian Richard Hofstadter called the 'Constitution-Against-Parties' (Hofstadter 1969). From the zenith of their power and influence in US politics in the late 19th century, parties as organizations have been in relative decline, having lost control of the ability to bestow party nominations and commanding allegiance among fewer and fewer voters. Progressive and New Deal era reforms undercut party solidarity and weakened party organizations as the US executive became the centralizing feature of US politics whereas parties in the early 2000s are in a 'late state of a century-long decline' (Shafer 2003). 'As the presidency evolved into a ubiquitous institution', noted Sidney Milkis, 'it preempted party leaders in many of their limited but significant tasks: linking the president to interest groups, staffing the executive department, policy development, and … campaign support' (Milkis 1999: 100). These reforms combined with what David Broder views as subsequent 'years of neglect' turned parties into little more than fundraising mechanisms for a candidate-centered polity (Broder 1971). In the 21st century, roughly 30 percent of the US electorate registers as 'independent' or 'no party'. Among the reasons for this de-alignment of voters is the decline of party organizations.

The decline of patronage, a result of civil service reforms and a more professionalized governmental work force, deprived the traditional system of its main source of support. Local party organizations, bereft of financial support and access to jobs, declined as well. As a result, party organizations became nationalized as the affairs of our politics became nationalized in scope during the mid-20th century. However, that greater outlook did not result in greater party power. Rather, parties served as devices for candidates to use to raise funds, hone their message and learn strategy. Their link to local organizations and citizens atrophied. Milkis reminds us that parties have always been a bulwark of local democratic forces and that the administrative aggrandizement and growth of presidential power in the mid-20th century further reduced the role of party organizations in American life. Despite frequent calls for a revival of strong parties, 'such calls for fundamental reorganization of political parties and their relationship to politics and government have fallen on deaf ears' (Milkis 1999: 185).

Parties, under the weight of national administrative power, strict campaign finance laws and primary elections to choose nominees, adapted. Newman (1994) details the transition of an older 'party concept' of campaign strategy where patronage and a 'lifetime of party affiliation' play a crucial role in a candidate's success, to a 'marketing concept' of strategy. In the latter, 'strategy originates from the voter and begins by breaking down the electorate into distinct and separate segments of voters'. Using the techniques of political consultants, once segmentation has been achieved, 'the candidate creates an image for himself and uses that to position himself.

The strategy is then executed through information channels based on the results of marketing research and polling' (Newman 1994: 38).

As for direct marketing, O'Shaughnessy and Peele (1985) is one of the few studies in political marketing, and this focuses on the use of direct mail in the 1980s. They note how it was used by previous presidential candidates including Barry Goldwater, George McGovern, Jimmy Carter, Edward Kennedy and Ronald Reagan, and argue that telemarketing works well in conjunction with a mailing or to approach lapsed supporters or donors: '*Americans for Reagan* in conjunction with a mailing raised seven million dollars by telephone in 1980' (O'Shaughnessy and Peele 1985: 115–16). This early study of direct mail noted the complexity of such tactics relative to party strength. On the one hand, the use of direct mail 'represents a way of mobilizing mass allegiance' but it does so in a 'personal way' and it is also a 'catalyst for political fragmentation in the United States, as maverick pressure groups innocent of party loyalty have employed it to carve out a national constituency' (O'Shaughnessy and Peele 1985: 119). Despite this, there is little doubt that advances in the targeting of direct mail were indispensable to parties and campaigns beginning in the 1970s. In the pre-electronic era, direct mail allowed party operatives to tap into a stream of new voters for electoral and financial support. Direct mail was conceived as a political mechanism less to benefit the Republican Party and more to galvanize a growing number of conservative activists around the country in the late 1970s who then successfully took over the party machinery. Pioneered by Richard Viguerie in the 1978 congressional election, direct mail was credited with assisting conservatives in 30 congressional races win an election, including future speaker Newt Gingrich of Georgia. The Republican National Committee (RNC) adopted the technique and aggressively used direct mail in an attempt to reach parity with Democratic lists of voters. It also allowed the national party to bypass state and local actors and to reinforce a political message directly to Republican and Republican-leaning voters. The appeal of direct mail to campaigns is that it can be targeted to distinct groups of voters by purchasing voter lists; it can allow campaigns to 'create a running narrative' with voters; and it provides a wonderful volunteer opportunity, infusing campaign organizations with energy (Shea and Burton 2006: 190).

Direct marketing requires a much greater level of active participation in the campaign or party apparatus. Also called multi-level or relationship marketing, direct marketing was pioneered as a business model that distributes products and services by using a process through which independent agents market to families and friends. Similar to a pyramid structure, the independent agents create their own sales force, called a downline, by recruiting others into the business. Profits earned reflect the sales activity of the sales force, with downline agents earning profits for themselves and their upline supervisors. All levels of the model earn greater profits based on the size and the activity of their team. Direct marketing firms rely on person-to-person advocacy, using personal networks of family, friends, churches and civic organizations as their recruiting ground.

However, in politics, direct mail as a campaign tactic opened the window to direct marketing by political parties since it allowed party and candidate organizations to move into a more direct relationship with voters. Of course, tactics that emphasize personal contact between political organizations and voters are not entirely new. During the heyday of party strength, personal tactics were part and parcel of precinct-by-precinct strength, but as direct marketing emerged in the 21st century as a multi-billion dollar, technologically savvy enterprise, major candidates for office took greater notice. The advent of social networking technology made the tactics easier to follow, though not all who try succeed, as the McCain campaign's failure to successfully navigate the new contours demonstrates. Obama's campaign beat McCain on every single measurement of online activity and at coordinating all of those who used social networking to engage the candidate. However, social networking is only one aspect of direct marketing and, as the unhappy experience of Howard Dean demonstrates, does not supplant get out the vote efforts. Still, it is the tactic du jour for campaigns for the same reason direct marketing firms continue to prosper: An analysis in the alternative online magazine *EnergyGrid* declared:

> The reason why MLM [multi-level marketing] can work so well is that people are much more likely to fall for a sales pitch from a friend or relative, or a stranger in a home setting, than they are from a stranger in a shop or market, or an advert in a paper, magazine or on the Internet.
>
> *(Energy Grid 2004)*

Here network marketing is quite similar to political marketing in terms of citizen participation in political parties. Paul Whiteley (2011) notes, in his research on the decline of political parties, that 'Membership and activism are stimulated by interest in politics, discussion of politics with friends and by civic norms'. An early research note on social pressure notes that 'social pressure messages are roughly an order of magnitude more influential than conventional partisan or nonpartisan appeals' (Davenport *et al.* 2010: 423). The authors define social pressure messages at those 'designed to encourage adherence to social norms by reminding people of their obligation to abide by these norms and indicating that compliance will be monitored and perhaps disclosed to others' (ibid.). Although political marketing has not focused on this development, this chapter will attempt to address that gap, and draw on literature within campaign and election studies, media sources and the accounts provided by practitioners during the key campaigns of 2000, 2004 and 2008 that saw a steady progression of direct and network marketing tactics.

New research: direct marketing by the Bush Republicans and beyond

When Republican President George W. Bush won re-election in 2004 over Massachusetts Democratic Senator John F. Kerry, he did so despite losing independent voters 49 percent to 48 percent, reversing a modern trend in presidential elections where independent voters decide who wins the White House. With both Bush and Kerry winning high percentages of strong partisan identifiers and Kerry winning the independent vote, it was an increase in Republican identifying voters who provided the margin of victory for Bush. The Republicans found and turned out more Republican voters. Abramson *et al.* note that:

> with fewer independents to woo and such an even balance, the battle becomes a contest for the remaining independents and the weak partisans, as well as one of 'strengthening the base', that is, appealing to those already predisposed to be supporters to motivate them to turn out.
>
> *(Abramson* et al. *2007: 216)*

In this environment, the Republicans relied on their growing fascination with direct marketing firms.

The gold standard of American network marketing companies is Amway. Founded in 1959 it is a privately held company that sells home health goods and a variety of household goods. By 2010 it had sales in excess of $9 billion in the US and it has expanded globally to all corners of the world. Its growth in sales is not due to traditional marketing. Amway bypasses the typical media environment by relying on independent business owners (IBOs) who market Amway's vast array of products directly to potential customers, beginning with their families and friends.

Success is achieved in part as IBOs convince their 'networks' to purchase products they already use in their households from the Amway distributor. IBOs also recruit and train other people, again drawing on their network of connections. The process repeats itself over and over again as pyramid-shaped structures grow and grow, all sparked by personal connections and influence.

Amway's success and its appeal to legions of supporters brought it a good deal of political attention. Amway formally met politics during the 2002 and 2004 Republican efforts to increase their majorities in Congress and ensure the re-election of George W. Bush. Voter segmentation and data processing have allowed campaigns and political parties to micro-target populations of voters with direct mail and, increasingly, direct outreach. This was achieved most effectively by the Republican Party under Bush and Karl Rove. Their near defeat in 2000 stimulated Rove's interest in these emerging tactics. Caught off-guard when his estimates for a 2000 victory hinged on turnout of about 20 million evangelical voters, about 4 million more than actually turned out for Bush, Rove set about recasting GOP (Republican Party) strategy. Rove and staffers at the Republican National Committee instituted the '72-Hour Task Force' which became the '72-Hour Project' designed to increase the number of Republican voters by using personal campaign teams to contact GOP-leaning voters within 72 hours of the polls opening on election day. In its implementation, the 72-Hour Task Force drew heavily on network marketing techniques to create a new organizational level of activism, the grassroots network, complete with 'upline' and 'downline' participants, who could more effectively reach prospective voters and increase turnout.

Mentoring young partisans

Dan Balz described these efforts as 'a throwback that both Democrats and Republicans have rediscovered as an antidote to television ads' (Balz 2003). However, this 'throwback' was applied with modern marketing techniques and direct marketing finesse. For example, the RNC ran experiments to test the claims of network marketing firms. According to Garance Franke-Ruta and Harold Meyerson, in 2002, as an experiment, 'four volunteers were pitted against a professional telemarketing firm, each with an identical script and separate lists of voter names. The four volunteers got almost 5 percent more people to the polls than the pros' (Franke-Ruta and Meyerson 2004). As Ken Mehlman noted:

> The most important thing you can do in politics is give someone a personal contact from a credible source. Not just a personal contact from a paid person on the ground, but someone in their church, their gun club or the PTA.
>
> *(Kondracke 2004)*

Armed with this data, volunteers were recruited by national, state, local and collegiate party organizations at rallies, meetings and, increasingly, through the internet. The new downline recruits were assigned to precincts in which they would network and would find mentors in more experienced campaign hands. All such volunteers reported to an RNC marshal who would organize them into small groups with mobile phones given to each one. The groups were assigned a specific task: to staff phone banks, canvass select precincts, or conduct campaign visibility. The training involved in this approach was rigorous, often occurring over a period of months and often targeted at specific goals of expanding the GOP coalition and registering new voters. Incentives were employed as well, such as receiving a signed picture of the president or tickets to major Bush re-election events.

The analysis of the network marketing tactics in the 2004 Ohio presidential campaign by Matt Bai illustrates the degree to which parties have mastered the techniques of network marketing. Campaign manager Ken Mehlman was one of the preeminent architects of what was referred to as 'the Plan'. Local parties and campaign organizations were to work in close consultation with the national party and Bush campaign to set goals for the volunteer aspect of the reelection effort. Said Mehlman:

> The lessons of reality TV are that people are into participatory activities … They want to have influence over a decision that's made. They don't want to just sit and passively absorb. They want to be involved, and a political program ought to recognize that.
>
> *(Bai 2004)*

The process of mobilizing voters in the 2004 Republican campaign was left in the hands of local volunteers, Bush Team Leaders. Bai was introduced to Todd Hanks, the Delaware County, Ohio Bush campaign chair. Bush won Delaware County with 66 percent of the vote in 2000, so it was a solidly Republican county where Bush needed to win big to offset expected Democratic gains in the urban areas of the state. In order to keep Ohio in the GOP fold, Hanks was committed to maximizing the Republican vote. As a downline participant, Todd Hanks was recruited and kept in the organization in the same way that someone is recruited and kept in a network marketing company. Despite his strong political preference for Bush, 'Hanks readily admitted that his ultimate goal is to rise through the ranks of local and even state politics', wrote Bai. 'For Hanks, the Bush campaign offers a chance to recruit a "downline" of new volunteers who will, ideally, remain loyal to him in future campaigns – including his own' (Eggen 2004). The old-style, patronage-based machine has thus been replaced by the pyramid goals of network marketing organizations.

The Bush brand

To provide a greater stimulus to their local campaign organizations, Bush's consultants developed an identifiable Bush brand. The branding was in part a product of Bush's unique moment in office during the terrorist attacks of 11 September 2001 and the ensuing rally of popular support around his presidency. Bush's rocky relationship with the American people, a lingering status due to the unusual circumstances of his election, ended with the terrorist attacks. The branding centered on issues of leadership, security and strength. W, the president's middle initial, was emblazoned on coffee mugs, cufflinks and apparel. Having a 'product' to 'sell' is, of course, critical to any marketing technique, and it is especially so for network marketing where the personal contact of the 'sales force' is on the line.

When Bush entered the congressional elections of 2002, he became the best upline salesman for the 'brand'. More than most recent presidents, he was relentless in these efforts, visiting 40 states and over 100 congressional districts on behalf of Republican candidates in 2002. While nearly all modern presidents engage the people during congressional elections, few dive as deeply as Bush. No president since Franklin Roosevelt in 1934 presided over a party that gained seats in their first midterm election.

The success of the 2002 campaign provided the evidence that Republican Party leaders needed of the effectiveness of not only Bush as party leader but also the network marketing of parties. Indeed, by 2004 Bush's efforts as party leader bore fruit because of the organizational network marketing techniques on the ground. According to Bush's chief strategist, Matthew

Dowd, 'We had good candidates, but also, we had such good tactics. But having a president with a 60 percent, 59 percent job approval helps' (Dowd 2005).

The GOP 'plan' in 2004 developed grassroots organizations in all 50 states, but with special emphasis on 16 'battleground states'. The top of the upline managers were at the campaign headquarters in Arlington, Virginia, followed by regional coordinators and state-level coordinators; these three levels were all paid campaign operatives. Beneath the state-level coordinators was the downline – county, city and precinct officials – who were volunteers. By election day, this cooperative operation had more than 1 million volunteers nationwide, a party machine for the modern era.

The upline managers set specific goals for the downline participants, including recruiting volunteers, organizing campaign events, registering and contacting voters. Participants at every level of the organization were held accountable for meeting these goals. Just as importantly, the Bush campaign provided highly targeted messages for the volunteers to deliver. This 'microtargeting' was produced by extensive and sophisticated research. As Dan Balz and Mike Allen reported:

> Once those people were identified, the RNC sought to register them, and the campaign used phone calls, mail and front-porch visits – all with a message emphasizing the issues about which they cared most – to encourage them to turn out for Bush.
>
> *(Balz and Allen 2004)*

The net result of the network marketing techniques was greater attention to the grassroots and more viral activity among potential Bush voters in 2004. According to state senator Jane Earll of Erie County, Pennsylvania, compared with past campaigns, 'There are more campaign people around, more coordination, more ground troops and grass-roots organizing' (Raum 2004).

After the 2004 election, RNC chair Ed Gillespie emailed his followers with the good news:

> 1.2 million volunteers made over 15 million contacts, knocking on doors and making calls in the 72 hours before the polls closed. 7.2 million e-activists were contacting their family, friends, and co-workers. The RNC registered 3.4 million new voters, enlisted 1.4 million Team Leaders, and contacted – on a person to person basis – 30 million Americans in the months leading up to and including Election Day, and in the final 72 hours we met 129 percent of our door-knocking goal; and met 120 percent of our phone-calling goal.
>
> *(East 2004)*

Beyond 2004

Direct marketing of campaigns was front and center in the Dean campaign of 2004 and the Obama campaign of 2008. Dean's was the first campaign to truly fashion the internet as a political force to be reckoned with. The increasingly unpopular war in Iraq fed Dean's insurgent campaign and provided it with a unifying message. His use of MeetUp and BlogforAmerica.com encouraged a small group of supporters to reach out to their networks. Dean began 2003 with a few hundred supporters on MeetUp, only to increase that number to 140,000 in the fall. He raised $15 million in contributions using these connections and innovative internet fundraising (Wolfe 2004). Going into the primary season, Dean had become the Democratic frontrunner due largely to his campaign's embrace of emerging technology and the direct marketing capabilities of social sites such as MeetUp. However, while the Bush campaign of 2004 would emerge successful for using direct marketing to identify new voters and get them to the polls, the Dean primary campaign faltered. His internet fundraising, MeetUp number and fundraising prowess could not motivate enough voters to get out the vote and he stumbled badly in early voting.

Two years after the Democrats failed to deny Bush re-election, the president's public standing was so low and sustained that Democrats came to appreciate how the direct marketing efforts advanced by their opponents and the effective use of the internet demonstrated by Howard Dean could be harnessed to help achieve victory at the ballot box.

Initially, the match-up between Democratic motivation and Republican direct marketing tactics was indeed an intriguing one. Robin Toner noted the continuing relevance of the 72-Hour Project to the Republicans in 2006, as well as the supreme confidence placed in it by many of the party's elite. Indeed, in an election where a sour national mood driven by an unpopular war in Iraq and a litany of high-profile Republican scandals was mounting against the GOP, many saw their voter outreach program as the biggest reason to remain hopeful going into the election. The ability of Republican strategists to target nearly every potential Republican voter through comprehensive computer databases and micro-targeting, and deliver an individually tailored message was considered an adequate compensation for a relatively unmotivated base. Party strategist Tom Cole described the 2006 midterms as 'a race where professionalism has to make up for enthusiasm' (Toner 2006).

However, the success of GOP efforts in 2004 faced a much more difficult environment in 2006. Still, they stuck to the same strategy that had helped them win the presidency in 2004 with a goal of adding roughly 2.2 million downline supporters to augment their 170 million member-strong Voter Vault database. On top of this were efforts to register over 400,000 new votes and recruit 2,000 more get out the vote coordinators along with thousands of precinct captains and roughly 100,000 new volunteers (Ambinder 2006). The GOP had also planned to invest roughly $26 million in its grassroots get out the vote efforts. The mechanics in terms of manpower and financial backing were in place to run a GOP mobilization campaign that was at the very least on par with the once vastly superior Republican efforts fielded in the previous two elections.

Democrats matched the Republican efforts and the most critical point of departure for them was to equalize Republican superiority with financial resources. According to the *National Journal*, the congressional and senate campaign chairs, Rahm Emmanuel and Charles Schumer, placed the 72-Hour Project firmly within their gaze and incorporated its capabilities into their campaign strategies over a year before the 2006 midterm elections. While dissention between Emanuel and Schumer and Howard Dean was well documented, Democratic strategic leadership was eventually able to coalesce around the need for a better-funded get out the vote effort. Dean, subsequently elected chair of the Democratic National Committee (DNC) after his presidential aspirations ended, loudly advocated a 50-state strategy whereas the congressional campaign chairs preferred a more targeted effort in states and districts where Democrats were truly competitive.

Voter outreach and targeting

Despite the tactical disagreements, the increased commitment to voter outreach helped open the possibility that combined Democratic efforts would actually be able to exceed those of their Republican rivals. This was aided by an assertive fundraising campaign on the part of Democrats which allowed them to enter into the final weeks of the campaign with nearly as much money as the Republicans. Prior to the election, the totals projected from the Democratic Senatorial

Campaign Committee (DSCC), the Democratic Congressional Campaign Committee (DCCC), and the DNC were expected to eclipse the $30 million budgeted for the 72-Hour Project. The DNC alone had budgeted around $12 million for voter outreach programs, setting a new high for a midterm election (Ambinder 2006). Increased funds for voter turnout helped the Democrats to bridge a crucial gap in micro-targeting in the 2006 election. Stephen Weismann at the non-partisan Campaign Finance Institute, noted that 'The big trend is micro-targeting, and that was used by Democratic-oriented groups to supplement their knowledge … they were trying to get more precise. Republicans were in this area first, but Democrats are catching up' (Vaida and Munro 2006).

Micro-targeting and the use of sophisticated internet databases were a crucial facet of the successful implementation of multi-level marketing strategies by the Republican Party in 2002 and 2004. In fact, the 72-Hour Project was essentially fueled by the information contained within the Republican database or the 'Voter Vault'. A massive collection of voter data, Voter Vault contained a wealth of information pertaining to individual voter biases, habits and points of view, and was accessible to GOP volunteers and organizers as well as the party leadership. As such, Voter Vault existed simultaneously as a means to monitor and organize party activity within the 72-Hour Project framework as well as a source of practically limitless data on potential voters. This voter data allowed the Republican Party to tailor specific messages to meet the preferences and persuasions of potential voters as well as deliver them with precision.

Obama's victory in 2008 has been remarked on at length and his successful use of the internet obscures the important permanence of the Bush strategies of 2002 and 2004. David Carr noted that:

> Like a lot of Web innovators, the Obama campaign did not invent anything completely new. Instead, by bolting together social networking applications under the banner of a movement, they created an unforeseen force to raise money, organize locally, fight smear campaigns and get out the vote that helped them topple the Clinton machine and then John McCain and the Republicans.
>
> *(Carr 2008)*

Obama had 290 percent more supporters on Facebook than John McCain, for example. Beyond the numbers, though, was the aggressive get out the vote mechanism. The characterization of the McCain campaign's ground effort is startling not just for its comparison to Obama's highly coordinated, energized effort, but also for the comparison to the Bush effort of 2004, noted for its high level of network activity. According to Sean Quinn, who visited both campaigns in the swing state of Missouri, '*We've observed no comparison between these ground campaigns*. To begin with, there's a 4–1 ratio of offices in most states. We walk into McCain offices to find them closed, empty, one person, two people, sometimes three people making calls' (Quinn 2008).

Quinn went on to add, 'The McCain offices are also calm, sedate. Little movement. No hustle. In the Obama offices, it's a whirlwind. People move. It's a dynamic bustle' (Quinn 2008). The contrast to the Bush efforts could not have been more striking.

The McCain campaign's failure to use advances in social media, its failure to integrate its web content and get out the vote mechanisms, and its relative disregard for the direct marketing tactics employed by the Bush Republicans are symptomatic of the candidate-centered, executive-dominated system of US elections. Despite centralization of certain key functions in their DC headquarters, political party organizations remain secondary to candidate influence and intra-party competition.

In sum, we can see that the Republican application of network marketing techniques to party organization paid off with party victories in 2002 and 2004. Significantly, however, Republican Party affiliation in the electorate has not changed since the 2000 election of Bush, hovering around 31 percent of the population, with Democrats declining from 36 percent to 33 percent (Harris Interactive 2005). It was also used beyond 2005 and direct marketing increased their share of the vote for the winning parties in 2004 and 2008. It is thus a significant tool for political parties and political campaigns but has also yet to become fully institutionalized.

Advice for practitioners

Direct marketing is to contemporary campaigns what direct mail was in the late 1970s: 'its role should interlock with other mediums so that the various elements of a campaign are mutually reinforcing' (O'Shaughnessy and Peele 1985: 122). The integration of marketing tactics needs to be adapted to the direct marketing environment perfected by the Bush, Dean and Obama campaigns. There are five key ways to effectively integrate direct marketing in modern political campaigns:

- Begin with voter targeting. In a political environment such as the US, where party membership is fluid and not formalized, where de-alignment has increased the numbers of independent voters, and where party identifiers of the two main parties are relatively equal, targeting sympathizers with a history of voting is a key first step in direct marketing of politics. If, as Davenport *et al.* (2010: 425) suggest, 'social pressure interventions have persistent effects', then finding likely voters to which one can directly market a candidate or party is vitally important.
- View the online campaign site as a portal for personal contact. Campaign consultants scrambled in the 1990s to develop websites to provide information to voters, but online presence is not an effective get out the vote mechanism unless thoroughly integrated into a direct marketing experience. Clicks on websites need to be evaluated and monitored for market integration: is the campaign connecting with the right prospective volunteers and voters and from where are these clicks emerging – Google searches, social media, etc. This information is important to campaigns looking to tailor a message to specific audiences.
- Social media integration. A modern campaign must take care to create a social media universe that does not dilute is message. A modern campaign must have a YouTube station, Facebook and Twitter accounts. It must be aware of emerging social media technologies and adapt accordingly. Ideally each page allows followers to post – particularly effective is a YouTube station that allows followers to create and post their own video, essentially campaign commercials for free. The social media environment allows prospective voters and volunteers to connect to likeminded individuals, an important solidary benefit.
- Mentorship. If campaigns want to turn new voters, donors and volunteers into long-term advocates, a system of mentorship and encouragement is necessary. Here the study of successful direct marketing firms, Amway, Tupperware, Discovery Toys, is essential. These firms have a well-honed system of mentorship that puts their most successful and proactive upline managers into an ongoing relationship with downline recruits. Shea and Burton's (2006: 182) study of modern campaigns notes that 'All the basic principles of new-style campaigning apply to the grassroots operation. Because the "soldiers" in the grassroots effort are generally untrained, they often need supervision.'
- Networking. Direct marketing is largely successful when new recruits tap into their existing networks. Here the solidary benefits of belonging to a party or working on a campaign are

used to advance the interests of a candidate into a cross-cutting array of groups: civic organizations, churches, volunteer or fraternal associations. Targeting prospective voters in these environments by properly trained campaign workers allows a candidate or party to buttress their messaging with a personal contact from a known and trusted source. The technology of voter identification 'adds efficiency to what used to be a time-sensitive process', notes Christine Pelosi (2007: 53), but 'the science of targeting numbers will always need the art of local wisdom. Micro targeting only works with input from people on the ground, in the communities.'

Impact on politics

Can direct marketing halt or reverse the decline of party organizations in the US? Although direct marketing is clearly an important tool in political marketing, hitherto it has not fundamentally reshaped the organizational contours of the US party system. Nevertheless, it may still do so. If direct marketing was used to its full potential it could help parties create more positive and long-lasting relationships with voters, and stimulate participation. The obstacles are high, as Whiteley (2011: 36) notes: 'Party activism and membership have been declining across most of the democratic world.' Of particular interest to Whiteley is the relationship of a political party to the state with a close relationship helping to weaken party activism: 'If party organizations become denuded of volunteers, then political parties are even more likely to become wholly dependent on the state.'

Any resurgence of party membership, activism and local organizational strength will come about from an increase in local membership. Here direct marketing can have the same impact in politics as it has had in business by fostering a downline of recruits sympathetic to the goals of the larger organization who enjoy the solidary benefits of being part of a team of likeminded individuals. However, the downline has a substantial impact on its upline supervisors and bad mentorship or a structure that impedes the solidary benefits enjoyed by members can stymie efforts at party renewal. Lilleker's work on New Labour is instructive: 'Those who Labour were relying on for unequivocal support felt the brand was no longer for them and so rejected the product entirely' (Lilleker 2005: 22).

A direct marketing approach that brings new recruits into the organization and continues to provide solidary benefits to more seasoned members and keeps both in a constant state of motion might be able to revive dormant organizations in support of a candidate or political party.

The way forward

The fascinating research to conduct may lie in the significance of what happens in those energetic campaign headquarters where network marketing techniques are utilized. New voters brought into the political process by the Bush and Obama campaigns experienced a new type of politics based upon older understandings of the importance of face-to-face encounters and networking. That socialization into politics at the local level has the potential to reshape local party and campaign organizations into a continuing force for renewing the US party system. Research could also study developments such as the creation of Organizing for America, which aims to bring volunteers into helping campaign in government, not just for an election, and other initiatives in parties around the world to involve party members. A useful next step is to figure out what happened to the new recruits into these organizations, to determine whether the experience with a formal direct marketing style of campaign had the long-term effect of keeping them politically active and responsive to party organizations and party politics.

Bibliography

Abramson, P.R., Aldrich, J.H. and Rohde, D.W. (2007) *Change and Continuity in the 2004 and 2006 Elections*, Washington, DC: Congressional Quarterly Press.

Ambinder, M. (2006) 'Know Thy Voter', *The Hotline*. Online, news.nationaljournal.com/articles/0915hotline.htm (accessed 15 September 2006).

Bai, Matt (2004) 'The Multilevel Marketing of the President', in *The New York Times Magazine* 25 April.

Baker, P. (2010) 'Obama Social Secretary Ran Into Sharp Elbows', *New York Times*, 11 March.

Balz, D. (2003) 'Getting the Votes – And the Kudos', *Washington Post*, 1 January.

Balz, D. and Allen, M. (2004) 'Four More Years Attributed to Rove's Strategy', *Washington Post*, 7 November.

Broder, D. (1971) *The Party's Over: The Failure of Politics in America*, New York: Harper & Row.

Carr, D. (2008) 'How Obama Tapped Into Social Networks' Power', *New York Times*, 8 November.

Cummings, J. (2006) 'Final Push: Hefty Democratic Fund Raising Vies with Clout of Incumbency', *Wall Street Journal*, 7 November.

Davenport, T.C., Gerber, A.S., Green, D.P., Larimer, C.W., Mann, C.B. and Panagopoulos, C. (2010) 'The Enduring Effects of Social Pressure: Tracking Campaign Experiments Over a Series of Elections', *Political Behavior* 32, 3: 423–30.

Dowd, Matthew (2005) *Interview with PBS Frontline's Karl Rove: The Architect*. Online, www.pbs.org/wgbh/pages/frontline/shows/architect, 5 September.

East, P. (2004) 'Notes from the Campaign Chair', *RWLC Blog*. Online, www.rwlc.net (accessed 4 October 2005).

Eggen, D. (2004) 'Policing Is Aggressive at Bush Events', *Washington Post*, 28 October.

Energy Grid (2004) 'Techniques of Persuasion in MLM or Network Marketing Companies'. Online, www.energygrid.com/money/2004/03ap-mlm.html (accessed 19 May 2011).

Franke-Ruta, G. and Meyerson, H. (2004) 'The GOP Deploys', *American Prospect Online*. Online, www.prospect.org (accessed 1 February 2004).

Ginsberg, B. and Shefter, M. (1999) *Politics by Other Means: Politicians, Prosecutors and the Press from Watergate to Whitewater*, New York: W.W. Norton & Co.

Granick, S. (2005) 'Membership Benefits, Membership Action: Why Incentives for Activism are What Members Want', in W. Wymer and J. Lees-Marshment (eds) *Current Issues in Political Marketing*, New York: Haworth Press.

Harris Interactive (2005) *The Harris Poll*, No. 19. Online, www.harrisinteractive.com (accessed 9 March 2006).

Hofstadter, R. (1969) *The Idea of a Party System: The Rise of Legitimate Opposition in the United States, 1780–1840*, Berkeley: University of California Press.

Jackson, J.S. (1992) 'The Party-as-Organization: Party Elites and Party Reforms in Presidential Nominations and Conventions', in J.K. White and J. Mileur (eds) *Challenges to Party Government*, Carbondale, IL: Southern Illinois University Press.

Kondracke, M. (2004) 'Registration Wars in Ohio, Florida Produce a Draw', *Roll Call* 28.

Lees, C. (2005) 'Political Marketing in Germany: The Case of the Social Democratic Party', in D. Lilleker and J. Lees-Marshment (eds) *Political Marketing in Comparative Perspective*, Manchester: Manchester University Press.

Lilleker, D.G. (2005) 'Political Marketing: The Cause of an Emerging Democratic Deficit in Britain?' in W. Wymer and J. Lees-Marshment (eds) *Current Issues in Political Marketing*, New York: Haworth Press.

Menn, J. (2004) 'The Race for the White House', *Los Angeles Times*, 28 October.

Milkis, S.M. (1999) *Political Parties and Constitutional Government: Remaking American Democracy*, Baltimore: The Johns Hopkins University Press.

Newman, B.I. (1994) *The Marketing of the President*, Thousand Oaks, CA: Sage.

O'Shaughnessy, N. and Peele, G. (1985) 'Money, Mail and Markets: Reflections on Direct Mail in American Politics', *Electoral Studies* 4, 2: 115–24.

Pelosi, C. (2007) *Campaign Boot Camp: Basic Training for Future Leaders*, Sausilito, CA: PoliPoint Press.

Pettitt, R. (2009) 'Case Study 6.4. Resisting Marketing: The Case of the British Labour Party under Blair', in J. Lees-Marshment (ed.) *Political Marketing: Principles and Applications*, London and New York: Routledge.

Quinn, S. (2008) 'On the Road: St. Louis County, Missouri', *Five Thirty Eight*. Online, www.fivethirtyeight.com/2008/10/on-road-st-louis-county-missouri.html (accessed 1 December 2008).

Raum, T. (2004) 'Bush Makes Gains in Battleground States', *Las Vegas Sun*, 14 September.
Reichley, A.J. (2007) 'The Future of the American Two-Party System in the Twenty First Century', in J.C. Green and D.J. Coffey (eds) *The State of the Parties: The Changing Role of Contemporary American Parties*, Lanham, MD: Rowman & Littlefield.
Shafer, B. (2003) *The Two Major Parties and the Puzzle of American Politics*, Lawrence: University Press of Kansas.
Shea, D.M. and Burton, M.J. (2006) *Campaign Craft: The Strategies, Tactics, and Art of Political Campaign Management*, third edn, Westport, CT: Praeger.
Toner, R. (2006) 'Democrats Have an Intensity, But G.O.P. Has Its Machine', *New York Times*, 15 October.
Vaida, B. and Munro, N. (2006) 'Reversal of Fortunes', *National Journal*, 11 November.
Whiteley, P.F. (2011) 'Is the Party Over? The Decline of Party Activism and Membership Across the Democratic World', *Party Politics* 17, 1: 21–24.
Wolfe, G. (2004) 'How the Internet Invented Howard Dean', *Wired* 12, 1.

15

The party official as political marketer

The Australian experience

Stephen Mills

A campaign is not a time for much original thought; it is a time for tactical manoeuvring and carrying out plans and procedures developed in an earlier more normal climate.

Andrew Robb, Federal Director Liberal Party of Australia (Robb 1996)

The topic: the party official as political marketer

Party officials – the full-time paid professional employees of the party organisation – are often overlooked in accounts of political marketing campaigns, in favour of the more high-profile elected party leaders and external consultants. Yet party officials can perform distinctive functions that the political marketing literature suggests are necessary if the party is to achieve sustained electoral success. This chapter describes these functions and presents examples, drawn from the Australian context, of party officials as political marketers. While party structures and campaign practices differ in democracies around the world, it is argued that greater attention to the role of party officials will provide a more complete understanding of the political marketing process.

Previous research

Party scholarship has long recognised that the 'party-as-organisation' represents a distinct element of a tripartite structure alongside the 'party on the ground' and the 'party in office'. The 'party-as-organisation' or 'party central office' includes the national executive, secretariat and paid party officials, and performs distinctive activities including managing and coordinating election campaigns (Key 1964; Katz and Mair 1993). As party membership declined, and communications technologies rapidly expanded and diversified, party officials transformed from bureaucratic administrators to become 'electoral professionals', with skills appropriate for post-ideological 'catch-all' campaign strategies (Kirchheimer 1966; Panebianco 1988; Farrell 1996; Henneberg and Eghbalian 2002; Negrine 2007; Smith 2009). Party officials manage campaign organisations and budgets, where volunteer labor and member subscriptions have been supplemented, and in some cases replaced, by professional staff and consultants, corporate donations and taxpayer subsidies (Ware 1996; Young and Tham 2006; Nassmacher 2009).

Yet party officials constitute 'one of the most under-researched fields in the study of political parties' (Webb and Kolodny 2006) – not least in the political marketing literature. In Britain, accounts of successful political marketing campaigns have tended to overlook party officials by aggregating their role within a broader narrative that features many other party and non-party actors: leaders, members of parliament, candidates, members, donors, supporters, activists within the party and aligned special interest groups and, not least, specialist external consultants (Lees-Marshment 2001; Wring 2005). Alternatively, US accounts have portrayed party officials as relics of a campaign model long superseded by the candidate-based campaign (Newman 1994; Sabato 1981; Scammell 1997; Medvic 2006), or perhaps as 'shadowy men of the political backrooms' (O'Shaughnessy 1990: 12); again, these accounts accord a prominent role to the external consultants.

However, an important contribution to the political marketing literature about party officials suggests that the sustained competitiveness of a political party can be analysed with the resource-based view (RBV). For Lynch *et al.* (2006), the competitive resources of a party include human resources (such as leaders, supporters and policy-developers), intellectual resources (policies) and organisational capabilities (such as campaign competencies, the skills and knowledge with which it crafts and communicates its messages for voters, deploys party activists at national and local levels, and targets voters). With this explicit introduction of the party organisation into the political marketing discussion, and its recognition of organisational skills as key competitive resources, the RBV invites closer consideration of the role of party officials. Critically, Lynch *et al.* distinguish between long- and short-term resources, asserting that short-term resources deployed in the immediate 'battle' of an election campaign will be 'more competitive if they have been nurtured in the years preceding the formal campaign' (Lynch *et al.* 2006: 86–87) – a view well articulated by the Australian party official Andrew Robb cited at the head of this chapter.

This chapter will argue that party officials can indeed play a key role in political marketing, and that this role extends well beyond the marketing communications functions, to include key decisions about the party's acquisition and deployment of long-term resources. It will do so by reference to the most senior officials of Australia's two major political parties – the national secretary of the Australian Labor Party (ALP) and the federal director of the Liberal Party. There has been no comprehensive or comparative study of Australian party officials, and the available material is scattered among party histories (Hancock 2000, 2007; McMullin 1991), published archives (Weller and Lloyd 1978; Starr 1980), organisational studies (West 1965; Parkin and Warhurst 1983; Warhurst and Parkin 2000), accounts of the new campaign technology deployed by party officials (Mills 1986; Young 2004) and journalist accounts of election campaigns. Despite contributions to the political marketing literature by Australian political marketing scholars (O'Cass 1996, 2001, 2009; Hughes and Dann 2009, 2010), there are few Australian case studies or discussions of Australian practitioners.

Party bureaucrats themselves are notoriously 'reticent' (Panebianco 1988: 221) about their role, and political marketing activities are difficult to perceive in real time (Lilleker and Negrine 2006) since parties developing rival political strategies seek to protect their plans against pre-emption. Yet successive national secretaries and federal directors have an interest, post-campaign, in explaining (or justifying) their strategic intentions. Certainly, national secretaries and federal directors have delivered post-election speeches at the National Press Club since 1993, and have participated in post-election academic collaborations (Bean *et al.* 1997; Simms and Warhurst 2000, 2005; Warhurst and Simms 2002; Simms 2009) and other conferences (for example, Young 1986). They have also acted as informants to post-campaign narratives and analyses by journalists (for example Williams 1997; Jackman 2008) and academics (Blewett 1973). These have together provided the basis for the following analysis.

New research: three party officials as political marketers in Australian federal elections

This analysis focuses on three Australian party officials: Mick Young, ALP federal secretary from 1969 to 1972; Andrew Robb, federal director of the Liberal Party from 1991 to 1997; and Tim Gartrell, ALP national secretary from 2003 to 2008. These officials were the most senior executives in their party organisations, elected (in the case of the ALP officials) and appointed (Liberal Party) by their national executive bodies to head the party's secretariat. In this capacity, each of them also held the title 'campaign director'. Each of them managed the opposition party's campaign in two successive elections, losing the first (in 1969, 1993 and 2004, respectively) and winning at their second attempt (in 1972, 1996 and 2007, respectively).

The analysis explores the activities of each official in relation to five distinctive functions that, according to the political marketing literature (Lees-Marshment 2001, 2009; Lynch *et al.* 2006), are necessary for a political party to achieve sustained electoral success. These are gathering market intelligence, designing the product (policy and leadership), building long-term campaign resources, deploying short-term campaign resources, and post-campaign product delivery.

Market intelligence

Gathering market intelligence has been identified as the necessary first stage of a political marketing campaign model, allowing the political marketing organisation to orient itself to voter preferences. Market-oriented parties have come increasingly to rely on market research; party officials play the central role in providing this intelligence.

Public opinion polling had been pioneered in Australian election campaigns by the ALP in its successful state campaign in South Australia in 1968; a key official in that campaign was Mick Young (Blewett and Jaensch 1971: 65–66, 204–5). Now as federal secretary and full-time campaign director, Young insisted that Labor 'use to the full the research and media techniques' that were available (Blewett 1973: 10, citing a planning memo written by Young nearly a year before the 1972 election). Young later acknowledged that national surveys had been used 'extensively' during the campaign, and were 'an integral part of all our decision making' (Young 1986: 98, 106). For example, polling identified weaknesses in the image of party leader Gough Whitlam, leading to a more effective communications style (Blewett 1973: 8) and was also used to pre-test the advertising slogan which carried Labor's message of change: 'It's Time' (Young 1986: 106). Polling was conducted through the party's advertising agency, the expenditure of which Young strictly controlled (Young 1986: 98).

In these early years, polling meant quantitative (random sample survey) research, conducted infrequently as funds permitted. Through the 1980s, both parties increased the frequency and intensity of this kind of polling while also embarking on qualitative (focus group) research, allowing them to segment the marketplace to track and target the attitudes of swing voters in marginal seats (Mills 1986). The frequency and reliability of national polls published in the media allowed both parties to focus their own survey work on marginal seats. While he was still deputy director of the Liberal Party, Andrew Robb had identified a promising young market researcher, Mark Textor; in 1991 he appointed him as the Liberals' in-house pollster. Textor's meticulous, extensive and innovative market research, both quantitative and qualitative, made a crucial contribution to the Liberals' development of a market orientation in the lead-up to the 1996 campaign. Robb distilled his campaign strategy not around a product description but around 'a distillation of swing voter sentiment' (Williams 1997: 100).

Textor's accumulation of attitudinal data allowed him to create what he termed a 'psychograph' of typical middle-Australian swinging voters. These fictional constructs, named 'Phil' and 'Jenny', represented a young married couple with one child, moderate incomes, a mortgage and a car in need of a service; 'Phil' and 'Jenny' had voted Labor in 1993 but their economic and lifestyle concerns made them open to changing their vote this time. This construct was created more than a year before the 1996 election campaign. Robb used it to help Liberal candidates in marginal seats identify and communicate effectively with the voters they needed for victory. He would ask the candidates: 'Have you spoken to Phil and Jenny lately?' According to the account by journalist Pamela Williams, to whom Robb granted privileged access during the campaign, 'Phil' and 'Jenny' became 'the subjects of endless discussion in party meetings, the template family every Liberal candidate needed to know about [and] a code for the entire campaign' (Williams 1997: 65). In all this, Robb's campaign underlines the validity of Lynch *et al.*'s (2006: 86) proposition that parties need to target their messages at voters of strategic significance; different voters – loyal voters as against swing voters – will have different views on the party's key messages. The Australian parties' focus on swing voters is perhaps intensified given that, under Australia's compulsory voting system, they are saved the expense of mobilising their loyalist voting base.

By the time of the 2007 election, Tim Gartrell was conscious of the Liberals' reputation for market research, admitting later 'much has been said about their crucial roles in victories, never defeats' (Gartrell 2007). Gartrell commissioned two separate research operations. For quantitative research, he continued to use the Australian-New Zealand firm UMR Research, whose principal, John Utting, had been engaged in federal and state Labor campaigns for the previous decade. UMR was commissioned to conduct quarterly telephone benchmark surveys of marginal seats; when a rapid response was needed, UMR conducted an 'e-panel' of online marginal seat respondents (Jackman 2008: 110, 151). For qualitative research, Gartrell appointed, on the advice of an earlier Labor research guru Rod Cameron, a new research group headed by Tony Mitchelmore (Jackman 2008: 35). Mitchelmore conducted intensive rounds of focus group discussions – for example, 16 group discussions in six centres around Australia in a fortnight. His techniques to probe the attitudes of swinging voters included using 'whimsical analogies', such as asking 'what kind of fathers' party leaders John Howard and Kim Beazley would make, or how a 'Labor factory' would differ from a 'Liberal factory'. He also asked voters to describe their hopes and fears for their children's future, as a way of assessing whether they thought the country was heading in the right direction (Jackman 2008: 37, 101).

Like Textor, Mitchelmore provided his client not just with reports of voter attitudes but with strategic advice on how to take advantage of this intelligence. This included suggesting words and phrases that Labor spokespeople could use that resonated with swing voters. Labor's description of their target swing voters as 'working families' was, like Textor's 'Phil' and 'Jenny', a product of market research. So was Labor's description of Prime Minister Howard as 'clever' and 'out of touch' (Jackman 2008: 59). On one occasion, Gartrell received a leaked copy of one of Textor's recent research reports for the Liberals (Jackman 2008: 142). Underlining the competitive environment of party research, Gartrell crowed in a speech to the National Press Club after Labor's victory that 'our researchers finally bested the other side' (Gartrell 2007).

In these examples party officials have identified market researchers, hired them as in-house or external agents, commissioned research, distilled communications messages and – particularly Robb and Gartrell – constructed campaign strategies and campaign messages from it.

Designing the product: policy

The second stage of a political marketing campaign is to use market intelligence to design the party's political product, including the policies it presents to voters. Lynch *et al.* identify as a critical resource the party's ability to develop policies that satisfy and attract current and future voters (Lynch *et al.* 2006: 83). Again, party officials can play a critical role in this process.

This was not an early development: in the early 1970s research was used for packaging purposes, and Young did not seek to influence policies. 'We did use slick marketing techniques, and did package Whitlam to a certain extent', Young conceded, '[b]ut we were only able to do that because there was something to be presented to the electorate. The policies had been hammered out over a number of years' (Young 1986: 107).

By the mid-1990s, however, Robb was closely involved in developing the Liberals' policy platform. At a critical meeting of party leaders and staff in January 1996, Robb addressed the meeting immediately after it was opened by party leader John Howard, and laid down the electoral framework within which policy should be selected. This was a research-driven framework. According to Williams' account, 'Each of the major policies, and its presentation, had to accord with the rhetoric of one or more of four campaign themes: 'to give certainty of security to families, to get small business back in business, to give hope to young people and to restore trust and honesty in government'. Robb also insisted that policies be accommodated in a planned 33-day campaign schedule to ensure a steady stream of announcements to feed the news cycle (Williams 1997: 160). Lynch *et al.* suggest that messages directed to 'swing' voters should be both persuasive (i.e. attracting voters to 'support your party') and dissuasive (i.e. making negative critiques of the other party). This accurately describes Robb's approach, which balanced positive messages around Howard with negative reminders of Prime Minister Keating (Williams 1997: 100).

In 2007 Labor's policies were developed by leader Kevin Rudd, his private staff and party strategists including Gartrell, to accord with the preferences of the 'working families' indentified in research. Seeking to position Rudd as 'the future' versus the Howard government as 'the past', Labor promoted fresh ideas, fiscal conservatism and opposition to the government's industrial relations legislation. Announcements of 'reviews' of government policy generated news during the campaign while retaining flexibility on the actual course to be followed if elected (Jackman 2008: 48–51, 110, 154).

Designing the product: leadership

Leaders are one of the primary party resources identified by Lynch *et al.* (2006: 83). Market research provides an intense focus on party leaders, measuring voters' approval of their performance and personalities; research on voting intentions provides a measure of a party's success at orienting itself to the preferences of the electorate. Market research accordingly influences party considerations about whether incumbent leaders are succeeding in their jobs or whether they should be replaced. Since market research is commissioned by, and presented in the first instance to, the party officials, they are in a position to influence these discussions.

Again, this was not the case during Young's time as federal secretary. Whitlam had been elected leader in 1967 and took Labor to victory in 1972 despite having lost the 1969 election. Both Robb and Gartrell, having lost their first campaigns (with John Hewson as leader in 1993, and Mark Latham in 2004, respectively), were closely involved in transforming their party's platforms and leadership, with a view to ensuring their electoral acceptability in the next election. Research commissioned by Robb and later leaked to the media from the party's secretariat, played an influential role in the dumping of Hewson by Alexander Downer. Subsequent research showing Downer's poor standing with voters led to his replacement by John Howard in 1995; Robb himself communicated the findings to Downer and within the party (Williams 1997: 15–21, 55).

Market research was likewise deeply implicated in Labor's dumping of Latham's replacement, Kim Beazley: market research, highlighting Beazley's inability to 'cut through' to voters, was being used internally to destabilise him by the end of 2005. Gartrell himself briefed Beazley on Mitchelmore's latest research on the leader's 'dismal' standing with voters (Jackman 2008: 35, 58). Later, Gartrell tellingly stated that it had been Rudd's replacement of Beazley in December 2006 that marked the start of the trend towards Labor. The implication is that none of the longer-term resources that the party had been developing under Beazley were relevant – a result that Lynch *et al.* would not have predicted. Beazley was an experienced parliamentarian and former senior minister, who had led the opposition to narrow defeat in the 1998 elections and again in 2001. Rudd was untried, a career bureaucrat elected to Parliament only in 1998, where his most senior political role had been foreign affairs spokesman. In fact, Beazley's accumulated experience was regarded in research as a negative, while Rudd's novelty became a campaign asset. Gartrell told the National Press Club: 'our research was telling us that people thought Kevin Rudd was different to the old Labor Party: a new style of Labor leader with an agenda that connected with people'. Labor built its entire campaign messaging including television commercials around introducing this new leader as 'Kevin '07' (Gartrell 2007).

Building the campaign's long-term resources

A critical element of political marketing is its time dimension. Lees-Marshment (2001) sees political marketing as a sequence of activities across the whole electoral cycle; Lynch *et al.* (2006) distinguish between long-term and short-term resources. The practical effect of this for campaigners is that the whole time between elections should be given over to strategic planning and resource development, such as acquiring the organisational skills to research, craft and communicate its message. The Australian examples indicate that party officials are the central players in building the long-term organisational resources of their party.

Young's approach to the 1972 campaign emphasised early planning, professional staffing, maximum possible use of market research and media techniques, expanded fundraising, centralised decision-making and consistent execution – all this in contrast to the 1969 campaign which was 'virtually a last minute effort' (Blewett 1973: 9–10, citing Young's planning memo). When Young was first appointed federal secretary, Labor's secretariat had 'no permanent staff'; he appointed three senior communications professionals and supplemented Labor's long-standing advertising agency with new sources of specialist advice. Young also assembled and, as campaign director led, a nationally coordinated campaign machine via a national campaign committee which included state branches, parliamentary leaders and their staff and agency representatives (Blewett 1973: 10). This was Labor's and indeed Australia's first national campaign structure and it met regularly in the year leading up to the 1972 election. Meanwhile, at the level of the 'party on the ground', 'some Labor stalwarts were aghast at the commercial slickness and fatuity of the "soft-sell" campaign' (Blewett 1973: 14).

Curiously, Lynch *et al.* do not mention financial capacity among the key party resources. Yet given the high cost of new campaign techniques, and the dwindling flow of member subscriptions in the 'catch-all' party model, access to secure funding is an essential party resource. In 1969 Labor had been 'many thousands of dollars' in debt from previous campaign costs (Young 1986: 96). Planning a much more expensive campaign for 1972, Young, along with Whitlam and others, set about raising new funds from unions, businesses, individuals, state and local party branches and – to fund the research survey in 1971 – an unnamed 'group of wealthy Whitlam supporters' (Blewett 1973).

Robb also assembled significant campaign resources for the Liberals' Head Office: in Williams' (1997) account, he hired new staff, including campaign experts from the US; upgraded the IT system and database on marginal seats; began 'overhauling' the party's advertising strategy and replacing its agency, George Patterson, with a bespoke team of creative and strategic professionals; and staffed a unit with special responsibility for marginal seat campaigns. Paying for these new campaign resources represented a significant challenge for Robb and the party organisation. The Federal Secretariat reportedly consumed an annual budget of $2.5 million, net of one-off election campaign costs. The leadership change to Howard had apparently helped re-ignite enthusiasm among the party's traditional corporate donor base, and the party's bank overdraft was renegotiated. Australian political parties had become eligible in 1984 to receive funding from the taxpayers commensurate to their voting support at the previous election. These funds were paid to state branches, however, and Robb needed to negotiate funding of campaign activities in each state.

As Robb and Young had done, Gartrell set about rebuilding Labor's organisational capabilities in the wake of the 2004 defeat, believing that Labor had been 'badly outgunned' both financially and 'in the way it developed and implemented strategy' (Jackman 2008: 78). In addition to hiring Mitchelmore and UMR, Gartrell appointed a new advertising strategist, Neil Lawrence, and brought in former British Labour politician Alan Milburn as adviser and sounding board. With the assistance of these advisers – Milburn providing copies of Tony Blair's 2005 campaign strategy – Gartrell wrote a 10-point plan for campaign management, which emphasised message discipline, centralised decision-making and close liaison with the parliamentary leader. The 'Kevin '07' theme was launched four months out from the expected campaign, building name recognition of the new leader and enforcing the 'past versus future' positioning (Jackman 2008: 87, 159). On funding, Gartrell as national secretary was the ALP's designated agent to receive the $22 million in public funding paid after the 2007 election (Australian Electoral Commission 2008; Orr 2010). Labor's campaign was also boosted by significant resources from the trade union movement: its 'Your Rights at Work' campaign, opposing the government's industrial relations legislation, included television advertising, rallies, workplace meetings and 22 full-time union organisers, at a total estimated cost of $28 million (Wanna 2010).

Deploying short-term resources

The corollary of the emphasis on long-term resourcing is that short-term resources are a less significant 'function of' the long term (Lynch *et al.* 2006: 85–86). This insight is borne out in practice by the examples of the three Australian party officials, for whom the election campaign – in Australia, typically of five or six weeks' duration between the issue of writs and polling day – was largely concerned, as Robb suggested, with 'tactical manoeuvring and carrying out plans and procedures developed … earlier'.

Labor used two electoral cycles to progressively develop its leadership and policy resources before the 1969 and 1972 elections. It built organisational resources, repaid its debt, built a professional team and developed campaign capabilities in the three years – especially, the final 12 months – before the 1972 election. Some 12 months before the election, Young ran a 'mini-campaign' that refined campaign themes and logistics. Four months out, the 'It's Time' theme had been selected and pre-tested, and most of the television commercials – involving a group of celebrities singing the 'It's Time' anthem – had been shot ready for broadcast (Young 1986: 107). Whitlam's policy speech, delivered at the outset of the campaign proper, was described by his speechwriter as 'simply a summary of the work of the previous six years' (Freudenberg 1977: 226).

However, in contrast to Labor's development over two electoral cycles under Whitlam, the Liberals in the 1990s and Labor in the following decade had much less time in which to develop their competitive resources, thanks to leadership instability and policy uncertainty. Robb and Gartrell built organisational capability in less than a single three-year electoral term. Once new leadership (Howard and Rudd, respectively) was in place, policy development proceeded, as we have seen, over a short, intense time frame in 1995–96 and 2006–07, respectively. Once the campaign 'battle' itself was underway, however, both Robb and Gartrell were able to deploy short-term resources effectively, in particular with intense marketing communications activity.

Robb rolled out the '50 or 60' policy announcements that had been agreed at the policy meeting in January (Williams 1997: 99). He created an operational headquarters in three floors of rented office accommodation in Melbourne. He enhanced staff resources with further short-term hires. He embarked on an intense program of television advertising designed to bring previous messaging to a sharp anti-government pitch. He intensified market research including marginal electorate surveys, and used it to rebalance campaign resources such as staff, advertising and direct mail. He prepared carefully for campaign set-pieces such as the policy launch and the leaders' debate.

Gartrell set up campaign headquarters in Sydney in readiness for the campaign and he, too, implemented a previously planned campaign schedule and advertising program. His campaign activities included authorising campaign advertising, arranging preference deals with minor parties and buying advertising. 'We went into those six weeks knowing every single day had to be a good day. No room for error. A gaffe-free zone', he recalled later (Gartrell 2007). Gartrell specialised in exploiting new opportunities for message dissemination during the last three days of the campaign when television advertising is forbidden, including skywriting, SMS texting, distributing DVDs and securing deals to run Labor advertisements on the homepages of popular websites and on the TVs for sale in the RetraVision retail chain (Jackman 2008: 193).

Delivery

Just as political marketing activity begins well before the campaign proper, so it extends long after voting day. Unsuccessful parties must return to the intelligence gathering and product design phases, to refine their offering for the next campaign; successful parties must set about delivering on their promises in government (Lees-Marshment 2001). While it remains unclear just how voters balance past performance with the promise of future gains, political marketing suggests that parties should work after every election to build a sustained relationship with voters over several election cycles, rather than relying for success on a one-shot transactional exchange at a single election.

Having identified political marketing functions performed by these Australian party officials before the elections, it is notable that less than a year after their respective electoral victories, all three of them had resigned. Young and Robb went on to significant parliamentary and ministerial careers; Gartrell remains a prominent social campaigner. None of them remained to assist their newly elected government with the delivery phase of the political marketing sequence. To the extent that the Whitlam, Howard and Rudd governments did deliver on their promises – and the record is somewhat patchy – this did not occur because of any contribution by the party officials who had been involved in winning the election.

Advice for practitioners

Party structures and campaign practices differ in democracies around the world. The campaign management role that in Australia is performed by party officials is typically performed in

US presidential campaigns by personal appointees of the candidate (Plouffe 2009: 24; Institute of Politics 2009) or in British campaigns by a Member of Parliament who is a trusted adviser of the leader (Blair 2010: 3; FT Reporters 2010). In Australia, party officials appear to have stronger institutional autonomy than in Britain: chosen by the party organisation, they are better able to survive differences with the parliamentary leader (for example compare Young 1986: 94–96, and Williams 1997: 57, 275, with Blair 2010: 82).

Yet professionalisation of campaigning has been a global phenomenon, driven by media and marketing revolutions that have transformed campaign management in Australia no less than in the US, Britain and elsewhere (Farrell 1996; Plasser and Plasser 2002). The three cases reported here suggest that party officials can be highly effective political marketers. As party executives and designated 'campaign directors', they exercised significant organisational power: they set electoral strategy, engaged market researchers and advertisers, marshalled financial resources including public funding, managed campaign headquarters, recruited staff and volunteers, and coordinated the campaign activities of the party 'in office' and the party 'on the ground'. Their campaign leadership bestowed personal influence on party resourcing across the board, including in policy development and the selection of parliamentary leadership.

Against this, it must be emphasised that they succeeded only as opposition campaigners. Successful opposition campaigns are rare, certainly in Australian politics where there have only been four changes of government at the ballot box in the 16 elections since 1972. Their performance over several years in opposition says nothing about their capacity to meet the political marketing challenge of government since, as we have seen, none of them attempted to do so.

The important point is that campaign managers of all varieties need to be aware of core political marketing concepts and develop expertise in applying them in campaigns. In the absence of formal training programs this can best be acquired through practical 'on the job' experience, as indeed was the case with these three examples. Parties seeking to ensure a future supply of campaign expertise should implement career development programs to rotate their officials through a variety of campaign roles and challenges (Mills 2010). This can include subordinate roles in the party organisation, exposure to specific campaign functions, electoral contests at state or local levels, or as volunteers or observers with affiliated parties in foreign countries.

Impact on politics

The impact of political marketing by party officials can be seen most obviously within the party itself. Contrary to the propositions advanced by Lynch *et al.* (2006: 85), party members and local activists do not represent an essential campaign resource. To be sure, there will always be some role for local volunteers, particularly in marginal seats, in doorknocking during the campaign and mobilising voters on election day. Yet a research-driven, capital intensive, nationally centralised style of political marketing places less reliance on bottom-up political expression and activism. Indeed, the centrist strategies arising from research-based marketing communications may serve to reduce levels of engagement and participation by members and activists driven by values or ideology. Thus while membership of Western political parties has been in decline, head offices have grown in size, resources, influence and specialisation.

In particular, the strategic significance of market research bestows organisational stature on whoever in the party controls that research. This can operate at the expense of the members (Smith 2009) and also of elected politicians, whose relative effectiveness and standing is measured by research in stark terms. It may be that in an environment of what has been termed a 'permanent' election campaign (Blumenthal 1980), activities across the entire party – by branch members as well as elected legislators – will be increasingly subjected to the centralising and coordinating role of Head Office. Party officials appear to have been granted – or, perhaps, they have seized – the mandate to make the pursuit of electoral success the overriding mission of the whole party organisation.

This implies a broader impact at the level of the electoral contest. Party officials are effective political marketers regardless of their partisan affiliation or personal political leanings. Of course, party officials may well share the broad values of their party and be personally committed to its success, but their effectiveness as campaign director depends on their professional skills, and they are employed for instrumental rather than ideological purposes: they seek electoral victory. They find political marketing strategies well suited to the task, and these are largely value-free and available to both sides of politics. Indeed, the RBV suggests that parties willing to make the necessary long-term investments in organisational capabilities such as campaigning skills can be expected to achieve more sustained electoral success than those that do not. The electoral contest, then, has shifted decisively beyond the traditional normative drivers of democratic choice – policy and leadership – to turn in part on a contest for campaigning skills, professional staffing and money.

Again, the limits of this transformation need to be noted. The evidence presented here suggests that different stages of the political marketing sequence are the responsibility of different parts of the party. While this requires further research, it seems that party officials – the 'party as organisation' – have clear responsibility for gathering market intelligence, building organisational resources and deploying them in the campaign contest. The product design phase is a more collective exercise involving the organisational and legislative components of the party, while delivery appears to be the exclusive preserve of the party 'in office'. Party members 'on the ground' have little role at any stage. Regardless of the attractions of market orientation as an opposition campaign strategy, a gulf may exist between the tasks of winning elections and of governing.

The way forward

The identification of party officials as central to political marketing opens up a challenging agenda of research questions with significant implications for practitioners. Political marketing research needs to include analysis of party officials when considering how campaign strategy and communication is developed. Further studies of party organisations and party officials are needed, including comparative studies across parties and, in particular, comparing parties in government and opposition. Establishing the framework of accountabilities within parties, including the organisational ownership of market research, appears central to understanding the broader process of political marketing. Further research is needed on the process of long-term resource development, expanded to include considerations of financial resources and brand.

Such research could throw light on a critical unresolved political marketing issue. Organisations seeking success in the electoral marketplace must be market oriented, that is, focused on understanding and satisfying the preference of consumers. This is a threshold requirement in the literature, yet its practical implications remain unclear. On the one hand, consumer-voter satisfaction is understood as essential but ultimately subordinate to the goal of the organisation itself (profitability, electoral success); relationship-building and product delivery are vehicles to further organisational success. On the other hand, consumer satisfaction is presented as a desirable end in itself, as it fundamentally considers 'society's well-being' (Henneberg and Eghbalian 2002: 81) or 'creates value for voter-citizens' (O'Cass 2009). Where do party officials fall in this debate? The evidence here would place them in the former camp, valuing voter preferences not for altruistic or normative purposes but for the instrumental purpose of defeating the competition and winning the electoral contest. Moreover, party officials appear to care less for relationship building or policy delivery, seeking instead to generate only just enough voter satisfaction to secure an electoral majority. Further research with practitioner reflection could establish the validity of these observations and consider their implications for political success and democratic health.

Bibliography

Australian Electoral Commission (2008) '2007 Federal Election Funding Payments'. Online, www.aec.gov.au/Elections/federal_elections/2007/election_funding_payment.htm (accessed 7 April 2011).

Bean, C., Simms, M., Bennett, S. and Warhurst, J. (1997) *The Politics of Retribution: The 1996 Australian Federal Election*, St Leonards: Allen & Unwin.

Blair, T. (2010) *A Journey*, London: Hutchinson.

Blewett, N. (1973) 'Labor 1968–72: Planning for Victory', in H. Mayer (ed.) *Labor to Power: Australia's 1972 Election*, Sydney: Angus and Robertson.

Blewett, N. and Jaensch, D. (1971) *Playford to Dunstan*, Melbourne: F.W. Cheshire.

Blumenthal, S. (1980) *Permanent Campaign: Inside the World of Elite Political Operatives*, Boston, MA: Beacon Press.

Farrell, D.M. (1996) 'Campaign Strategies and Tactics', in L. Le Duc, R.G. Niemi and P. Norris (eds) *Comparing Democracies: Elections and Voting in Global Perspective*, Thousand Oaks, CA: Sage Publications.

Freudenberg, G. (1977) *A Certain Grandeur*, Melbourne: Macmillan.

FT Reporters (2010) 'A-Teams assemble in battle to woo voters', *Financial Times* FT.com, 8 March.

Gartrell, T. (2007) 'Labor Won the Campaign, Outright', Paper presented at the National Press Club, Canberra, Australia, 4 December.

Hancock, I. (2000) *National and Permanent: The Federal Organisation of the Liberal Party of Australia 1944–1965*, Carlton: Melbourne University Press.

—— (2007) *The Liberals: A History of the NSW Division of the Liberal Party of Australia 1945–2000*, Annandale: Federation Press.

Henneberg, S. (2002) 'Understanding Political Marketing', in N. O'Shaughnessy and S.C. Henneberg (eds) *The Idea of Political Marketing*, Westport, CT: Praeger.

Henneberg, S. and Eghbalian, S. (2002) 'Kirchheimer's Catch-all Party: A Reinterpretation in Marketing Terms', in N. O'Shaughnessy and S.C. Henneberg (eds) *The Idea of Political Marketing*, Westport, CT: Praeger.

Hughes, A. and Dann, S. (2009) 'Political Marketing and Stakeholder Engagement', *Marketing Theory* 9, 2: 243–56.

—— (2010) 'Australian Political Marketing: Substance Backed by Style', in J. Lees-Marshment, J. Stromback and C. Rudd (eds) *Global Political Marketing*, London: Routledge, 82–95.

Institute of Politics, John F. Kennedy School of Government, Harvard University (2009) *Campaign for President: The Managers look at 2008*, Lanham, MD: Rowman and Littlefield.

Jackman, C. (2008) *Inside Kevin 07*, Carlton: Melbourne University Press.

Katz, R.S. and Mair, P. (1993) 'The Evolution of Party Organisations in Europe: The Three Faces of Party Organisation', *American Review of Politics* 14: 593–617. [Reprinted in S. Wolinetz (ed.) (1998) *Political Parties*, London and New York: Ashgate Dartmouth.]

Key, V.O. (1964) *Politics, Parties and Pressure Groups*, New York: Crowell.

Kirchheimer, O. (1966) 'The Transformation of the Western European Party Systems', in J. La Palombara and M. Weiner (eds) *Political Parties and Political Development*, Princeton, NJ: Princeton University Press.

Lees-Marshment, J. (2001) *Political Marketing and British Political Parties. The Party's Just Begun*, Manchester: Manchester University Press.

—— (2009) *Political Marketing – Principles and Applications*, London: Routledge.

Lilleker, D. and Negrine, R. (2006) 'Mapping a Market Orientation: Can We Detect Political Marketing only Through the Lens of Hindsight?', in P.J. Davies and B.I. Newman (eds) *Winning Elections with Political Marketing*, New York: The Haworth Press.

Lynch, R., Baines, P. and Egan, J. (2006) 'Long-Term Performance of Political Parties: Towards a Competitive Resource-Based Perspective', *Journal of Political Marketing* 5, 3: 71–92.

McMullin, R. (1991) *The Light on the Hill: The Australian Labor Party, 1891–1991*, Melbourne: Oxford University Press.

Medvic, S. (2006) 'Understanding Campaign Strategy: Deliberate Priming and the Role of Professional Political Consultants', *Journal of Political Marketing* 5, 1/2: 11–32.

Mills, S. (1986) *The New Machine Men: Polls and Persuasion in Australian Politics*, Ringwood: Penguin Books.

—— (2010) 'Contrasting Paths: Political careers of Labor and Liberal State Party Officials', Paper presented to the Australian Political Science Association. Online, apsa2010.com.au/full-papers/pdf/APSA2010_0157.pdf (accessed 8 April 2011).

Nassmacher, K.-H. (2009) *The Funding of Party Competition: Political Finance in 25 Democracies*, Baden-Baden: Nomos.

Negrine, R. (2007) 'The Professionalisation of Political Communication in Europe', in R. Negrine, P. Mancini, C. Holtz-Bacha and S. Papathanassopoulos (eds) *The Professionalisation of Political Communication*, Bristol: Intellect.

Newman, B. (1994) *The Marketing of the President: Political Marketing as Campaign Strategy*, Thousand Oaks, CA: Sage.

O'Cass, A. (1996) 'Political Marketing and the Marketing Concept', *European Journal of Marketing* 30, 10/11: 45–61.

—— (2001) 'Political Marketing: An Investigation of the Political Marketing Concept and Political Market Orientation in Australian Politics', *European Journal of Marketing* 35, 9/10: 1003–25.

—— (2009) 'A Resource-based View of the Political Party and Value Creation for the Voter citizen: An Integrated Framework for Political Marketing', *Marketing Theory* 9, 2: 189–208.

Orr, G. (2010) *The Law of Politics: Elections, Parties and Money in Australia*, Sydney: Federation Press.

O'Shaughnessy, N.J. (1990) *The Phenomenon of Political Marketing*, London: Macmillan.

Panebianco, A. (1988) *Political Parties: Organization and Power*, Cambridge: Cambridge University Press.

Parkin, A. and Warhurst, J. (eds) (1983) *Machine Politics in the Australian Labor Party*, North Sydney: George Allen & Unwin.

Plasser, F. and Plasser, G. (2002) *Global Political Campaigning: A Worldwide Analysis of Campaign Professionals and Their Practices*, Westport, CT: Praeger.

Plouffe, D. (2009) *The Audacity to Win*, New York: Viking.

Robb, A. (1996) 'Lessons from the 1996 Campaign', *The Sydney Papers* (Autumn).

Sabato, L.J. (1981) *The Rise of Political Consultants*, New York: Basic Books.

Scammell, M. (1997) 'The Wisdom of the War Room: US Campaigning and Americanization', Research Paper R-17, Cambridge, MA: Joan Shorenstein Center for Press, Politics and Public Policy, Harvard University.

Simms, M. (ed.) (2009) 'Kevin 07: The 2007 Australian Election', *Australian Cultural History* 27/28, 2/1.

Simms, M. and Warhurst, J. (eds) (2000) *Howard's Agenda: The 1998 Australian Election*, St Lucia: University of Queensland Press.

—— (2005) *Mortgage Nation: The 2004 Australian election*, Perth: API Network.

Smith, J.K. (2009) 'Campaigning and the Catch-All Party: The Process of Party Transformation in Britain', *Party Politics* 15, 5: 555–72.

Starr, G. (ed.). (1980) *The Liberal Party of Australia, A Documentary History*, Richmond: Drummond/Heinemann.

Wanna, J. (2010) 'Business and Unions', *Australian Cultural History* 28, 1: 15–22.

Ware, A. (1996) *Political Parties and Party Systems*, Oxford: Oxford University Press.

Warhurst, J. and Parkin, A. (2000) *The Machine: Labor Confronts the Future*: St Leonards: Allen & Unwin.

Warhurst, J. and Simms, M. (2002) *2001: The Centenary Election*, St Lucia: University of Queensland Press.

Webb, P. and Kolodny, R. (2006) 'Professional Staff in Political Parties', in R.S. Katz and W. Crotty (eds) *Handbook of Party Politics*, London: Sage Publications.

Weller, P. and Lloyd, B. (eds) (1978) *Federal Executive Minutes 1915–1955: Minutes of the Meetings of the Federal Executive of the Australian Labor Party*, Melbourne: Melbourne University Press.

West, K. (1965) *Power in the Liberal Party: A Study in Australian Politics*, Melbourne: F.W. Cheshire.

Williams, P. (1997) *The Victory: The Inside Story of the Takeover of Australia*, St Leonards: Allen & Unwin.

Wring, D. (2005) *The Politics of Marketing the Labour Party*, Houndmills, Basingstoke: Palgrave Macmillan.

Young, M. (1986) 'The Build-up to 1972', in *The Whitlam Phenomenon: Fabian Papers*, Ringwood: McPhee Gribble/Penguin Books.

Young, S. (2004) *The Persuaders: Inside the Hidden Machine of Political Advertising*, North Melbourne: Pluto Press.

Young, S. and Tham, J.-C. (2006) *Political Finance in Australia: A Skewed and Secret System*, Canberra: Democratic Audit of Australia, Australian National University.

Part IV
Communicating and connecting with the public

16

Campaigning in the 21st century

Change and continuity in American political marketing

Dennis W. Johnson

The topic: campaigning in the 21st century

Political marketing strategies and techniques have transformed campaigns and elections in the US during the first decade of the 21st century. What was creative and new in 2000 was surpassed in 2004; what was exciting and unique in 2008 was improved upon in 2010. Because of the immense changes brought about by technology and online communication over the past decade, a new model of professional political campaigning has been emerging: one that is far less top-down and controlled by political consultants and has greater engagement of ordinary citizens. This chapter describes and evaluates the enormous changes that have occurred in American political marketing, especially with the advent of online communication, and presents a model for 21st-century campaigning, looks at what works and what does not, and suggests areas for future inquiry and scholarly research.

Previous research

For most of American history, political parties have been dominant forces in campaigns and elections. They recruited candidates, made campaign funds available, assessed public opinion and mobilized voters (Herrnson 2005: 19–36). By the mid-1960s, however, party-centered campaigns had given way to candidate-centered campaigns, with individual candidates hiring their own teams of experts, political consultants and operatives (Menefee-Libey 2000; Herrnson and Campbell 2008). Scholars began noting the growing importance of a new fixture in election campaigning: the political consultant (Sabato 1981; Medvic 2001; Burton and Shea 2003; Dulio 2004; Johnson 2007). By the late 1960s and early 1970s, political consultants routinely worked for individual candidates and in the last two decades of the 20th century, they became permanent fixtures in US elections.

An example of a well-funded US Senate campaign held during the 1990s would illustrate the extent to which candidates relied on professional assistance. The senatorial candidate would hire a full range of consultants and operatives: a campaign manager, a media team, private polling firm, researchers, fundraisers, voter identification and targeting specialists, get out the vote, direct mail and telephone operatives. In order to pay for the consultants, the polling, phone banks, television advertising, direct mail, staff and office, and countless other expenditures, the campaign would probably need to raise $5 million, depending on the size and number of media markets (Johnson 2007).

This senate campaign and thousands like it would have been conducted using the 20th-century model of campaigning.

The 20th-century model of campaigning in the US

During the last 35 or 40 years of the 20th century, candidates for major political office in the US retained the services of political consultants. Those campaigns shared several common features.

First, political consultants were in command-and-control mode. They would be the dominant voice in defining the contest, creating strategy and in maintaining message discipline. Candidates, of course, would have the last word and were ultimately responsible for the conduct and tone of the campaign, but often the decisions were driven by the experience and knowledge of the senior consultants.

Second, the consultants and strategists would employ a top-down method of communicating. They would gather information from likely voters, guided by survey research results, through polls, focus groups and dial meter sessions, but would not involve individual voters or activists in the critical decisions of the campaign, such as what the candidate says, the shape and content of the candidate's television commercials, where the candidate goes and what issues should be emphasized.

Third, campaigns relied on television as the chief medium of communication. For many secondary races in major media markets which could not afford television, direct mail became the communication weapon of choice. Campaigns also relied on radio advertising, billboards, phone banks and newsprint to get their message across to voters (West 2010).

Fourth, campaigns had time to craft messages, days and even weeks to put together television advertising, time to absorb an opponent's attack and then respond in kind. However, with the advent of all-news television and radio channels and 24/7 news cycles, campaign messaging and communications were compelled to go on all-day and all-night alert. Polling results became more easily available and their results were aided by advances in software technology.

Fifth, much of the campaign was based on guesswork, instinct and past experience. Campaigns relied on past voting data and census figures, but did not factor in other elements such as lifestyle choices, intensity of support for issues or candidates, and other matters.

Sixth, fundraising was conducted primarily through big ticket events, where a small number of contributors would 'max out' – give the largest amount of money permitted by law. Direct mail was the vehicle of choice for reaching those contributors who gave less money, but it was very expensive to cast about for potential donors. Small-dollar donations, $25 or so, were also received, but it was difficult and expensive to rely on such small givers. Except for special events, it was very hard to raise large amounts of money in short periods of time.

Seventh, except in presidential and other high-profile campaigns, voters were basically spectators. They would be asked primarily to do one thing, show up on election day and cast their ballot. Few voters contributed money, volunteered on campaigns or interacted with the campaign in any way.

New research

Scholars from the disciplines of political science, political communications and political marketing increasingly are turning their attention to modern campaigning and professional campaign management. They have seen over the past decade a number of critical, even transformative, changes in the way US campaigns are conducted. The changes have come in fundraising, survey research, television advertising, targeting and mobilizing voters, and the nationalization of campaigns (Semiatin 2005; Semiatin 2008; Johnson 2010). Most profoundly, however, the changes have come from the explosion of online communication, which will be the focus of this chapter.

The new media

Just as online communication has fundamentally changed the way we interact with one another, so, too, have political campaigns made enormous changes in the way they communicate with people, the way people communicate with campaigns, and the way citizens, activists and voters communicate with one another about elections and campaigns. What has changed during the past decade?

Getting information about elections

Just like much of the industrialized world, the US has become a much more wired nation. At the end of 2009 a total of 74 percent of American adults stated that they used the internet, 60 percent used broadband and 55 percent connected to the internet wirelessly (Rainie 2010). While online communications have become more accepted by younger, better-educated citizens, still the majority of Americans rely on the local television news (40 percent), cable news networks (38 percent) and the nightly network television news (32 percent) to 'regularly learn something' about presidential politics. The internet was relied on by 24 percent of those surveyed (Pew Research Center for the People and the Press 2008).

Campaign websites

As new online technologies have emerged, they have been incorporated into political campaigns, sometimes quickly and, at other times, hesitantly and cautiously. By the 2000 US presidential campaign and the 2002 midterm elections, campaign websites and online communications had become common features (Johnson 2006). Some online activists and observers were talking about the profound changes that online communications would bring, changing forever the way campaigns are run. In their assessment of the place of the internet in future elections, political scientists Bruce Bimber and Richard Davis took a sober look, and concluded that internet campaigning helped to reinforce political attachments, helped mobilize activists to contribute funds and to volunteer their time, and 'just maybe – to vote'. They recognized that the internet was a niche communication tool, directed at highly specific audiences, which would become highly effective to mobilize those who are politically active and interested, but they predicted that the internet would 'not produce the mobilization of voters long predicted' (Bimber and Davis 2003: 165).

Political scientists Stephen Schneider and Kristen Foot examined the growth of US presidential campaign internet site features from 2000 to 2004. They found that websites grouped features in four common areas: informing (with features presenting issues, campaign news, biography speeches, photos and campaign advertisements); involving (online donations, volunteer, sign up for email, campaign calendar events and campaign store); connecting (endorsements, links to government, civic and advocacy groups, political parties, and comparisons with other candidates); and mobilizing (sending links from the site, e-paraphernalia, offline distribution of campaign materials, letters to the editor, action management sites or sections) (Schneider and Foot 2006; also Foot and Schneider 2006). The authors found a slight increase from 2000 to 2004 in informing, a sharp increase in the practice of involving, a slight increase in the proportion of campaigns engaged in connecting, and mobilization was just beginning to emerge in 2004.

The innovations in online communication first came in the 2003–04 Democratic presidential primary season from the Howard Dean campaign. Dean connected with the social networking site MeetUp.com, created the first presidential candidate blog site, its own social network (Deanlink), a personalized page for fundraising (Deanspace) and a virtual community for young people (Generation Dean). Several on the Dean online technology team created Blue State Digital, an online technology firm, and later worked directly on the Obama 2008 presidential campaign or as consultants to it. The Dean campaign led scholars to examine the impact of online technology in the pre-Obama era (Williams and Tedesco 2006).

YouTube and web videos

With the creation of the video website YouTube in 2005, it was not long before campaigns began using this convenient platform for free media. YouTube hit its stride in the 2008 presidential campaign. Barack Obama made the most use of this vehicle, posting 1,839 videos with an astounding 132.8 million viewers; by contrast, John McCain posted 329 videos with 26.3 million viewers. YouTube became a platform for candidates to bypass the established media and go directly to viewers online (Frantzich 2009). Many of those viewers, of course, were too young to vote or were not registered, were not American citizens, or were repeat viewers. YouTube also joined up with CNN to produce two presidential debates, where questions posted online by viewers were used, rather than those posed by a panel from the mainstream media.

Email, cell phones and Twitter

One of the older technologies is still one of the most important: electronic mail. Online expert Michael Cornfield observed in 2004 that email would outperform a website 'ninety-nine days out of a hundred'. Email is sent to a defined address, it is read, it is easier to respond to, and it is harder for the press and the political opposition to monitor than a campaign website (Cornfield 2004: 27). Over the years, campaigns have become more interactive: posting pictures, videos, links to other information and, not surprisingly, including 'Donate Now' buttons.

One of the innovations of the 2000 presidential election came from the Al Gore campaign. Through emails to supporters and followers, it encouraged them to text message or email their

Table 16.1 First use of selected online communication tools in US political campaigns

Campaign websites	1992
Email	1992
Political advertising on the web	1998
Text messaging	2000
Blogging	2003
Social networking	2004
Online videos (YouTube)	2006
Microblogging (Twitter)	2008

own friends, to get them interested in Gore's campaign. By 2008, and particularly in the Obama campaign, text messaging and friend-to-friend contacts were used on a massive scale.

Not until the mid-2000s did US campaigns begin to understand the potential of cell phones as communication devices. Mobile phone communication had caught on in other parts of the world, helping to bring down the government of Joseph Estrada in the Philippines in 2001 and mobilizing democracy protestors during the Ukrainian 'Orange Revolution' in 2004 (Institute for Politics, Democracy and the Internet 2005). With the creation of the smartphone, particularly the RIM BlackBerry, the Apple iPhone, the Nokia N900 and phones running Google's Android operating systems, campaigns have been able to develop smartphone applications to help mobilize volunteers, and facilitate fundraising and other campaign functions.

The microblog Twitter was created in early 2006 and soon went public. Several 2008 presidential candidates, starting with John Edwards, Joe Biden and Barack Obama, used Twitter to communicate with followers. Since then, candidates have been routinely adding Twitter to their repertoire of online communication devices.

Political and campaign blogs

Political blogs have fundamentally changed the way citizens interact with candidates and others. Blogs, first used in presidential campaigns by Howard Dean in 2003, were then used extensively by John Kerry and George W. Bush in the 2004 general election (Trammell 2006). Since that time, presidential and many other national and state candidates have used blogs to communicate with followers.

Social networking

Social networking as a political communication tool first appeared during the 2004 Democratic primaries, when Howard Dean's campaign used MeetUp.com; then other campaigns both at presidential and congressional levels in 2006 began to use social networking. Presidential candidate John Edwards signed up on more social networks than any other candidate in 2008: at least 23 sites. However, it was Barack Obama's campaign that had a huge presence on social network sites. There were over 2.2 million supporters on the various Obama Facebook sites, 800,000 on MySpace and a substantial following on LinkedIn and other social networking sites. More than 2 million people logged on to MyBO (My.BarackObama.com) and through it were able to contribute funds, raise funds, develop communities and reach out to like-minded groups. Through MyBO, there were 400,000 blog postings, 35,000 volunteers were recruited and 200,000 off-line events were held. Obama had 'friended' more than 7 million supporters (Vargas 2008a).

Online advertising

Political advertising on internet sites began in 1998 and has grown slowly since. During the 2004 presidential campaign, the candidates, parties and major interest groups spent roughly $2.6 million on online banner advertisements. Yet this figure was less than 1 percent of that spent on television buys in the 100 largest media markets during the same time. By the end of the 2008 presidential election, the Obama campaign had spent some $16 million on online media – a tiny fraction of the complete media buys (Kaye 2009).

A relatively new marketing theory, Long-Tail Marketing, argues that businesses and political candidates can communicate better with those they are trying to reach by going to small, niche markets rather than relying on broadcasting to larger audiences (Anderson 2006). The 2008 US Senate campaign of Minnesota Democrat Al Franken used long-tail nanotargeting to reach voters. It targeted more than 125 niche groups with more than 1,000 pieces of persuasive online advertising, for less than $100,000. For example, when a Minnesota farmer used the search engine Google, the Franken campaign had bought keywords and phrases, hundreds of them, like 'farm supply', 'feed stores', or 'large animal veterinarian'. When the farmer entered those words in his search, up would pop a Franken for Senate advertisement geared toward agricultural interests (Koster 2009).

Impact of online communication

Increase in online news consumers

We might mark the 1996 presidential election as the beginning of online political campaigning in the US. During one of the presidential debates, Republican candidate Robert Dole announced his website address to a nationwide audience. His presidential website was rudimentary and he botched the address; nevertheless, over a million people responded the next day. Looking back on 1996, it seems almost light years away when thinking about online communication. First came email and websites, then blogs, social networking, web videos, smartphone applications and the rest. The best of presidential, congressional and statewide campaigns began adopting all of these communications tools; so, too, did advocacy groups, the old media and others. By the mid-2000s, the attentive public had an incredible, bewildering array of information available about presidential campaigns. During the 2004 campaign, for example, the Pew Research Center estimated that there were 63 million 'online news consumers' in the US (Rainie *et al.* 2005). That number rapidly expanded during the 2008 campaign, as indicated in Table 16.2.

Instant, unfiltered communication

Online communication meant instant communication and campaigns, especially in the crucial final weeks, can run at warp speed. A campaign can be attacked at all times of the day or night,

Table 16.2 Online metrics for the 2008 presidential campaign

	Obama	*McCain*
Facebook friends on election day	2,397,253	622,860
Unique visits to campaign websites in week ending 1 November	4,851,069	1,464,544
Online videos mentioning candidate	104,454	64,092
Campaign-made videos posted on YouTube	1,822	330
Total hours people spent watching campaign videos (as of 23 October)	14,600,000	488,000
Cost of equivalent purchase of 30-second advertisements	$46.9 million	$1.5 million
References to campaign's voters contact operation on Google	479,000	325

Note: These figures should be observed with caution, since there is no way to know the number of repeat viewers, those who live outside of the US, and those not eligible to vote.

and in the pinball-like atmosphere of a heated contest, particularly in its final days, bad news can come with the speed of digital communication. It could be a blog posting, an email charge gone viral, a nasty video posted on YouTube, or any one of a variety of online sources. This also means that rumor and innuendo, unchecked and unverified, can abound. Rumors during the 2008 presidential contest were bountiful. Whisper and rumor campaigns have always been part of political campaigns, but the online nature took them to a different, more sinister level. Psychology professor Nicholas DiFonzo, who had been studying political rumor-mongering for 20 years, observed that he had never seen so many rumors as seen in 2008 (DiFonzo 2008). Many of the falsehoods and ugly rumors were directed against Obama, in particular.

Is the internet the culprit? It is certainly the vehicle. Cass R. Sunstein argues that people increasingly are getting their information not from the major news channels, like network television, but from online sources. They subscribe to email listservs or RSS feeds for their favorite sites. Liberal blogs tend to link to other liberal blog sites, and conservative blogs, to an even greater extent, link to other conservative blogs (Adamic and Glance 2005). Sunstein argues that the internet 'serves, for many, as a breeding group for extremism, precisely because like-minded people are deliberating with greater ease and frequency with one another'. He calls this process 'cyberpolarization' (Sunstein 2009; Kolbert 2009).

The ever-present camera and the viral response

Today, no candidate is safe from the prying eye of the television lens, the video recorder, or the cell phone camera. A gaffe, an errant word or gesture, can be immediately captured by a campaign volunteer or by anyone holding a cell phone. During the early 2008 presidential primaries, Hillary Clinton was caught singing the national anthem horribly off-key at a campaign stop; John Edwards was caught primping for two full minutes in a television station's green room, meticulously combing his hair before an on-camera appearance. Journalists Chris Cillizza and Dan Balz mark the 2006 mid-term election as one that changed the rules of the game. This was the year of the 'rogue videographers' (Cillizza and Balz 2007). Probably the most damaging was an errant comment made by Senator George Allen of Virginia, running for re-election. His slur of an Indian-American campaign worker reached YouTube, went viral, and was probably a central factor in his close loss. The Allen defeat meant the end of his possible presidential bid, but also a key loss for Republicans in the US Senate, leading to a turnover in party control.

The open-source campaign

Taking its name from open-source software, the term 'open-source campaigning' or 'open-source politics' emphasizes citizen involvement and direct online participation in elections and campaigns (Sifry 2004). Veteran Democratic pollster Peter Hart summed up the impact of technology on the 2008 presidential campaign: 'This is a big transformation in how campaigns operate, and it boils down to the power of one, the feeling that one individual can make a difference' (Vargas 2008b). Successful, professionally driven campaigns have always been driven from the top down, but now with the enormous opportunities and challenges of online communication, a new model is appearing, with citizen input encouraged and fostered.

This is probably the most important aspect for new media and online communication in election politics: in the best of campaigns (and with the best of candidates) activists and even casual voters can feel a sense of sharing and participation. Through online communication, they share their ideas with candidates, are encouraged to volunteer, meet and talk with others, share their experiences and take some measure of ownership in the campaign.

Advice for practitioners

The 2008 presidential campaign offered us the most technologically savvy presidential candidate in history, Barack Obama. Armed with his two BlackBerrys, Obama first had to do battle against Hillary Clinton, who announced her candidacy over the internet but then ran a much more traditional 20th-century campaign, and in the general election against John McCain, who didn't even use email and whose campaign, while it used some of the bells and whistles of online communication, didn't have the same remarkable effects as Obama's. The Obama campaign set the standard for the use of online technology, the integration of offline and online elements, and the innovative usage of social media, cell phones, the internet and television.

Obama campaign manager David Plouffe stated that 'technology was core to our campaign from Day One and it only grew in importance' (Plouffe 2009: 237). The campaign invested heavily in staff and equipment. Digital campaign veterans from the Howard Dean campaign, like Joe Rospars and Jascha Franklin-Hodge, both of whom then worked for Blue State Digital, Chris Hughes, who along with Mark Zuckerberg had co-founded Facebook, and a number of executives from technology companies teamed up to form the backbone of the online campaign team. Nearly 90 staffers were hired, and millions were spent on servers, email systems, web development and text messaging. A single database, with terabytes of information, was created, integrating all aspects of fundraising, social networking and activism from MyBO – something never done before in presidential campaigns (Graff 2009).

Aided by online communication, Obama supporters held more than 100,000 events throughout the country; more than 10,000 people applied to become one of the 3,000 Obama 'organizing fellows' who would go out in their communities to register voters; more than 3 million phone calls were made by Obama supporters during the last four days of the campaign alone (Graff 2009).

The Obama campaign oversaw more than 100 different websites, had 57 different profiles on MySpace, created nearly 2,000 YouTube videos, including the most successful YouTube entry, Obama's 37-minute speech on race relations during the 2008 primary season, which was watched by more people online than seen on television.

What the Obama team had done could have been done by any of the 20 major party candidates for president that year. There was nothing radically new about the technology; there was no secret formula. The key was the integration of online campaigning into the overall campaign: in fundraising, field organizing and communications (Cornfield 2010; Germany 2009). Garrett M. Graff, a veteran of the Dean presidential bid, observed that 'the game-changer in the Obama campaign … was that technology and the Internet was not an add-on for them. It was a carefully considered element of almost every critical campaign function' (Graff 2009: 38).

Impact on politics

The 21st-century campaign model

Compared with the presidential campaign of 2008 and the congressional elections of 2010, the US campaigns of a decade earlier on the surface may seem antiquated. With the maturing of online communication techniques, it seems like a whole new ball game for candidates, political consultants, political activists and voters. The reality, however, is more complicated. A new campaign model is emerging, but in many ways it still fits into the contours of the 20th-century model.

First, political consultants will still dominate in defining the campaign, setting its objectives, laying out the strategy for victory. Consultants will be in much greater demand because of their ability to cut through the clutter of both new and old media communication. With many more voices involved, there is the need for a clear, determined voice to define the race and state the case for the candidate. Campaigns will forever need to focus on fundraising, developing and communicating their message, mobilizing voters and getting them to vote. Campaigns in the 21st century will rely heavily on campaign managers, general consultants, pollsters, media teams, direct mail and other specialists. What will change, however, is the acceptance and the integration of online media into the core of the campaign. As the online component began to mature, campaigns realized the importance of having a webmaster, a blog specialist, a director of social media, an online advertising group, an online staff with equal strategic importance as any other component of the campaign. Ultimately, in the best-run campaigns, the online component will be a seamless, integral part of all campaign functions.

Second, the top-down, command-and-control model will give way to a more fluid model, which encourages citizen input and involvement. However, this can be tricky. On the one hand, it sounds like a clearly desired goal to have more people involved with the campaign, with more ideas flowing, with greater participation. On the other hand, it can be chaotic: following the whims and wishes of the moment instead of concentrating on a consistent, long-term strategy; listening to the loudest voices rather than the voices of those voters who could carry the candidate to victory; having a thousand messages and no clear message at all; and, like online media-savvy 2004 presidential candidate Howard Dean, being overtaken by the demands of supporters and losing control of the campaign.

Third, television will continue to be an important medium for campaign advertising, but, perhaps in the most fundamental transformation, online communications have created whole new ways of reaching voters. Free media, once confined to television, radio or newspaper coverage, now finds an unlimited home on YouTube and other web video sites. Likely voters are now reached through internet advertising, RSS feeds, podcasts, interactive websites, social media platforms, blogs, microblogs (like Twitter), text messages and that old standby, email.

Fourth, campaigns have speeded up dramatically. The campaign must expect to be engaged 24 hours a day. Polling results, field information, targeting and early voting data can all be received, analyzed and put into action in hours rather than in days or weeks. The campaign now sleeps only when the election is over.

Fifth, guesswork, instinct and experience are still key, but they are supplemented by research, metrics, and advances in market research and data collection. It now becomes easier for a campaign to know if a series of advertisements is working through focus group and dial meter research, by the click-through rates of online advertising, by the analysis of microtargeting information, and other techniques.

Sixth, campaigns still rely on big-dollar givers, but now can also have inexpensive access to small-dollar donors, thanks to online contributing solicited through email, texting, websites and online advertising. The universe of money givers can expand many-fold, using techniques often seen in public radio or other nonprofit fundraising schemes.

Seventh, thanks to online communication, voters can have a greater sense of participation in a campaign. They can be mobilized, they can mobilize themselves, meet with like-minded activists, and more easily contribute time, money and energy to a campaign. Of all the aspects of the 21st-century campaign model, this is the most promising for bringing about greater participation.

The 21st-century model recognizes the continuing need for consultants and campaign specialists, but it also recognizes that campaigns stuck in the old traditions and practices of the 1980s and 1990s are destined to be left behind and ultimately will become non-competitive. Likewise, those campaigns that fail to appreciate and use the craft and techniques of the 20th-century model are destined to become non-competitive.

Table 16.3 20th-century and 21st-century campaign models compared

20th-century model	*21st-century model*
Consultants dominate in creating strategy, in maintaining message discipline, in communicating with the public, and getting voters out to vote on election day	Consultants dominate; online component becomes integral part of campaign
Top-down approach	More fluid, with ideas, direction and support from grassroots
Television as most important communication medium	Television is important, but explosion of new media, free media online
Relatively more time to craft messages, responses and analysis	Campaign speeds up, running 24/7
Much of campaign based on guesswork, instinct and past experience	Heavier reliance on research, data and metrics to guide the campaign
Fundraising through big-ticket items; expensive direct mail solicitations; few small-amount donors	Big-ticket fundraising important; small-amount donors opening up through inexpensive online technology
Except for presidential contests, limited involvement of citizens beyond voting	Greater involvement of citizens, activists; sense that campaign is directly connected to them

The way forward

The 21st-century campaign offers many research opportunities for political management and political marketing scholars. With a new model of campaigning emerging and dynamic new ways to reach people, there are many challenges and opportunities for scholars and practitioners to examine and explore. Here are a few questions concerning new media communications and other aspects of 21st-century campaigning in the US:

The shape and direction of professional campaigning

How have the various segments – campaign generalists, pollsters, media, fundraisers, targeting specialists – of the political consulting industry adjusted to the new reality of technology and online communication? Is there a disconnect between the manner in which voters want to be informed and contacted and the way political consultants inform and contact them?

Just what works?

Green and Gerber (2008) have examined the impact of get out the vote techniques and found most of them wanting. What about other areas of communication, persuasion and identifying voters – are the current practices of political consultants effective and efficient uses of scarce time and money? What new technologies and online communication tools hold out the most promise for connecting with voters?

Integration of old and new media in campaigns

How will online media be integrated into other forms of communication? Is the technological revolution in campaigning at a plateau, or will there be new advances in communication and in identifying and contacting voters? Will there be a grand convergence of media platforms?

New media advertising

If we are in the 'prehistoric age' (Cornfield and Kaye 2009) of online advertising, what are the possibilities and opportunities for such advertising? What is the impact of such advertising? With the ability to measure click-throughs, do such metrics give researchers a clearer insight into the impact and effectiveness of online advertising?

Television

Is the 30-second spot a relic of 20th-century advertising? With more people watching more television (and more television channels), how can consultants strategically target their paid television advertising? How will television advertising be transformed in the next decade?

Polling, cell phones and reaching people

How can the inherent problems of cell phone-survey research be resolved? Can automated polls (robocalls) and brushfire polls yield results that are statistically reliable and valid as survey instruments? Will private political pollsters find online polling an inexpensive and reliable alternative to telephone-based polling? Is random digit dialing (RDD) too expensive a method for reaching voters; should it be replaced with voter lists?

The opportunities and limitations of microtargeting

Microtargeting in political campaigns came of age during the first decade of this century. Is there a more cost-effective way of conducting microtargeting analysis? With more and more demographic, lifestyle and psychographic information loaded into databases, does this information yield more accurate and sophisticated portraits of the electorate?

Campaigning at the local level and 21st-century techniques

As Chapman Rackman (2009) has observed, local-level campaigns seem to be a decade or so behind in developing the state-of-the-art campaign techniques that are seen at the presidential or major statewide level. How have local, small-budget contests been able to tap into new technologies and online communication? What are the optimal tools that a small-budget campaign can use most effectively?

A better way to fund political campaigns

Thanks to online contributions, it becomes easier to both solicit funds and contribute them. Are there ways in which structural and legal barriers to small-amount campaign financing can be broken down further? Is democracy better served by having strict limits on campaign contributions and by encouraging small-dollar donors through online giving? Is the legislation for public funding of presidential candidates in need of a major overhaul?

Better campaigning or merely louder voices

How can online technology and online communication bring about better citizen participation, a more informed electorate and more democratization of the electoral process? How can it do so without merely succumbing to the loudest, most persistent voices rather than the true wishes of the greater majority?

These and other questions face us in the decade ahead, as the 21st-century model of professional campaigning becomes more evident, and as technology and online communication both reinforce and transform our ways of electing candidates to office.

Bibliography

Adamic, L. and Glance, N. (2005) 'Divided they blog'. Online, www.blogpulse.com/papers/2005/AdamicGlanceBlogWWW.pdf (accessed 10 June 2010).

Adkins, R.E. and Dulio, D. (2010) *Cases in Congressional Campaigns: Incumbents Playing Defense*, New York: Routledge.

Anderson, C. (2006) *The Long Tail: Why the Future of Business is Selling Less of More*, New York: Hyperion.

Baker, F.W. (2009) *Political Campaigns and Political Advertising*, Santa Barbara, CA: Greenwood Press.

Bimber, B. and Davis, R. (2003) *Campaigning Online: The Internet in U.S. Elections*, New York: Oxford University Press.

Burton, J.B. and Shea, D.M. (2003) *Campaign Mode: Strategic Vision in Congressional Elections*, Lanham, MD: Rowman & Littlefield.

Cillizza, C. and Balz, D. (2007) 'On the electronic campaign trail', *Washington Post*, 22 January.

Cornfield, M. (2010) 'Game-changers: new technology and the 2008 presidential election', in L. Sabato (ed.) *The Year of Obama: How Barack Obama Won the White House*, New York: Longman.

—— (2004) *Politics Moves Online: Campaigning and the Internet*, New York: Century Foundation.

Cornfield, M. and Kaye, K. (2009) 'Online political advertising: The prehistoric era continues', *720 Strategies*. Online, www.720strategies.com/site/page/online_political_advertising_the_prehistoric_era_continues (accessed 1 June 2010).

Corrado, A., Malbin, M.J., Mann, T.E., and Ornstein, N.J. (2010) *Reform in an Age of Networked Campaigns: How to Foster Citizen Participation Through Small Donors and Volunteers*, Washington, DC: Campaign Finance Institute, American Enterprise Institute, and Brookings Institution.

Corrado, A., Ortiz, D.R., Mann, T.E. and Potter, T. (2005) *The New Campaign Finance Sourcebook*, Washington, DC: Brookings Institution.

DiFonzo, N. (2008) 'Political rumors in the 2008 election', *Psychology Today*, 29 October.

Dulio, D.A. (2004) *For Better or Worse? How Political Consultants Are Changing Elections in the United States*, Albany: State University of New York Press.

Foot, K. and Schneider, S. (2006) *Web Campaigning*, Cambridge, MA: MIT Press.

Frantzich, S.E. (2009) 'E-Politics and the 2008 presidential campaign', in W.J. Crotty (ed.) *Winning the Presidency 2008*, Boulder, CO: Paradigm Publishers.

Germany, J.B. (2009) 'The online revolution', in D.W. Johnson (ed.) *Campaigning for President 2008: Strategy and Tactics, New Voices and New Techniques*, New York: Routledge.

Graff, G.M. (2009) 'Barack Obama: How content management and Web 2.0 helped win the White House', *Infonomics*, March–April. Online, aiim.org/Infonomics/Obama-How-Web2.0-Helped-Win-Whitehouse.aspx (accessed 28 May 2010).

Green, D.P. and Gerber, A.S. (2008) *Get Out the Vote: How to Increase Voter Turnout*, second edn, Washington, DC: Brookings Institution.

Herrnson, P.S. (2005) 'The evolution of political campaigns', in P.S. Herrnson (ed.) *Guide to Political Campaigns in America*, Washington, DC: CQ Press.

Herrnson, P.S. and Campbell, C.C. (2008) 'Modern political campaigns in the United States', in D.W. Johnson (ed.) *Routledge Handbook on Political Management*, New York: Routledge.

Institute for Politics, Democracy and the Internet (2005) *The Politics-To-Go Handbook: A Guide to Using Mobile Technology in Politics*, Washington, DC: George Washington University.

Jagoda, K.A.B. (ed.) (2009) *About Face: The Dramatic Impact of the Internet on Politics and Advocacy*, San Diego, CA: e-Voter Institute Press.

Johnson, D.W. (2006) 'Campaigning and the Internet', in S.C. Craig (ed.) *The Electoral Challenge: Theory Meets Practice*, Washington, DC: CQ Press.

—— (2007) *No Place for Amateurs: How Political Consultants Are Reshaping American Democracy*, second edn, New York: Routledge.

—— (ed.) (2008) *Routledge Handbook on Political Management*, New York: Routledge.

—— (ed.) (2009) *Campaigning for President 2008: Strategy and Tactics, New Voices and New Techniques*, New York: Routledge.

—— (2010) *Campaigning in the Twenty-First Century: A Whole New Ballgame?* New York: Routledge.

Kaye, K. (2009) 'Google grabbed most of Obama's $16 million in 2008', *ClickZ*, 6 January. Online, www.clickz.com/3632263 (accessed 20 May 2011).

Kerbel, M.R. (2009) *Netroots: Online Progressives and the Transformation of American Politics*, Boulder, CO: Paradigm Publishers.

Kolbert, E. (2009) 'The things people say', *New Yorker*, 2 November.

Koster, J. (2009) 'Long-tail nanotargeting', *Politics*, February. Online, www.politicsmagazine.com/magazine-issues/february-2009/long-tail/nanotargeting (accessed 28 May 2010).

Malchow, H. (2003) *The New Political Targeting*, Washington, DC: Campaigns and Elections.

Medvic, S.K. (2001) *Political Consultants in U.S. Congressional Elections*, Columbus: Ohio State University Press.

Menefee-Libey, D. (2000) *The Triumph of Campaign-Centered Politics*, New York: Chatham House.

Panagopoulos, C. (ed.) (2009) *Politicking Online: The Transformation of Election Campaign Communications*, New Brunswick, NJ: Rutgers University Press.

Pew Research Center for the People and the Press (2008) 'Internet's broader role in campaign 2008', 11 January. Online, people-press.org/report/384/internets-broader-role-in-campaign-2008 (accessed 15 August 2009).

Plouffe, D. (2009) *The Audacity to Win: The Insider Story and Lessons of Barack Obama's Historic Victory*, New York: Viking.

Rackman, C. (2009) 'Trickle-down technology: The use of computing and network technology in state legislative campaigns', in C. Panagoupolos (ed.) *Politicking Online: The Transformation of Election Campaign Communications*, New Brunswick, NJ: Rutgers University Press.

Rainie, L. (2010) 'Internet, broadband and cell phone statistics', *Pew Internet and American Life Project*, 5 January. Online, www.pewinternet.org/Reports/2010/Internet-broadband-and-cell-phone-statistics.aspx (accessed 12 January 2010).

Rainie, L., Cornfield, M. and Horrigan, J. (2005) *The Internet and Campaign 2004*, Washington, DC: Pew Internet and American Life Project and Pew Research Center for the People and the Press.

Sabato, L. (1981) *The Rise of the Political Consultants: New Ways of Winning Elections*, New York: Basic Books.

Schneider, S.M. and Foot, K.A. (2006) 'Web campaigning by U.S. presidential primary candidates in 2000 and 2004', in A.P. Williams and J.C. Tedesco (eds) *The Internet Election: Perspectives on the Web in Campaign 2004*, Lanham, MD: Rowman & Littlefield.

Semiatin, R.J. (2005) *Campaigns in the 21st Century: The Changing Mosaic of American Politics*, Boston: McGraw Hill.

—— (ed.) (2008) *Campaigns on the Cutting Edge*, Washington, DC: CQ Press.

Sifry, M.L. (2004) 'The rise of open-source politics', *The Nation*. Online, www.thenation.com/issue/november-22-2004 (accessed 15 August 2010).

Stonecash, J.M. (2008) *Political Polling: Strategic Information in Campaigns*, Lanham, MD: Rowman & Littlefield.

Sunstein, C.R. (2009) *On Rumors: How Falsehood Spread, Why We Believe Them, What Can Be Done*, New York: Farrar, Strauss & Giroux.

Trammell, K.D. (2006) 'The blogging of the president', in A.P. Williams and J.C. Tedesco (eds) *The Internet Election: Perspectives on the Web in Campaign 2004*, Lanham, MD: Rowman & Littlefield.

Vargas, J.A. (2008a) 'Obama's wide web', *Washington Post*, 20 August.

—— (2008b) 'Something just clicked', *Washington Post*, 10 June.

West, D.M. (2010) *Air Wars: Television Advertising in Election Campaigns, 1952–2008*, fifth edn, Washington, DC: CQ Press.

Williams, A.P. and Tedesco, J.C. (eds) (2006) *The Internet Election: Perspectives on the Web in Campaign 2004*, Lanham, MD: Rowman & Littlefield.

17

Selling Sarah Palin

Political marketing and the 'Walmart Mom'

Robert Busby

The topic: selling candidates

The emergence of Sarah Palin as an iconic figure for the Republican party in the 2008 election was testament to the interplay of several issues central to an understanding of the contemporary nature of political marketing. Her personal brand utilised elements of her personal values and her lifestyle choices, the emotive use of the history of the Republican party to symbolise her as the inheritor of a distinctive Republican mandate, and the expression of populism through the exploitation of her autobiographical past and regional location. On its own the Palin brand was sufficient to create an identifiable and marketable political product which attracted attention on both a state and a national stage. However, other factors were significant. Palin's 'mediagenic' presence granted her a disproportionate amount of coverage in the 2008 election race in comparison with her opponents and indeed her running mate. Her brand of marketing, while targeting a perceived swing voting group in the form of the 'Walmart Mom', appeared to marginalise rather than expand the base from which she aspired to gain votes. While her marketing strategy in the first instance appeared to aspire towards a sales approach in an attempt to attract swing voters, it became clear as the 2008 campaign progressed, and indeed beyond its conclusion, that she became increasingly embroiled in a product-oriented approach, shoring up the right wing of the Republican party and advancing forcefully her personal brand.

Previous research: existing marketing theory and selling the individual

The US approach to political marketing is distinctive, increasingly candidate- rather than party-centred, and is highly dependent upon the interaction between polling information and media images (Lock and Harris 1996). Existing theory on individual brand marketing has concentrated on a range of attributes considered essential to effective political brand construction and marketing. Among the most important attributes of candidate branding are consistency of brand (Butler and Harris 2009), the manufactured image (Newman 2001), authenticity and consistency (Needham 2006; Holt 2002), the substance of the candidate (Henneberg *et al.* 2009), and market segmentation and appeal (Henneberg and O'Shaughnessy 2007; Baines 1999). Of associated importance in terms of the branding of character are the integration of human characteristics and brand identity (Smith 2009), emotional bonds between elector and elected (Newman 1999), and the integration of hard and soft political issues (Scammell 2007). These elements as individual components are instrumental to effective political marketing.

In addressing the dynamics of appealing to voters in the 2008 presidential election, market segmentation and targeting were important to creating a successful electoral coalition. As evidenced by Clinton's election wins, voters respond to the image and messages advanced by candidates in several ways, emotional, rational and social (Newman 1999: 263). Targeted messages to specific voting groups work to make campaigning more efficient and meaningful to the intended recipient. Voter breakdown goes beyond simple messages, however. Additional features include geographical identification, association with particular behavioural traits of a group, psychographic issues relating to lifestyle choice and beliefs, and demographic facets reflecting social locators (Smith and Saunders 1990). In modern election campaigns segmentation has been increasingly detailed and has worked to target sub-categories to further afford narrow targeted campaigning (Penn 2007). Segmentation works in partnership with the attempted mobilisation of voting blocks central to the creation of winning majorities. Existing understandings of a segmented electorate played an important part in the selection of Palin as a candidate, and in her marketing to narrow sections of the voting block in both a social and ideological manner.

Candidate branding receives mainstream media coverage and a reciprocal relationship between the two is evident. In addressing political marketing, Bruce I. Newman identified:

> In politics, the application of marketing centers on the same process [as commercial marketing], but the analysis of needs centers voters and citizens; the product becomes a multifaceted combination of the politician himself or herself, the politician's image, and the platform the politician advocates which is then promoted and delivered to the appropriate audience.
>
> *(Newman 1999: 3)*

Branding is multidimensional in its form and assists in the political positioning of candidates (Scammell 2008). Political figures are now increasingly, alongside political parties, considered as an individual brand in modern politics (Guzman and Sierra 2009: 208). Existing consideration of the importance of brands in politics suggests that they are important in creating positive images of leadership, instilling the values of a product, and 'are aspirational and evoke a positive vision for a better way of life' (Needham 2005: 347–48). Branding can also be used to create bonds of association with the electorate through the use of language designed to evoke emotional association in the political realm, for example Bush's use of '"moms and dads" in place of parents' (Fritz *et al.* 2004).

Acting as a further element in the successful marketing placement of a candidate is the effort to place the individual in an appropriate market niche. The identity of the candidate conjoined with an awareness of their role and function in selling the political product is an important element in an appreciation of the realities of selling leadership to the electorate. In the case under consideration, the selling of Palin as a vice-presidential candidate, this is significant. Collins and Butler identified theories of market positioning with respect to candidates, challengers and leadership options. They pinpointed positions relating to the 'market leader', the position of the 'challenger', the 'follower' and the 'nicher' (Collins and Butler 2002: 7–13). The role of a vice-presidential candidate in the contemporary election cycle presents theoretical challenges of brand placement and positioning. The role, dependent upon the variables employed to market the candidate, appears suited to the positioning of the nicher; that is, it serves to address niche market needs and complements the product position of the market leader who is best placed to appeal to a broad range of voters. The problem of the 'nicher' placement is that it serves to cater to a narrow product identity in the electoral marketplace and can be limited in its electoral appeal. An additional feature of placement is a consistency of position, that it remains identifiable to the consumer in a sustained form (Bannon 2004). In the context of 2008 and the economic downturn, consistency of position, market placement and credibility were important variables in marketing a successful vice-presidential candidate.

New research: marketing Sarah Palin

McCain was aware, at an early pre-Palin stage of the election process, that the Republican party had a problem confronting Bush's legacy, arguing 'we've got a brand problem' (Ramsay 2008). Incorporating Palin onto the Republican ticket offered an opportunity to address issues relating to branding, market positioning, segmentation, and to appeal to important social locators. On paper and in her prior experiences in Alaska, Palin's selection appeared to fulfil many of the theoretical requirements underpinning political marketing and the selling of an individual candidate.

America Online identified the issue of personal market branding, familiar from business applications, and how this applied to Sarah Palin. It stated:

> A person's brand is their mission statement. What are your core values? When people hear your name, what do you want them to think? These are the questions brand consultants say Palin should be asking at this crossroads of her career.
>
> *(Pendlebury 2009)*

On CNN John Quelch, a marketing professor at Harvard Business School, considered the McCain–Palin ticket to be 'an example of what good marketing and brand-building are all about' (Keck 2008; Ramsay 2008). Quelch considered that the 2008 election had a twist which accentuated the importance of the individual candidate brand at the expense of that of the political party. He observed:

> What is relevant is the brand image of the candidate. I don't think that there is a GOP brand issue relevant to the outcome of this presidential election. It is going to be a matter of McCain–Palin, Obama–Biden. Those are the brands in play for the swing voters, regardless of party affiliation.
>
> *(Keck 2008)*

McCain worked in particular to distance himself from the past Republican brand of Bush, yet he was thought to have generally failed to offer the voter 'a different direction' (Pew Research Center for the People and the Press 2008a). Moreover, consumers expect there to be a consistent quality of product to be correlated under a brand name, in this case the Republican brand (Phipps *et al.* 2008). McCain also appeared to lack consistency of brand identity across the course of the campaign (Butler and Harris 2009). Bruce I. Newman argued:

> Just as companies need to partner with each other to be effective, so too do politicians. A candidate must get all partners to share his or her vision of the future. The focus should be on what can be, not what is. One must never lose sight of one's customer.
>
> *(Newman 1999: 85)*

A problem for the Palin candidacy was that while in theory she could support McCain and fulfil a 'nicher' position in market placement, in practice her brand became excessively narrow and her product limited in its appeal. McCain argued, when he introduced Palin as his running mate on the ticket, that she appealed as someone 'who reached across the aisle and asked Republicans, Democrats and independents to serve in government' (Thornburgh 2008). This proved to be increasingly erroneous as the election progressed and suggested a problem of brand and market placement.

Alongside her Alaskan politics, Palin's physical appearance became an issue which determined her brand. Newman identified the importance of the manufactured image as a core facet in the acceptance of a political candidate (Newman 2001). In parallel Needham identified the need for consistency of brand identity and authenticity, and the basis for success in this area: 'brands must be perceived as authentic and value-based, necessitating congruence between the internal values of the product or company and its external message' (Needham 2006: 419). The collision of these two elements ultimately caused problems in selling Palin's message. Her physical appearance was a focus of media attention from the outset. Susan Scafidi, a law professor from Fordham, perceived of Palin: 'In our image-based society, the packaging of a candidate requires strategic spending on visuals, from stage make-up to backdrops to podiums at a flattering height – and yes costumes' (cited in Thee 2008). The authenticity of Palin's brand was questioned when it was disclosed that she had received $150,000 from the Republican Party for clothing. News of expensive clothes offered a stark contrast to Palin's brand as a 'hockey mom' (Stacy and Wangrin 2008). Ed Rollins, who ran Reagan's re-election campaign in 1984, argued on similar grounds, 'It just undercuts Palin's whole image as a hockey mom, a "one-of-us" type of candidate' (Healy and Luo 2008). This had the impact of confusing Palin's brand, creating division between the internal and external values of the brand, and presented an inconsistent message to the voter.

There were problems in accommodating Palin onto the Republican ticket in the election race. Accommodating her brand with McCain's brand as both a Republican and a political maverick created confusion. She served in part as a focal figure for the Republican right, but was presented as earthy and authentic so as to appeal to potential swing voters. Steve Schmidt, key campaign strategist for the McCain team, identified the requirements of the vice-presidential candidate. They had to support McCain's '"maverick" credentials', attract women voters, distance the ticket from the Bush presidency and mobilise the base of the core Republican movement (Brox and Cassels 2009: 352; Mohan-Neill and Neill 2009: 24) There was some success in this realm. Chris Cillizza, writing in the *Washington Post*, observed:

> There is no brand in Republican politics as powerful – or as tenuous – as that of Alaska Gov. Sarah Palin. She is simultaneously the hottest commodity on the Republican fun-draising circuit and a figure of ridicule among the Democrats (and even many independents) who believe that her status as a national figure is entirely undeserved.
>
> *(Cillizza 2009)*

Palin's position as a vice-presidential nominee, however, made the attainment of Schmidt's objectives demanding, particularly as she perceived herself to be constrained by the mandate of the McCain agenda. She aspired to imprint her own brand as she desired during the campaign. She appeared to err towards a 'market leader' concept as opposed to the 'nicher' position that she had been selected to fulfil.

The selection of Palin initially aspired towards co-branding alongside McCain on the Republican ticket. Howard Belk, co-president and chief creative officer at branding agency Siegel and Gale in New York, observed:

> Each partnered a complementary personality who would overcome their own shortcomings and reach new audiences. It's a good strategy, but it panned out very differently for each … McCain's appointment of Sarah Palin, on the other hand, looked smart initially – she is young and a woman – but she became a bigger focus of media attention than McCain himself, which was confusing.
>
> *(Simms 2008)*

In this instance the fusion of two distinctive brands created confusion as to the identity value and meaning of the party ticket. In this instance media coverage acted as a variable on the balance of the co-branding strategy.

Palin's individualism made the relationship with the Republican party and McCain difficult to sustain across the duration of the campaign. The manufacturing of the McCain–Palin brand revolved around political and cultural populism and a rejection by the Republicans, and Palin in particular, of any trappings of elitism. This went hand-in-hand with an anti-intellectual platform. This was the bedrock for Palin's preferred style of political marketing. It was instinctive, revolved on an appealing personality and valued emotion above reason. Palin's interaction with the voter was to have a relational approach to the overall construct of political marketing, utilising social media as a route through which to interact with her consumer groups. However, as identified by Henneberg *et al.*, there are problems with this approach as it 'has to go beyond the cosmetic and superficial' (Henneberg *et al.* 2009: 170).

McCain was identified as a 'maverick' candidate – giving him an ill-defined ideological position within the race. Palin ultimately followed a similar path. She declared that she was 'going rogue' and forged her own identity within the campaign. This, however, blurred further her brand image and that of the party. An unnamed McCain source complained that Palin:

> is a diva. She takes no advice from anyone. She does not have any relationships of trust with any of us, her family or anyone else. Also, she is playing for her own future and sees herself as the next leader of the party.
>
> *(Bash* et al. *2008)*

Increasing disputes and overt tensions between Palin and McCain created a campaign where the precise nature of the party brand became unclear (Palin 2009: 318–21). It was relatively easy to pinpoint individual ideas and political aspirations, but as a singular entity the brand became ill-defined and problematic, suggesting tensions between party identity and the contemporary branding of individual candidates.

Palin's marketing brand during 2008 became heavily interwoven with an identification with a perceived swing voting group, the Walmart Mom. This was testament to an understanding of market segmentation and the use of Palin's background as a marketable commodity. Market research underpinned an appreciation of the importance of the Walmart Mom as a pivotal swing group with split electoral loyalties. Walmart Moms represented a distinctive brand of their own during the campaign. Henneberg and O'Shaughnessy identified that market segmentation allowed an identification to cater to 'what voters want, and how they want it …' (Henneberg and O'Shaughnessy 2007: 18). With an ongoing economic recession, a directed appeal to an identifiable consumer group on the grounds of gender and socio-economic status appeared to be of strategic benefit to the Republican party, catered to swing voters who received concentrated media attention, and addressed microtargets in marketing.

The Walmart Mom was defined as a lower-middle-class white woman who shopped at discount retailer Walmart at least once a week. *Business Week* identified the statistical bracket within which this group fell:

> They're not as well off as average Americans: Some 41% of frequent Wal-Mart shoppers have incomes below $35,000 vs. 25% of the population at large. They're less educated than their neighbors: 31% of U.S. voters have a high school education or less, vs. 39% for Wal-Mart Women. Those characteristics set them apart from the firmly middle-class Soccer Moms so closely tracked in past election.
>
> *(Sasseen 2008)*

This target group had three attributes. They were squeezed by the prevailing downturn in the economy, they were likely to vote, and polls indicated that they, as an aggregate grouping, were undecided about who to vote for. This is important to the theory on segmentation and microtargeting. The targeting strategy was overt. This segment was given a niche label, it was talked about openly in the campaign and it shaped the interpretation of Palin's candidacy and brand appeal.

The Palin product dovetailed with this target group. Palin was presented as a political manifestation of the Walmart Mom. Although wealthy, she was by far the poorest of the four candidates competing for office. The *New York Magazine* considered the rationale for the prominence of Palin in the race:

> in picking Palin as his V.P., McCain had introduced into the electoral equation a set of variables – gender, class, celebrity, ideology – at once powerful, combustible, and unpredictable. They presaged a fall campaign in which the most wretched sort of identity politics will apparently prevail. And they reflected a new strategic dynamic that may well determine the outcome: the fierce and frantic pursuit by sides of this year's 'It' demographic, the so-called Wal-Mart moms.
>
> *(Heilemann 2008)*

For example, a single mother from Florida who worked as a waitress argued that there were connections between her prior support for President Bush and her new-found support during the campaign for Palin: 'He [Bush] was really good for my family … We're hurting financially, but he shares our values just like Sarah Palin does' (Bosman 2008). Thus, it was not just the case that Palin targeted key groups, but that she was marketed, with pronounced psychographic meaning, as the embodiment of the social group she sought in part to represent. The integration of the political product with consumer identity was transparent and marketed prominently.

In addressing market segmentation there were problems of Palin's appeal becoming limited rather than fulfilling the broader brand considerations desired by campaign strategist Schmidt. Her product became intrinsically linked to a narrow target segment. It fulfilled a 'nicher' role in this context, but worked to narrow her appeal. Conservative columnist William Kristol, writing in the *New York Times*, mused over the political considerations used to pick vice-presidential running mates and how this impacted on the selection of Palin:

> McCain didn't just pick a politician who could appeal to Wal-Mart Moms. He picked a Wal-Mart Mom. Indeed he picked someone who, in 1999, as Wasilla mayor, presided over a wedding of two Wal-Mart associates at the local Wal-Mart. 'It was so sweet' said Palin, according to the Anchorage Daily News. 'It was so Wasilla.' A Wasilla Wal-Mart

> Mom a heartbeat away? I suspect most voters will say, 'No problem.' And some – perhaps a decisive number – will say, 'It's about time.'
>
> *(Kristol 2008)*

The justification of Palin's placement in targeting a narrow market segment appeared to be ratified by poll statistics. Alignment between product identity and market outcomes appeared to initially work. McCain experienced pronounced alterations in demographic support across the period of the Republican convention in 2008. The benefits of targeting a market were evident. *Time* reported:

> where 55% of white women voted for Bush in 2004, only 50% voted for Republican candidates in the 2006 midterm elections, which was one of the reasons the party lost both houses of Congress … as much as Palin pleased the conservative base of the party, white women were the real target audience McCain was aiming at with his surprise pick of the Alaska governor. The campaign hopes female voters will relate to her thoroughly modern and complicated everywoman story, even if they don't agree with her on the issues.
>
> *(Tumulty 2008)*

Through the Republican convention, according to a *Washington Post/ABC News* poll, 'McCain enjoyed a 20-percentage point turnaround against Obama among white women, going from an eight-point deficit before the Republican National Convention to a 12 point advantage after it' (Tumulty 2008).

Across the longer term Palin made little inroad into solidifying a female vote. She was viewed in a similar light by men and women in poll samples. In September Pew reported, 'Men and women offer nearly identical ratings of Palin; 56% of men and 53% of women say they have a positive view of the vice presidential candidate' (Pew Research Center for the People and the Press 2008b). Over time Palin appealed less and less to women voters, especially those identified as Walmart Moms. By the third week of October, 38 percent of women sampled by Pew had a 'favorable impression' of Palin, as contrasted with 50 percent of men. The early poll figures, where Palin fared best, indicate that she appealed, in socio-economic brackets, mostly (61–34 percent) to those who earned between $50,000 and $75,000, and much less (46–35 percent) to those who earned less than $30,000 (Pew Research Center for the People and the Press 2008c).

Interpretation of candidate personality is important to the creation of brands and in marrying human characteristics with brand identity (Smith 2009). Furthermore, Palin's Alaskan identity allowed geographic segmentation in the marketplace. Her candidacy and personality did not have to be reinvented to play to a national audience. Marketing involved subtle refinement and accentuation on aspects of her background which had already proven to be viable and electorally popular in Alaska. Early poll evidence suggested that the selection might bode well. Following her acceptance speech, Palin was viewed favourably by 58 percent of a Rasmussen poll sample, a rating which put her ahead, albeit marginally, of both McCain and Obama (Rasmussen Reports 2008).

Palin's authenticity was central to her brand. She was portrayed as a person who genuinely represented the person she was in real life. In looking for a distinctive brand identity within the ticket, the Pew Research Center asked poll respondents for a single word that best described the vice-presidential nominees. Although 'inexperienced' was the highest one-word response for Palin, there were additional issues which contributed towards the positive branding of Palin. Pew observed, 'For Palin "strong", "fresh" and "interesting" are among the most commonly mentioned terms. Voters also say Palin is "smart", "confident" and "energetic"' (Pew Research Center for the People and the Press 2008b).

Underscoring Palin's market placement for a targeted socio-economic group, her candidacy was imbued with populist attributes. It was sold as a clear and distinct form of her appeal, and contrasted with the more subtle populist mandates of her opponents, including Obama (Greenberg 2009). Modern populism embodied 'a language whose speakers conceive of ordinary people as a noble assemblage not bounded narrowly by class, view their elite opponents as a self-serving and undemocratic, and seek to mobilize the former against the latter' (Kazin 1995: 1). Eleanor Clift in *Newsweek* identified the challenges facing voters when considering the information presented by the vice-presidential candidates of each party: 'Palin is wooing the same working-class constituency that could decide the election in battleground states like Ohio and Pennsylvania with her pro-gun, family and religious down-to-earth values' (Clift 2008). Her life story afforded her many advantages in branding herself as a populist, serving to fuse psychographic segmentation with demographic and behavioural elements. She reflected in her autobiography on what she and her husband conveyed: 'We felt our very normalcy, our status as ordinary Americans, could be a much needed fresh breeze blowing into Washington D.C.' (Palin 2009: 220–21).

The major television networks labelled her as a 'perfect populist' (Bauder 2008), her rhetoric was consistent to this end, and her opponents criticised her for celebrating the merits of ordinariness at the expense of elites and political leaders. Selling her as a person worked effectively. Selling her as a prospective political leader proved more problematic. Pew reported that:

> By a wide margin (70% to 50%), more swing voters say Palin is down-to-earth. While nearly identical percentages of all voters see both candidates as honest, more swing voters say this trait describes Palin (67%) than say it applies to Biden.
>
> *(Pew Research Center for the People and the Press 2008a)*

Marketing the person as an individual brand was an important element in selling Palin to the Walmart Mom; however, she was strongly linked to the right of the Republican Party and this proved more difficult to present as a marketable asset during the campaign (Salam 2009).

In summary, the impact of Palin's candidacy in the 2008 presidential election was pronounced and significant. A range of elements central to the modern campaign were used and exploited to good effect by Palin and her campaign strategists. Her authenticity, psychographic profile and the exploitation of geographic and behavioural elements of her background and character fused to great effect in presenting her as a product of appeal and market impact. The gender component was utilised to provide contrasts with Hillary Clinton and suggested that Palin's experiences as a woman were relevant to her ability to sell herself as a political product. Individual brand elements were strong. However, such strengths also created weaknesses, or were undermined during the campaign:

- Her prominence in the span of media coverage far surpassed that generally afforded a vice-presidential candidate. Her position as a 'nicher' in the formation of a working ticket which had a target audience morphed into a scenario where she appeared to be the market leader, and this changed the dynamics of media campaign coverage, and thereafter popular interpretation.
- Her brand proved controversial and divisive, thus losing as well as attracting support. Her ability to sell herself as the embodiment of the contemporary working woman had pronounced limitations, because despite her emotional appeal she appeared unable to mobilise her target market into actual votes.

- The emphasis on her personal life cast doubt on her leadership ability and thus suitability for vice-president. Scammell (2007) pinpointed the importance of interweaving hard politics and soft social attributes into the building of a political brand and the challenges afforded by this fusion.
- Media exposure of issues, such as her clothing choices and their cost, lent credence to beliefs that Palin's image was manufactured and thus created confusion about her brand identity.

Advice for practitioners

The marketing of Palin's political brand has distinctive lessons for leadership and strategy:

- Do not allow vice-presidential candidates to become the market leader as their position is then vulnerable to attack.
- Avoid developing a brand that only appeals to a distinctive psychographic populism, which whilst successful initially, can also alienate mainstream supporters and thus lose votes overall. The integration of personal attributes and a populist mandate, where the candidate is presented as being a mirror of the target voting segment, builds ultimately superficial support in elections.
- Take care to protect initial brand strengths, and do not let them be undermined by other presentational tools or campaign activities.
- Exhibit both leadership and personal attributes; both skills and emotional connections with voters.
- Caution should be exercised with market strategies that interweave economic variables with the social and lifestyle characteristics of candidates.
- Gender can have a positive role in creating a distinctive brand identity, but also changes the type and tone of coverage afforded a candidate.
- The difficulties of incorporating individual brands into an embedded party brand identity are pronounced, and suggest that short-term rebranding of both candidates and party is difficult to accomplish.

Impact on politics

Marketing individual candidates is not straightforward, but both the success and the difficulties faced by the candidate in this case study suggest positive implications for democracy. The success of authenticity in this case suggests that politicians need to be 'normal' and reflect ordinary citizens. Populism is important in branding, but it has limits in its market appeal. Whilst tools such as branding, positioning and targeting offer politicians the means to attract support at the early stages of the campaign, and connect emotionally with the public, voters still require to be shown leadership skills and that a candidate can connect with a range of support groups, not just one target market. This may be good for democracy, because it shows the limitations of pragmatic strategising to win support.

Individual candidate brands are clearly an enticing realm for media coverage, with evidence of elongated coverage on personal considerations throughout election campaigns. Yet candidate-centred coverage appears to demonstrate limitations on the willingness of the voter to accommodate wall-to-wall coverage on individuals as central components in election races. Voter exhaustion suggests that candidate branding, while important in informing voters of election choices, can be detrimental to popular engagement with politics and create weariness during election cycles.

The fusion of multiple individual brands with a party brand, particularly one that is entrenched, is a challenging task. In seeking to alter brand identity the consumer requires time to accommodate and understand new identities and to appreciate consistency of the brand product. Multilevel branding, if not delivered with precision and clarity, runs the risk of presenting the voter with a range of competing identities which acts to the detriment of the political party and candidates. Long-term rebranding is evidently an important consideration for candidates who aspire to, or have to, modify the underlying party brand.

The failure of a strong recognisable brand to generate the support it was chosen to target suggests that the current means by which political organisations, with sophisticated techniques of market research, make decisions may need reconsideration. The appeal of candidates at local or state level of government may not necessarily be transferable to a national stage, and the variables that propel candidate branding at the sub-national and national positions evidently demonstrate different challenges in mobilising voters and presenting a legitimate brand identity.

The way forward

There exist clear avenues for further exploration in the field of candidate branding and political marketing strategies. Further research is needed on party and candidate branding, and how the two interconnect. After the election Palin extricated herself from the limitations of a tight party brand and took steps to place herself in a political position where she could develop her own personal brand via media devices which cut the linkage with the mass media. Separation between candidate branding and party branding is clearly necessary. Yet they are inevitable bedfellows in the pursuit of political office. In political coalitions, and in scenarios where minor parties or political individuals are able to sell themselves with more effectiveness than the prime candidate, there are similar conundrums. The challenge faced by Cameron and Clegg in representing themselves as party leaders, as prime minister and deputy prime minister in the UK, and as individual political figures in their own right, poses questions about how political balance can be successfully achieved. While individual candidate branding is clearly evident and of importance in the contemporary campaign, how internal candidate brands are accommodated alongside one another in both campaigns and government is an aspect of importance, particularly given the increasing focus on individuals as candidates and the slow diminution of party brands as prime product locators.

Gender remains an important consideration in political branding. Continued attention given to gender-related candidate branding underscores a need for further research into whether differing expectations of brands across male and female candidates are generated by the candidates themselves, the media or the voter. Similarly, the presence of men and women on the same political platforms presents issues about brand balance. In the case study evaluated here the female candidate's brand received disproportionate coverage and attention. The increasing number of women in pursuit of high political office creates opportunities for comparative analysis about whether there are similar gender-skewed brand mechanisms in place in comparative democratic systems.

Market intelligence and product placement have become increasingly sophisticated in the contemporary era. Market segmentation and microtargets suggests that the selection of candidates who can appeal to swing voters have a pivotal place in influencing voter choice and election outcomes. Yet it is clear that selecting a candidate on this account has limitations and that while market placement is important, there exist peripheral market spheres which have to be addressed to ensure a breadth of appeal. How non-target groups can be engaged and mobilised in the context of leadership and candidate-centred brand politics remains a pressing marketing concern.

Bibliography

Baines, P.R. (1999) 'Voter Segmentation and Candidate Positioning', in B. Newman (ed.) *Handbook of Political Marketing*, New York: Sage.

Bannon, D. (2004) 'Marketing Segmentation and Political Marketing', paper presented to the UK Political Studies Association conference, University of Lincoln, Lincoln, UK.

Bash, D., Hamby, P. and King, J. (2008) 'Palin's "Going Rogue", McCain Aide Says', CNN, 25 October. Online, edition.cnn.com/2008/POLITICS/10/25/palin.tension (accessed 21 July 2010).

Bauder, D. (2008) 'Palin Provides a "Perfect Populist Pitch" ', *USA Today*, 4 September. Online, www.usatoday.com/news/politics/2008-09-03-2226980962_x.htm (accessed 20 April 2010).

Bosman, J. (2008) 'Palin Plays to Conservative Base in Florida Rallies', *New York Times* 8 October. Online, www.nytimes.com/2008/10/08/us/politics/08palin.html?scp=1&sq=Plays%20to%20Conservative%20Base%20in%20Florida%20Rallies&st=cse (accessed 12 July 2010).

Brox, B.J. and Cassels, M.L. (2009) 'The Contemporary Effects of Vice-Presidential Nominees: Sarah Palin and the 2008 Presidential Campaign', *Journal of Political Marketing* 8, 4: 349–63.

Butler, P. and Harris, P. (2009) 'Considerations on the Evolution of Political Marketing Theory', *Marketing Theory* 9, 2: 149–62.

Cillizza, C. (2009) 'The Protectors of the Palin Brand', *Washington Post*, 17 March. Online, www.voices.washingtonpost.com (accessed 13 July 2010).

Clift, E. (2008) 'Palin Reignites The Culture War', *Newsweek*, 3 October.

Collins, N. and Butler, P. (2002) 'Considerations on Market Analysis for Political Parties', in N. O'Shaughnessy and S. Henneberg (eds) *The Idea of Political Marketing*, London: Praeger.

Dowd, M. (2008) 'Sarah's Pompom Palaver', *New York Times*, 5 October. Online, www.nytimes.com/2008/10/05/opinion/05dowd.html?scp=1&sq=Sarah%E2%80%99s%20Pom%20Pom%20Palaver&st=cse (accessed 13 May 2010).

Fritz, B., Keefer, B. and Nyham, B. (2004) *All the President's Spin: George W. Bush, the Media, and the Truth*, New York: Touchstone.

Greenberg, D. (2009) 'The Populism of the FDR Era', *Time*, 4 July.

Guzman, F. and Sierra, V. (2009) 'A Political Candidate's Brand Image Scale: Are Political Candidates Brands?' *Brand Management* 17, 3: 207–17.

Healy, P. and Luo, M. (2008) '$150, 000 Wardrobe for Palin May Alter Tailor-Made Image', *New York Times*, 22 October. Online, www.nytimes.com/2008/10/23/us/politics/23palin.html?scp=1&sq=%91%24150,%20000%20Wardrobe%20for%20Palin%20May%20Alter%20Tailor-Made%20Image&st=cse (accessed 14 March 2010).

Heilemann, J. (2008) 'The Wal-Mart Frontier', *New York Magazine*, 14 September. Online, nymag.com/news/politics/powergrid/50277 (accessed 21 July 2010).

Henneberg, S.C. and O'Shaughnessy, N.J. (2007) 'Theory and Concept Development in Political Marketing', *Journal of Political Marketing* 6, 2: 5–31.

Henneberg, S.C., Scammell, M. and O'Shaughnessy, N.J. (2009) 'Political Marketing Management and Theories of Democracy', *Marketing Theory* 9, 2: 165–88.

Herbert, B. (2008) 'Palin's Alternate Universe', *New York Times*, 4 October. Online, www.nytimes.com/2008/10/04/opinion/04herbert.html?scp=1&sq=Palin%E2%80%99s%20Alternate%20Universe&st=cse (accessed 15 March 2010).

Holt, D.B. (2002) 'Why Do Brands Cause Trouble?' *A Dialectical Theory of Consumer Culture and Branding* 29, 1: 70–90.

Kazin, M. (1995) *The Populist Persuasion: An American History*, revised edition, London: Cornell University Press.

Keck, K. (2008) 'Palin Power Recharges GOP Ticket', *CNN*, 17 September. Online, edition.cnn.com/2008/POLITICS/09/17/mccain.palin.marketing/index.html?iref=allsearch (accessed 22 July 2010).

Kristol, W. (2008) 'A Heartbeat Away', *New York Times*, 8 September. Online, www.nytimes.com/2008/09/08/opinion/08kristol.html (accessed 12 February 2010).

Lock, A. and Harris, P. (1996) 'Political Marketing – Vive la Difference!' *European Journal of Marketing* 30, 10/11: 14–24.

Mohan-Neill, S. and Neill, I. (2009) 'Executive Decision-Making and Marketing Research: The Choice of Sarah Palin as 2008 Republican Vice-Presidential Nominee', *Proceedings of the Academy of Marketing Studies* 14, 1: 23–28.

Needham, C. (2005) 'Brand Leaders: Clinton, Blair and the Limitations of the Permanent Campaign', *Political Studies* 53, 2: 343–61.

—— (2006) 'Brands and Political Loyalty', *Brand Management* 13, 3: 178–87.

Newman, B.I. (1999) *The Mass Marketing of Politics: Democracy in an Age of Manufactured Images*, London: Sage.

—— (2001) 'Image-manufacturing in the USA: Recent US Presidential Elections and Beyond', *European Journal of Marketing* 35, 9/10: 966–70.

Noonan, P. (2008) 'A Servant's Heart', *Wall Street Journal*, 5 September. Online, online.wsj.com/article/SB122059352189503479.html (accessed 21 June 2010).

Palin, S. (2009) *Going Rogue: An American Life*, New York: HarperCollins.

Pendlebury, S. (2009) 'Will Sarah Palin Reinvent Herself?' *AOL News*, 25 July. Online, www.aolnews.com/story/sarah-palins-brand/588403 (accessed 21 July 2010).

Penn, M., with Zalesne, E.K. (2007) *Micro-Trends: The Small Forces Behind Tomorrow's Big Changes*, London: Twelve.

Pinker, S. (2008) 'Everything You Heard Is Wrong', *New York Times*, 4 October. Online, www.nytimes.com/2008/10/04/opinion/04pinker.html?scp=1&sq=Everything%20You%20Heard%20Is%20Wrong&st=cse (accessed 15 March 2010).

Pew Research Center for the People and the Press (2008a) 'Obama Boosts Leadership Image and Regains Lead over McCain: Growing Concerns About Palin's Qualification', 1 October. Online, people-press.org/2008/10/01/obama-boosts-leadership-image-and-regains-lead-over-mccain (accessed 21 March 2010).

—— (2008b) 'McCain Gains on Issues, but Stalls as Candidate of Change', 18 September. Online, people-press.org/2008/09/18/mccain-gains-on-issues-but-stalls-as-candidate-of-change (accessed 20 March 2010).

—— (2008c) 'Growing Doubts About McCain's Judgment, Age and Campaign Conduct', 21 October. Online, people-press.org/2008/10/21/growing-doubts-about-mccains-judgment-age-and-campaign-conduct (accessed 23 March 2010).

—— (2008d) 'Many Say Press Has Been Too Tough on Palin', 9 October. Online, people-press.org/2008/10/09/many-say-press-has-been-too-tough-on-palin (accessed 21 March 2010).

—— (2008e) 'Palin Fatigue Now Rivals Obama Fatigue: SNL Appearance, Wardrobe Flap Register Widely', 29 October. Online, people-press.org/2008/10/29/palin-fatigue-now-rivals-obama-fatigue (accessed 22 March 2010).

Phipps, M., Brace-Govan, J. and Jevons, C. (2008) 'The Duality of Political Brand Equity', *European Journal of Marketing* 44, 3/4: 496–514.

Ramsay, K. (2008) 'McCain: If the Election was Ttomorrow, GOP Would Lose', *CNN*, 26 June. Online, politicalticker.blogs.cnn.com/2008/06/26/mccain-if-the-election-was-tomorrow-gop-would-lose/www.cnn.com (accessed 21 July 2010).

Rasmussen Reports (2008) 'Palin Power: Fresh Face Now More Popular than Obama, McCain', *Rasmussen Reports*, 5 September. Online, www.rasmussenreports.com/public_content/politics/elections/election_ 2008/2008_presidential_election/palin_power_fresh_face_now_more_popular_than_obama_mccain (accessed 14 July 2010).

Salam, R. (2009) 'The Last Culture Warrior', *Forbes*, 4 July. Online, www.forbes.com/2009/07/04/governor-alaska-republican-white-house-opinions-columnists-sarah-palin.html (accessed 13 March 2010).

Sasseen, J. (2008) 'The Wal-Mart Sisterhood', *Business Week*, 17 April. Online, www.businessweek.com/magazine/content/08_17/b4081089044593.htm (accessed 17 April 2010).

Scammell, M. (2007) 'Political Brands and Consumer Citizens: The Rebranding of Tony Blair', *Annals, AAPSS* 611, 1: 176–92.

—— (2008) 'Brand Blair: Marketing Politics in the Consumer Age', in D. Lilleker and R. Scullion (eds) *Voters or Consumers: Imaging the Contemporary Electorate*, Cambridge: Scholars Publishing.

Simms, J. (2008) 'What UK Marketers Learn from the US Presidential Election', *Marketing*, 11 November.

Smith, G. (2009) 'Conceptualizing and Testing Brand Personality in British Politics', *Journal of Political Marketing* 8, 3: 209–32.

Smith, G. and Saunders, J. (1990) 'The Application of Marketing to British Politics', *Journal of Marketing Management* 5, 3: 295–306.

Stacy, M. and Wangrin, M. (2008). 'Palin Says Expensive Clothing not Her Property', *Breitbart*, 26 October. Online, www.breitbart.com/article.php?id=D942H6SO0&show_article=1 (accessed 14 June 2010).

Thee, F. (2008) 'Palin Clothing Bill Up, Poll Standing Down', *Boston Globe*, 22 October. Online, www.boston.com/news/politics/politicalintelligence/2008/10/palin_clothing.html (accessed 26 June 2010).

Thornburgh, N. (2008) 'Mayor Palin: A Rough Record', *Time*, 2 September. Online, www.time.com/time/politics/article/0,8599,1837918,00.html (accessed 12 June 2010).

Tumulty, K. (2008) 'Can Obama Win Back Wal-Mart Moms?' *Time*, 9 September. Online, www.time.com/time/politics/article/0,8599,1839930,00.html (accessed 12 June 2010).

18

Populism as political marketing technique[1]

Georg Winder and Jens Tenscher

The topic: populism

Populism is a widely used communicative strategy in politics that seems to have become more and more important in recent years. Since the mid-1980s populism has entered the political stage of some established Western democracies; to name but a few: Jörg Haider (Austria's Freedom Party) in Austria; Jean-Marie Le Pen (Front National) in France; Silvio Berlusconi (Forza Italia) in Italy; Josef Blocher (Swiss People's Party) in Switzerland; and Geert Wilders (Freedom Party) in the Netherlands. Their success has been perceived by some scholars as a typical symptom of fundamental political transformation or political crisis (Taggart 2000: 5), or reflective of disenchantment with established, 'old-fashioned' political parties (Mudde 1996). However, populism is not only a symptom of crisis but also a strategy of managing communicative relationships.

Against this backdrop, it is time to reflect on populism as a political marketing technique. So far, this has neither been done in political marketing studies nor in populism research. Yet, we assume that populism is a political marketing technique in its own right, one that offers a specific form of political communication, organization and mobilization. This chapter will discuss the concept and contextual factors which facilitate or impede the introduction of populist actors and the development of populism as a political marketing technique. Furthermore, we will test its practical relevance by examining case studies from the US (long-time established democracy), Austria (relatively young but strong democracy) and Venezuela (emergent, unstable democracy).

Previous research

Political marketing research has not previously focused on populism (Lederer *et al.* 2005), although it is of course the subject of significant and controversial debate elsewhere in political science (see, for example Ionescu and Gellner 1969; Canovan 1981). There is very little consensus in this literature about how to define populism: some see it as a political ideology with roots in a cohesive social concept of the democratic society (Mény and Surel 2002: 40 ff.), while others tend to qualify populism as a 'thin centered ideology' (Freeden 1998; Mudde 2004: 544) that misses an elaborated vision of society and 'only gives a precise meaning and priority to certain key concepts of political discourse' (Abts and Rummens 2007: 408). In this understanding, populism possesses an ideological core that considers society to be ultimately separated into two homogeneous and antagonistic groups, 'the pure people' versus 'the corrupt elite', and which argues that politics should be an expression of the *volonté générale* (general will) of the people (Mudde 2004: 562). A second research strand emphasizes the communicative dimension of populism: here, populism is characterized as a communication instrument or a political style (Taguieff 2002: 80; Jagers and Walgrave 2007). Political actors make use of the same principles as in the ideological approaches to populism but deploy populist communication in order to be more successful while ideological concepts assume that the populist elements form an essential part of a political actor's policies. Both approaches to populism, as well as those that point at its organizational components (Weyland 2001: 12), refer to the two key criteria of 'the people' and 'the elites'. We therefore argue that *populism is a political communication style that is strategically deployed by political actors in order to mobilize potential voters and to establish stable relationships with specific target groups*.

Populism has two key dimensions: inclusion and exclusion. Inclusion refers to the fact that populist communicators claim to speak *for the people* in the meaning of 'representing the whole democratic sovereign' (Canovan 1999: 4). Jagers and Walgrave (2007: 3) explain that 'populism is a communication frame that appeals to and identifies with the people, and pretends to speak in their name'. When politicians are being inclusive, they frame their political messages in a way that conveys both the message of proximity to a broad range of potential 'clients' and the pretended advocacy for their needs and concerns. Exclusion is used to stress inclusion – if some people are 'in', then others must be 'out', and thus they are a perceived menace to those within the 'in' group. Populist discourse attempts to introduce, consolidate and frame such threats. Respective political leaders challenge the existing order and thus stigmatize 'the elites' as people's principal opponents. Thus, what we can draw from this literature is that populism is a communication style where politicians frame proximity to and identification with 'the people' and simultaneously purport to advocate their interests against a highly privileged elite that is out of touch with the citizens' needs. To reach their goals populist communicators routinely refer to notions of civic identity, including terms like 'the state', 'the nation' or 'religious feelings' – especially when branding threats from outside.

New research: marketed populism

The theory: populism and the stages of political marketing

Populism as a communication strategy can be connected with political marketing concepts and market orientation. Market orientation discusses how techniques (such as market research and product design) and concepts (such as the desire to satisfy voter demands) can be used to reach specific goals such as winning elections, but lacks detailed ideas for an effective communication strategy, without which any political marketing objectives and any efforts to establish and stabilize external relationships are doomed to fail. This section puts forward new concepts by adapting Lees-Marshment's (2001) concept, which differentiates between product orientation, sales orientation and market orientation.

Product-oriented political parties tend to 'set policies and expect others to support the organization on the basis that the policy is right' (Lilleker and Lees-Marshment 2005: 7). Sales-oriented parties also start with well-established political products, i.e. a set of realistic policies, but additionally make use of 'market intelligence to design their communication strategy in order to persuade voters to support the party' (ibid.). In contrast, market-oriented parties first turn to the 'customer's' concerns, behaviors, needs and demands before designing a product that is delivered in accordance to specific market conditions. Obviously, such market orientation requires not only the highest degree of sophistication and professionalization within political parties but also a maximum of ideological flexibility to effectively mold political products and promises. We assume that populist parties hold such an ideological flexibility since they often lack a clear-cut, long-established profile and position within the electoral market. Furthermore, populist parties are keen to adjust their communicative strategies to their customers' needs and feelings. Their organizational structure, normally hierarchical and leader-oriented, makes it easy to incorporate political marketing techniques. As a consequence, we argue that populism best suits market-oriented political parties and less suits a sales orientation. Product-oriented parties would not turn to populism as a communicative strategy. How populism and market orientation match becomes obvious when we refer to the nine stages of a political marketing process that Lees-Marshment's (2010) model identifies. We merge those stages into three crucial phases (see Figure 18.1).

Phase 1 – market intelligence

Market research could be considered as the initial stage of every marketing process. Before developing and designing a product it is necessary for political parties to identify most prospective target groups, their needs, desires and feelings (Lilleker and Lees-Marshment 2005: 10). Even though this stage is crucial for all political competitors nowadays, populist parties do have a special interest in ascertaining potential customers' orientations since their communicative strategy is explicitly supposed to procure 'closeness to the people'. Such an approach asks for an in-depth-knowledge of 'the people's' needs and worries. Actually, it is not 'the people' as a whole who are targeted by populist parties but especially the 'ordinary, decent people' (Canovan 1999: 5), who feel not sufficiently addressed by the governing elites and frustrated by the established parties. It is the common people, namely the 'losers of modernization', people who are or at least feel to be economically or culturally deprived, that are foremost open to populist pledges (Spier 2006: 36; Decker 2006: 13). These people are 'counter-consumers' (Butler and Collins 1994: 26) on the political market; they rather vote *against* than in favor of political supplies. The first step of

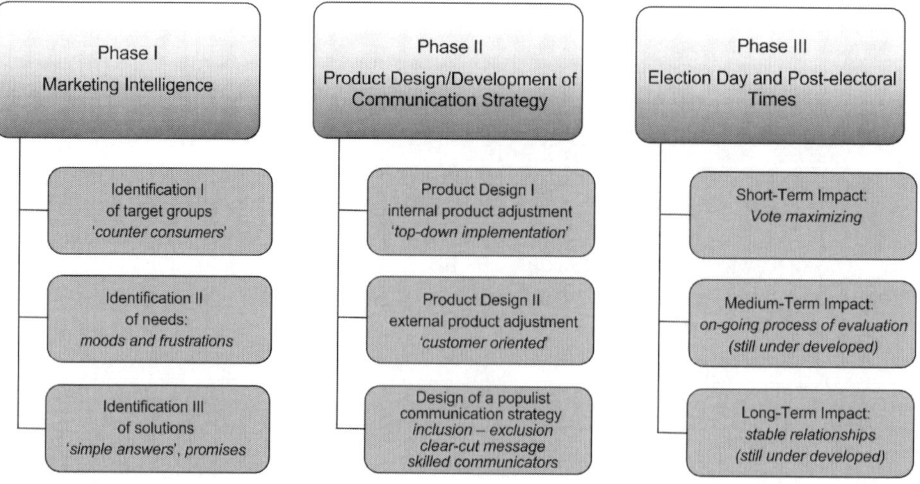

Figure 18.1 Model of marketed populism (populism-specific elements are in italic)

populist market intelligence is to locate these people and to get detailed information about their moods, feelings and policy demands. At this stage, populist parties and candidates, like their competitors, make use of a broad set of opinion research instruments, including opinion polls and focus groups.

Phase 2 – product design and development of a communication strategy

Based on marketing intelligence data about prospective consumers, political parties develop a product, adjust to it and implement it internally, i.e. within the political party. Afterwards, a strategy on how to communicate the (new) product externally to prospective supporters, voters, competitors and media, has to be designed. Compared with other parties, the process of product development, adjustment and implementation seems to be much easier for populist parties because they are to a large extent exempt from ideological or policy-related standpoints, which makes it easier for them to react to current moods and to design products that are easy to grasp and to communicate. While established parties have to take care of their party history and former political decisions, populist actors have the edge over their competitors in simply *being against* (the elites, the other parties, etc.) and *being in favor* of something/somebody (the underprivileged, frustrated 'counter-consumers'). Consequently, populists usually turn to *position issues* (Stokes 1966) that are most important for their potential voters and in which established parties' records or promises are non-satisfying. Populist answers to burning problems are for the most part rather vague and simplistic, and populist products usually appear as simple solutions to complex problems. This is where positive role models, leaders, frontrunners and skilled communicators to whom people can refer as being the product come in. Therefore, populist products are basically composed of two main components: clear-cut (and mostly just a few) messages covering the most prominent issues, plus the image of a strong and charismatic frontrunner or party leader. Other aspects of political products that are crucial for the success of competing political parties – namely the political party and its ideology (Butler and Collins 1994: 21) – are of minor importance.

When it comes to product adjustment and its internal implementation, populist parties benefit from their hierarchical structure: party members, candidates and parties' representatives do not have to be *convinced*, they just have to *accept* and follow the parameters and decisions of the party leaders. In this process the leaders of populist parties (and their advisors) play a crucial role as they do when it comes to developing a campaign strategy. Obviously, populist parties are privileged concerning the centralization of strategy development and strategy conducting, often regarded as a key element of successful political campaigning (e.g. Plasser and Plasser 2002; Strömbäck 2010). They have always and inherently focused on communicating externally with 'the people' and not on internal discussions. This focus usually unfolds as a 'pro/con' or a 'good/bad' strategy reflecting the two dimensions of inclusion and exclusion. The charismatic leader thereby serves as focal point between framing of closeness and comprehension towards the people (*inclusion*) and framing of the advocacy for the people's concerns against the ruling establishment and perceived menaces (*exclusion*).

In sum, a populist communication style is characterized by simplified standpoints, primarily communicated through a charismatic, rhetorically skilled and supposedly credible character. Such an approach has to be perpetuated – during an election campaign and beyond – to have a lasting impact on potential voters and consumers. That includes permanent observation of contextual campaign dynamics (e.g. issue cycles, public mood, oppositional strategies, political decisions, etc.), which are essential for a cyclical process of readjusting and communicative implementing of product-related standpoints. In this campaign-related perspective populism as a political marketing technique also requires continuous proactive communication efforts and the ability for short-term reactions. Once again, we assume that the organizational, leader-focused, hierarchical and lean structures (Taggart 2000: 102) of populist parties facilitate this process of continual modulations and quick reactions.

Phase 3 – election day and post-electoral times

Due to the pivotal importance of elections within liberal democratic systems and political markets, populist parties' success and acceptance is essentially measured in electoral votes: votes obtained for their product and counter-votes 'stolen' from established parties. Vote-seeking is the primary imperative of populist parties while most of their opponents strive for policy-making as well. That might explain why populist parties are extremely focused on electoral campaigns and why they tend to concentrate on short-term success instead of long-term sustainability. Therefore, political marketing's cyclical dimension (Lees-Marshment 2010: 8), i.e. the process of building up stable relationships with consumers, seems to be underdeveloped.

That explains both rapid uprisings and electoral successes of populist parties, and their abrupt disappearances (Heinisch 2003). In addition to that, populists' propensity to 'anti-communication', especially against competing political parties and the governing class, casts their potential for a pragmatic parliamentary oppositional role and, even more, for governing positions into doubt. Ironically, populists' electoral success therefore often stimulates their parliamentary disappearance at the next elections. The rationale behind this up and down with which populist parties are universally confronted is that parliaments inherently constrain politicians both with respect to policy standpoints and their communicative performances. Therefore, populists in parliament often become what they initially pretended to stand against: a part of the political elite. As a consequence, populist parties habitually tend to become less populist or even show a tendency to collapse as a result of internal frictions. However, there is one structural feature that impedes populist parties' rupture: namely, once again, a strong, internally undisputed, charismatic leader (Canovan 1999: 5) who takes the chance of an oppositional role to present himself and his party as solitary advocate of people's needs in parliament.

Such a strategy repeatedly malfunctions if transferred to governmental roles. At least in well-established democracies with multi-party systems and a politically independent press, long-term reigning populists are still exceptions that prove the rule (e.g. Italy's current prime minister Silvio Berlusconi). The lack of enduring success of most populist parties might, however, not only result from their disqualification and unwillingness to form coalitions with political opponents (and vice versa), rising frictions between pre-election promises and post-election performances and tangible deficits in political decision-making. It is, as we argue, not least a consequence of weak cyclical marketing efforts and populists' self-reduction to sales-orientation.

Contextual impacts on the applicability of populism as a political marketing technique

Although populism might be universally applied to any political markets, there are some intervening factors – beyond the political product itself discussed above – that have an impact on the probability of successfully relying on populism as a political marketing technique. Such factors are located both on the meso level of the political party involved and on the macro level, i.e. the 'environment' shaping the political market conditions. The latter ones primarily result from a country's (a) political system (including its institutional framework, electoral system and party system), (b) social and cleavage structure and political culture, (c) media system and journalistic culture, and (d) situational contingencies (issue cycles, public mood, etc.). These contextual factors do not only affect political marketing orientations in general (Strömbäck 2010), but we assume that they also have a significant impact on the emergence and success of populist parties incorporating political marketing techniques.

When we first look at the meso level in particular, there are numerous factors that facilitate a party's turn to populism as a communicative, marketing-oriented strategy. As mentioned above, these factors root in a party's internal structure and culture on the one hand and its governmental and parliamentary role on the other hand. In short, political parties with a top-down structure and a leader-focused hierarchy are privileged to turn to populism.

Long-established political parties with clear-cut ideological profiles, deeply rooted in the cleavage structures of societies, are insufficiently flexible to turn to populism – even more so if they reflect rather (in a Western sense) left-wing, socialist or post-material positions which somehow contradict business-type practices of marketing (Kavanagh 1996).

Catch-all parties are less prone to use populist communicative strategies – which might alienate large portions of their prospective voters – than niche or clientele parties attracting specific voter segments.

As a consequence, young parties, lacking ideological burdens and expectations, with strong, internally undisputed leaders who publicly 'stand for' the party almost exclusively, and with a strong marketing or sales orientation (Lees-Marshment 2001), backed by sufficient financial resources, are most likely to turn to populist techniques. Even more so if they start from an oppositional, at best non-parliamentary position, which facilitates the use of attack strategies, undifferentiated simplifications and popular critique against 'the political class'.

With regards to the macro level, the most important factors facilitating populism are:

- *Candidate-centered democracies* (i.e. presidential and semi-presidential systems): a high degree of polarization and a weak fragmentation of the political party system supports the rise of populist actors. In such an environment with only small numbers of political competitors the probability of getting a spot on the political landscape is much bigger compared with already crowded, highly fragmented and extremely polarized party systems (Wring 2002; Strömbäck 2010: 20). However, there are some exceptions that prove the rule, such as Jörg Haider (FPÖ) in Austria, who managed to enter the political stage, backed by a clear-cut populist communicative strategy in a parliamentary system with proportional representation and a seemingly established and polarized multi-party system.
- Countries with strong traditions of a *subject culture*, i.e. societies with a dominating focus on the political output (achievements and performances of the political elite) and low levels of internal or external efficacy of the people (Almond and Verba 1963; Balch 1974) such as Austria, tend to be much more open to populists than participation or civic cultures. Ultimately, as recent victories of populist parties in the Netherlands or Belgium have shown, even post-industrial and democratically stable societies are not immune to rising populism, especially when growing skepticism towards established political elites and parties, declining partisanship and growing electoral volatility come together with strong national or regional sentiments and latent fears of being overrun by globalization or modernization processes (including rising immigration, unemployment, etc.).
- In liberal, highly *competitive media systems* (e.g. the US, UK), in which political actors are exceptionally urged to adjust to media logics, populist communication strategies would have a better chance to prevail than in democratic corporatist media systems (e.g. Germany) or polarized pluralist media systems (e.g. Spain). In such media environments governmental actors can directly control the media organizations (and sometimes even their coverage). In

addition to that, *television-oriented societies* (e.g. the US, Italy) tend to be more open to populist communicative strategies than newspaper-oriented societies (e.g. Scandinavian countries) because of the specific constraint of the audiovisual medium which asks – more than other media – for personalization, simplification, visualization and reduction (Mazzoleni *et al.* 2003; Mazzoleni 2008): the exact components of populist leaders' communicative strategies. With the advent of the Internet they have gained yet another audiovisual platform – independent from journalistic gatekeepers – which has been rapidly sprawling throughout society. As a consequence, it is likely that the dissemination of populists' thoughts will become easier in the future.

Populist political marketing in practice

To test the impact of each of such a broad set of party-related and environmental factors we rely on three case studies that cover not only three different geographical regions (North America, South America and Europe), but also three kinds of political cultures – respectively, three stages of democratization. The US is a long-established democracy and 'civic culture', Venezuela is an emerging, still unstable democracy and 'subject culture', and Austria is a relatively young, but fairly stable democracy, with a political culture somewhere between civic and subject. While the two American countries represent presidential systems, Austria is a parliamentary political regime (with a tendency to semi-presidentialism). Finally, with regards to media systems, these countries cover the whole spectrum from liberal (US), democratic corporatist (Austria), to polarized pluralist (Venezuela).

The US: the Perot phenomenon

In the US, the majoritarian electoral system has been an important obstacle to the establishment of a national populist party, as it has been for the emergence of other parties beneath the Democrats and Republicans. Populism has therefore always been located primarily on the individual level of candidates and not on the meso level of political parties, which are traditionally weak in the US. However, a recent exception to this was Ross Perot, an entrepreneur and self-made billionaire from Texas who ran as an independent candidate for president in 1992 and as frontrunner of his own Reform Party in 1996. It was above all Perot's electoral campaign in 1992 that caught public and academic attention (e.g. Post 1995). It had a direct impact on the campaign as a whole and especially on Bill Clinton's campaign and first presidential election victory. Ultimately, Perot's campaign affected and mobilized 18.9 percent of voters in a presidential system with two historically strong parties.

Perot's communication strategy in 1992 fitted perfectly into a time in which Americans were disillusioned with their political elite and frustrated after 12 years of Republican governance. Against this backdrop and respective market intelligence efforts, Perot repeatedly stressed his and 'the American people's' disaffection with the way the 'political class' exercised their political power (Black and Black 1994: 162). His anti-establishment discourse primarily focused on economic and financial policy issues that he claimed were urgent and needed action on. As a successful businessman he could present himself as a strong leader, who was indisputably competent in economic and financial affairs and thus capable to balance the national budget. Issue and candidate image were perfectly integrated into one message. In addition, Perot benefited from his politically fresh, aggressive, but rhetorically skilled appearance. This made it easier to enter free media platforms such as the CNN talk show *Larry King Live*, in which he announced his candidacy, presumably motivating Bill Clinton and subsequent candidates to enter this free media platform too.

Despite his personal wealth, Perot's campaign was effective in presenting him as in touch with ordinary people's needs and fears (inclusion) and against the ruling class (exclusion). This case illustrates the potential for populist marketing techniques even in traditionally 'closed', polarized electoral markets, and especially on the federal state level. His messages well reflected the growing dissatisfaction and cynicism among the people. However, Perot's campaign also stands for a rather sales-oriented approach, as it did not have an enduning impact, either for him or in the political landscape, as a market-oriented approach might have had.

Venezuela: populism as a presidential phenomenon

Populism in the Latin American context dates back to the 1930s and 1940s when the first populist leaders, namely Getulio Vargas (Brazil), José María Velasco Ibarra (Ecuador) and Juan Perón (Argentina), entered the political stage in response to deep-felt social and economic crises and political deadlocks (Coniff 1999: 7). Their early success, partly supported by military upheavals, was not least a consequence of not yet established democratic structures and missing democratic traditions. Since then, populism has remained an integral part and omnipresent phenomenon of Latin American politics.

One of the most prominent examples is the rise of a new 'anti-party movement' (Hawkins 2003: 1137) built around the figure of Hugo Chávez. Although the way in which Chávez came into political power in 1999 (military coup) cannot be considered related to any marketing techniques, the efforts that he has made to maintain and institutionalize his political power since then do meet the criteria. Hugo Chávez Frías undoubtedly comes close to what can be described as the epitome of a populist charismatic leader (Weyland 2003; Roberts 2003). Since the first day of his reign, his rhetoric has combined elements of an anti-elite discourse (against the economic elites within Venezuela) and an anti-system discourse (mainly directed against capitalism and US imperialism). In addition, he has repeatedly presented himself as an instrument ('the humble soldier') that will unselfishly fight for the rights of the people (he refers to them as 'el pueblo') in Venezuela and in other Latin American countries. Claiming to represent the voice of the people, Chávez has called several times for voter support in referenda that fundamentally target the institutional setting of the Venezuelan political system, including the annulment of the president's limited term of office and a strengthening of governmental rights. Although not all of these constitutional changes gained sufficient support, overall Chávez was successful in strengthening his own position as president. Accordingly, both national and international criticism about the democratic progress in Venezuela has been increasing (Hawkins 2003: 1156).

Chávez's popularity and three electoral victories have been based strongly on his capacity for gaining support and mobilizing voters in a kind of 'permanent campaign'. In that campaign, the political product, i.e. policies, promises and constitutional transformation, has been connected closely with the leader himself. It has been Chávez and a handful of his advisors who have designed the product and developed the campaign strategy that gained public support. In a political marketing sense, Chávez's approach has slowly turned from product orientation to sales orientation. There are three main factors that have facilitated his ongoing success:

- The political culture in Venezuela, as in many other Latin American countries, is rather subject-oriented and is not yet consolidated. Venezuelans traditionally ask for a strong state, they look for strong leaders, they are mainly focused on the political output and are seldom party-aligned (Lagos 2006; Dalton *et al.* 2007). As a consequence, the floor is wide open to charismatic, populist leaders.

- Chávez has successively expanded control over the most important media in Venezuela. Therefore, large, constant and mostly positive coverage has been guaranteed.
- Chávez's political record has been convincing due to enormous investment in social programs funded by earnings of the state-owned oil company.

In sum, Chávez's populism can be considered highly successful. The Venezuelan presidential system, media control, a sedated opposition and the country's political culture have simplified a product- and sales-oriented marketing approach for a strong leader. In such a democratically transitory and unstable context, clear-cut marketing orientation seems unnecessary and inappropriate.

Austria: the Haider phenomenon

In the European context, populism is a rather new phenomenon that emerged in the late 20th century as a result of an increasing number of constituents who no longer felt represented by established political parties (Taggart 2000: 73). The majority of the European neo-populist parties have taken rightist and often nationalist positions. This also applies to the Austrian Freedom Party (FPÖ), one of the most successful and persistent populist parties in Europe ever. Founded in 1956, the FPÖ initially positioned itself as a protest party against the two catch-all parties, the Social Democrats (SPÖ) and the conservative Austrian's People Party (ÖVP). Until the 1980s, however, the FPÖ's impact on Austrian politics remained marginal (Betz 1994: 11; Riedlsperger 1998: 32).

That changed substantially when Jörg Haider took over the FPÖ's leadership in 1986. He immediately started a process of rebuilding and centralizing the party's organizational structure. Lean and hierarchical structures, led by Haider himself and a handful of his loyal associates, made the introduction of modern political marketing techniques easy. Step by step, Haider transformed the FPÖ from a formerly product-oriented party to a market-oriented one (Lederer *et al.* 2005: 132). With regards to issue positions, Haider's FPÖ trusted in a variable mix of anti-establishment and anti-EU discourse in combination with nationalist-xenophobic standpoints. Haider, a young, charismatic and rhetorically skilled politician, set a new tone in Austria's political discourse. He was successful in presenting himself as advocate of the people, pointing out the most important socioeconomic and political grievances. A strategy of continuous, but unreckoned populist communication including simplifications and personal attacks finally led to the best result a populist radical right party in Western Europe could ever achieve (Mudde 2004): it was in 1999 when the FPÖ got 26.9 percent of the vote in the national elections, coming second (after the SPÖ) and entering into a coalition government with the ÖVP – an unprecedented event that caused national and international protests. In its governmental role, which was prolonged in 2002, the FPÖ had to readjust some of its original populist ambitions giving concessions to its governing partner, and it lost significant support in state and European elections. Finally, Haider and his associates separated from the FPÖ and founded a new party, the Alliance for the Future of Austria (BZÖ) in 2005. While the FPÖ's new party leader, Heinz-Christian Strache, copied Haider's leadership style and market-oriented populist strategy, Haider received a last and unanticipated victory in the snap elections of 2008: the FPÖ gained 17.5 percent of the vote and the BZÖ – basically a leader-oriented, sales-oriented movement at that time – got 10.7 percent. However, just two weeks later Haider died in a car accident. Not surprisingly, this marked the beginning of the BZÖ's rapid disappearance from the political landscape, culminating in internal conflict between leading members in 2010.

In conclusion, the Austrian political environment turned out to be a fertile ground for the rise and enduring success of populist parties. Its political culture is still a mixture of subject and civic orientations, with strong xenophobic tendencies including a widespread aversion to the European Union. Those tendencies have become even more vivid in the 1990s due to the parallel processes of modernization and Europeanization (rising numbers of unemployed, immigrants, etc.). Relying on up-to-date market intelligence, a long-term strategy and a handful of professional marketers, the FPÖ has turned into to a marketing-oriented party and it has been successful in filling the gap that the SPÖ and ÖVP left open (Kickl 2008). In doing so, Haider and Strache, two strong, charismatic and eloquent leaders, have put populist discourse on the political stage in Austria. A media system in which the tabloid *Kronen Zeitung* possesses a universally unique scope has alleviated this process. Today, it seems very likely that the FPÖ will hold its position as the third strong force and that the FPÖ's techniques of populist political marketing could serve as a role model for other populist parties in Europe.

Advice for practitioners

Although it is widespread, populism is still not a universally applicable marketing technique. It is a universally reoccurring, non-lasting phenomenon. There are numerous environmental factors that have to collude both on the macro level and on the meso level. Still, we assume that chances for populists are increasing, even in consolidated liberal democracies. There are three main factors that might facilitate a rise in populism: (a) people are departing from 'old-fashioned' political parties, instead opening themselves to short-term influences and convincing products; (b) fundamental changes in the media environment have just begun and in future rhetorically skilled populists will be able to reach consumers directly and interactively via hybrids of mass and new media (Mazzoleni 2008); (c) marketing strategies are becoming more accepted in politics, and political actors have started to look for approaches that have proven successful.

Populism has repeatedly turned out to be an efficient way to get the message out and to attract a notable share of voters. However, in most cases populism has been a short-term phenomenon and populists have failed to build up stable relationships with their supporters. We assume that such failures reflect the insufficient information held about potential supporters and their needs, the inadequate way in which cohesive and convincing political alternatives are developed and implemented, and – probably most important – the continuous effort needed in market orientation, self-reflection and evaluation. Thus, if we were to advise politicians on how to use populism as a political marketing technique, we would suggest starting with professional market analysis. As a next step, qualitative research (i.e. focus groups) might help to create the right 'products' and develop the most appropriate communication mix. A special focus should be placed on the political leader himself/herself – you simply need an internally undisputed and externally assertive politician with charisma and excellent media skills. Finally, as the Austrian case demonstrates, populist actors are able to build lasting relationships if they do not cease their activities on election day. Backed-up by market and opinion research, a continuing process of product readjustment has to be structurally guaranteed.

Impact on politics

An evaluation of the impact of populism as a political marketing technique depends on the political context on the one hand (i.e. the political system and political culture) and our understanding of democracy on the other hand. Taking the position of participatory or deliberative theory, populism must be considered dysfunctional, since it undermines equal participation of the people as well as rational discourse. Only the liberal, representative model of democracy, which stresses the importance of intermediary forces such as political parties, would consider populism as a generally acceptable mode of political communication. In that sense, the effects of rising populism are ambivalent. On the one hand, it could spoil democracy and political culture, as it threatens not only established political parties but also public cultures of constructive controversy which are vital to any liberal democracy. On the other hand, rising populism might have a positive impact on politics: populist parties have always been an integral element of modern democracy and they are often seen as a necessary barb for competing political parties, which tend to readjust in response and thus move closer to people's demands more quickly (e.g. Decker 2006).

The democratic issue for the future will be whether populist parties move closer towards the market-oriented model and thus achieve longer-term success. Populists' adjustment to market orientation could prolong their existence compared with product- or sales-oriented populist parties. In the long run, we would argue, it is only market orientation that could guarantee lasting success for populist parties here too, particularly when control over the media is fading. After all, compared with 'old' democracies, populism is not only more accepted in most transitory societies, but it is also one of the biggest obstacles to democratization. Ultimately, it is this normative dimension for democratization and the people that has to be taken into account when we look at the spread of populism as a political marketing technique in the future.

The way forward

Although we assume that populist actors have been increasingly keen to adapt political marketing techniques, our assumption has been until now primarily based on single case studies. There is a major deficit in empirical analyses that would either longitudinally or cross-sectionally compare culture-specific variants of populism (e.g. Betz 1994; Mény and Surel 2002; Albertazzi and McDonnell 2008). This deficit becomes even more obvious when we look at populism from a political communications or marketing perspective. Therefore, our integrative approach is rather novel. To back our argument, some empirical research would have to be done. Such research should take the complexity of potentially relevant macro and meso variables into account. Thus, we need empirical studies that use a *most dissimilar design* when looking at the independent variables. Ideally, those studies would look at the dependent variable, i.e. the development and transformation of political communication of populist parties within and between countries. We are not interested in explanations for the rise and disappearance of populist actors, but we need to sharpen our understanding of the impact that communication matters have on populist parties.

Such empirical findings are indispensable when it comes to the practical applicability of our concept. Practitioners simply need reliable information about the conditions under which a populist approach to political marketing might ensure political success. They have to be aware of the risks with which successful populists are confronted, both politically and publicly. Therefore, we not only have to strengthen our empirical research in that field, but also our ethical and normative considerations. It will not be enough to provide practitioners with a 'how to do populism as political marketing technique' kit. What is also desperately needed are theoretical, ethical and normative discussions about the practical relevance of populists and their marketers' actions. We hope that this chapter has opened the field for further research and discussion.

Note

1 We would like to thank Iris Höller, Lore Hayek and the two anonymous reviewers for their input on an earlier version of this chapter. This research was carried out under the auspices of the Austrian National Election Study (AUTNES), a National Research Network (NFN) sponsored by the Austrian Research Fund (FWF) (S10904-G11; S10905-G11).

Bibliography

Abts, K. and Rummens, S. (2007) 'Populism versus Democracy', *Political Studies* 55: 405–24.

Albertazzi, D. and McDonnell, D. (eds) (2008) *Twenty-First Century Populism. The Spectre of Western European Democracy*, Basingstoke: Palgrave.

Almond, G.A. and Verba, S. (1963) *The Civic Culture. Political Attitudes and Democracy in Five Nations*, Princeton, NJ: Princeton University Press.

Balch, G.I. (1974) 'Multiple Indicators in Survey Research. The Concept "Sense of Political Efficacy"', *Political Methodology* 1: 1–43.

Betz, H.-G. (1994) *Radical Right-Wing Populism in Western Europe*, New York: St Martin's Press.

Black, G.S. and Black, B.D. (1994) *The Politics of American Discontent. How a New Party Can Make Democracy Work Again*, New York: John Wiley & Sons.

Butler, P. and Collins, N. (1994) 'Political Marketing. Structure and Process', *European Journal of Marketing* 28, 1: 19–34.

Canovan, M. (1981) *Populism*, London: Junction Books.

—— (1999) 'Trust the People. Populism and the Two Faces of Democracy', *Political Studies* XLVII: 2–16.

Coniff, M.L. (1999) *Populism in Latin America*, Tuscaloosa: The University of Alabama Press.

Dalton, R.J., Shin, D.C. and Jou, W. (2007) 'Understanding Democracy. Data from Unlike Places', *Journal of Democracy* 18, 4: 142–56.

Decker, F. (2006) 'Die populistische Herausforderung. Theoretische und ländervergleichende Perspektiven', in F. Decker (ed.) *Populismus. Gefahr für die Demokratie oder nützliches Korrektiv*, Wiesbaden: VS, 9–32.

Freeden, M. (1998) 'Is Nationalism a Distinct Ideology', *Political Studies* 46, 4: 748–65.

Hawkins, K. (2003) 'Populism in Venezuela. The Rise of Chavismo', *Third World Quarterly* 24, 6: 1137–60.

Heinisch, R. (2003) 'Success in Opposition – Failure in Government. Explaining the Performance of Right-Wing Populist Parties in Public Office', *West European Politics* 26: 91–130.

Ionescu, G. and Gellner, E. (eds) (1969) *Populism. Its Meanings and National Characteristics*, London: Weidenfeld and Nicholson.

Jagers, J. and Walgrave, S. (2007) 'Populism as Political Communication Style. An Empirical Study of Political Parties' Discourse in Belgium', *European Journal of Political Research* 46, 3: 319–45.

Kavanagh, D. (1996) 'New Campaign Communications. Consequences for British Political Parties', *The Harvard International Journal of Press/Politics* 1, 3: 60–76.

Kickl, H. (2008) 'Unterwegs in Richtung 20 Prozent', in T. Hofer and B. Toth (eds) *Wahl 2008. Strategien – Sieger – Sensationen*, Vienna: Molden, 55–64.

Lagos, M. (2006) 'A Apearse a la Fantasía. Hugo Chávez y los Liderazgos en América Latina', *Revista Nueva Sociedad* 205: 92–101.

Lederer, A., Plasser, F. and Scheucher, C. (2005) 'The Rise and Fall of Populism in Austria. A Political Marketing Perspective', in D. Lilleker and J. Lees-Marshment (eds) *Political Marketing. A Comparative Perspective*, New York: Palgrave, 132–47.

Lees-Marshment, J. (2001) 'The Marriage of Politics and Marketing', *Political Studies* 49, 4: 692–713.

—— (2010) 'Global Political Marketing', in J. Lees-Marshment, J. Strömbäck and C. Rudd (eds) *Global Political Marketing*, New York: Routledge, 1–15.

Lilleker, D.G. and Lees-Marshment, J. (2005) 'Introduction. Rethinking Political Party Behaviour', in D.G. Lilleker and J. Lees-Marshment (eds) *Political Marketing. A Comparative Perspective*, Manchester: Manchester University Press, 1–14.

Mazzoleni, G. (2008) 'Populism and the Media', in D. Albertazzi and D. McDonnell (eds) *Twenty-First Century Populism. The Spectre of Western European Democracy*, Basingstoke: Palgrave, 49–64.

Mazzoleni, G., Stewart, J. and Horsfield, B. (eds) (2003) *The Media and Neo-Populism. A Comparative Analysis*, Westport, CT: Praeger.

Mény, Y. and Surel, Y. (2002) *Democracies and the Populist Challenge*, New York: Palgrave Macmillan.

Mudde, C. (1996) 'The Paradox of the Anti-Party', *Party Politics* 2, 2: 265–76.

—— (2004) 'The Populist Zeitgeist', *Government and Opposition* 39, 3: 541–63.

Plasser, F. and Plasser, G. (2002) *Global Political Campaigning. A Worldwide Analysis of Campaign Professionals and Their Practices*, Westport, CT and London: Praeger.

Post, J.M. (1995) 'The Political Psychology of the Ross Perot Phenomenon', in S.A. Renshon (ed.) *The Clinton Presidency. Campaigning, Governing, and the Psychology of Leadership*, Boulder, CO, San Francisco and Oxford: Westview Press, 37–56.

Riedlsperger, M. (1998) 'The Freedom Party of Austria. From Protest to Radical Right Populism', in H.G. Betz and S. Immerfall (eds) *The New Politics of the Radical Right. Neo-Populist Parties and Movements in Established Democracies*, London: Macmillan Press, 27–44.

Roberts, K.M. (2003) 'Social Correlates of Party System Demise and Populist Resurgence in Venezuela', *Latin American Politics and Society* 45, 3: 35–57.

Spier, T. (2006) 'Populismus und Modernisierung', in F. Decker (ed.) *Populismus. Gefahr für die Demokratie oder nützliches Korrektiv*, Wiesbaden: VS, 33–58.

Stokes, D.E. (1966) 'Spatial Models of Party Competition', in A. Campbell, P.E. Converse, W. Miller and D.E. Stokes (eds) *Elections and the Political Order*, New York: Wiley, 161–79.

Strömbäck, J. (2010) 'A Framework for Comparing Political Market-Orientation', in J. Lees-Marshment, J. Strömbäck and C. Rudd (eds) *Global Political Marketing*, New York: Routledge, 16–33.

Taggart, P. (2000) *Populism*, Buckingham: Open University Press.

Taguieff, P.A. (2002) *L'illusion Populiste*, Paris: Berg International.

Weyland, K. (2001) 'Clarifying a Contested Concept. Populism in the Study of Latin American Politics', *Comparative Politics* 34, 1: 1–22.

—— (2003) 'Economic Voting Reconsidered. Crisis and Charisma in the Election of Hugo Chávez', *Comparative Political Studies* 36: 822–48.

Wring, D. (2002) 'Conceptualising Political Marketing. A Framework for Election-Campaign Analysis', in N. O'Shaughnessy and S.C. Henneberg (eds) *The Idea of Political Marketing*, Westport, CT: Praeger, 171–86.

19

Something old, something new?

Modelling political communication in the 2010 UK general election

Jenny Lloyd

The topic: political communication

It might be argued that political communication is one of the primary drivers of an effective democracy (Cook 1998) and, as such, an understanding of the political communication process is essential to those seeking to work within one. In its most simple form, 'political communication' has been defined as the transmission of political messages between government and voters (Baek 2009). However, it is clear that the contemporary political communication landscape is much more complex than this. According to Manheim (2011), in addition to conventional sources, modern political communication has also evolved to include messages from non-governmental sources such as advocacy groups, corporations, international organisations and even insurgent and terrorist groups. These touch every aspect of contemporary political life with their aim to not only inform but to influence and persuade.

It is not only the nature of the participants in the communication process that have developed; the media channels and vehicles through which political messages flow have also altered significantly over recent decades. It has been noted that the growth and proliferation of digital technology has resulted in an increasingly fragmented media landscape (Jenkins 2006) and a greater propensity for consumers to be more selective in their media choices (Bennett and Iyengar 2008). Furthermore, public disillusionment with political institutions (Mortimore 2002) and with conventional media and journalism (Hamilton 2004) suggests a propensity for voters to look to non-conventional sources of information, which they believe have greater authenticity.

It is thought that the structure and organisation of the media affects political actors' ability to diffuse their messages amongst the voting public and, as such, has the potential to negatively impact upon the voters' ability to cast informed votes (Bennett 1990; Bennett *et al.* 2007; Bennett and Iyengar 2008). This being the case, it becomes imperative that those who see the media as an essential pillar in the support of effective democracy understand the logistical implications posed by the new media landscape so that they can plan their media campaigns in a way that can target specific voter groups but also can proactively respond to the non-conventional political influences in the contemporary communication environment.

Previous research: conceptualising the communication process

In political marketing literature, scant attention had been paid to modelling the contemporary process of political communication (see Lloyd 2009). Even in the broader field of marketing communication, there appeared to have been only limited attempts to model pathways of message transmission.

Where references to the process of communication do exist in political marketing literature, they are limited and tend to relate to Katz and Lazerfeld's (1955) two-step flow process of communication with a focus on the content (i.e. influence) as opposed to the physical, logistical transmission of a message.

Discussions pertaining to the physical transmission of messages tend to draw upon classic models of the communication process such as that of Shannon and Weaver (1949) (see Figure 19.1). This model is very reflective of its era in that it conveys the physical and mechanical process of message transmission. Despite this, it clearly underpins many of the subsequent developments in the field, none less than that of Westley and MacLean (1957) (see Figure 19.2) whose model of mass communication not only recognises the fact that messages are often compiled on the basis of information derived from multiple sources (X1, X2, X3), but also that messages may travel via multiple media (A, C) before they reach their final destination (B). Additionally, it recognises the potential existence of feedback from the receiver once the message has been received.

In the field of politics, discussions pertaining to issues of communication tend to focus on specific areas such as the impact of communications, its role in agenda setting (Scheufele 2000), priming (Mendelson 1996) and framing (Scheufele 1999; Entman 2006), and its link or influence on voter engagement or participation (Norris *et al.* 1999; Norris 2000). Alternatively, bodies of literature consider issues in relation to the function, role or impact of emergent communications channels or vehicles such as the internet (Best and Krueger 2005) and blogs (Lawson-Borders and Kirk 2005; Eveland and Dylko 2007).

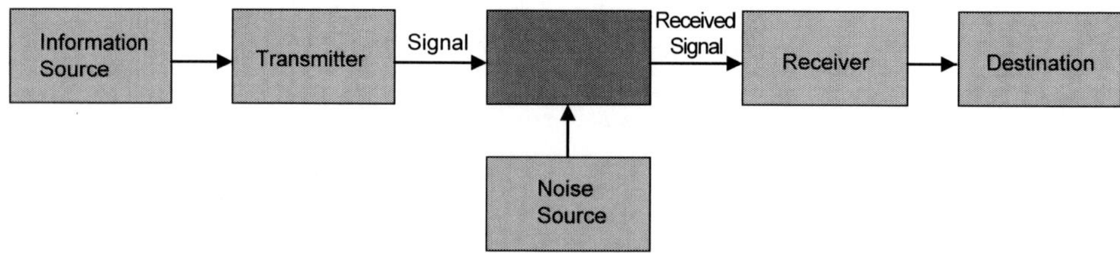

Figure 19.1 Shannon and Weaver's (1949) model of communication

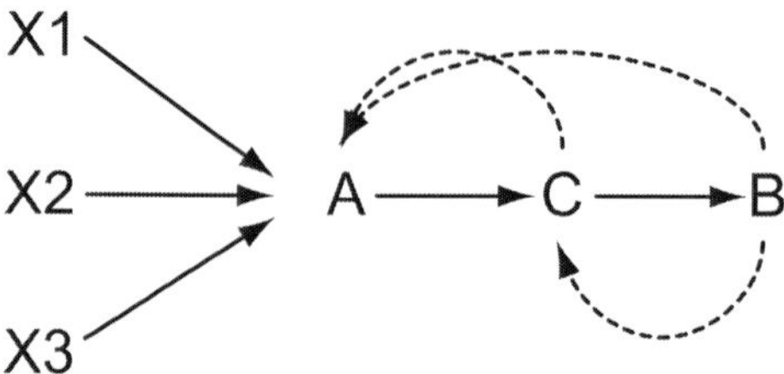

Figure 19.2 The Westley and MacLean (1957) model of mass communication

New research: using constructivist grounded theory to create a contemporary model of political marketing communication

To address this apparent theoretical gap, a constructivist grounded theory approach was adopted to explore and interrogate the political communications process by considering the receiver perspective and interviewing the voters themselves. This approach clearly coincides with a political market-oriented approach (Lees-Marshment 2001), places the 'market' (i.e. the voter) at the centre of the research and reflects Shimp's (2000) view that when working within the context of an integrated marketing communications process, one should start at the consumer and work backwards towards the communicator.

Grounded theory was thought the most appropriate for this study because of the paucity of current models and its acknowledged ability to generate new theory (Glaser and Strauss 1967; Charmaz 2000; Goulding 2002). By taking a 'constructivist' perspective it was hoped that issues and criticisms associated with apparent methodological conflicts of positivism versus objectivism (Goulding 1998; Allen 2003) might be addressed.

Prior to the 2005 general election, twenty-four respondents were interviewed using a political 'life history' technique. According to Goulding (1998) the number of interviews required for any single study is arbitrary as it should be determined by that point at which subsequent interviews fail to yield new insight, known as the point of 'saturation'. However, depending upon the focus of the topic, Riley (1996) suggests that a sample size of between eight and twenty-four interviews are likely to be sufficient to reach a point of saturation and this was proven to be the case in this instance.

Mariampolski (2001: 53) defines 'life history' interviews as 'a mode of in-depth interviewing which focuses on the evolution of behaviours and attitudes over the life course'. It was the research method of choice in this case because its long-term focus not only lent insight into the current media consumption behaviour and preferences of the respondents, but also their evolution over time, thus giving some idea of the potential trajectory of consumption changes. The assumption of a clear political focus in the interview meant that it was possible to avoid one of the frequently cited problems associated with both grounded theory and life history interviews: unmanageable volumes of data (Chicchi 2000).

Transcripts of interviews were analysed on an ongoing basis throughout the research process and the results were used to inform subsequent sample selection. This process is in line with the theoretical tenets of grounded theory, which state that respondents should be purposefully selected on an ongoing basis according to category development and emergent theory (Goulding 2002). Following each interview, the transcript was analysed and coded on a line-by-line basis and the results were grouped together under the headings known as 'conceptual codes'. Recurring themes were identified and the conceptual codes were further grouped into the 'core categories' which were used to underpin the creation of the theoretical framework and, ultimately, a model of contemporary political communication, depicted in Figure 19.3.

Following the 2010 UK general election, eight of the original respondents were contacted for follow-up interviews. In the period between 2005 and 2010 there had been a number of significant events that had the potential to affect the electorate's interaction with the political communication process. The emergence of broadband and increased access to computer technology had broadened the channels of communication whilst the worldwide recession and the collapse of the banks together with scandals pertaining to MPs' expense claims and other allegations of political corruption had potentially affected the electorate's ability to accept and process political communications once transmitted. Therefore, the aim of this additional research was to check the validity of the original model and also to determine whether developments in the economic and technical landscape had altered political communications'

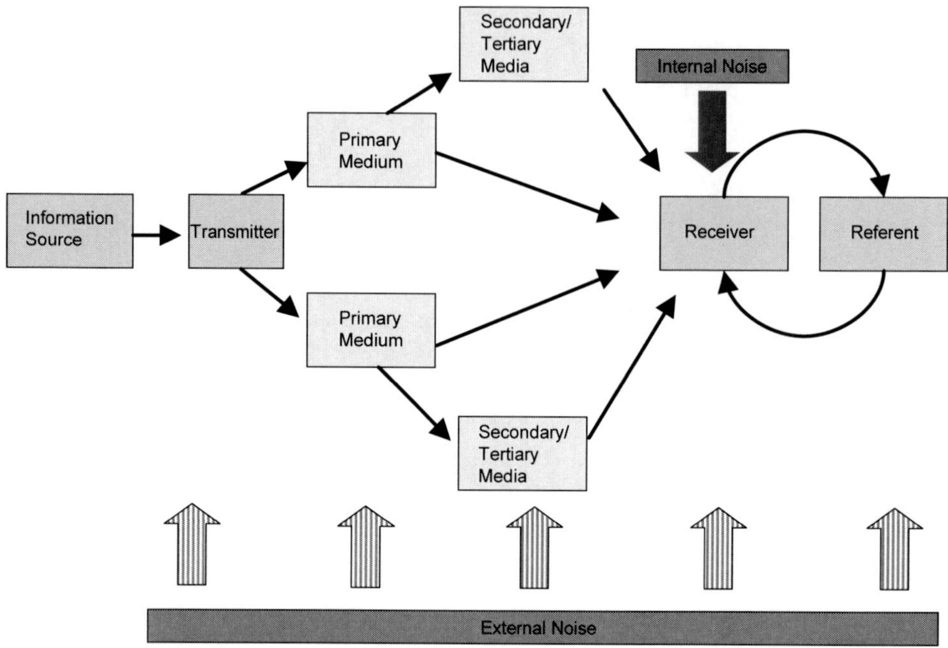

Figure 19.3 The UK general election in 2005: A model of political communication

structure and behaviour. These interviews were conducted in a similar 'political life history' fashion using constructivist grounded theory. However, in this instance the respondents were asked to give an account of the period starting from the 2005 UK general election until the present day.

The model generated on the basis of the 2005 data showed that many of the basic characteristics of the classical models by Shannon and Weaver (1949) and Westley and MacLean (1957) still applied. It was clear that the communication process possessed five key characteristics.

Lack of direct contact

None of the respondents interviewed had experienced unmediated contact with their MPs, prospective parliamentary candidates or any member of local or national government. None had received a visit from canvassers or the electoral candidates themselves. The closest thing to direct contact that the respondents appear to have experienced was political interviews and speeches on television or radio, but their credibility as political messages appeared undermined with respondents repeatedly used words like 'false', 'stage managed' or 'spin'. Further, it was felt that the credibility of political interviews often undermined the personal agenda of the interviewer and the overly forceful style of interviewing by journalists and presenters like Jeremy Paxman was particularly disliked. According to one respondent:

> It'd be all right if he'd let them get their answers out – but he won't … he just keeps on interrupting them and goes on and on. You lose track. I just feel like screaming 'will you shut up' … but I just switch off instead.

Multiple media stages

Instead of direct contact, political communications received by respondents have generally travelled via multiple media before reaching their final destination. Respondents said that it was often the case that the communications they received and gave most credence to were actually commentaries or editorials that were themselves commenting on news reports. These, it was felt, offered clarity in an information landscape considered by most respondents to be complicated and ambiguous. One respondent particularly liked 'Littlejohn', a correspondent in the UK newspaper the *Daily Mail*:

> I always read Littlejohn. He's for people like me and you know where he stands. I like it simple and to the point – none of this fannying around – simple and straight to the point.

The impact of noise

A factor of particular importance to emerge in the contemporary communications process is the impact of 'noise', defined as factors that may inhibit the effectiveness of the communications process. There are a number of different types of noise but the research suggested that they can be broadly divided into two: internal factors, which relate to the individual's psychological state and ability to process communication; and external factors, which originate from factors outside of the individual.

The data analysed in this study supported Wu and Newell's (2003) proposition that an individual's state of mind can affect their ability to process information. In particular, it became clear that the emotions of fear, stress and anger surfaced during elections, particularly amongst the older respondents, as political parties discussed policy platforms pertaining to social security, national security and pensions. When talking about pensions policy and her savings, one elderly respondent felt desperate:

> I don't know how I'm going to cope. One party says one thing and another says another. I can't make head nor tail of it, you see. All the time I see my little income dwindling and I don't know what to do.

These results concur with the findings of Mundorf *et al.* (1991) which suggest that intense mood states of all types, and particularly negative ones such as anger, can result in the creation of 'blocks' upon stimuli. The impact of such blocks, or internal noise is that, potentially, certain messages are only partially received or, at times, their reception is blocked completely.

With regard to external noise, it became clear that one particular form, 'clutter', had a major impact upon the respondents' ability to receive and accurately process information sent to them, particularly during election time. Clutter is defined by Tellis (1998: 354) as the 'proliferation of ads that compete for an audience's attention within a particular time period or printed space'. Quite simply, the greater the number of communications received by an individual, the less time he or she has to give to process each one. Within the context of a general election, the sheer volume of media coverage together with the leaflets, posters and other promotional material issued by each of the parties, naturally creates clutter. In this study it was clearly the case that many of the respondents felt overwhelmed by the volume and sometimes contradictory nature of the communications and, as a result, looked for information shortcuts such as the aforementioned Littlejohn, or simply decided to ignore the communications completely.

Another form of external noise, 'semantic' noise, was identified by the research as a potential barrier to communication. Defined by Fiske (2002) as the extent to which meaning is distorted during the course of the communication process, semantic noise can occur either intentionally or unintentionally. In political communications, the research results support Watson's (2003) proposition that semantic noise can be the result of the use of ambiguous language, overly technical terms or jargon, or a simple lack of explanation. One respondent was adamant:

> I can't understand it. *New* Labour? *New* Labour? What's *new* about it? I simply don't understand. [Respondent's own emphasis.]

A final type of external noise identified by the study is that of external distraction. According to Watson (2003), because of the high quality of modern-day message transmission, this type of noise has replaced the 'mechanical' noise originally identified by Shannon and Weaver (1949). The busy lives of the respondents resulted in almost all stating that they did not have the time or the inclination to read party manifestos, campaign leaflets or sit down and watch party political broadcasts. In particular, the two youngest respondents, aged 17 and 18, respectively, felt that politics had no relevance to them. This was evidenced by one of the respondents who, when talking about the eventual election result, said:

> Like, I'm not a home owner and I don't have a job so it really doesn't matter … does it?

The importance of reference groups

On receipt of a message, it became clear that reference groups had a major part to play when determining whether the receiver accepted the message as originally intended by the information source. In this study, 'reference groups', defined as 'an actual or imaginary individual or group conceived of having significant relevance upon an individual's evaluations, aspirations, or behaviour' (Cohen and Golden 1972: 54), generally took the form of family or close friends for the younger respondents. In these cases, referents tended to be seen to possess what Cohen and Golden (1972) term 'information power' – the power to give meaning to the message by filling in any gaps in knowledge or understanding. However, as the respondents grow more knowledgeable it appears that there was a greater tendency to seek reinforcement of their existing views by referring to people or bodies they felt to be credible commentators on the subject and thus possessed 'expert power'. One young respondent reflected on the regular references made to past Conservative prime minister Margaret Thatcher during the election campaign:

> I know stuff about her … but because I was too young, I don't know. Loads of people have said different things, like my family who said she was good because she did all this stuff. But now I'm at work, I'm hearing that she did other things and I'm not sure.

The lack of feedback

An interesting feature of the model was the perceived lack of opportunity for feedback. Respondents felt that they were subject to communications from politicians and political parties but there were few if any opportunities to respond. The lack of opportunity for feedback was frequently cited as a source of frustration. This feeling was typified by one respondent when discussing his feelings regarding government policy and, in particular, the Iraq War:

> I will be quite angry and it's just sickening. But what can you do? I don't think there is a way of showing your dissent any more.

Political communications in 2010: the findings updated

Analysis of the voters' 2010 transcripts revealed that two of the basic principles of the 2005 model still remained. First, it was clear that the multisource, multistage model still applies. Responses indicated that information about the 2010 election was gleaned from multiple sources and that the multistep model of mass communication applied to the majority of the information consumed. All of the respondents stated that they formed their opinions through the assimilation of information from multiple sources and that the majority of these sources took the form of reporting and editorials. Older respondents tended to favour the more traditional media. For example, one respondent stated:

> I liked the BBC and *The Telegraph*. Sometimes I listened to the radio too. That John Pinaar is nice … I like his voice. He explains things.

Whilst younger respondents also assimilated information through the traditional media, it was more incidental and the information derived took the form of 'soundbites'. However, if they encountered a topic of interest, they would actively research it, usually through the internet.

Second, there was still a distortion of message transmission by noise. A consistent theme to emerge from the transcripts was the increasing impact of noise, both internal and external, upon the effectiveness of political communications. Four of the respondents said that they felt overwhelmed by noise in the form of clutter through the sheer volume of coverage that the election achieved in the media, together with leaflets, posters and other promotional material. One respondent was adamant:

> It's too much. Every time you turn on the telly they're there saying the same old 'yak yak'. They don't say anything new. I don't listen … I just switch off.

The presence of internal noise was also apparent in this study. The recessionary economic climate and debate about cuts in public spending had a clear effect upon the respondents' willingness and ability to listen to and process messages. In analysing the transcripts, the respondents expressed fear and anger in their response to economic discussion in the media. 'I don't want to listen but I feel I have to …' and 'It's so scary …' and 'I just want to bury my head in the sand or run away' are typical of respondents' expressions of fear, whilst anger was directed at politicians on all sides for their apparent impotence.

> They should have known what was happening … it's their job, isn't it? And now … the bankers, they walk away scot free and they're not doing anything … none of them. It's disgusting.

However, analysis of the transcripts revealed some interesting developments that appear to emerge as a result of the introduction of a series of televised party leaders' debates, technological developments and environmental factors.

Perceived increase in 'direct' communication and dialogue

The televised debate made a big impression on all of the respondents and, without exception, it was felt to be a very positive addition to the election campaign. In particular, the opportunity for 'normal' people to visibly pose questions to the respective leaders and for the leader to immediately respond was perceived not only as a form of direct communication but of dialogue. One respondent put it succinctly:

> It wasn't so much us watching them talk … it was like us talking to them and them talking back.

Perceived opportunity for feedback

Unlike the 2005 UK general election, most of the respondents felt that there was far greater scope to respond to both politicians and political parties. 'Talk' radio and the radio 'phone-in' were identified by all of the respondents as media offering potential for feedback. All but one cited both the telephone and email as offering vehicles for immediate feedback, whilst the youngest two respondents also cited Twitter. Interestingly, Facebook and the political parties' own websites were not seen as particularly useful. In the case of the party websites, none of the respondents had considered even accessing them for information let alone using them as a vehicle for feedback. When party websites were suggested as a potential vehicle for feedback, the general feeling appears to have been that party websites were not a useful vehicle for two-way communication. In contrast, three of the respondents had tried to access Facebook pages on one or more occasions, but found them unsatisfactory. Finding the right pages took more time than the respondents were willing to give up, as there were a number of 'spoof' pages. In addition, two of the respondents commented on the apparent lack of dialogue or reasoned discussion on the Facebook pages. According to one respondent, when he finally found the page he wanted, he gave up because, he said, 'it was just full of idiots with an axe to grind'.

Active creation of perceptual barriers

A recurring theme to emerge from the data was that respondents found the intensity of the media campaign associated with the general election to be overwhelming or, as one respondent put it, she felt 'positively stifled'. In light of the sheer volume of coverage that the election received in the media paired with the length of the campaign, several of the respondents actively sought to avoid anything directly related to it. Television coverage, in particular, was singled out as being particularly invasive.

> Every time you switched it [the television] on it was someone talking election this or election that … I just got to the point where I couldn't stand the sight of it.

Perceptual selectivity, defined by Solomon *et al.* (2002: 587) as 'the process in which people attend to only a small portion of the stimuli to which they are exposed', is a natural and unconscious defence mechanism employed to stop individuals being overwhelmed by stimuli. However, far from being unconscious, what became clear was that the respondents reached a tipping point at which they consciously established barriers to avoid unsolicited political communication.

The impact of novelty

Whilst it became clear that there was a tendency amongst the respondents to actively enforce barriers against what they felt to be an intrusive level of media coverage, what also emerged was that where an entity was perceived to be 'novel', not only did it successfully overcome perceptual barriers, but many of the respondents actively sought it out.

There were three elements to the 2010 UK general election that were perceived as novel. The televised 'leaders' debates' were particularly well received. As previously stated, not only did respondents feel that they provided a direct channel of communication between the main political parties and voters, but also that they provided a simple vehicle for comparison between their respective offerings. The 'hype' surrounding the fact that it was the first time that a three-way televised political debate had taken place in the UK also heightened the novelty, which made it a 'must watch' event for almost all of the respondents.

An outcome of the first debate that provided an additional source of novelty was the emergence of the Liberal Democrats as a viable third option. Liberal Democrat leader Nick Clegg's strong performance made a positive impression on one of the respondents in particular:

> I've never thought much of the Libdems. Too soft. But he [Nick Clegg] was like a breath of fresh air ... he talked straight and he made sense ... like he actually knows what he was doing.

The presence of a third option was seen as a particularly positive development because the respondents felt that it gave them an option they previously hadn't considered useful before.

> I never bothered with the Liberals. Bit of a waste of space, really. A wasted vote. Might as well not have bothered getting my coat on ... not going out to vote. Now, though, you think 'they might just do it'. It's worth a punt just to put one in the eye of old Cameron.

The outcome of the 2010 UK general election provided the final element of novelty: the coalition government. Interestingly, despite the perceived negative coverage in the press, most of the respondents saw its existence as a sign of hope. This was clearly expressed by one of the respondents:

> The man on the telly said it would never work ... that we might have to have another election in the autumn. But I don't see why ... why can't they get along ... work together, like? I think it's good.

For the female respondents, the youthful appearance of Conservative leader David Cameron and Liberal Democratic leader Nick Clegg also proved a draw. When talking about their appearance, one of the oldest respondents commented:

> Such nice looking boys ... yes, it might actually be worth tuning into Prime Minister's Questions!

In addition to breaching the perceptual barriers erected by respondents, another effect of the perceived novel aspects to the communication process was an increased level of engagement. All of the respondents alluded to the fact that the debates had prompted them to think about the issues discussed and the parties' relative responses to questions posed. Further, all of the respondents said that they had discussed the content of the debates with friends or family, who themselves had discussed the debates with other people. After the debates, half of the respondents said that they had actively sought to read or listen to coverage and the media reaction, and particularly sought out editorials or broadcasts by journalists and other sources that they trusted or liked.

The result of this research suggests a new, post-2010 model of political marketing communications, which is illustrated in Figure 19.4. The updated model accommodates voters' perception that 'direct' channels of communication exist between political parties, politicians and voters, together with the potential for voters to return feedback, have been added to the original model. In addition, a perceptual barrier has been added to reflect respondents' strategies when trying to reduce their exposure to the volume of election coverage by the media. Finally, the number of 'referents' have increased and the interrelated flows of communication have been highlighted to reflect the communal nature of the respondents who, post debates, spent time discussing the content with friends or family or gained perspective from other individuals and sources whom they saw as referents.

Obviously, some of the technology that has become so central to much of today's communication processes may be seen to be new in a 'new to the world' sense, but these relate to the mechanical processes of communication. As such, the question must then arise: how and in what way is this updated model of the communication *process* itself 'new'?

In truth, one must say 'very little'. None of the components in the model depicted in Figure 19.4 are new to the world, as they have long existed in other fields such as marketing, communication studies and psychology. Instead, the 'newness' of this model comes from the components' assemblage and application within the context of the field of politics.

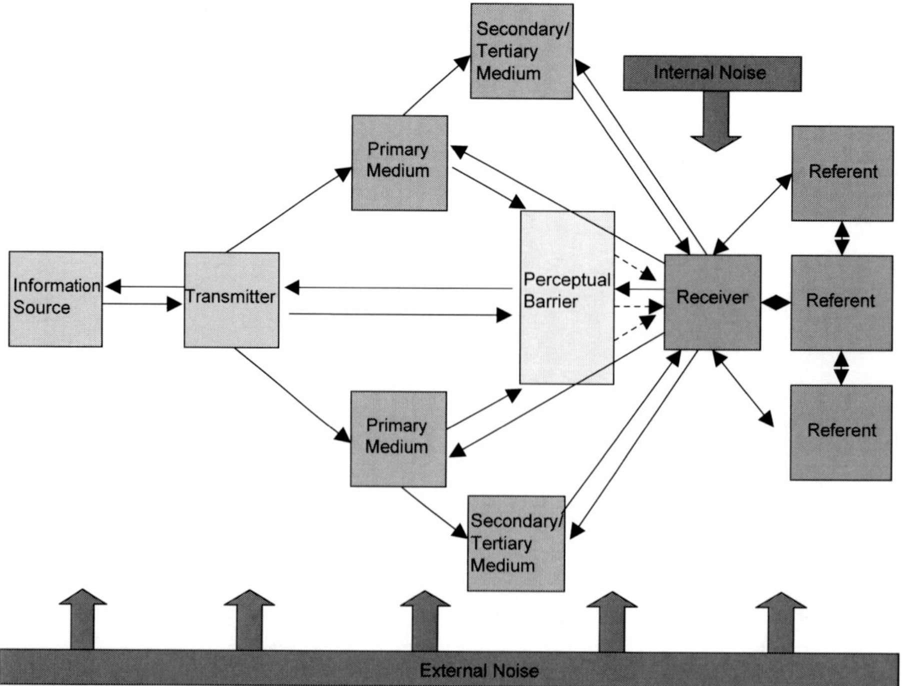

Figure 19.4 The 2010 model of political marketing communications

Furthermore, what became clear over the course of the study was that the true source of novelty in the 2010 UK general election came largely from the televised series of leaders' debates. Whilst political debate can hardly be considered new, newness did stem from the fact that, in this election, there seemed to be greater capacity for dialogue. Unlike previous elections, the respondents felt that they had experienced a form of communication from party leaders that actually appeared to address the issues that were important to them. The presence of all three main parties gave them a clear, simple and accessible vehicle with which to compare the 'brands' of politics on offer, and the presence of an audience of 'normal' people together with interactive digital media meant that avenues for meaningful and immediate feedback were perceived to exist. Ultimately, what was truly new about this election was that, for the first time in many years, the electorate was offered political debate in a format with which they could actively engage and respond, and they appeared to grasp the opportunity with gusto.

Advice for practitioners

At party level, the high volumes of communications involved in any electoral campaign together with voters' resulting tendency to selectively access and process information, means that the more broadly based communications – those lacking in a 'hook' – are unlikely to engage the receiver and are thus unlikely to reach their destination. In a tough economic climate where party finances are restricted, this is a complete waste of time, effort and money. Therefore, this research suggests that, when constructing a political communications strategy, the following principles should be observed:

Insight is everything

Effective political communication depends upon a message actually being received and understood by its target audience. A programme of voter insight will not only reveal the most effective combinations of media, but lend valuable insight into what aspects of the communications process are most important to specific target groups. Starting from the voter and working backwards through the communication chain, a clear understanding should be established as to which combination of media is consumed, which is considered the most credible and what aspects of noise disrupt the passage of communication at every stage.

Composite profiles enhance segmentation strategy

When segmenting the political market it is essential to go beyond the classic bases of demographic and geographic data. Voters' media consumption patterns and preferred sources of information are often driven by lifestyle factors which are best analysed using the traditional bases paired with attitudinal and behavioural data. Undertaken effectively, segments profiled using composite data have the potential to generate insight in support of a variety of communications functions, from the formulation of message content and creative approach to the most effective media combinations to ensure message delivery.

Use targeting to support the provision of tailored information packages

Within a multisource, multistage communications landscape, it is essential to establish the relative role and value of each member of the communications chain either individually or in tandem with other sources. Individual members or groups can then be targeted with tailored communications packages that correspond specifically to their information needs in terms of both content and format. This will reduce the need for 'editing' and thereby increase the likelihood that the message will move along the communications chain in a form intended by the information source.

Keep it simple, keep it real, keep it relevant – and don't patronise

During elections it is extremely difficult for voters to draw clear comparisons between the variety of political options on offer. Simple vehicles like the televised leaders' debates proved extremely popular in the 2010 general election as it allowed comparison of the political leaders and their party policies side by side.

In addition, voters are more likely to pay attention to a political message if they think that it has relevance to their everyday lives. Political messages that have resonance locally as well as nationally are likely to draw the attention of the voter. To maximise engagement, the language used should be clear and unambiguous and the use of political clichés avoided wherever possible. When explaining the benefit of political policies, it is just as important to address voters' fears or concerns. Where politicians dismiss or 'gloss over' concerns, such behaviour is likely to be perceived as patronising and result in the erection of perceptual barriers against future attempts at communication.

Don't be afraid to be different

Novelty proved to be a major vehicle for voter engagement in the 2010 UK general election. The opportunity to try something different – from a new forum for televised political debate to a new coalition government – excited interest amongst the media and the electorate alike. Going forward, political parties should show themselves more willing to embrace change and engage the electorate in conversations as to what the nature of that change should be.

Build meaningful mechanisms for feedback

It is clear that, given the opportunity, the electorate want to engage with the electoral process. However, channels for feedback must be accessible, meaningful and, ideally, enjoyable to access. Voters' perception that direct, two-way communication exists is very important to the process. Whilst relevance appears an essential requirement in order for a message to breach perceptual barriers, the opportunity for recipients to respond not only potentially engages them, but appears to empower them. To this end, political communication strategies should be designed in a way that offers the recipient the opportunity to offer meaningful feedback and some acknowledgement that it has not only been received but reflected upon and, ideally, acted upon in some way.

Impact on politics

Whilst the model cited here offers little that is truly revolutionary in the fields of politics or political marketing, it does highlight a potential strategy to address the political malaise that has plagued UK democratic processes over recent years. The model as it stands behoves political agents to obtain a deeper and more powerful understanding of the people who they seek to govern. It requires that they understand their issues and concerns and make a genuine effort to establish a positive and meaningful dialogue. In turn, such a targeted communications strategy has the potential to foster a clearer understanding amongst the electorate as to the complexities and challenges faced in government and the potential political choice on offer. The creation of channels for two-way communication offers voters a voice where previously it was felt that none existed, and the opportunity for those in power to hear the unmediated response to their political actions. Ultimately, what this model signals is a potential system that not only fosters greater levels of informed political debate between the political elite and the political electorate, but is also likely to result in greater levels of political engagement and participation at both local and national levels.

The way forward

In the UK the 2010 general election gave many voters a perceived, if not real, taste of participatory democracy and they appear to have responded positively. Moving forward, political establishments should seek to build upon this through the development of local and national dialogues. Using old established media and what may be considered truly new technology, there is now great scope to explore and develop the concept of participative democracy and the creation of dialogue at local, national and international levels, with the aim of encouraging civil engagement and political participation. From an academic perspective, there is significant scope to develop knowledge in this field. It is clear that larger-scale tests should be undertaken to establish the generalisability of this model. Additional work on the nature and process of voter engagement with political messages is clearly also needed to identify how effective political dialogue can best be fostered. To conclude, whilst it is clear that the basic mechanics associated with the process of communications have little changed over decades, technological advances offer great prospects to reverse the trend towards falling political engagement and participation. It is now up to those involved in the process of political communications to make it a reality.

Bibliography

Allen, G. (2003) 'A Critique of Using Grounded Theory as a Research Method', *Electronic Journal of Business Research Methods* 2, 1: 1–9.

Baek, M. (2009) 'A Comparative Analysis of Political Communication Systems and Voter Turnout', *American Journal of Political Science* 53, 2: 376–93.

Bennett, W.L. (1990) 'Toward a Theory of Press-State Relations', *Journal of Communication* 40: 103–25.

Bennett, W.L. and Iyengar, S. (2008) 'A New Era of Minimal Effects? The Changing Foundations of Political Communication', *Journal of Communication* 58: 707–31.

Bennett, W.L., Lawrence, R.G. and Livingston, S. (2007) *When the Press Fails: Political Power and the New Media from Iraq to Katrina*, Chicago: University of Chicago Press.

Best, S.J. and Krueger, B.S. (2005) 'Analyzing the Representativeness of Internet Political Participation', *Political Behaviour* 7, 2: 183.

Charmaz, K. (2000) 'Grounded Theory – Objectivist and Constructivist Methods', in N.K. Denzin and Y.S. Lincoln (eds) *Handbook of Qualitative Research*, London: Sage Publications Ltd.

Chicchi, F. (2000) 'Grounded Theory and the Biographical Approach: An Attempt at an Integrated Heuristic Strategy', *International Review of Sociology* 10: 5–23.

Cohen, J.B. and Golden, E. (1972) 'Informational Social Influence and Product Evaluation', *Journal of Applied Psychology* 56, 1: 54–59.

Cook, T. (1998) *Governing with the News*, Chicago: University of Chicago Press.

Entman, R.M. (1993) 'Framing: Toward Clarification of a Fractured Paradigm', *Journal of Communication* 43, 4: 51–58.

—— (2006) 'Framing Bias - Media in the Distribution of Power', *Journal of Communication*, Volume 57, Issue 1: 163–73.

Eveland, W.P. and Dylko, I. (2007) 'Reading Political Blogs During the 2004 Election Campaign: Correlates and Political Consequences', in M. Tremayne (ed.) *Blogging, Citizenship, and the Future of Media*, New York: Routledge.

Fiske, J. (2002) *Introduction to Communication Studies*, London: Routledge.

Glaser, B. (1992) *Basics of Grounded Theory Analysis: Emergence v Forcing*, Mill Valley, CA: Sociology Press.

Glaser, B. and Strauss, A. (1967) *The Discovery of Grounded Theory: Strategies for Qualitative Research*, New York: DeGruyter.

Goulding, C. (2002) *Grounded Theory: A Practical Guide for Management, Business and Market Researchers*, London: Sage.

—— (1999) 'Consumer Research, Interpretive Paradigms and Methodological Ambiguities', *European Journal of Marketing* 33, 9/10: 859–73.

—— (1998) 'Grounded Theory: The Missing Methodology on the Interpretivist Agenda', *Qualitative Market Research: An International Journal* 1, 1: 50–57.

Hamilton, J. (2004) *All the News That's Fit to Sell*, Princeton, NJ: Princeton University Press.

Jenkins, H. (2006) *Convergence Culture: Where Old and New Media Collide*, New York: New York University Press.

Jobber, D. (2007) *Principles and Practice of Marketing*, fifth edn, New York and London: McGraw-Hill.

Katz, E. and Lazarsfeld, P.F. (1955) *Personal Influence: The Part Played by People in the Flow of Communication*, New York: Free Press.

Lawson-Borders, G. and Kirk, R. (2005) 'Blogs in Campaign Communication', *American Behavioural Scientist* 49, 4: 548–59.

Lees-Marshment, J. (2001) 'The Marriage of Politics and Marketing', *Political Studies* 49: 692–713.

Lloyd, Jenny (2009) 'Keeping Both the Baby and the Bathwater: Scoping a New Model of Political Marketing Communication', *International Review on Public and Non-Profit Marketing*, 6 (2): 119–35.

Manheim, Jarol B. (2011) *Strategy in Information and Influence Campaigns*, New York: Routledge.

Mariampolski, H. (2001) *Qualitative Market Research: A Comprehensive Guide*, London: Sage.

Mendelson, M. (1996) 'The Media and Interpersonal Communications: The Priming of Issues, Leaders, and Party Identification', *Journal of Politics* 58, 1: 112–25.

Mortimore, R. (2002) 'Trusting the Politicians', *MORI Research Review*. Online, www.ipsos-mori.com/newsevents/ca/292/Trusting-The-Politicians.aspx (accessed 10 April 2011).

Mundorf, N., Zillman, D. and Drew, D. (1991) 'Effects of Disturbing Televised Events on the Acquisition of Information from Subsequently Presented Commercials', *Journal of Advertising* 20, 1: 46–53.

Norris, P. (2000) *A Virtuous Circle – Political Communications in Postindustrial Societies*, Cambridge: Cambridge University Press.

Norris, P., Curtice, D., Sanders, M., Scammell, M. and Semetko, H.A. (1999) *On Message: Communicating the Campaign*, London: Sage Publications.

O'Callaghan, J. (1996) 'Grounded Theory: A Potential Methodology', *Counselling Psychology Review* 11, 1: 23–18.

Riley, R. (1996) 'Revealing Socially Constructed Knowledge through Quasi-structured Interviews and Grounded Theory Analysis', *Journal of Travel and Tourism Marketing* 15: 21–40.

Scammell, M. (1999) 'Political Marketing: Lessons for Political Science', *Political Studies* 47, 4: 718–38.

Scheufele, D.A. (2000) 'Agenda-Setting, Priming, and Framing Revisited: Another Look at Cognitive Effects of Political Communication', *Mass Communication and Society* 3, 2: 297–316.

—— (1999) 'Framing as a Theory of Media Effects', *Journal of Communication* 49, 1: 103–22.

Shannon, C. and Weaver, W. (1949) *The Mathematical Theory of Communication*, Urbana, IL: University of Illinois Press.

Shimp, T.A. (2000) *Advertising Promotion: Supplemental Aspects of Integrated Marketing Communications*, fifth edn, Fort Worth, TX: Dryden Press.

Solomon, M., Bamossy, G. and Askegaard, S. (2002) *Consumer Behaviour – A European Perspective*, Upper Saddle River, NJ: Prentice Hall.

Tellis, G.J. (1998) *Advertising and Sales Promotion Strategy*, Reading, MA: Addison Wesley.

Watson, J. (2003) *Media Communication – An Introduction to Theory and Process*, Basingstoke: Palgrave Macmillan.

Westley, B. and MacLean, M. (1957) 'A Conceptual Model for Communication Research', *Journalism Quarterly* 34: 31–38.

Wu, B.T. and Newell, S.J. (2003) 'The Impact of Noise on Recall of Advertisements', *Journal of Marketing*, Spring: 56–65.

20
Interacting leaders

Claire Robinson

The topic: interaction with leaders

For most people interaction with political leaders is not physically experienced. It is largely at a distance and mediated, generally through news and internet channels, but also through forms of advertising and by the opinions of others. While it would be ideal for every citizen to have a one-on-one relationship with their leader, this is difficult in contemporary politics. The greater the physical distance between an incumbent or aspiring head of government and others, the more likely it is that people's experiences of political leadership are influenced by what they see, hear and read about a political leader. How do people translate the messages they see, hear and read into attributes that enable them to form a judgment about a political leader? Bean and Mughan (1989: 1176) point to people receiving stimuli that trigger pre-existing mental images or schema of 'what a leader should be like'. To arrive at these schema 'voters abstract from their experience of past [leaders] those features and behaviors they associate with political success, and then evaluate other candidates with respect to these same characteristics' (Miller *et al.* 1986: 535). Leadership characteristics that have been found to matter to voters include effectiveness, trustworthiness, strength in leadership, attractiveness, likability, integrity, reliability, listening to reason, caring, sticking to principle and competence (Banducci 2002; Ballew and Todorov 2007; Bean 1992; Bean and Mughan 1989; Leathers and Eaves 2008; McAllister and Bean 2006; Miller *et al.* 1986). What is not widely understood, however, is how citizens arrive at assessments of competence or trustworthiness, for example, when so much of the stimuli they receive about a political leader or potential leader are messages about the state of their marriage, what brand of clothing they wear, or whether they cook and clean at home – personal, often trivial, information that on the surface has very little direct relevance to the qualities of leadership that matter. This chapter combines recent shifts in leadership theory with relationship marketing theory and research into nonverbal behavior and political persuasion to contextualize the importance of the leader image, defined here as the mediated presentation of a political party leader or leadership candidate. It offers a social interaction framework to contextualize how media audiences translate what is being observed in a leader image into a leadership judgment. The chapter proposes that leader image is fundamental to the offer, exercise and acceptance of political leadership in today's political environment.

Previous research

Over the past 40 years politics has become increasingly personalized. Television and other mass media changes including greater newspaper competition, tabloidization and the popularity of newer digitized forms of social networking have enabled the news media to give greater coverage and scrutiny to the appearance, behavior, private lives and narratives of political leaders and leadership candidates. Alongside this has been the rise to prominence of professional image consultants and brand strategists – people employed to manage the image of political leaders. Scholars have been increasingly worried that this 'personalization of politics' has become more important than ever before, to the point of taking precedence over principle, policy and the rational deliberation of objective information, in determining the outcome of democratic elections (Brader 2006; Dean and Croft 2009; Erickson 2008; Mutz 2007; Postman 1987; Street 2004). Despite the attention accorded leaders' personal lives in the media, however, researchers have found that leadership personality factors are still not as significant an influence on voter decision-making as party predisposition and policy preference (Bean 1992, 2003; Bean and Mughan 1989; Hayes 2009; King 2002; Senior and Onselen 2008; Vowles and Aimer 2004; Poguntke and Webb 2005). Having said that, King's (2002) study found that it is possible for even a small leadership effect to influence an election outcome in extremely close and competitive elections, and Poguntke and Webb found leader effects on voters significant and/or increasing in 11 out of the 14 countries examined in their 2005 study. Outside the campaign period leadership effects have the potential to inflict even more damage, with the public's reported opinions of the traits and popularity of political leaders affecting leaders' levels of support from within their own party. Over the past few decades, for example, a number of New Zealand and Australian party leaders (most recently Australian prime minister Kevin Rudd in 2010) have been 'rolled' by their own caucuses outside election campaign periods, with a decline in their personal popularity measured by public opinion polls often cited by caucuses as justification for the leadership change (Robinson 2009).

What does political marketing offer to this discussion? Where political leader image is discussed in the literature it is principally in the context of political marketing management (Henneberg and O'Shaughnessy 2007); that is, in relation to the processes and tactics political parties and strategists devise to satisfy voters. Leader image is regarded as part of the marketing mix, a 'tool' in the armory of political strategists (Kotler 1975; Lees-Marshment 2001; Newman 1999); a product controlled, packaged and styled to appeal to the electorate (Campus 2010; De Landtsheer *et al.* 2008; Scammell 1995; Smith 2009). Somewhat problematically, this concept of packaging implies that there is no intrinsic content in a leader image. This devalues the contribution that political marketing can make to an understanding of contemporary political leadership, a subject that is normally claimed for study by political science. Henneberg and O'Shaughnessy (2007: 21) have called for more theory and concept development in the area of leader image, writing that 'political marketing can succeed with repackaging, repositioning, and makeovers … but we lack a clear conceptual understanding of how this affects voters, the media and other stakeholders. Political marketing theory needs to address this issue and the specific impact that leadership perceptions have.'

Relational leadership

However, recent business leadership studies literature does provide a way to conceptualize the link between the political leader image and leadership judgment. For a long period leadership studies was dominated by the need to define the qualities and characteristics that business leaders should have: the traits, behaviors, intelligences, skills and competencies needed to lead, and the extent to which certain leaders possess these qualities. While this shed light on the 'what', 'why' and 'who' of leadership, researchers and scholars have recently begun to question the 'how' – how leaders enact leadership behavior, and how those experiencing leadership recognize and judge leadership qualities from that behavior. Studies have focused on such areas as the practice of leadership (Carroll *et al.* 2008; Crevani *et al.* 2010), aesthetic leadership (Duke 1986; Hansen *et al.* 2007; Ladkin 2008; Smith 1996), relational leadership (Uhl-Bien 2006) and embodied leadership (Sinclair 2005). While nuanced differently (and there is not the space here to detail each area), there are commonalities in the way these researchers and scholars conceptualize leadership. Theirs is a social constructivist view (Fairhurst and Grant 2010). They argue that the behavior of a leader does not constitute leadership until it is perceived to be so by a follower. That perception is generated in the interaction between people and a leader over time. There is a relational aspect to this interaction that will be embodied, experienced and/or sensed through communicative practices.

There are parallels between this conception of leadership and theories of relationship marketing (RM) and customer relationship management (CRM). The field of marketing has in recent times shifted to a greater appreciation of the relationship between suppliers and customers – equivalent to leaders and followers – as it recognizes that customers rather than suppliers determine the long-term worth of a product or service. According to these theories customers look to a supplier's desire and efforts to enter into a relationship with them before they put their trust in, and make a long-term commitment to, that supplier, their product or the services they offer. It is the quality of interactions between customer and the supplier over time that determine the extent of a customer's satisfaction with a product or supplier. Businesses that are alert to this put effort into the development of long-term relationships with existing customers, considering this to be of greater economic value than constantly chasing new customers (Aurier and N'Goala 2010; Finne and Grönroos 2009; Grönroos 1999; Gummesson 2008; Harwood *et al.* 2008).

What happens when these ideas are applied to political leader image and political leadership? Political leadership is more commonly thought of as a power, rather than a social relationship, so considering it through the lens of social interaction is a novel approach. However, social interaction provides a useful framework for appreciating the significance of the images that citizens are observing and from which they are generating leadership meaning. A cursory scan of leader images in any media channel will show that audiences are in constant exposure to images of leaders interacting with and relating to others: be it with a child, a partner, a voter, another politician, a celebrity, an official, a journalist, a photographer, a world leader, a competitor, an audience, party members, colleagues, or protestors. Most leader images also have a relational aspect, be it as friend, foe, guest, guide or messenger, and most images contain a sensed aspect: whether it be a leader listening to someone speaking to them, chairing a meeting, talking down the barrel of a camera to an audience at home, or shaking hands with people at a rally. Framing leader image in terms of social interaction enables evidence-based research into nonverbal behavior to be drawn upon to help explain how people relate their understandings of the rules and conventions of social interaction with political leadership schema when processing and negotiating meaning from leader images. The next section will set out a new framework, building on this literature.

New research – proxemic interaction framework

The framework presented here provides for analysis of the nonverbal messages conveyed by leader images. Nonverbal messages are the primary method by which relationships are communicated in the still or moving media image (Adler *et al.* 2007; Remland 2004; Surawski and

Ossof 2006). Recognizing this is an increasing body of research into the connection between nonverbal cues and political perception and decision-making, particularly the link between appearance-based trait inferences and voting (see Grabe and Bucy 2009; Olivola and Todorov 2010; Riggio and Riggio 2010; Stewart *et al.* 2009).

The framework is divided into four categories based on proxemic zones, or the distances people maintain between each other in social situations that signal their degrees of interest, involvement and attraction to others in Western cultures. Each of these spatial zones lends itself to the enactment or embodiment of different social behaviors and actions and each carries a distinctive set of meanings that people interpret using their understanding of the conventions of social interaction (Adler *et al.* 2007; Leathers and Eaves 2008; Remland 2004). The idea of proxemics was developed by anthropologist Edward T. Hall (1966). Hall identified four types of proxemic distance: Intimate distance – beginning with skin contact and ranging out to about 18 inches (0cm–45cm); personal distance – defined as anything from 1.5 feet to around 4 feet (45cm–1.2m); social distance – extending from approximately 4 to 12 feet (1.2m–3.7m); and public distance – running outwards from 12 feet (3.7m). Hall's proxemic definitions were devised in the 1960s as a method of understanding relationships when people were in the same physical vicinity as each other. To apply them to the messages of social interaction presented by political leaders in a mediated environment, awareness of the actual physical distance between leaders and observers has to be suspended, and in its place a mimicry of interpersonal distance has to be applied. This is a phenomenon created by the moving or still camera shot length minimizing the actual distance between audience and presenter (Meyrowitz 1985). Once a mimicry of interpersonal distance is applied, it is possible to equate each proxemic zone with the social situations in which a Western political leader will be most commonly observed in mediated images interacting with people – in face-to-face, one-on-one, small and large group contexts.

In the section below the following questions are examined for each proxemic zone: How is the leadership message enacted nonverbally? Through what form of communication and media channel is the message transmitted? What is the mimicked interpersonal distance and role of the observer? How much control does a political leader have over their image? Between whom is the observed relationship? What is the leader's/strategist's intent? What are audiences looking for? How does this translate into a leadership judgment? What is the relative importance of this? Each proxemic zone is illustrated with an empirical example.

Intimate distance: face-to-face

How is the leadership message enacted nonverbally?

At face-to-face distance, the leadership message is most commonly conveyed in a close-up head and shoulders image of a leader making a direct appeal to the audience down the barrel of a still or moving image camera. Messages are primarily communicated through eye contact, appearance, clothing, facial expression and body posture.

Through what form of communication and media channel is the message transmitted?

The image may be found in a television address or election broadcast, a web video, social networking site, poster, billboard, newsprint advertisement, brochure, newsletter or book cover. In the 2010 British general election campaign, leader of the Conservative Party David Cameron utilized the face-to-face address as his primary means of communicating with British voters in two of the party's five election broadcasts. He spoke direct to camera in a front-on head and shoulders camera shot. He wore a blue shirt with no tie and the top button undone, suggesting a conservative but relaxed and friendly nature. He was located in a tidy backyard with symbols of middle-class domestic aspiration – children's wooden play equipment and trees in blossom – visible in the background. He also utilized the direct address in videos posted on the Conservative Party website, under the heading 'webcameron', where he would pull aside from events on the campaign trail and talk to viewers about matters of the day (see www.conservatives.com/Video/Webcameron.aspx). It was a significant point of difference between Cameron and Labour leader Gordon Brown, who did not engage in any face-to-face address with voters in Labour's election broadcasts, and very little in any other social media.

What is the mimicked interpersonal distance and the role of the observer?

The actual distance is between the leader and the camera lens, and the transmitted/published image/screen and the receiver. The mimicked distance is directly between the leader and the audience in their homes or offices.

How much control does a leader have over their self-presentation?

Leaders and their media strategists have total control of the leader's appearance, words, setting, length of broadcast and choice of transmission channel.

Between whom is the observed relationship?

It is a direct relationship between a leader and individual members of an audience. At this distance the audience is both an active participant as well as an observer, which makes it harder for audiences to be detached.

What is the leader/strategist's intent?

To convey the leader's desire for an honest, friendly and trusting relationship with individual members of an audience (Messaris 1997). They want audiences to like them.

What are audiences looking for?

Subconsciously, audiences are looking for physical signs that establish whether a leader is benign. The more attractive the appearance of the leader, the less of a threat they are perceived to be.

How does this translate into a leadership judgment?

Researchers have found that people use appearance to make instant and instinctive trait judgments of politicians and that physical attractiveness exerts a major influence on impression formation, strongly affecting the personality traits and qualities that are attributed to people (Leathers and Eaves 2008). Attractiveness has a 'halo effect', causing observers to infer other positive behavior and personality traits like competence from a good looking political candidate (Ballew and Todorov 2007; Riggio and Riggio 2010; Surawski and Ossof 2006).

What is the relative importance of this?

While appearance is perhaps the most contentious aspect of personality politics because it attracts much public attention and has the least direct connection to issues or policy, it is not as influential on most people's voting behavior as is assumed. Researchers have found that, when faced with no information, when partisanship is weak and when voters are low involved, appearance may be used by audiences as a heuristic so that they can make instant and instinctive trait judgments of leaders. When an election becomes more controversial and contentious, however, and with greater voter involvement and partisanship, appearance becomes less important as an influence on voter behavior (Ballew and Todorov 2007; Miller *et al.* 1986; Riggio and Riggio 2010; Riggle *et al.* 1992).

Personal distance: one-on-one

How is the leadership message enacted nonverbally?

At personal distance relationships between political leader and others are manifest in one-on-one television interviews. The interviewer and leader will usually be facing each other, both at the same height. The background setting is usually visible. Camera shots are mid to close-up. Tone of voice, facial expression and hand gestures help carry the message.

Through what form of communication and media channel is the message transmitted?

Interviews may take place in a television studio, on a talk show set, or at a radio station; they may also take place in informal or stand-up press conferences. Interviews may be published on news media websites and may virally spread to blog and social networking sites. Edited versions will appear on television news.

What is the mimicked interpersonal distance and the role of the observer?

Individual members of an audience are normally at a substantial physical distance from the event (except for members of a live studio audience). However, they will observe a relationship enacted at personal distance between interviewer and leader.

How much control does a leader have over their self-presentation?

At this distance there is substantial media framing of context, and control over timing of broadcast. Leaders and strategists have little control over interviewer attitude, production and editorial decisions, which camera shot is used, what is edited in and out, and what happens to the media clip after publication. They do have control over the leader's appearance, verbal and nonverbal responses to questions. They also exercise control over acceptance of interview and interviewer, time, location and subject areas for discussion, and will often agree to interviews when it suits their longer-term objectives. In July 2010 US president Barack Obama agreed to appear on *The View*, a US daytime talk show broadcast on ABC. This was the first time a sitting US president had appeared on a daytime talk show. Obama presented himself as relaxed, and engaged in much friendly banter with the female presenters. It was a strategic move on Obama's part, who needed to re-engage with a demoralized US public dealing with the aftermath of the BP oil crisis, the worsening of the situation in Afghanistan and the faltering US economy. It became the most-watched episode ever, with 6.59 million viewers, and the most watched telecast of any daytime show on ABC, CBS or NBC (Buckman 2010).

Between whom is the observed relationship?

Despite the interaction taking place between leader and interviewer, the relationship that conveys the meaning is between the leader and the viewing audience.

What is the leader/strategist's intent?

The leader wants the audience to consider them as relaxed, credible and knowledgeable about the subject matter, prepared for difficult and unpredictable questions. Leaders sometimes invite interviewers into their homes to demonstrate their affinity with the lives of ordinary people.

What are audiences looking for?

Audiences are looking for reassurance that the leader is able to select appropriate coping behaviors in a situation they do not ostensibly control (Stewart *et al.* 2009). As they observe interviews over time people will look for signs that the leader is able to retain a sense of balance and awareness of appropriate behaviors, despite the pressures of office.

How does this translate into a leadership judgment?

Assessments of a leader as socially aware lead to judgments of strength in leadership, sticking to principle and competence (Stewart *et al.* 2009).

What is the relative importance of this?

After the direct address, one-on-one interviews are any leader's primary means of communication with a mass audience. While audiences may learn a lot about a leader in a single interview, and may find a leader's characteristics on that day endearing or appalling, the overall impact or relevance of the interview is a longer-term phenomenon. The more an audience is exposed to leader interviews, the more familiar they will be with the leader's body language, verbal language and facial expressions. As time goes by leadership judgments are more likely to be based on signs of change from the norm – out-of-character behaviors and responses that might signal a lack of coping with the responsibility of leading the nation.

Social distance: small group

How is the leadership message enacted nonverbally?

At social distance leadership is enacted in images of political leaders meeting with small groups of people: usually family, members of the public, staff, colleagues, supporters and other leaders. The small group could number anything from one to ten, depending on how many people can fit within the camera frame. Leadership will be communicated through the leader's use of hand gestures (like handshaking, waving), physical contact (patting a shoulder or knee, hugging, kissing), and facial expressions (smiling, laughing together, frowning) (Bucy and Grabe 2008; Knapp and Hall 2006).

Through what form of communication and media channel is the message transmitted?

The mediated image will most commonly be a full or three-quarter body camera shot, most commonly transmitted in a still image in a newspaper, on a media website, on a party or social networking website. It could also be in a political campaign advertisement, or on the television news.

What is the mimicked interpersonal distance and the role of the observer?

Audiences are observers of a relationship enacted between leader and small groups of people.

How much control does a leader have over their self-presentation?

Leaders and strategists have significant control of appearance, verbal and nonverbal behavior; who and where the leader meets people; who is permitted to photograph or film them and from which angle; and which images are published on their own party websites and advertisements. Leaders do not have control over editorial choice of which image or clip or part thereof is used by a news outlet or what happens to the media clip after publication. They do not have control over the response of some of the people they meet.

Between whom is the observed relationship?

On the face of it this is a relationship occurring between leader and people in small groups, but this is still very much a presentation of themselves for evaluation by their more distant audience.

What is the leader/strategist's intent?

The leader wants to convey their ability to have empathy, to relate socially to and to care for others.

What are audiences looking for?

Humans are instinctively primed to look for caring body language to assess whether a leader is friend or foe. They are seeking reassurance in a leader's ability to relate to 'real' people. Touch becomes an important signifier of this.

How does this translate into a leadership judgment?

Small group relationships communicate important information about a leader's affinity with and orientation towards people. These assessments translate into judgments of caring, likability, trustworthiness and effective leadership (Riggio and Reichard 2008), compassion and benevolence (Grabe and Bucy 2009).

What is the relative importance of this?

Images of leaders interacting at small group distance are important for the communication of a leader's ability to relate to real people. Although strategists like to control these situations, it is the gaffes and unscripted moments that often convey more meaning: when the leader meets someone on the campaign trail who says something unexpected, when they make an inappropriate gesture, when someone throws something at them. In the 2010 British election campaign, a television station caught then Labour leader Gordon Brown with his microphone still on, in his car, calling a member of the public a 'bigoted woman' after a chat on camera in the street, surrounded by a large media entourage. Brown visibly crumpled, head in his hands, when he learned of the gaffe as he was being filmed taking part in a live interview at a radio station later that day. Although the British media described the episode as a disaster for Brown, Labour's percentage vote did not decline further as a result of this particular incident. While some observers would have seen his behavior as duplicitous, others would have appreciated that the 'real' Brown was simply expressing his frustration at having to regulate his behavior in a situation in which he had been tested by someone with whom he did not have empathy.

Public distance: large group

How is the leadership message enacted nonverbally?

At this distance leadership messages are conveyed in images of public events like leaders' debates during an election campaign, and large public meetings, to which audiences choose, are invited or pay to attend. Camera shots move between long range, at which members of the audience are seen, and medium close-ups on the speaker.

Through what form of communication and media channel is the message transmitted?

Debates will be televised and streamed live on television and internet news sites. Public meetings will be covered in news stories or included in campaign advertising.

What is the mimicked interpersonal distance and the role of the observer?

Camera length of shots and angles will mimic the point of view of a viewer actually attending a live event. Audiences at home have the added benefit of being able to see close-up camera shots of leaders that live audiences may not see in detail. In a debate, the audience's role is not as benign observer. Audiences at home are active participants judging the competition.

How much control does a leader have over their self-presentation?

Leaders and strategists have significant control over the clothes leaders wear, the tone and manner in which they deliver an address, the setting and presence of cameras. In a debate they have control over their self-presentation and acceptance of the debate format. They will have advance knowledge of question themes and will have rehearsed their performance, but they will not always know in advance the precise questions asked. They will not have control over the actions and responses of the other debaters, nor of the audience.

Between whom is the observed relationship?

In public addresses the relationship observed is between the leader and the live audience. In debates the relationship observed is between a leader and their competition.

What is the leader/strategist's intent?

In debates leaders want to communicate that they have the confidence and strength to fight off any 'pretenders to the throne'. Ultimately they want to be judged the debate winner. In public addresses the leader's intent is to communicate their popularity – that they have the charisma to attract and control a large group of followers.

What are audiences looking for?

Debate audiences will be looking for signs of how leaders respond to threat from a competitor; who handles a complex and stressful social confrontation the best (Baker 2009; Leathers and Eaves 2008) in a situation where there is a live audience and nowhere for the leader to hide. In the 2008 US presidential debates Obama, on the whole, demonstrated better control over his nonverbal responses to threat than his Republican rival Senator John McCain. Summarizing this in a post-debate analysis on CNN, communications coach Bill McGowan explained:

> what you've seen from [Obama] in the first two debates is no great risk-taking, no big chances he's taken. I think he's played it pretty safe, he's not trying to fix what's not broken, and what I think he's done extremely well is, when he's under attack from Senator McCain he's sat very serenely, very placidly on the front of his chair, not twitching, not fidgeting, not wincing, not scribbling notes, but looking him directly in the eye with a confident look on his face. He has seemed really unflappable under attack … Obama has a strategy on what to do physically when he is under attack.
>
> *(CNN 2008)*

How does this translate into a leadership judgment?

Presentation of a confident self in relation to competition directly influences assessments of credibility, strength in leadership (Leathers and Eaves 2008; Remland 2004), competence, character, composure and sociability (Seiter *et al.* 1998 cited by Remland 2004).

What is the relative importance of this?

Relationships are not always benign. They can also be threatening. Just as people make trait assessments from the direct address about whether a leader is going to be a personal threat, they also want to know if the leader can be trusted to protect against threat to themselves and others. Being judged as not coping with threat, manifest in assessments of who lost a political debate, can be very damaging to someone's political leadership aspirations.

Advice for practitioners

Recognize that enacting leadership behavior requires a leader to relate and be seen to relate to people

Leader image is much more than simply packaging. It is fundamental to the establishment and maintenance of a relationship between leader and people, which is necessary if people are to put their trust in, and make a long-term commitment to that leader or their party in today's mediated political environment. It is through the leader image that most people experience leadership, and recognize and judge leadership qualities. Political parties will increasingly need to select leadership candidates for their ability to sustain meaningful interactions with publics.

When relating to people, ensure that all proxemic zones are covered

As social beings audiences are attuned to reading social behavior in all proxemic contexts. The more the leader is seen to relate in each context, the broader and deeper the leadership impression will be. Leader images at intimate distance covey information about whether the leader is a personal threat; at personal distance leader images demonstrate the leader's ability to relate to another, allowing observers to choose whether they, too, want a (mediated) personal relationship with that leader; leader images at social distance convey the leader's ability to relate more widely to and care for others; and public distance images allow audiences to gauge how well the leader is able to fend off challengers, and assess whether they have the skills to overcome threats and become leader. Leaders need to demonstrate their ability to relate to people in all four proxemic zones, in a wide variety of media contexts, in order to be accepted by as wide an audience as possible.

This is a long-term phenomenon

To be properly appreciated the expression and impression of leadership needs to be considered as something that builds over time and is experienced in a wide variety of contexts, not simply in election campaigns. Those who consult on leaders' images need to accept that their task is a long-term process to create and maintain a positive relationship between leader and people over time, rather than see it in terms of singular events and the use of certain tools. As leaders become busier with the business of running countries, they tend to become less focused on being seen out and about. It is a gift for challengers because they can present themselves as being more 'in touch'.

Don't try to control everything

Ironically, the greatest barriers to leaders benefiting from the meaning that audiences attribute to leader images are their own strategists. So aware are they of the importance of their employer making a good impression that they spend a large amount of time trying to avoid a leader being seen in contexts that cannot be controlled easily. The more the leader image is managed, the more audiences will look for signs of the 'real' leader in the way they respond to unmanaged moments. If the commitment to the relationship is not genuine, the public will read this in their nonverbal behavior, and shift their attention to a candidate or party that is showing more desire for a relationship.

Don't worry about the odd gaffe

The reality is that gaffes are rarely sustained, and peoples' deeper impressions of political leadership are not formed over a single incident, or even a few. The longer audiences are exposed to the behavior, careers and personalities of political leaders and leaders in general, the more likely they are to appreciate single incidents in context – the incidents may be amusing, unusual, embarrassing even, but not always terminal to the protagonist's career.

Impact on politics

Critics of political marketing will need to reassess the relative importance of what they are observing in the media, so the next time a leader changes their hair color, goes on a daytime talk show, or uses a social networking site it can be better appreciated in the context of the exercise, perception and acceptance of political leadership as a longer-term phenomenon, and not as something heralding the end of democracy and rational choice, or as a symptom of the dumbing down of politics!

The way forward

Further cross-disciplinary research should combine marketing theory with recent leadership theory to enable a broader discussion about political leadership, and increase the value that a marketing perspective can make to a subject normally considered as belonging to the more established field of political science. The relationship concepts discussed here could be taken further into the study of social media. Facebook and Twitter, for example, are newer vehicles for the communication of a social relationship at intimate or personal distance. Observation to date suggests that these channels are not well used to sustain relationships once a leader is incumbent, so there is un-mined potential for the study and practice of relationship-building in social media spaces.

Practitioners are advised to prepare for further predicted technological changes in large-format, high-definition (Bucy and Grabe 2008), 3D and eventually holographic in-home media display systems. Relationships that are currently perceived at a tele-mediated distance will soon be perceived through immersion in an experience that realistically and intimately mimics an embodied relationship between political leaders and individual citizens. Expressions and impressions of a relationship enacted between a leader and others are going to become more, not less, important as time and technology march on. This will not enthuse scholars and commentators, who think that there is too much emphasis on personality politics already in the media. However, the potential for new technologies to lessen the physical distance between leader and others is far reaching.

Bibliography

Adler, R.B., Rosenfeld, L.B. and Proctor, R.F. (2007) *Interplay: The Process of Interpersonal Communication*, New York: Oxford University Press.

Aurier, P. and N'Goala, G. (2010) 'The Differing and Mediating Roles of Trust and Relationship Commitment in Service Relationship Maintenance and Development', *Journal of the Academy of Marketing Science* 38: 303–25.

Baker, F.W. (2009) *Political Campaigns and Political Advertising: A Media Literacy Guide*, Santa Barbara, CA: Greenwood Press.

Ballew II, C.C. and Todorov, A. (2007) 'Predicting Political Elections from Rapid and Unreflective Face Movements', *Proceedings of the National Academy of Sciences of the United States of America* 104, 46: 17948–53.

Banducci, S. (2002) 'Gender and Leadership', in J. Vowles, P. Aimer, J. Karp, S. Banducci, R. Miller and A. Sullivan (eds) *Proportional Representation on Trial*, Auckland: Auckland University Press.

Bean, C. (1992) 'Party Leaders and Local Candidates', in M. Holland (ed.) *Electoral Behaviour in New Zealand*, Auckland: Oxford University Press.

—— (2003) 'Leadership and Voting: The Connection at the State Level', *Australian Journal of Political Science* 38, 3: 465–78.

Bean, C. and Mughan, A. (1989) 'Leadership Effects in Parliamentary Elections in Australia and Britain', *American Political Science Review* 83, 4: 1165–79.

Brader, T. (2006) *Campaigning for Hearts and Minds*, Chicago: University of Chicago Press.

Buckman, A. (2010) 'From Praise to Palin: Obama's "View" Visit Draws Many Viewers', *Xfinity.tv*. Online, xfinitytv.comcast.net/blogs/2010/tv-news/from-praise-to-palin-obamas-view-visit-draws-many-views/?cmpid=FCST_hero (accessed 10 April 2011).

Bucy, E.P. and Grabe, M.E. (2008) '"Happy Warriors" Revisited: Hedonic and Agonic Display Repertoires of Presidential Candidates on the Evening News', *Politics and the Life Sciences* 27, 1: 78–98.
Campus, D. (2010) 'Mediatization and Personalization of Politics in Italy and France: The Cases of Berlusconi and Sarkozy', *The International Journal of Press/Politics* 2010, 15: 219–35.
Carroll, B., Levy, L. and Richmond, D. (2008) 'Leadership as Practice: Challenging the Competency Paradigm', *Leadership* 2008, 4: 363–79.
CNN (2008) 'Political Posturing. Obama – McCain Debate: Body Language Analysis', *CNN,* 15 October. Online, www.youtube.com/watch?v=elQNgSO_leI&feature=related (accessed 17 January 2010).
Conservative Party (2010) 'Vote Conservative Today, Get Change Tomorrow'. Online, www.conservatives.com/Video/Webcameron.aspx?id=220cb871-b6cf-4f89-87b6-f30d99f87d8c (accessed 17 September 2010).
Crevani, L., Lindgren, M. and Packendorff, J. (2010) 'Leadership, not Leaders: On the Study of Leadership as Practices and Interactions', *Scandinavian Journal of Management* 26: 77–86.
De Landtsheer, C.L., De Vries, P. and Vertessen, D. (2008) 'Political Impression Management: How Metaphors, Sound Bites, Appearance Effectiveness, and Personality Traits Can Win Elections', *Journal of Political Marketing* 7, 3: 217–38.
Dean, D. and Croft, R. (2009) 'Reason and Choice: A Conceptual Study of Consumer Decision Making and Electoral Behaviour', *Journal of Political Marketing* 8, 2: 130–46.
Duke, D.L. (1986) 'The Aesthetics of Leadership', *Educational Administration Quarterly* 22, 1: 7–27.
Erickson, K.V. (2008) 'Presidential Rhetoric's Visual Turn: Performance Fragments and the Politics of Illusionism', in L.C. Olson, C.A. Finnegan and D.S. Hope (eds) *Visual Rhetoric: A Reader in Communication and American Culture*, Thousand Oaks, CA: Sage Publications.
Fairhurst, G.T. and Grant, D. (2010) 'The Social Construction of Leadership: A Sailing Guide', *Management Communication Quarterly* 24, 2: 171–210.
Finne, Å. and Grönroos, C. (2009) 'Rethinking Marketing Communication: From Integrated Marketing Communication to Relationship Communication', *Journal of Marketing Communications* 15, 2–3: 179–95.
Grabe, M.E. and Bucy, E.P. (2009) *Image Bite Politics: News and the Visual Framing of Elections*, New York: Oxford University Press.
Grönroos, C. (1999) 'Relationship Marketing: Challenges for the Organization', *Journal of Business Research* 46: 327–35.
Gummesson, E. (2008) *Total Relationship Marketing*, third edn, Oxford: Butterworth-Heinemann.
Hall, E.T. (1966) *The Hidden Dimension*, New York: Doubleday.
Hansen, H., Ropo, A. and Sauer, E. (2007) 'Aesthetic Leadership', *The Leadership Quarterly* 18, 6: 544–60.
Harwood, T., Garry, T. and Broderick, A. (2008) *Relationship Marketing: Perspectives, Dimensions and Contexts*, Maidenhead: McGraw-Hill Education.
Hayes, D. (2009) 'Has Television Personalized Voting Behavior?', *Political Behavior* 31: 231–60.
Henneberg, S.C. and O'Shaughnessy, N.J. (2007) 'Theory and Concept Development in Political Marketing', *Journal of Political Marketing* 6, 2: 5–31.
—— (2009) 'Political Relationship Marketing: some macro/micro thoughts', *Journal of Marketing Management* 25, 1–2: 5–29.
King, A. (ed.) (2002) *Leaders' Personalities and the Outcomes of Democratic Elections*, Oxford: Oxford University Press.
Knapp, M.L. and Hall, J.A. (2006) *Nonverbal Communication in Human Interaction*, sixth edn, Belmont, CA: Thomson Higher Education.
Kotler, P. (1975) 'Overview of Political Candidate Marketing', *Advances in Consumer Research* 2, 1: 761–69.
Ladkin, D. (2008) 'Leading beautifully: How Mastery, Congruence and Purpose Create the Aesthetic of Embodied Leadership Practice', *The Leadership Quarterly* 19: 31–31.
Leathers, D. and Eaves, M.H. (2008) *Successful Nonverbal Communication: Principles and Applications*, fourth edn, Boston: Pearson.
Lees-Marshment, J. (2001) 'The Marriage of Politics and Marketing', *Political Studies* 49: 692–713.
McAllister, I. and Bean, C. (2006) 'Leaders, the Economy or Iraq? Explaining Voting in the 2004 Australian Election', *Australian Journal of Politics and History* 52, 4: 604–20.
Messaris, P. (1997) *Visual Persuasion: The Role of Images in Advertising*, Thousand Oaks, CA: Sage Publications.
Meyrowitz, J. (1985) *No Sense of Place: The Impact of Electronic Media on Social Behavior*, New York: Oxford University Press.
Miller, A.H., Wattenberg, M.P. and Malanchuk, O. (1986) 'Schematic Assessments of Presidential Candidates', *American Political Science Review* 80, 2: 521–40.

Mutz, D.C. (2007) 'Political Psychology and Choice', in R.J. Dalton and H.D. Klingemann (eds) *The Oxford Handbook of Political Behavior*, Oxford: Oxford University Press.
Newman, B.I. (1999) 'A Predictive Model of Voting Behavior: The Repositioning of Bill Clinton', in B.I. Newman (ed.) *Handbook of Political Marketing*, Thousand Oaks, CA: Sage Publications.
O'Donoghue, G. (2010) 'Is This a Car-crash Campaign Moment for Gordon Brown?' *BBC*, 28 April. Online, news.bbc.co.uk/2/hi/8649578.stm (accessed 29 April 2010).
Olivola, C.Y. and Todorov, A. (2010) 'Elected in 100 Milliseconds: Appearance-Based Trait Inferences and Voting', *Journal of Nonverbal Behavior* 34: 83–110.
Poguntke, T. and Webb, P. (2005) *The Presidentialization of Politics*, Oxford: Oxford University Press.
Postman, N. (1987) *Amusing Ourselves to Death: Public Discourse in the Age of Show Business*, London: Methuen.
Remland, M.S. (2004) *Nonverbal Communication in Everyday Life*, second edn, Boston: Houghton Mifflin Company.
Riggio, R.E. and Reichard, R.J. (2008) 'The Emotional and Social Intelligences of Effective Leadership', *Journal of Managerial Psychology* 23, 2: 169–85.
Riggio, H.R. and Riggio, R.E. (2010) 'Appearance-Based Trait Inferences and Voting: Evolutionary Roots and Implications for Leadership', *Journal of Nonverbal Behavior* 34: 119–25.
Riggle, E.D., Ottati, V.C., Wyer, R.S., Kuklinski, J. and Schwarz, N. (1992) 'Bases of Political Judgments: The Role of Stereotypic and Nonstereotypic Information', *Political Behavior* 14, 1: 67–87.
Robinson, C. (2009) '"Vote for Me": Political Advertising', in C. Rudd, J. Hayward and G. Craig (eds) *Informing Voters? Politics, Media and the New Zealand Election 2008*, Rosedale: Pearson.
Scammell, M. (1995) *Designer Politics: How Elections are Won*, New York: St Martins Press.
Senior, P. and van Onselen, P. (2008) 'Re-examining Leader Effects: Have Leader Effects Grown in Australian Federal Elections 1990–2004?', *Australian Journal of Political Science* 43, 2: 225–42.
Sinclair, A. (2005) 'Body Possibilities in Leadership', *Leadership* 1: 387–406.
Smith, G. (2009) 'Conceptualizing and Testing Brand Personality in British Politics', *Journal of Political Marketing* 8, 3: 209–32.
Smith, R.A. (1996) 'Leadership as Aesthetic Process', *Journal of Aesthetic Education* 30, 4: 39–52.
Stewart, P.A., Salter, F.K. and Mehu, M. (2009) 'Taking Leaders at Face Value', *Politics and the Life Sciences* 28, 1: 48–74.
Street, J. (2004) 'Celebrity Politicians: Popular Culture and Political Representation', *British Journal of Politics and International Relations* 6: 435–52.
Surawski, M.K. and Ossof, E.P. (2006) 'The Effects of Physical and Vocal Attractiveness on Impression Formation of Politicians', *Current Psychology* 25, 1: 15–27.
Uhl-Bien, M. (2006) 'Relational Leadership Theory: Exploring the Social Processes of Leadership and Organizing', *The Leadership Quarterly* 17: 654–76.
Vowles, J. and Aimer, P. (2004) 'Political Leadership, Representation and Trust', in J. Vowles, P. Aimer, S. Banducci, J. Karp and R. Miller (eds) *Voters' Veto: The 2002 Election in New Zealand and the Consolidation of Minority Government*, Auckland: Auckland University Press.

21

Underused campaigning tools

Political public relations

Nigel A. Jackson

The topic: public relations

The use of public relations (PR) enables the sender of a message to identify who to target, how to reach them and the appropriate message. It therefore constructs persuasive messages, enters into dialogue and builds relationships to raise interest in a product, organisation or idea. Political PR is not restricted to promoting a specific political product, but also includes building and maintaining positive relationships with key audiences. It can include developing dialogue, considering the receiver of the communication, raising interest in a candidate or party, and managing reputations. This chapter will outline a model of political PR and explore to what extent it was used during the 2010 UK general election at local candidate level. We will then suggest how it could be developed, assessing the broader potential of PR to create more positive long-term relationships between government and the public.

Previous research

Public relations is a well-established discipline in its own right, but Strömbäck *et al.* (2010) suggest that previous references to it in political marketing do not fully understand the concept. Where political marketing has addressed political PR, it has largely done so by equating it primarily with media relations (Gaber 2000; Esser *et al.* 2000; Xifra 2010). The focus on spin and media management (Heffernan 2006), suggests that the role of public relations is merely to gain visibility, and hence relegates it to a minor short-term tactic. A more useful approach is to divide public relations into marketing PR (MPR) and corporate PR (CPR) (Moloney 2006). MPR is the view of political PR outlined above, namely to gain visibility by using, for example, media relations, pseudo-events and events management to gain attention for what political actors have to say (Brissenden and Moloney 2005). This is a legitimate use of PR, but one that is narrow, tactical and short term. CPR supplements political marketers' use of MPR, because it is much more strategic, longer term and seeks to influence corporate reputation (Fombrun 1995) through tools such as issues management, crisis management and internal communication. Whilst there is a considerable body of academic work on the meaning and use of public relations in general, there is very little on how it applies to the political sphere.

Previous research has only explored a rather narrow conception of PR in the political sphere, hype and persuasion, with the latter the single most popular, with broader concepts such as relations in public and community building being largely absent within political PR literature. For example, Xifra (2010) interviewed the professional communicators for Spain's political parties and identified two key findings in their use of public relations. First, respondents stressed the tactical nature of their work, relying on MPR techniques. Such one-way, publicity-led tactical communication was, Xifra found, consistent with Grunig and Hunt's (1984) press agentry model. Second, the other model that his respondents reflected was personal influence. This might imply a relational approach, but it did not because their focus was primarily with journalists. Both findings reflect that his respondents, all paid employees, viewed media management as their prime job. This chapter seeks to address this omission by creating a broader conceptual model of the tools or approaches that can be used in politics, drawing on non-political PR literature, and then testing it empirically.

New research: political public relations conceptually and in practice

Conceptual framework: a new model of political public relations

A number of definitions of public relations exist, with Harlow (1976) identifying 472, yet the meaning of political PR has attracted far less attention. Indeed, a number of authors have used the term political PR without actually defining it (Davis 2000; Strömbäck *et al.* 2010). Whilst media relations is stressed (Moloney and Colmer 2001; Froehilch and Rudiger 2006), some authors have attempted to construct a useable meaning of political PR. Strömbäck and Kioussis (2011) suggest that as a management process, political PR aims to shape relationships with key publics to help achieve political goals, so that Jackson (2010) notes that political PR reaches a much wider range of audiences than political marketing. Political PR presents the views of political actors to other political publics in a positive light. It does so by raising awareness, engaging in dialogue and building relationships.

To assess how political actors might use political PR, we shall apply Jackson's (2010) theoretical framework based upon eight different possible approaches (Table 21.1). To create a model of effective political PR we will identify and evaluate core concepts within this framework, using four features: purpose; tools used; where applied; intended effect.

Relations with publics

Public relations is about the relationship that political elites have with their publics, and thus public relations practitioners should identify, reach and manage the relationship with their key audiences. They can apply situational theory, to seek to identify who and why will be active communicators seeking information, and therefore more likely to respond to messages received (Grunig 1997). One obvious example of this situational-type analysis is market research, and political marketing literature has shown how political parties have increasingly sought to collect data on voters through polling and focus groups (Lees-Marshment 2001). The use of polling was believed to have helped re-position Clinton in 1994 (Worcester and Baines 2006), and make the UK Labour Party electable in 1997. Research can also be used to ascertain voter response to an existing position, so that Sherman and Schiffman (2002) suggest that in the US 2000 election this was not so much parties researching their key audiences, as trying to make sense of what the electorate were thinking and their likely voting behaviour.

Table 21.1 Model for effective political PR

School of thought	*Purpose*	*PR tools used*	*Application*	*Intended effect*
Relations with publics	Identify, reach and communicate with key audiences. The management of relationships between an organisation and its publics.	Research – the focus is not on the PR tools but matching the most appropriate message to the correct segmented audience.	To support all forms of PR activity, both strategic and tactical.	To use finite resources efficiently and effectively. Neutral in terms of effect on wider society.
Grunigian paradigm	Mutual understanding. Mutual benefit?	Symmetrical two-way communication based upon feedback.	Research-focused. Relational. Strategic.	Win-win. Develop conversations. Encourage a strategic approach to PR. Inclusive culture (internal and external). To benefit society as well as the organisation.
Hype	Reaching consumers by 'making a noise' through publicity.	Media relations. Online PR.	MPR. Getting bums on seats. Press agentry.	Increase awareness. Increase sales. Short term. Benefit essentially the organisation.
Persuasion	To inform and then change attitudes and/or behaviour.	Media relations. Promotional campaigns. Lobbying. Community affairs/ CSR. Issues management. Uses both logic and emotional messages.	MPR – tactical CPR – strategic.	To represent an interest. To inform the wider public. To primarily benefit the organisation, but logic-based campaigns may also benefit wider society.
Relational	Develop influential relationships. Mutual benefit.	Target key influencers. Build networks. Personal interaction. Sponsorship. CSR. Online PR. Media relations. Lobbying. Corporate communications. Quanxi.	Issues management. Crisis management.	Long-term benefits. Build reputation. To benefit wider society as well as the organisation.

Table 21.1 (continued)

School of thought	*Purpose*	*PR tools used*	*Application*	*Intended effect*
Reputation management	Manage corporate image, brand and reputation. Shape public opinion.	Corporate communications. Investor relations. Lobbying. CSR. Community affairs. Issues management. Crisis management. Media relations. Online PR.	CPR – shape all audiences' perspectives of an organisation.	Build reputation. Create competitive advantage. Enhance profitability. Ensure long-term survival. A side-effect of enhancing reputation may be benefits for wider society.
Relations in public	Relations in the public (sphere) and of the public (sphere). Encourage a free flow of information to society. Development of the public sphere.	Issues management. Internal communications. Persuasion based on negotiated connection between audiences. Boundary spanning role. Uses both communication and relational tools.	Strategic – internal and external communications (but probably not customers). Business ethics.	Increase the public sphere. Free flow of information. Encouragement of freedom of speech. Minority opinion is heard. Reflective.
Community building	By helping to create a broad sense of community, this in turn benefits organisations.	Concept of 'general public'. Interaction. Community affairs. CSR. Issues management. Two-way symmetrical communication.	To subjugate interest and segmentation to enhancing community. Globalisation. Multicultural societies.	Enhancement of a communitarian approach. Increased social capital. Improved commercial sector within a more stable community.

Grunigian paradigm

PR can also be used to establish mutual understanding between an organisation and its publics (Newsom *et al.* 2000), and also, to create mutual benefit (Grunig and Hunt 1984). This involves not so much communicating to the public, but developing dialogue. Despite the dominance in the generic PR literature of the Grunigian paradigm, there is as yet limited evidence of dialogical PR in politics. The one exception is the internet (Jackson and Lilleker 2004).

Hype

Hype is perhaps the most commonly known aspect of public relations, creating publicity that makes 'noise' through media relations to generate interest and therefore reach consumers. As a result, it is mostly associated with unethical 'press agentry', but the internet can be another means of gaining publicity through viral marketing, as can MPR. Hype can help increase the visibility of products (see Grunig and Hunt 1984; Xifra 2010), but without it having to be simply spin, which attracts criticism (see Esser *et al.* 2001; Heffernan 2006).

Persuasion

The purpose of persuasion is to reach, inform and then change the attitudes/behaviour of key audiences, and to make it effective, practitioners consider the source of the message, the message itself and the personality of the message receiver (Perloff 2004). Persuasive techniques and messages need to be ethical to be distinguished from propaganda (Messina 2007). Whilst clearly political actors seek to use rational argument to persuade, there is evidence that they use a much wider range of persuasive techniques. Many political messages are couched in emotional terms. Indeed, Westen (2007) suggests that the emotional side of the brain is more influential in determining voting behaviour than the rational side. Within a plural system, political actors use persuasion to represent an interest.

Relational

Public relations can also be used to build relationships with key, influential stakeholders (see Ferguson 1984) to help build the reputation of an organisation (Ledingham and Bruning 1998). This approach is often used by pressure and lobbying groups who seek to influence government policy (Kovacs 2001). A relational approach, by maximising ideas, contacts and political 'muscle', can be the means by which individual activist groups become part of the policy community. It could also be used by government, political parties and individual politicians.

Reputation management

This approach focuses on identifying, managing and changing the reputation of an organisation. Whilst it is a rather intangible concept, it could have a tangible effect (Fombrun 1995; Griffin 2008). In politics, political parties that have lost a series of elections often turn to reputation management as the solution to their problems. Studies of political market orientation and campaigning have observed how the UK Labour Party, for example, sought to repair its image, which could be seen as reputation management (Lees-Marshment 2001). Having lost four elections, Wring (1998) suggests that the Labour Party developed new policies and organisational reforms to make it electable by changing its corporate reputation. Individual elected representatives also seek to develop their reputation (Negrine and Lilleker 2004), driven by a belief that it may help develop a personal vote, and so buck any national voting behaviour trends. Reputation management may be particularly useful in politics where there is crisis, scandal and delivery problems.

Relations in public

The historical background to this approach is discussions in the 18th and early 19th centuries concerning political representation. This European approach, therefore, is consistent with pluralism (Ihlen and Van Ruler 2007), and is closely associated with the concept of the public sphere (Vercic *et al.* 2001). The purpose of relations in public is to encourage the flow of information within society, and consider relations within the broader public sphere (Ruler and Vercic 2002). There are few examples of this in politics.

Community building

Community building is about creating and maintaining a sense of community, and enhancing and improving society by reducing conflict (Kruckeberg and Starck 1998). There is limited evidence that political PR has been used to encourage community building. Taylor (2000) noted that media relations was used to assist relationship building between groups and individuals within Bosnia. She suggests that media relations, by encouraging a free press and debate, can help developing countries to build civil society. Thus, so far at least, the ability of public relations to build political communities seems to be more one of potential than actuality.

These concepts are not necessarily mutually exclusive, and political actors could apply several at the same time. Considering the literature on political PR, only some of the approaches have been applied to public relations activity within the political sphere. The two most dominant approaches, in terms of amount of literature, are hype and persuasion, with the latter the single most popular. Four of the approaches appear to occupy a political niche: relations with publics, Grunigian paradigm, relationship management and reputation management. These four approaches tend to be applied for either specific purposes, or to meet the needs of those who have limited political power and influence. Two approaches – relations in public and community building – are largely absent within political PR literature.

Empirical application: political PR in practice in a local campaign in the UK 2010 election

In terms of methodology, a pilot study was conducted during the 2010 UK general election of parliamentary seats in the county of Devon. Interviews of prospective parliamentary candidates (PPCs) were conducted from July to September (see the list of interviewees at the end of the chapter). There were 75 candidates standing in the 12 Devon seats, and Table 21.2 shows that the 14 interviewed, representing just over one in five of the total, reflected a range of factors. The sample was slightly weighted towards the bigger parties and marginal seats. Marginality was decided using Finer *et al.*'s (1961) percentage of majority model, where seats were divided into those that were safe (11 percent of votes over the next highest candidate), near-marginal (5.1 percent to 10.9 percent) or marginal (5 percent or under). The interviewer was unable to arrange interviews with any of the candidates from the English Democrats (1), British National Party (5), Communist Party of Great Britain (1), and Socialist Labour Party (2). This did limit a little the ideological range of parties, but in all cases none of these candidates generated enough votes, or had a presence, to effect either the campaign or its results.

The data were operationalised using Jackson's four features: purpose; tools; application; intended effect. Factor analysis was applied to respondents' communication objectives, communication channels used and impact on their campaign.

Purpose of communication

Not unsurprisingly, two approaches appear to dominate: hype and persuasion. Several candidates made reference to gaining visibility or making noise. For example, Peter Milton, challenging to

Table 21.2 Breakdown of sample interviewed

Factor	*Number of respondents*
Incumbent	3
Conservative	3
Labour	5
Liberal Democrat	2
Green	2
United Kingdom Independence Party (UKIP)	1
Independent	1
Marginal	5
Near-marginal	1
Safe	8
First	3
Second	5
Third	2
Other	4

Note: Devon Central, a new seat, was based on the notional 2005 result provided by ukpollingreport.co.uk.

win, said 'This reflects the belief, especially in close run contests, that reputation of the candidate may have an effect'. Luke Pollard used noise to help another candidate: 'I wanted to use symmetric communications as much as we could to make noise, and to appear bigger than we were. We wanted to detract some Conservative activity moving into Linda Gilroy's seat'. A theme common to most interviewees, irrespective of whether they could expect to win the seat, was the desire to win votes. Therefore, candidates tried to persuade voters to actually vote, and then to choose them. For example, Oliver Colvile, who beat the incumbent MP, noted that 'I had to communicate with the electorate in order to give them a reason to vote for me'. Persuasion was not just to external audiences, but also to motivate activists, so Darren Jones wanted 'to build up a local organisation'. Essentially, candidates sought to gain attention as an important component in persuading people to vote for them.

After hype and persuasion, the next most used approach is reputation management, where several candidates suggested that they wanted to promote particular aspects of their character. Typical of this was that candidates wished to stress that they were local, so, for example, Vernon Whitlock noted that 'our communication was primarily about promoting myself as someone who was born and bred in the local area, and understood local issues'. Similar sentiments were also stressed by John Underwood, Peter Milton, Luke Pollard and Gary Streeter. The three incumbents all stressed the amount of constituency work in which they had engaged during the previous five years or more. There was limited evidence of both relations with publics and the Grunigian paradigm. Whilst it may be inherently implied that candidates will seek to identify, reach and manage their relationship with their publics using finite resources, this was not mentioned overtly by the sample. In terms of identifying and reaching publics, candidates seem to have divided these into two different types. First geographically, so that they would focus on particular wards, towns or villages in the seat, usually where their strength was. Second they focused on voting behaviour, for example Alison Seabeck commented that they 'wanted to reach out to core Labour support', though it is worth noting that Labour candidates reflecting that they represented the incumbent government were more likely to focus on their core vote. Some candidates were also aware of publics in future elections, so that Lydia

Somerville focused her efforts in two target wards for the 2011 local county council elections: 'so I was trying to find out how many people would vote for the Green Party'. The purpose of communication for candidates was weighted towards being heard rather than listening.

Tools used

We might expect that if the tools used are indicative of hype and persuasion, media relations might dominate. In fact, all candidates believed that the two most important means of communication were knocking on doors and putting leaflets through doors, suggesting little evidence for hype. The next level of tools, but lagging far behind, was the internet and media relations; moreover, there was a consistency of view on face-to-face communication and leaflets, which was not the case with the second-level tools. Some candidates, typically in the more rural seats, where the local print media showed an active interest in the campaign, did invest time and effort in media relations. However, an almost equal number, especially in the suburban and urban seats with different local media, did not. Similarly, candidates' use of the internet varied from the pioneers, such as Luke Pollard, Linda Gilroy and Peter Milton, through to the laggards, including two who did not even have a website. Candidates relied upon a small range of channels that they could control.

Given the focus by candidates on direct communication, the two most commonly found approaches were the Grunigian paradigm and persuasion. All candidates knocked on doors or telephone canvassed, but this was especially important for those hoping to win, do better than in 2005 or build up their strength in targeted areas. For example, Phil Hutty's parliamentary agent believed that his candidate knocked on 9,000 doors during the four weeks of the campaign. Although canvassing might appear a form of opinion polling, it inherently encourages two-way symmetrical communication. As Alison Seabeck notes, it is 'about finding out … people's voting intention, what issues are important to them'. Luke Pollard made such sentiments central to his campaign: 'the message (on the doors) was we are here and listening'. Indeed, all of the candidates who invested time in knocking on doors recounted examples of in-depth, two-way conversation. At a far lesser level, the internet encouraged some interaction, but candidates suggested that this was essentially at the margins. For example, a typical response of those using Facebook was from Darren Jones, who stated 'a lot of people on this were family and friends, but it did help me engage with some people'. Similarly, Twitter does not appear to have encouraged significant levels of mutual understanding, so that Colin Matthews said: 'I tweeted on issues I thought were interesting, and hoped would build up dialogue. But they did not lead to much dialogue, which was disappointing'. The levels of interaction encouraged by canvassing, and to a lesser extent the internet, were inherently persuasive as candidates tried to get core voters to vote, or undecideds to vote for them. Indeed, Linda Gilroy appeared to suggest that her key role was a persuasive one: 'the job of the team was to work across the constituency and to get our voters to turn out on the day. My role was to speak to the swing voters'. Dialogue was at the heart of candidates' campaigning; the difference was whether this encouraged mutual understanding, or sought to 'sell' the candidate.

Hype is at best the third most identified approach, reflecting the fact noted above that media relations and the internet were a secondary channel. There was evidence of relationship building from most candidates prior to the campaign. For example, when selected, Oliver Colvile deliberately sought to have a presence with the civic and business community in his local church, the local professional rugby club and a yacht club. Yet, once the election campaign began such targeted relationships were less important, whereas number of individual voters contacted mattered. Labour candidates tended to build relationships with those within trade unions and local community groups. All of the serious candidates who were running an active campaign, as opposed to 'paper candidates' (candidates who although they may do some work locally, are by and large standing just so that the party has a presence), also sought to build relationships with local print journalists. Only one respondent – Colvile – explicitly made reference to relationships during the campaign, but we can assume that it was based on work beforehand.

There is evidence of relations with publics amongst only a few candidates, such as Luke Pollard, Oliver Colvile and Linda Gilroy. The last two used software (Mosaic) to identify possible supporters, though with more financial support from headquarters Colvile probably made the most use of it. Prior to the election Pollard conducted surveys to identify where best to focus his efforts, and as a result changed his target both geographically and socially. Reputation management can be inherently assumed to be present and we return to this shortly, but in terms of communication tools the main evidence is that of internal communications to mobilise supporters and activists. There is virtually no evidence for relations in public and community building.

In terms of the six tools we identified that might indicate either an MPR or CPR approach, there is very limited evidence. Of the three MPR tools on which we focused, only media relations is a common tool, but even here only six of the respondents took an active approach and sent out press releases. Most waited for the media to contact them. Whilst all candidates attended hustings (where all the candidates are brought together in one meeting to discuss their policies and answer questions from members of the public), organised by local civic groups, very few organised events themselves during the actual campaign. One held a rally in a local shopping centre and several had candidate launches for party members, intended to raise funds. Only Dr Steven Hopwood appears to have given a high priority to events, when he arranged a number of public meetings. This probably reflects the fact that as an Independent he had no party organisation. Only two appear to have constructed pseudo-events designed to gain media coverage. Lydia Somerville paddled in a canoe to canvass some constituents as a photo opportunity, and Dr Hopwood 'stormed' the local castle to launch his campaign, and gained considerable local media coverage. In terms of CPR, there is no overt evidence of either issues or crisis management, though we note the importance of reputation management. All the party candidates viewed their internal audiences as very important; this was especially the case with those who needed to mobilise volunteers for leafleting and canvassing.

Application

If we assume that 'strategic' includes seeing the bigger picture and putting each individual campaign in context, then there is some evidence for it. For example, the two Green Party candidates were clearly following national party strategy in two key areas. First, their messages deliberately stressed non-environmental issues, because the party was less well-known for these. Second, following the party's Target to Win strategy, both focused their efforts in target wards for local elections in 2011. Several candidates, irrespective of their result in 2005, saw this campaign as part of a much larger one. For example, Jonathan Underwood, in second place, wanted 'to build up our strength for future campaigns'. There is also clear evidence that Gary Streeter, Luke Pollard, Darren Jones and Peter Milton had half an eye on the effect of their campaign on another key target seat, with at least three sending helpers to campaign in nearby seats. Conversely, if 'tactical' means focusing on immediate issues of vote winning, then clearly this was the norm for all candidates, as it effectively comes with the territory. All candidates appear aware of tactical issues, and most also considered strategic issues.

There is some evidence of MPR, in terms of seeking to get their voters out, so Oliver Colvile was typical when he stated: 'our first priority was to identify who our supporters were, and then the second priority was to get them out to vote'. However, as noted above, few candidates relied upon press agentry high-visibility tactics. There is evidence of CPR in terms of trying to manage overall reputation. This was fairly obviously the case with those hoping to win, so that incumbent Gary Streeter noted:

> the reputation of Gary Streeter PLC is very important to me. I think I know what it is, that I am local, works hard, is a committed Christian and people know what this means in terms of principles and he gets things done.

Reputation was also important to other candidates, so challenger Phil Hutty commented that, 'as a candidate there is a lot of pressure as the face of the party'. Candidates also sought to tackle long-held images of their party, so Lydia Somerville said: 'I do think that people tend to label the Green Party, and have this view of sandals and beards. So I wanted to address this'. This implies that party candidates believe that their own personal reputation impacts voting behaviour.

Overall, the level of activity amongst our sample appears weighted towards the tactical and MPR, yet a number of candidates also took a strategic and CPR approach. Overall, this suggests evidence of relations with publics, persuasion and probably the strongest being reputation management, and there is less evidence for hype and the Grunigian perspective. Whilst clearly an election campaign encourages participation and may support enhanced communities, there is very limited evidence of relations in public and community building. It could be argued that Dr Hopwood's whole 'outsider' campaign was based on ethical objectives which would enhance communities, but only Darren Jones, when he mentioned in his election address that he wanted people to vote whether for himself or not, might be taking an overtly ethical approach.

Intended effect

The two strongest approaches are hype and persuasion. All candidates clearly seek to raise awareness of themselves and their policies; this is an inherent component of being a candidate. They certainly all want to gain votes and although several, as noted above, have long-term goals, all are concerned with the immediate campaign. Whilst all candidates would argue that their policies would ultimately benefit society, they view the impact of their communication primarily in terms of the benefit for themselves and their party, not wider societal concerns. We can assume that candidates are largely concerned with using finite resources effectively, implying some use of relations with publics. Several candidates view reputation management as providing them with a competitive edge. It is arguable that within a pluralist society candidates' use of direct communication (leaflets, canvassing and the internet) does help to increase information within the public sphere, though this may only be at an individual not a community level. There is no evidence that social capital will be enhanced. The intended effect is on candidates' own campaigns, rather than any wider questions affecting the body politic.

Conclusion

Political PR essentially represents an interest, but it also encourages a rich interaction at a range of different levels between those active, interested or even uninterested in political discourse. As Figure 21.1 shows, the data support existing literature that there are three categories: the dominant, the niche and the unused. Far and away the dominant approach is persuasion, which is either the single strongest or in the strongest group on each of the four features. This suggests that candidates view elections as essentially a battle in which there is one winner, and so political PR is

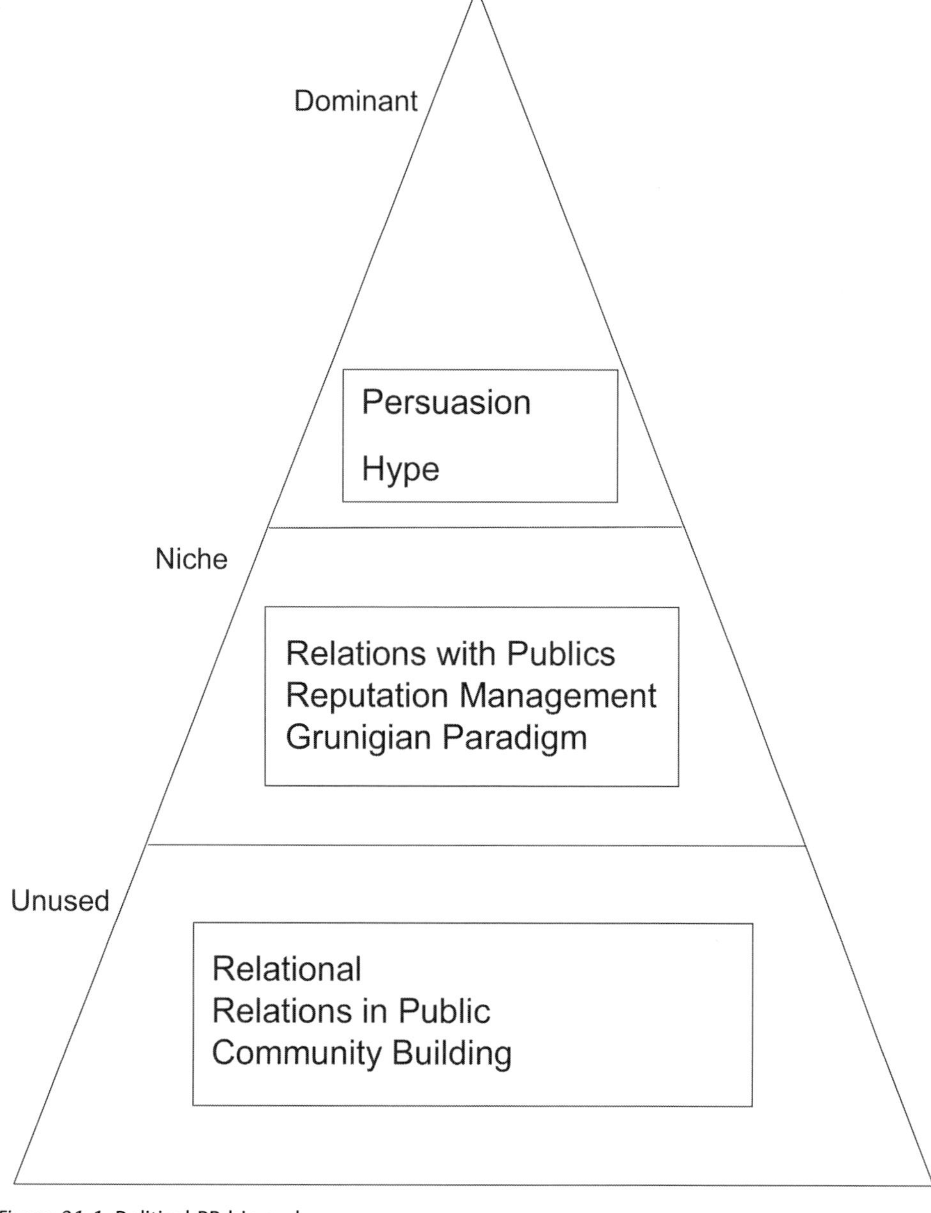

Figure 21.1 Political PR hierarchy

used to support one interest at the expense of another. Just below persuasion is hype, which is clearly limited by the fact that media relations plays less of a role at a local as opposed to a national level. The second niche level is relations with publics, the Grunigian paradigm and reputation management. There is evidence that candidates seek some understanding of their audience, but respond with asymmetrical communication to enhance their brand. The third grouping, with very limited evidence, is the relational: relations in public and community building. However, it would be too simplistic to suggest that candidates use only one approach. It could be argued that relations with publics and the Grunigian perspective by focusing on the needs of the audience is the direct opposite of the persuasive. Yet there is clear evidence that candidates follow a number of different strategies and these may appear contradictory.

The data suggest that at a local level politicians have an awareness of the value of CPR. With an absence of a reliance on mass media channels, local politicians have to be more adaptive in how they reach their audiences. Hence, they appear more likely to use a wider range of approaches. They use MPR, but are also aware that some CPR approaches, especially reputation management, open up a space that they control in which they can reach voters. The enhanced use of direct communications at a local level has two effects. First, it changes the nature of persuasion as it is primarily one to one, rather than one to many. Second, it also encourages candidates to consider a wider range of approaches. Local candidates may be leading national campaigners in their application of political PR.

Xifra's (2010) sample at a national party level, encompassing a narrow role and with limited freedom of action, leads to very different conceptual findings from our data. There may also be a cultural and political difference between Spain and the UK. A more local nature, during elections and with politicians who are effectively their own boss, leads to a much broader and strategic use of political PR to reach a wider range of audiences directly. This suggests that our understanding of political PR will be shaped, to some degree, by the nature and role of the sample, the characteristics of the political and electoral culture and systems they inhabit, and the political context. However, we can assume that there is common ground between both samples, in that they view political PR as essentially persuasive.

Advice for practitioners

Our model of political PR, although essentially descriptive of current practice within a narrow set of political circumstances, may provide political practitioners with a template. The model suggests two key lessons which might direct political actors' communications behaviour. First, whilst they may rely on a particular approach, they would be wise to supplement this with a niche strategy which might add to any dominant approach. Second, we suggest that the hierarchical structure identified within the confines of this research project will be different within different political contexts. In an election situation candidates and political parties may well be advised to focus on using PR to present their campaign in the best light in a primarily monologic way. In such a situation the purpose of political PR is essentially to provide information and persuade. However, between elections the same actors would be better advised to use political PR in a very different way, in encouraging long-term dialogue. Political PR would then utilise more interactive two-way communication as with relationship building and the Grunigian paradigm. For governments, political PR also offers a range of opportunities based on purpose. Where governments try to build support for their policies, then the relational and dialogic approaches should be dominant, to build-up support for policies. This implies that governments should encourage, listen and respond to such feedback. However, once governments are seeking to implement agreed policies where the purpose is to inform and bring about changes in behaviour, then persuasion and hype should be dominant. By using the appropriate dominant and niche strategy at the right time, political actors are more likely to gain political support at key times, and at the same time avoid unnecessary crisis.

Impact on politics

Political PR used by prospective parliamentary candidates is primarily persuasive in nature, reflecting their need to gain competitive advantage. It provides politicians with a means of reaching, and sometimes interacting with, citizens and voters in a range of different ways. Political PR encourages political actors to reach a wider audience including internal audiences, competitors and even those not necessarily overtly interested in politics. As a result, candidates recognise the value of combining both the tactical (MPR) and strategic (CPR) uses of public relations. Political PR is perhaps more capable of presenting the human side of politics than political marketing alone. Where political marketing tends to use MPR as a means of shouting in a loud voice, political PR can also use CPR to effectively apply a 'softer' approach to communication.

The impact of political PR, then, is centred upon a human face to politics, namely understanding the impact of policies on individuals, and then knowing how best to communicate this. We would suggest that most politicians are unlikely to fully follow the political PR model. They may in the context of elections, but potentially lack the sophistication to switch approaches to non-election situations. Political PR is not then a single rigid model; rather it can help politicians consider what is the appropriate communication approach in different situations. Using the right combination of political PR approaches may not just help win elections, but also potentially encourage better governmental decisions and ultimately build trust in politics.

The way forward

This is a small exploratory project designed to test a new conceptual framework. As such, there are limitations to the project. First, it was of a small sample, and a much wider one geographically would open up new data. Second, it focused at the local level, and a comparative with national-level strategies would provide a clearer picture. Third, it was conducted during the 'wartime' of an election campaign, and the results in 'peacetime' may well be different. This might explain the slightly surprising fact that the relational approach played such a limited role, as might addressing other political actors such as pressure groups. Fourth, although an initial comparison was made with existing data from Spain, a comparative study is required across political and electoral systems. Further tests of the model are required to apply it to different political situations such as policy development and implementation, different countries and at different levels. However, overall this project suggests that political actors, in trying to reach key audiences both during peace and wartime, should make greater use of political PR.

Bibliography

List of interviewees

Colvile, Oliver (2010) British Conservative Party MP, Plymouth Sutton and Devonport. Interviewed 9 August.

Gilroy, Linda (2010) British Labour Party, Plymouth Sutton and Devonport. Interviewed 7 September.

Hopwood, Stephen (2010) Independent, Totnes. Interviewed 19 August 2010.

Hutty, Phil (2010) Liberal Democrat, Devon Central. Interviewed 17 August 2010.

Jones, Darren (2010) British Labour Party, Torridge and West Devon. Interviewed 10 August 2010.

Matthews, Colin (2010) British Green Party, Devon Central. Interviewed 29 July 2010.
Milton, P., private correspondence, 7 September 2010.
Pollard, Luke (2010) British Labour Party, Devon South West. Interviewed 13 August 2010.
Seabeck, Alison (2010) British Labour Party MP, Plymouth Moor View. Interviewed 26 July 2010.
Somerville, Lydia (2010) British Green Party, Totnes. Interviewed 11 August 2010.
Streeter, Gary (2010) British Conservative Party MP, Devon South West. Interviewed 30 July 2010.
Underwood, Jonathan (2010) Liberal Democrat, Tiverton and Honiton. Interviewed 30 July 2010.
Whitlock, Vernon (2010) British Labour Party, Tiverton and Honiton. Interviewed 17 August 2010.
Williams, Hugh (2010) UKIP, Devon South West. Interviewed 15 July 2010.

Academic references

Brissenden, J. and Moloney, K. (2005) 'Political PR in the 2005 UK General Election: winning and losing with a little help from spin', *Journal of Marketing Management* 21, 9–10: 1005–20.

Davis, A. (2000) 'Public Relations, News Production and Changing Patterns of Source Access in the British National Media', *Media Culture & Society* 22, 1: 9–59.

Esser, F., Reinemann, C. and Fan, D. (2000) 'Spin Doctoring in British and German Election Campaigns: how the press is being confronted with a new quality of political PR', *European Journal of Communication* 15, 2: 209–39.

—— (2001) 'Spin Doctors in the United States, Great Britain and Germany: metacommunication about media manipulation', *Harvard International Journal of Press/Politics* 6(1): 16–45.

Ferguson, M. (1984) 'Building Theory in Public Relations: inter-organisational relationship', paper presented to Association for Education in Journalism and Mass Communication, Gainesville, FL. August.

Finer, S., Berrington, H. and Bartholowmew, D. (1961) *Backbench Opinion in the House of Commons, 1955–59*, New York: Pergamon.

Fombrun, C. (1995) *Reputation: realizing value from the corporate image*, Boston, MA: Harvard Business School Press.

Froehilch, R. and Rudiger, B. (2006) 'Framing Political Public Relations: measuring success of political communications strategies in Germany', *Public Relations Review* 32, 1: 18–25.

Gaber, I. (2000) 'Government by Spin: an analysis of the process', *Media, Culture and Society* 22, 4: 507–18.

Griffin, A. (2008) *New Strategies for Reputation Management*, London: Kogan Page.

Grunig, J. (1997) 'A Situational Theory of Publics: conceptual history, recent challenges and new research', in D. Moss, T. MacManus and D. Vercic (eds) *Public Relations Research: an international perspective*, London: International Thomson Business.

Grunig, J. and Hunt, T (1984) *Managing Public Relations*, New York: Holt, Rinehart and Winston.

Harlow, R. (1976) 'Building a Public Relations Definition', *Public Relations Review* 2, 44: 34–42.

Heffernan, R. (2006) 'The Prime Minster and the News Media: political communication as a leadership resource', *Parliamentary Affairs* 59, 4: 582–98.

Ihlen, O. and Van Ruler, B. (2007) 'How Public Relations Works: theoretical roots and public relations perspectives', *Public Relations Review* 33, 3: 243–48.

Jackson, N. (2010) 'Political Public Relations: spin, persuasion or reputation building?' paper presented at the Political Studies Association annual conference, Edinburgh.

Jackson, N. and Lilleker, D. (2004) 'Just Public Relations or an Attempt at Interaction? British MPs in the press, on the web, and "in your face"', *European Journal of Communication* 19, 4: 507–34.

Kovacs, R. (2001) 'Relationship Building as an Integral to British Activism: its impact on accountability in broadcasting', *Public Relations Review* 27: 421–36.

Kruckeberg, D. and Starck, K. (1998) *Public Relations and Community: a reconstructed theory*, New York: Praeger.

Ledingham, J. and Bruning, S. (1998) 'Relationship Management in Public Relations: dimensions of an organisation-public relationship', *Public Relations Review* 24, 1: 55–65.

Lees-Marshment, J. (2001) *Political Marketing and British Political Parties*, Manchester: Manchester University Press.

Messina, A. (2007) 'Public Relations, the Public Interest and Persuasion: an ethical approach', *Journal of Communication Management* 11, 1: 29–52.

Moloney, K. (2006) *Rethinking Public Relations*, second edn, Abingdon: Routledge.

Moloney, K. and Colmer, R. (2001) 'Does Political PR Enhance or Trivialise Democracy? The UK general election 2001 as a contest between presentation and substance', *Journal of Marketing Management* 17, 9–10: 957–68.

Negrine, R. and Lilleker, D. (2004) 'The Rise of a Local Media Strategy in British Political Communication: clear continuities and evolutionary change 1996–2001', *Journalism Studies* 4, 2: 199–211.

Newsom, D., Turk, J. and Kruckeberg, D. (2000) *This Is PR: the realities of public relations*, seventh edn, London: Thomson Learning.

Perloff, R. (2004) *The Dynamics of Persuasion*, Hillsdale, NJ: Lawrence Erlbaum.

Rose, R. (2008) 'Political Communication in a European Public Sphere', *Journal of Common Market Studies* 46, 2: 451–76.

Ruler, B. and Vercic, D. (2002) *The Bled Manifesto on Public Relations*, Ljublijana: Pristop Communications.

Sherman, E. and Schiffman, L. (2002) 'Political Marketing Research in the 2000 U.S. Election', in B. Newman and D. Vercic (eds) *Communication of Politics: cross-cultural theory building in the practice of public relations and political marketing*, London: Haworth, 53–68.

Strömbäck, J. and Kioussis, S. (eds) (2011) *Political Public Relations: principles and applications*, New York: Routledge.

Strömbäck, J., Mitrook, M. and Kiousis, S. (2010) 'Bridging Two Schools of Thought: applications of public relations theory to political marketing', *Journal of Political Marketing* 9, 1/2: 73–92.

Taylor, M. (2000) 'Media Relations in Bosnia: a role for public relations in building civil society', *Public Relations Review* 26, 1: 1–14.

Vercic, D., Ruler, B., Butschi, G. and Flodin, B. (2001) 'On the Definitions of Public Relations: a European view', *Public Relations Review* 27: 373–87.

Westen, D. (2007) *The Political Brain: the role of emotion in deciding the fate of the nation*, New York: Public Affairs.

Worcester, R. and Baines, P. (2006) 'Voter Research and Market Positioning: triangulating and its implications for policy', in P. Davies and B. Newman (eds) *Winning Elections with Political Marketing*, New York: Haworth Press, 11–32.

Wring, D. (1998) 'The Media and Intraparty Democracy: "New" Labour and the clause four debate in Britain', *Democratization* 5, 2: 42–61.

Xifra, X. (2010) 'Linkages Between Public Relations Models and Communication Managers' Roles in Spanish Political Parties', *Journal of Political Marketing* 9, 3: 167–85.

22

Political marketing in an online election environment

Short-term sales or long-term relationships?

Nigel A. Jackson, Darren G. Lilleker and Eva Johanna Schweitzer

The topic: online political marketing

The practical application of both political marketing as a concept and the internet as a campaigning tool share a similar time frame, with both gaining attention in the 1990s. However, apart from a few individual authors (Bowers-Brown and Gunter 2002; Jackson 2006), the two have not been generally pulled together conceptually. Indeed, Coleman (2001) was quite dismissive over the use of the internet in the UK 2001 general election, implying that because it only appeared to have been used for marketing purposes, and not to enhance democracy, that this was a less worthy use. Yet the construction of the so-called Web 2.0 era, which is based on a more interactive, bottom-up approach (O'Reilly 2005), opens up new marketing possibilities. This chapter will seek to assess whether the internet is supporting an essentially sales-based political marketing strategy, or one based on longer-term relations that encourages dialogue and public expressions of opinion. We will do this by considering the relevance of the concept of online political marketing, a child whose parentage is conceptually political marketing and at a campaign level the internet. We will first outline the relevant literature on political marketing and the internet, then introduce our methodology for examining how the internet was used in four elections between 2007 and 2010, covering four different countries: France, the US, Germany and the UK. The main findings are summarized in the conclusion, and discussed with regard to their implications for the current state of online political marketing.

We suggest that *online political marketing* describes the sustainable, goal-oriented and strategy-based management of relationships between political actors and their stakeholders, by the means of new information and communication technologies. In essence, political marketing is a curious mixture of the application of marketing practice to politics online and offline, especially electoral behaviour. It has been criticized for being neither true to politics nor marketing, but it can also be viewed as a discipline in its own right (Lees-Marshment 2009). In fact, the link between the two was first made by Kotler and Levy (1969), who famously suggested that candidates used the same principles as marketers selling commercial goods. This principle has been debated for some time; we suggest that of relevance to our debate is an understanding of political marketing practice.

Political marketing practice is not uniform; rather we can identify two different approaches to how political actors use marketing. The first is transactional marketing where the political party or candidate focuses on the immediate sale, or gaining the vote, which appears to be the dominant approach of politicians (Mauser 1983; O'Shaughnessy 1990; Johansen 2005). Indeed, Wring (1997) noted how easily traditional marketing applied to politics. This form of political marketing would use the internet as a one-way promotional tool. Transactional marketing has been challenged by relationship marketing, where the emphasis is on building longer-term relationships, which inherently requires two-way communication. Bannon (2005) suggests that as a service industry, politics applies a relationship marketing approach. Moreover, Henneberg (2002) argues that political marketing is moving away from a sales orientation, towards one which seeks to build long-term relationships with voters. This form of political marketing would use the internet as a means of facilitating such dialogue (e.g. in blogs, discussion forums or chats). Potentially, the internet provides a simple and cost-effective means of reaching external and internal audiences over a long period of time. This can have positive side-effects on political participation in general (see Hardy and Scheufele 2005; Mossberger *et al.* 2008), which Henneberg and O'Shaughnessy (2010) suggest may encourage citizen re-engagement with politics.

From a conceptual viewpoint, the linkage of the internet to a transactional marketing approach is associated with the static content of websites used within the Web 1.0 era (e.g. information about the candidate, party or election programme, campaign paraphernalia, etc.). However, the inherently more interactive approach implied within the Web 2.0 era suggests that relationship marketing is more achievable. The rationale is that with Web 2.0 the stress is on gaining feedback, and interacting within an 'architecture of participation' (O'Reilly 2005). Web 2.0 makes it easier for parties to encourage interactivity, since they can build on the technical infrastructures and services that are already established, such as Facebook, Twitter and MySpace. This is a 'rational choice' for them as they do not have to rely on inventing anything from scratch. Recent literature suggests that in the era of Web 2.0 the internet offers a means of enhancing the relationship between those seeking election and voters (Anderson 2007; Chadwick 2009), though often the reality is that participation is used for the purposes of endorsements, aiding brand management as opposed to relationship management (Jackson and Lilleker 2009). It is through private and targeted communication by email or e-newsletters where attempts are made to build relationships with supporters (Jackson 2006). To assess which forms of participation are currently employed in American and European elections, we will summarize the present state of the discipline and explore ways of measuring different approaches in online political marketing.

Previous research

Online political marketing can apply to both the 'peacetime' in legislative periods, when it is often associated with the permanent campaign, and the 'wartime' of political competitions. Our focus is on elections due to their societal relevance, higher adoption rate of campaign innovations, and the greater focus by parties and candidates on political marketing as a vote-winner.

Empirical work

The internet has become a standard marketing tool in modern election campaigns. Its rapid diffusion around the world is attributed to the unique technical features of online communication (i.e. capacity, efficiency, hypertextuality, interactivity, multimediality, topicality and ubiquity), which provide political actors with new strategic options to respond to today's electoral challenges (e.g. unparalleled degrees of political cynicism, voter de-alignment and civic apathy in the

Western democracies) (see, for example Dalton and Wattenberg 2002). Social scientists are interested in questions of how these features affect the style and substance of modern political communication. To this end, they conduct quantitative and qualitative content and structural analyses of e-campaigns in different electoral settings and various political cultures (for an overview, see Ward *et al.* 2008).

Their results are astonishingly similar: they prove a standardization, a professionalization and a normalization in online political marketing. Parties and candidates increasingly rely on the same web-based features and successively integrate new formats (like blogs, Twitter and social networking sites) into their overall e-campaigns (*standardization*) (e.g. Kluver *et al.* 2007). The US is said to be a role model in this international standardization process since the sheer number and frequency of their elections, the competitiveness of their political system and the advanced consultant industry foster technical campaign innovations (Chadwick 2009). These developments inspire similar adoptions in other countries (Howard 2006; Schneider and Foot 2006). Moreover, e-campaigns have been found to become more professionalized over time (*professionalization*). In different electoral contests, parties and candidates advance their existing web presences by including more information, offering more multimedia content, and providing more sophisticated means for user involvement and navigation (Druckman *et al.* 2007; Carlson and Strandberg 2008; Schweitzer 2008a). This increases the overall usability, readability and design of the web presences, which in turn has been found to positively affect party and candidate evaluations and voter knowledge (e.g. Hansen and Benoit 2005; Rittenberg and Tewksbury 2007).

These qualitative advancements, however, have not changed the traditional focus of online political marketing. All around the world, party and candidate websites have been found to rely on traditional offline campaign strategies that override any internet-specific style of communication (Rohrschneider 2002; for an overview see Schweitzer 2008b). In particular, political actors refrain from employing extensive interactivity and bottom-up features that could encourage a genuine two-way dialogue with citizens (e.g. Kluver *et al.* 2007). Instead, they continue to focus on information-heavy, centralized and neatly presented top-down web content so as to retain their message control and save human and financial resources (Stromer-Galley 2000). The current use of the internet as a political campaign tool thus resembles a transactional marketing approach that remains locked into styles and modes of communication synonymous with the Web 1.0 philosophy of 'we will build it and they will come' (Birdsall 2007).

With the emergence of Web 2.0 and its successful utilization in the 2008 Obama campaign, however, this normalization in e-campaigning might be under threat. The integration of the social web features demands a 'they will come and build it' philosophy, which prioritizes interactive co-production and empowers the user as civic producer ('produser' or producer-user). To effectively adopt this new means of political communication thus implies that parties and candidates need to move from a transactional to a more relationship approach of online political marketing. To test whether this assumption holds true, we will review past conceptual works on how to measure different paradigms of e-campaigning.

Conceptual work

Historically, the internet has played a set range of key functions within election campaigning. These can be related to either the transactional or the relationship mode of political marketing (Gibson *et al.* 2003). Based on Gibson and Ward's (2000) established schema, the following tasks can be distinguished:

- Information provision both on civic issues (e.g. on the electoral procedures) and on the campaign (e.g. candidates, programme or the party);
- Promoting persuasive messages to mobilize supporters and undecided voters: this could be a discrete message written for the site, or it could be linking, and so amplifying, a message within other media such as advertisements or policy documents;
- Negative campaigning (see also Schweitzer 2010): that is, the deliberate attacks on opponents so as to cast doubt on their suitability for office;
- Generating resources: usually donations but also encouraging activism so as to increase the logistical power of the organization and its competitiveness;
- Networking, providing spaces for supporters and activists to discuss issues and tactics and for the party to communicate directly to their supporters: historically this has taken place on password-protected intranets or via email to closed lists (Norris 2000); and
- Encouraging participation, traditionally limited to getting out the vote.

These functions are not exclusive, but the first three imply a transactional marketing approach, the sixth a relationship marketing approach, and the fourth and fifth could be central to either.

Web 2.0 challenges these functions; the philosophy underpinning the technologies (O'Reilly 2005; Anderson 2007; Chadwick 2009) suggests that the internet presents opportunities for the user as well as those who create websites. Web 2.0 technologies enable the building of participatory architectures, which provide space for individual production and user-generated content. Users are able to easily upload comments, pictures and videos with minimum effort and technological ability, and these can all become part of an online milieu of campaign communication. Parties can harness 'produsers', first identified by James (1991), to enhance the campaign as creators of supportive material and endorsers through comments and sharing. Harnessing the power of the crowd enhances activism, creating a win-win situation for both organizations and supportive publics. Thus, theoretically, the internet becomes one huge archive of co-created data which is open and accessible to everyone. While this data can meet campaigning functions, Web 2.0 is bottom-up and non-hierarchical; the opposite is traditionally the case with political communication.

The existence of such data encourages interactivity, a process by which face-to-face communication is replicated through the use of online tools. These can be asynchronous, such as email, discussion forums and the participatory spaces within social networks; alternatively they can be synchronous chat facilities that allow one-to-one or many-to-many conversations to take place. While technologies that facilitate using the online environment are often discussed in terms of being interactive, Stromer-Galley (2004) offers a useful distinction in types of interactivity. *Interactivity-as-product* refers to the ability of the user to click links, play videos and dovetails neatly with McMillan's (2002) definition of user-to-document interactivity, where users have choices over reading only. *Interactivity-as-process* replicates conversation and is contiguous to definitions of user-to-user interactivity. While this dual distinction is useful, Ferber *et al.* (2007) suggested a refinement of definitions of online communication. Supporting notions of user-to-document and product-driven interactivity, they discuss the notion of one-way, top-down communication. Asynchronous and private communication is two-way, but the host retains control over the process of communication. In contrast, three-way participatory communication can involve multiple users in an open forum and conversations can be either synchronous (ideally), or asynchronous with users contributing at numerous points within what some refer to as a global conversation. One-way clearly links to transactional marketing while three-way is clearly relational; two-way communication offers some degree of hybridity depending on feature usage. Asynchronous communication such as email can be highly relational, yet features such as frequently asked questions or aggregated data from offline or online interaction are essentially one-way, as they are packaged in a persuasive format for consumption. Our intention is to assess the extent to which candidate and political party website use of interactivity encourages a transactional or relationship management approach.

Case study: US, French, German and UK elections 2007–10

Our methodology will apply Ferber *et al.*'s (2007) model (Figure 22.1), as operationalized by Lilleker and Malagon (2010) to test for conversations taking place within the selected four countries, and to consider the outcomes of such interactivity. The first step in the data collection was to archive the websites so that they could be analysed later in the research. For this purpose, the content of the websites was converted through PDF Professional and Web Dumper Software at a key point towards the end of the campaign when the sites were fully mature.

Operationalization

As outlined above, Ferber *et al.* suggest that there are two key dimensions to understanding the use and impact of the internet within politics. First, they assess the direction of communication. One-way is traditional promotion; two-way involves some level of interaction, but it is largely held in private between user and political actor; and in three-way such dialogue is held in public

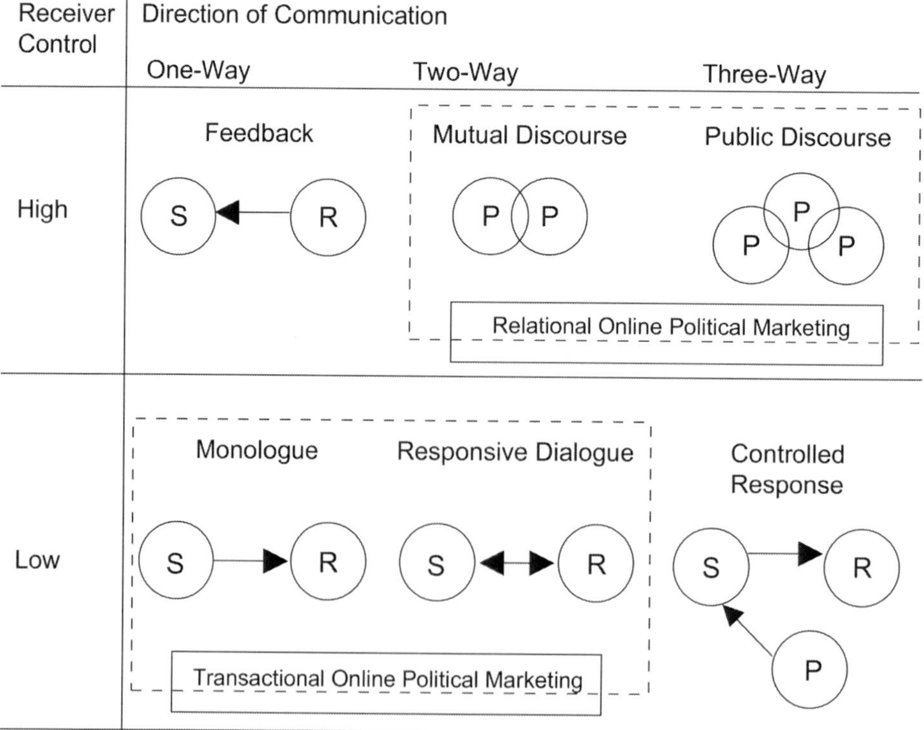

Figure 22.1 Ferber *et al.*, six-part model of cyber-interactivity

Table 22.1 Scale for measuring levels of receiver control

Category	*Scale*	*Definition*
Low receiver control	1	One-way hyperlink with unclear destination
	2	One-way hyperlink with defined destination
	3	Hyperlinks created with user input, language is dynamic using second person
	4	User has control over read and link options, video play is optional, content can be downloaded
	5	Users have control over interfacing with content (above) and can send information
	6	Users can send and receive information, i.e. debate forums
	7	Users have multiple options to send and receive information, their input has transformational power – can be seen, i.e. text-only chat
High receiver control	8	Users can upload content, questions, including videos, and can receive answers from receivers
	9	User can choose time, type and amount of information sent and received; the information sent is transformed by the receiver and the transformation is transparent. Communication is asymmetrical
	10	Sender and receiver have equal levels of control; communication is conversational

and open to all. Second, within each direction they suggest that the internet user has different levels of control, from low to high. Table 22.1 identifies a 10-point scale for the measurement of receiver control. This was based on a slightly revised form of Gibson and Ward's (2000) methodology, which sought to code 51 elements present or absent in websites across four functional groups (downward information flows; upward information flows; lateral information flows; interactive information flows). High-level two- and three-way communication indicates evidence of a relationship marketing campaign; low-level one- and two-way implies a purely persuasive transactional sales approach (see indications in Figure 22.1). Both suggest the existence of political marketing, but of different styles.

Through a comparison of feature use, and the user experience potentiated by their inclusion within the architecture of the site, we are able to assess progression in the use of the internet as a campaign tool by our sample, as well as the adoption of new communication technologies. Furthermore, we compare the overall averages for the sites to assess the extent to which website visitors in each of the four countries are encouraged to participate, and the extent they allowed control over the ways in which they participated. This is mapped onto an axis which measures the degree to which the websites offer an open participatory structure, or remain propagandistic tools. The former, by helping to build relationships through interaction, is indicative of a relationship marketing approach. The latter, by stressing one-way, top-down, content-heavy information, indicates a transactional marketing approach.

Sample

We will apply this methodology to four elections: the 2007 French presidential election; the 2008 US presidential election campaign; the 2009 German national election; and the 2010 UK general election. We will specifically assess to what extent these four campaigns provided voters with space to talk to one another and talk to the campaign, and to what extent a collaborative campaign diegesis was presented to website visitors. The style of this communication will then be used to assess the nature and type of online political marketing, as employed by the primary political actors in these four election campaigns.

The nations were selected for comparison on the basis that the elections were a standard distance apart, were national contests and would see a high degree of professionalization (Negrine 2008). The countries – France, the US, Germany and the UK – are all advanced industrial nations with high internet penetration rates[1] and established democratic institutions. The US and France share a presidential system with a separately elected lower chamber. We therefore chose to analyse the main *candidate* websites in these countries (i.e. of Ségolène Royal and Nicolas Sarkozy in France; Barack Obama and John McCain in the US). The UK and Germany, on the other hand, are parliamentary systems where the party or coalition with the most seats builds government. Here we focused on the websites of the main *parties* in the election (i.e. the Christlich Demokratische Union Deutschlands (CDU), the Christlich-Soziale Union (CSU), the Sozialdemokratische Partei Deutschlands (SPD), the Freie Demokratische Partei (FDP), Gruene (Bündnis 90/Die Grünen) and Die Linke in Germany; the Conservative Party, Labour Party, Green Party, Liberal Democrats, British National Party (BNP) and United Kingdom Independence Party (UKIP) in the UK).

In general, the countries have independent traditions of campaigning, with specific national constraints as regards the electoral system, the respective laws for political advertising or the overall political culture (Plasser 2002). However, there has also been a significant amount of cross-fertilization of ideas and practices. For example, the Americanization debate has been related to all four nations within research articles (Swanson and Mancini 1996; Negrine *et al.* 2007). There has also been a crossover of personnel working within nations. One of Sarkozy's online strategists, Loic le Meur, went to work with the US Democratic Party in 2007; Blue State Digital, the creators of Obama's website, were prominent in the UK and worked with both the Conservative and Labour parties in an advisory capacity; similarly, a number of strategists from the US were present in Germany in the years preceding the campaign, with all the major parties showing an interest in what lessons could be learned from the Obama campaign. This cumulatively suggests that looking across these elections is a useful way to understand the evolution of online political marketing in practice.

Results

Table 22.2 shows the percentage of features that fit into the five categories identified by McMillan (2002) and operationalized for the purposes of website analysis (Gibson and Ward 2000; Lilleker and Malagon 2010; Lilleker and Jackson 2011). This data refutes the expectation of a gradual evolution towards a more Web 2.0 style, showing neither an overall progression, nor stasis in terms of online political campaign communication. Instead, this evidences an ebb and flow in adoption of Web 2.0 features, with party and candidate websites showing a range of differences and similarities in the overall design of website architectures. What we suggest is that innovations in the use of website features are adopted in order to fit with a strategy and the campaign context, with resources appearing to have a strong mediating role.

To take a sequential approach we see the lowest level of interactivity, and consequently the most transactional marketing strategy, within the French presidential contest of 2007. This is perhaps consistent with the lower levels of internet penetration in France as well as greater reliance on modern, as opposed to postmodern (Norris 2000), tools of campaign communication. In 2008 Obama, building on innovations from the 2003–04 Howard Dean failed bid for

Table 22.2 Features present across websites 2007–10 by category (in %)

Party/candidate	*Downward flows*	*Upward flows*	*Lateral flows*	*Asymmetrical flows*	*Symmetrical flows*
Royal (FR)	94.3	0.1	0.3	5.4	0.6
Sarkozy (FR)	94.7	0.1	0.1	4.1	0.9
McCain (US)	78.3	0.2	1.7	2.8	17.1
Obama (US)	3.6	<0.1	0.2	0.1	96.0
CDU (DE)	4.6	0.2	85.1	0.7	9.3
CSU (DE)	4.2	0.4	93.3	1.1	0.9
FDP (DE)	61.0	0.8	21.8	2.6	13.8
Gruene (DE)	36.9	1.4	54.9	3.8	2.9
Linke (DE)	62.1	1.3	8.5	4.0	24.1
SPD (DE)	12.0	0.5	68.9	1.4	18.2
BNP (UK)	1.1	<0.1	0.3	0.8	97.9
Conservative (UK)	58.9	<0.1	0.5	0.8	39.7
Green (UK)	70.9	0.1	5.3	4.1	11.2
Labour (UK)	29.4	0.3	34.1	5.1	31.1
Liberal Democrat (UK)	18.8	<0.1	6.1	3.1	71.6
UKIP (UK)	94.2	0.3	3.9	1.7	0.0

the Democrat party nomination, made a significant step forward in allowing participation within his website. Key innovations adopted were community-based tools of mobilization within his bespoke network, my.barackobama.com (MyBO), and his leveraging of social networks to promote his campaign – in particular Facebook but also a range of other niche networks popular among ethnic minority, same sex or political interest groups. Obama's delivery of all campaign news in weblog format, presenting literally thousands of participatory opportunities alongside his network, forum and social network presences, clearly offered new dimensions to campaigning and relationship marketing in online environments. That Obama reached out to different communities online probably reflected his background as a community campaigner as well as his more left-wing ideological position and branding as the outsider and people's champion. McCain, though traditional in comparison with Obama, equally made attempts to leverage online networks as well as adopting a range of weblog tools.

The parties in Germany and the UK show rather mixed approaches to online campaigning, and so a more diverse approach was adopted within both nations. While in Germany hyperlinks dominated many sites compared with the number of other features included, one can see a range of both transactional marketing tools alongside Web 2.0 innovations. Communities such as www.meineSPD.de and www.team2009.de were used to draw supporters closer to the SPD and CDU, respectively. CDU leader Angela Merkel, in particular, tried to leverage social networks to increase communication reach and levels of support. Weblog tools also were prominent, with the Linke website being dominated by this feature. Similarly, in the UK parties created a range of communities, though unlike their German counterparts most were public throughout. The largest was the Liberal Democrat Act area (www.act.libdems.org.uk), but both www.myconservatives.org.uk and Labour's www.members.labour.org.uk represented large areas of the party's websites and replicated to varying extents the relational concept behind Obama's site. Interestingly, the far-right BNP was the most interactive, providing spaces to participate within every aspect of the site from the news weblog to sharing facilities on every page and providing a forum. The site, www.bnp.org.uk, acted as a hub for a minority with marginalized ideas, and so provided the party with an active group who co-created their campaign to a far greater extent than Obama or any other of the party community sites.

Comparing the overall architectures one finds that the websites that predominantly supplied information were those of Sarkozy and Royal, where little else was provided; UKIP, McCain and the British Green Party, then Linke, the FDP and the British Conservative Party. Except for the sites of the Conservatives, Linke and John McCain, all these sites contained few Web 2.0 features and so offered little opportunity for interactivity. Royal apart, these also presented the greatest number of negative arguments, in particular UKIP and the German opposition parties, the FDP, Gruene and SPD. Linke and John McCain both had small weblogs that did allow site visitors to add comments and interact with one another and the host. This provides the sense of being at the centre of a websphere, and the Labour Party in particular used hyperlinks to network with a range of supportive groups from internal associations to trade unions and other non-governmental organizations and pressure groups. These sites tend to adhere to traditions of political communication and serve only campaigning functions, paying only lip service to philosophies of Web 2.0. The websites offering symmetrical information flows has the BNP ranked first, closely followed by Barack Obama; these were true Web 2.0 participatory architectures. British parties the Liberal Democrats, Conservatives and Labour demonstrated a mixed strategy of supplying information balanced by features that offered interactivity. In all three cases the size of the network created within the website determined the number of opportunities to interact, and so the overall percentage of symmetrical communication permitted. The reason that the use of StudiVZ profiles and other German social network communities such as meineSPD and teamDeutschland did not increase the extent to which the sites offered symmetrical communication was due to them being protected by registration procedures and passwords. Obama's MyBO area and all the British party communities were visible to all visitors, although posting and commenting was limited to members only. This positions these communities as fundamental features of an impression management strategy, as well as having a mobilization function and so demonstrating the dual function of Web 2.0 within the context of a campaign. This mixed strategy combines campaigning with co-production and suggests a shift away from a purely transactional marketing strategy.

In Figure 22.2 we compare the political marketing approaches of parties and candidates testing for relational or transactional strategies and the extent to which sites are informational or interactive. As expected, Figure 22.2 shows that Obama's website was both interactive in terms of receiver control and highly participatory in terms of communication direction. Less expected is the fact that the BNP also followed a relationship marketing approach, though this was very controlled and to a very small internal audience. There is, then, a series of parties in the UK and Germany that can be found in a middle ground, Web 1.5 (Jackson and Lilleker 2009), which offer the architecture for a relationship marketing approach, but seek to project sales messages. We then find candidates such as Sarkozy and McCain and parties such as UKIP and Gruene in a purely Web 1.0, transactional marketing space.

The unexpected level of adoption of Web 2.0 by Barack Obama represents an outlier in terms of all other parties and candidates within this study except for the BNP; though Obama sought to build relationships with a mass network, the BNP maintained a conversation among their minority of like-minded supporters. Mainstream German and UK parties created communities based around their existing members and supporters, and the latter, in particular, appear to have drawn ideas from MyBO. They also built on their existing uses of databases and

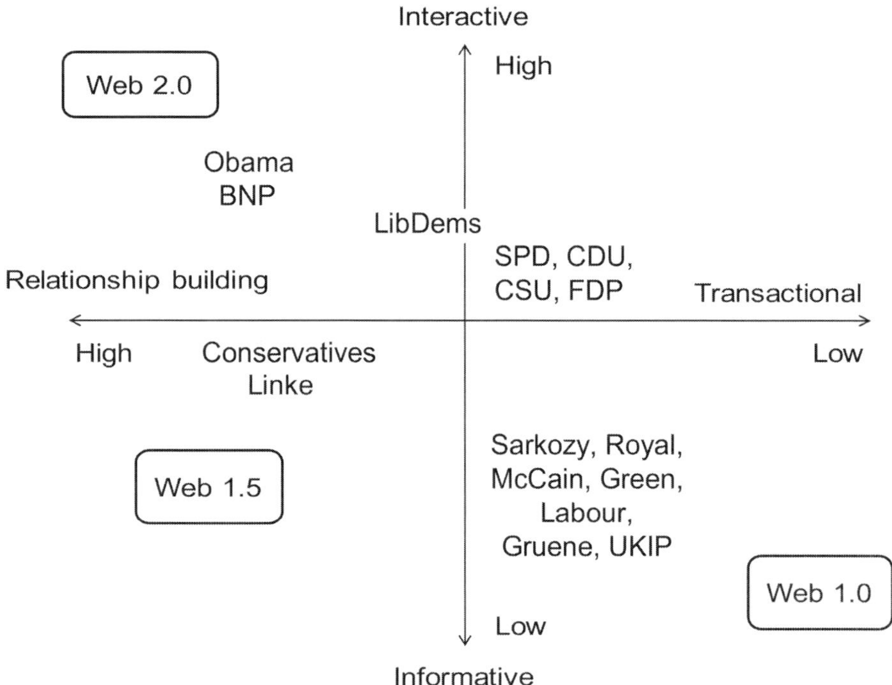

Figure 22.2 Use of transactional or relationship marketing 2007–10

email lists, and whilst this implied some level of relationship marketing, it was targeted at internal audiences. The outreach to the general public was closer to a transactional approach. This implies that the two basic modes of online political marketing (transactional versus relationship) can in fact co-exist, depending on the type of stakeholders that will be addressed on the internet. Obama, in contrast, used the internet to gain new supporters. His relational style of online political marketing thus encompassed both internal and external audiences. However, he did not start with a blank canvas. After his 2004 speech to the Democrat Party Convention a Facebook group was created independently called Obama for President. Its membership increased to almost a million over the three years prior to Obama declaring his intention to stand for the presidency. This was a clear indicator that there was a supportive, online crowd whose power the campaign could harness. This was not the case elsewhere; Royal built a network slowly around her Notebooks of Hope which were co-created in the two years prior to the contest but also had a party network in place. German and UK parties have similar traditions of mass membership and, though in decline, these remain the lifeblood of the organizations. Thus networks were created to draw these members closer as opposed to focusing on reaching out to the masses.

Moreover, the French election was at a time when the ideas of Web 2.0 were nascent and so Sarkozy's and Royal's approach reflects both this fact and the political outlook. In fact, of our sample, Sarkozy is the only one whose approach is essentially transactional to both internal and external audiences. In the wake of the Obama success, though, there seemed to be a shift in European elections towards relational modes of online campaigning. While Web 2.0 features may not have been embedded, as for Obama, parties in Germany and the UK clearly sought to embrace social networking. In Germany, this happened in a rather restrictive manner so as to retain the party's overall message control. As a consequence, the public response was rather meagre. Whilst we cannot fully compare the number of fans on candidate and party sites, they provide an interesting snapshot. Chancellor Angela Merkel could only gain 14,000 fans to her Facebook site during the campaign, suggesting that there was limited interest. In the UK the Conservative Party's Facebook profile gained 70,732 fans, suggesting that there was a stronger response to the more open-minded Web 2.0 approach of British parties. However, Obama had an online audience in place, and his number of fans was millions strong, topping 8 million globally by election day. Such levels of support enhance an external relationship marketing approach.

Advice for practitioners

The data across our four countries suggests that there is not a single answer as to what works, and hence no simple universal lesson as to how politicians and campaigners should direct their online activities. This absence of one size fits all reflects in part differences between these countries in terms of their electoral procedures, political systems and cultures. The lack of uniformity in our data also reflects factors individual to the key players in each country, such as resources and skills available to make use of marketing knowledge and internet technology. However, we suggest that there are certain lessons which may have a practical impact upon political marketing strategies and tactics. First, practitioners need to take into account national approaches to politics and the internet. There is some evidence that political campaigners in Germany and the UK tried to adopt Obama's campaign, but we suggest that campaigners need to cherry-pick from how the internet is used and not import it wholesale. Start with an understanding of the national political scene and apply the technology to this, not the other way around. Second, we would suggest that there is some evidence that political campaigners would extend their understanding and use of political marketing principles to include a discrete online approach. This would not mean different aims and objectives, but would recognize the potential unique benefits that the internet as a communication channel offers them. In particular, we would suggest that as a marketing communication channel the internet provides political campaigners with flexibility, so that it can be used as both a broadcast and narrowcast tool at the same time. Third, we suggest that political campaigners would be best advised to use different marketing styles at the same time as they meet different audience needs. The discussion has been primarily whether the internet is being used as part of a transactional marketing strategy or a relationship marketing approach. Normatively, we might suggest a relationship marketing approach, but the evidence suggests that both are perfectly acceptable. The persuasive and information-based transactional approach is probably most appropriate for reaching external audiences who know little about the party or candidate. In contrast, relationship marketing is probably more effective for internal audiences, such as members or stakeholders with strong party identification and high levels of knowledge and political interest. We suggest, therefore, that the ebb and flow data we identified indicates that political actors should be marketing agents using a range of approaches, depending on the circumstances.

Impact on politics

The impact of online political marketing can be described in three ways: in a communicational dimension; in a logistical dimension; and in a civic dimension. As a communication channel the internet has helped political actors to deliver persuasive and alternative messages to the public without journalistic interventions or presentational constraints. This increases their message control and provides a compensation for the lack of attention in the traditional mass media. Another impact on politics is found in the options to generate new funds and to mobilize and coordinate activists. This applies not only to candidate-centred systems where there is more scope/need, but also to party-centred systems. In this way, the internet has become a vital logistical backbone in modern political marketing that increases the competitiveness even of smaller organizations. Finally, the interactivity we identified within Web 2.0 has the potential to transform the relationship between political actors and citizens. In particular, parties and candidates are able to rely on direct voter input as regards their policy standpoints or their campaign strategies. In turn, they can provide opportunities for lasting civic participation so as to enhance the responsivity and legitimacy of the democratic system. This is especially so if a long-term relationship marketing approach is applied between elections which encourages an ongoing two-way dialogue. At present, however, the external impacts on democratic discourse between governed and governing is more a theoretical construct than a reality. For now, the evidence suggests that the internet is primarily affecting the communicational and logistical dimensions of political communication, and less so the civic foundation.

The way forward

This project used the same methodology to assess four different elections at the very beginning of the Web 2.0 era. For finesse, the analysis requires a wider sample as regards the number and type of political actors and the countries that are included. Moreover, research should strive to cover both election and routine periods to learn more about the conditional factors that influence the adoption of different marketing styles. Finally, longitudinal comparisons are warranted that allow for conclusions about the development of online political communication in relation to their offline environment. Apart from these scientific desiderata, there are also future considerations for the practice of e-campaigning. At present, political consultants are actively looking at the technology, but are primarily interested in its vote-winning potential within a transactional marketing approach. We suggest that not enough practitioners are considering the wider conceptual issues of how they can use the internet to enhance democratic participation within a relationship marketing approach. We suspect that most believe that elections, in particular, are not the time to consider wider participation. However, we suggest that the embeddedness of the internet within political marketing communication strategies, both before and during elections, may actually bring powerful electoral benefits to parties and candidates.

Note

1 According to the database www.internetworldstats.com, France had an internet penetration of 51.8 percent in 2007. In the US 74.7 percent of all citizens were online in 2008, while in Germany 75.3 percent used the web in 2009. In the UK internet penetration was 76.4 percent in 2010.

Bibliography

Anderson, P. (2007) *What is Web 2.0? Ideas, Technologies and Implications for Education*, JISC Technology and Standards Watch Report, February.

Bannon, D. (2005) 'Relationship Marketing and the Political Process', *Journal of Political Marketing* 4, 2: 73–90.

Birdsall, W.F. (2007) 'Web 2.0 as a Social Movement', *Webology* 4, 2. Online, www.webology.ir/2007/v4n2/a40.html (accessed 1 July 2008).

Bowers-Brown, J. and Gunter, B. (2002) 'Political Parties' Use of the Web during the 2001 General Election', *Aslib Proceedings* 54, 3: 166–76.

Carlson, T. and Strandberg, K. (2008) 'Plus ça change, plus c'est la même chose? The evolution of Finnish Web campaigning 1996–2004', in J. Strömbäck (ed.) *Communicating Politics. Political Communication in the Nordic Countries*, Göteborg: Nordicom, 61–79.

Chadwick, A. (2009) 'Web 2.0: new challenges for the study of e-democracy in an era of informational exuberance', *I/S: Journal of Law and Policy for the Information Society* 5, 1: 9–41.

Coleman, S. (ed.) (2001) *2001: Cyber Space Odyssey – The Internet at the UK Election*, London: Hansard Society.

Dalton, R. and Wattenberg, M. (eds) (2002) *Parties Without Partisans: Political Change in Advanced Industrial Democracies*, New York: Oxford University Press.

Druckman, J., Kifer, M. and Parkin, M. (2007) 'The Technological Development of Congressional Candidate Web Sites: how and why candidates use web innovations', *Social Science Computer Review* 25, 4: 425–42.

Ferber, P., Foltz, F. and Pugliese, R. (2007) 'Cyberdemocracy and Online Politics: a new model of interactivity', *Bulletin of Science, Technology and Society* 27, 1: 391–400.

Gibson, R., Römmele, A. and Ward, S. (2003) 'German Parties and Internet Campaigning in the 2002 Federal Election', *German Politics* 12, 1: 79–104.

Gibson, R. and Ward, S. (2000) 'A Proposed Methodology for Measuring the Function and Effectiveness of Political Websites', *Social Science Computer Review* 18, 3: 301–19.

Hansen, G.J., and Benoit, W.L. (2005) 'Presidential Campaigning on the Web: the influence of candidate World Wide Web sites in the 2000 general elections', *The Southern Communication Journal* 70, 3: 219–29.

Hardy, B.W. and Scheufele, D.A. (2005) 'Examining Differential Gains from Internet Use: comparing the moderating role of talk and online interactions', *Journal of Communication* 55, 1: 71–84.

Henneberg, S. (2002) 'Understanding Political Marketing', in N. O'Shaughnnessy and S. Henneberg (eds) *The Idea of Political Marketing*, Westport, CT: Praeger, 93–170.

Henneberg, S. and O'Shaughnessy, N. (2010) 'Political Relationship Marketing: some macro/micro thoughts', *Journal of Marketing Management* 25, 1: 5–29.

Internet Worlds Stats (no date) Online, www.internetworldstats.com/stats.htm (accessed 20 July 2009).

Howard, P. (2006) *New Media Campaigns and the Managed Citizen*, Cambridge: Cambridge University Press.

Jackson, N. (2006) 'Banking Online: the use of the Internet by political parties to build relationships with voters', in D. Lilleker, N. Jackson and R. Scullion (eds) *The Marketing of British Politics: Political Marketing at the 2005 General Election*, Manchester: Manchester University Press, 157–84.

Jackson, N. and Lilleker, D. (2009) 'Building an Architecture of Participation? Political parties and Web 2.0 in Britain', *Journal of Information Technology and Politics* 6, 3/4: 232–50.

James, M.G. (1991) *PRODUSER: PROcess for Developing USER interfaces*, San Diego, CA: Academic Press.

Johansen, H. (2005) 'Political Marketing: more than persuasive techniques, an organizational perspective', *Journal of Political Marketing* 4, 4: 85–105.

Kotler, P. and Levy, S. (1969) 'Broadening the Concept of Marketing', *Journal of Marketing* 33, 1: 10–15.

Kluver, R., Jankowski, N.W., Foot, K.A. and Schneider, S.M. (2007) *The Internet and National Election: A Comparative Study of Web Campaigning*, London: Routledge.

Lees-Marshment, J. (2009) *Political Marketing: Principles and Applications*, London: Routledge.

Lilleker, D.G. and Jackson, N.A. (2011) *Political Campaigning, Elections and the Internet*, London: Routledge.

Lilleker, D. and Malagon, C. (2010) 'Making Elections Interactive: online discourse during the 2006 French presidential election', *European Journal of Communication* 25, 1: 25–42.

Mauser, G. (1983) *Political Marketing: An Approach to Campaign Strategy*, New York: Praeger.

McMillan, S.J. (2002) 'A Four-part Model of Cyber-interactivity: some places are more interactive than others', *New Media and Society* 14, 2: 271–91.

Mossberger, K., Tolbert, C.J. and McNeal, R.S. (2008) *Digital Citizenship: The Internet, Society, and Participation*, Cambridge, MA: MIT Press.

Negrine, R. (2008) *The Transformation of Political Communication*, Basingstoke: Palgrave Macmillan.

Negrine, R., Mancini, P., Holtz-Bacha, C. and Papathanassopoulos, S. (eds) (2007) *The Professionalisation of Political Communication*, Bristol: Intellect Books.

Norris, P. (2000) *A Virtuous Circle: Political Communication in Post-Industrial Societies*, New York: Cambridge University Press.

O'Reilly, T. (2005) 'What is Web 2.0: design patterns and business models for the next generation of software', *O'Reilly*. Online, www.oreillynet.com/pub/a/oreilly/tim/news/2005/09/30/what-is-web-20.html (accessed 10 April 2011).

O'Shaughnessy, J. (1990) *The Phenomenon of Political Marketing*, London: Macmillan.
Plasser, F. (2002) 'Global Political Campaigning: a worldwide analysis of campaign professionals and their practices', Westport, CT: Praeger.
Rittenberg, J. and Tewksbury, D. (2007) *The Effects of Campaign Website Viewing on Candidate Evaluations*, paper presented at the 60th Annual Meeting of the World Association for Public Opinion Research, Berlin, September.
Rohrschneider, R. (2002) 'Mobilising Versus Chasing: how do parties target voters in election campaigns?' *Electoral Studies* 21, 3: 367–82.
Schneider, S. and Foot, K. (2006) 'Web Campaigning by U.S. Presidential Primary Candidates in 2000 and 2004', in A. Williams and J. Tedesco (eds) *The Internet Election. Perspectives on the Web in Campaign 2004*, Lanham, MD: Rowman & Littlefield, 21–36.
Schweitzer, E.J. (2008a) 'Germany: Online campaign professionalism in the 2002 and 2005 national elections', in S. Ward, D. Owen, R. Davis and D. Taras (eds) *Making a Difference: A Comparative View of the Role of the Internet in Election Politics*, Lanham, MD: Lexington Books, 235–55.
—— (2008b) 'Innovation or Normalisation in E-campaigning? A longitudinal content and structural analysis of German party websites in the 2002 and 2005 national elections', *European Journal of Communication* 23, 3: 449–70.
—— (2010) 'Global Patterns of Virtual Mudslinging? Comparing the use of attacks on German party websites in state, national, and European parliamentary elections', *German Politics* 19, 2: 200–21.
Stromer-Galley, J. (2000) 'Online Interaction and Why Candidates Avoid It', *Journal of Communication* 50, 4: 111–32.
—— (2004) 'Interactivity-as-product and Interactivity-as-process', *The Information Society* 20, 5: 391–94.
Swanson, D. and Mancini, P. (1996) *Politics, Media and Modern Democracy: An International Study of Innovations in Electoral Campaigning and Their Consquences*, Westport, CT: Praeger.
Ward, S., Owen, D., Davis, R. and Taras, D. (eds) (2008) *Making a Difference. A Comparative View of the Role of the Internet in Election Politics*, Lanham, MD: Lexington Books.
Wring, D. (1997) 'Reconciling Marketing with Political Science: theories of political marketing', *Journal of Marketing Management* 13, 7: 651–63.

Part V

Government marketing – delivery, policy and leadership

23

Delivering in government and getting results in minorities and coalitions

Anna Esselment

The topic: delivery in government

A key component of political marketing principles is the 'product'. In the ideal market-oriented party (MOP), the product has been carefully crafted based on market intelligence gathered from extensive consultation with both the public (through focus groups and polling surveys), and party members and volunteers (Lees-Marshment 2001). The product itself is multifaceted and can include, among other aspects, the image of the leader (for example, open, accessible, trustworthy), type of party candidates (competent and responsive), the logo of the party, and policy commitments contained in the campaign platform (ibid.). While much of the literature on political marketing has focused on its techniques to help parties win elections, less emphasis has been placed on whether, or how, the product (particularly election promises) is delivered in government. Considering the design of the product has been informed by market intelligence, success in power is often dependent on the ability to implement the identified policy preferences of voters. In other words, if a party wishes re-election, delivering on commitments is crucial.

The focus of this chapter is on product delivery. First, it will provide an overview of the literature on delivery in government within the political marketing context. Express attention will be devoted to 'delivery units', specialized structures within the centre of government initially designed by the British New Labour Party to oversee the implementation of policy priorities. Have these implementation units been successful in translating electoral commitments into government policy? If so, are they a new necessity to the machinery of government, particularly for a MOP that wants to maintain its market-orientation in power?

Second, this chapter will analyze product delivery in a minority government. A minority parliament (or 'hung' parliament as it is called elsewhere) occurs when no political party has won a majority of seats in the House of Commons (the lower House in a bicameral parliamentary system). In this type of parliament usually the party that has won the most seats, but not a majority, forms the government. That party must govern with the help of opposition parties in order to pass legislation. If important legislation fails (for example, supply measures), this is considered a loss of confidence in the government and, in most cases, Parliament is dissolved and new elections are called.

Canada has had a succession of minority governments since 2004. By comparing product delivery under Paul Martin's Liberal minority (2004–06) with that of Conservative prime minister Stephen Harper's first term (2006–08), we will learn that product implementation can be successful even without commanding a majority of parliamentary seats. The sheer prospect of an unexpected election appears to galvanize minority governments into action and assists in maintaining a tight focus on accomplishing their goals. What differentiates the Liberal minority from the Conservative minority is not so much implementation per se, but the ability to effectively communicate that delivery. On the other hand, MOPs that form majority and coalition governments could benefit from the use of implementation units in order to stave off 'drift' for the former, and keep the latter connected over the course of their coalition agreement. The chapter will conclude with lessons about the nature of marketing and delivery in government that can be more widely applied to other countries with similar political and electoral systems.

Previous research

Studies of policy implementation are plentiful. Scholars in the field of public administration, in particular, have a fascination with how policy is delivered, although interest has admittedly ebbed and flowed (Bardach 1977; Gunn 1978; Hill and Hupe 2002; Howlett 1991; Mazmanian and Sabatier 1983; Pressman and Wildavsky 1984). Apparent in this literature is the lament that problems of implementation identified in the 1970s are still posing challenges to governments today. Governments must wrestle with issues that transgress departmental boundaries, thereby requiring a greater degree of horizontal coordination (Bakvis and Juillet 2004). In some cases, governments are no longer the direct provider of services, which also contributes a layer of complexity to the issue of delivery (Hamburger 2007). What does this mean from a political marketing perspective? Since the structure and processes of government have changed little, a MOP, despite its intent to remain responsive to voters, faces the same implementation hurdles as parties in the past. Unlike the 1970s, however, voters take the commitments made by parties much more seriously. There is an expectation that 'governments need to identify commitments and demonstrate results' (Lindquist 2006: 430). As a consequence, campaign platforms have become serious documents, evidenced by the Liberal Party of Canada's 'Red Book' in 1993, the US Republicans' 'Contract with America' in 1994, the UK Labour Party's 'pledges' to Britons in 1997, and the Conservative Party of Canada's 'five commitments' in 2006. Voters are invited to toss out the government if it fails to achieve its goals.

Lees-Marshment's study of the UK and New Zealand governments demonstrated that the difficult and slow pace of delivery tests the ability of MOPs to remain that way in power (Lees-Marshment 2009a: 533). Implementation has also hampered market-oriented leaders in the US, such as Bill Clinton, who had the political will to resolve certain problems facing the middle class but faced institutional and financial restraints (Newman 1999). The gap between the expectations of voters from a new government and the form a promised policy may actually take after its roll out can also work against the market orientation of parties if voters are disappointed with the final outcome (Newman 1999). Marland (2005) has noted that some MOPs revert to being sales-oriented parties (SOPs) after time in government, perhaps in order to 'sell' what it was they were able to accomplish even though it may differ substantially from what they had initially promised voters. Because of these difficulties, the management and communication of product delivery must be a priority of any MOP in power (Lees-Marshment 2009b: 212–13). Creating greater capacity at the centre of government – that is, directly in the office of prime minister – is one way in which parties, particularly MOPs, have addressed the issue of delivery. By linking the first minister's office to the bureaucratic level through an oversight role that assists in identifying and solving delivery problems, party leaders are able to track their progress on key election commitments.

Delivery/implementation units

The advent of a 'delivery unit' to assist governments with their implementation goals was first created by the Labour Party under Tony Blair. Labour became a savvy, market-oriented party prior to the 1997 election and used market intelligence to shape a product responsive to voters' needs (Lees-Marshment 2001). New Labour shaved most of its hard left ideological edges and embraced a 'third way' of doing politics in Britain (Labour Party 1997). Wildly successful in its first election, New Labour also garnered a second and then a third majority government. In 2001, despite the party's second victory at the polls, Prime Minister Blair noted that a number of the government's initiatives had not been achieved. In short, delivery had stagnated. This was perhaps unsurprising since, as elsewhere, academics have observed that '[t]raditionally in British government, there has been a sharp separation of responsibilities for developing policy and delivering it' (Boaz and Solesbury 2007).

In the context of political marketing, however, the lack of delivery was especially concerning since it contributed to a public perception of the government as 'out of touch' and unable to follow through on its promise of public service reform (Richards and Smith 2006: 333). As part of a larger effort to reconnect with voters and demonstrate new capacity for policy implementation, Prime Minister Blair created the Prime Minister's Delivery Unit (PMDU). This dedicated political unit at the centre of government was staffed with 40 individuals and reported directly to the prime minister. It was tasked with monitoring the implementation of policies that the prime minster himself had identified as personal priorities, such as health, education, crime and transport (ibid.: 338). The primary focus of the PMDU was to ensure that the government met its targets in these policy areas through early identification and anticipation of potential implementation problems at the bureaucratic level (ibid.: 338). If problems did arise, the PMDU would work with the department responsible for the policy and help resolve issues of delivery. The Delivery Unit was successful in the sense that it created new capacity at the centre of government to drive implementation. It also renewed and strengthened relationships between the centre and the departments on matters pertaining to delivery and achieving policy outcomes (Barber 2007: 285–86). As a result, a number of the government's policy targets were either achieved or had vastly improved (in literacy and numeracy in public schools, for example, and in managing road congestion). The largest impact of the PMDU, in Barber's view, was that of momentum in government:

> the longer 2004 went on, the more it became clear that we had that intangible but vital force of change – momentum. Indeed, in modern government – as with aircraft – the only alternative to moving forward is falling out of the sky. Advance or fail. Momentum or drift … [w]e were able to review thoroughly every area of delivery in our portfolio and assist in removing blockages and generating results.
>
> *(Barber 2007: 213)*

The delivery unit in the UK was a valuable tool for New Labour because it assisted the party in government to generate tangible results. It kept the government focused on its priorities and, to a great extent, staved off second- and third-term drift that can work against a market orientation in government.

Governments in other countries took a favourable view of the PMDU. In 2003 John Howard, the prime minister of the Australian National/Liberal coalition government, created a Cabinet Implementation Unit (CIU) with the hope of emulating the delivery successes of the UK PMDU. Prime Minister Howard's interest in a CIU was due to several factors, not the least of which was a concern that coalition governments can disintegrate after several years because of 'indecision and a lack of ability to make decisions stick' (Wanna 2006: 350). Like the PMDU, the CIU was placed in the centre of government and charged with tracking the progress of key government commitments. Unlike the PMDU, the CIU was staffed by civil servants, not political advisors (ibid.: 363). Furthermore, Australia's CIU was not focused on ensuring that specific policy targets were met, but instead on anticipating implementation problems in cabinet submissions and highlighting them using a traffic light signal system. Initiatives with amber or red lights posed implementation challenges (because they involved sensitive issues, for example, or were expensive, or involved the agreement of sub-national units) and were monitored carefully, with reports made to the prime minister and Cabinet on implementation progress every few months (Shergold 2007: 13; Wanna 2006: 359). In general, the effect of the CIU has been viewed positively. The traffic light system is a simple way of monitoring and reporting on difficulties in delivery. Prime Minister Howard noted that the CIU is 'one of the necessary central mechanisms to assist a mature government to focus on forward strategy and on implementation' (Wanna 2006: 364). This is perhaps especially important for a long-term coalition government that must, as do all multiple-term administrations, continue to deliver on its promises, thereby ensuring a fruitful and effective partnership.

The UK and Australian governments are not the only jurisdictions that have created a delivery unit model to assist with policy implementation. This unit has been replicated at the sub-national level in Australia (Queensland in particular), as well as in Indonesia, Malaysia, the US state of Maryland and the city of Los Angeles, among others.

New research

The greater capacity for implementation and delivery provided by the 'units' described above is relatively clear. They have, to greater and lesser degrees, provided parties in power with an extra tool to ensure that promises made in an election have a better chance of being delivered because of central oversight of critical commitments.

That delivery units have not been replicated in most representative democracies suggests that implementation problems may vary depending on the strength of other coordinating departments and agencies already in place, and the type of administration in power. Tony Blair, John Howard and Premier Peter Beattie of Queensland led either majority or coalition governments. These types of governments face two major challenges: first, the mid-term or multiple-term 'malaise' can result in policy drift because of detachment from voters due to a variety of factors, including daily crises and constraints with which the government must contend (distracting them from their main policy agenda), and longevity in power that can lead a party towards arrogance and complacency with regard to the public (Lees-Marshment 2009a: 533; Kent 2006: 14; Tiernan 2006: 371; Wanna and Williams 2005). Second, coalition governments must ensure that their agreements hold firm in order to form a more perfect partnership. These agreements can be quite detailed, particularly with regard to the policy initiatives to be pursued (Müller and Strøm 2008: 159–60). Delivery units can thus keep a majority government focused, even in its second or third mandate, and can assist coalition partners by doggedly pursuing the implementation of its agreed-upon agenda, thereby minimizing conflict between the parties and contributing to a productive government partnership.

Minority governments and delivery

What happens if the government is in a minority? Since 1920 Canada has had 13 minority governments, three of which have been in power since 2004. This section will examine the ability of the Liberal minority under Paul Martin (2004–06) and the Conservative minority under Stephen Harper's first term (2006–08) to deliver on their commitments in government.

Paul Martin and the Liberal Party were reduced to a minority government in the 2004 election.[1] The party had previously won three straight majority governments in 1993, 1997 and 2000 under leader Jean Chrétien. While majority governments also face delivery constraints, they have at least two advantages over minority governments: the luxury of time between elections and control over the Commons. Having governed with some ease in Parliament for a decade, the Liberals now found themselves in newer parliamentary territory. The 2004 Liberal campaign platform was styled similarly to previous Liberal Red Books containing detailed promises for what a Paul Martin government would accomplish. Of the 42 election promises, arguably only a few were memorable, set out in Table 23.1.

While none of those particular promises was easy to achieve, Martin's minority was still very productive. On the big campaign promises, such as a national system of childcare (which required the cooperation and consent of the sub-national governments), the Liberals were able to bring all 10 provinces on board and had started to flow the funds for the expansion of childcare spaces by the end of 2005. On the democratic deficit, the government passed whistleblower protection legislation and allowed a greater number of free votes in Parliament (Clarkson 2006: 27; Seidle 2004). The government also signed a health accord with the provincial premiers that included an additional C$41 billion from the federal government over the course of the ensuing 10 years (CBC News Online 2006). In its 2005 Budget, C$600 million was diverted from the federal gas tax to cities in order to fulfil the promise of the 'new deal' for cities (Department of Finance Canada 2005a: 14). Martin's minority also facilitated the legalization of same-sex marriage, the inclusion of tougher provisions of the criminal code, and improvements on Aboriginal issues (Clarkson 2006: 27).

Several reasons contributed to the productivity of the Martin government, even in the absence of a dedicated 'delivery unit'. First, Prime Minister Martin had experience in power. As the finance minister to former prime minister Jean Chrétien, Martin had skilfully eliminated Canada's deficit in the 1990s and the exercise gave Martin and his staff an intimate knowledge of the machinery of government. When the Liberal majority was reduced to a minority, the prime minister's familiarity with government assisted in strategic planning vis-à-vis delivery. Second, his long tenure as an elected member and then minister also meant that he had built relationships with the leaders of provincial governments. These personal relationships helped the government in its negotiations on the childcare agreements, particularly with provincial governments led by Liberal administrations (Esselment 2009). Third, money helped. The government did not lack for financial resources and spreading the wealth around, particularly to the provinces, garnered support from Parliament for certain initiatives such as greater funding for

Table 23.1 Liberal Party of Canada key campaign promises, 2004

1. Eliminate the 'democratic deficit'
2. A national, publicly funded childcare system
3. Fix healthcare 'for a generation'
4. A 'new deal' for cities to assist with transportation and infrastructure costs

Source: Liberal Party of Canada, 2004.

healthcare, enriched equalization for two Atlantic provinces and reduction of the 'fiscal gap' in Ontario (CBC News Online 2006; Department of Finance Canada 2005b; Goar 2007). Managing competing demands and following through on spending pledges is easier when the government has a budget surplus.

Fourth, the Martin government quickly learned that working with the opposition parties would be an integral part of staying in power. The prime minister and Cabinet accepted a number of revisions from the Bloc Québécois to the government's first Throne Speech in fall 2004 (Axworthy 2004: 1) and the 2005 Budget won the support of the New Democratic Party (NDP) because of the inclusion of new spending measures important to the NDP's socially progressive constituency (CBC News Online 2005). In May 2005 the Liberals were able to survive a non-confidence measure by wooing Belinda Stronach, a Conservative MP, across the floor with the promise of a cabinet position, and her crucial vote kept Parliament in session. Finally, a government in a minority situation often results in greater political pressure brought to bear on the public service to implement key items from the party's election manifesto. The PM and Cabinet themselves become a 'delivery unit' of sorts; time is of the essence to demonstrate the ability of the government to be efficient and effective in implementing the product it promised.

Unfortunately for the Liberals, productivity in government did not equate to longevity in power. Within 17 months of winning its minority, the government fell on a motion of non-confidence. The party's downfall was not due to a lack of delivery of their promises; indeed, in their short time in power the Liberals were able to achieve much of their agenda (Clarkson 2006). Instead, the Martin government failed to effectively *communicate* its agenda, a critical part of delivery overall (Lees-Marshment 2009b: 213). This misfiring can be largely attributed to the 'sponsorship' investigation, a scandal from the previous Liberal administration involving mis-appropriated funds from a government program that were filtered into the bank accounts of Liberal-friendly advertising agencies in Quebec (Canada 2006). The judicial inquiry into the scandal hung like an anvil around the necks of the Liberals, detracting from the policy successes achieved under Paul Martin while simultaneously eroding the Liberal 'brand' of being competent fiscal managers. Other mistakes, such as ignoring the input of the opposition for the fall 2005 economic update, led to the government's collapse on 28 November.

With the black cloud of sponsorship hanging over the Martin government, Stephen Harper and the Conservative Party of Canada (CPC) were victorious in the 2006 election.[2] The party's platform document contained numerous commitments but focused on five main priorities, set out in Table 23.2.

As an untested government viewed sceptically by many Canadians, the new prime minister was keen to demonstrate to Canadians that his government was competent, legitimate and trustworthy by moving quickly on a few campaign promises. Immediate action would help to move public perception in this direction. Fortunately for the Conservatives, disappointed and

Table 23.2 Conservative Party of Canada key campaign promises, 2006

1. Reduction in the goods and services tax (from 7 percent to 5 percent)
2. Childcare allowance for families with children aged five and under
3. Stronger government accountability measures
4. Criminal justice reform
5. Patient wait times guarantee

Source: Conservative Party of Canada, 2006.

exhausted opposition parties had less appetite to mobilize against government initiatives so soon after an election.[3] The initial GST point reduction and the childcare allowance were put into the government's first Budget (which passed through Parliament with the support of the Bloc Québécois) and took effect 1 July 2006 (Department of Finance Canada 2006). The Federal Accountability Act (FAA) was the Conservative government's response to the sponsorship scandal and it was one of the first pieces of legislation introduced in the legislature. Among other changes, the new legislation reduced limits on financial donations to political parties, placed strict parameters and rules around lobbying the government, and strengthened the role of the ethics commissioner and auditor-general (Government of Canada 2006). Because of the political salience of that particular issue with all the parties, the FAA passed quickly through the legislative process and was enacted into law in December 2006. It is noteworthy that within the first year of power the Conservatives were able to pass three major policy items. These 'quick wins' gave the minority Conservative government a record of achievement on which it could rely if an unexpected election were to occur.

The CPC government had more difficulty delivering its two remaining promises of criminal justice reform and a patient wait times guarantee. The justice reforms, introduced as 11 separate pieces of legislation, became bogged down in the committee system. In a minority Parliament, opposition parties hold the majority of seats on committees and this can be a stumbling block for government, particularly on contentious issues. To face this challenge, the government repackaged the 11 separate bills into one large bill called the Tackling Violent Crime Act. Playing a much tougher legislative hand, the government then framed the issue as either 'for or against' crime in Canada. Introduced in October 2007, the bill was given royal assent just four months later (Government of Canada 2008).

Arguably, the patient wait times guarantee was never fully realized. Dependent on the agreement of the provincial governments (which are responsible for healthcare in Canada's federal system), the Harper minority was unable to fully realize the commitment it made in the election. Instead, the government allowed some flexibility on the 'guarantee' portion of the promise, asking the provinces to meet just one wait time guarantee from a list of five areas.[4] When this agreement was secured, the Harper administration declared the promise delivered and moved on to other items in its agenda (CTV.ca 2007). Thus of the five main promises, three could be characterized as delivered 'cleanly'. While the Conservatives had promised action on many other items that were ultimately left unfulfilled, they went into the 2008 election with a record of achievement in their minority government and won re-election, albeit with a second minority mandate.

Both of these minority governments – the Liberals and the Conservatives – have been praised for being unusually productive. At least one (the CPC) has also been characterized as a market-oriented party and thus, by extension, should want to remain responsive to voters while in government (Paré and Berger 2008). Part of being responsive in power is putting the party's policy agenda into effect. While both minorities obtained relative success in their task, neither the Liberal nor the Conservative government chose to emulate the UK's 'delivery unit' model. How were these minorities different from either majority or coalition governments?

Paradoxically, much of these governments' electoral agendas were achieved *because* of their minority status. It makes intuitive sense that, without majority control of Parliament, passing legislation and delivering on campaign promises should be more difficult. At the same time, delivery takes on heightened importance since the government is at the mercy of Parliament; a vote of no confidence is a continuing threat and, should the governing party be thrust into an early election, a record of some achievements is critical to a new campaign. In other words, a minority government does not suffer as much as majority governments from fatigue, inaction, or lack of momentum; instead, time itself is the precious resource that must be maximized in order to fulfil key commitments. Other factors came into play too: both the Liberal and Conservative governments had policies that appealed to at least one opposition party in order to secure passage of legislation and stave off defeat in the House of Commons; both governments had to be flexible on some issues in order to ensure their delivery; both governments had ample financial resources to put their promises into effect and secure 'quick wins' should an election be called; and both governments kept a watchful eye on the strategic manoeuvres available to their opposition and pounced on weaknesses to strengthen their own position, such as wooing members to cross the floor.

The differences between the two minority administrations also impart valuable lessons for students of political marketing interested in delivery. Influential factors in successful delivery for the two governments are listed in Table 23.3.

As a fully fledged MOP, the Harper government was able to maintain its market orientation throughout its first term in power and was more adept at doing so than the Liberals under Paul Martin. In particular, the Conservatives rarely underestimated the strength of the opposition, trod carefully in Parliament, made splashy announcements when campaign promises had been fulfilled (CityNews.ca 2007), used the Privy Council Office (PCO) as their own 'implementation-driving machine',[5] and continued to gather market research while in government (*Ottawa Citizen* 2007).

The Liberals were responsive to the opposition at first, but by the fall of 2005 they ignored the other parties in Parliament and had difficulty communicating the delivery of their priority policies because of the prominence of the sponsorship scandal. Policy achievements by government were often hijacked by reporters wanting to know more about the scandal and

Table 23.3 Influential factors in successful delivery

Paul Martin Liberal government	*Stephen Harper Conservative government*
Prime Minister Martin had extensive experience in power. As an elected member and finance minister, Martin had built relationships with provincial premiers – this helped with some policy commitments that required sub-national coordination. The government worked with opposition parties on budget matters, which later aided delivery. More pressure was put on the public service to implement key platform items. The government was in a strong financial position.	The government moved quickly to implement campaign promises, which gave it a record of achievement, a perception of competence and greater legitimacy in the eyes of the public. The Privy Council Office became an implementation-driving machine, the equivalent of a delivery unit. This helped the government maintain focus on its priorities. Important government legislation was consolidated and clearly framed ('for' or 'against' crime, for example) to increase its chances of passage through the Commons. The government always assumed opposition strength, not weakness. Implementation of campaign items was communicated effectively through staged photo opportunities so that Canadians would know that the Conservatives had 'delivered'. Gathering market intelligence continued when in government. The government was in a strong financial position.

Table 23.4 A political marketing model of successful delivery

1. Create a separate 'delivery unit' or focus a central agency on driving implementation. This is especially important for coalition governments in order to ensure the most fruitful partnership.
2. Ensure that a few campaign promises can be delivered almost immediately for 'quick wins' and an early record of achievement if an election is called.
3. Work with opposition parties and always remember that they have the upper hand in Parliament.
4. Communicate delivery of policy promises with memorable events and photo opportunities.
5. If necessary, repackage promises and frame them in terms that make opposition to them publicly unpopular.
6. Continue market research while in government to monitor public perception of delivery progress, stay responsive to voters and develop new policy ideas – the goal is to form a majority government in the next election.
7. Build relationships with key figures in government departments, opposition parties and lower levels of government such as provinces, states or devolved parliaments, as many of these relationships will be leaned on to ensure effective implementation.

Martin's role in it (Gregg 2005). Due to different perceptions of the proper role of the PCO, Paul Martin did not wield it in the same way as Stephen Harper. As Lindquist (2006: 431) warns, 'having an implementation unit working out of the cabinet office might be inconsistent with its mission as a pure co-ordinating agency', and thus using it as a quasi-delivery unit was unappealing to a party that had long governed with the aid of the PCO solely in a coordinating function. Finally, while the Liberals consulted polls and focus groups, the investment in and use of market research was not to the same degree as the Harper Conservatives in their first years in power.

Advice for practitioners

From the examination of these cases, several recommendations emerge vis-à-vis delivery in minority governments, as set out in Table 23.4.

This model of delivery, while not exhaustive, provides a base from which further research can develop and cases across jurisdictions can be compared. A key component is the use of some kind of *implementation tool*, but if we recall that a minority situation, and the electoral uncertainty that comes with it, is itself an impetus to keep a government focused on delivery, where do mechanisms such as implementation units best fit? Arguably the UK and Australian examples demonstrate that delivery units are uniquely suited to majority and coalition governments. This is not to suggest that greater capacity is unwarranted in a minority government, but implementation units as part of a political marketing model of successful delivery appear to provide an additional focus to governments that are either more susceptible to policy drift, or those that need to keep a partnership together. For market-oriented parties in these two types of government, delivery units can assist by concentrating on the implementation of priority commitments, identifying potential problems and assisting with horizontal coordination where commitments overlap departmental areas.

Impact on politics

Failure to implement campaign commitments can have negative reverberations for democratic government. Peter Shergold, former secretary to the Department of the Prime Minister and Cabinet in Australia, observed that:

> Poor delivery … risks public dissatisfaction. It can reduce trust not only in public service but in the government it serves. The quality of the implementation of government policy is central to community support for the institutions of democratic governance.
>
> *(quoted in Tiernan 2007: 116)*

Shergold views the Cabinet Implementation Unit in Australia as 'a vehicle for communicating more effectively between those implementing government policy, public service leadership and government' (Shergold 2007: 14). Strengthened relationships between these branches leads to better delivery in government and, by extension, improves citizen confidence in their government. This can have a positive impact on democratic government.

At the same time, 'delivery units' are located at the centre of government, directly under the auspices of the prime minister. The centralization of control in the PMO is a concern for scholars (Savoie 1999) and delivery units appear to add another layer to the power of the centre which privileges downstream decision-making. If the implementation unit is staffed by political advisors (as it was in the UK PMDU), this also raises questions of accountability and answerability since we know little about the role of partisan staff in government (Savoie 2008; Blick 2004; Eichbaum and Shaw 2010). Viewed this way, implementation or delivery units contribute to the growth of the centre of government and this squeezes the notion of democratic government.

The way forward

Political marketing examines how parties use market intelligence to design a product that responds to the needs and wants of voters. How market-oriented parties are able to deliver that product in government is deserving of more attention. There are a few complicating factors to this task, however. First, becoming 'market-oriented' is still a new concept to many parties and the stages involved have only been embraced by a small handful. Second, a party that sets out to be market-oriented may not remain that way in power (Marland 2005). Third, even if a MOP maintains its market orientation in government, it faces the same implementation obstacles that challenge all parties in power. The crucial point is whether a MOP will take advantage of tools such as a 'delivery' or 'implementation' unit to help ensure the success of its priority initiatives. Last, the use of such a unit may turn on the type of government in place – minority, majority or coalition.

The Canadian example of minority governments has demonstrated that such units may be superfluous. Working under severe time constraints, minority governments do not appear to lose sight of their goals or experience policy drift. On the other hand, as demonstrated by the UK and Queensland examples, majority governments appear to have difficulty staving off malaise, and a delivery unit provides needed focus and oversight to their product delivery. Coalition governments, such as in Australia under John Howard, can also make use of implementation units. The ability to cooperate is of benefit to both partners in a coalition and a delivery unit can help to ensure that agreed upon policies come to fruition.

More research along these lines is sorely needed. The new UK coalition government between the Conservatives and the Liberal Democrats is one place to start. David Cameron has brought an end to the PMDU in an effort to 'decentralize' decision-making (Cameron and Clegg 2010). Whether such a move will facilitate implementation and hold the coalition together is debatable. Observers are already questioning the stability of the coalition (O'Sullivan 2010) and without a delivery unit to keep the parties focused on the key aspects of their agreement, their time in office may not be viewed favourably. Likewise, the Australian federal government should also be monitored closely. The Labour government won a minority in the August 2010 election. The Canadian example suggests that an implementation unit may no longer be necessary – Prime Minister Julia Gillard and her Cabinet should have enough momentum to keep policies on track because of the parliamentary situation alone. Arguably, the Cabinet Implementation Unit has become institutionalized at the federal level. Will its role still be of benefit to the new minority government? New lessons regarding the benefit or detriment of an established implementation unit for a minority government could be learned from this case.

It is evident that there is much work to be done in political marketing regarding the delivery of the party's product. Further examination of implementation units as well as other means of keeping promises is particularly important, including the consequences of non-delivery, or delivery in the context of weakening brand values (as faced by the Liberal Party of Canada, for example, from which it has yet to recover). Further exploration in all of these areas will continue to broaden this particular branch of political marketing studies.

Notes

1 The Liberals won 135 seats, the Conservatives 99, the Bloc Québécois 54, and the New Democratic Party 19.
2 The CPC won 124 seats, the Liberals 103, the Bloc Québécois 51, and the New Democrats 29.
3 This was not true after the 2008 federal election. The 'economic update' from the Conservative government included items that were unacceptable to the opposition. This resulted in a 'constitutional crisis' where the opposition parties threatened to topple the Conservatives and form their own coalition government.
4 The five areas were cancer care, hip and knee replacement, cardiac care, diagnostic imaging and cataract surgeries.
5 Personal interview with a former senior advisor to the prime minister.

Bibliography

Axworthy, T.S. (2004) 'Addressing the Accountability Deficit: Why Paul Martin's Minority Government Must Pay More Attention to the Three A's', *Working Paper Series* 11, Kingston: Institute for Research on Public Policy.

Bakvis, H. and Juillet, L. (2004) *The Horizontal Challenge: Line Departments, Central Agencies and Leadership*, Ottawa: Canada School of Public Service.

Barber, M. (2007) *Instruction to Deliver: Fighting to Transform Britain's Public Services*, London: Politicos.

Bardach, E. (1977) *The Implementation Game: What Happens After a Bill Becomes Law*, Cambridge, MA: MIT Press.

Blick, A. (2004) *People Who Live in the Dark*, London: Politicos.

Boaz, A. and Solesbury, W. (2007) 'Strategy and Politics: The Example of the United Kingdom', in T. Fischer, G.P. Schmitz and M. Seberich (eds) *The Strategy of Politics: Results of a Comparative Study*, Gutersloh: Bertelsmann Stiftung.

Cameron, D. and Clegg, N. (2010) 'David Cameron and Nick Clegg: We'll Transform Britain by Giving Power Away', *Telegraph.co.uk*, 12 July. Online, www.telegraph.co.uk/news/newstopics/politics/david-cameron/7884681 (accessed 10 August 2010).

Canada (2006) 'Who is Responsible?' *Commission of Inquiry into the Sponsorship Program and Advertising*, Ottawa: Public Works and Government Services Canada.

CBC News Online (2005) 'Liberal-NDP Budget Deal', *CBC News Online*, 24 June. Online, www.cbc.ca/news/background/budget2005/liberal-ndp-deal.html (accessed 2 September 2010).

—— (2006) 'In Depth: Health Care', *CBC News Online*, 22 August. Online, www.cbc.ca/news/background/healthcare (accessed 25 September 2010).

CityNews.ca (2007) 'Harper Ends Year by Cutting GST to 5 per cent', *CityNews Toronto*, 31 December. Online, www.citytv.com/toronto/citynews/news/local/article/19441-harper-ends-year-by-cutting-gst-to-5-percent (accessed 10 April 2011).

Clarkson, S. (2006) 'How the Big Red Machine Became the Little Red Machine', in J. Pammett (ed.) *The Canadian Federal Election of 2006*, Toronto: Dundurn Group.

Conservative Party of Canada (2006) *Stand Up For Canada*. Online, www.cbc.ca/canadavotes2006/leadersparties/pdf/conservative_platform20060113.pdf (accessed 19 August 2010).

CTV.ca (2007) 'Critics Say Wait-times Deal Falls Short of Promise', *CTV News*, 4 April. Online, www.ctv.ca/servlet/ArticleNews/story/CTVNews/20070403/wait_times_070404/20070404?hub=TopStories (accessed 5 April 2010).

Department of Finance Canada (2005a) 'Delivering on Commitments', *The Budget in Brief 2005*, Ottawa: Her Majesty the Queen in Right of Canada.

—— (2005b) 'Government of Canada Reaches Offshore Agreement with Newfoundland and Labrador', *News Release*. Online, www.fin.gc.ca/n05/2005-7-eng.asp (accessed 15 September 2010).

—— (2006) 'Focusing on Priorities: Canada's New Government Turning a New Leaf', *The Budget Speech 2006*, Ottawa: Her Majesty the Queen in Right of Canada.

Eichbaum, C. and Shaw, R. (eds) (2010) *Partisan Appointees and Public Servants: An International Analysis of the Role of the Political Advisor*, Cheltenham, UK: Edward Elgar.

Esselment, A. (2009) 'Family Matters: The Role of Partisanship in Federal-Provincial Relations in Canada'. Unpublished doctoral dissertation. London, Ontario: The University of Western Ontario.

Goar, C. (2007) 'Ontario's Disappearing Fiscal Gap', *TheStar.com*. Online, www.thestar.com/comment/article/244867 (accessed 1 October 2010).

Government of Canada (2006) *Federal Accountability Act*, C-2, 39th Parliament, 1st Sess.

—— (2008) 'Canadian Communities Now Safer as Tackling Violent Crime Act Receives Royal Assent'. Online, www.tacklingcrime.gc.ca/nr/nr20080228-eng.aspx (accessed 12 March 2010).

Gregg, A. (2005) 'Desperately Seeking Ideas', *Walrusmagazine.com*. Online, www.walrusmagazine.com/articles/2005.06-politics-party-political-system (accessed 8 May 2010).

Gunn, L. (1978) 'Why is Implementation so Difficult?' *Management Services in Government*, November.

Hamburger, P. (2007) 'The Australian Government Cabinet Implementation Unit', in J. Wanna (ed.) *Improving Implementation: Organizational Change and Project Management*, Canberra: ANU E Press.

Hill, M. and Hupe, P. (2002) *Implementing Public Policy*, London: Sage.

Howlett, M. (1991) 'Policy Instruments, Policy Styles, and Policy Implementation: National Approaches to Theories of Instrument Choice', *Policy Studies Journal* 19, 2: 1–21.

Kent, T. (2006) 'The Pearson Decade: How Defeat Foretold Victory', *Policy Options* 27, 2: 13–17.

Labour Party (1997) *New Labour: Because Britain Deserves Better*, London: Labour Party.

Lees-Marshment, J. (2001) *Political Marketing and British Political Parties: The Party's Just Begun*, Manchester: Manchester University Press.

—— (2009a) 'Managing a Market-orientation in Government: Cases in the UK and New Zealand', in D.W. Johnson (ed.) *The Routledge Handbook of Political Management*, New York: Routledge.

—— (2009b) 'Marketing After the Election: The Potential and Limitations of Maintaining a Market Orientation in Government', *Canadian Journal of Communication* 34: 205–27.

Liberal Party of Canada (2004) *Moving Canada Forward: The Paul Martin Plan for Getting Things Done*, Ottawa: Liberal Party.

Lindquist, E. (2006) 'Organizing for Policy Implementation: Comparisons, Lessons and Prospects for Cabinet Implementation Units', *Journal of Comparative Policy Analysis* 8: 421–35.

Marland, A. (2005) 'Canadian Political Parties: Market-oriented or Ideological Slagbrains?' in D.G. Lilleker and J. Lees-Marshment (eds) *Political Marketing: A Comparative Perspective*, Manchester: Manchester University Press.

Mazmanian, D.A. and Sabatier, P.A. (1983) *Implementation and Public Policy*, Glenview, IL: Scott Foresman.

Müller, W.C. and Strøm, K. (2008) 'Coalition Agreements and Cabinet Governance', in K. Strøm, W.C. Müller and T. Bergman (eds) *Cabinets and Coalition Bargaining: The Democratic Life Cycle in Western Europe*, Oxford: Oxford University Press.

Newman, B.I. (1999) *The Mass Marketing of Politics: Democracy in an Age of Manufactured Images*, Thousand Oaks, CA: Sage Publications.

O'Sullivan, J. (2010) 'Tip of the Coalition Iceberg', *Globe and Mail*, 18 August: A19.

The Ottawa Citizen (2007) 'Tories Spend Big on Polls', *Ottawa Citizen*, 4 December. Online, www.canada.com/ottawacitizen/news/story.html?id=5947b76e-5e86-4b0d-8ba0-e95f2d1e5bb2 (accessed 26 April 2010).

Paré, D.J. and Berger, F. (2008) 'Political Marketing Canadian Style? The Conservative Party and the 2006 Federal Election', *Canadian Journal of Communication* 33, 1: 39–63.

Pressman, J.L. and Wildavsky, A.B. (1984) *Implementation: How Great Expectations in Washington are Dashed in Oakland*, third edn, Berkley, CA: University of California Press.
Richards, D. and Smith, M. (2006) 'Central Control and Policy Implementation in the UK: A Case Study of the Prime Minister's Delivery Unit', *Journal of Comparative Policy Analysis: Research and Practice* 8: 325–45.
Savoie, D. (1999) *Governing From the Centre*, Toronto: University of Toronto Press.
—— (2008) *Court Government and the Collapse of Accountability in Canada and the United Kingdom*, Toronto: University of Toronto Press.
Seidle, F.L. (2004) 'Explanding the Federal Democratic Reform Agenda', *Policy Options*, October: 48–53.
Shergold, P. (2007) 'Driving Change to Bring About Better Implementation and Delivery', in J. Wanna (ed.) *Improving Implementation: Organizational Change and Project Management*, Canberra: ANU E Press.
Tiernan, A. (2006) 'Working with the Stock We Have: The Evolving Role of Queensland's Implementation Unit', *Journal of Comparative Policy Analysis: Research and Practice* 8, 4: 371–91.
—— (2007) 'Building Capacity for Policy Implementation', in J. Wanna (ed.) *Improving Implementation: Organizational Change and Project Management*, Canberra: ANU E Press.
Wanna, J. (2006) 'From Afterthought to Afterburner: Australia's Cabinet Implementation Unit', *Journal of Comparative Policy Analysis: Research and Practice* 8: 347–69.
Wanna, J. and Williams, P. (2005) 'Peter Beattie: The Boy from Atherton', in J. Wanna and P. Williams (eds) *Yes Premier*, Sydney: UNSW Press.

24

Advocacy coalitions strategies

Tensions about legitimacy in environmental causes

Émilie Foster, Raymond Hudon and Stéphanie Yates

The topic: marketing and advocacy coalitions in environmental causes

In a context where authorities are pressed worldwide to maintain a balance between ever growing demand for energy and resources and the preservation of natural areas (Aldrich 2008: 6), public infrastructure projects raising environmental concerns, such as nuclear installations or dams, have sparked off, in the last decades, a series of popular protest movements (Hudon *et al.* 2009). In most instances, protesters, increasingly reunited in amateur advocacy coalitions, have been quick to claim that they represent the general will and promote the common good with the objective of influencing decisions to be made. In this perspective, they have occasionally relied on political marketing techniques.

In this chapter, we examine the extent and the form of political marketing techniques used by advocacy coalitions, through five cases raising environmental concerns that took place in Quebec (Canada) over the recent decades back to the 1970s. First, we briefly develop our theoretical framework. Second, we introduce our five cases and sketch our methodology. Third, we analyze and compare the political marketing techniques used by each of the advocacy coalitions involved in our cases and assess their impacts in term of the coalitions' legitimacy. Finally, we draw general lessons from our cases, and assess the impacts of political marketing on politics.

Previous research

Political marketing has traditionally been studied by reference to parties and elections, but a few researchers have recently expanded the field to include interest groups (King 2006; McGrath 2006; Lees-Marshment 2003), associating political marketing with lobbying by interest groups. For Mack (1997: 4), both marketing and lobbying aim at persuading policy-makers. Andrews (1996: 79) argues that businesses are successful in influencing public policy not because they buy influence but because they apply appropriate marketing strategies in their lobbying activities. For his part, McGrath (2006: 108) notes that 'the persuasion function of lobbying can be bound into political marketing theory'. Despite these close links between the two fields of practice, Lock and Harris (1996: 318) observe that political marketing techniques are still neglected by scholars studying lobbying.

Even if they pertain to a comparable logic, political marketing strategies elaborated by interest groups remain different from those used by political parties. Interest groups have no ambition to govern: they are rather empowered to represent certain values (and interests) and to persuade rulers and the public that their stand is legitimate and socially (and politically) acceptable (Foster and Hudon 2010: 5). Accordingly, groups are prone to think of their strategies in terms of political compromises to prevent being subjected to unilateral solutions imposed by political authorities and to attract and retain members and donators. So, they regularly, in relation to 'upstream marketing' mechanisms, have to build compromises internally before attempting to influence the rulers. Since parties aspire to become the rulers themselves, they have broader incentives to attract members and supporters and, structurally, they appear to have an advantage over interest groups in their strategies to influence policy outcomes, referred to as 'downstream marketing'. Similarly to parties, interest groups can be considered as offering a 'product' (in fact, a message or a position) in competition with other groups' 'products'. Comparatively, however, they must establish their legitimacy and the validity of the claim that they speak for a majority of citizens and, by extension, promote the common good.

The multiplication of advocacy coalitions (Hudon *et al.* 2008; Hula 1999) since the beginning of the 1980s has played a significant role in the articulation and aggregation of citizens' interests and their translation into political demands. We define advocacy coalitions as at least two organizations, sometimes joined by lay citizens, working together, often on a limited basis, to influence a specific policy outcome (Hudon *et al.* 2009: 7). By their very existence, coalitions can encourage political dialogue and compromises both internally – between the members of the organizations involved – and externally – with public authorities.

The legitimacy of groups (and coalitions) relies, on the one hand, on the proceedings allowing internal discussions and expressions of dissent prior to their downstream strategies to influence policy outcomes and, on the other hand, on mechanisms and dialogue intended to making arguments or action accepted by the members of a society (Guibentif 2005: 262). In this context, legitimacy can be understood as 'a sense that an organization is lawful, proper, admissible and justified in doing what it does, and saying what it says, and that it continues to enjoy the support of an identifiable constituency' (Edwards 1998: 258).

Political marketing techniques can powerfully contribute in establishing a group's or an advocacy coalition's legitimacy. Lees-Marshment (2001: 1074–76) has developed a comprehensive political marketing model, (CPM) accounting for the extent to which an organization has included political marketing techniques in its operation. She emphasizes that '[m]arketing concepts as well as techniques can be applied not just to how political organizations communicate with their market, but how they determine their behavior or product' (Lees-Marshment 2001: 1074–76). In her model, she makes a distinction between a 'product-oriented' approach, a 'sales-oriented' approach and a 'market-oriented' approach. As for political marketing theory in general, these concepts were developed first and foremost to examine political parties' strategies and positions. However, it turns out that they also appear particularly relevant for the analysis of interest groups' tactics and actions. The three approaches (Table 24.1) make it possible to classify groups on the basis of their strategic thinking and, more specifically, of their use of political marketing techniques. They also make it possible to compare groups between themselves by referring to the different steps that characterize each approach.

In a first category, we find groups adopting a 'product-oriented' approach. These groups typically put their 'cause' at the forefront of their decisions and stick to the initial message promoting this cause. Indeed, these groups, ideological in nature, appear especially reluctant to

Table 24.1 Ideal types of political marketing approaches used by interest groups

1. Product-oriented group	*2. Sales-oriented group*	*3. Market-oriented group*
Step 1: Product design	Step 1: Product design	Step 1: Market intelligence
Step 2: Communication	Step 2: Market intelligence	Step 2: Product design
Step 3: Campaign	Step 3: Communication	Step 3: Product refinement
Step 4: Delivery	Step 4: Campaign	Step 4: Communication
	Step 5: Delivery	Step 5: Campaign
		Step 6: Delivery

Source: (Lees-Marshment 2004: 99–105).

fit their message to their audience, which could be helpful to increase their membership, obtain financial support, or heighten public awareness about their cause. In fact, it seems that they do not care about developing long-term strategies to ensure larger support.

In a second category, 'sales-oriented' groups also tend to stick to the message promoting their cause, regardless of the demands emerging from 'their' political market; however, they appear more prone to resort to marketing techniques. According to Lees-Marshment (2004: 99), groups generally choose this approach to cope with highly competitive conditions for raising funds and holding public attention. Furthermore, the decline of traditional social networks (Putnam 2000) makes it plausible that a number of groups have realized that mass communication has become the most profitable means to reach a maximum of potential supporters.

Finally, in a last category, 'market-oriented' groups try to find 'the best means by which to attract and maintain supporters', using 'market intelligence' to 'identify supporters' demands, design a "product" to reflect the results, and communicate campaign progress to retain their support' (Lees-Marshment 2003: 359). Despite the relevance of the comparison between the business and the interest groups' universes, there are non-trivial limits to this exercise. While market-oriented businesses create products that meet the needs and requirements of their potential clients, interest groups do not create products *per se*: they rather react to given situations (such as a public infrastructure project). This reaction mainly consists of a message, the formulation of which can follow a market-oriented approach (i.e. that groups articulate their message according to the results of a preliminary market intelligence exercise). Hence, these groups can identify the new circumstances they face, through focus groups, surveys, or media monitoring, and adapt their strategy accordingly in order to secure their support. Therefore, they devise strategies very different from the traditional 'product-sales-market-orientation cycle' (Keith 1960, in Lees-Marshment 2003: 360) by making market analysis a central factor of their decisions.

The objective of this chapter is to explore in greater detail how Lees-Marshment's CPM model can be applied to interest groups and, by extension, to advocacy coalitions, through five cases of public infrastructure projects marked by tensions over environmental concerns.

New research: advocacy coalitions' strategies in five cases

Our five cases took place between 1972 and 2009 and involve amateur advocacy coalitions opposing developers' infrastructure projects. The five cases are presented in greater detail in Table 24.2. For each case, our data were collected by means of an extensive survey of media

Table 24.2 Details of the five cases

Case	*Project outline*	*Protest movement*	*Outcome*
Beauport highway project 1970–78	Build a motorway between Beauport (then a suburban municipality east of Quebec City) and downtown Quebec City.	A coalition of citizens called *Sauvons les battures!* (Save the strands) was formed in 1978 on the initiative of the *Association des biologistes du Québec* (Quebec Biologists Association).	The highway layout was substantially modified to take into account environmental concerns.
Champigny project 1972–73	Build a power station in the Jacques-Cartier River Valley, north of Quebec City.	As soon as the project was announced, residents from local communities at the outskirts of the site created the *Comité pour la conservation de la Jacques-Cartier* (Jacques-Cartier River preservation committee), to prevent the destruction of a unique natural heritage.	The developer withdrew its project.
Mont Orford project 2002–07	Develop a pedestrian village with condominiums at the foot of the Orford mountain, within the Mont Orford National Park, located near Sherbrooke (about 150 km from Montréal).	In Spring 2006 the coalition *SOS Parc Orford* urged the government to stop the developer's project in order to protect the provincial park from residential developments.	The developer withdrew its initial project.
Rabaska project 2004–08	Build a liquefied natural gas (LNG) terminal on the south shore of the Saint Lawrence River, in front of Quebec City.	A few months after the developer presented its project, opponents joined under an umbrella coalition called *Rabat-joie*, determined to stop the project.	Governmental authorities have approved the project, which is still pending for gas supply considerations.
Sept-Îles uranium exploration project 2007–10	Prospect for uranium at Lac Kachiwiss, located 20 km north from Sept-Îles, a small town on the north shore of the Gulf of Saint Lawrence.	In December 2007 about a dozen citizens formed a coalition, *Sept-Îles sans uranium* (SISUR, or Sept-Îles free of uranium), which called for the end of the project and ultimately a provincial moratorium on uranium exploration and exploitation.	The developer withdrew its project.

Note: Information and data about our cases were collected in the context of a research grant from the Social Sciences and Humanities Research Council of Canada (Raymond Hudon and Christian Poirier, *Coalitions et groupes d'intérêt au Canada. Dynamiques, enjeux et reconfigurations de l'action politique*).

coverage and of interviews with selected stakeholders. The press clipping was made of more than 1,600 articles for the Orford case, 1,000 articles for the Rabaska case, 170 articles for the Sept-Îles uranium project, 50 articles for the Champigny case and about 30 for the Beauport case. Some 32 interviews were also conducted from February 2008 to July 2010, with an average of five or six interviews for each case. Three additional interviews were done with 'general observers', selected on the basis of their in-depth historical knowledge of environmental issues in Quebec. The interviews were recorded and transcribed (except for the Sept-Îles case), and interviewees were guaranteed anonymity.

For each case, we examine the advocacy coalition's use of 'market intelligence' (research, strategic positioning/targeting), the message developed by the organization (the elaboration phase), and the means deployed to persuade citizens (the 'communication' phase). As already seen, a given organization gives more or less importance to these various elements, and tackles them in a different order, depending on its approach to political marketing. We conclude each case by highlighting the links between the advocacy coalition's approach to political marketing and its perceived legitimacy, which is closely linked to success or failure to stop or modify the developer's project.

Beauport project opponents' strategy as a 'product-oriented' approach

In the Beauport case, the group called *Sauvons les battures!* (Save the strands) appears to have adopted a 'product-oriented' approach. In terms of market intelligence, opponents were on a reactive mode, intervening belatedly in the process – the highway was almost completed! – to mitigate the anticipated impacts on the environment. Their organization was mainly 'amateur', composed of about 30 people, academics and members of different environmental groups, who gathered once a week in a restaurant to discuss the actions to be undertaken. There was no official leader or spokesperson.

In their message, opponents focused on the protection and preservation of the strands; however, their slogan, *Sauvons les battures!*, was not strongly echoed in the population. In a vast majority, citizens in the region were rather enthusiastic about finally being given the possibility to drive freely to the city. In fact, opponents did not devote resources to get information about their political environment, like surveying public opinion or monitoring the government's actions. Having done so, they would have found that their message was going against the tide of public opinion: back in the 1970s, the construction of a highway was considered an essential asset to foster regional economic development.

In terms of communications, opponents did not specifically target publics who would likely sympathize with their message. They gave a few interviews to media and benefited from some press coverage, but again, without a clearly devised strategy. In fact, it appears that the cause was insisted on alive in the public with the help of two local journalists who had insisted on questioning the government's plans. The fact that the issue of the environment was still a new item on the political agenda in Quebec at the end of the 1970s (a Ministry of the Environment was created in 1978) could explain their professional interest in the cause: the protest offered them a good occasion to establish their own reputations and make alliances with this new movement.

On that basis, the project became highly salient. The rightfulness of the project began to be doubted and the government agreed to organize public consultations. More than 300 people showed up at the audiences organized by the newly created environmental public hearings office, the *Bureau d'audiences publiques sur l'environnement* (BAPE). Hence, the degree of local mobilization did not mainly result from action orchestrated by opponents, but was due to the media coverage.

Indeed, protestors never claimed to be representative of citizens and, as such, never put forward upstream marketing techniques that could have helped them to recruit supporters. At one point, they produced a poster showing their slogan (*Sauvons les battures!*) which could have created the impression that the movement was well organized. In reality, protesters called upon people who were part of their own network, such as university professors, public servants, or intellectuals active in a few learned societies. They gathered, in so doing, different types of expertise that provided them with some legitimacy in the eyes of the two local journalists already mentioned.

In view of the number of participants at the BAPE public hearings, public authorities could not help but acknowledge that the protestors' claims were representative of lay citizens' views; accordingly, they modified the highway layout. Hence, despite their weak marketing approach and thanks to the credibility granted by two journalists, the opponents won their battle.

The Rabaska project opponents' strategy as a 'sales-oriented' approach

Opponents of the Rabaska project formed a coalition called *Rabat-joie*. Their action seems to have corresponded to a 'sales-oriented' approach, since they mainly focused on the promotion of their message – or product – without developing a coherent strategy in terms of market intelligence. With several spokespersons and, generally, a weak coordination between the different groups within the coalition, opponents were mainly on a reactive mode that led to some muddled actions. Given their lack of market intelligence, the opponents had no particular targeting or positioning strategies: they just opposed the project, multiplying their communications, but generating little impact, if any. Apart from some efforts to document the risks associated with natural gas terminals (as exemplified by similar projects around the world), the opponents did not have the resources to conduct reliable research and analysis.

Rabat-joie had a central message and stuck to it for the most part of the protest. As such, the coalition's main argument revolved around security concerns such as risks of spills or explosion. From the outside, this message was repeatedly interpreted as a typical NIMBY (not in my backyard) syndrome. This impression was reinforced as one prominent organizer resided on the Orleans Island, a natural heritage area well known for its tranquility and its stunning view.

Nevertheless, opponents of Rabaska tried everything they could to promote their cause and disseminate their message: they multiplied media contacts and interviews, organized concerts to raise funds, created a website, wrote many opinion letters in newspapers, distributed pamphlets to citizens and circulated a number of press releases. In brief, they used many 'media-attention-seeking campaigning techniques' (Lees-Marshment 2004: 99) to 'sell' their message.

At the end of 2007, with the help of national environmental groups like Greenpeace, opponents modified their approach by adopting some principles pertaining to 'market intelligence'. Hence, they tried to operate a 'rise in generalization', a process that turns an argument or an issue that is essentially local and limited into a phenomenon having a general impact, whether at the local, regional, national or international levels (Trom 1999; Lolive 1997). The rise in generalization also enables actors to 'politicize the singular', or to expand the political arena, multiply the actors interested and mobilize more supporters. In that perspective, opponents claimed that the project presented a real danger for the region as a whole, and that it should be an issue involving all Quebec inhabitants. Opponents also argued that Canadian sovereignty in the energy sector was at stake, since the project would require a foreign supply of gas, most likely (if ever) from the Russian Gazprom. The very energy needs of Quebec were further questioned in the climate change context. The rise in generalization was also reflected, finally, by pointing to foreign counter-examples: according to the opponents, the project would never get approval elsewhere, especially in the US, because of its proximity to residential areas.

However, the generalization process appeared severely impaired by the highly complicated nature of the Rabaska project, with experts hired by the developer bringing a counter expertise to the opponents' argument. Moreover, as often observed in this kind of collective action (Chetkovich and Kunreuther 2006: 161), there was strife among environmental groups, some of them giving their support to the natural gas industry, viewed as an acceptable alternative to more polluting energy sources. Finally, as the rise in generalization came very late, it appeared difficult to block decisions already made.

As a result, despite the fact that the population was mainly distrustful of the project during the first year and a half in which it was discussed, Rabaska was later accepted by a majority of citizens (according to all polls realized in 2006–07 in the Quebec region). The developer, who could be considered the winner in this struggle, finally obtained, in early 2008, all the approbations required from local, provincial and federal authorities.

In retrospect, it appears that in the first months of their protest, opponents tried some upstream marketing strategies to recruit supporters, such as the distribution of pamphlets; however, because their main argument, pertaining to security concerns, was viewed as a typical NIMBY reaction, they were not able to make their claim legitimate in the eyes of the public authorities. They did not succeed in being considered representative of the 'silent majority'. Even though opponents relied on volunteer experts to put their arguments forward, their amateurism could not counterbalance the expertise of the developer, well prepared to discredit any opposition to the project.

The shift in the opponents' argument, which followed the market intelligence analysis brought in by national environmental groups, allowed them to make some gains in terms of legitimacy, their struggle having become associated with broader environmental concerns and relying on more solid expertise. As a result, opponents received greater and more positive media coverage and more citizens rallied to the cause. Combined with the huge amount of briefs (more than 600) presented at the BAPE, the protest movement made significant gains in terms of perceived representation.

Champigny, Orford and Sept-Îles uranium exploration projects: examples of 'market-oriented' approaches

The Champigny, Orford and Sept-Îles uranium exploration projects seem to have adopted a market-oriented approach.

Champigny

From the beginning, opponents to the Champigny project demonstrated a position that took account of the limited environmental concerns in the population at large. In such a context, they focused on the importance of preserving the Jacques-Cartier national park, arguing that the developers were infringing the National Parks Law (*Loi sur les parcs*). This message was easy to understand, and movement leaders did everything they could to control it. They also looked for allies, obtaining support from important and credible political or social actors such as the mayor of Tewkesbury (municipality located near the Jacques-Cartier park), who was directly concerned by the project, and the *Corporation des ingénieurs forestiers du Québec* (CIFQ, or the Quebec Forest Engineers' Corporation).

A group of about five people orchestrated the whole protest campaign. They planned concerted actions, using the diversity of their expertise to gather different kinds of information and to target a variety of stakeholders and publics prone to hearing their message. In terms of market intelligence, opponents proved to be constantly conscious of their political environment, seizing every opportunity to quickly react to every move from the developer. With his own international scientific network, one of the opponents helped to build a credible argument. Contrary to Rabaska, the developer was not ready to fight back with proper counter-expertise.

In terms of communication, opponents to the Champigny project were among the first in Quebec to make a systematic use of the media as part of a political strategy aimed at blocking a public infrastructure project raising environmental concerns. One of them was particularly instrumental in ensuring privileged access to local and regional media. In fact, one journalist in the local media was personally involved as an unofficial opponent! He organized – and covered – a press conference that resulted in a decisive shift in the protest campaign: on that occasion, the CIFQ presented a scale model that ridiculed the developer's plan of nature preservation.

Since the Champigny project took place in a context when citizen mobilization in defense of the environment was only just emerging (the BAPE was created a few years after the Champigny case), lay citizens did not appear especially concerned by the preservation of this natural area. In fact, opponents had to struggle against a popular tide of sympathy for the project and its developer (Hydro Quebec, the state-owned enterprise in charge of developing hydro-electricity in Quebec). In reality, despite some upstream marketing techniques to drum up support, such as circulating a petition to visitors in the park, opponents in the Champigny case remained mainly local and confined to interest groups concerned with nature preservation.

Although citizens were not directly involved in the protest, opponents succeeded in creating the impression of general disapproval, and of a huge protest movement supported by public opinion. These downstream marketing strategies increased the legitimacy of the protestors' claims, particularly in the eyes of some public office holders (elected and non-elected), who were paramount in the decision to stop the developer's project. Since citizen involvement in the policy process was only emerging in the 1970s, the protestors' representation was not thoroughly examined by public authorities to shed light on their decision.

Orford

From the outset of its protest action, the coalition *SOS Parc Orford* made use of techniques characteristic of market intelligence by forming a committee in charge of strategic planning. Thus, a few people made all the decisions pertaining to protest actions and citizen mobilization. These decisions were based on public opinion 'surveys', realized through open meetings held on a regular basis with local citizens, wherein the opponents' official position was discussed and debated. Opponents made a thorough analysis of their position in the political environment. Based on this analysis, they set up sub-committees and, relying on volunteer experts from different fields, developed environmental, economic and legal arguments. Fully aware of their insufficient financial resources, they also formed a strategic alliance with *Nature Québec*, a provincial ecology group, which gave them access to more funding.

SOS Parc Orford adapted its message from the outset to rally a broader array of citizens, including those living outside the immediate region in which the project was planned. Through a rise in generalization, the coalition claimed that the Mont Orford Park was public property and that all people of Quebec should feel concerned by the project. Then it was suggested that the privatization of a part of the Mont Orford Park would inevitably lead to the privatization of other national parks. Furthermore, there were efforts to stretch the debate across the Canadian scene by referring, for instance, to the problem of climate change (due to increased automobile traffic). The fact that the Mont Orford Park is geographically close to metropolitan Montreal likely helped the rise in generalization, by 'montrealizing' the case, which brought about broader support for the opponents, notably from national environmental groups.

In terms of communication, the coalition strategically involved well-known personalities with the intention of winning a friendly attitude towards the cause from citizens, which was witnessed by two successful public demonstrations, a petition signed by thousands of people and concerts organized to raise funds. The coalition also developed an exemplary media strategy that ensured steady coverage, with arguments regularly renewed. In retrospect, *SOS Parc Orford* achieved success in 'selling' its message both locally and on a provincial scale.

The coalition's legitimacy relied essentially on a perceived representation of a vast array of lay citizens opposed to the developer's project. Indeed, in its analysis, the BAPE stated that the final approval of the project was conditional upon getting support from environmental groups, municipal authorities and citizens in the region. Thanks to a market-intelligence analysis, opponents were able to develop different types of arguments and elaborate an upstream marketing strategy. Consequently, they were able to recruit thousands of supporters and make it convincing that they were representing a vast protest movement, gathering citizens from across the province. In terms of downstream marketing strategies, opponents went as far as having one of them elected mayor of Orford. Thus, they got a direct say in the authorization process (for zoning, for example), and exerted a great influence on other elected and non-elected public office holders.

Sept-Îles uranium exploration project

From the beginning, opponents in the Sept-Îles uranium exploration case, united under the SISUR (*Sept-Îles sans uranium*) umbrella, were well organized in terms of market intelligence. On a daily basis, the coalition's founder and a few collaborators were making decisions, but a small board of 'governors' was holding monthly meetings to confirm or modify all these decisions. Thus, the opponents' leaders were making sure that they were in-tune with citizens in the region. In terms of messaging, SISUR's leaders wanted to make it clear that they were not against mining development in general, but against uranium mines in particular. They attempted a rise in generalization when appealing to a provincial moratorium on uranium development activities (this appeal was rejected by governmental authorities).

SISUR devoted resources to monitor its political environment and, in particular, to figure out who had to approve or reject the project. The coalition also kept an eye on every government move concerning the project, and based its decisions on this socio-political watch. The opponents rapidly entered into an alliance with other provincial groups concerned by the mining exploration project in Sept-Îles, such as the *Coalition pour que le Québec ait meilleure mine*, *Radon* and *Fondation Rivières*. Physicians from the Sept-Îles regional hospital were also of invaluable help.

Benefitting from these allies, SISUR gathered the expertise necessary to put together a solid scientific background to its stand; however, with the aim of having as much media exposure as possible, SISUR deliberately chose to publish its own press releases, hence multiplying the possibility of being noticed by journalists. Hence, in terms of communication, the coalition's leaders were very active in the media, targeted them according to their high visibility, and made sure that they had regular coverage every week or every two weeks. Opponents managed to be heard and seen by using, apart from press releases, a broad array of tools such as press conferences, petitions, demonstrations, creation of an official website, extensive use of social media (Twitter and Facebook), and dissemination of videos on YouTube. These websites allowed opponents to segment their public by regularly collecting data from their visitors.

The results of this communication strategy were quite impressive: in December 2009, according to a Leger Marketing survey commissioned by the Sept-Îles municipality, 100 percent of people surveyed were aware of the uranium exploration project, and 91 percent expressed their opposition to it (Dupont 2010). Thus, the opponents were successful in raising the public attention and winning citizen support. As such, they won the battle for legitimacy over the developer. Their credibility arose, on the one hand, from the physicians of the region, who rallied to the opposing forces: their argument that uranium exploration poses a threat for citizens' health – and that of children in particular – could hardly be set aside. On the other hand, the collaboration with provincial environmental groups like the *Fondation Rivières* and *Nature Québec* also allowed another set of credible arguments revolving around environmental concerns to be put forward. Furthermore, the opponents' legitimacy was strengthened by their main spokesperson becoming advantageously known in the region, while being also well-articulated and liked: witness the mailing of Christmas cards by citizens who encouraged him to keep fighting against the developer. Finally, SISUR's legitimacy was reinforced by the apparent representativeness of the coalition: the street demonstration against the project, which gathered thousands of people, including the children and babies who were more vulnerable to health hazards caused by uranium, being a tangible sign that the coalition's view was shared by a great portion of the Sept-Îles population.

By contrast, the developer, though sufficiently credible to be allowed by the government to start the exploration phase, was virtually absent in the region. No communication plan was implemented, to the point that interviews solicited by in the media to explain the project were declined. In the end, the project did not arouse any significant support within the Sept-Îles region, with no groups speaking in favor of it. The developer finally discreetly moved away with all its machinery.

Advice for practitioners

Even if our small-*n* study precludes us from overly generalizing our conclusions, our cases show clear tendencies from which we can draw general lessons to be learned by opponents of other public infrastructure projects that raise environmental concerns, in Canada or elsewhere. We believe that a market-oriented approach provides advocacy coalitions with the legitimacy required to influence the decision-making process, while purely sales-oriented or product-oriented approaches seem inappropriate to provide this legitimacy. From this assumption, we suggest that advocacy coalitions could find it advisable to follow five principles relating to market intelligence, organization, message and communication. These principles, presented in more detail below, would enhance their chances to reorient the course of decision in their favor.

First, market intelligence (segmenting, targeting and positioning) should always be prioritized. Before elaborating their message and undertaking communication actions, opponents should review existing polls and the press coverage on the issue at stake. They should also make an assessment of their strengths and weaknesses and identify their potential allies and enemies. After these preliminary operations, opponents should be able to define the most attractive message to rally as many people as possible to their cause.

Second, in terms of organization, leadership should be centralized to be more efficient. Advocacy coalitions should designate a small group of people, ideally fully dedicated to the cause, in charge of orchestrating the whole protest campaign with the mandate to make strategic decisions when necessary. As long as it has the legitimacy to act on behalf of the whole coalition, this 'executive core' is paramount in order to avoid internal disagreements and to manage more or less fierce disputes between big 'egos', thus saving precious resources, energy and time.

Third, opponents should develop a credible message based on thorough expertise in order to counterbalance that of the developer. As shown in our case studies, developers have devoted, over the years, a growing amount of resources to build expertise about their projects. Since opponents' resources are generally more limited, coalitions should take advantage of building a solid network with other environmental groups, which could provide expertise thanks to their larger financial and technical resources.

Fourth, again in terms of messaging, opponents should aim at generalization by pointing out that the project has an impact larger than immediately envisioned, with broader consequences regionally or nationally. If they neglect to do so, opponents are at risk of being tagged with the NIMBY label, which makes it more difficult to gather support from citizens and public officials who are not directly concerned by a given project, a condition to be perceived as a vast protest movement.

Finally, in terms of communication, opponents should be constant in their media appearances by feeding journalists weekly – if not daily – with diverse material (press releases, announcements, presentation of a new study, demonstrations, etc.). Equally important, a coalition should prevent multiple and sometimes contradictory messages by designating one spokesperson. Combined with an effective rise in generalization strategy, continuous contact with the media should lead to national media coverage. The involvement of national media usually marks a point of no return where advocacy coalitions are granted enough legitimacy 'to appear on mainstream political and cultural agendas and register in the collective mind' (Castells 2000: 365), hence being in a position to exert tangible influence.

Impact on politics

The general use of political marketing techniques by interest groups and advocacy coalitions concerned with public infrastructure projects that raise environmental concerns, and the 'market-oriented' approach in particular, can be seen as having both positive and negative impacts on the decision-making process.

On the one hand, a political marketing approach leads interest groups – and coalitions – to care not only about the needs and interests of their own members, but also to take into account trends in the general public and among other social (and political) actors. As already seen, the legitimacy of a group mainly relies on its ability to demonstrate that its claim corresponds with the views of a broad array of citizens. In that sense, we could assert that a 'market-oriented' approach is instrumental in making sure that lay citizens are genuinely represented by advocacy groups, the work of which can help to find a better balance between economic development and environmental considerations when reacting to a new public infrastructure project.

On the other hand, a well-thought out political marketing strategy can also have some pernicious effects, by blurring the dichotomy between general and particular interests (Jordan *et al.* 1996: 72). As such, 'what is done in [supposedly] everyone's interest was harmful and disastrous consequences and is contrary to the ultimate goal pursued' (Hirschman 1991: 67). Indeed, the defense of special interests can be easily hidden beneath the virtuous claim to defend the environment and thus the public good. In these cases, an advocacy coalition's legitimacy follows its ability to make decision-makers believe that it speaks for the majority of citizens, often referred to as the 'silent majority'. As seen above, marketing techniques can help to 'sell' this idea of a broad representation. However, one could be left with the impression of an instrumentalization of the so-called silent majority.

The way forward

In exploring how Lees-Marshment's CPM model could be applied to advocacy coalitions intervening in public infrastructure cases raising environmental concerns, we found that the model is relevant to characterize the political marketing approaches used by these groups. Of course, many avenues could be further explored to refine and develop this type of analysis.

First, our results remain limited since none of the organizations we have examined fits entirely into one or the other of the three ideal types of political marketing approaches (product-oriented, sales-oriented or market-oriented). Future efforts should be devoted to developing more refined indicators to associate an approach with a given organization, based on its actions and positioning.

Second, our five cases pertain to advocacy coalitions opposing infrastructure projects that raised environmental concerns, which is quite a specific field of investigation. Further research could explore the use of political marketing by advocacy coalitions opposing – or supporting – other types of political decisions in different fields: health, economy, education and so on. Extending the field of research into other countries could also provide a useful comparative perspective.

Finally, it could be interesting to study the impact of political marketing on the survival and transformation of advocacy coalitions. Indeed, groups do not aim only at influencing political decisions; they are also preoccupied with their own continuity as an organization in recruiting new supporters and finding funds (Hudon and Yates 2008: 388). Political marketing could be an efficient tool to foster and consolidate these precious assets.

Bibliography

Aldrich, D.P. (2008) *Site Fights: Divisive Facilities and Civil Society in Japan and the West*, Ithaca, NY: Cornell University Press.

Andrews, L. (1996) 'The Relationship of Political Marketing to Political Lobbying. An examination of the Devenport campaign for the Trident Refitting Contract', *European Journal of Marketing* 30, 10/11: 68–91.

Castells, M. (2000) *The Rise of the Network Society*, second edition, Oxford: Blackwell.

Chetkovich, C. and Kunreuther, F. (2006) *From the Ground Up: Grassroots Organizations Making Social Change*, Ithaca, NY: Cornell University Press.

Dupont, N. (2010) '91 % des Septiliens s'opposent à l'exploration de l'uranium', *Canoe.ca: Le Nord Est*, 4 January. Online, nordest.canoe.ca/webapp/sitepages/content.asp?contentid=124005&id=1267 (accessed 8 January 2011).

Edwards, M. (1998) 'Legitimacy and values in NGOs and voluntary organizations: some skeptical thoughts'. In D. Lewis (ed.) *International Perspectives on Voluntary Action: Reshaping the Third Sector*. London: Earthscan.

Foster, É. and Hudon, R. (2010) 'The Use of Political Marketing by Interest Groups', Paper presented at the Annual Meeting of Canadian Political Science Association, Montreal.
Guibentif, P. (2005) 'La légitimité des mouvements sociaux. Un exercice conceptuel dans le prolongement de Habermas et Luhman', in M. Coutu and G. Rocher (eds) *La légitimité de l'État et du droit. Autour de Max Weber*, Québec: Les Presses de l'Université Laval, 259–98.
Hirschman, A.O. (1991) *The Rhetoric of Reaction. Perversity. Diversity. Jeopardy*, Cambridge, MA: Belknap Press.
Hudon, R., Poirier, C. and Yates, S. (2008) 'Participation politique, expressions de la citoyenneté et formes organisées d'engagement: la contribution des coalitions à un renouvellement des conceptions et des pratiques', *Politique et Sociétés* 27, 3: 165–85.
Hudon, R. and Yates, S. (2008) 'Lobbying et patronage: Modes de médiation en contexte démocratique', *Revue Canadienne de Science Politique* 41, 2: 375–409.
Hudon, R., Yates, S. and Poirier, C. (2009) 'Protest Movements and Their Self-Assertions about Representation: four cases related to environmental concerns', Paper presented at the International Political Science Association, Santiago.
Hula, K.W. (1999) *Lobbying Together. Interest Group Coalitions in Legislative Politics*, Washington, DC: Georgetown University Press.
Jordan, G., Maloney, W.A. and Bennie, L.G. (1996) 'Les groupes d'intérêt public', *Pouvoirs* 79: 69–85.
King, S. (2006) *Pink Ribbons, Inc.: Breast Cancer and the Politics of Philanthropy*, Minneapolis: University of Minnesota Press.
Lees-Marshment, J. (2001) 'The Product, Sales and Market-oriented Party. How Labour learnt to market the product, not just the presentation', *European Journal of Marketing* 35, 9/10: 1074–84.
—— (2003) 'Marketing Good Works: New trends in how interest groups recruit supporters', *Journal of Public Affairs* 3, 4: 358–70.
—— (2004) *The Political Marketing Revolution. Transforming the Government of the UK*, Manchester: Manchester University Press.
Lock, A. and Harris, P. (1996) 'Machiavellian Marketing. The development of corporate lobbying in the UK', *Journal of Marketing Management* 12, 4: 313–28.
Lolive, J. (1997) 'La montée en généralité pour sortir du NIMBY. La mobilisation associative contre le TGV Méditerranée', *Politix* 10, 39: 109–30.
Mack, C.S. (1997) *Business, Politics, and the Practice of Government Relations*, Wesport, CT: Quorum.
McGrath, C. (2006) 'Grassroots Lobbying: Marketing politics and policy beyond the beltway', in P.J. Davies and B.I. Newman (eds) *Winning Elections with Political Marketing*, Binghampton, NY: The Haworth Press, 105–30.
Putnam, R. (2000) *Bowling Alone: Civic Disengagement in America*, New York: Simon and Schuster.
Trom, D. (1999) 'De la réfutation de l'effet NIMBY considérée comme une pratique militante. Notes pour une approche pragmatique de l'activité revendicatrice', *Revue française de science politique* 49, 1: 31–50.

25

Branding public policy[1]

David Marsh and Paul Fawcett

The topic: branding public policy

Branding is often thought of as being about the branding of politicians and parties, but in this chapter we explore the branding of public policy and what this means for democracy and governance.

Branding has attracted relatively little interest even in the field of political marketing, although that may be changing (see French and Smith 2008: 210). Holt makes this point most effectively:

> Today branding is a core activity of capitalism, so must be included in any serious attempt to understand contemporary society and politics. Yet, despite its social significance, branding has rarely been subject to concerted empirical examination and theoretical development outside of business schools.
>
> *(Holt 2006: 300)*

Even those, like Savigny (2008), who argue that marketing and branding hinder democracy, nevertheless recognise that we should aim to develop a better and more critical understanding of how these techniques are used, given their increased popularity amongst political actors.[2]

However, before we examine this link in further detail, one other point is important here, namely the relationship between marketing and branding, which is not an entirely uncontentious issue in the marketing literature.[3] Whilst the branding of a city, party or policy is a key feature of the marketing of it, this is a relationship that is not as straightforward in the public sector as it is in the private sector. In the private sector, branding is probably best seen as a marketing tool designed to increase a company's market share/sales revenue. To an extent, the same is true of country and city branding where, in part, the aim is to market a country/city to increase revenue from tourism. However, in the case of the branding of politicians or parties, the aim is to market them to increase support and, particularly, vote share. Finally, the branding of public policy is different again. Policies are marketed, but the aim is usually not to increase revenue, but rather to ensure the adoption and success of a particular policy.

Previous research: branding and politics

The limited literature on politics and branding is not systematic and most of it is, in essence, a sub-set of the political marketing literature, concentrating upon the branding of parties and politicians. In contrast, we develop a heuristic, which identifies four different areas in which branding and politics intersect. A summary of this heuristic is shown in Table 25.1 below (for a fuller development of the heuristic see Marsh and Fawcett 2011).

In what remains of this chapter, we focus on the branding of public policy.

Table 25.1 Four areas wherein politics and branding intersect

Public sector organisations that use branded products and services	*Branding countries, sub-national governments and government departments/ agencies*	*Branding parties, leaders and governments*	*Branding public policy*
Description			
Public sector organisations have developed both their own branded products and services, and have used products and services that have been branded by the private sector, particularly in the HR, IT and finance sectors.	Successful place branding is increasingly viewed as a key competitive asset and can be linked to the move towards a post-modern or late-modern world. Its increased importance is reflected in Anholt-GfK Roper's decision, in 2005, to begin producing an annual Nation Branding and City Branding Index based on 1,000 interviews with respondents in 20 developed countries. Government departments and agencies also increasingly brand themselves and their activities.	The branding of parties, politicians and governments is a key concern of the political marketing literature, which has grown rapidly in the last decade.	Public policies are sometimes, perhaps increasingly, branded either by international organisations or government departments and agencies.
Examples			
Examples include: the Investors in People Standard, which is now used worldwide in over 20 countries, and the European Foundation for Quality Management Excellence Model, which was first developed by industry in 1988, but which has since been adopted by a number of public sector agencies.	Examples of place branding are frequent and range from the national (Australia, Canada and Singapore) to the local (South Australia). The branding of government departments and agencies is just as frequent. To choose one example, the Office of Government Commerce (OGC) in the UK is	Two of the most prominent examples are Clinton and Blair, who are noted for not only branding themselves, but also their parties and the governments that they led.	Examples include: the Truth Campaign in the US; the World Health Organization's (WHO) Direct Observation of Treatment, Short-Course Chemotherapy Programme (DOTS) for tuberculosis control;

Table 25.1 (continued)

Public sector organisations that use branded products and services	*Branding countries, sub-national governments and government departments/ agencies*	*Branding parties, leaders and governments*	*Branding public policy*
	branded and has also used branding to promote its activities, including its 'Best Practice Portfolio'. It owns the intellectual property and trademarks to the generic swirl logo that is used in all of its promotional material.		the UNAIDS Red Campaign; and the Gateway Review Process, which we discuss below.

Example sources

Civil Service College Singapore 2006; Emberson and Winters 2000; Evans *et al.* 2005; George *et al.* 2003; Hides *et al.* 2004; Nabitz *et al.* 2000; Nimijean 2006; Ogden *et al.* 2003; Sanchez *et al.* 2006; Temple 2005.

New research: policy transfer and branding – the Gateway Review Process

Branding appears to play an increasingly important role in the development and implementation of public policy, but it can also feature as part of the process of policy transfer, which is an increasingly important development in public policy (see Dolowitz and Marsh 1996, 2000; Evans 2009). In this section, we examine the case of the Gateway Review Process (henceforth Gateway), which was first introduced by the UK's Office of Government Commerce (OGC) in February 2001 (for more detail on Gateway see Fawcett and Marsh forthcoming; Marsh and Fawcett forthcoming). At the time that interviews were conducted for this chapter, the OGC was an independent office of HM Treasury with responsibility for, amongst other things, public sector procurement and project management (from 15 June 2010 the OGC was based in the Efficiency and Reform Group in the Cabinet Office). Gateway was introduced with the aim of improving the public sector's capacity in both of these areas. It is a particularly interesting case in the context of this discussion because it is an example of a public policy that has been branded and franchised to other jurisdictions both within and outside of the originating country. In addition, whilst the focus of the policy transfer literature has been on why and how a country imports policy models from another country to solve a policy problem, the Gateway case turns our attention to why and how a country tries to export its policies and the role of branding and franchising in this process.[4]

Three critical reports focused on the issue of public procurement policy between 1995 and 1999, including the Gershon Review, which was published in April 1999 (Gershon 1999). In response, the government created the OGC in April 2000 and introduced a new set of best practice guidance for the procurement of major projects in the public sector, which became known as Gateway. In its initial stages, the Gateway process involves the creation of a risk profile, which determines whether the Department can conduct its own review or has to call in an independent team of reviewers nominated by the central Gateway Unit. All reviewers are accredited by the OGC and many are drawn from the private sector. Each project is then assessed at six key decision points or 'gates': start up; business justification; procurement strategy; investment decision; readiness for service; and benefits evaluation. At the end of each review, which lasts between three and four days, a short report is produced for the Department's Senior Responsible Owner (SRO). Initially, these reports would grade projects Red, Amber or Green, although that process has subsequently changed. The report is discussed with the SRO and forwarded to OGC within seven days, with all actions agreed before the Gateway team departs.

Gateway was conceived as a brand from the outset, after a brand consultant gave a three-hour presentation to its first head, Ian Glenday, and his colleagues (Glenday 2007). Given that it was branded, it is clear that it was intended to 'market' Gateway, initially to UK partners and then overseas. As such, franchising was also a key element of Gateway's strategy. These two features of Gateway are clearly reflected in both the trade-marking of the Gateway brand and in the quality of the promotional literature that they produce, which is adopted, but also adapted to varying extents, by all the franchisees.

In the UK, Gateway is overseen by the Gateway Unit in the OGC and operates in central government, local government, the National Health Service (NHS), the Ministry of Defence, the police force, and in the sub-national governments in Scotland and Wales. It is widely seen as a success in the UK (see Fawcett and Marsh forthcoming for a discussion of its putative 'success'), and has been transferred to Australia, first to Victoria and, subsequently, to the Commonwealth, New South Wales, Queensland and Western Australia. There has also been transfer to other sub-state jurisdictions in Australia, notably Brisbane City Council, which has established itself as a leader in this area and is attempting to market itself as a centre of excellence among councils in northeastern Australia. In 2008 it was introduced to New Zealand and the Netherlands.

However, we argue here, and it is a point that we develop at further length elsewhere (see Fawcett and Marsh forthcoming), that there is strong prima facie evidence that, other factors notwithstanding, the way in which Gateway has been branded and franchised helps to explain not only the success of the policy itself, but also the success of its subsequent transfer to other jurisdictions. Certainly, our interviewees in the Gateway Units in the UK and Victoria emphasised this point (see Fawcett and Marsh forthcoming). Interestingly, however, Gateway wasn't branded and franchised in order to raise revenue, as would clearly be the case in the private sector. Rather, the initial intention was to ensure that Gateway was used in a consistent and comprehensive manner as it spread to different parts of the UK public sector. Subsequently, as the transfer became international, franchising was regarded as crucially important to 'preserve the brand' and to ensure that: first, failures, which might reflect back adversely on the process in the UK, were less likely; and second, best practice could be exchanged within a common framework.

The importance that the OGC attached to Gateway, as a brand, was most clearly demonstrated in 2007 when it established a Brand Assurance Team. The Brand Assurance Team was created to protect the integrity of the brand, deal with requests for information about Gateway from other jurisdictions, and encourage the exchange of best practice, or lesson drawing from hubs, including the international hubs. In addition, the Brand Assurance Team was also responsible for conducting a review of each of the hubs every three years. To date, of the international hubs, only Victoria has been reviewed. This occurred in 2007 and it was a light touch review. The franchisee bears the cost of the review, but no other payment is involved.

As emphasised, Gateway is also franchised. Again, franchising is more common in the private sector. Alon (2005) argues that franchising in the private sector is most successful in companies with strong and continuing profitability and for businesses that can be easily duplicated. There has also been considerable work identifying the putative advantages and disadvantages of franchising for both franchisors and franchisees. Most of these factors are not relevant in relation to franchising in the public sector, but some are important. So, it is argued that franchisers benefit from the opportunity to spread their business model at limited cost and from the fact that franchisees have more incentives than employees to make a brand work. The main disadvantage is that franchisers lose control unless they have a careful vetting procedure and regular checks on performance. As far as franchisees are concerned, they are seen as benefitting from the knowledge of, and training by, the franchiser, but the main disadvantage is the loss of control, compared with the option of launching their own brand.

These arguments about franchising have some, if limited, resonance in the case of Gateway. Franchising has enabled Gateway UK to spread the model with limited cost, but the benefits it has enjoyed have not been financial. In most cases, what franchising has helped Gateway UK to do is reinforce its claims about its success and, to a limited, if growing, extent, gain from the exchange of best practice. As far as the borrowing jurisdictions are concerned, the benefits are more obvious. Their costs have been reduced by the fact that the Gateway model and the accompanying documentation were already available, and indeed tried and tested. In addition, the fact that it was widely seen as a success in the UK made it less of a risk. At the same time, borrowing jurisdictions have also retained significant control as UK Gateway has, to date, given then significant flexibility over the way in which they have implemented the model enabling them to adapt it to suit local circumstances.

Advice for practitioners

Measuring the success of branding in the public sector is much more difficult than it is in the private sector. In the private sector, success is judged in terms of factors such as sales, profit and market share, but in the public sector indicators of success are much more problematic. In the case of parties or politicians, the success of branding might be measured at election time or by opinion polls between elections. However, the problem is, perhaps, more complex in relation to the branding of public policy. A public policy may be branded and marketed in order to ensure effective implementation or greater take-up, but it is not usually sold or charged for, so we cannot assess success in monetary terms. Overall, this raises a set of broader questions about how to assess policy success, but this is an under-analysed area within public policy (for attempts to address the issues involved, see Marsh and McConnell 2010; McConnell 2010). However, our key argument here is that success in the public policy field, whether or not branding is involved, is a contested issue. This point can be briefly illustrated by returning to two cases, one based on our research into Gateway and the other based on Ogden *et al.*'s research into the World Health Organization's (WHO) Direct Observation of Treatment, Short-Course Chemotherapy Programme (DOTS) campaign, which was referred to briefly in Table 25.1.

Ogden *et al.* (2003) examine how branding was used by the WHO as part of their DOTS programme for tuberculosis control, which was introduced in the early 1990s. DOTS was strongly contested and resisted by academic and scientific communities, despite Ogden *et al.* (2003: 184) argument that the policy package was explicitly developed with the aim of making it 'simple and marketable to policy makers and programme implementers'. This meant that:

> a strongly political approach characterized what is usually thought of as a technical health policy process. The DOTS campaign was extremely successful in emphasizing advocacy and the marketing of an idea. ... [T]he Global TB Programme managed effectively to

> exploit an important window of opportunity (a TB outbreak in New York) in order to come up with a branded solution by which to solve it. Their success can be measured in the number of countries adopting the DOTS policy to date – 127 out of 211.
>
> *(Ogden* et al. *2003: 186)*

Ogden *et al.* focus on programmatic success: whether the policy achieved its intended outcomes and whether it was implemented as per its objectives. This is perhaps the most common measure of success. For example, it is the same measure used by Evans *et al.* (2005) in their study of the Truth Campaign, which was launched in the US to establish an anti-smoking brand with teenagers. They note that: 'There was a marked decline in youth tobacco use associated with the Truth Campaigns in the states of Florida and Massachusetts' (Evans *et al.* 2005: 188). Again, success is equated here with whether the outcomes of the programme have been achieved.

However, Ogden *et al.*'s analysis also highlights other measures of success (or, to be more accurate, lack of success). For example, they point out that: 'While the marketing of DOTS was, in many ways, hugely successful, in terms of attracting attention and resources for TB, branding had disadvantages and led to further contestation' (Ogden *et al.* 2003: 185). They continue: 'the overt political approach of branding and marketing DOTS led to considerable contestation within a normally technical and relatively consensual policy community, with disagreements between academic, scientists and programme managers at WHO' (ibid.: 186). This suggests that other aspects of the programme were less successful. Hence, the lack of success to which they refer here is less about whether the outcomes of the programme were achieved (indeed, on most counts it appears that they were), and more about process success, or, in other words, the extent to which the programme had legitimacy amongst relevant stakeholders. It is therefore insufficient to concentrate only on financial output measures, or even the outcomes of a programme, when it comes to assessing the success of branding in public policy.

Of course, the problems associated with assessing policy success mean that identifying what makes the branding of a public policy more or less likely to be successful is difficult. Basu and Wang's (2009) work on the branding of public health programmes is important here. Their main concern is to explain why branding in the public sector is less likely to be as successful as branding in the private sector, with particular reference to public health. The weaknesses that they identify include: 'fuzzy brands' that don't sustain interest or retain sufficient loyalty; a bias within public health communication towards one-way, top-down promotion; a reliance on standard communication tools that lack tactical excellence and effectiveness; dominant health control frameworks that fail to accommodate the culture and context of the target audience in the planning, design and implementation of campaigns; and a lack of organisational resources and managerial commitment towards the promotion, protection and ongoing success of the brand (Basu and Wang 2009).

Applied to the public sector more broadly, many of Basu and Wang's conclusions still hold. For example, some of the reason for the success of Gateway as a brand can be explained by the way in which it addressed many of the weaknesses identified by Basu and Wang. First, Gateway is certainly not a 'fuzzy brand'. The jurisdictions that franchise the Gateway Review system are all well aware of the nature of the system and only adopt it after extensive consultation. Second, the documentation associated with Gateway is extensive, thorough and professional, and franchising means that it is used by all jurisdictions. Certainly, no one can mistake the brand. Third, the quality of the documentation, along with the establishment of a Brand Assurance Team, reflects the continued commitment of the OGC and the UK Gateway

Unit to the brand. Here, the Brand Assurance Team plays a key role in ensuring that all of the relevant stakeholders are involved in the process of brand development. For example, reviewing each of the hubs every three years is one way in which the OGC can exchange best practice. This enables policy learning and further strengthens the brand through a process of ongoing revision to the documentation that is produced. This exchange of best practice, and consequent brand development, is also encouraged by the UK Gateway Governance Board, which includes representatives from the international stakeholders group. Of course, the latter is, by its very nature, a virtual group, but this does not stop an extensive exchange of ideas, experience and best practice from taking place (see Fawcett and Marsh forthcoming). Finally, whilst all of these factors are important, perhaps the key reason for the success of the Gateway brand lies in brand communication. While Gateway is branded and franchised, the UK allows the borrowing jurisdictions to adapt the Gateway process to meet their needs, as long as they accept the 14 broad principles of the system. As such, the management of the brand is not top-down and takes account of the different contexts that exist across jurisdictions.

In short, the factors outlined above help to explain the role that branding has played in ensuring the success of Gateway as a public policy. However, what they also do is contribute towards our understanding of the role that branding has played in ensuring that Gateway's transfer to other jurisdictions has been a success. Building on this, the following principles could be suggested for how to make the branding of public policy effective:

- The brand should only be adopted after all relevant stakeholders are aware of its nature and have been extensively consulted.
- Extensive, thorough and professional documentation must be provided about the brand, especially for franchising, so that the brand is clear.
- A Brand Assurance Team should be established, so that all relevant stakeholders can be involved in the process of brand development.
- The government department needs to show continued commitment to the brand.
- There should be a review of the policy at appropriate intervals to enable the exchange of best practice and policy learning; this can help reinvigorate and strengthen the brand.
- Franchisees need to be free to adapt the overarching brand to meet their needs as long as they accept the broad principles of the system, which need to be established at the outset of the programme.

Impact on politics: branding, governance and democracy

Much of the work and growing interest in the intersection between branding and politics has been rooted in an argument about the putative move towards a post-modern or late-modern world. As van Ham (2002: 252) puts it: 'The importance public relations has taken on in public diplomacy implies a shift in political paradigms, a shift from the modern world of geo-politics and power to the postmodern world of images and influence'. This suggests that the links that are developing between branding and politics are probably best understood as part of a longer-term process in which political systems and political actors adapt to the technological, social and political changes associated with what is most often termed late-modernity. As such, the increased use of branding in politics raises immediate questions about the nature of modern governance and the operation of contemporary democracy. Here, we consider the two issues separately.

Branding and governance

Sociologists argue that we have moved into a period of late-modernity characterised by increased complexity and broad changes in economic, socio-cultural and political processes. This debate has permeated political science, particularly in the literature on governance (Pierre and Peters 2000; Bell and Hindmoor 2009) and its relation to late-modernity. Here, the work of Henrik Bang (2003, 2004, 2005, 2007, 2008; Bang and Sørensen 2001) is particularly interesting. Bang sees the politics of late-modernity as characterised by: the replacement of hierarchy by networks as the dominant mode of governance; the hollowing out of the state; a move from politics-policy to policy-politics; the increased fluidity of identity, including political identities; greater reflexivity; changing forms of political participation; the increased importance of the discursive arena for network governance and the associated rise of the role of the media and celebrity politics; and the changing nature and role of parties. These are crucial claims which, to the extent that they are true, change the nature of politics and the political and, perhaps most crucially of all, contemporary democracy.

We are not concerned with Bang's overall argument here (see Marsh *et al.* 2010; Li and Marsh 2008; Marsh 2011), but it is easy to see how branding might play a role in the changes that he describes, particularly in the move from politics-policy to policy-politics (Bang 2007, 2008). For Bang, politics-policy was rooted in an input-output model, in which the focus was upon how pre-constituted political agents, individuals, but also groups, gained access to, and recognition in, political decision-making processes. In contrast, policy-politics is rooted in what Bang terms a 'flowput' model, in which the focus is upon how political elites from the public, private and voluntary sectors are networking in order to produce and deliver the policies wanted by the reflexive individuals characteristic of late or high modernity.

Bang (2007) further contends that the contemporary governance networks that he identifies operate in three arenas: parliamentary, corporatist and discursive. He argues that the discursive arena is becoming more important because it is crucial for attempting to resolve the tension between the complexities of late-modernity and the imperative involved in the need to produce effective public policy. The idea here is that contemporary states are under more pressure to deal with increased complexity and, for that reason, incorporate more elites into the policy-making process.

In Bang's view, in contemporary network society, policy emerges through this networking process, as a result of discursive engagement among the network elite, which utilises their media expertise, in order to convince citizens that they have the answers to the problems that they face. As such, Bang (2007: 8) identifies a shift from an input-output model of politics, in which inputs from citizens, via parties and interest groups, are negotiated and aggregated into policy outputs by government (in his terms a period of politics-policy), to a recursive one in which the network elite, operating through the political system, acts 'in its own terms and on its own values, thereby shaping and constructing societal interests and identities' (in his terms a period of policy-politics).

Bang also argues that the move from politics-policy to policy-politics has led to a significant change in the nature and role of political parties. In his view, parties are no longer channels of representation; rather, they are the means by which governments, and, indeed, oppositions, attempt to convince citizens that they have the best leaders and the best policies. From this perspective, the branding of parties, politicians and policies is increasingly necessary to convince citizens of the quality of the product produced by the party/government.

If Bang is right, then his conclusions raise important issues about the relationship between political branding, governance and democracy. In short, if it does appear that branding is being increasingly used to legitimise policy decisions taken in expert networks, then one might suggest that this may well undermine the foundations of representative and parliamentary democracy. Overall, there is little doubt that the growing prominence of political branding in politics has implications for the nature and future of democracy and this is an issue that a number of authors have discussed, particularly in the political marketing literature.

Branding and democracy

Moufahim and Lim (2009: 764) argue that the branding/marketing literature 'has, for the most part, taken an "instrumental" approach to marketing, focusing on practical, rather than methodological or philosophical, issues'. Consequently, they contend that 'political marketing scholars continue to wrestle with the narrowly pragmatic nature of much of the research conducted by their peers and colleagues' (Moufahim and Lim 2009: 764). This is partly because most of the mainstream literature on political branding/marketing essentially treats it as almost totally analogous to branding/marketing in the business sector, although, as we saw earlier, that is problematic. As Moufahim and Lim (2009: 765) put it, 'Applied to political processes, commercial marketing becomes "political marketing", i.e. the application of business practices to politics and the mindset of "voter-centeredness"'. In contrast, there are two distinct streams in the more critical literature: authors who see branding as involving control by parties/politicians/governments, rather than increased participation/involvement by citizens (Moufahim and Lim 2009; Savigny 2008; Smith 2009); and authors who think that branding/political marketing could extend democracy but, to date, does not (Lees-Marshment 2004). Most of this work, however, has focused exclusively on the branding/marketing of political parties and politicians.

As such, much of this literature tends to avoid the hard, but very important, question of whether this process constrains democracy. Yet, at the same time, what also underpins much of the same literature is the implicit view that branding makes it easier for citizen customers to make a choice between parties/politicians/policies, etc., which subsequently helps to expand democracy, because it engages more people in the political process. In addition, treating citizens as consumers means that parties will be more responsive to their wishes, so branding and marketing can contribute to a better representation of constituents (Lees-Marshment 2001).

Many authors are critical of this view and, indeed, the broader orientation of the political marketing and branding literature. Here, Smith (2009) makes an important point by identifying the tension between the focus on voters as consumers, which is crucial to political marketing/branding, and the need for parties to be 'responsible', particularly in government. Indeed, it could be argued, in a way that fits with Bang's analysis, that this tension is resolved by parties using brands as a means of control, 'selling' policies made in expert networks to citizens.

This argument is developed by Jansen (2008: 131), who argues that nation branding normalises market fundamentalism, with few benefiting. As Jansen (2008: 134) puts it, 'The primary impetus for branding products, companies and nations, like cattle and slaves, is control'. As such, Jansen contends that there is little room for democratic control of a nation's brand identity: 'nation branding is a monologic, hierarchical, reductive form of communication that is intended to privilege one message, require all voices of authority to speak in unison, and marginalize and silence dissenting voices' (Jansen 2008: 134).

This link between neo-liberalism, or economic rationalism, and political marketing/branding is developed by Savigny (2004; see also Scammell 1999: 726). Savigny contends that marketing, and thus branding 'is not adopted to enhance the democratic process; rather, it is a means to an end [the election of political parties/politicians], as such [sic] usage does not necessarily entail democratic outcomes' (Savigny 2007b: 133; our addition in brackets). Consequently, Savigny suggests that political marketing/branding effectively depoliticises the democratic process.

More specifically, Smith and French, who are generally more positive, argue that:

> when branding has been applied in the political marketplace, it can produce unwanted effects such as narrowing the political agenda, increasing confrontation, demanding conformity of behaviour/message and even increasing political disengagement at the local level (Scammell 1999; Lilleker and Negrine 2003; Needham 2005). For some at least, political parties are not soap powder brands and should not be treated as such.
>
> *(Smith and French 2009: 210)*

In contrast, a number of authors are less sceptical, seeing marketing and branding as capable of extending democracy, but currently failing to do so (Smith and French 2009). Much of this argument originates from a post-structuralist position and suggests that late-modernity, with increased information and reflexivity, can give rise to a consumer counter-culture, in which affluence and choice empowers consumers in the marketplace and citizens in the polity. So, Smith and French argue that:

> Even accepting that greater pluralism is possible within the system, achieving greater connection (with a distant political elite), a greater sense of community (in an increasingly atomised society) and authenticity (in a combative political system concerned with point scoring) calls for a root and branch re-think as to what the political brand is for. For example, for consumers to see a political brand as authentic requires it to be seen as 'disinterested'. That is, driven, not by a self-serving motive to achieve power and govern, but core brand values that are of relevance and use to consumers in living their lives and fulfilling their ambitions.
>
> *(Smith and French 2009: 219)*

As such, Smith and French's argument is that marketing and branding can improve democracy, but only if the focus of the political brand is upon authenticity:

> The prize of a more connected electorate, involved in politics and gaining benefits at a number of levels from their brand of choice, is critical for the democratic process. The danger is that an increasingly alienated electorate, for whom political brands have nothing of real value, won't engage enough to let them.
>
> *(Smith and French 2009: 220)*

To date, this discussion about the relationship between branding/marketing and democracy has focused on the branding of parties and politicians, because this is the main concern in the literature. However, it is worth briefly considering how the branding of public policy affects democracy.

Again, this is inevitably a contested area. So, we might see the branding of public policy as positive if it brings increased attention to public health issues like AIDS, or means that the policy is easier/cheaper to implement, because it is accepted by more citizens (who 'buy into the brand'). However, the branding of one policy by drawing attention to that area may lead to more finance for that policy area at the expense of another equally/more important area. More broadly, if one follows Bang's reasoning, policies may be developed in unrepresentative expert networks, which are then marketed to citizens using branding: not a very democratic process.

The way forward

We conclude by suggesting three areas for further research. First, there is a need to engage more systematically with the relationship between branding/marketing and governance and democracy. More specifically, we agree with Moufahim and Lim (2009; see also Savigny 2004, 2007a, 2007b, 2008) that it is essential to develop a more critical political marketing/branding agenda, which is much less instrumental in its research concerns and draws on a broader range of epistemological and theoretical perspectives. This should start with a far more thorough interrogation of the critical relationship between political marketing/branding and democracy.

Second, the branding of public policy appears to be a growing phenomenon. This suggests that the public sector, as well as researchers, need to take it more seriously. Research in this area should start with more empirical work on the different uses of branding in public policy, why we have seen a growth in its use, and its potential benefits and drawbacks for the public sector.

Finally, we need more work on what it means to say that public policy is 'successful', as this is obviously an essential precursor to any attempt to assess whether, and why, a branded policy is successful or not. A better understanding of the factors that contribute to policy success will also help us to better assess what leads some brands to be more effective than others and why.

Notes

1 We are grateful to Carsten Daugbjerg, Jennifer Lees-Marshment, Catherine Needham, Heather Savigny and the two anonymous referees for their useful comments on earlier versions of this chapter.
2 We are grateful to Heather Savigny for this point.
3 We are grateful to both Catherine Needham and Heather Savigny for drawing our attention to the need to, briefly at least, make this point.
4 We are grateful to Carsten Daugbjerg for this important point.

Bibliography

Alon, I. (2005) 'Key Success Factors of Franchising Systems in the Retailing Sector', *Management and Change* 9, 2: 29–36.

Bang, H. (ed.) (2003) *Governance as Social and Political Communication*, Manchester: Manchester University Press.

Bang, H. (2004) 'Culture Governance: Governing Self-reflexive Modernity', *Public Administration* 82, 1: 157–90.

—— (2005) 'Among Everyday Makers and Expert Citizens', in J. Newman (ed.) *Remaking Governance: Peoples, Politics and the Public Sphere*, Bristol: The Policy Press, 159–79.

—— (2007) 'Parties in the Swing: Between Democratic Representation and Communicative Management' Mimeo, Department of Political Science, University of Copenhagen.

—— (2008) 'Between Democracy and Good Governance', *Journal on Political Excellence*, serial online, jpox.eu/component/streams/view,content/cid,211 (accessed 11 April 2011).

Bang, H. and Sørensen, E. (2001) 'The Everyday Maker: Building Social Rather than Political Capital', in P. Dekker and E. Uslaner (eds) *Social Capital and Participation in Everyday Life*, London: Routledge, 148–61.

Basu, A. and Wang, J. (2009) 'The Role of Branding in Public Health Campaigns', *Journal of Communication Management* 13, 1: 77–91.

Bell, S. and Hindmoor, A. (2009) *Rethinking Governance: The Centrality of the State in Modern Society*, Melbourne: Cambridge University Press.

Civil Service College Singapore, Institute of Policy Development Research Unit (2006) *Nation Branding and National Identity: Desperately Seeking Singapore*, Singapore: Institute of Policy Development. Online, www.cscollege.gov.sg/cgl/pdf/Nation%20Branding%20and%20National%20Identity.pdf (accessed 11 April 2011).

Dolowitz, D. and Marsh, D. (1996) 'Who Learns What from Whom: A Review of the Policy Transfer Literature', *Political Studies* 44, 2: 343–57.
—— (2000) 'Learning from Abroad: The Role of Policy Transfer in Contemporary Policy Making', *Governance* 13, 1: 5–24.
Emberson, M. and Winters, J. (2000) 'Investors in People: How a Large Public Sector Organization in the UK Dealt with a New National Training Initiative', *International Journal of Training and Development* 4, 4: 259–71.
Evans, M. (2009) 'Policy Transfer in Critical Perspective', *Policy Studies* 30, 3: 243–68.
Evans, W.D., Price, S. and Blahut, S. (2005) 'Evaluating the Truth ® Brand', *Journal of Health Communication* 10, 2: 181–92.
Fawcett, P. and Marsh, D. (forthcoming) 'Policy Transfer and Policy Success: The Case of The Gateway Review Process', *Government and Opposition*.
French, A. and Smith, I.G. (2008) 'Measuring Political Brand Equity: A Consumer Approach', *Proceedings of the 5th International Conference on Political Marketing*, Manchester Business School, March.
George, C., Cooper, F. and Douglas, A. (2003) 'Implementing the EFQM Excellence Model in a Local Authority', *Managerial Auditing Journal* 18, 2: 122–27.
Gershon, P. (1999) *Review of Civil Procurement in Central Government*. Online, archive.treasury.gov.uk/docs/1999/pgfinalr.html (accessed 11 April 2011).
Glenday, I. (2007) 'Governments Can Deliver: Better Practice in Project and Program Delivery, in J. Wanna (ed.) *Improving Implementation: Organisational Change and Project Management*, Canberra: ANU E Press, 189–98.
Hides, T., Davies, J. and Jackson, S. (2004) 'Implementation of EFQM Excellence Model Self-Assessment in the UK Higher Education Sector – Lessons Learned from Other Sectors', *The TQM Magazine* 16, 3: 194–201.
Holt, D.B. (2006) 'Towards a Sociology of Branding', *Journal of Consumer Culture* 6, 3: 299–302.
Jansen, S.C. (2008) 'Designer Nations: Neo-Liberal Nation Branding – Brand Estonia', *Social Identities* 14, 1: 121–42.
Lees-Marshment, J. (2001) 'The Marriage of Politics and Marketing', *Political Studies* 49, 4: 692–713.
—— (2004) *The Political Marketing Revolution*, Manchester: Manchester University Press.
Li, Y. and Marsh, D. (2008) 'New Forms of Political Participation: Searching for Expert Citizens and Everyday Makers', *British Journal of Political Science* 38: 247–72.
Lilleker, D. and Negrine, R. (2003) 'Not Big Brands but Corner Shops: Political Marketing Politics to a Disengaged Electorate', *Journal of Political Marketing* 2, 1: 55–75.
Marsh, D. (2011) 'Late Modernity and the Changing Nature of Politics: Two Cheers for Henrik Bang', *Critical Policy Studies* 5, 1, April: 73–89.
Marsh, D. and Fawcett, P. (forthcoming) 'Branding and Franchising a Public Policy: The Case of the Gateway Review Process', *The Australian Journal of Public Administration*.
—— (2011) 'Branding, Politics and Democracy', *Policy Studies*, available early online: http://www.tandfonline.com/doi/abs/10.1080/01442872.2011.586498.
Marsh, D., Hart, P. and Tindall, K. (2010) 'Celebrity Politics: The Politics of Late Modernity', *Political Studies Review* 8, 3: 322–40.
Marsh, D. and McConnell, A. (2010) 'Towards a Framework for Establishing Policy Success', *Public Administration* 88, 2: 564–83.
McConnell, A. (2010) *Understanding Policy Success: Rethinking Public Policy*, Houndmills: Palgrave.
Moufahim, M. and Lim, M. (2009) 'Towards a Critical Political Marketing Agenda?', *Journal of Marketing Management* 25, 7–8: 763–76.
Nabitz, U., Klazinga, N. and Walburg, J. (2000) 'The EFQM Excellence Model: European and Dutch Experiences with the EFQM Approach in Health Care', *International Journal for Quality in Health Care* 12, 3: 191–201.
Needham, C. (2005) 'Brand Leaders: Clinton, Blair and the Limitations of the Permanent Campaign', *Political Studies* 53, 2: 343–61.
Nimijean, R. (2006) 'The Politics of Branding Canada: The International-Domestic Nexus and the Rethinking of Canada's Place in the World', *Revista Mexicana de Estudios Canadienses* (neuva epoca) 11: 67–85. Online, redalyc.uaemex.mx/pdf/739/73901104.pdf (accessed 11 April 2011).
Ogden, J., Walt, G. and Lush, L. (2003) 'The Politics of "Branding" in Policy Transfer: the Case of DOTS for Tuberculosis Control', *Social Science and Medicine* 57, 1: 179–88.
Pierre, J. and Peters, B.G. (2000) *Governance, Politics and the State*, Houndmills: Palgrave.

Sánchez, E., Letona, J., González, R., García, M., Daprón, J. and Garay, J.I. (2006) 'A Descriptive Study of the Implementation of the EFQM Excellence Model and Underlying Tools in the Basque Health Service', *International Journal for Quality in Health Care* 18, 1: 58–65.

Savigny, H. (2004) 'Political Marketing: a Rational Choice?', *Journal of Political Marketing* 6, 2: 33–47.

—— (2007a) 'Ontology and Epistemology in Political Marketing: Keeping It Real', *Journal of Political Marketing* 6, 2: 33–47.

—— (2007b) 'Focus Groups and Political Marketing: Science and Democracy as Axiomatic?', British *Journal of Politics and International Relations* 9, 1: 122–37.

—— (2008) *The Problem of Political Marketing*, London: The Continuum International Publishing Group.

Scammell, M. (1999) 'Political Marketing: Lessons for Political Science', *Political Studies* 47, 4: 718–39.

Smith, G. (2009) 'Conceptualizing and Testing Brand Personalities in British Politics', *Journal of Political Marketing* 8, 3: 209–32.

Smith, G. and French, A. (2009) 'The Political Brand: A Consumer Perspective', *Marketing Theory* 9, 2: 209–26.

Temple, P. (2005) 'The EFQM Excellence Model®: Higher Education's Latest Management Fad?' *Higher Education Quarterly* 59, 4: 261–74.

van Ham, P. (2002) 'Branding Territory: Inside the Wonderful Worlds of PR and IR Theory', *Millennium* 31, 2: 249–69.

26

The use of public opinion research by government

Insights from American and Canadian research

Lisa Birch and François Pétry

The topic: government public opinion research

Political marketing research has previously discussed the use of focus groups and polling by political parties, but it has neglected to consider the substantial opinion research commissioned and conducted by government agencies. Government public opinion research (POR) is not well publicised, but provides a significant resource for politicians that can influence policy development, decisions and communication. Paraphrasing the Communications Policy of the Government of Canada (Treasury Board of Canada 2006), we define government POR as applied social science and marketing research using surveys and focus groups, commissioned by government agencies to map the attitudes and perceptions of citizens in order to produce policy-relevant information that will respond to the knowledge and marketing intelligence needs of policy-makers and managers. This definition of government POR includes the gathering of information from civil society for evaluations; however, it excludes citizen consultations involving two-way communication between government and civil society through public hearings, web-based consultations or memoirs, even though some political actors view these state-citizen interactions as legitimate ways of knowing about public opinion on a given issue. Government POR is intended primarily for internal use to improve the knowledge base on which policy-makers and public managers conduct policy. Unlike political polling, which is not government-regulated, government POR is regulated at the federal levels in both Canada and the US to ensure political neutrality and methodological quality. Political neutrality requirements preclude government polling about voter preferences for political parties or candidates. Many of the uses of market research for a 'permanent campaign' presented by Sparrow and Turner (2001) would not be acceptable uses of government POR under current Canadian and US rules and regulations. This chapter will explore this hitherto neglected area of market research by considering government POR within a political marketing context.

Previous research

The existing literature within the political science discipline that links public administration, public opinion and public policy provides a basic starting point for bridging this research gap. Overall, there have been relatively few empirical studies of how executive agencies and bureaucracies actually use POR commissioned by the government. Instead, there is a vast literature on government responsiveness (or lack thereof) to public opinion at the macro-policy level. Three schools of thought can be distinguished within this literature depending on whether public opinion is seen as influencing policy-makers (see Page and Shapiro 1983 and Monroe 1998 for US evidence; see Johnston 1986 and Pétry 1999 for Canadian evidence), or as being influenced by policy-makers (Bourdieu 1979; Chomsky and Herman 1988; Ginsberg 1986; Hoy 1989; Margolis and Mauser 1989), or whether the relationship is seen as reciprocal, with public opinion influencing and being influenced by policy-makers at the same time (Geer 1996; Jacobs 1992; Soroka and Wlezien 2004; Stimson 1998; see Eisinger 2008 for a recent review). This literature relies mostly on data from mediatized polls[1] commissioned by non-governmental policy actors and by the media. The problem is that there is no solid proof that policy-makers use or trust mediatized polls when it comes to elaborate and decide public policy (the government responsiveness literature implicitly assumes this without providing the evidence). In fact, the evidence suggests that policy-makers do not trust mediatized polls and prefer to use other sources of information about public opinion when they make policy decisions (Herbst 1998; Pétry 2007). As we will see, one of the other sources of information on public opinion that policy-makers trust is government-sponsored POR.

A more directly relevant research program focuses on the use of government-sponsored POR by the executive branch of government for strategic communication purposes. In the US, qualitative studies have shown how presidents commission public opinion polls not so much to change policy toward majority opinion, but rather to better promote actions that they believe will improve society, and to steer presidential policy initiatives through the legislative process (Canes-Wrone 2006; Eisinger 2003; Heith 2004; Morris 1997). Cox *et al.* (2002) document the way in which US presidents, members of Congress and interest groups have invoked public opinion about social security. They conclude that these invocations often fail to be based on evidence, and are rarely contested even when they have little factual basis. Jacobs and Shapiro (2000) show how polls were used by President Clinton to 'craft talk' in ways that appealed to the public by appearing to show responsiveness, while enabling the pursuit of his preferred policy objectives.

In Canada, no systematic study of the strategic polling done by central executive agencies (the Office of the Prime Minister and the Privy Council Office) has been published. Roberts and Rose (1995) have studied how the Conservative government of Brian Mulroney used polls to try to change public opinion about the Goods and Services Tax (GST) (but failed to do so). Lachapelle (1996) has shown how Prime Minister Jean Chrétien used polling for strategic purposes in the decision to join the 1991 Gulf War. Ponting (2006) has documented the strategic use of POR and the subsequent invocation of public opinion by the New Democratic Party (NDP) government of Premier Glen Clark in its campaign to 'sell' the Nisga'a Treaty to British Columbia's electorate. Work by Kiss (2009) traces the development of the 'public relations state' in Alberta and shows how government POR activity became centralized and structured during Premier Ralph Klein's era. He argues that the Klein government used POR mainly as a tool for public relations despite democratic responsiveness rhetoric. Finally, in his study of the use of government-sponsored POR on constitutional renewal, the GST and gun control in Canada, Page (2006) argued that the primary purpose of POR was to help policy-makers influence government communication. Since POR was commissioned too late to influence policy design, he argued that the only useful role left for POR was one of marketing the policy and informing the public about it. This begs the question of whether POR may be commissioned early in the policy process in other cases.

While POR may be limited to facilitating political communication in some cases, this is far from being the sole or even the primary role of government POR. Hastak *et al.* (2001) argue that POR use occurs throughout the policy process, although the intensity and the nature of use vary from stage to stage. They analyze three case studies of patient package inserts, direct-to-consumer advertising, and environmental marketing guides. They found that US government agencies use POR to 'build policy mandates' at the agenda-setting stage, during which the government chooses which problems will require state action. They argue that policy-makers tend to commission large-scale conventional surveys at that stage in order to match the competing influence of polls commissioned by other policy actors. They show that US government officials use survey research to variable degrees at the subsequent policy formulation, execution and enforcement stages, depending on factors such as the amount of controversy and the degree of complexity associated with the policy initiative. Similarly, in a study of the use of public opinion research by the Canadian Biotechnology Secretariat, Medlock (2005) finds that POR is used in communication (to inform senior management and to shape future communication strategies) as well as in policy development (to provide background information and context, to supply evidence to support policy decisions and to forecast areas of controversy). Rothmayr and Hardmeier (2002) analyze polling by the Swiss government and find that public relations is only one of four functions of the government POR utilization process, the others being essentially information functions for planning for future policy decisions, evaluating existing policies essentially to gather information to plan future policy decisions, and observing the development of certain problems in a specific policy area. They found that the impact of polls on decisions was more likely when the commissioning department had the power to implement decisions based on poll results.

Inspired by scientific work in the field of knowledge utilization, Birch and Pétry (2010, 2011b) show how policy-makers use POR findings for strategic, instrumental, conceptual and managerial purposes to develop, design, implement and evaluate policies and their instruments. This includes a surveillance function following implementation. They find that there is a link between POR utilization, the knowledge needs at each stage in the policy cycle, and the nature of the decisions involved at each stage of the policy cycle, just as Fafard (2008) theorized. Their demonstration is based on the analysis of POR utilization by Health Canada in tobacco control. Their work in progress extends the analysis to other health policy issues. To explain how government POR is used and the kind of impact it has on policy, future research needs to explore explanatory factors such as the level of opposition to an initiative, the activities of interest groups, the complexity of an initiative, the time factor and perceptions of citizens' knowledge and competency regarding an issue as well as the organizational capacity of the government agency for research uptake.

New research: government POR in Canada and the US in practice and theory

Since government POR is a relatively new area of research, this section simply explains and illustrates the nature, source and implications of government POR conceptually and also empirically with Canadian and US examples.

Types of government POR

In practice, government POR is quite varied in nature by the research objectives pursued, the methods used and the data produced. Government POR sometimes comes in the form of survey questions purchased from syndicated polls. In Canada, a moratorium on new syndicated contracts was imposed in 2008 to ensure better coordination of syndicated POR across departments to avoid duplication. At the time of writing, all Canadian government POR comes in the form of custom research tailored to particular objectives that are associated with specific policy needs which range from better understanding a problem or target group, to designing possible policy solutions then monitoring and evaluating the impact of policy decisions. Custom POR entails quantitative, qualitative and mixed research designs, some of which can be quite sophisticated and most of which defies preconceived ideas that equate POR with syndicated polls. The examination of hundreds of government POR reports led us to conclude that this POR is a form of applied social and marketing research.

Unlike multi-client syndicated POR, custom POR is exclusively sponsored by single government agencies that own the property rights (the rights to syndicated polls are owned by polling houses). US and Canadian regulations governing this POR activity have similar objectives to guarantee the quality of the research, the transparency and the political neutrality of government-sponsored custom POR. US regulation seems preoccupied with 'paperwork reduction' and over-soliciting citizens for information, whereas recent Canadian regulation appears focused on value-for-money considerations. Since 2008, all custom POR proposals must have ministerial approval. In the US (less in Canada) it is not uncommon to find custom POR reports that present a secondary analysis of POR commissioned by the media or non-governmental actors made available through the Office of Management and Budget Information Collection Services at the White House.

To prevent the party in power from using government POR resources to collect politically sensitive information, periodic independent assessments of government POR are performed by the Auditor-General of Canada or by independent advisors (Paillé 2007). In the US, the Comptroller-General has not investigated the federal government's POR activity. However, a detailed examination of the content of government POR reports suggests that safeguards similar to those found in Canada are enforced. In Canada, unlike the US, the administrative guidelines for POR include the obligation to make all reports available to the public. There is evidence of POR production in the Canadian provinces and US states, but research on its utilization is sparse and what is available suggests that there seems to be considerable variation in the regulations and disclosure rules for government-sponsored POR across jurisdictions.

Sources of government POR

POR may be conducted internally within government agencies or externally through contracts to private suppliers. In Canada, the dominant pattern is to contract-out to private suppliers. Only the largest agencies have the capacity to commission the data collection and then conduct their own analysis. Private suppliers in Canada are almost exclusively polling firms. There are specializations among these firms by type of research (e.g. general POR or advertising) and by type of clientele (e.g. youth, first nations). In the US there is a wide variety of supply options. In addition to internal production capacity, federal departments contract-out to private research firms according to their area of expertise as well as to university-based POR centres. In Canada, academic research centres and think-tanks are increasingly left out of government POR activity, at least at the federal level (it was not always like that), whereas in the US government agencies are more willing to share government POR with private think-tanks and university-based research centres.

How government POR differs from mediatized POR

Government-sponsored POR seems to differ from mediatized POR by its higher overall level of quality. For example, a systematic inquiry of over 200 Canadian health surveys sponsored by Health Canada, private interest groups and by the media reveals that the frequency of measurement errors (ambiguous survey questions, unbalanced answer choices, absence of split sample rotation) is lower in government polls (Birch and Pétry 2011b). The difference in the level of quality can be attributed in part to the fact that pollsters often get larger amounts of time, money and resources to conduct government-sponsored POR than what they get to conduct surveys sponsored by interest groups and the media. Another consideration is the credibility of government-sponsored surveys. The accuracy of government POR, and the credibility of the pollster who does the research, is ultimately sanctioned by the success of the policy, program or instrument that it helped achieve. This ultimate sanction may constitute an incentive to produce survey results that are valid and accurate. By contrast, political polls conducted for media release are followed by no tangible outcome. Often the results of privately sponsored polls are mobilized in the media as 'news' by policy actors seeking to influence the public agenda and debate on a particular issue. However, there is very little really to test the validity and accuracy of their results, or to sanction the credibility of the pollsters who administer these polls, and the policy actors who sponsor them. The incentive to achieve and maintain high quality standards may not be as elevated in mediatized polls, since their purpose is to influence agendas, not to produce policy-relevant knowledge for policy decisions and implementation. One last consideration is that government polls are strictly regulated, whereas polls conducted on behalf of private actors or as a joint-venture between a polling firm and a media network are not subject to regulations requiring political neutrality, periodic and independent reviews of POR practices, and full transparency through the public disclosure of POR reports.

Government POR in Canada and the US

In Canada, federal government POR expenditures have rapidly expanded since the mid-1990s. The annual cost of POR increased from C$4 million in 1993–94 to C$31 million in 2006–07. Since then, the POR budget has been drastically reduced by the Harper government, which has also imposed new, stricter POR contracting rules. Regrettably, comparable data is not readily available for the US because there is no overarching institution that gathers and centralizes information about government POR in the US.

The rapid rise of POR capacity in the Canadian federal government coincided with new discourses on governance, result-based management, citizen consultation and engagement and, more recently, evidence-based policy. Organizational thinking and arrangements in the Canadian federal government have incorporated many of these ideas into public management policies such as the Communications Policy of the Government of Canada (Treasury Board of Canada 2006). These policies encouraged the institutionalization of POR through the development of specialized POR units within departments and the creation of the Public Opinion Research Directorate of Public Works and Government Services (PWGS). The PWGS directorate acts as a broker for POR for all departments, provides best practices guidelines, offers webinar training and publishes annual reports on government POR activity. POR institutionalization in the Canadian public sector was seen as a means of 'focusing on citizens, embracing a clear set of public service values, managing for results and ensuring responsible spending' (Treasury Board of Canada 2000). Despite this institutionalization of POR, the link between POR capacity and political marketing as well as the potential of POR for political marketing and strategic management escaped most of the Canadian public officers who were surveyed by Mintz *et al.* (2006). Yet the Communications Policy, which is easily accessible online, specifically identifies government POR as policy tool in the following passage:

> Public opinion research helps the government to better understand Canadian society and to identify citizen needs and expectations. It is used to assess the public's response to proposals or to possible initiatives; to assess the effectiveness of polices, programs and services; to measure progress in service improvement; to evaluate the effectiveness of communication activities such as advertising; and to plan and evaluate marketing initiatives, among other applications.
>
> *(Treasury Board of Canada 2006)*

Recent research using a mixed method design with interviews, document analysis, content analysis of government POR reports, and cross-analysis of POR reports relative to policy decisions suggests that there is such utilization, although the practitioners may not employ political marketing lingo to describe their activities (Birch and Pétry 2010, 2011a; Birch 2010). Let us illustrate this with a discussion of salient findings from a case study of Health Canada's internationally acclaimed health warning messages (HWM) on cigarette packages.

The case of graphic health warning messages

Between the late 1990s and 2010 extensive, pioneering POR activity guided the development of the first generation of HWM implemented in 2000, monitored their impact on the general public and smokers, then contributed to the design of the second generation of HWM announced in 2010. In this case, POR is first used conceptually to allow decision-makers to acquire a better understanding of problems surrounding cigarette labelling and to appreciate the range of possible solutions. There is also evidence of conceptual use during the early stages of the HWM program, when extensive use of POR took place to understand smokers and what motivates them to smoke and to quit. Interestingly, HWM were rated by Canadians as less effective than smoking cessation instruments (tax breaks for cessation) and exhortation instruments (information campaigns and TV advertisements). This did not deter Health Canada from moving forward to impose new warning messages on the basis of scientific evidence of labelling effects.

After it was decided to proceed with the HWM program, POR was used extensively to assist in micro decisions about the design of the new graphic messages. This use of POR can be characterized as instrumental use in which one is able to link specific POR findings to the adoption of discrete decisions about specific policy instruments. As many as 68 distinct messages and graphics were tested through a series of 35 focus groups across Canada in 1999–2000. The data show that two-thirds of the messages that were favourably assessed by focus group participants were retained, while virtually all the retained messages that had received mixed or negative reviews were modified according to focus groups' recommendations, which does suggest some instrumental use of POR findings (the χ^2 test for favourably reviewed messages retained vs. negatively reviewed messages rejected was statistically significant at $p = .05$). The opinion research design was carefully constructed to also study how different target groups within the population understood and responded to HWM using focus groups, surveys and mixed research methods. This reflects a sophisticated understanding of who needs to be reached if the overall policy objectives of tobacco control are to be achieved. It also shows an application of marketing notions in policy instrument design.

There was also some strategic use of POR to justify regulatory change for tobacco labelling. The policy actors who we interviewed all ranked the HWM among the top policy instruments for an effective, comprehensive tobacco control strategy, alongside taxation, other retail controls and smoking bans. Notwithstanding this ranking, comments from some non-governmental organization (NGO) actors indicate that they would have preferred even more audacious labels, some of which were pre-tested through their own POR. The story of Canadian HWM is cited on the World Health Organization's website as a 'best practice' in tobacco control. The effectiveness of the Canadian warnings is supported by empirical evidence from their own quasi-experimental scientific work, as well as POR commissioned by the Australian government and independent scientific studies.

POR was also used for surveillance purposes. Successive waves of survey research preceded and followed implementation, with the main objective being 'to provide information to assist in the evaluation of the impact of HWM on tobacco packaging'. Time-series analyses of survey data trends led policy-makers to anticipate the eventual wear-out of some warning messages. This prompted the government's decision to begin a new regulatory proposal process in 2004. A first round of focus groups allowed the testing of a dozen new warning concepts. The concept that came out the strongest in these focus groups inspired the creation of some 50 messages, which were subjected to subsequent testing in 40 focus groups to determine which ones, in the words of one policy actor, 'are the most effective, which are the most noticeable and resonate more with smokers'. Subsequent POR studies examined the impact of the size of warning messages and the impact of 50 mock-ups of potential health warnings and 24 mock-ups of potential health information messages. Every last detail of the content and visual packaging of these messages was subjected to extensive testing with the target groups. There were tensions behind the scenes as the tobacco industry lobbied against new labels and anti-tobacco groups pressured for even larger ones. Nonetheless, on 30 December, 2010 (a year and a half after the last POR work was completed), Leona Aglukkaq, the Canadian minister of health, presented new regulatory submission with 16 new health warnings and health information messages which will cover 75 percent of the cigarette packages as opposed to 50 percent, and which will be used on a rotational basis. These new messages will include more health information with links to free cessation services by phone and internet as suggested in the POR.

This example demonstrates how the surveillance work is linked proactively to work in regulatory development and thus overall policy management. The POR activity that led to the successful first generation of HWM provided a model for subsequent POR to design the second generation of messages. Again, the results of the first focus groups influenced the choice of marketing concepts retained for the new HWM. These concepts were transformed into 50 mock-ups of health warnings and 14 mock-ups of health information messages which were subjected to extensive quantitative and qualitative testing with smokers, who were classified into various market segments by variables such as gender, age and language to assess the effectiveness of these final mock-ups and their ability to resonate with each target group. Similar work is in progress to develop warning messages for smokeless tobacco products. This case attests to instrumental use through a rigorous, structured approach to policy development. It also demonstrates how POR data gathered for surveillance use loops back into the policy process. Similar stories can be told for policy initiatives for smoking cessation, second-hand smoke and smoking bans, as well as the regulation of 'light' and 'mild' descriptors.

Preliminary work exploring the use of POR in US tobacco control suggests very similar patterns. We identified US equivalents of the Canadian wave surveys designed for the monitoring and surveillance of smoking behaviour among adults and youth. We also found evidence of survey and focus group work to better understand the target audiences, to design campaign tools and to evaluate their impact in the context of social marketing initiatives. Whereas in Canada this work is linked to Health Canada's tobacco control program, in the US the Centers for Disease Control is the key federal agency. In both contexts, tobacco control is a policy matter that benefits from a permissive consensus among the electorates (Studlar 2002), which may facilitate the utilization of POR for instrumental and conceptual purposes in policy design, implementation and evaluation. However, POR utilization patterns may be quite different in contexts where there is more controversy.

What does the case of graphic health warning messages tell us?

From this discussion, it is clear that governments use POR in more varied and complex ways than to slavishly pander to or cynically manipulate public opinion as is often assumed. Granted, policy-makers sometimes use POR to craft their messages – to promote and legitimize their own preferred policy choices; however, they also use POR for the very different purpose of helping in the design, implementation and evaluation of policy instruments. This includes analyses of target clienteles for policy initiatives, customer/citizen satisfaction surveys, social marketing activities and, occasionally, public relations tools. Second, contrary to popular belief, even if governments still use POR commissioned by private actors for media release, governments sponsor their own POR more and more frequently. The fact that custom government POR results are not reported in the media suggests that this type of POR is needed less for public relations activities and more for improving the quality and effectiveness of public policies.

Advice for practitioners

There is no guarantee that the use of government POR will improve the quality and effectiveness of public policies as it did in the HWM case, but the case provides useful indications as to how the appropriate use of government POR may contribute to better policy-making. If governments are to use POR effectively as a tool for policy decisions and management, they must first formally recognize POR as a means of producing valuable, policy-relevant knowledge. To adapt marketing language, they must come to see how POR can be a powerful tool for policy (marketing) intelligence. In other words, they must see POR as more than just a tool for improving communications and public relations. Second, they must institutionalize POR in ways similar to the institutionalization of the policy evaluation process (Furubo *et al.* 2002). This entails four important elements, as follows:

- requiring that POR becomes a compulsory policy input and establishing clear standards for the quality of research, the presentation and the disclosure of final reports;
- developing POR expertise within the bureaucracy through training, networking among POR specialists and sharing of lessons learned through POR production and use in different policy areas with various clienteles and target groups;
- fostering a learning-oriented organizational culture that values research entrepreneurship and quality data gathered through rigorous methodology over anecdotal evidence about the attitudes, opinions and behaviour of citizens; and
- last but not least, allocating adequate, reliable funding for research initiatives and programs.

To protect democratic values by preventing the use of public funds for POR that would confer an unfair advantage to the governing party rather than contributing to the higher goal of serving the public interest through better designed and more effective policies, government POR activity must be subject to public scrutiny. This requires clear restrictions on partisan uses of POR as well as easy, transparent, public access to government POR reports within a reasonable time delay.

Impact on politics

Government POR can produce highly specialized knowledge about the beliefs, attitudes, opinions and behaviours of the general public as well as the specific groups targeted by any given policy. This knowledge can facilitate bringing evidence into policy and thus developing policies and mixes of policy instruments that are grounded firmly in the empirical reality of each particular policy context. It can also facilitate the policy management process through enhanced monitoring of the effectiveness of policy instruments and of general trends in the policy environment. When government POR is carefully designed to provide data throughout the policy cycle, it contributes to more effective, responsive and responsible policies, which in turn may enhance the legitimacy of policy decisions. When the government must decide whether to act or not in response to a new issue, its final decision will gain legitimacy in three cases. These arise when: (1) the government adopts policies that reflect citizens' preferences; (2) the government offers good explanations for choosing a different option; (3) the government benefits from a permissive consensus and thus adopts a policy that is within the public's zone of acquiescence for government intervention (Birch 2010, 2012; see Stimson 1998 for zones of acquiescence). In all three cases, POR conducted to understand citizens' preferences and their thresholds or comfort zones for state action (or inaction) can provide useful input into the decision-making process. In cases where a decision to act is rendered, legitimacy will depend on how the policy is designed, implemented and evaluated. The legitimacy of policy decisions at these stages depends on the state bureaucracy's respect of accepted regulatory procedures including public consultations as required, its capacity to justify decisions regarding policy instruments, often using scientific knowledge, and the subsequent effectiveness of these instruments in attaining policy objectives (Schrefler 2010). Again, POR can generate specialized knowledge to guide the bureaucracy in its decisions and actions by generating policy-specific data about what works with whom in which context and what does not, as well as data about policy outcomes and ways to improve them.

In political marketing lingo, government POR can enlighten decision-making and enhance governance by clarifying the wants and needs of citizens, identifying the characteristics of market segments (policy target groups) and their special needs, developing the best product (policy) to meet those needs, determining the best delivery channels (implementation), assessing the product's impact, refining the product as needed, facilitating market-oriented communication, producing market (policy) intelligence and ensuring continual market consultation. To conclude, then, government POR has the potential to contribute to policy decisions that are both responsive and responsible – that is, responsive to citizens' policy needs and responsible given the presumed preference of citizens for the effective and efficient use of public funds to attain legitimate policy goals.

The way forward

The scientific study of the government-sponsored POR and its utilization is an emerging field of study situated at the crossroads between political marketing, political science, political communication, but also public administration. The study of POR has much to gain by borrowing from the vast public administration literature, particularly on the utilization of knowledge, scientific research and evaluation. By considering POR as one of the means of producing applied policy-relevant knowledge for government, research in this field may also contribute to larger questions about knowledge utilization in policy-making. In particular, we believe that categorizing government POR use as either instrumental, conceptual or strategic opens new avenues of research about government POR and enables comparisons with studies on the utilization of evaluation, scientific research and knowledge in policy. Future studies could analyze the production and utilization of government POR as well as the organizational capacity for knowledge utilization and the POR apparatus of government at the executive and bureaucratic levels. The guiding questions for these future studies could be: When, how and why is government POR utilized (or ignored) by public managers and decision-makers? What are the determinants of POR utilization by government? What are the implications of government POR utilization for the quality or effectiveness of public policies, for legitimating these policies and, ultimately, for democracy?

Conceptually, future research on the use of government POR ought to distinguish between macro political decisions about whether to act or not, which are usually made at the executive level, and micro political decisions about the fine details of policy instruments, which are usually made at the bureaucratic level. Conceptual designs must include a clear distinction between policy instruments, such as regulations, incentive schemes and social marketing, which are linked to specific policy goals, and communication activities focused strictly on state-citizen or state-media relations. Finally, our early explorations of this field suggest that the following variables may influence POR utilization: the nature of the policy area, the degree of conflict around the issue or sub-issue, the ideological orientation of the government, POR budgets and regulations, the distribution of competencies between orders of government, the policy environments and organizational capacity of government departments, the level of decision, the type of policy instrument, the stage in the policy cycle, the dynamics of policy actors in networks, issue salience and election proximity.

As for study, training and practice, while specific courses introduce students to the theories and empirical research on public opinion and democracy, it is amazing to note that very few political science departments offer courses on knowledge utilization and political and social marketing. After examining the current offer of social marketing courses in the US, Kelly (2009) suggested that this field would benefit greatly from the development of a bank of detailed case studies illustrating the different ways in which social marketing is applied in the real world. She found that most courses teach the methods of social marketing and require students to produce a social marketing plan as a main assignment. Desphande and Lagarde (2008) surveyed 477 practitioners, mainly in Canada and the US, who clearly expressed the need for training regarding marketing basics, research issues such as audience analysis, formative and evaluation research methods, marketing strategy, the application of the four Ps of marketing, and managerial issues linked to budgeting, funding and ethics. Although these studies focused on training for social marketing, we expect that similar training needs apply for POR when it is associated with political marketing or with public administration. If Lees-Marshment's (2003) vibrant plea in favour of integrating political science and management science is to become a reality, academics and practitioners will need tailored training that explicitly shows how to bridge the two.

Thus, the development of applied courses on POR as a tool of governance and management may facilitate bridge-building efforts. Such courses should offer modules on POR methodology, technical quality standards and POR utilization for policy decisions, be they in the context of political and social marketing, routine program management or policy innovation. We would encourage the development of a bank of case studies of POR utilization with specific examples of social and political marketing as well as a bank of decision-making simulations which would require students to determine POR needs for a given policy issue, to assess the quality of POR, and then to use POR results to make policy decisions at the macro and micro levels.

Note

1 By mediatized polls, we mean surveys that are publicized through any form of mass media. In most cases, one of the primary purposes of such surveys is to gain media attention.

Bibliography

Birch, L. (2010) L'utilisation de la recherche sur l'opinion publique dans les politiques publiques: Le cas du programme du contrôle du tabagisme. Doctoral Dissertation, Université Laval, Quebec City, Canada.

—— (2012, forthcoming) 'Does Public Opinion Research Matter: The Marketing of Health Policy', in T. Giasson, J. Lees-Marshment and A. Marland (eds) *Political Marketing in Canada*, Vancouver: UBC Press.

Birch, L. and Pétry, F. (2010) 'Exploring the Use of Public Opinion Research in Canadian Tobacco Control', *Alert! Magazine of the American Marketing Research Association*, March: 19–21.

—— (2011a) 'L'utilization des entretiens de groupe dans l'élaboration des politiques de santé', *Recherches qualitatives* 29, 3: 103–32.

—— (2011b, forthcoming) 'Exploring the Use of Polls and Focus Groups in Healthcare Policymaking'.

Bourdieu, P. (1979) 'Public Opinion Does Not Exist', in A. Mattelart and S. Siegelbaum (eds) *Communication and Class Struggle: Vol. 1 Capitalism, Imperialism*, New York: International General, 1240–59.

Canes-Wrone, B. (2006) *Who Leads Whom? Presidents, Policy, and the Public*, Chicago: University of Chicago Press.

Chomsky, N. and Herman, E. (1988) *Manufacturing Consent: The Political Economy of the Mass Media*, New York: Pantheon Books.

Cox, F.L., Barabas, J. and Page, B.I. (2002) 'Invoking Public Opinion: Policy Elites and Social Security', *Public Opinion Quarterly* 66, 2: 235–64.

Desphande, S. and Lagarde, F. (2008) 'International Survey on Advanced-Level Social Marketing Training Events', *Social Marketing Quarterly* 14, 2: 50–66.

Eisinger, R.M. (2003) *The Evolution of Presidential Polling*, New York: Cambridge University Press.

—— (2008) 'The Use of Surveys by Governments and Politicians', in Wolfgang Donsbach and Michael Traugott (eds) *The Sage Handbook of Public Opinion Research*, Thousand Oaks, CA: Sage Publications, 487–195.

Fafard, P. (2008) *Evidence and Healthy Public Policy: Insights from Health and Political Sciences*, Quebec: National Collaborating Centre for Healthy Public Policy, Canadian Policy Research Networks.

Furubo, J.E., Rist, R.C. and Sandahl, R. (eds) (2002) *International Atlas of Evaluation*, New Brunswick, NJ: Transaction Publishers.

Geer, J. (1996) *From Tea Leaves to Opinion Polls: A Theory of Democratic Leadership*, New York: Columbia University Press.

Ginsberg, B. (1986) *The Captive Public: How Mass Opinion Promotes State Power*, New York: Basic Books.

Hastak, M., Mazis, M.B. and Morris, L.A. (2001) 'The Role of Consumer Surveys in Public Policy Decision Making', *Journal of Public Policy and Marketing* 20, 2: 170–85.

Heith, D.J. (2004) *Polling to Govern: Public Opinion and Presidential Leadership*, Stanford, CA: Stanford University Press.

Herbst, S. (1998) *Reading Public Opinion: How Political Actors View the Democratic Process*, Chicago: University of Chicago Press.

Hoy, C. (1989) *Margin of Error. Pollsters and the Manipulation of Canadian Politics*, Toronto: Key Porter.

Jacobs, L. (1992) 'The Recoil Effect: Public Opinion and Policy Making in the United States and Britain', *Comparative Politics* 24: 199–217.

Jacobs, L. and Shapiro, R. (2000) *Politicians Don't Pander: Political Manipulation and the Loss of Democratic Responsiveness*, Chicago: University of Chicago Press.

Johnston, R. (1986) *Public Opinion and Public Policy in Canada: Questions of Confidence*, Toronto: University of Toronto Press.
Kelly, K. (2009) 'Social Marketing Education: The Beat Goes On', *Social Marketing Quarterly* 15, 3: 129–41.
Kiss, S. (2009) 'The Public Relations State in Alberta: Participatory or Post-Democracy?' Paper presented at the Annual Conference of the Canadian Political Science Association, Carleton University, Ottawa.
Lachapelle, G. (1996) 'Public Opinion and the Gulf War: Its Influence on the Decision-making Process', The McNaughton Papers, *The Canadian Journal of Strategic Studies*: 81–99.
Lees-Marshment, J. (2003) 'Political Marketing: How to Reach the Pot of Gold', *Journal of Political Marketing* 2, 1: 1–32.
Lilleker, D.G. and Lees-Marshment, J. (eds) (2005) *Political Marketing: A Comparative Perspective*, Manchester: Manchester University Press.
Margolis, M. and Mauser, G.M. (1989) *Manipulating Public Opinion: Essays on Public Opinion as a Dependent Variable*, Pacific Grove, CA: Brook/Cole.
Medlock, J. (2005) *The Role of Public Opinion Research in Federal Public Policy Development*, Calgary: University of Calgary.
Mintz, J.H., Church, D. and Colterman, B. (2006) 'The Case for Marketing in the Public Sector', Optimum on-line, *The Journal of Public Sector Management* 36, 4: 40–48.
Monroe, A. (1998) 'Public Opinion and Public Policy, 1980–93', *Public Opinion Quarterly* 62: 6–28.
Morris, D. (1997) *Behind the Oval Office. Winning the Presidency in the Nineties*, New York: Random House.
Page, B. and Shapiro, R. (1983) 'Effects of Public Opinion on Policy', *American Political Science Review* 77: 175–90.
Page, C. (2006) *The Roles of Public Opinion Research in Canadian Government*, Toronto: University of Toronto Press.
Paillé, D. (2007) *Public Opinion Research Practices of the Government of Canada*, Independent Advisor's Report, Public Works and Government Services Canada.
Pétry, F. (1999) 'The Opinion-Policy Relationship in Canada', *The Journal of Politics* 61, 2: 540–50.
—— (2007) 'How Policymakers View Public Opinion', in L. Dobuzinskis, M. Howlett and D. Laycock (eds) *Policy Analysis in Canada: The State of the Art*, Toronto: University of Toronto Press, 375–98.
Ponting, J.R. (2006) *The Nisga'a Treaty: Polling Dynamics and Political Communication in Comparative Context*, Toronto: University of Toronto Press.
Roberts, A. and Rose, J. (1995) 'Selling the Good and Services Tax: Government Advertising and Public Discourse in Canada', *Canadian Journal of Political Science* 28: 311–30.
Rothmayr, C. and Hardmeier, S. (2002) 'Government and Polling: Use and Impact of Polls in the Policy-Making Process in Switzerland', *International Journal of Public Opinion Research* 14, 2: 124–40.
Schrefler, L. (2010) 'The Usage of Scientific Knowledge by Independent Regulatory Agencies', *Governance: An International Journal of Policy, Administration and Institutions* 23, 2: 309–30.
Soroka, S. and Wlezien, C. (2004) 'Opinion Representation and Policy Feedback: Canada in Comparative Perspective', *Canadian Journal of Political Science* 37, 3: 531–60.
Sparrow, N. and Turner, J. (2001) 'The Permanent Campaign: The Integration of Market Research Techniques in Developing Strategies in a More Uncertain Political Climate', *European Journal of Marketing* 35: 984–1002.
Stimson, J. (1998) Public Opinion in America: Moods, Cycles, and Swings, Boulder, CO: Westview.
Studlar, D.T. (2002) *Tobacco Control: Comparative Politics in the United States and Canada*, Peterborough, ON: Broadview Press Inc.
Treasury Board of Canada (2002) '*Results for Canadians: A Management Framework for the Government of Canada*'. Online pamphlet, www.tbs-sct.gc.ca/report/res_can/rc_bro-eng.asp (accessed 23 February 2007).
—— (2006) 'Communications Policy of the Government of Canada'. Online, www.tbs-sct.gc.ca/pol/doc-eng.aspx?id=12316§ion=HTML (accessed 10 April 2011).

27

Making space for leadership

The scope for politicians to choose how they respond to market research

Jennifer Lees-Marshment

The topic: leadership and political marketing

Leadership is an important part of democratic politics. Not only are political leaders a key focus of the political offering at election time, but they are the ones who make the final decisions as a president or prime minister with the potential to affect not just an individual country but the world. Leadership and political marketing both encompass many different activities and concepts, but this chapter focuses on how leaders respond to one aspect of political marketing, market research, which is a crucial part of political marketing. Market research offers politicians the opportunity to understand public opinion, and can help politicians demonstrate a feeling of being in touch. However, it could also prevent them making the 'right' decisions on policy against the findings of market research. Towards the end of his leadership, Tony Blair, once critiqued for being a follower of focus groups, commented:

> The easy thing to do, frankly, is to hit the button on exactly what the public wants to hear … The responsibility, though, in the end, particularly in the case of war, is to do what I believe to be the right thing for the country. I can't do it simply on the basis of the number of people who demonstrate, or on the basis of this opinion poll or that opinion poll. You've got to do, on an issue like this, what you genuinely believe to be right for the country, and then pay the price at the election if people disagree with you.
>
> *(Tony Blair,* Tony and June, *Channel 4, 30 January 2005)*

If politicians do not feel free to act against market research, then they do not have the space for leadership. Without entering a big debate about what constitutes leadership generally, the issue for this chapter is to what extent leaders have scope to make a range of policy decisions in response to market research findings, and be free to be the kind of leader they choose. Previous literature and new concepts will conceptualise how leadership might be exercised when using market research, and new empirical research demonstrates how politicians and their advisors have sought to exercise leadership in response to market research.

Previous research: political marketing is a threat to leadership

One of the previous dominant themes in political marketing research was the rise of market-oriented politics, where politicians researched the market to identify demands and then created political products – and policy promises – to suit them. This suggested that politicians ended up following market research too much. Paleologos (1997: 1184) argues that 'a poll-driven society … ignores creativity. It overlooks new ideas. It prohibits change and true reform'. Smith and Saunders (1990: 298) contended that 'pandering to the prejudices of the majority might herald a tyranny of the ill-formed. Capital punishment, forced repatriation and other lowest common denominator issues could become important if marketing research showed a short-term benefit in courting them.'

However, on a theoretical level Henneberg (2006: 17) explained that politicians can choose to lead or follow; indeed, 'leading and following can happen simultaneously as part of political marketing management'. An empirical example of using research to achieve change is provided by Allington *et al.* (1999), who demonstrate that marketing was used to help politicians sell a policy of privatization in the UK in the 1980s. In order to gain support, communication was aimed not at typical shareholders but at the general public, with communication designed to appeal to their interests and perspectives. When selling British Gas the campaign used the slogan 'Tell Sid' to convey the message that 'privatisation represented good news for ordinary people because they could now get a piece of the action' (Allington *et al.* 1999: 634). It was attractive to individuals because it implied that share buying was a higher-class activity but one that was open to all. Responsive marketing communications can therefore be used to change opinion: Allington *et al.* (1999: 636) conclude that 'marketing … has the power to change things and even to change the world order'. Presidential studies such as Jacobs and Shapiro (2000: 11) observed how 'the proliferation and visibility of public opinion polling during the Clinton administration … led many critics of American politics to fear that poll taking, focus groups and the like has permanently replaced political leaders', but their own studies concluded that generally politicians do not pander to polls and that 'presidents can use polls to determine how to explain and present already determined proposals and policies to the public' (ibid.: 13). Goot (1999: 237) studied how the Australian Liberal leader John Howard used market analysis to make the proposal to sell the publicly owned telecommunications company Telstra more attractive to the public. Goot concluded that it is not true 'that on every issue, or even on all the important ones, polling necessarily commits politicians to the position of the median voter'. Murray's (2006: 495) study of the Reagan presidency concluded that whilst some party-driven issues were sidelined, and changes were made if too much opposition was encountered, survey data were also used to find potential 'overlap' between the leadership goals and public opinion, 'to thereby identify political opportunities where it could accomplish some of its ideological goals and satisfy some of its partisan constituents, while staying within broad constraints established by majority opinion'. The use of research does not dictate the decision that leaders make; it merely informs it. With the benefit of practitioner experience, Mortimore and Gill (2010: 259) argue that despite the value of market research, 'the leadership function is crucial, and that leader must exercise judgement when to follow the dictates of the market and when to defy it'. This literature provides insights into the complexity surrounding market research and leadership, which this chapter builds on by putting forward new theories for the different responses politicians can make to market research, and exploring them empirically through interviews with political advisors.

New research: market research and the space for leadership

On a conceptual level, it can be theorised that whilst market research and strategy are utilised in politics by all leaders, this does not mean that they simply have to follow the public and have no room to achieve changes. Instead, research can be used more proactively, to understand and overcome opposition, and create space for leadership. Market research can therefore be used in a range of ways by leaders: see Figure 27.1.

However, we still need to know to what extent this more nuanced use of market research occurs in practice. Some 100 in-depth interviews were conducted with a range of staff in all areas of political marketing in 2005–09 in the UK, US, Australia, New Zealand and Canada. The complete findings are presented in Lees-Marshment (2011), but here discussion focuses on what practitioners said about how they conduct and use market research. The interviewees included consultants and advisors to political leaders including US Presidents Bill Clinton and George Bush, UK Prime Minister Tony Blair, Canadian Prime Ministers Paul Martin and Stephen Harper, New Zealand Prime Minister Helen Clark and Australian Premier Bob Carr. Data were collected inductively – i.e. without any starting position or theory in mind. Interviews were qualitative, unstructured, soft and intensive, with content led by the participant (see Lees-Marshment 2011 for further discussion of methodology).

The research found that practitioners are aware of the need to avoid relying on market analysis for product ideas. From his UK Labour experience, Carter (interviewed in 2007) said, 'there was never a decision taken on this single fact or on that piece of research. It's never a focus group has said go and do this so somebody went and did that.' Evans (interviewed in 2006) argued that:

> research is essential in politics, but it can only tell you where you've been and where you are. It can't really tell you where you want to get to … It shouldn't affect where you ultimately want to get to but it can affect maybe how you get there. You have to believe in something in politics before you can go out and sell it.

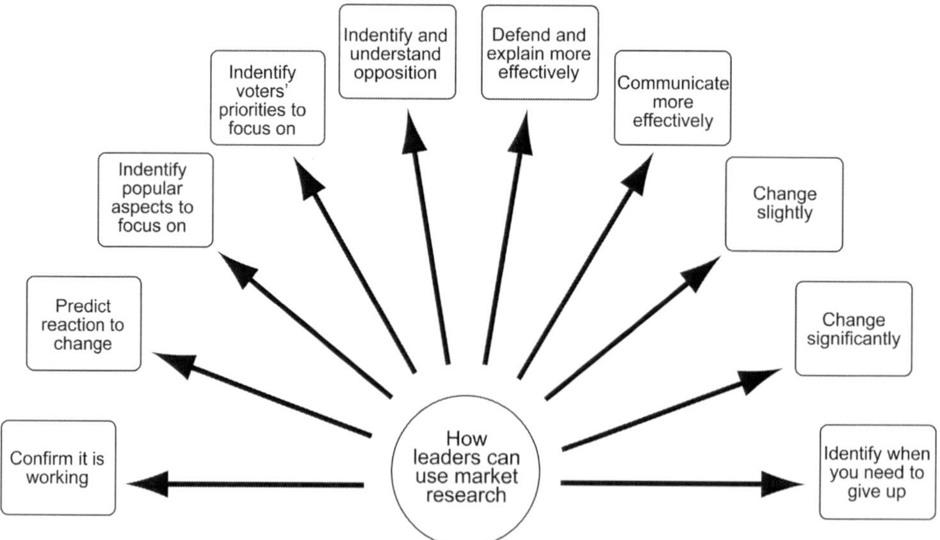

Figure 27.1 Leaders' options for how to use market research in politics

Mortimer (interviewed in 2006) explained that:

> the public can't tell you new policies because they actually don't know much about politics. Politicians have to be able to come up with the new answers and the new solutions … we can tell you what percentage of the public are running around flapping about an issue, but it's not going to tell you what the policy solution to that problem should be.

They therefore use market research in many different ways. It can simply be used to communicate existing decisions more effectively, thus not impacting on leadership at all. Mills (interviewed in 2009) argued that 'overwhelmingly, polling is used to work out how to communicate policies or even how to prioritise which policies are communicated in election campaigns rather than determine policy'. Mellman (interviewed in 2007) said:

> we want to use the data analysis we're generating to answer sort of three questions. And if we've answered those three questions, we've gone a long way towards developing their strategy. Where do we want to say it, who do we want to say it to, when do we want to say it?

It can be used to identify the most popular aspects of a product that should feature strongly in communication. As Rennard (interviewed in 2006) explains,

> the policy we had of increasing income tax by a penny in the pound to pay for more investment in education was very successful. And market research confirmed that was a very popular policy. Therefore we would emphasise that fairly heavily in communication in '92, '97 and 2001. Market research gave us confidence that it was a particularly good thing.

More recently,

> on foreign affairs, the Iraq war, our policy was very popular, particularly of course for minority communities and for traditional Labour voters. So … the degree to which we emphasised the Iraq war was strengthened by market research and guided us in Brent, and in Liverpool, and in Birmingham and by-elections like that. Having tested people's feeling on it, it was a good card to play.

Research also helps to ensure that MPs and candidates talk about issues that local people care about: Noble (interviewed in 2009) notes how:

> you can't just govern your principles from opinion research, but you can certainly refine them. You might have 100 things that you stand for, but no single voter, no collective voting block is going to be able to process them. So, we did a lot of market research to hone in on the things that we were talking about that really mattered to people. What are going to be their ballot drivers? What are they going to go to the polls and actually cast their ballot deciding? What are the most important issues for them?

Research helps to communicate issues about which the politician cares: Taylor (interviewed in 2008) recalled how in the White House:

> The research was very useful in helping us communicate the messages which the president wanted to talk about. President Bush is not somebody who was interested in sort of just,

> he just doesn't take a poll and decide what to talk about; he says here's what I'm saying, if you can help me articulate it in a way that resonates with people better, I'm all ears … We knew kind of instinctively what issues he wanted to talk about and then it was conducting focus groups, doing traditional survey research and figuring out exactly what it is, the nuances, how to communicate. How to best utilise examples.

Just because politicians use market research does not mean that they follow it blindly. Indeed, Reid (interviewed in 2009) noted that:

> even if you were wholly venal and shallow as could be, and you came to the job with no preconceived notion of what you wanted to do and you would be more than happy to be directed solely on the basis of what appears most popular – you actually can't always make that – there's a million issues that confront you on a daily basis, a thousand decisions, and frequently people don't have a point of view about a particular topic.

Carter conceded the value of research but again said:

> there is a gap here which is for judgment. And the leader has to make their decisions on the basis of judgment and on the basis of good advice and sound evidence, high-quality research – yes, but also on the basis of good judgment.

Market research can therefore be used in a range of ways by political leaders: it is a tool to inform, not dictate, decisions.

Research does still influence decisions, however, as it can identify when politicians can't change opinion, with Carr (interviewed in 2008) noting how 'qualitative polling can help you, sometimes in identifying ideas that simply don't work'. Politicians who ignore polls do so at their peril: as Harris (interviewed in 2006) noted, '[Michael, leader UK Conservatives 2003–05] Howard ended up running a very nasty right-wing campaign, and yet that's not something that anyone advising him at the beginning would have recommended' – and they lost against the then unpopular Labour incumbent, Tony Blair. Similarly, another politician who lost an election, John Kerry, was noted to be anti-polls: Mellman described how:

> Kerry wasn't that interested in polls per se … the candidate wasn't all that interested in the polling, so it was probably less useful to him because it just wasn't his thing … on the message side, I mean, you know, there are certainly various points where, you know, he was not, you know, particularly enamoured of what it is we were suggesting for various reasons, had his own things he wanted to do, what he's talking about, we wanted to talk about.

Leaders need to be 'sufficiently flexible when clearly an announcement or a policy or an issue has not gone down well', and have 'the courage to acknowledge that maybe it wasn't the right issue, if the weight of the community reaction or other stakeholder reaction is such that you know that they're suggesting that this isn't doable at this time' (Tyson, interviewed in 2008).

Research helps to prevent leaders becoming too remote and dismissive of the public. Griffin (interviewed in 2006) notes how:

> what you have to do when going into an election campaign as an incumbent Prime Minister is swallow your pride, forget you are the Prime Minister, and go back and petition

> people – you are asking people to vote for you, that's not a mandate for you to tell them how clever you are, and how well your Government has done. You have to engage at a far different level.

However, this is not easy. As Callingham (interviewed in 2009) notes:

> they get out of touch, they have to. They may meet thousands of people, but they're still meeting them as a Prime Minister. They're not meeting them as Joe Blog in a caff; they're not meeting them as someone in a queue in a post-office.

Reid noted how:

> incumbency becomes a real threat because it is isolating the apparatus of government … so incumbency starts to equal complacency, and complacency starts to equal self-interest, and you can start taking it for granted, and suddenly you don't seem like you're well motivated, so you don't communicate that you get it. And maybe you don't … it is sufficiently isolating that if you are in government for too long that people tend to conflate their own opinion with the national interest.

Similarly Campbell (interviewed in 2005) noted how Westminster is 'in a political bubble', and 'it's very hard' to stay in touch; it is particularly hard to be the prime minister, as you're 'surrounded by security' and 'lots of people talking to you all the time telling you their own ideas and agenda'. Being in power works against responsiveness: 'it's a trait of government that the longer they go on, the less they remember to think about that. The more ministers become ministers, they think as ministers rather than thinking as politicians' (Robertson, interviewed in 2006).

However, whilst leaders need to be flexible and willing to change position if a new idea is not accepted, this does not mean that politicians should simply follow public opinion. Research can encourage politicians to make adjustments, rather than wholesale change: 'more and more, I would see candidates understanding the value of research, and then really sending the results, and adjusting their policies, or programme-manning efforts, or their positioning overall based on research' (Braun, interviewed in 2009). Moreover, whilst research may point out the need to give up on certain policies, it can also help guide leaders as to when they can sell something and not be too cautious. Somerville (interviewed in 2007) noted how:

> serious politicians have a good rule of thumb, which is, if you give me something that I think I can sell, then I will, if it is going to make sense. But if I don't think I can sell it, then I won't sell it … leadership is saying what I can sell … it is much more an instinctive judgment – Asylum liberalization, no that's gonna kill my party. Baby bonds – that's not going to be popular in certain areas, but I think I can sell that.

Research identifies the space for leadership: former premier Bob Carr said: 'there are some issues where the public attitude might affect you and doesn't count; one because it's something you want to pursue, and two, because by leading you can change public opinion'. Carr said:

> a strong leader can shape public opinion. You might look at a bit of polling information that shows 55–45 division, but by simply staking your case and heading the media, you can

> see that flip over. Secondly, the issue might not be in the media for that long. So even if you're behind, it may not hurt you.

Response to research therefore needs to vary depending on the issue, and effective leadership includes both leading and following and somewhere in between. When discussing the Blair government, Gould (interviewed in 2007) conceded that 'it may be a fair criticism to say in the early days that it was poll-driven or too much, I don't know, public opinion-driven', although 'in the later stages … almost nothing Tony Blair did was popular. Everything was based on conviction.' However, Blair lost support when he adopted a more conviction-based strategy. Gould argues that:

> The art of politics, modern politics, is kind of being able to perfectly blend these two together and to make them work. I mean, if you become too much of a listening party you just get nowhere. If you become too much of a leadership government, then you start to disconnecting your voters, which is bad also. If you're too flexible it's bad, if you're too inflexible it's bad, so you need to balance these … it's absolutely crucial to listen in modern politics, but equally important to lead … you have to balance flexibility and resolution. What I call soft-hard politics. You have to be soft, you have to be flexible, you have to be listening … you have to be participatory. But you also have to have the courage and your convictions. Now that's very hard.

In practice, research is used alongside other considerations such as the party itself, because as Utting (interviewed in 2008) explained,

> politicians aren't slaves to opinion polls because politicians are slaves to other more substantial interests like … the internal dynamic level in their party … what their support level is in caucus, what the attitudes of some of their big donors are, the cultural institutional things … they're the kind of real things that they have to sort of balance.

Politicians must aim to position themselves in relation to both internal and external opinion to both maintain support and achieve progress. Polling is more of 'a stepping off point for political strategy' (Gould) – it does not set the goal itself.

Furthermore, it is also pragmatic to avoid following research at all costs. Leaders need some kind of position and should not just follow, not least because voters want them to have some kind of integrity: 'it's much better to have a consistent position and I'd say be slightly out of centre than make that desperate dash to the centre and weaken any kind of credibility that you've got' (Utting). Harris, who was marketing director for the UK Conservatives, argued that you need positive vision to win:

> you need vision … Howard never ever created a sense of belief in what his overall vision was and all he did was get stuck into the negatives, and then with IDS he also had no clear sense of purpose. I think that without a noble purpose you're sunk.

Lavigne (interviewed in 2009) recalls how he worked on Canadian New Democratic Party (NDP) leader Jack Layton's leadership campaign for the 2003 election, and:

> when we sat down at the kitchen table at the very beginning, and we started to talk about the kind of party we wished to build and the kind of country we wished to build, that's

> where the vision of where you want to take the party, and where you want to take the country, that's where it starts.

Evans said that marketing needs to be driven:

> by a vision and a set of values. As long as it is about political ideas and doesn't become reduced to a tactical squabble for power. Anyone involved in that game will get outflanked. Another party provision will come along and will get traction with vision as to where people want to get next. Politics and marketing have a bad reputation individually, put the two together and it is deeply mistrusted. But without that compass, you'd get found out. You wouldn't go to tap into people's aspirations.

Political marketing need not result in creating politicians who just follow – not only is it problematic democratically it is also problematic on a pragmatic level.

Practitioners suggested that any changes in position to suit polls need thinking out and justifying. Sparrow (interviewed in 2007) recalled how research tells the politicians in the UK that the public 'love the NHS and they want the politicians to love it as well', and that even if it's not something politicians feel passionate about:

> they go out and talk about it, they do what the researchers and strategists tell them to do, but they do it without the conviction that they have for the things that they do actually feel really passionate about. So they don't actually get the message across.

Evans argued that 'if you are not authentic you will fail, maybe not initially, but ultimately … I wouldn't go as far as to say there is a collective intelligence but the public tend to figure out what's going on'. Reid said that it is not enough to show responsiveness to the public, the message had to be authentic. Changing position to suit polls all the time can backfire: Mills noted how 'polling may show that right now 75 percent of voters favour Policy A but if you had declared passionately against Policy A a few months back you can't now advocate Policy A without a cost to your personal credibility'. Duncan-Smith (interviewed in 2006) commented how in his experience as a party leader 'if we attack something one day we are considered as hypocrites if we then go back to that position later on and say we are in favour of it now.'

Advisors, therefore, take into account the politician's history and beliefs. Ulm (interviewed in 2007) said that he had:

> never had a candidate ask me 'What should I believe on this?' Never had. Never had it once. Usually the candidate has a core history, a core set of beliefs, and you're trying to figure out of all those, what's the best way to win? Is the history both good and bad?

The same works for communication: Mellman explained how 'if your message is we need someone who's tough and you have a wimpy sort of candidate – doesn't work so well. That can't really be your message … you have to work with the material you have'. Despite the use of research and advice, politicians need to be genuine otherwise 'you get found out pretty quick. There's no doubt about that' (Fitzpatrick, interviewed in 2008).

Furthermore, leaders can use research proactively to help them achieve change in public opinion, rather than just change their position. Tyson explained how research can be used to work out how to sell something, to tailor the message, and then on a continual basis so that politicians are 'finding out what will appease people, to get them to back down'. Similarly, Mellman said:

> my view is you shouldn't base public policy on polling in particular. On the other hand, sometimes politicians come to us and say well, this is what I've decided to do, what I need you to do is tell me how do I sell that? How do I get people to support that, given that this is what I want to do? That's perfectly appropriate and responsible in my view, because our job isn't to dictate public policy to them, but it is to help them figure out how to sell their policies for the maximum impact.

Market intelligence can be used to advise on a predetermined, locked-in position without changing the product. Duffy (interviewed in 2009) said that 'the best use of market-research, in my experience, is … it can show you a pathway through what appears to be an insurmountable barrier'. Research can help suggest a way forward through opposition:

> it tells you 'Well actually if you link your agenda – if you call it that you'll have a problem, but if you don't call it that, if you call it something else, and if you present the motive behind what you are doing as being conservation in aid of environmental best-practices, then the public will buy it.' So, that's what market research does. It gives you some quantifiable basis on which you can venture your opinions.

Gill (interviewed in 2007) said that his experience at Mori showed that 'public opinion can be led and changed very substantially on a lot of issues, because most of the time most people aren't thinking about these issues that politicians and government are thinking about very much'. Research helps to understand the level of support or opposition, and who supports or opposes, and what might make them change. Nanos (interviewed in 2009) argues that the best politicians use research by 'saying I have an objective, then they are on the right track. Can it be achieved? Is it the right objective? What are the resources that are going to be needed to achieve that objective? How relevant is it?' It helps identify potential risks. It can predict how voters might change or react to changes. Utting explained that although traditional research simply researches where people are right now, more sophisticated sensitivity modelling can explore what impact a politician changing position on something will have on public opinion: 'you can almost create a kind of black box situation where you can try different options within your model, and just see how it affects things like vote choice or other outcomes you're interested in'. Research can help identify the potential room for politicians to lead public opinion.

Research remains useful even when leaders adopt a position that is, or becomes, anti-market, helping politicians to understand opposition to their positions and show respect for public opinion even if they do not agree with it. In 2004–05 more innovative research by the company Promise for the UK Labour/Blair government identified that the problem wasn't just Blair's policy on Iraq, but that people felt neglected by Blair, that he hadn't listened to them and became too focused on international rather than domestic issues. This then informed a reconnection strategy, which as Carter explained,

> involved taking the Prime Minister to studios after studios and putting him in front of live audiences that could engage and talk with him and put their concerns, those events helped to show that the Prime Minister had not moved off the key agendas that he had been elected on, but indeed remained very focused on them, even though there had been other things going on.

When the public have negative perceptions of politicians who have already been elected or are known to them, practitioners can work to offset them. When former first lady Hillary Clinton stood for the Senate as well as president, she conducted a listening, conversation tour to combat concerns that 'people were weary of her, they didn't know her, they believed in the negative stereotypes about her, and the way to dispel them was to appear personally in small groups that were open, so people could report on them' (Blumenthal, interviewed in 2007). It is important to use research to identify the real source of any weakness so that it can be managed more effectively.

Overall, this research demonstrates that, as suggested by previous literature, political marketing does not lead politicians to simply follow market research. Instead, research is used to inform a variety of positions and decisions. Indeed, for both pragmatic and principled reasons, politicians should use market research more reflectively. Taking our understanding beyond theoretical assertions, this gives us a rare insight into the thinking of politicians and their advisors who conduct and use market research when making leadership decisions about policy.

Advice for practitioners

Practitioners would be wise to understand that market research is only part of the decision-making process, and politicians should not simply follow the results of research. Market research needs to be used carefully, to guide leaders to make decisions which will both maintain support and help politicians achieve policy change: see Box 27.1.

Box 27.1 How political leaders should use market research in politics

1 Try to achieve a few changes and use market analysis to help identify how to change opinion
2 Manage anti-market positions: continue to conduct market analysis; show awareness of and respect for opposition; and conduct listening exercises to get back in touch
3 Use market analysis proactively to inform, not dictate decisions
4 Balance leading and following the public
5 Ensure changes are justifiable and credible
6 Adopt a proactive, visionary position: do not just follow

Impact on politics

What this means for politics is that there is still room for politicians to take a range of policy decisions in relation to market research. Whilst political marketing is clearly a prevalent force in politics, it need not be a constraining force in democracy that prevents politicians taking up certain policies. Yes, they do need to stay in touch and they do need to listen, but that does not mean they need to do everything the public wants. It is about nuance – leaders can take a range of positions in response to research, and research can be used to find a way to create public support for change as well as stop politicians doing something that is deeply against the public will. There may be a maturing of political leadership which could help to create a more positive relationship between government and citizens, but this positive impact will only happen in practice if politicians choose to use political marketing more effectively. Ultimately the decision rests with them.

The way forward: for research, study, training and practice

Whilst political marketing has extensively researched how politicians follow market demands, there needs to be more research that explores how marketing might be used to create space for leadership decisions that go against public opinion and managing anti-market decisions more effectively. The leadership literature itself needs to be integrated, and it would be beneficial if a model of reflective leadership were created and tested on specific empirical cases. Practitioners need to be aware of the need to utilise market research in a proactive way to help create the room for leadership, and to spend time reflecting on how to respond to the public. Political marketing will then help leaders not just win elections but help meet public long-term needs and be beneficial for society as a whole.

Bibliography

List of interviewees

Blumenthal, Sidney (2007) former advisor to President Bill Clinton, Third Way advocate, and advisor to Hillary Clinton's presidential nomination campaign. Interviewed in Washington DC, USA, September.

Braun, Alex (2009) PSB (Penn, Schoen and Berland) Associates New York. Telephone interview from Auckland, New Zealand, January.

Callingham, Judy (2009) media advisor to former New Zealand prime minister Helen Clark. Interviewed in Auckland, New Zealand, January.

Campbell, Alastair (2005) former chief press secretary to UK prime minister Tony Blair. Interviewed at Millbank, London, UK, October.

Carr, Bob (2008) former premier of NSW, Australia. Interviewed in Sydney, Australia, February.

Carter, Matt (2007) former UK Labour general secretary and managing director London branch of Penn, Schoen and Berland Associates. Interviewed at PSB London, UK, 7 September.

Duffy, John (2009) advisor to Canadian prime minister Paul Martin, currently principal at Strategycorp. Interviewed in Toronto, Canada, 20 May.

Duncan Smith, Iain (2006) former leader of the UK Conservatives 2001–03. Interviewed at the House of Commons, London, UK, 18 April.

Edwards, Brian (2009) media advisor to former New Zealand prime minister Helen Clark. Interviewed in Auckland, New Zealand, January.

Evans, David (2006) The Campaign Company. Interviewed in London, UK and by telephone from Auckland, New Zealand, April.

Fitzpatrick, Eammon (2008) former media advisor, state level; current consultant Hawker Brittain. Interviewed in Sydney, February.

Gill, Mark (2007) former head of political research at Ipsos Mori, current Director of Woodnewton Associates, UK. Interviewed in London, UK, 5 September.

Gould, Phillip (2007) Labour strategist/pollster and advisor to the Blair New Labour opposition and government. Interviewed in London, UK, 10 September.

Griffin, Richard (2006) former chief press secretary to Prime Minister Bolger in New Zealand. Interviewed in Wellington, New Zealand, 29 November.

Harris, Will (2006) former director of marketing for the UK Conservative Party. Interview at The Bank, London, UK, 19 April.

Lavigne, Brad (2009) national director of the New Democratic Party of Canada and former advisor to the NDP leader. Interviewed in Ottawa, Canada, 28 May.

Mellman, Mark (2007) Kerry 2004 campaign advisor and senatorial advisor. Interviewed in Washington DC, USA, October.

Mills, Stephen (2009) UMR pollster to New Zealand Labour Party since the 1990s to present day. Interviewed in Auckland, New Zealand and written comments provided subsequently, March.

Mortimer, Roger (2006) MORI polling company UK, interviewed in London, UK, 11 April.

Nanos, Nik (2009) pollster and CEO of the Nanos Research Corporation. Interviewed in Ottawa, Canada, 28 May.

Noble, Leslie (2009) strategic advisor to the Progressive Conservatives and campaign manager for Ontario premier Mike Harris in 1995 and 1999, and current principal in Strategy Corp. Interviewed in Toronto, Canada, 20 May.

Reid, Scott (2009) senior advisor and director of communications to Canadian prime minister Paul Martin and director of communications for the 2004 and 2006 Liberal Party election campaign, currently principal of Feschuk Reid. Interviewed in Toronto, Canada, 19 May.

Rennard, Chris (2006) chief executive of the UK Liberal Democrats. Interviewed in London, April.

Robertson, Grant (2006) former senior advisor to former New Zealand prime minister Helen Clark. Interviewed in Wellington, New Zealand, 28 November.

Somerville, Will (2007) senior policy analyst, Migration Institute, Washington, DC and former IPPR, UK. Interviewed in Washington DC, USA, October.

Sparrow, Nick (2007) pollster ICM UK/former pollster Conservative Party 1995–2001, and 2003–04. Interviewed in London, UK, 5 September.

Taylor, Sara (2008) strategist on the 2004 Bush-Cheney campaign and former political director in the White House. Telephone interview from Auckland, New Zealand, 11(US)/12(NZ) March.

Tyson, Brian (2008) political advisor, Gavin Anderson and company, Australia. Interviewed in Sydney, Australia, February.

Ulm, Gene (2007) political consultant for Public Opinion Strategies. Interviewed in Alexandria, VA, USA, 24 October.

Utting, John (2008) UMR pollster, Australia. Interviewed in Sydney, Australia, February.

Academic references

Allington, N., Morgan, P. and O'Shaughnessy, N. (1999) 'How Marketing Changed the World. The Political Marketing of an Idea: A Case Study of Privatization', in B. Newman (ed.) *The Handbook of Political Marketing*, Thousand Oaks, CA: Sage, 627–42.

Goot, M. (1999) 'Public Opinion, Privatization and the Electoral Politics of Telstra', *Australian Journal of Politics and History* 45, 2: 214–38.

Henneberg, S.C. (2006) 'Strategic Postures of Political Marketing: An Exploratory Operationalization', *Journal of Public Affairs* 6, 1: 15–30.

Hughes, A. and Dann, S. (2010) 'Australian Political Marketing: Substance Backed by Style', in J. Lees-Marshment, J. Strömbäck and C. Rudd (eds) *Global Political Marketing*, London: Routledge, 82–95.

Jacobs, L.R. and Shapiro, R.Y. (2000) *Politicians Don't Pander: Political Manipulation and the Loss of Democratic Responsiveness*, Chicago, IL: University of Chicago Press.

Lees-Marshment, J. (2011) *The Political Marketing Game*, Houndmills, Basingstoke, Hampshire: Palgrave Macmillan.

Lees-Marshment, J., Strömbäck, J. and Rudd, C. (eds) (2010) *Global Political Marketing*, London and New York: Routledge.

Mortimore, R. and Gill, M. (2010) 'Implementing and Interpreting Market Orientation in Practice: Lessons from Britain', in J. Lees-Marshment, J. Strömbäck and C. Rudd (eds) *Global Political Marketing*, London and New York: Routledge, 249–62.

Murray, S.-K. (2006) 'Private Polls and Presidential Policymaking: Reagan as a Facilitator of Change', *Public Opinion Quarterly* 70, 4: 477–98.

Paleologos, D.A. (1997) 'A Pollster on Polling', *American Behavioral Scientist* 40, 8: 1183–89.

Smith, G. and Saunders, J. (1990) 'The Application of Marketing to British Politics', *Journal of Marketing Management* 5: 295–306.

28

Conclusion

New directions in political marketing practice, political marketing and democracy, and future trends

Jennifer Lees-Marshment

This chapter will draw together main findings from this *Handbook*. Drawing on the material presented in each chapter, it will set out new directions in political marketing practice, discuss political marketing and democracy, and outline future trends in political marketing research and practice.

New directions in political marketing practice

The *Handbook* has discussed a range of tools and concepts that politicians and advisors can use when formulating a strategy, developing a product or brand, organising volunteers, managing staff, communicating to the public and marketing in government.

From researching voter demands to co-creation of the political product

Understanding the market is the first step in political marketing. This includes market research and more innovative forms of listening to, and working with, the public. Opinion research is obviously the starting point for a campaign or political strategy. However, for it to be valuable, the research must be high quality, generate ideas for action not just data, and be interpreted carefully. Different research is done at different stages of the campaign, with the initial benchmark poll assessing the current situation, and subsequent research developing or updating positioning and messaging, timing, sequencing, intensity and the means of its communications.

Segmentation needs to be used strategically and respond to changes in the market. One of the examples in this *Handbook* was segmenting by age by understanding the role of differing generational characteristics and the influence of an individual's progress through the life cycle, as in each stage individuals have different experiences, social interactions, relationships, networks and economic circumstances. Practitioners need to understand the importance of older voters as not only is this segment expanding, but older voters are more active and likely to vote. Detailed segmentation of this group is necessary because they still make their own decisions as opposed to voting en masse, and hold a range of views and values. A long-term relationship with seniors that allows for their development during this time will be more effective, such as understanding that their internet and social media usage is growing and expectations go beyond simple old-age benefits. The segment has widely varying resources in terms of health, money and family support, so segmentation needs to combine data on lifestyle, social attitudes, local political intelligence, life stage, generational identities and aspirations, and not just focus on age. More generally, although targeting is a tactical tool, to make it most effective voters should be selected strategically – considering the specific situation and context, to create a customised strategy. Voter selection needs to consider what segments are politically meaningful, and then choose targets on the basis of what will be most cost-effective to achieve the overall goals.

In addition to these formal methods which tend to research voters' existing views on a political product, elites can bring the political consumer into the production process. Deliberative forms of consultation can be used for a decision which has not already been made, to create new solutions to political problems. Deliberative marketing needs a clear leader to give it strategic importance, but it also needs to fit in with the strategy of the party or politician, and it needs to be communicated effectively. Most importantly, practitioners need to plan for managing the output, to ensure that people who deliberate know the time they are investing in a deliberative governance arena is worthwhile. The leadership will need to explain their final decision, so that stakeholders can understand why the leader prefers one possible solution over another.

Similarly, co-creation offers a range of techniques that involve the voter in creating the solution to the problem, rather than simply voicing their demands. As with deliberative marketing, there needs to be a plan made for what will happen to the results. Voters know politicians listen at election time, but co-creation exercises, if executed effectively, could reassure the public that politicians will listen once in power. Different methods are used during the actual process to ensure participant comfort, including discussion, sharing of perspectives in large and small groups, individual reflection, games, and using verbal but also visual expression. Exercises are employed to open up selfish and social sides of human beings, encourage awareness of other people's perspectives, and allow room for different opinions and divisions, but groups then work to explore their consequences and find ways to work around them. Exercises are also carried out to identify where past experience is restricting consideration of future options, and create a clearing to allow space for new information and creativity. This is particularly important in politics where cynicism about politicians can prevent new possibilities emerging. Action from there on is concerned with developing creative – but realistic – solutions that take into account conflicts and restrictions, but move outside the box without being pie in the sky. Ideas can come in different forms: visionary, process, doing things and small improvements that make a big difference. People are given permission and made to feel safe to contribute. The goal is that everyone learns together and that all knowledge is combined to become a resource for the entire group. Structuring them into an action plan comes later, as it is a very different process to creation. Even here, listening is one of the most important activities, and helps to create consensus instead of conflict, even between experts and ordinary individuals. The findings are then written up to provide different options for elites to consider.

From 'market-oriented party wins all' to situation-dependent strategic options to build long-term relationships with voters and supporters

Previously, literature argued that major parties needed to adopt a market orientation – which put at it simplest means designing the political product to satisfy voter demands – in order to win elections. However, this *Handbook* suggests that practitioners, politicians and parties have a choice: they can and do choose to retain a sales-oriented strategy that focuses marketing efforts on communicating elite-driven decisions. Moreover, sales-oriented parties do still win and maintain power against other non-market-oriented parties – so the effectiveness of a particular orientation is situation-dependent rather than universal. Whilst a market orientation can aid electoral success, and be adopted in any country/political system, the leadership must drive the process and manage internal markets effectively otherwise they risk being thwarted by party figures and members. Once in power, if parties want to maintain support they need to maintain a market orientation or try to reconnect – but as yet, few succeed at this. Thus whilst we may see market-oriented parties develop around the world in every country at some stage, it is not the case that all parties will become market oriented in order to win.

Strategy is therefore much more unique to the particular situation. Niche marketing is another option for parties. A niche market-oriented party focuses its products on a particular segment of the electorate, rather than the whole market. Parties can market the leader rather than the whole party, win support in lower levels of government to gain credibility at a national level, and utilise rules of the electoral system – such as regional list voting and proportional systems – to gain support, rather than trying to compete head-to-head with mainstream parties. However, this is more likely to be successful for a minor rather than a major party.

Branding is another approach that can help the politician to develop a positive relationship with the voter. It also allows more flexibility than designing a specific product to suit voter demands, as a market orientation suggests political elites need to do. Nevertheless, practitioners need to ensure that the brand is built around a strong product, is used consistently, and that it is used to build a long-term relationship with voters. The product may change from one election to the next, but the brand can work beyond the vote at election time. It connects with people's values and emotions rather than simply offering tangible benefits. Political brands can also encourage volunteers and members to be more active. Furthermore, branding can and should involve the political party, not just a candidate or leader. Party branding requires responsiveness to internal stakeholders as well as voters, seeking to build a long-term relationship that involves the internal market. This also reflects the research findings that market-oriented strategies only succeed if the internal market is on board. Effective party branding ensures that volunteers support the new brand and interact with the public through this prism. Thus, strategy is complex, involving consideration of different markets to develop and maintain productive long-term relationships.

From ignoring members to viewing the internal stakeholders and staff as integral to successful political marketing, and building a relationship that not only recruits volunteers but donors – and ultimately voters

Relationship marketing offers important tools for parties to increase the activism amongst their volunteers, involving consideration of the incentives on offer to supporters. However, there are costs and benefits involved in offering incentives, and a balance to be struck between meeting internal and external demands. To make the right choice, and build an effective relationship with supporters, parties and campaigns need to research the concerns and views of their internal market, not just voters, so that they can make informed decisions about meeting often conflicting demands. As with branding and party orientation, choices need to be strategic and suit the particular situation and circumstances facing the party.

Despite these challenges, party members and party staff can become helpful 'part-time marketers'. Research also shows that in some parties, members may actually be more representative of voters and not exhibit diverging views. In this case, volunteers can play an important role in being active in the interests of the party or campaign. They can also provide effective but cheap market intelligence if parties set up structures to gather their views regularly. This is what the Democrats did in the US under the chairmanship of Howard Dean, training volunteers to speak to the party brand in a unified manner, and build up face-to-face contact with voters before the presidential nominee – Barack Obama – was selected. Furthermore, it creates a long-term relationship between parties and voters which can work after an election, through government and beyond the campaign of a single candidate. Similarly, the growing importance and duties of party staff means that they also commission market research, influence strategy and policy development, commission communication consultants, and recruit and manage volunteers. Parties therefore need to train them in political marketing so that they can use it expertly.

Direct marketing can be used to motivate supporters, not just voters. It can target not just the usual floating voter but potential party sympathisers who would be open not just to vote but to volunteer for a party's candidate. This merges get out the vote (GOTV) initiatives with membership marketing, or the external with the internal market. Online communication should be designed to allow supporters to connect with likeminded individuals and create their own campaign materials. A mentorship scheme should be created to deepen volunteers' relationship with the party and turn them into party advocates, offering training and support. Additionally, direct marketing can link new supporters into networks and thus increase the solidary benefits. Effective fundraising also builds on internal marketing efforts. Active and satisfied volunteers who already have a positive relationship with their party or campaign are also more likely to respond favourably to calls for donations. However, both the concept and mechanics of donor marketing have to be adapted to suit divergent volunteer and donor cultures and regulatory frameworks within each political system.

From short-term sales to long-term, mutual, interactive communication relationships

Trends in campaigning methods have changed in obvious ways, with the increased use of technology, but the same principle applies: integrate all communications methods with the overall strategy. When marketing candidates, the brand needs to work for both presidential and vice-presidential candidates and the party, and communications need to support existing brand strengths. Whilst personal characteristics such as authenticity and the common touch are important, communication of leadership and governing skills remains crucial. The market leader candidate will always be subject to greater attack and scrutiny, and female candidates, whilst able to create distinctiveness, can face problematic coverage. Campaigns need to ensure that the target markets will produce actual votes, otherwise segmentation can just risk alienating mainstream support. Populist marketing enables short-term products utilising new media to attract significant support quickly. To turn immediate success from a populist approach into a more stable position, politicians need to reflect and respond to market research and thus readjust the product over time to build up positive relationships in the long term.

Communication is becoming more participatory and interactive. Using new technology, politicians can engage in local and national dialogue to encourage civil engagement and political participation. Leaders need to convey that they are open to a meaningful interaction with people, not just being seen to relate to but care for the public, and capable of holding a positive – if mediated – relationship that develops over time. Thus leadership communication needs to be managed beyond the election as part of a long-term process, not one-off events or singular use of tools. Like individual relationships, leader-public relationships can't be completely controlled, and voters are alienated by signs of over-management – better to let the odd gaffe occur than erode any potential for authenticity.

Political public relations need to be developed to suit the particular context and purpose. It should involve long-term and two-way dialogue which builds relationships. In government, relational and dialogic approaches help to build up support for policies. Governments can encourage, listen and respond to public feedback, but more persuasion and hype is appropriate when governments are seeking to implement agreed policies.

In online or e-marketing, as with all global knowledge transfer, practitioners need to adapt ideas from other countries – such as Obama in the US – to suit the local context, rather than import it wholesale. They also need to understand the potential of applying political marketing principles to online communications, understanding the advantages it brings such as flexibility to be used as a broadcast and narrowcast tool at the same time; offer different marketing styles to suit each audience; and develop either a transactional or relationship marketing approach depending on the goals. A persuasive and information-based transactional approach will help to reach untapped markets who know little about the party or candidate, whereas relationship marketing suits members or stakeholders.

From campaigning to governing: the expansion of political marketing into policy delivery and leadership

For political marketing to succeed in the long term, politicians need to think about delivery before election, creating promises in the campaign that can be easily achieved once in power, which should be communicated in memorable ways to help to establish credibility with voters. Creating a central unit focused on delivery can help to lead progress, especially in a coalition government, along with efforts to create positive relationships that work with coalition partners, lower levels of government and government staff. Promises made in a campaign may need to be repackaged in power to help increase public support and make it harder for the opposition to oppose them.

Interest groups who seek influence over government decisions can take a market-oriented approach to make their advocacy more effective. They need to use market intelligence (segmenting, targeting and positioning) to assess their strengths and weaknesses, identify their allies and enemies and help to create the most attractive message to gain public support for their cause. Organisationally they need to create a focused leadership team that can make strategic decisions and keep everyone on board, to avoid reducing resource effectiveness through internal disagreements. They should utilise expertise when devising the message, drawing on networks, and generalise the argument to expand the potential impact of any government decision. Communication should be continual and unified, to promote national media coverage.

Policies themselves can be branded to widen their influence within one country but also abroad, but several steps need to be taken to make this process successful. Stakeholders affected by the potential brand need to be consulted and involved before rebranding takes place, and a brand assurance team created to help this process. Comprehensive documentation provided about the brand, especially where franchising will be allowed, and the government department involved need to show continued commitment to the brand. Government should also plan a review of the policy brand which can enable adaptation over time to suit changing circumstances, new knowledge and policy learning, with franchisees free to adapt the brand within the parameters set at the outset of the branding process.

Returning full circle to market research, once in government, politicians have access to government public opinion research, which provides highly specialised knowledge about the beliefs, attitudes, opinions and behaviours of the general public as well as the specific groups targeted by any given policy. They can therefore use this knowledge to improve the potential of a policy to achieve the desired outcomes when implemented, arguably helping achieve delivery of those initial promises – such as cutting crime – made in the campaign. Such research can also be used to monitor the effectiveness of policies once implemented, making the overall policy process more responsive. However, it can also be used to help politicians show leadership and make decisions that are not so reflective of voter preferences whilst maintaining support, by helping them explain why they have chosen a different option. Additionally, it can identify the space for leadership by exploring citizens' preferences and their thresholds or comfort zones for government decisions. Market research, both partisan and governmental, is only part of the decision-making process, however, and politicians should not simply follow the results of research. Research needs to be used carefully, to guide leaders to make decisions that will both maintain support and achieve policy change, by identifying how to change opinion and manage unpopular decisions.

Summary

Political marketing is clearly taking different directions in the early period of the 21st century, compared with the end of the 20th century. Whilst market research in politics was previously seen as being all about polls and focus groups to find out what people wanted, this *Handbook* shows that a more varied range of research tools are used, for different purposes, and not just to identify existing demands, but to involve the political consumer in creating the solution to how to meet those demands. This elevates citizens further in the political decision-making process, but doesn't simply mean that elites pay more attention to what they want out of elections. Instead, the public is asked to step into the decision-makers' shoes and help to solve the problems. Whilst deliberative political marketing and co-creation will of course need further research, not least to explore how they fit into existing government institutions and campaign practices, this means that we need to be open to new parameters when debating the impact of market analysis on citizenship and democracy.

Political marketing strategy is more varied, and focused on long-term relationships that may be both internally and externally oriented. Internal marketing is developing and expanding, and is concerned with building positive and mutually beneficial relationships that show respect for, and offer support to, volunteers and staff to help them become effective political marketers in their own right.

Communication is becoming more relationship-focused with interaction, connectivity, emotions and authenticity helping to create success for politicians. However, that does not remove the need for traditional communication of leadership skills and product offerings, or the success of short-term populist and persuasive communication to gain quick voters or pass legislation. Instead, it depends on the particular goals and context. Practitioners should choose carefully, opting for more dialogical and transformational approaches to achieve and maintain relationships with political consumers over the long term.

In government, political marketing is not just about doing what the media voter wants; it is a much more mutualistic, organic, nuanced process, which aims to build a constructive relationship between the public and government, and which can potentially improve policy-making and debate within the political system.

Building on this knowledge, Table 28.1 provides a list of lessons for practitioners when using political marketing.

Table 28.1 Lessons for practitioners using political marketing

Understanding the market
1. Be aware of the wide range of market research tools available and choose them to suit your goals and purposes.
2. Political marketing research is not just about researching what people want; consider viewing the political market as a co-producer of solutions to problems rather than just a course of demands.
Strategy
3. Political marketing strategy is about building long-term, internal and external relationships.
4. Choose the right strategy to suit your party/politician and unique circumstances. A sales-oriented party might not win against other market-oriented competitors, but if your goal is not to win, or the opposition is sales oriented or product oriented, then you do not need to adopt a market orientation.
5. Choose a niche marketing approach for a minor party seeking initial support and influence.
6. Develop not just the product but an effective brand that allows more flexibility than designing a specific product to suit voter demands as a market orientation suggests that political elites need to do, focusing on connecting with voters rather than just promising tangible benefits.
7. Ensure that branding and market-oriented strategies respond to and involve the internal market to build effective loyal relationships and support with volunteers.
8. Maintain and deliver the brand and market orientation in government.
Internal marketing
9. Parties need to research the internal market of volunteers, supporters and members.
10. Where internal and external market views differ, make careful trade-offs between involving the internal market to gain their valuable support and meeting conflicting demands from voters.
11. Where members are more representative of voters, engage them as part-time marketers, to both provide useful market intelligence and campaign on behalf of the party, and build long-term relationships that outlast the campaigns – and governments – of political candidates and leaders.
12. Train party staff in political marketing as they have increasing influence on marketing activities.
13. Use direct marketing to encourage party sympathisers to be involved in a party, designing e-marketing to enable them to campaign for the party.
14. Offer mentors and training to volunteers to support them in becoming long-term advocates for the party, and plug them into networks to increase their solidary benefits from volunteering.
15. Target online fundraising messages to suit the audience to make them more effective, and aim fundraising at active and satisfied volunteers.
16. Adapt both the concept and mechanics of donor marketing to suit the volunteer and donor cultures and regulatory frameworks within the political system.
Communication
17. Utilise online methods of campaigning in the same way that you would for non-online methods, and ensure that all forms of communication fit the overall strategy.
18. Identify initial brand strengths and ensure that campaign activities protect these.
19. Short-term branding of political candidates needs to be interwoven with long-term party brands.
20. Don't convey 'the common touch' at the neglect of leadership and governing skills; both are important.
21. When targeting market segments, ensure that this will generate voters, rather than just alienate cross-segment support.
22. If populist marketing achieves initial success, more reflective, market-oriented responses to adjust the product over time are needed to secure more long-term support.
23. Use technology to engage in local and national dialogue with voters in campaigns.
24. Ensure that communication and PR becomes more relationship-focused, which enables two-way dialogue and interaction over the long term, avoiding over-control in favour of authenticity and developed understanding of the challenges facing political leaders.

Table 28.1 (continued)

25. In government choose the PR strategy to suit the goals; whilst listening and responding to feedback helps to build positive relationships, if the goal is to implement chosen policies, persuasive and hype approaches are more suitable to help maintain support and avoid crisis.
26. Design e-marketing to suit communication goals, the market and environment. Do not just copy Obama's use of technology. Use more traditional transactional styles to reach new voters, but a relationship approach to maintain existing relationships with internal marketers.
Governing
27. Even in the campaign, create promises that can be delivered easily once in power to help build initial support to help mitigate more difficult delivery.
28. Once in power, build positive relationships that support delivery and attract positive public evaluation for initial success through delivery units, effective communication and re-framing of promises if necessary.
29. Interest groups can influence government decisions – they need to create market-researched, unified and effectively resourced campaigns which make the general impact of any decision beyond particular segments clear, and use continual communication to generate national media coverage.
30. Brand public policy to increase the chances of implementation both nationally and internationally, ensuring success by consulting and involving stakeholders, creating a brand assurance team, providing effective documentation about the brand, showing continued commitment to the brand at government department level, and leaving room for review and adaption of the brand over time.
31. Use government public opinion research to understand the needs of groups at which the policy is targeted, explore general public support for proposed policies, scope out potential for change, improve policy development and monitor implementation to ensure that it meets original aims, and make adjustments over time if necessary.
32. In government, use market analysis proactively to inform, not dictate decisions, and create room for leadership that balances leading and following the public to ensure that politicians can still take a proactive, visionary position.

Political marketing and democracy

It is clear from the discussion above that political marketing is moving in new directions: from researching voter demands to co-creation of the political product; from 'market-oriented party wins all' to situation-dependent strategic options to build long-term relationships with voters and supporters; from ignoring members to viewing the internal stakeholders and staff as integral to successful political marketing and building a relationship that not only recruits volunteers but donors – and ultimately voters; from short-term sales to long-term, mutual, interactive communication relationships; and from campaigning to governing with the expansion of political marketing into policy delivery and leadership. We therefore need to revisit the democratic implications of political marketing.

Previous research on political marketing and democracy

Previous research critiqued political marketing for potentially causing damage to democracy on several fronts. Savigny asserted that:

> politics, as both elite-level activity and the dissemination of this to the public, has predominantly become a process of marketing … this use of marketing has played a key role

> in contributing to the existence of a political malaise as marketing subverts the democratic process and disconnects the public from politics.
>
> *(Savigny 2008a: 1)*

Academics debate whether politicians should collect voters' views at all, as well as whether market research is a good way to identify those views. For example, Coleman takes issue with the suggestion:

> that voters' views and preferences are sufficiently consistent to be suited to strategic reasoning. Most of the empirical evidence suggests that voters are promiscuous and rationally irresponsible in the range of inconsistent views they hold at any one time, and rarely think about long-term policy consequences in ways that politicians and their advisors are required to do.
>
> *(Coleman 2007: 181)*

A range of literature criticises voters for being changeable in their opinions; selfish, acting in their own interests and not those of the whole country; highly emotional, prejudiced and irrational; short-term in focus; lacking the necessary experience, knowledge and capacity to make appropriate judgements, and led by media. There is, of course, the potential for elites to shape preferences and thus control the opinions they are listening to. Savigny (2008a: 38–40) notes how political marketing theory seems to omit consideration of preference shaping that can be carried out by elites, whether by politicians or the media or politicians influencing the media (see also Temple 2010; Savigny and Temple 2010).

Segmentation and targeting are also criticised for leading elites to only listen to some consumers and not others, disenfranchising the electorate. Savigny (2008a: 57) argued that 'the "product" is only targeted towards those groups who are in marginal seats, those groups for whom it is necessary to win the election' (see also Temple 2010: 271). Similarly Steger (1999: 680) argues that in the US, 'legislators are disproportionately attentive and responsive to those subsets of society that contribute most heavily to their re-election'. This threatens the democratic ideal of egalitarianism. Lilleker (2005a: 23) claimed that segmentation and targeting 'are to some extent responsible for causing a division in society: those to whom politics belongs and those whom politics has abandoned'. Savigny (2008a: 54–55) argues that focus groups are not conducted 'in accordance with standard sampling techniques, which seek to ensure some kind of demographic equality, rather focus groups comprise tactically significant voters', meaning that any responsiveness is only to 'selected members of the electorate' (see also Savigny 2007 and Wring 2007). Segmentation and targeting can also enable parties to concentrate their efforts and can help smaller parties and new candidates to gain support and power. This may help to reduce the effect of incumbency. The negative side is that extremist parties might use it. McGough detailed that Sinn Fein used research, segmentation, profiling and sales-oriented communication. He suggested from this that:

> there is clearly an opportunity here for extremists to achieve a 'fair' advantage but use it in an undemocratic manner … the same tactics have the potential to allow groups like Al Qaeda to gain a democratic position … the extremists may gain far more advantages through democracy than they ever did through the bomb and the bullet.
>
> *(McGough 2009: 190)*

More broadly, consumerism seems to threaten traditional notions of citizenship. Lilleker and Scullion (2008: 4) explain how 'voting is implicitly an act with ethical values and morals attached as any individual choice will also take into account the broader impact on others of that choice'. In contrast, consumerism encourages people 'to be selfish, vain and individualistic' (ibid.). Needham (2003: 7) argued it has 'turned democracy into a marketplace' and downgraded citizenship, and Savigny (2008b) stated that it encourages self-interest (see also Walsh 1994: 67; Slocum 2004: 744). Consumer and customer concepts ignore the big issues of politics such as distribution of power, fairness and social justice (Aberbach and Christensen 2005: 236).

The emphasis on professionalism which seems to accompany the use of marketing in communications can also reduce the importance of internal members whilst increasing that of unelected advisors (see Sackman 1996). Lilleker (2005b: 573) argues that political marketing can change internal power: as strategists together with the leadership determine policy direction in relation to market intelligence, this 'can leave ordinary members feeling alienated' if they see no response to their demands within that product development process.

There are a number of potential problems with marketing-informed communication. Academics argue that political marketing communication can increase distrust depending on how it is used. It can be seen as manipulative, as research enables political elites to get inside the heads of voters. Scammell (2008: 111) noted 'the danger of misleading the public through an increasingly sophisticated understanding of consumer psychology' in branding. Dermody and Hamner-Lloyd (2006: 128) suggested that 'the way in which promotional marketing tools and concepts are being used in election campaigns, with the emphasis on creating distrust and suspicion of the competing parties, does not bode well for the future of democracy in Britain'. Branding can also simplify discourse, so the public relies on the brand without detailed scrutiny of elite behaviour and play on emotion, reducing debate (see Scammell 2008; Needham 2005; Barberio 2006).

Academics have also argued that market analysis causes declining turnout and participation in the public sphere. Lees-Marshment and Lilleker (2005) argued that the sudden fall in turn-out in the UK 2001 election suggested that the greater the use of targeted marketing techniques, such as voter segmentation, the more likely it is that non-target groups are demobilised, so political marketing could cause the problem. Washbourne (2005) argued that political marketing could reduce debate within the public sphere: 'what is missed out is the idea of public discussion and debate being central to, even representative of, politics … replacement of (some part of) public discussion by polls and focus groups bypasses democratic politics rather than engages it', but whilst the more varied market analysis methods are acknowledging this.

Other discussion focuses on the concern that politicians' use of market analysis threatens leadership and could undermine creativity and new ideas. Jacobs and Shapiro (2000: 11) observed that 'the proliferation and visibility of public opinion polling during the Clinton administration … led many critics of American politics to fear that poll taking, focus groups and the like has permanently replaced political leaders' (see also Slocum 2004: 770; Newman 1999: 41). Paleologos (1997: 1184) argues that 'a poll-driven society … ignores creativity. It overlooks new ideas. It prohibits change and true reform'. In political marketing research, Paré and Berger's (2008: 58) conclusion from analysing how the Conservative Party of Canada was elected in 2006 as a minority government after using marketing, was that in doing so they strategically chose to avoid 'engagement with contentious policy considerations that appeal directly to contending social values'. Coleman (2007) contended that 'a culture of mutual trust between parties and citizens is not achievable (and certainly not sustainable) by simply repeating to voters what they already think'. Smith and Saunders (1990: 298) conclude that 'pandering to the prejudices of the majority might herald a tyranny of the ill-formed. Capital punishment, forced repatriation and other lowest common denominator issues could become important if marketing research showed a short-term benefit in courting them'. Watt argued that:

> treating democratic elections as if they were akin to purchases, the culmination of a marketing exercise, mistakes the function and purpose of elections. Elections are designed to provide the country with a government to represent the public will for a period of up to five years. Not many commercial transactions are designed to last for that length of time in the face of changing circumstances and it may well be that a government which starts out with one set of political priorities is obliged to change them in the face of ensuing events … The government may well have to adopt unpopular and painful policies to deal with these problems.
>
> *(Watt 2006: 19–23)*

However, other research has suggested that political marketing techniques and tools can be used for more positive effect. Segmentation can be used positively to help politicians identify and understand the concerns of smaller groups which might otherwise be neglected, such as those less likely to vote, and those who don't normally participate in consultation and mechanisms and services developed to target them and help their involvement in the political process. As Davidson (2005: 1190) noted, there is an argument that 'where levels of party identification and trust in the political system as a whole are in decline, simplistic categorizations of voters is an inadequate response'. Segmentation of the pensioner or retiree market has shown significant variation in the needs of those who have retired. Emerging minorities may be found earlier because of organisations using market segmentation than if they were just left to grow over time until they were powerful and established enough to get their issues placed on the agenda.

Academics have also conceded that citizenship-type values can be integrated within consumerist behaviour. Consumers of commercial goods have integrated ethical and environmental factors when making purchasing decisions: as Slocum (2004: 767) notes, 'personal wellbeing may be at the heart of much consumer action, but it is doubtful that people only think of themselves when they consider the safety of food, water, and other goods: they think of kids, family, and even community'. Similarly, Scullion (2008) suggested that citizenship and consumerisation can work alongside each other. People can take on 'citizenly roles' whilst in the market as consumers and retain responsibility (see also Lane 1991, 1996, 2000; Lilleker and Scullion 2008). Lees-Marshment's (2011) interviews with practitioners suggest that there are ways to overcome the potential problems and that politicians can choose to use marketing with positive impact on democracy.

Whilst the traditional sources of the public sphere may be in decline, it is developing elsewhere and run by the consumers themselves. Jackson (2008: 154–57) explored how a more consumerised media combined with technological tools such as texting and RSS feeds enables the public to have 'a more personalised experience of news and current affairs'. E-marketing supports interactive and two-way communication, consultation and citizen involvement. This may lift the citizen from passive consumer to active participant not just in political communication, but political decision-making. Geiselhart *et al.* (2003: 216–17) argue that it could be developed to create a 'truly user-driven interactive democratic model that offers multiple modes for feedback, civic dialogue and participation'. Similarly, Morison and Newman (2001: 177) argued that 'the possibilities that a more thoughtful engagement with the new technologies on offer accord very well with a range of approaches within recent political theory which suggest ways in which traditional democracy can be renewed'. Whilst this area has to be developed further in political practice, it is an area for potential growth. Henneberg *et al.* note the use of such tools in the London mayoral campaign that Boris Johnson won, and argue that:

> while none of this really amounts to political relationship marketing in any finished sense, and it may be seen as fostering the illusion of participation, it nevertheless establishes the trajectory along which we are being driven towards relational interactions in politics.
>
> *(Henneberg* et al. *2009: 170)*

Pragmatically as well as normatively elites should consider their internal market. Positioning and branding requires differentiation and therefore enhances public choice (see Scammell 2008; Needham 2005; Barberio 2006; Lilleker 2005a). Although some academics were concerned that party branding was removing the freedom of candidates to respond to local voter needs, with Needham (2005: 356) recalling how Freedland (1999) noted that 'Number 10 officials insist that Labour is a "brand" and they cannot let just anybody go into the marketplace with that precious label', more recently parties have learnt the importance of allowing diversification at local level.

Political marketing can also be used by elites to exercise leadership, as research helps understand and move opinion to overcome the problem. Goot argued that market intelligence:

> may be just as effective as a means of working out how to galvanise support, neutralise opposition or convert those who might otherwise be reluctant to see things the party's way ... it is not true that on every issue, or even on all the important ones, polling necessarily commits politicians to the position of the median voter.
>
> *(Goot 1999: 237)*

Murray's (2006: 495) study of the Reagan presidency concluded that whilst some party-driven issues were sidelined, and changes were made if too much opposition was encountered, survey data were also used to find potential 'overlap' between the leadership goals and public opinion, 'to thereby identify political opportunities where it could accomplish some of its ideological goals and satisfy some of its partisan constituents, while staying within broad constraints established by majority opinion'. The Promise work on reconnecting Tony Blair for the 2005 election suggested that there should be a 'Mature Tony' including both conviction and reflection. Mortimore and Gill (2010: 255) thus argue that 'leadership judgment is also indispensable' to a party using marketing: 'even a party with no ideological principles would need sometimes to defy public opinion', and marketing can help to 'create appropriate communication to make them more tolerated'.

Thus, whilst acknowledging the potential problems in the way political marketing is used, the reality is more varied and there is room for it to have a positive impact. We also need to take account of the realities of politics. Savigny (2008a: 3–5) conceded that problems have to be reconciled 'more practically, within contemporary politics', and Henneberg *et al.* (2009: 166) caution that 'political marketing should not be judged against ideal and impossible standards of a perfectly informed, knowledgeable and participating electorate, but rather against the real world of relatively low interest and knowledge in politics'. Henneberg and O'Shaughnessy (2009: 13) argue that a political relationship marketing approach would lead to positive implications for democracy, whereby 'voters would be consulted more often (and not only for election purposes), party members turned into stakeholders'. Scullion (2008) suggested that political consumers will also expect 'a share of responsibility and blame when things go wrong, if they appreciate a link between their own choice and the resultant conclusion'. This suggests support for the development of a more mutual, interactive, dually responsible, long-term relationship between voter and politicians. Many chapters in this *Handbook* suggest a changing relationship, with the chapters on deliberative marketing and co-creation supporting a link between political marketing and deliberative democracy, already suggested by Lees-Marshment and Winter (2009) and Henneberg *et al.* (2009: 176–79), and Lees-Marshment's (2011) notion of a partnership democracy. As Henneberg *et al.* (2009: 166) conclude, we may see in the future a new genre of political marketing 'which focuses on the goals of information, persuasion and reciprocity, rather than attack and defence', heralding a very different future for political marketing and democracy.

New possibilities – the results of this Handbook

Reflecting the debate in the literature, the research presented in this *Handbook* suggests the need to reflect further on our understanding of how marketing is used in politics, sometimes confirming problems previously raised but in other instances challenging the extent of that problem in practice.

A lot of the criticism about opinion research can be rebutted for being misinformed about the reality of practice. Despite the importance of market research, politicians retain the right to choose how they use it, and it does not always lead to a change in position or policy, but just how pre-determined decisions are communicated, to a range of contrasting market segments. There are democratic benefits from research informing political elites about what people think, and if there remains debate about this, it is not whether research should be used in politics, but how politicians in the 21st century can achieve both progress-initiating principled leadership and responsiveness to people's needs.

Segmentation can be used to reach under-represented groups. When applied to older voters, it has helped to ensure that elected representatives are conscious of the increasingly diverse needs of this growing section of society. This helps to correct inaccurate assumptions, such as older voters only caring about pensions and healthcare and how well they will be looked after by the state, instead of wider issues and opportunities for them to continue to contribute to society. Segmentation helps to promote more effective dialogue and debate between government and this changing section, and prevent neglect of a minority group. Of course, like any other marketing tool, segmentation can be abused. Political elites need to avoid preferencing – or being seen to preference – one segment over others, particularly important when the interests of seniors may need to be met by long-term solutions paid for by younger or future older generations. However, it can be used to inform policy and governing decisions, rather than simply the targeting of direct mail in election campaigns.

Strategic voter selection can be criticised for causing exclusion of large numbers of voters from political communications and thus political debate. This could erode the legitimacy of elections. On the other hand, targeting voters who have not yet made up their mind whether or how to vote maximises the potential benefits of political information, and GOTV on both floating and core voters increases participation amongst those who might otherwise not participate in elections.

Deliberative consultation can help to improve the value of voter opinion gathered by market research. Deliberative marketing could potentially lead to the development of a new leadership style, merging market research with governance, but it would require new collaborative skills employed within new arenas that can be reconciled with existing decision-making processes. Deliberative political marketing is not just about a market research tool, but is almost a new philosophy. It could increase trust between politicians and the public and thus have a very positive impact on democracy, but it would not be easy to implement deliberative marketing within the current reality of politics and government.

Co-creation similarly suggests that there could be a change in the relationship between government and the people. It is a very different approach to market research, asking the public to play a constructive role in solution creation, instead of simply letting them voice their demands. It opens up politicians to a broader range of possibilities. Politicians are no longer set up to fail – because they are not expected to find the answer to everything. They become judges and managers of solutions suggested by the market itself, thus increasing trust between the citizen and state. This moves traditional politics away from the 'elites know best' idea, but also political marketing from 'the market is king' approach to 'we need to work together to figure this out'. Politicians and public are both creators of the solution.

When choosing how to approach elections, politicians can choose a range of strategies. Political marketing is a global activity, which may seem to threaten ideology and value by treating elections like a commercial translation. However, politicians still have room to choose how they are going to respond to the electorate, which leaves room for leadership and creativity. Minor parties can adopt niche market-oriented behaviours without destroying their identity, thus retaining more choice for voters and continuing debate. Marketing can encourage niche parties to gain a better understanding of their voters and thus provide a more effective representation of minority interests.

Branding has the potential to help politicians communicate more effectively with citizens, and works well to introduce a new political candidate, movement or policy, but is less helpful in government or for re-branding. It can undermine trust if it is shown to be inauthentic or used manipulatively, but a positive brand can maintain long-term ties between the citizen and the politician. Effectively branded parties can help generate and maintain support for individual candidates when internal supporters are included in the process, but if ignored, centralised branding can alienate volunteers.

Relationship and direct marketing can be used to mobilise volunteers, activists and members, which can increase participation in the political system, and challenges the usual 'party and participation decline' thesis in non-political marketing literature. When used internally, political marketing can increase engagement with the public either as voters or as party activists at local and national level, improving party ties with civil society. For this benefit to be realised, internal relationship marketing needs to be carried out effectively and carefully, taking account of the potential impact on the balance between party responsiveness to its external voter and internal supporter market. A strategy that prioritises maximising the activism of volunteers could lead to a product that repels many voters and thus results in a highly participatory but entirely unelectable party. Instead, parties need to create a more emotional relationship with their supporters that can survive varying product formations over the long term. If parties involve supporters in product design, making them aware of what is required to create a product that is electorally attractive, and noting the potential value of influence in government for idealist ends, this could mobilise both members and voters, creating a lasting positive relationship. Where members are more in line with voters anyway, they can be employed as part-time marketers and be involved not so much as foot soldiers but as co-producers of the campaign. This fits both with the theoretical ideals of a participatory democracy and the pragmatism of political marketing. Political marketing is not necessarily in conflict with traditional party activism, and a centralised organisation can help coordinate members' work as part-time marketers have little chance of being truly effective. Similarly, direct marketing can be used to identify and mobilise supporters if aimed not just at floating voters but party sympathisers, thus stimulating participation.

Recognising the party official as a part-time marketer as well can ensure that they receive appropriate training in political marketing and are thus more effective. However, this could encourage the centralisation of marketing in politics and thus reduce levels of engagement and participation by members and activists. The growth in use of market research by party HQ may threaten the role not just of members but elected politicians. It also emphasises instrumental goals of victory rather than ideological aims such as policy influence, and instead of leadership, organisational resources in terms of skills, staffing and money.

In fundraising, marketing can be used ethically but practitioners have to balance high ethical ideals with the practical need to gather funds to pay for all other marketing activities, and achieve a strategy that collects donations within what is broadly acceptable both ethically and legally. Using e-marketing for fundraising purposes can ensure that ordinary people are involved in donating to political parties and campaigns instead of obscured back room deals between monied and political elites, and thus increase civic involvement. This does not prevent fraud or abuse, or donor fatigue, due to the ease and low cost of executing online fundraising, or prevent high-level donor marketing. Equally, though, it does not prevent practitioners aiming to provide donor satisfaction in a way which has beneficial societal implications and thus fits within the social marketing concept, encouraging a positive relationship between donor and recipient rather than alienating citizens from contributing financially towards the political process.

In communications there have been significant changes that open debate as to the democratic consequences of political marketing in the early 21st century. First, changes in campaigning in turn affect participation. Whilst political consultants still play a profound role in campaigns, organisationally they will become more flexible, with greater volunteer involvement but also influence and self-mobilisation. Voters are partners in campaigns, rather than foot soldiers. This can help parties and candidates connect more with supporters, and increase participation, but could also make campaigns harder to control and thus open politicians to crisis and attack. Campaigns communicate with voters via multiple media, which could help to reach voters in new ways and thus increase engagement between politicians and the public. However, the instant nature of communications exposes politicians to unexpected critique, encouraging a focus on tactics which makes it harder to stick to more nuanced and thought-out strategies. The greater availability of market research and data means that campaign decisions are more informed, but could restrict the ability of candidates to make high-impacting leadership decisions. Online forms of campaigning open up volunteering, as voters can contribute more easily in a way that suits them, and this both increases and diversifies political participation.

Communicating with individual candidates and political leaders is not easy, but this has positive implications for democracy. Micro-management by advisors can cause problems, and voters desire and reward authenticity, so politicians need to be capable of forming a relationship with ordinary voters. However, they also need to exhibit traditional leadership skills and connect with a range of support groups, not just one target market. Whilst branding can be used to gain initial support and media attention for a new candidate, politicians remain subject to serious scrutiny over their knowledge and policies and fit with the party brand during a campaign, and thus cannot assume to attract votes in the final election. Leaders need to be as interactive as possible, offering a long-term relationship to voters, with less emphasis on lower-level attributes such as their hair colour and media appearance, and more on their performance within a political and governmental context.

When politicians succeed with more populist marketing, whilst they enjoy short-term success, if they want to maintain support in the long term they also have to revert to more traditional forms of political marketing, adjusting their product in a reflective and market-oriented manner.

Thus, whilst the immediate effectiveness of populist marketing raises democratic concerns because it threatens constructive dialogue, it ultimately results in adaptation by either the populists themselves or established parties who create a more mainstream response to the previously ignored demands.

Election communication needs to suit the recipient, not just the producer, to be effective, and thus start with the voter not the politician. This means keeping it 'real' and relevant, such as averting not ignoring voter fears, and linking a national issue with the local context. Communication should also allow feedback and dialogue, and ensure the creation of avenues that allow the electorate to engage with the electoral process in a way that suits them and is two-way, so that they are part of the conversation instead of just being a passive recipient. This can then increase public participation and engagement with politics.

Political public relations used in elections to gain power, and to sell policy once in government, tends to be persuasive and thus open to the usual criticism of marketing communications as being manipulative. However, over the long term – and once politicians are in power – it can help representatives reach and interact with citizens and voters including those not normally interested in politics, making political communication more human, responsive and dialogic. This can help to build trust in politics and government.

Online marketing can similarly be used both to sell a message and a product without media interference, and more profoundly to engage in a more transformational relationship form of two-way communication. The potential interactivity of online and other forms of communication means that political marketing now holds the potential to create more positive relationships between political actors and citizens, especially if a long-term relationship marketing approach is applied between elections which encourages an ongoing dialogue.

The rise of delivery marketing has encouraged politicians to place more focus on action rather than just promise. Failure to deliver impacts re-election prospects; success improves citizen confidence in their government. This can have a positive impact on democratic government. However, it could also lead to over-centralisation with delivery units being placed under the prime minister's office, and therefore increasing top-down decision-making. Such offices also tend to be staffed by partisan appointments, increasing the role of unelected advisors which could limit democracy.

Interest group marketing encourages organisations to reach out beyond their narrow segment and think about how their proposals influence the rest of society, to create a broader support group. They try to gain greater legitimacy for their actions and thus become more responsive to society as a whole. However, an effective marketing strategy can then increase the influence of what are, at heart, special interests rather than the public good, and could hinder the implementation of market-driven policies.

The branding of public policy reflects an overall change in governance, whereby branding is needed in politics to convey to citizens that the product produced by governments is valuable because political parties are no longer seen as effective representative channels. Branding helps to justify policy decisions taken by elites, which whilst helpful to those in power, could undermine traditional representative democracy. Rather than involving citizens, used in this way branding gives elites more control over the public. Whilst it could help citizens to make a choice, branding of policy by government occurs after that choice – the vote – has been made. Branding thus narrows choice, and constricts debate, requiring uniformity. The alternative argument is that branding of government policy is about branding to elites within government and thus securing support for the implementation of policies that politicians have offered and received a mandate for in elections, which could be good for democracy. The branding of public policy, such as that on AIDS, can make the policy easier to implement and achieve public good. Simply getting elites to think of politics as a brand can encourage them to connect more effectively and create a more authentic offering built on core values of relevance to the public. Perhaps, as with many areas, it is a case whereby there is the potential for political marketing to extend and expand democracy, but practice has not yet realised this possibility.

Lastly, returning again to the use of research, but in government, there is an acknowledgement that it can be used with negative impact. However, there are also positive options: government opinion research can improve the information used to design and implement policies so that they achieve the desired output, enhancing the link between citizen choices in an election and government action. Despite the use of research by politicians in power, there is still room for politicians to take a range of policy decisions in relation to market research. Whilst political marketing is clearly a prevalent force in politics, it need not be a constraining force in democracy that prevents politicians taking up certain policies. Yes, they do need to stay in touch and they do need to listen, but that does not mean that they need to do everything the public wants. It is about nuance – leaders can take a range of positions in response to research, and research can be used to find a way to create public support for change as well as stop politicians doing something that is deeply against the public will. There may be a maturing of political leadership which could help to create a more positive relationship between government and citizens, but this positive impact will only happen in practice if politicians choose to use political marketing more effectively. Ultimately the decision rests with them.

Summary: the potential, if not the reality, of political marketing

Whilst there are clearly problems with political marketing's impact on democracy, this *Handbook* has also noted examples of positive effects and the overall evidence suggests that the change in direction also leads to a change in impact on democracy, at least potentially if not yet in reality. This leads us to discuss where next, and thus future trends for research and practice in political marketing.

The way forward: future trends in political marketing research and practice

Research

This *Handbook* has presented new ideas and conclusions about political marketing. Like all good research, it also suggests many avenues for future research. Below is a list that highlights a selected summary of those found in individual chapters.

- The impact that research-based campaigns have both on political practice and on voter behaviour;
- How research-based strategies are actually used in reality;
- Which voter selection procedures tend to be most useful across campaign timing and jurisdictions;
- How to work with large groups in deliberative governance arenas and build decision-making processes in which participatory action is possible with a fully engaged leadership group that can still make effective decisions;
- How more innovative research tools, especially co-creation, are used in politics;

- Use of a broader range of methods when studying comparative political marketing-orientation research, including quantitative analysis using standardised research instruments that can be applied in different settings rather than just qualitative case studies;
- Applying a version of the Long Tail model to niche parties;
- How party and candidate branding interconnect, whether in presidential elections or in coalition government;
- Gender branding – whether differing expectations of brands across male and female candidates are generated by the candidates themselves, the media or the voter, and opportunities for female candidates;
- Which incentive and recruitment strategies build long-lasting relationships with local activists beyond a single campaign – after 'yes we can', what next?
- Bringing volunteers into helping campaign in government, not just for an election (e.g. Organizing for America);
- To what extent new recruits attracted through direct and network marketing remain politically active after a campaign;
- Comparative studies of the role of party organisations and party officials in political marketing, including in government and opposition;
- What actually works in campaigning – the cost and benefits of different techniques such as micro-targeting, online and telemarketing research, new technologies and online communication tools that hold out the most promise for connecting with voters;
- Longitudinal or cross-sectional comparisons of populist marketing to enable informed theoretical, ethical and normative discussions about the practical relevance of populists and their marketers' actions;
- Applying the political PR model to different political situations such as policy development and implementation, in different countries and at different levels;
- A larger study of the use of Web 2.0 with a wider sample of countries and actors for not just the election but routine politics;
- Delivery by minority governments such as the UK coalition government elected in 2010 and the Australian federal government elected in 2010, and the consequences of non-delivery;
- The use of political marketing by advocacy coalitions opposing – or supporting – other types of political decisions in different fields such as health, economy and education, and the impact on their survival;
- The different uses of branding in public policy, why we have seen a growth in its use, the effectiveness of policy branding, its potential benefits and drawbacks for the public sector, and impact on governance;
- The appropriate use of government opinion research and how it might contribute to better policy-making;
- Discussion about political leadership and sustainable relationships especially once a leader is in power; and
- How we can create space for leadership within a political marketing environment.

Practice

A number of areas of development were also identified for practice:

- Become more informed about the strengths and weaknesses of voter research and understand how to conduct it properly;

- Use segmentation to discover the political needs and aspirations of the aging electorate, and provide the evidence base for the communicative and policy responses from governments and parties;
- Consider using research and processes that are co-creative and move beyond the simple focus group or poll, and develop more positive long-term relationships with the public;
- Continue to share ideas through global knowledge transfer, but adapt techniques and strategies to suit not even just the particular country, but the particular election;
- Green parties in particular need to consider marrying a market-oriented mindset with more pragmatic electoral strategies to improve the niche parties' ability to tap into existing supporters and gain their vote;
- Take the brand premise more seriously – design a party brand story that responds to and reflects the concerns, issues and aspirations gleaned from potential target audiences;
- Transparently inform donors about how their funds will be used and offer civic engagement as benefits for donating. Ask for money to support the promotion of specific policy proposals that funding can help implement which outlines how the money will be used and engages them in the policy campaign;
- Obtain a deeper understanding of the people you seek to govern; understand their issues and concerns and create a meaningful dialogue;
- Use communication to convey the complexities and challenges faced in government and the actual choice on offer given to voters;
- Prepare for further predicted technological changes such as 3D or holographic in-home media display systems, which will lessen the physical distance between politician and citizen and make the relationship on offer more important;
- Make greater use of political PR between elections and in government;
- Use the internet to enhance democratic participation within a relationship marketing approach rather than just at election time;
- Take the branding of public policy more seriously;
- Require that public opinion research (POR) becomes a compulsory policy input; develop expertise for its use amongst the bureaucracy (such as developing and using applied courses on POR as a tool of governance and management), and allocate funding for research; and
- Be aware of the need to utilise market research in a pro-active way to help create the room for leadership, and spend time reflecting on how to respond to the public.

The *Routledge Handbook of Political Marketing* therefore provides us with a sense of where the field is moving in the future. Political marketing offers modern insights into the age-old question of how political elites listen, respond to and deliver for the public. At the turn of the century, political marketing moved from being focused on communication to a strategic orientation that puts the voter at the heart of political decisions to produce market-led products. Currently, it is going through further change as practitioners and politicians seek to modify their behaviour to maximise its potential benefit not just to winning elections but to ensuring societal progress and positive democratic impact. Politics needs to use marketing methods to understand an increasingly diverse and unpredictable electorate and market research and segmentation offer new tools to do this, but it is not easy to satisfy market demands. Politicians are now realising that voters want a more nuanced and reflective leader who will consider the realities, constraints and long-term needs of the country, rather than just public desires identified by focus groups. In this case, politicians also need conceptual tools such as branding to help develop not just a product but a sense of direction and vision, and more mature conversational market research tools such as co-creation and deliberation. There is also more emphasis on marketing in government and delivery. If politicians focus on delivery, this holds the potential to create longer-term trust between politicians and the public. Political marketing is now more about relationships and mass–elite interaction through organisational development. In communications, the focus is now on interactive online communication and longer-term relations with the public: in party organisation avenues for participation are being created to suit the volunteer; and in strategy politicians are exploring the room to both lead and follow. Without denying that political marketing can be used problematically, this *Handbook* has explored and projected a more mature and reflective form of political marketing which holds the potential to create a more positive relationship between citizen and state. It is up to practitioners to turn this vision into reality.

Bibliography

Aberbach, J.D. and Christensen, T. (2005) 'Citizens and Consumers', *Public Management Review* 7 2: 226–45.

Barberio, R.P. (2006) 'Branding: presidential politics and crafted political communications' paper presented at the 2006 Annual Meeting of the American Political Science Association, Philadelphia, Pennsylvania, 31 August–3 September.

Coleman, S. (2007) 'Review of Lilleker and Lees-Marshment (2005) Political Marketing: a comparative perspective', *Parliamentary Affairs* 60, 1: 180–86.

Davidson, S. (2005) 'Grey Power, School Gate Mums and the Youth Vote: age as a key factor in voter segmentation and engagement in the 2005 UK general election', *Journal of Marketing Management* 21, 9/10: 1179–92.

Dermody, J. and Hamner-Lloyd, S. (2006) 'A Marketing Analysis of the 2005 General Election Advertising Campaigns', in D.G. Lilleker, N.A. Jackson and R. Scullion (eds) *The Marketing of Political Parties: Political marketing at the British 2005 general election*, Manchester: Manchester University Press, 101–31.

Freedland, J. (1999) 'The Trashing of Ken', *Guardian*, London, 17 November.

Geiselhart, K., Griffiths, M. and FitzGerald, B. (2003) 'What Lies Beyond Service Delivery – an Australian perspective', *Journal of Political Marketing* 2, 3/4: 213–33.

Goot, M. (1999) 'Public Opinion, Privatization and the Electoral Politics of Telstra', *Australian Journal of Politics and History* 45, 2: 214–38.

Henneberg, S. and O'Shaughnessy, N. (2009) 'Political Relationship Marketing: some macro/micro thoughts', *Journal of Marketing Management* 25, 1/2: 5–29.

Henneberg, S.C., Scammell, M. and O'Shaughnessy, N.J. (2009) 'Political Marketing Management and Theories of Democracy', *Marketing Theory* 9, 2: 165–88.

Jackson, D. (2008) 'Citizens, Consumers and the Demands of Market-driven News', in D.G. Lilleker and R. Scullion (eds) *Voters or Consumers: Imagining the contemporary electorate*, Newcastle: Cambridge Scholars Publishing.

Jacobs, L.R. and Shapiro, R.Y. (2000) 'Polling and Pandering', *Society* 37, 6: 11–13.

Lane, R.E. (1991) *The Market Experience*, Cambridge: Cambridge University Press.

—— (1996) 'Losing Tough in a Democracy: demands versus needs', in J. Hayward (ed.) *Elitism, Populism and European Politics*, Oxford: Clarendon Press.

—— (2000) *The Loss of Happiness in Market Democracies*, New Haven, CT and London: Yale University Press.

Lees-Marshment, J. (2011) *The Political Marketing Game*, Houndmills, Basingstoke, Hampshire: Palgrave Macmillan.

Lees-Marshment, J. and Lilleker, D.G. (2005) 'Political Marketing in the UK: a positive start but an uncertain future', in D.G. Lilleker and J. Lees-Marshment (eds) *Political Marketing: A comparative perspective*, Manchester: Manchester University Press, 15–38.

Lees-Marshment, J. and Winter, S. (2009) 'Figure 10.5 Reconciling Political Marketing Market-oriented Party Theory with Deliberative Democracy: initial conceptual thoughts', in J. Lees-Marshment (ed.) *Political Marketing: Principles and applications*, London and New York: Routledge, 282.

Lilleker, D.G. (2005a) 'Political Marketing: the cause of an emerging democratic deficit in Britain?' in W. Wymer and J. Lees-Marshment (eds) *Current Issues in Political Marketing*, Binghamton, NY: Best Business Books, 5–26.

—— (2005b) 'The Impact of Political Marketing on Internal Party Democracy', *Parliamentary Affairs* 58, 3: 570–84.

Lilleker, D.G. and Scullion, R. (eds) (2008) *Voters or Consumers: Imagining the contemporary electorate*, Newcastle: Cambridge Scholars Publishing.

McGough, S. (2009) 'Case Study 10.3 Political Marketing, Democracy and Terrorism: Ireland highlights the dangers', in J. Lees-Marshment (ed.) *Political Marketing: Principles and applications*, London and New York: Routledge, 288–90.

Morison, J. and Newman, D.R. (2001) 'On-line Citizenship: consultation and participation in New Labour's Britain and beyond', *International Review of Law, Computers and Technology* 15, 2: 171–104.

Mortimore, R. and Gill, M. (2010) 'Implementing and Interpreting Market Orientation in Practice: lessons from Britain', in J. Lees-Marshment, J. Strömbäck and C. Rudd (eds) *Global Political Marketing*, London and New York: Routledge, 249–62.

Murray, S.-K. (2006) 'Private Polls and Presidential Policymaking: Reagan as a facilitator of change', *Public Opinion Quarterly* 70, 4: 477–98.

Needham, C. (2003) *Citizen-consumers: New Labour's marketplace democracy*, London: Catalyst.

—— (2005) 'Brand Leaders: Clinton, Blair and the limitations of the permanent campaign', *Political Studies* 53, 2: 343–61.

Newman, B.I. (1999) *The Mass Marketing of Politics: Democracy in an age of manufactured images*, Beverley Hills, CA: Sage Publications.

Paleologos, D.A. (1997) 'A Pollster on Polling', *American Behavioral Scientist* 40, 8: 1183–89.

Paré, D.J. and Berger, F. (2008) 'Political Marketing Canadian Style? the conservative party and the 2006 federal election', *Canadian Journal of Communication* 33, 1: 39–63.

Sackman, A.I. (1996) 'The Learning Curve towards New Labour: Neil Kinnock's corporate party 1983–92', *European Journal of Marketing* 30, 10/11: 147–58.

Savigny, H. (2007) 'Focus Groups and Political Marketing: science and democracy as axiomatic?' *British Journal of Politics and International Relations* 9: 122–37.

—— (2008a) *The Problem of Political Marketing*, New York: Continuum International Publishing Group.

—— (2008b) 'The Construction of the Political Consumer (or politics: what not to consume)', in D. Lilleker and R. Scullion (eds) *Voters or Consumers: Imagining the contemporary electorate*, Newcastle: Cambridge Scholars Publishing.

Savigny, H. and Temple, M. (2010) 'Political Marketing Models: the curious incident of the dog that doesn't bark', Political Studies 58, 5: 1049–64.

Scammell, M. (2008) 'Brand Blair: marketing politics in the consumer age', in D. Lilleker and R. Scullion (eds) *Voters or Consumers: Imagining the contemporary electorate*, Newcastle Cambridge Scholars Publishing, 97–113.

Scullion, R. (2008) 'The Impact of the Market on the Character of Citizenship, and the Consequences of this for Political Engagement', in D. Lilleker and R. Scullion (eds) *Voters or Consumers: Imagining the contemporary electorate*, Newcastle: Cambridge Scholars Publishing.

Slocum, R. (2004) 'Consumer Citizens and the Cities for Climate Protection Campaign', *Environment and Planning* 36: 763–82.

Smith, G. and Saunders, J. (1990) 'The Application of marketing to British Politics', *Journal of Marketing Management* 5: 295–306.

Steger, W. (1999) 'The Permanent Campaign: marketing from the hill', in B. Newman (ed.) *The Handbook of Political Marketing*, Thousand Oaks CA: Sage, 661–84.

Temple, M. (2010) 'Political Marketing, Party Behaviour and Political Science', in J. Lees-Marshment, J. Strömbäck and C. Rudd (eds) *Global Political Marketing*, London and New York: Routledge, 263–77.

Walsh, K. (1994) 'Marketing and Public Sector Management', *European Journal of Marketing* 28, 3: 63–71.

Washbourne, N. (2005) '(Comprehensive) Political Marketing, Expertise and the Conditions for Democracy', Paper presented at the Political Studies Association Political Marketing Group Conference, London, UK.

Watt, B. (2006) *UK Election Law: A critical examination*, London Routledge-Cavendish.

Wring, D. (2007) 'Focus Group Follies? Qualitative research and British Labour Party strategy', *Journal of Political Marketing* 5, 4: 71–97.

Index